THOSE
WHO
FORGET
THE
PAST

EDITED AND WITH AN INTRODUCTION BY

RON ROSENBAUM

Afterword by Cynthia Ozick

THOSE
WHO
FORGET
THE
PAST

The Question of Anti-Semitism

RANDOM HOUSE TRADE PAPERBACKS | NEW YORK

A Random House Trade Paperback Original
Introduction copyright © 2004 by Ron Rosenbaum
Afterword copyright © 2004 by Cynthia Ozick

Library of Congress Cataloging-in-Publication Data

Those who forget the past: the question of anti-semitism / edited and
introduced by Ron Rosenbaum ; afterword by Cynthia Ozick.
  p.   cm.
Contents: Awakenings—Something old, something new—One death,
one lie—The ultimate stakes: the Second-Holocaust debate—The facts
on the ground in France—The shift from right to left—The deicide
accusation—Some new forms of anti-Semitism—Anti-Zionism and anti-
Semitism—Israel—Muslims
ISBN 0-8129-7203-1
  1. Anti-Semitism—History—21st century. 2. Israel—Public opinion.
3. Jews—Public opinion. I. Rosenbaum, Ron.
DS145.K485 2004
305.892'4'0090511–dc22   2003065542

Random House website address: www.atrandom.com

Printed in the United States of America

9 8 7 6 5 4 3 2 1

CONTENTS

PART THREE: ONE DEATH, ONE LIE

One Death

One Lie

PART FOUR: THE ULTIMATE STAKES: THE SECOND-HOLOCAUST DEBATE

PART FIVE: THE FACTS ON THE GROUND IN FRANCE

PART SIX: THE SHIFT FROM RIGHT TO LEFT

PART SEVEN: THE DEICIDE ACCUSATION

PART EIGHT: SOME NEW FORMS OF ANTI-SEMITISM

INTRODUCTION

RON ROSENBAUM

Kidnapped by History

---

1) A BAD JOKE, OR HALITOSIS OF THE SOUL

It is a mystery whose magnitude calls for humility—why anti-Semitism, why the persistence, the recurrence, of this particular hatred? "The longest hatred," Robert Wistrich, one of the foremost analysts of that long history, called it.

I feel an even greater humility now, writing this final draft of an introduction, than when I began the first draft several months ago. Back then I had only just begun the process of assembling the pieces in this book, one of the most difficult challenges I've faced. There was so much to include, so much that space constraints forced me to leave out.

I wouldn't claim this collection is exhaustive, but the level of thought, of argumentation, the number of challenging perspectives in the essays herein, cumulatively exceeded my expectations. And left me feeling, when looking at my original introduction, that it didn't do justice to the scope and complexity of the work within. It still doesn't. So it won't hurt my feelings if you stop reading this now and skip to Jonathan Rosen's essay and all that follow.

I mention Jonathan's essay not merely because it opens the book but because rereading it, fifteen months after it was first published, gave me the idea for this book.

I had met Jonathan when he was cultural editor of *The For-ward,* had been deeply impressed by his book-length essay/memoir *The Talmud and the Internet.* We had served on a panel discussion about *Shadows on the Hudson,* I. B. Singer's post-Holocaust novel, and I had taken to having occasional lunches with him at that temple of secular Jewish culture on New York's Upper West Side, Barney Greengrass ("The Sturgeon King").

It was at one of those lunches early in 2003 that Jonathan asked me if I could fill in for him at a speaking engagement at a Connecticut temple, because his wife was about to give birth, and I asked him for a copy of the piece he had written for the November 4, 2001, issue of *The New York Times Magazine.*

I'd wanted to refer to it in my substitute talk, and I was stunned at how prescient it seemed, reading it this time. Less than two months after 9/11 he'd seen the shape of things to come with remarkable acuity: the eruption of violence, physical and rhetorical, against Jews in the Middle East and Europe, that would soon become endemic. And I was struck by the precision with which he expressed feelings I'd begun to have on what he called "The Uncomfortable Question of Anti-Semitism."

Although his family experience was tragic in a way mine wasn't—his father had escaped Hitler's Vienna on one of the *Kindertransport*s that rescued Jewish children, most of whose families, like Jonathan's father's family, were later murdered—the feeling he described, in 2001, of being "kidnapped by history," spoke to me and many people I knew.

He wrote at one point of having been born in 1963, part of the first generation or two of Jews to live, in America at least, without anti-Semitism as a significant fact of life, and now suddenly having Jews—as Jonathan put it—"being turned into a question mark once again." If not here, then in much of the rest of the world.

A question mark again . . . a chilling phrase. The Question

of Anti-Semitism contains within it several questions. Among them: What, if anything, is new about the so-called "new anti-Semitism"? Why does anti-Semitism seem to have migrated from Right to Left? How does one define the difference, when there is one, between anti-Semitism and anti-Zionism?

By that time, there had appeared a significant number of essays, polemics, and exemplary reports on these questions, and it occurred to me that it would be worthwhile to attempt to collect them—to document both the phenomenon of contemporary anti-Semitism and the responses to it, in a book such as this. Now that you know how this endeavor began, go, begin if you'd like. Go read Jonathan Rosen or Jonathan Freedland or Berel Lang or Ruth R. Wisse or David Mamet, or skip to the fiery Afterword that Cynthia Ozick was gracious enough to write for this book. I won't complain. I won't be taking attendance. And no penalties for not reading consecutively: yes, there's a logic behind the ordering of the sections, and some of the opposing polemics are paired off, but nothing prohibits your skipping around in the book.

Meanwhile I'll just press forward here, for those who remain and those who return, with some observations, some contentions, some conjectures, some controversy.

I'd like to begin by talking about a little-known site on the Web I'd become fascinated with—and its metaphoric resonance. It's called "Exposing the Exposer."* It's a site run by two guys named Zachary and Mo and is entirely devoted to exposing *another* website, run by a guy they call "Mickey." It seems that Mickey (real first name Michael) began *his* website by promoting post–9/11 conspiracy theories about Jews masterminding the World Trade Center attacks—remember the spectral "4,000 Jews" (or Israelis) who were supposedly told to stay home that day by that secret cabal behind it all, the Elders of Zion?

---

*http://www.sicmuse.com/weblog/

Post–9/11 anti-Semitic conspiracy theories soon became a portal for Mickey to enter the underworld of *pre*–9/11 anti-Semitic theories. So his website lurched from the false announcement "NPR NEWSCASTER: ISRAEL HAD ADVANCE KNOWLEDGE OF SEPT. 11" to a defense of the ancient "blood libel" charges that Jewish ritual called for using the blood of murdered Christian children to make pastry for religious feasts. New anti-Semitism, old anti-Semitism: it was one-stop shopping for the Web-surfing Jew-hater or credulous recruit at Mickey's site.

But Zachary and Mo weren't having it; they weren't letting him get away with it so easily. On *their* website, "Exposing the Exposer," they ceaselessly do just that: expose every myth, every poisonous slur Mickey posts, however many times it has been exposed before. They just won't let the sad, silly fellow (Mickey's other cause, aside from slandering Jews, is public nudity—thus, perhaps, the added resonance of their nickname for him: "The Exposer") have a free ride on the information superhighway. Not without their cleansing ridicule.

There's something appealing about the spirit of their mission. As Simon Schama recently pointed out in a talk at a YIVO Institute conference, the Web can be a "verification-free" environment, and trying to fight the tide of Internet anti-Semitism is a Canute-like task. And yet Zachary and Mo, the two guys who run the "Exposing the Exposer" website, take a zestfully comic approach to pulling the rug out from under the crude and stupid slurs that "Mickey" propagates. Somehow by using the diminutive "Mickey" they not only invoke the cartoon mouse, but make it seem as if the guy they're addressing is not a bad sort, just a bit mentally challenged—like the slow one in *Of Mice and Men*: "Tell me about the rabbits, George." For poor "Mickey," the Jews are like "the rabbits"—an illusion that makes sense of a world confusing to his undernourished (let's say) intellect. "Tell me about the rabbis, George."

At first I wondered, indeed *you* might wonder: why pay attention to this obscure website that exposes another website? There are worthy organizations that take on the Big Lies and the Big Distortions, such as the Anti-Defamation League and the Simon Wiesenthal Center. On the Internet there's the indispensable Tom Gross, former Middle East reporter for the U.K. *Telegraph* (and son of the London literary couple John and Miriam Gross), who is a one-man army when it comes to exposing the hypocrisies and prejudices of the mainstream press for his media-centric weblist. There's the remarkable MEMRI, the Middle East Media Research Institute, which has devoted itself to translating what's being said about Jews in Arabic and Islamist media. There are webloggers like Andrew Sullivan, Jeff Jarvis, and Meryl Yourish, who keep close track of American developments. The Web is the New Frontier of the new anti-Semitism, the realm where the future of the struggle of truth against fiction may be won or lost in a universe of ever-proliferating linked sites such as those of Mickey and his exposers.

Maybe it's futile, maybe lies will always outrun the truth. But I came to admire the guys for trying to keep up. The mistake of underestimating the power of lies and incitement has already been made once. They exist like a subterranean river of poison that occasionally breaks to the surface. And reading "Exposing the Exposer" gives one a chance to put the mind behind the very model of a modern anti-Semitic Internet site under the microscope. You can sense that Zachary and Mo, in addition to being jocularly contemptuous of Mickey, are fascinated by him. Cancer researchers do not *like* cancer, but they're deeply intrigued by the way tumors work. So it is with the study of anti-Semitism.

One of the things that can be gained, for instance, from the study of Mickey's site is a reminder of the continuing malign power of *The Protocols of the Elders of Zion,* that czarist fraud that purportedly exposed a secret Jewish conspiracy to rule the world.

It is, alas, one of those lies that have become immune to disproof, a template always awaiting some traumatic public or personal tragedy with the appeal of a "knowing insider's" insight.* And so for Mickey there was a ready-to-hand way of explaining 9/11: it was all the work of a secret cabal of Jews—here, the Mossad, Israeli intelligence—manipulating things from behind the scenes, in this case engineering the hijacking of the jetliners, the murder of thousands, in order to blame it on "innocent" Islamist terrorists.

The *Protocols* and their updated version, distributed by Henry Ford as *The International Jew,* became (in German translation) a basis for Hitler's vision of "Jewry" and the Jewish conspiracy as well: Jewish capitalists were secretly in league with the Jewish Marxist anti-capitalists to make puppets of everyone else. The *Protocols* is not just a silly conspiracy theory: in Hitler's hands it became what the historian Norman Cohn called "a Warrant for Genocide."

And now the *Protocols* are back with us, not just in Western Web media, not just in disguised form in 9/11 conspiracy theories, but in widespread Arabic translation of the original Russian version and, of course, in a forty-one-part TV series broadcast on Egyptian television in 2002.

The study of this sort of phenomenon is important, yes, but still, it's demoralizing; especially if, like me, you're Jewish and you spent a decade or so working on a book about Hitler and you thought you'd left the whole hideous subject behind

---

*Just as this book was going to press, I had an interesting discussion with Jonathan Alter, the *Newsweek* and *Washington Monthly* writer. He suggested there are two types of anti-Semitic utterances: those that come from an almost unconscious resort to a preexisting external "template," one such as the *Protocols,* and those that come from within, where they are embedded in the consciousness of the utterer like a "virus" (his word), or meme. It's important to remember: just as not all Jews are alike, neither are all anti-Semites.

and then you find yourself spending months immersed in the recent literature on anti-Semitism.

When I was working on the book that eventually became *Explaining Hitler,* a kind of intellectual history of postwar theories about the origin and nature of Hitler's anti-Semitism, friends would ask me, "Isn't it depressing spending so much time on the subject?" Of course it was, I'd say, trying to put a brave face on it, but the debates about the source of evil, the theodicy of the Holocaust, the modes of explaining the particular virulence of Hitler's anti-Semitism, the question of degrees of evil—*these* weren't depressing, they were intellectually stimulating arguments. Here were some of the best minds of the century in deep disagreement about some of the most important issues of history and human nature.

Anyway, that's what I'd say for the first five years. For the next five years until publication in 1998 the intellectual stimulation was outweighed by the emotional drain. I lost some of the zest for the task that the "Exposing the Exposer" website guys still display. (I hope they don't get tired.)

So I understand if some might approach a collection of essays about anti-Semitism—more suffering! more despair! many Holocaust references!—with a certain reluctance or weariness. A reluctance or weariness probably equaled or exceeded by my own when I approached this project—and now, as I'm writing this, as I approach its conclusion.

Finishing the Hitler book had left me in a black hole of despair: the historical record was too fragmentary to offer any certainty, the mysteries were unresolvable, the images unshakable. It was a hole I'd begun to crawl out of by beginning a book about Shakespearean scholars and directors.

By early 2003 I had handed in half that book; as a writer I was having the time of my life, exploring challenging questions with brilliant Shakespeareans. I felt I'd earned these pleasures.

But something happened. As Paul Berman put it, "something's changed." It was all the more shocking, coming at a moment, a brief, now lost moment at the end of the twentieth century when the signs seemed to point to normalization. In America a Jew had been nominated for the vice presidency with almost negligible backlash. That same summer, at Camp David, Israelis and Palestinians seemed close to a dramatic breakthrough to a two-state compromise that would allow both peoples, both in their own ways victims of history, to live in peace.

Then everything began to unravel: the peace talks broke down, the Second Intifada with its terror tactic of "suicide bombings" began, European demonstrators, and increasingly many in the United States, began to turn against the Jewish state, denouncing its efforts at self-defense while "explaining" the acts of those who murdered its children.

For a time I tried to ignore it and to look away, and then that became impossible. For me I guess it culminated with the March 27, 2002, Passover massacre in Netanya when twenty-nine worshippers were blown apart by a so-called suicide bomber (a misleading term; I'm not fond of the alternative "homicide bomber," because of its redundancy. I prefer the simple term "mass murderer").

What made this mass murder different from other mass murders? The astonishing leap by much of the world to demonize the response, blame the victims. When the Israeli Army rolled into Jenin, in early April 2002, to dismantle the terrorist infrastructure responsible for the mass murder at Netanya, the world seemed to me shockingly eager to believe fraudulent claims of a "massacre" committed by Israelis while all too often ignoring the original massacre that prompted the self-defense measures.

The obvious and unashamed longing to be able to accuse Israelis of "Nazi-like" crimes, of creating "an Auschwitz" in Jenin, was disturbing to me and many others. It was a phenomenon I have heard described before: "Europe killed the Jews and would never forgive them for it," someone once observed bleakly. The Holocaust had become a kind of defining shame for European civilization that was intolerable to bear without some form of displacement, of "balancing" the scales: "See, the Jews commit mass murder too." It was just too much, especially as objective inquiries soon discredited the "Jenin massacre" reports. And yet, despite all the evidence to the contrary, Jenin remained, in the rhetoric of many "anti-Zionists," their analogue for Auschwitz. It was like witnessing the very birth of a classic anti-Semitic myth with—who knows?—the potential destructive power of the *Protocols*.*

About that time, I began to write about the subject, reluctantly at first. I'd written and spoken on Hitler questions for several years, but I'd always felt I was speaking about something safely in the past. This new rage of the world against the idea of Jews defending their children was something I was reluctant to engage; it was just so inhuman, so far beyond the pale, so to speak, that it made you want to look away or wish it away. But it kept getting worse. How much worse might it become? It was in asking that question that I touched off a debate about the potential for a "second Holocaust."

That moment, spring 2002, now seems like a turning point in many ways. Not just the resurgence of anti-Semitism, and the awareness of it, but the debate over how much to be con-

---

*That was what I found so fascinating in Dr. David Zangen's account. He was someone who was an eyewitness in Jenin, now witnessing the unveiling of a film that would perpetrate the lie about Jenin: a slick, deceptive propaganda "documentary" that would soon be shown throughout the world. It was as if he were there to watch the composition of the *Protocols*. He seeks to speak the truth, knowing it may be too late, and is shouted down. Jenin is one of a number of moments that you will find described from various perspectives by various authors herein, such as the incident at San Francisco State University and the Egyptian TV dramatization of the *Protocols*. I don't consider these recurrences repetitious; I'd call them cumulative testimony to the iconic status these events attained, and the grim reality they represented.

cerned about it. Some chose to speak out; some chose to tell those who spoke out they were alarmists, panicky.

LET ME SEEK to put that moment in the perspective of post-Holocaust anti-Semitism—the nearly sixty years since Hitler's death camps were shut down. Chronological divisions, like just about every other aspect of anti-Semitism, are a subject of contention (including how one spells it. There is a school of thought that believes the compound word "anti-Semitism" is unsatisfactory to one degree or another because it was a term invented *by* an anti-Semite, the nineteenth-century German "racial theorist" Wilhelm Marr. Some argue for other terms, such as "Judeophobia" or just plain "Jew-hatred," because it's not about all Semitic people (Arabs, for instance) but about all Jews. Even the hyphenation of the word "anti-Semitism" is argued over, with some believing that a hyphen and a capital *S* mimic Wilhelm Marr too closely and that "antisemitism" is to be preferred. The Random House style has long been to spell it "anti-Semitism," and "antisemitism" doesn't entirely escape the shadow of Marr, so I've gone with the more familiar form.*

In any case, one of the key contentions involves chronology. I'd suggest there is not just one new anti-Semitism in the post-Holocaust period, but that there are two. The Israeli scholar Yehuda Bauer makes a case for *four* postwar waves, and no doubt his typology offers greater specificity, but I'd suggest that there are roughly two qualitatively different periods: the post-Holocaust period and the post–9/11 period.

The passage of nearly six decades since 1945 makes post-Holocaust anti-Semitism not exactly new but new in the scale of centuries. One minor but telling way in which post-

---

*There are similar arguments over whether "Holocaust" is the preferable term, as opposed to "Shoah" (Hebrew for "destruction"), "Final Solution," or just plain "genocide." I have some reservations about the sacralizing origin of "Holocaust" (Greek for "burnt offering in a religious ritual") but have gone with it because it has become the most familiar, and now historically specific, usage for Hitler's crime.

Holocaust anti-Semitism differs from the pre–1939 variety is the way the fact of the Holocaust shadows and stains what might have been, before World War II, "casual" anti-Semitic remarks, slurs, jokes. All of which now, alas, must be construed as part of the culture of prejudice and persecution that permitted the execution of the Final Solution—and the world's indifference to it.

After such knowledge, for one thing, "casual" is not casual anymore. What do I mean by "casual anti-Semitism"? Well, there was the phrase that the president of the United States Holocaust Memorial Museum used in July 2003 when he reacted to disclosures of anti-Jewish comments in Harry Truman's private diary. He called them "the typical sort of cultural anti-Semitism that was common at the time."

That's something of a stretch, since Truman was writing in 1947—I think he meant "common at the time Truman was growing up." But the phrase "the typical sort of cultural anti-Semitism" is useful when distinguishing pre-Holocaust country-club anti-Semitism from what I'd call "post-Holocaust anti-Semitism of the first type." The events of 1939–1945 can't help but give a different gravity to what had once been casual.

Here's a relatively trivial but, I think, useful example of the change, which I experienced myself at an upscale Upper East Side book party in the mid-1990s. In the crush of conviviality I was approached by a colleague who had suffered some criticism for what some had seen as anti-Semitic stereotypes in his fiction. He was a writer who specialized in preening rants against "New Money" types—preening in the sense that he customarily implied that people from *his* circle of exquisitely well-bred Old Money types would not be guilty of the supposedly vulgar and unscrupulous practices of New Money.

If many of his New Money characters were Jews, he'd insist his animus was not that they were Jews, but that they were new. The most charitable interpretation of his attitude was not prejudice but condescension: he looked down at people who hadn't the time to attain the stainless ethical gentility of those in his circle.

There is a vast historical naïveté and double standard in this view—the idea that Old Money in America was somehow cleaner, when in fact many Old Money fortunes came from plunder and murder (of Native Americans), from enslavement and murder (of black people), and from the merciless exploitation of generations of wage slaves of all colors, who in effect paid with their immiseration for the self-congratulatory gentility that allowed certain Old Money types to sneer at the New and the Jew.

Still, I had always felt this fellow was basically a good-natured sort, not a hater. Despite what was, to me, his irritating, almost willfully ahistorical ingenuousness about the superior moral status of Old Money, I'd been willing to accept his word that when he portrayed a stereotyped Jew behaving badly, he didn't necessarily believe "the Jews" were to be despised as a people. It's an important distinction, as Berel Lang argues herein. Jews, like others, needless to say, are capable of all manner of wrongdoing. One definition of an anti-Semite is someone who insists that when Jews do wrong, it's because they are Jews, not because they are human.

But I'll never forget the moment he approached me at this book party with a glow in his cheeks, a glass in his hand, and, if not a slur in his voice, a slur in a joke. He proceeded to single me out, with no preliminaries, for a hugely self-entertaining rendition of a joke in his idea of a Yiddish accent. It was about two small-time Jewish businessmen, I forget the names, something like Abie and Mendy, and basically it was about how they wanted to cheat their creditors out of what they owed.

"I found the solution to our problems," Abie tells Mendy, or Mendy tells Abie, in this joke. "It's in da Bible."

"In da *Bible*? Vut in da Bible?"

"*Chapter Eleven!*"

As the Old Money writer brayed in my ear at his own joke, I felt I was being somehow challenged to show I could rise above harmless ethnic humor and join him in a laugh. But I must admit I couldn't find this brilliant joke funny. Jews chortling about the Bible and bankruptcy to cheat people out of money: I couldn't help thinking how easily it could have been a comic strip from Julius Streicher's odious *Der Stürmer,* circa 1934.

It was about as funny as if he had donned blackface and told an Uncle Remus story to one of the black writers in the room. Ah yes, the exquisite manners of Old Money. I've never felt the same about him again.

Still there was a sense, before September 11, that post-Holocaust anti-Semitism—because of the revulsion that this kind of heedlessness usually has attached to it—was, more than anything, a bad joke, a halitosis of the soul, a breach of decorum, but essentially harmless. It seemed to lack consequence—Jews in America were never more secure (witness the Lieberman nomination). Even Jews in Israel had the illusion that a "peace process" offered the promise of security in the future. And Jews in Europe were, well, just Jews in Europe, not yet victims of violence again—there didn't seem to be a threat of consequence; there wasn't a threatening *context.* So, in most cases—when they did not involve murder, as in the case of Alan Berg, the outspoken talk show host murdered by neo-Nazis, or Yankel Rosenbaum (no relation), murdered by a Brooklyn mob that chanted, "Kill the Jew!"—most expressions of anti-Semitism could be regarded as exceptions that proved a rule.

Let us conjecture, then, that one thing that distinguished post-Holocaust anti-Semitism of the first kind from post-Holocaust anti-Semitism of the post-9/11, or post-millennial, kind is the return of a *threatening context* for anti-Semitism: the return to what Yehuda Bauer, who served as head of Yad Vashem Holocaust Center in Jerusalem, has called a "genocidal" threat, to the five million Jews of the State of Israel. Indeed, one thing I've noted in reading the post–9/11 literature about Jews and Israel and anti-Semitism is the recurrence of a phrase, rarely seen before: "existential threat."

In a way it's a euphemism. The more commonly used sense of "existential" is, of course, as shorthand for a French philosophic tendency, and it's hard, when one hears "existential threat," to avoid conjuring up the image of Sartre and de Beauvoir shaking puny fists at the universe.

But "existential threat" as it is used these days, alas, goes back to a more primal meaning of the word: an existential threat means a threat to a state's, or a people's, very *existence*. And so when people speak of an "existential threat" to the Jewish state or the people of Israel, they are speaking of nothing less than annihilation.

The existential threat was given shocking immediacy by the September 11 radical Islamist attacks on the United States, by the escalating suicide attacks on Israeli citizens, a proliferation of exterminationist, often Hitler-worshipping rhetoric in the media of the Middle East, and the procurement of nuclear capability and delivery systems by Islamic states surrounding Israel. A capability easily transferrable to terrorist groups.

There could be little doubt that those capable of committing mass murder by suicide in the United States would not hesitate, given the chance, to carry out an attack on an even larger scale on their other declared enemy, the Jewish state— and that it would be far easier to essentially end the existence of the Jewish state than it would be to do such profound damage to the far vaster realm of the United States.

What September 11 demonstrated also was that Israel's possession of a nuclear deterrent—like that of the United States—while it might still deter other *states,* would no longer protect it from a suicidal terrorist cell in possession of a suitcase nuclear weapon, or a nuclear-tipped missile launched from the Bekaa Valley. In August 2002, when the chief of staff of the Israel Defense Forces explicitly used the phrase, conceded the presence of an "existential threat" to the State of Israel, it was the realism of an experienced military man speaking.

Indeed, the terrorist forces behind individual "suicide bombers" in Israel and their supporters among radical Islamists in the Arab world spoke openly of their desire to eliminate the State of Israel and, increasingly, its people as well.

The sense of a new dimension to the existential threat is what makes post–September 11 anti-Semitism a phenomenon of a different order of magnitude from what came before. And yet there is one distinctive invention of post–1945 anti-Semitism that persists in curious ways in the post–September 11 period, one that has mutated just as anti-Semitism itself has mutated in that period: Holocaust denial. Old-fashioned Holocaust denial certainly persists, but one could almost say there is a denial of a new type: the one that takes the form of equanimity. It is not technically Holocaust denial; it is the denial of Holocaust consequences. Let me explain.

2) AGAINST EQUANIMITY

I wish I could regard Holocaust denial as merely a bad joke, a parody of an anti-Semitic theory. One of the most interesting discussions I had on this question was with the philosopher Berel Lang, author of an extremely thoughtful consideration of the nature of Nazi evil, *Act and Idea in the Nazi Genocide*. In the course of interviewing him for *Explaining Hitler* I brought up the question of whether one could posit an *evolution* of evil. Professor Lang had recently published a journal article on that question in which he proposed the notion that human evil, like other aspects of human culture, may have undergone a kind of evolution, or at least a changing history, from a theoretical first murder to mass murder. Should we consider Hitler's genocidal Final Solution the *final* step on a ladder down into the abyss, or just the *latest* step? And if the latter, what might the *next* step be?

I had posited to Lang that Holocaust denial was the next

step, because of what you might call its demonic ingenuity, the cruel sophistry of those who propagate it. For the most part, they *know* it happened (the testimony of apostate neo-Nazi Holocaust deniers confirms this); they're *glad* it happened; they take sick satisfaction in denying it happened only because it offers a novel way to add insult to injury: to murder not just the body but the soul, the memory, of the dead. To become, in effect, accessories after the fact, by the very act of denying the fact.*

But Lang countered with another, more subtle and persuasive argument about the next step in post-Holocaust evil: the evil of equanimity. He cited a monograph he was researching on the postwar writings of Martin Heidegger, the preeminent German philosopher of the twentieth century (subsequently published as *Heidegger's Silence*).

Essentially, Lang said, the Holocaust didn't exist for Heidegger. He didn't *deny* it, but he might as well have: it wasn't a factor in his thought; it did not affect his view of history and human nature, despite the Hitler-friendly spin he gave to his philosophy in order to advance his academic career in the 1930s. After the war, Heidegger was more outspoken about the depredations of mechanized agriculture than he was about the mechanized mass murder that had happened under his nose. It was this . . . *knowing equanimity* that incensed the ordinarily mild-mannered Lang.

"Heidegger knew it happened and he didn't care," Lang said. "His silence—it wasn't even denial. For him, it wasn't *important*!

"It wasn't important," Lang repeated. And then again, "It wasn't important."

His silence wasn't even denial. . . . Already, even in the pre–

---

*I suspect this is why Robert Jan van Pelt, historian of Auschwitz, prefers the term "negationism" to "Holocaust denial." Negationism is a cynical, knowing attempt to erase something that happened, while "denial" pretends to believe it never happened at all.

September 11 period, one could sense a curious kind of back-lash, one might call it, against speaking of the Holocaust. It took various forms. While hard-core Holocaust denial was itself off the grid for most minimally educated people, it was clear that there were some who were tired of being reminded it had happened, some who resented references to it. Some consigned all memorializing to the derisive phrase "Holocaust industry" to deny there could be any good-faith reason for seeking to remember the Holocaust: It was all part of the Zion-ist agenda to exploit Hitler's crime for the supposedly Nazi-like crimes of the State of Israel.

But even among those who didn't use that particular nox-ious phrase "Holocaust industry" (with a not-so-subtle anti-Semitic stereotype of "mercenary Jews" embedded in it) there had evolved a new, more sophisticated way of seeking to ban-ish the Holocaust from contemporary discourse or relevance: the attempt to delegitimize and silence any attempt to assert that there are historical *consequences* to the Final Solution. Con-sequences the Jewish state should take into account in assess-ing the dangers it faces today. The past indifference—if not complicity—of much of the world to Hitler's genocide might for instance be a factor in assessing how much to rely on "in-ternational guarantees" of the Jewish state's safety as opposed to its reliance on active self-defense.

Cynthia Ozick singles out an instance of what you might call "inconsequentialism" when she cites a writer who took Menachem Begin to task for invoking the memory of the mil-lion children murdered during the Holocaust when Begin de-fended the 1981 Israeli destruction of Saddam's Osirak nuclear reactor. A facility clearly intended to produce weaponizable nuclear material for a tyrant who would later threaten to "burn half of Israel." Saddam made that threat during the first Gulf War, and who's to say that if Begin hadn't acted in defiance of world opinion, one of Saddam's Scuds, the ones he fired at Tel Aviv (as well as at American forces in Kuwait), would not have carried nuclear explosives. Should the fact that a previous genocidal threat (Hitler's) was in fact carried out have no consequences, deserve no mention from decision-makers?

Should Begin be shamed posthumously for telling the world one of his motives was, in effect, to save his people and their children from a second Holocaust, for seeking to avoid giving Hitler a posthumous victory?

This is not denial in the usual sense. It doesn't assert the event didn't *happen*. It just denies that it should have an *effect* on how one thinks about history and human nature in general, the fate of the Jewish state and its attempts to defend itself in particular. It is Heidegger's equanimity: It happened but . . . "It wasn't important. It wasn't important."

3) LOOKING AWAY

I'd argue that another distinctive feature of post–9/11 anti-Semitism, in addition to the existential threat, is the recurrence of emblematic moments of Looking—and Looking Away. I know I've been guilty of looking away.

When asked to speak at Jewish institutions such as the Simon Wiesenthal Center, at colleges, synagogues, and shuls on the nature of Hitler's anti-Semitism, I did not focus much on *contemporary* anti-Semitism. With one exception—Holocaust denial—it seemed incommensurable with Hitler's crime. After all, Hitler was history, Hitler was past, Hitler was dead.

And yet some ugly truths were hard to avoid. And writing about the culture of anti-Semitism that helped give license to Hitler clearly sensitized me to the situation in the Middle East. My reaction to one controversy in particular—Netanyahu and "incitement"—was a sign of that change.

Back in 1996, you'll recall, Benjamin Netanyahu, then newly elected Israeli prime minister, came under attack from just about everyone here in America (and on the left in Israel) for his alleged stubbornness in not "moving forward with the peace process." His particular stubbornness was said to consist in his demanding that the Palestinian side live up to its commitment in the Oslo accords to remove references from Palestinian textbooks which incited hatred of Jews and Israel. Everyone, it seemed, wanted Netanyahu to move on—to move forward to the next step in "the process," to give up another chunk of West Bank land to the Palestinian Authority as part of the "land-for-peace" peace process—and ignore the incitement issue, and the Palestinians' failure to address it.

Up till then, I had been a hopeful believer that the Oslo peace process would bring about two states—and peace. But Netanyahu was being portrayed in terms that bordered on ancient Christian anti-Semitic stereotypes. The Jews, in the New Testament, are a stubborn people for not bowing to Jesus as Messiah; Netanyahu was being stubborn for making a fuss over incitement, over the Palestinians' failure to live up to the other, less tangible, side of the "land-for-peace" agreement: peacefulness. He was portrayed as ignoring the Big Picture in favor of—again the shadow of the stereotype was there—Semitic pettifogging.

I found myself surprised to be in agreement with the position of the supposedly stubborn Netanyahu. Anti-Semitic incitement was no minor issue, no window dressing. Incitement to hatred *was* the Big Picture. Anyone who has studied the history of the twentieth century knows that "incitement" is the heart of the matter, the source of the hatred that spills over into mass murder. And incitement of children to hate is even more lasting in its damage. But instead, everyone was telling Netanyahu, essentially: Ignore the incitement, get on with "the process." Look away. We are now witnessing the consequences of ignoring a generation of incitement.

AND THEN THERE WAS the matter of two televisuals: the lynching of two Israeli Jews in Ramallah and the videotaped throat-slitting murder of American Jewish journalist Daniel Pearl in Pakistan. To look, or look away?

In the fall of 2000 I was watching CNN when the footage of the lynching at Ramallah was broadcast. Do you recall? Two Israeli reservists heading home from duty took a wrong turn near that West Bank town. They were seized and taken to the town's Palestinian police headquarters, which was soon surrounded by an angry mob demanding their death. They were slaughtered in an upper room, under the eyes, if not by the hands, of the Palestinian Authority, and then their bodies thrown to the cheering crowd below. Following which their murderers appeared in the upper windows of the killing room and brandished their bloody hands to further cheers.

In some ways I had no choice whether or not to watch the lynching in Ramallah. I would have actively had to switch away from CNN. That was not the case with the Daniel Pearl video. The actual sequence of events in that video is somewhat unclear, but at one point one can see Daniel Pearl telling his captors and their camera: My father is Jewish, my mother is Jewish, I am Jewish. Following which the video presents his throat being slit, his head being severed, the severed head held up by the gloating killer.

When the video subsequently became available on certain websites in the United States, a debate broke out over whether one should watch. Daniel Pearl's wife and parents argued that to watch it was to serve the terrorists' purposes, to become accessories after the fact to murderous terrorist propaganda. On the other hand, many respected figures argued that one must not avoid watching: one has to face the truth of the nature of this hatred. "Truth is more important than taste," *The New Republic* argued in an editorial entitled "The Face of Evil."

"Don't Look Away," Samuel G. Freedman entitled his essay. And while I see his argument, while I tend to *agree* with his argument in the abstract, I have yet to bring myself to watch the video. There is a line in Jonathan Rosen's piece about the "private balancing act" one has to engage in, in this as in all grim realities: "You don't have to read much Freud to discover that the key to a healthy life is the ability to fend off reality to a certain extent. Deny reality too much, of course, and you're crazy; too little and you're merely miserable."

And thus in my private balancing act, I guess, I have looked away from the horrid spectacle of Daniel Pearl's death and dismemberment. In part perhaps because I've spoken on the phone about this question with Daniel Pearl's father, Judea Pearl. Dr. Pearl is a man of extraordinary strength in the face of extraordinary pain, and I felt somehow that to watch his son being slaughtered would be a kind of personal betrayal. But I won't say that's the only reason. The philosopher Berel Lang argues in his book *Holocaust Representation* that there are some aspects of the death camp process that, by an almost universal human consensus, should just not be represented. Or, if they are, not watched. But I'll admit my reluctance is not entirely philosophical; it's part of my "private balancing act."

You'll recall that in the classical myth, those who gazed on the Medusa's head turned to stone. In some respects I think of the savagely severed head of Daniel Pearl as something like the Medusa's head of contemporary anti-Semitism.

So, I understand the reluctance of some to gaze too deeply into such acts of darkness. I've felt it. I just don't think it should become a principle, a general rule.

Looking and looking away. How much does one want—need—to know? I had a curious experience, one I've come to think of as inadvertently emblematic of this dichotomy, in compiling this anthology.

One of the most important and influential, if dispiriting, examples of reporting I read in the months after September 11 was Jeffrey Goldberg's "Behind Mubarak" in *The New Yorker*. It was a courageous piece of reporting in which Goldberg, who did not disguise his Jewishness, walked into mosques, madrasas, and media centers in Cairo and asked mullahs and newspaper columnists to talk about 9/11, America, and the Jews. It was about this time that an influential mullah in Cairo (who was also head of the Islamic Cultural Center in New York City) advanced the claim that the World Trade Center attack was the work of Jews and added, "If it became known to the American people, they would have done to the Jews what Hitler did." He did not make this sound like an unattractive prospect to him.

It was the first instance I'd come across of what began to blossom into a kind of subgenre of radical Islamist rhetorical appeals and encomiums to Hitler. These began to surface in English through the important efforts of the Middle East Media Research Institute. It was an organization founded to promote understanding by translating Arabic media into English. But one of the less savory themes MEMRI* brought to light was a disturbing tendency one could find in Islamist rhetoric: the apostrophe to Hitler.

Goldberg cites one example, a tribute to Hitler written by a columnist in a self-described "very moderate publication" in Cairo: "Thanks to Hitler, of blessed memory, who on behalf of the Palestinians took revenge in advance, against the most vile criminals on the face of the Earth. . . ."

"Revenge in advance": retrospectively "justified" genocide. But he doesn't stop there. He feels Hitler did not do enough: "[W]e do have a complaint against him [Hitler], for his revenge was not enough. . . ." In other words, he failed to kill every single Jew. This, again, in a "moderate" Egyptian newspaper.

This was exceeded in vile ingenuity by another quote from the Egyptian media, courtesy of MEMRI's translation. An-

*www.memri.org/

other kind of complaint against Hitler: "French studies have proven that [the Holocaust] is no more than a fabrication. . . . But I . . . complain to Hitler, even saying to him from the bottom of my heart: 'if only you had done it, brother, if only it had really happened . . . so the world could sigh in relief.'"

"Sigh in relief," knowing all the Jews were dead. A unique and groundbreaking fusion of Holocaust denial and Holocaust craving. Even "mainstream" Holocaust deniers at least publicly imply that the mass murder of Jews would have been a bad thing (otherwise why bother to defend Hitler from the charge?).

But the laments about Hitler's failure to be ruthless enough were not the most disturbing aspect of Goldberg's piece. That honor goes to Mustafa Bakri's dream. Bakri is the editor of another Cairo newspaper, and Goldberg says he had "wanted to meet him for some time, ever since I read a translation of a column in which he described a dream. The dream began with his appointment as one of Ariel Sharon's bodyguards, assigned to protect the Israeli Prime Minister at Cairo's airport [during a state visit], and in the column . . . he wrote:

> The pig landed; his face was diabolical, a murderer; his hands soiled with the blood of women and children. A criminal who should be executed in the town square. Should I remain silent as many others did? Should I guard this butcher on my homeland's soil? All of a sudden, I forgot everything . . . and I decided to do it. I pulled my gun and aimed it at the cowardly pig's head. I emptied all the bullets and screamed. . . . The murderer collapsed under my feet. I breathed a sigh of relief. I realized the meaning of virility, and of self-sacrifice. . . . I stepped on the pig's head with my shoes and screamed from the bottom of my heart: Long live Egypt, long live Palestine, Jerusalem will never die and never will the honor of the nation be lost."

A columnist for an Islamist newspaper in a nation with which Israel is ostensibly at peace. A culture in which such a murderous excrescence is celebrated rather than despised. In which such a "dream" was—it was fairly clear—thinly disguised incitement to *real* Egyptian bodyguards to "realize the meaning of virility" and carry out the assassination Bakri "dreamed."

What made it more disturbing was its metaphoric import: the Jewish state was in effect being asked by the international community to put its trust in the good faith, put its very fate in the hands of "bodyguards" such as this. By "trading land for peace," as they were incessantly being urged to do, they'd be trading defensible borders and, in effect, giving themselves over to "bodyguards" who had not given up dreams like that. Making themselves, making their children's lives, hostage to the "bodyguard" of purported Islamist goodwill.*

Again, Egypt was a land officially "at peace" with Israel. That's why the bodyguard murder-fantasy, that one paragraph in a six-thousand-word *New Yorker* report, touched such a nerve in those of us who had wanted to believe there was a simple, attainable, trustable, *reasonable* solution to the Middle East crisis. That's why it gave one—gave me—such a sense of hopelessness, a profound historical pessimism about the possibility of peace.

But as I said, something curious happened to Bakri's dream, to that single paragraph in its transmission to the world.

In preparing this volume I'd asked a researcher to fax me a copy of Goldberg's *New Yorker* article she had downloaded from the LexisNexis database, the source that most commentators, journalists, and essayists consult, the one that—in practical effect—defines, describes the contours of the public debate on any given issue, internationally.

---

*As Christopher Caldwell put it recently, "Land once ceded is hard to reclaim; peace can be revoked by merely changing one's mind."

As I read over the LexisNexis version of the Goldberg piece for the first time since it came out in *The New Yorker* of October 8, 2001, and came to the portion where Bakri's ugly dream is recounted, I was stunned. It wasn't there anymore. The text came to the place where Goldberg quoted from the dream—"in the column . . . he [Bakri] wrote:"—and after the colon, there was a space break and the text picked up: "Bakri offered me an orange soda. . . ." The existence of the murderous dream from beginning ("The pig landed") to end ("I stepped on the pig's head . . .") was erased.

I called both Goldberg and LexisNexis: neither was aware of the omission. The man at LexisNexis investigated and reported back that it appeared to be a technological glitch, not a deliberate political or ideological erasure. The dream passage was preserved on one *New Yorker* website version of the piece (not the "printer-friendly" one) but *not* on LexisNexis. The LexisNexis man said he believed that because the dream was printed in smaller type in *The New Yorker,* it may have dropped out in the scan that transferred it to the LexisNexis database. So it appears to be an inadvertent omission. Inadvertent, but emblematic of the way that dream of slaughter—and the widespread sentiment it spoke for—had dropped off the scan of discourse on the question.

When I wrote the first draft of this introduction, it had not been restored. Which allowed anyone reading the piece to avoid facing an unsavory truth. Now it's back again on LexisNexis; the murderous dream has been restored, although of course in reality it was never gone.

But the two versions of the Goldberg story, the one with and the one without the dream, represented two versions of the world—two ways of looking at the world, and looking away.

4) SPEAKING ABOUT THE UNSPEAKABLE

Those two ways of looking at the world: I suppose that's what I evoked—even if it wasn't what I set out to do—when I touched off a controversy by putting into print a phrase that some found transgressive, disturbing, and virtually taboo: "a second Holocaust."

I had set out to write something about the revival of European anti-Semitism masquerading as anti-Zionism. The kind of anti-Semitism that could feature a child wearing a mock "suicide-bomber" explosive bandolier in a "peace" march. And the emerging phenomenon of "Holocaust inversion," as Melanie Phillips called it, the pernicious rhetorical device in which Nazi imagery is used to depict Jews. There was Tom Paulin's famous formulation "the Zionist SS"—merely the most egregious. Holocaust inversion took Holocaust denial one step further: the Jews were not victims, not even "fake" victims, as the deniers contended; the Jews were now portrayed as the perpetrators of the kinds of crimes that had been committed against them.

In any case, the fact that I uttered the phrase "second Holocaust" was, in truth, inadvertent, a Web-surfing happenstance. Safe in America, yet suffering with each new report of a "suicide bombing" in Israel, one morning I followed a link from the popular "InstaPundit" website to a site I'd never visited before, one operated by a Canadian political commentator, David Artemiw.

On that day, he happened to quote a deliberately shocking passage from a Philip Roth novel, the 1993 work called *Operation Shylock*. It's a novel that is set mainly in Israel, in 1988, during the first Intifada, and begins with a comic doppelgänger premise that turns—lurches at times—into moments of terrifying seriousness. (And ends in, of all places, the back room of Barney Greengrass.) I don't want to anticipate the excerpt published herein. But in sum, the "real" Philip Roth hears that an impostor calling himself "Philip Roth" is ensconced in the King David Hotel in Jerusalem giving talks about an ideology he calls Diasporism.

This is the belief that exile, Diaspora, the historic dispersion of the Jews, had by that year become a better solution to the problem of Jewish survival than their dangerous "concentration," so to speak, in the State of Israel. "The Diasporist" argues that the in-gathering to Israel, while it served a purpose in the immediate aftermath of the Holocaust, now threatens to lead to an unthinkable catastrophe. Unthinkable but not unspeakable. He speaks it. He calls the dread possibility "a second Holocaust."

The phrase comes in the context of an argument he gets into with the "real" Philip Roth about the danger posed to the Jewish state, not merely from stone-throwing Palestinians but from powerful Islamic states that will someday—a day not too distant—have nuclear weapons. Indeed, Pakistan would soon have the first "Islamic bomb"; Iran was developing missiles with the range to deliver such bombs or hand them off to terrorists.

In fact, when I reread the "second-Holocaust" passage, which Roth wrote in 1992, it was hard not to think of the Iranian leader who (some ten years after Roth wrote the passage) was thinking about the same arithmetic as the Diasporist. In December 2001, Hashemi-Rafsanjani, former president of Iran, gave us an insight into the calculations of mass murder that were going on in certain quarters of the world. He gave a speech in which he estimated that in a nuclear exchange with the State of Israel, Iran might lose fifteen million people, but that would be a sacrifice of fifteen million out of a billion Muslims worldwide. And in return, the five million Jews of Israel would be no more. He seemed pleased with the possibility of such a trade-off (regardless of the cost to Palestinian and Israeli Arabs). Perhaps it was just bluster, but less than a year after that speech, Iran announced that it had missiles capable of reaching Tel Aviv.*

Perhaps that was just bluster as well; nonetheless, Rafsan-

---

*News report, November 21, 2003: "Israeli Deputy Chief of Staff Ashkenazi warns: 'Iranian nuclear threat to Israel is a matter of time.'"

jani was speaking casually of the elimination of the Jewish state and up to five million Jews. The language of extermination— of a second Holocaust—was not entirely new. Indeed, after I'd read and quoted the "second-Holocaust" passage, I recalled a conversation I'd had ten years ago in Jerusalem about the run-up to the Six-Day War with Emil Fackenheim, the late much-admired "theologian of the Holocaust." Fackenheim was describing the apprehension of an existential threat he'd felt at the time of Purim, in April 1967, two months before the outbreak of the war. Purim is a holiday celebrating Jewish deliverance from slaughter, but (as I'd described it in *Explaining Hitler*) with "Nasser about to blockade Israel's ports, a growing threat of a three-front attack to come, with the world indifferent if not hostile, it looked to Fackenheim as if a second Holocaust was in the works."

"That was the crisis," Fackenheim told me, "where I first put forward the 614th commandment," as it has come to be known (an addition to the 613 rules of Jewish orthodoxy): "Jews are forbidden to grant posthumous victories to Hitler." (In a sense, every postwar act of anti-Semitic violence or incitement—or indifference to them—can be considered a posthumous victory for Hitler.)

It was that crisis that prompted Fackenheim, an escapee from Hitler's Sachsenhausen concentration camp, to take an action quite the opposite from Roth's "Diasporist": he left Canada, where he'd been living and teaching since the end of World War II, and went to live in imperiled Jerusalem. Nonetheless, what Fackenheim and the Diasporist (who advocated a reverse migration—the return of European Jews in Israel to their homelands) had in common was a willingness to face the possibility, to think about the unbearable and speak the unspeakable. Here's what Roth's Diasporist said—these are the lines from the novel which I found on David Artemiw's website and quoted in my *New York Observer* column:

The meanings of the Holocaust are for us to determine, but one thing is sure—its meaning will be no less tragic than it is now if there is a second Holocaust and the offspring of the European Jews who evacuated Europe for a seemingly safer haven [Israel] should meet collective annihilation in the Middle East. . . . But a second Holocaust could happen here all too easily, and, if the conflict between Arab and Jew escalates much longer, it will—*it must.* The destruction of Israel in a nuclear exchange is a possibility much less farfetched today than was the Holocaust itself fifty years ago.

"Much less farfetched." Say what you will about the Diasporist's outrageous "solution" to this prospect. Is it in fact utterly "farfetched" *now* to say that a second Holocaust is possible? Not if you listen to the rhetoric in the mosques and media of the Middle East these days.

Reports of Hitler's Final Solution were, of course, considered "farfetched" at the time. Anyone who reads David S. Wyman and Rafael Medoff's heartbreaking book *A Race Against Death,* about the efforts of a small group of Jews to alert the American government to the mass murder being planned and executed in Europe—and the incredulity, obstinacy, and yes, equanimity they found in response—will come to understand that the prospect of a genocide, even as it was happening and as escapees from the death camps were testifying to it, was dismissed as "farfetched," as "atrocity stories," as self-interested propaganda, ethnic special pleading.

As Bill Keller pointed out in a piece in *The New York Times Magazine* (May 26, 2002) about the possibility of terrorist use of nuclear weapons, "The best reason for thinking it won't happen is that it hasn't happened yet, and that is terrible logic." But when something has already happened once, in secrecy, and is now advocated openly, gleefully, it is less improbable that it will happen again. To let the words "second Holocaust" frighten away consideration of a worst-case scenario seems foolish, "terrible logic." The best way to avoid the "worst case" is not to deny it but to study how to prevent it.

Yet the words seemed to be at the heart of the controversy. There were three kinds of reactions to my essay quoting Roth's "Diasporist." Some found merit in my argument that one hidden source of resurgent anti-Semitism in Europe is the burden of guilt Europeans feel about their culture's widespread complicity with the Final Solution.

Another reaction, especially important to me, came from certain Holocaust survivors. Some wrote or called to express relief that someone had raised the issue. Somehow, having faced the abyss once, they tended to be the ones who were unafraid—or perhaps unsurprised—to face the possibility again. They would not look away.

But a more curious reaction was the purported shock and horror at uttering the words "second Holocaust" at all. Obviously I was not the first; nor, it turns out, was Roth. In Michael Oren's important book *Six Days of War,* he speaks, in a postscript interview, of his parents believing back in 1967 that "a second Holocaust was about to occur." Every all-out war poses this threat to the people of Israel.* An existential threat, a "genocidal" threat (Yehuda Bauer's term), a "worst-case scenario"—again, the words are less important than the possibility they describe.

In some respects, I could understand the resistance to the phrase: it was akin to my reaction to the video of Daniel Pearl's murder. I didn't want to watch it. I suspect at some level I was angry not just at those who made it but at those here who made it available: it represented an ugly truth I preferred not to have to gaze at directly. In addition, peremptory rejection of a

---

*It has been said that the Arab states can lose a thousand wars and still survive; Israel will not survive if it loses one.

worst-case scenario gave those who did so the excuse of not having to consider the many less-than-worst-case scenarios—however horrific—and permitted a return to equanimity. (Another evasion was the false identification of Palestinian "suicide bombers," rather than, say, Iranian and Pakistani nukes, as the source of the worst-case threat.)

"Second Holocaust." It was almost as if some numinous taboo had been broken; it was as if it evoked a superstitious dread—that to speak of it was to bring it closer. (Of course silence hadn't done much good for the victims of Hitler's Holocaust.) It violated a comforting precept: that history repeats itself, the first time as tragedy, the second time as farce. It suggests instead: first time tragedy, second time even *worse* tragedy. Or perhaps it was an aspect of the mystification of the Holocaust that removes it from history.

So unwillingness to contemplate an unbearable possibility was understandable, even if it led some to project that fear upon those who spoke of it. Whatever the cause, many found unusual versions of denial when reacting to it. While I have no wish to watch the dismemberment of Daniel Pearl's body, I don't try to deny that it *happened* to Daniel Pearl—or that it's possible something like it could happen again.

It is perhaps an interesting problem in scholastic or Talmudic logic: whether a second Holocaust would in any way be "worse" than Hitler's because of (for want of a better word) its secondness. It wouldn't make a difference to the victims of either one. But it might say something even more unspeakable than we knew, or were willing to admit, about human nature, just as we learned more than we wanted to know from the first one.

Interesting questions, but these weren't the questions raised. Still, I was surprised about the ways in which some chose to avoid the question entirely.

There was what I came to think of as the "displacement

syndrome," for instance. Some sought to avoid considering whether it could happen in the one place it was most likely to happen.

Clearly, in my *Observer* essay, I'd been speaking of the possible consequences of a nuclear exchange, or a nuclear terrorist attack, in the Middle East—on the State of Israel. But when asked to discuss the question on a talk show, I found myself assailed by a leftist critic of the Jewish state, who said I was mistaken to suggest the possibility of a second Holocaust in *Europe*. (After I corrected that rather disingenuous geographical displacement, he later proceeded to astonish me further by claiming that Europeans felt no guilt about complicity in the Holocaust. When I challenged him on *that* assertion, he replied that, well, some European nations, like Portugal, were not complicit. Thank God for the Portuguese!)

So that was the European displacement of the worst-case scenario. Then there was the American displacement. There was, for instance, the implication by a columnist at a New York paper that I was concerned that a second Holocaust might take place in *America*. In July 2002 he wrote a column calling essentially for *more equanimity* among American Jews. He cited some recent survey which showed that the rise in anti-Semitic incidents in the past year *in America* had been relatively small. He cited Leon Wieseltier's May 27, 2002, *New Republic* essay "Against Ethnic Panic: Hitler Is Dead." So American Jews should stop fretting, the columnist lectured us, and not get all *concerned,* like that fellow in the *Observer* who, he left the impression, believed that we were in danger of a second Holocaust *in America*.

It was a variation on the displacement syndrome: displacing the locus of concern about a second Holocaust from Israel, where it might actually happen, to America, where there was no suggestion (not from me) that it would.

All of which allowed him to preserve *his* equanimity—

which, stunningly, seemed to extend to the denial that the nuclear extermination of five million Jews would even *be* a Holocaust. I'm not making this up. After I read his column I called him up, since I'd had lunch with him once, in Jerusalem in fact. It turned out to be a strange conversation, one that revealed an even more desperate desire for equanimity than I could have inferred from his column. It was Holocaust displacement by means of redefinition.

When I questioned him about his characterization of my "second Holocaust" column and went over key passages, he conceded I wasn't suggesting the possibility of a mass murder in America, but in the Middle East, in Israel. But, he added, even if a nuclear weapon was detonated in Tel Aviv, wiping out most of Israel's five million Jews, it would be inaccurate to call this "a Holocaust."

Huh?

That's right, a *true* Holocaust involved "rounding up people," he maintained, the way the Germans did, before killing them. That was the key, he explained to me, the "rounding up." A missile strike or terrorist-nuke scenario would not involve rounding up and therefore could not be called a "Holocaust" no matter how many million Jews it killed. He seemed almost touchingly fixated in an ingenuous way on the notion that the *essence* of a Holocaust was to be found in the "rounding-up" process, not the mass murder to follow. No rounding up, no Holocaust, apparently, no matter how many millions were deliberately murdered.

But isn't the point of a missile strike to kill the maximum number of people without the inconvenience of rounding them up? I asked him, a bit incredulous that he would be advancing this as somehow a consequential distinction.

No, he insisted, a missile strike that wiped out the Jews of Israel wouldn't be a Holocaust; it would be "an act of war." How could he know? A handoff of a nuke to a terrorist group and its detonation wouldn't necessarily be an act of war. It would be an act of terrorism, of deliberate extermination. "Act of war" implies a *response*, at the very least mutual combat. But he was insisting that a nuclear strike on Israel could result only from "an act of war"—implying the mutual tragedy of combat. It was the moral relativism of those who use the phrase "cycle of violence." He was in effect displacing the blame—or at least half of it—to the victims. In any case, it appeared he was more *comfortable* thinking of the death of five million Jews as coming from an "act of war" than from one of those old-fashioned "rounding-up" Holocausts. Equanimity at all costs—even at the cost of intelligibility.

Until that moment I hadn't realized just how frightening the very phrase "second Holocaust" could be. I'm tempted to say superstitious fear of these words was the real "ethnic panic." I dwell on this because it occurred to me that this desperation to avoid conceding that another Holocaust, by any definition, was *ever* possible, even in Israel, was akin to pre–World War II equanimity and denial. The voice of those Jews who urged other Jews to be quiet about reports of death camps in Europe for fear of arousing anti-Semitism here. The mind-set that buried the reports from the death camps on page 12, as Deborah Lipstadt* has demonstrated. Don't be too "ethnic," too ethnically conspicuous. Was the fear of ethnic panic really panic over ethnicity?

Perhaps accusing Jews of ethnic panic may have made the columnist feel more tough-minded, more steady-nerved than all those allegedly panicky Jews whose concerns he dismissed. But I was hearing echoes of the past: the voice of those

---

*Beyond Belief: The American Press and the Coming of the Holocaust, 1933–1945. See also *The Terrible Secret: The Suppression of the Truth About Hitler's Holocaust*, by Walter Laqueur, as well as Wyman and Medoff's *A Race Against Death*. In his new book, *The Return of Anti-Semitism*, Gabriel Schoenfeld calls the phenomenon "anti-Semitism denial."

Jews who were somewhat embarrassed about other Jews' speaking up on behalf of fellow Jews. The journalist Ben Hecht (co-author of *The Front Page*), who worked with Peter Bergson in the early forties to bring Hitler's Holocaust to the attention of the world, wrote bitterly about such behavior. *The New York Times*, to its credit, apologized for not following up on the ominous reports.

Most cruelly—and wrongly—however, this "rounding-up" columnist made those who raised a voice of concern sound as if they were afraid for *themselves* here in America rather than concerned for families in Israel who had to worry when they saw their children go out for a pizza that they might not come back. (Was that ethnic panic?)* His column implied that since American Jews had nothing to fear for *themselves* at this point, why should they get all upset on behalf of the fate of fellow Jews half a world away? (I'm alright, Jack.)

This was one of the earliest manifestations of a phenomenon I've come to think of as "Holocaust shame." It begins with Holocaust inconsequentialism—one shouldn't mention the far, far distant past, in which Hitler murdered six million, in discussing the fate of the five million Jews of Israel. But the columnist— and others who take this line—goes on to try to shame those who *do* refer to the Holocaust for having done so.

Often, the word "shame" in one of its forms is used: as Tony Judt did in an October 23, 2003, *New York Review of Books* piece calling for the dissolution of the Jewish state. American Zionists, Mr. Judt wrote, have "shamefully" exploited the Holocaust in arguing that Israel should be a refuge for Jews.

Leon Wieseltier didn't use the word "shame" in his "Ethnic Panic" essay, but using the word "panic" (and the phrase "the fright of American Jewry" as well) was a similar attempt to

---

*Daniel Gordis's piece captures the emotional reality of those living under this threat.

shame those who believed the past should have admonitory consequences for the present.

I will let readers consider for themselves the differences between me and Wieseltier and between Wieseltier and Ruth R. Wisse on these questions. (I have refrained, out of fairness, from reprinting herein my own June 10, 2002, response to the Wieseltier essay, but those interested can find it on the *Observer* website, at http://observer.com/pages/story.asp?ID=5949.)

Nonetheless, I've come to feel that "the second-Holocaust debate," as it's been called, raised an important question: how much weight *should* be given to the Holocaust in influencing the policy of the Jewish state—and the world's opinion of that policy?

To some, no Hitler and Holocaust comparisons are allowed. It happened, but it shouldn't have any policy implications. Arab media could laud Hitler and the Holocaust (when they weren't trying to deny it happened), but Jews in Israel should not take it into account when deciding on measures of self-preservation.

And was it true that "Hitler is dead"? Not in Islamist media. Was the re-legitimization of Hitler by prominent voices in the Middle East something to be dismissed as merely trivial, then? Ruth Wisse makes the point that in certain crucial ways the hatred in the Middle East for Israel, for Jews, for the Jewish state, is far *worse* than the hatred that preceded and made possible Hitler's genocide.

For one thing, Hitler never advertised, never boasted about, and never celebrated his mass murder of Jews. He broadcast his *hatred*, but he did not broadcast the ongoing extermination process. In fact he took pains to distance himself from the death camps. To carry on the killing process in great secrecy and official denial. Hitler was, as I pointed out in my book, the first Holocaust denier.*

---

*See Hitler's "Table Talk," October 24, 1941.

But today in the Middle East, Hitler's mass murder of Jews is publicly celebrated by some, and a second mass murder openly sought by others. Today in the Middle East the murder of Jews by a "suicide bomber" is marked by parties for the families who receive blood-money bonuses for their child's hideous act. It is not just an individual act of fanaticism spurred by the false promise of paradise, it is a practice backed by an entire culture.

How much *should* the Holocaust be used as a rationale for a Jewish state's existence, for its attempts at self-defense? It would seem that self-defense by any people is a legitimate goal, whether they've had a Holocaust in the past or not.

But to ignore that particular past is, to say the least, difficult. Of course it is possible to make too much of the Holocaust in the sense of sacralizing and mystifying it. Making it an event beyond all comparison, Jonathan Rosen has suggested, removes it from history almost as effectively as the Holocaust deniers.* This may be the source of the misconception of those who believe no Hitler comparisons should be allowed; Hitler is dead, there will never come another one in the same category of evil as Hitler, and therefore we can learn no lessons, make no contemporary comparisons to Hitler and his Holocaust—they must inevitably be disproportionate with the graven image of evil some turn Hitler into. A mystifying inversion of worship.

But there *are* lessons to be learned from Hitler and the Holocaust. Some of them are just common sense. In the *Observer* essay that initiated the controversy, I cited the old proverb "Fool me once, your fault. Fool me twice, my fault." In other words, Jews had been told to remain calm once before—not to "panic," not to escape Germany, say, because Hitler was noth-

---

*See Yehuda Bauer's important challenge to the "mystifiers" in "Is the Holocaust Explicable?," originally published in the journal *Holocaust and Genocide Studies* and reprinted in *Rethinking the Holocaust,* Yale University Press, 2001.

ing new; Jews had lived through anti-Semitic regimes before. Jews in America were told by some of their fellow Jews not to make too much fuss about Jews in Europe in the years before (and during) the Final Solution. Not to make themselves conspicuously "ethnic" by expressing alarm. This turned out to be terribly wrong. (Fool me once, your fault.)

Today Jews are being told not to get alarmed, because "ethnic panic" will "undermine a political solution," undermine the trust they are asked to place in the benign intent of regimes and societies that promote the spread of Hitlerian rhetoric and celebrate the massacre of Jewish children.

They're being told they must trust, otherwise they'll be called "unreasonable." They're being asked (after making unprecedented negotiating concessions) to ignore subsequent years of mass murder of their children and look to the good faith of their "negotiating partners" to shift from subsidizing suicide killers of Jews to ensuring the safety of Jews. (Fool me twice, my fault.)

5) INTENT AND EFFECT

To return to the question of the weight of the Holocaust, I'd argue that in fact it has *not* been overemphasized. It may have been over-mystified, perhaps over-museumized, but its significance to our estimation of the dark potential of human nature and the merciless, unredemptive processes of history has only *begun* to be taken into account. As George Steiner put it in an interview for my Hitler book, the Holocaust "removed the reinsurance on human hope." Tore away the safety net beneath which our estimates of human nature's lowest depths had not previously plunged.

I think this helps explain something else relatively new in what has been called the new anti-Semitism: the recent shift of anti-Semitism from Right to Left. The Left, for one thing, may have put its faith too blindly in an optimistic view of the power of Reason in human nature, one that looks away from those depths.

This shift was the not-so-buried implication of the warning that Lawrence Summers delivered in September 2002 to the Harvard community in now-famous remarks he made at Memorial Chapel.

Summers was reacting to an accumulation of incidents in the year since 9/11. Not just synagogue burnings in Europe or the "suicide bombings" in Israel but disturbing developments in some left-wing rhetoric here in America. Chiefly on campuses, in the "Israel divestiture" movement, for instance, which seeks to delegitimize (as well as disinvest from) Israel. It was there as well in the "anti-globalist" and "peace" demonstrations that, after 9/11, prominently featured anti-Israel, anti-Zionist, and sometimes anti-Semitic rhetoric and imagery.

What Summers focused on was not just that a point had been reached at which anti-Zionism tipped over into anti-Semitism, but that it came from an unexpected place. He defined himself as not an alarmist, not a victim of "ethnic panic," so to speak, described himself as not the kind of person who hears "the sound of breaking glass," of *Kristallnacht,* in every insult or slight to Jews.

Nonetheless, he said, he felt compelled to sound an alarm:

"[W]here anti-Semitism and views that are profoundly anti-Israel have traditionally been the primary preserve of poorly educated right-wing populaces, profoundly anti-Israel views are increasingly finding support in progressive intellectual communities. Serious and thoughtful people are advocating and taking actions that are anti-Semitic in their effect if not intent." The perception of a new anti-Semitism, he continued, is "less alarmist in the world of today than [in the world of a] year ago."

It is that phrase—anti-Semitic in "effect if not intent"— that may have been even more provocative than his description of the shift from Right to Left in the debate that followed.

It spoke to the question of when anti-Zionism became anti-Semitism.

"Effect if not intent . . ." I believe it's clear what Summers was trying to say. The effect/intent relationship was elucidated this way by the British historian Peter Pulzer:* Some anti-Zionists deny their *intent* is anti-Semitic, and are thus heedless of the *effect* of their double standard in singling out the Jewish state for human rights opprobrium ignored elsewhere. "Effect simply consists," Pulzer wrote, "ultimately of the resurfacing of the underground repertoire of anti-Jewish stereotypes, instinctively understood by both the utterer and their recipient." Effect was evident in indisputably anti-Semitic incidents growing out of "anti-Zionist" activism on American campuses such as those reported on by eyewitnesses such as Dr. Laurie Zoloth at San Francisco State and Eli Muller at Yale.

I'd tend to agree with Pulzer. Purportedly "anti-Zionist" criticism of Israel increasingly couched in the rhetoric of ancient anti-Semitic stereotypes—"grasping" Jews, hook-nosed caricatures of money-grubbing Jews—is not mere anti-Zionism. Consider the cartoon that appeared in the *Chicago Tribune* in 2003 that featured Ariel Sharon crossing a bridge labeled "peace" *only* because the bridge had been "baited," so to speak, with dollar signs (symbolizing U.S. subsidies). That would surely persuade the stiff-necked but money-grubbing Jew Sharon (drawn with an exaggeratedly hooklike beak for a nose) to be reasonable! I think one can safely say this is no longer simple anti-Zionism. Whatever the "intent," the effect is anti-Semitic.†
It is here that one finds special relevance in Berel Lang's reflec-

---

*In an important British anthology called *A New Anti-Semitism? Debating Judeophobia in 21st-Century Britain* (ed. by Paul Iganski and Barry Kosmin), the source of Jonathan Freedland's essay.

†In November 2003 the U.K. Political Cartoon Society gave its annual first prize to a depiction (in *The Independent*) of a bloodthirsty Ariel Sharon biting off the bloody head of a Palestinian child. "Mere" anti-Zionism or repulsive anti-Semitism?

tions on the very popular defense that denying one is anti-Semitic proves that one *can't* be anti-Semitic.

But to return to the question of the shift in the locus of anti-Semitism from Right to Left, I don't mean to imply that more traditional right-wing anti-Semitism has evaporated. There are of course old-fashioned white racists and neo-Nazis scattered throughout the Western world. As Andrew Sullivan put it, "It's important to realize that old far-Right anti-Semitism has not been replaced by the new far-Left variety. Just supplemented." One can find it among some "paleoconservatives," as they're called. And while there is some reason to welcome the apparent philo-Semitism of the fundamentalist movement in America, there is also some reason for concern about the doctrine beneath some of the philo-Semitism: the belief in the ultimate conversion, or self-erasure, of the Jews in the eschatology of the Last Days.

But the appearance of anti-Semitism on the Left is, at least on the surface, paradoxical. The Left is, or was supposed to be, about Tolerance, against prejudice, the friend of the Jews (or, as the more cynical have said, on the side of the Jews as long as they were victims). Many Jews, including to some extent myself, saw democratic socialism as embodying some of the ethical spirit of Judaism's prophets and sages.

But there is another side to the Left's relationship to Judaism. Something that became apparent in that year 2002 when some icons of the Left, such as Naomi Klein and Todd Gitlin, felt compelled to speak out about it, sought to separate the Left from "the socialism of fools," as anti-Semitism has been called.*

There were those who argued that in some ways anti-

---

*I had sought to reprint herein the whole text of Ms. Klein's important caution to the Left, about "all the recent events I've gone to where anti-Muslim violence was rightly condemned, but no mention made about attacks on Jewish synagogues, cemeteries and community centers," but permission was not granted.

Semitism found a *natural home* on the Left. At the heart of that argument was the notion of Reason. The Left's Enlightenment faith in human perfectibility had replaced God with an almost religious faith in Reason. And (as the writer David Samuels suggested to me) for the first Enlightenment philosophers, such as the notoriously anti-Semitic Voltaire, religion represented un-Reason, and Jewishness was the fount of all religion and thus of all un-Reason.

Paul Berman put the Left's devotion to Reason at the heart of his analysis of the double standard the Left applied to the "suicide bombings" in Israel. Deploring them, of course (with some exceptions), but always with a "but": *but* they are understandable in some way. They *must* be. And to understand all is to forgive all, we're told by Enlightenment *philosophes.*

What Berman argued was that, confronted with a "suicide bomber" blowing himself and dozens of men, women, and children to bits, the Left in effect could not look directly at the act, because it's so unbearable, because to take it all in might lead to admitting that some things can't be contained or explained within the framework of Reason—especially murderous religious fanaticism. That not all problems are soluble. That some, history suggests, are ineluctably tragic. Left theories of history, from Whig Progressivism to Marxist dialectical materialism, tend to lack a tragic sense of life—and of history.

And so one saw variations on "looking away" again—explaining it, distancing it, "contextualizing" it with "reasons." This accomplished two goals: first, it removed the element of unreason from the "suicide bomber's" act itself. Made it "understandable" in both senses of the word. And second, it allowed a shift of blame to the victims of the blast. Made them part of the oppressive hegemony that in some abstract—horribly abstract—way "deserved it." Thus, there *was* Reason behind their death. Thus, there *was* a measure of justice to it. As there was to those who responded to the attacks of September 11 by saying, in one way or another, "Sorry about the three thousand dead, but America had it coming," or, alternately, "America needed the lesson."

Another, deeper connection of the Left to anti-Semitism is to be found in Marxism itself. I'm not the first to point out that much Marxist imagery is a kind of universalized version of anti-Semitic imagery. The greedy capitalist is substituted for the greedy Jew, the suffering proletariat for the suffering Jesus scourged by Jews. The promised Marxist future dissolution of the state and universal peace, once the exploiter (read, Jewish) class is eliminated, is substituted for the promise of Heaven for the Elect.

In fact I'd suggest there is a darker element in some of the Left's willingness to demonize Israel. It has to do with a different kind of denial, not the neo-Nazi Holocaust denial but the denial of—and then the equanimity about—the *Marxist* holocausts of the twentieth century. The reaction—or lack of reaction—to the emerging evidence for mass murders in the millions in Stalin's Russia, in Mao's China, in somewhat lesser numbers (but greater percentage of the population) in Pol Pot's Cambodia. None of which has resulted in many on the Left questioning whether there might be some *connection* between Marxist ideology and the frequency of mass murder in Marxist regimes. Well, they're not *really* Marxist regimes—they weren't doing Marxism *right,* some will say. Or even if there were mass murders, they came from *good intentions,* utopian aspirations that somehow seemed to go awry—so it's not like Hitler's mass murder at all.

Well, there are certainly differences. But the Heideggerian equanimity, the deafening silence, the lack of outrage of much of the Left about the mass murders and the gulags in Marxist regimes—during *and* after—has its most practical and disheartening effect in the way it has not succeeded in altering the long-standing *corollary* perception on the Left that the locus of greatest evil in recent history is the United States. Only by ig-noring Marxist genocides can one come to this conclusion.*

U.S. allies, such as Israel, thus tend to be judged by the same a priori prejudice, as agents of intrinsically evil American impe-rialism. So anti-Zionism, along with the anti-Semitism it en-courages or shades into, is, in some instances, a derivative of a kind of ahistorical, knee-jerk Left anti-Americanism which ig-nores Marxist genocides and still views the United States as *the* evil empire—and lacks the willingness to question judgments that proceed from that. Such as the Left judgment on Israel.

I was particularly impressed by the analysis of the anti-Semitism of the Left by Melanie Phillips in London's *Spectator*. She suggests an even deeper, more provocative source of Left anti-Semitism, one elucidated by a Polish intellectual at a Jeru-salem conference who argued: "The Left could not face the fact that they had totally misconstrued the Middle East because this would undermine their whole philosophy . . . founded on the premise that reason could reconcile all differences; all that was needed in Israel was an enlightened government for reason to prevail. The evidence that we are facing a phenomenon which is not susceptible to reason would destroy that world view."

Whether you agree or not with this take on the subject, it has become apparent to me that Reason, reasonableness, un-reasonableness, and how they're defined are central to the argument over what is mere anti-Zionism and what is anti-Semitism. To many anti-Zionists, there can be no *reasonable* explanation for Israelis' "unreasonableness"—their unwilling-

---

*This enrages certain figures on the Left, whose most fervent political belief seems to be that they've always been *right*, ever since, as undergraduates, they accepted Marxism as a "science of history," and see no need to reexamine this premise as more genocidal history emerges. There are some, however, such as Tony Judt, who *will* concede that such history is "the demon in the family closet of the Left." It's no accident that Harvey Klehr and John Earl Haynes call their account of the re-sponse of Left academics to Marxist genocide *In Denial*. They could have called it *It Wasn't Important*.

ness to trust the 300 million Muslims surrounding them—except for some unreasonable stiff-necked character apparently intrinsic to Jewish nature. Or a malign Jewish disposition to torment those who share their land. Thus anti-Zionism elides into anti-Semitism. To me the most pernicious implication of some anti-Zionists, the heart of anti-Zionist anti-Semitism, is in the implication that, somehow, malevolent Jews enjoy imposing an occupation with its attendant restrictions and suffering on Palestinians. Jews want to live in peace, but three wars in which Arab states tried to drive them into the sea, and a terror campaign by Palestinians who reject the idea of a Jewish state, have left Israelis with the tragic choice between self-defense and self-destruction. The root cause of Palestinian suffering has been the rejection by Arab and Palestinian leadership of the Jewish state's right to exist at all.

To many Israelis and many Jews, their people are asked to be "reasonable" under a definition of "reasonableness" that once again puts the existence of their state, of their people, in peril. This is why Amos Oz's essay is so important. Important because, however brief, it appeared in a Left publication such as *The Nation*.

It is, in fact, the shortest piece in this collection, but it says something very significant, from a very significant standpoint. Oz, the celebrated Israeli novelist, has been well known as a founder of Peace Now. And while he still supports the Palestinian right to statehood and has opposed the occupation and the Jewish settlements in the disputed territories, he recognizes that things have changed. That one can't just look narrowly at Israel, Palestine, and the lovely vision of a two-state solution in isolation.

Rather, Oz writes that one must take into account the war "waged by fanatical Islam from Iran to Gaza and from Lebanon to Ramallah, to destroy Israel and drive the Jews out of their land."

He then asks the difficult question that goes to the heart of the "reasonableness" issue, the issue that is itself at the heart of the mutation of anti-Zionism into anti-Semitism. This is Amos Oz's question: "[W]ould an end to occupation [of the West Bank] terminate the Muslim holy war against Israel?"

His answer: "This is hard to predict. If jihad comes to an end, both sides would be able to sit down and negotiate peace. If it does not, we would have to seal and fortify Israel's logical border, the demographic border, and keep fighting for our lives against fanatical Islam." (This is why the discussion of the origin and reformability of Muslim anti-Semitism, engaged in here by Bernard Lewis and Tariq Ramadan, is so important: is jihad against unbelievers intrinsic to Islam?)

Here are Amos Oz's final words: "If, despite simplistic visions, the end of occupation will not result in peace, at least we will have one war to fight rather than two. Not a war for our full occupancy of the holy land, but a war for our right to live in a free and sovereign Jewish state in part of that land. A just war, a no-alternative war. A war we will win. Like any people who were ever forced to fight for their very homes and freedom and lives."

I wish I could share his optimistic certainty about the outcome of such a war. But what is most important is that Oz doesn't look away from the harsh reality shadowing the easy talk of a reasonable "two-state" solution: the holy war against Jews.

AFTER NEARLY TWO DECADES of reading the literature of anti-Semitism—both the thing itself and the analysis of the thing itself—I have yet to find a satisfactory explanation for its persistence. Not a single-pointed answer, anyway. In *Explaining Hitler* I explored theological anti-Semitism with Hyam Maccoby, who believes it is not so much the Christ-killing accusation that kept the flame of Christian anti-Semitism burning—although it certainly has been a factor—but the more insidious

Judas story, the Jew as betrayer and backstabber. (Hitler rode to power on the fraudulent "stab-in-the-back" myth, the one that had the supposedly near-victorious German armies in World War I stabbed in the back by Jewish Marxist Judases on the home front.)

I've explored Daniel Goldhagen's belief in the primacy of what he calls "eliminationist" anti-Semitism, the racially rather than religiously based anti-Semitism that arose in nineteenth-century Germany and helped mold Hitler. There's truth there as well. As there is in Saul Friedlander's contention that Wagner's fusion of religious *and* racial anti-Semitism was crucial in shaping Hitler's psyche.

But why the always ready market for anti-Semitism, religious and racial, medieval and modern, and now postmodern?* I gave respectful if skeptical attention to George Steiner's view that the world continues to hate the Jews for their "invention of conscience"—for what Steiner calls the Jews' threefold "blackmail of transcendence." Which is how Steiner characterizes Moses's demand for perfect obedience, Jesus's demand for perfect love, and Marx's demand for perfect justice. Three demands for perfection made by Jews that are unfulfillable by fallible human beings—and thus, Steiner believes, the source of bitter and recurrent resentment toward the people who dreamed up these impossible demands. As I suggested, this can, even if it's not intended to, devolve into a blame-the-victims argument.

Others say it's because Jews have long chosen to be "a

---

*Could it be, as one of Roth's characters suggests in *Operation Shylock,* that a better model for anti-Semitism than template or virus might be alcoholism, which has components of organic disease and psychological syndrome? (You can see it in the way some anti-Semites literally seem to get drunk on their hatred.) Roth offers (apparently) in jest one character's notion that the only way anti-Semitism can be cured is by a quintessentially modern self-help solution: the twelve-step program. And he gives us, in the novel, the steps he suggests for "Anti-Semites Anonymous." Step One: "We admit that we are haters and that hatred has ruined our lives." If only.

people apart," with an unwillingess to assimilate or submerge their identity in modernity's universalism. Others maintain it was the Jews' *invention* of modernity. The explanations multiply and contradict one another.

And perhaps—and this might sound at first like a radical suggestion—*it doesn't matter anymore.* The reasons, the origins, no longer matter. At this point anti-Semitism has become so embedded in history, or in sub-history, the subterranean history and mythology of hatred, that it will always be there, a template for whatever hurts need to find an easy answer, a simple-minded balm: the Jews are responsible. The explanation of renewed anti-Semitism is anti-Semitism: its ineradicable pre-existing history—and its efficacy. It has become its own origin.

What is to be done? One answer was suggested by Leon Wieseltier at a conference he helped organize under the auspices of YIVO, the New York–based Jewish cultural institution, in May 2003. The conference was called "Old Demons, New Debates: Anti-Semitism in the West," so apparently it was now no longer panicky to speak of such matters. And it brought together an impressive group of speakers.

In any case, although out of town at that time I was impressed by the tape I later heard of the opening address by Wieseltier. He said a number of very important things, I thought. Some had been said before by others, but he said them especially well.

One important thing he said is that those who consider that anti-Semitism is a problem only for Jews ought to reconsider: "If anti-Semitism is to vanish from the earth it will be from the transformation of non-Jewish rather than Jewish [peoples]. . . . In this sense it is not a Jewish problem at all . . . it is a prejudice whose object is not its cause . . . if you wish to study racism, study whites, not blacks." But he also said that the struggle against anti-Semitism is "a requirement of self-interest and of dignity" for Jews.

I'm pleased to cede virtually the last word in this essay to the "Ethnic Panic" author, because it seemed to me he had learned much from the events of the year that followed his "Ethnic Panic" polemic—and perhaps from Ruth Wisse's critique of it.*

But I wouldn't say all non-Jews have abandoned that responsibility Leon Wieseltier spoke of, for anti-Semitism in our culture. I have been impressed by the seriousness with which some Christians and Muslims have addressed the question. Andrew Sullivan's "Anti-Semitism Watch" on his weblog has been invaluable in spotlighting shameful incidents. As has Glenn Reynolds's "InstaPundit" website and Jeff Jarvis's "buzzmachine." So have George Will's columns and commentaries, and those of Stanley Crouch and Christopher Caldwell. Harold Evans and Oriana Fallaci were early and important voices. I'm sure there are more Christians on the Left who have spoken out, even if for some reason none come instantly to mind. (Unless you count Christopher Hitchens, who, while half Jewish—and only half Leftist now according to the more rigid ideologues—deserves credit for popularizing a brilliantly compressed polemical coinage for Jew-hating Middle Eastern terrorists: "Islamo-fascists." As in, isn't the Left supposed to *oppose* fascism?)

But to return to the question of optimism I first raised in regard to Amos Oz. I wish I could find an upbeat way of concluding this essay. As I write this draft, two Turkish synagogues and a Jewish school in France have just been bombed. The world is discussing whether the pronouncements of the retiring Malaysian prime minister that Jews rule the world is more than "merely anti-Semitic" but somehow a voice for reform in the Islamic world.

---

*And Wieseltier's dissection (in the October 27, 2003, issue of *The New Republic*) of Tony Judt's proposal, in *The New York Review of Books,* to dismantle the Jewish state was Wieseltier at his best.

And a new cinematic version of the Passion Play, the depiction of the Gospel story of the death of Jesus, is upon us. By an auteur who claims he is not making a movie so much as presenting "history." Perhaps it is history, perhaps not; there seems a certain amount of disagreement even among Christians, even among the Gospels, as to what is or what isn't "history." But Mel Gibson thinks he knows.

But still, I was surprised by the savagery of his attack on Frank Rich for raising questions about the project. "I want to kill him," taken alone, might be angry hyperbole, but the primitive specificity of "I want his intestines on a stake," particularly in this context, could not help but recall the New Testament image of the death of Judas, who, in one Gospel at least, is depicted, after betraying Jesus, as taking a violent fall and literally spilling his intestines in what is later called a "field of blood." The wish to see Rich's "intestines on a stake" sounds to me like more than an accidental coincidence of imagery.

Rich's response was both deft and dignified, but why the lack of outrage from others? A death threat, however rhetorical, because a Jew raised questions about a movie about the death of Jesus? Has the rhetorical bar been lowered that far?

History. One thing that is history—undeniable, documented, bloodstained history—is the effect if not the intent of the Passion Play in the past. For those unfamiliar with these effects, I recommend the scholar James Shapiro's book *Oberammergau: The Troubling Story of the World's Most Famous Passion Play.* The deicide—or "Christ-killer—accusation lives to incite anew, in effect if not intent.

Once, I actually attended a Passion Play, the surprisingly elaborately mounted "Passion Play of the Ozarks" presented by the Christ of the Ozarks theme park in Eureka Springs, Arkansas. In addition to boasting it had the tallest statue of Jesus in the Northern Hemisphere, the theme park featured many miniature Shetland ponies that were the favorite of Gerald L. K.

Smith, the anti-Semitic demagogue who founded the Christ of the Ozarks project and peddled his anti-Jewish propaganda through its gift store.

Smith had enjoyed some success as a "populist" acolyte of Huey Long after Long died. Populism turned to anti-Semitism, and watching the Passion Play, one could understand his enthusiasm for it.

For those wondering what I was doing there, it was the early 1980s and I had an idea for a novel (which I never wrote) in which the Passion Play of the Ozarks would be a setting. So it was "material" in a sense, and perhaps it's changed since then, but I found it discomfiting to watch the Passion Play, with its black-bearded Jewish caricatures in villainous makeup and sinister black robes scheming with Judas to get Christ killed through betrayal. It wasn't presented as "history" so much as the Gospel Truth.

I'm sorry for the digression. The question I was addressing —or avoiding—was optimism. As in: any hope for it? I'll admit I'm not constitutionally predisposed to optimism. The study of modern history is not a source of optimism.* At the very least, though, I'm the sort of pessimist who seeks out sources of hope. This is something I did when I was preparing to give a talk on contemporary anti-Semitism—that fill-in talk for Jonathan Rosen in fact (to bring things full circle). I e-mailed Ruth Wisse at Harvard, where she is a professor of literature, and asked her if she saw any basis for hope for the situation in Israel. She replied that a distinction must be made between false hope and real hope. That false hope means trusting sworn enemies for your security. That for true hope, one has to draw faith from the continued survival of the Jewish people for three

---

*The single most pessimistic remark on this subject may be the one uttered by the Max von Sydow character in *Hannah and Her Sisters*. Denouncing Holocaust documentaries on TV, he says, "Given what people are, the question is: Why doesn't it happen more *often*? Of course it does, in subtler forms."

millennia despite anti-Semitism. From their continuing determination to fight for their survival, and not hide their faces from the truth.

I do not suggest that the truth will set us free from anti-Semitism; perhaps nothing will. But there are a couple of glimmers of hope, even to this pessimist. First is the fact that people are no longer denying there's cause for concern. In addition to Leon Wieseltier's YIVO conference, there was the turnabout of *New York* magazine, which, in that spring of 2002, when some people were speaking out, published a piece by Amy Wilentz that looked down its nose at those who did. A year and a half later, the same magazine published a cover story, "The New Face of Anti-Semitism," which was subtitled "In much of the world, hating the Jews has become politically correct. How did this happen?" In addition, there were books by Phyllis Chesler, Alan Dershowitz, Abraham Foxman, Kenneth Timmerman, and Gabriel Schoenfeld which sounded an alarm. (Readers are entitled to ask why is this book different from all those other books, and I'd suggest that, while I certainly have a point of view, I wanted to include a multiplicity of perspectives, some of them clashing, on the questions within the question of anti-Semitism. That and also the presence of Cynthia Ozick, who writes on this subject with the incandescent clarity of a biblical prophet.)

But perhaps the most surprising suggestion of an optimistic development in the situation itself (as opposed to the kind of attention paid to it) could be found in a May 7, 2003, article by Yigal Carmon, the founder of MEMRI, the Middle East Media Research Institute, in Washington. It's a report entitled "Harbingers of Change in the Anti-Semitic Discourse of the Arab World."

It's a startling document* because it suggests that the light

---

*The whole text will appear in a forthcoming MEMRI anthology.

MEMRI has thrown on the dark utterances of the most extreme Islamist anti-Semites is actually having some effect: causing *some* of the more responsible intellectuals, commentators, and political figures in the Arab Middle East to condemn the worst excrescences of such rhetoric as embarrassments to the image of Islam in the civilized world.

Carmon cites the following four developments:

- "Calls to Cancel the Beirut Holocaust Deniers' Conference": The conference "is, in effect, a conference against the truth," a columnist in *Al-Hayat*, a London-based Arabic language paper, said scornfully. "This is a conference against consciousness."
- "Saudi Editor Apologizes for Publishing Blood Libel": The editor of the Saudi government paper *Al-Riyadh* apologized for publishing "an idiotic and false news item regarding the use of human blood" in Jewish religious rituals, a practice that "does not exist in the world at all."
- "Criticism of Anti-Semitic Series [on *The Protocols of the Elders of Zion*] on Egyptian Television": The secretary-general of the Palestinian Ministry called the *Protocols* "a stupid pamphlet full of nonsense," and important Egyptian government officials called the *Protocols* "a fabrication," "an example of racist literature and hate literature."
- "A New Recommendation by Al-Azhar [University Institute for Islamic Research]: Stop Calling Jews 'Apes and Pigs.'"

"It appears," Carmon writes, "that the increase in anti-Semitic propaganda in the Arab media since the beginning of the al-Aqsa Intifada . . . has led some Arab intellectuals to rethink the matter and reject anti-Semitic statements."

While some of this may stem from opportunistic concerns about image, even such concern is a cause for some tempered optimism.* Calling attention to this kind of incitement—facing rather than denying it—might help forestall it. It's too early to hope such a process might work, considering the crude and savage incitement of radical Islamist anti-Semitism. But the MEMRI report suggests that *memory*—not dismissing the phenomenon, not looking away out of some exaggerated panic over "panic"—might be at least a source of some hopeful change.

So any optimism I can muster comes from those who do face the facts and fight the good fight: the translators at MEMRI; those dedicated souls at the Anti-Defamation League, at CAMERA, and at the Simon Wiesenthal Center, among others, who deal with the depressing day-to-day reality of anti-Semitism; intrepid reporters such as Jeffrey Goldberg; weblist media critics like Tom Gross; brave local cops like the one in the Paris *banlieue*s that Marie Brenner chronicles; "bloggers" like Meryl Yourish, Jeff Jarvis, and Roger Simon, to name a few; the "Exposing the Exposer" website guys Zachary and Mo; non-Jews such as Oriana Fallaci and Harold Evans who speak out because they understand that anti-Semitism *is* a problem of and for non-Jews as well. All people who refuse to look away. All people who believe that facing the threat directly will make a difference. I hope they're right.

As Lawrence Summers put it: "I would like nothing more than to be wrong. It is my greatest hope and prayer that the idea of a rise of anti-Semitism proves to be a self-denying prophecy—a prediction that carries the seeds of its own falsification. But that depends on all of us."

No more posthumous victories for Hitler.

January 5, 2004

---

*Well-tempered optimism, alas. The morning I first reviewed this draft, a report appeared in *The New York Sun*, which described the dramatic depiction of the ritual-murder "blood libel" on Hizbollah TV, based in Lebanon, broadcast throughout the Arab world. The drama depicted "the murder of a 12-year-old Christian boy to make the unleavened bread" for a Jewish ritual.

POSTSCRIPT

I can't resist making note of a remarkable essay that appeared after the bound galleys of this book went to press: one by Holocaust scholar Omer Bartov, in the February 2, 2004, issue of *The New Republic*. It was a review of Hitler's so-called second book, the one he wrote after *Mein Kampf* but decided not to publish. Bartov's review was entitled "He [Hitler] Meant What He Said." And speaking of contemporary Jew-haters, Bartov added, "These are people who mean what they say." In other words, when terrorist groups use exterminationist rhetoric, we must face the possibility that they are not just making idle threats. As Bartov says, "There are precedents for this." On the cover of *The New Republic,* the Bartov essay was billed as "Hitler Is Dead, Hitlerism Lives On." My point exactly. Those who forget the past . . .

February 5, 2004

PART ONE

AWAKENINGS

JONATHAN ROSEN

The Uncomfortable Question
of Anti-Semitism

WHEN I WAS GROWING UP, my father would go to bed
with a transistor radio set to an all-news station. Even
without a radio, my father was attuned to the menace of history. A Jew born in Vienna in 1924, he fled his homeland in
1938; his parents were killed in the Holocaust. I sometimes
imagined my father was listening for some repetition of past
evils so that he could rectify old responses, but he may just
have been expecting more bad news. In any event, the grum-
bling static from the bedroom depressed me, and I vowed to
replace it with music more cheerfully in tune with America.
These days, however, I find myself on my father's frequency.
I have awakened to anti-Semitism.

I am not being chased down alleyways and called a Christ
killer, I do not feel that prejudicial hiring practices will keep me
out of a job, and I am not afraid that the police will come and
take away my family. I am, in fact, more grateful than ever that
my father found refuge in this country. But in recent weeks I
have been reminded, in ways too plentiful to ignore, about the
role Jews play in the fantasy life of the world. Jews were not the
cause of World War II, but they were at the metaphysical center of that conflict nonetheless, since the Holocaust was part of

Hitler's agenda and a key motivation of his campaign. Jews are not the cause of World War III, if that's what we are facing, but they have been placed at the center of it in mysterious and disturbing ways.

I was born in 1963, a generation removed and an ocean away from the destruction of European Jewry. My mother was born here, so there was always half the family that breathed in the easy air of postwar America. You don't have to read a lot of Freud to discover that the key to a healthy life is the ability to fend off reality to a certain extent. Deny reality too much, of course, and you're crazy; too little and you're merely miserable. My own private balancing act has involved acknowledging the fate of my murdered grandparents and trying to live a modern American life. I studied English literature in college and in graduate school, where I toyed with a dissertation on Milton, a Christian concerned with justifying the ways of God to man. I dropped out of graduate school to become a writer, but I always felt about my life in America what Milton says of Adam and Eve entering exile—the world was all before me.

Living in New York, pursuing my writing life, I had the world forever all before me. I chose within it—I married and had a child. For ten years I worked at a Jewish newspaper. But my sense of endless American possibility never left me—even working at a Jewish newspaper seemed a paradoxical assertion of American comfort. My father's refugee sense of the world was something that both informed me and that I worked to define myself against. I felt it was an act of mental health to recognize that his world was not my world and that his fears were the product of an experience alien to me. I was critical of the Holocaust Museum in Washington. I didn't want ancient European anti-Semitism enshrined on federal land. But now everything has come to American soil.

Recently, I read an interview with Sheik Muhammad Gemeaha—who was not only the representative in the United

States of the prominent Cairo Center of Islamic Learning, al-Azhar University, but also imam of the Islamic Cultural Center of New York City. The sheik, who until recently lived in Manhattan on the Upper West Side, explained that "only the Jews" were capable of destroying the World Trade Center and added that "if it became known to the American people, they would have done to Jews what Hitler did." This sentiment will be familiar to anyone who has been watching the news or reading the papers. In Kuwait, there were reports that New York rabbis told their followers to take their money out of the stock market before September 11; in Egypt, the Mossad was blamed for the attack. It is easy talk to dismiss as madness, I suppose, but because so many millions of Muslims seem to believe it, and because airplanes actually did crash into the World Trade Center, words have a different weight and menace than they had before.

So does history, or rather the forces that shape history—particularly the history of the Jews. It would be wrong to say that everything changed on the eleventh of September for me. Like the man in the Hemingway novel who went bankrupt two ways—gradually and then suddenly—my awareness of things had also been growing slowly. My father's sister escaped in the 1930s from Vienna to Palestine—now, of course, called Israel—and I have a lot of family there. I grew up knowing that Israel, for all its vitality, was ringed with enemies; I knew how perilous and bleak life had become after the collapse of the Oslo peace process a year ago and how perilous and bleak it could be before that.

I knew, too, that works like "The Protocols of the Elders of Zion," the Russian forgery about demonic Jewish power, have been imported into Arab society, like obsolete but deadly Soviet weapons. By grafting ancient Christian calumnies onto modern political grievances, Arab governments have transformed Israel into an outpost of malevolent world Jewry, viewing Israelis and Jews as interchangeable emblems of cosmic evil. So when the Syrian defense minister recently told a delegation from the British Royal College of Defense Studies that the destruction of the World Trade Center was part of a Jewish conspiracy, I wasn't really surprised.

I'd gotten a whiff of this back in early September, while following the United Nations conference on racism and discrimination in Durban, South Africa, where the Arab Lawyers Union distributed booklets at the conference containing anti-Semitic caricatures of Jews with fangs dripping blood—a mere sideshow to the isolation of Israel and the equating of Zionism with racism that ultimately led to the United States' withdrawal. Singling out Israel made of a modern nation an archetypal villain—Jews were the problem and the countries of the world were figuring out the solution. This was hardly new in the history of the United Nations, but there was something so naked about the resurrected Nazi propaganda and the anti-Semitism fueling the political denunciations that I felt kidnapped by history. The past had come calling.

I felt this in a different form reading coverage of Israel in European papers. Though public expressions of anti-Semitism are taboo in a post-Holocaust world, many Europeans, in writing about Israel, have felt free to conjure images of determined child killers and mass murderers. Earlier this year, the Spanish daily *La Vanguardia* published a cartoon depicting a large building labeled "Museum of the Jewish Holocaust" and behind it a building under construction labeled "Future Museum of the Palestinian Holocaust." The cartoon manages to demonize Jews and trivialize the Holocaust simultaneously. Tom Gross, an Israel-based journalist, recently pointed out to me that a BBC correspondent, Hilary Andersson, declared that to describe adequately the outrage of Israel's murder of Palestinian children one would have to reach back to Herod's slaughter of the innocents—alluding to Herod's attempt to kill Christ in the cradle by massacring Jewish babies. After leading an editor from *The Guardian* on a tour of the occupied territories, Gross was astonished at the resulting front-page editorial in that highly influential British paper declaring that the establishment of Israel has exacted such a high moral price that "the international community cannot support this cost indefinitely."

I understood that the editorial, speaking of the cost of the establishment of Israel—not of any particular policies—implied that Israel's very right to exist is somehow still at issue. (One cannot imagine something similar being formulated about, say, Russia, in response to its battle with Chechen rebels, however much *The Guardian* might have disagreed with that country's policies.) And this reminded me inevitably of the situation of the Jews in 1940s Europe, where simply to be was an unpardonable crime.

I had somehow believed that the Jewish Question, which so obsessed both Jews and anti-Semites in the nineteenth and twentieth centuries, had been solved—most horribly by Hitler's "final solution," most hopefully by Zionism. But more and more I feel Jews being turned into a question mark once again. How is it, the world still asks—about Israel, about Jews, about me—that you are still here? I have always known that much of the world wanted Jews simply to disappear, but there are degrees of knowledge, and after September 11 my imagination seems more terribly able to imagine a world of rhetoric fulfilled.

There are five million Jews in Israel and eight million more Jews in the rest of the world. There are one billion Muslims. How has it happened that Israel and "world Jewry," along with the United States, is the enemy of so many of them? To be singled out inside a singled-out country is doubly disconcerting. There are a lot of reasons why modernizing, secularizing, globalizing America, whose every decision has universal impact, would disturb large swaths of the world; we are, after all, a superpower. Surely it is stranger that Jews, by their mere presence in the world, would unleash such hysteria.

And yet what I kept hearing in those first days in the aftermath of the attack on the World Trade Center is that it was our support of Israel that had somehow brought this devastation down on us. It was a kind of respectable variant of the belief that the Mossad had literally blown up the World Trade Center. It could of course be parried—after all, the turning point in Osama bin Laden's hatred of the United States came during the Gulf war, when American troops were stationed in Saudi Arabia. But it had a lingering effect; it was hard to avoid a certain feeling that there was something almost magical about Israel that made it toxic for friends and foes alike.

This feeling will not go away, if only because our support of that nation makes it harder to maintain our coalition. Israel has somehow become an obstacle to war and an obstacle to peace simultaneously.

Lately, of course, bin Laden has added treatment of Palestinians to his list of grievances, and this may revive the sense that Israel bears some measure of responsibility. Large lies can be constructed out of smaller truths. The occupation of the West Bank by Israel, though it grew out of a war Israel did not want, has been a nightmare for the Palestinians and a disaster for Israel morally, politically, and spiritually. It is a peculiar misery to feel this way and to feel, at the same time, that the situation has become a weapon in the war against Israel. Bin Laden would not want a Palestinian state on the West Bank, because he could not abide a Jewish state alongside it.

Neither could many of our allies in the Muslim world, who keep euphemistically suggesting that if only the "Mideast crisis" were resolved, terrorism would diminish. It has a plausible veneer—and indeed, it would be an extraordinary achievement if the Palestinians got a homeland and Israel got safe borders. But since most of the players in the Middle East do not accept the existence of Israel, since "solving the Mideast crisis" would for them entail a modern version of Hitler's final solution, the phrase takes on weird and even sinister overtones when it is blandly employed by well-intentioned governments calling for a speedy solution. And this Orwellian transformation of language is one of the most exasperating and disorienting aspects of the campaign against Israel. It has turned the word "peace" into a euphemism for war.

I grew up in a post-Holocaust world. For all the grim weight of that burden, and for all its echoing emptiness, there was a weird sort of safety in it too. After all, the worst thing had already happened—everything else was aftermath. In the wake of the Holocaust, American anti-Semitism dissipated, the church expunged old calumnies. The horror had been sufficient to shock even countries like the Soviet Union into supporting a newly declared Jewish state. Israel after 1967 was a powerful nation—besieged, but secure. American Jews were safe as houses.

I am not writing this essay to predict some inevitable calamity but to identify a change of mood. To say aloud that European anti-Semitism, which made the Holocaust possible, is still shaping the way Jews are perceived; Arab anti-Israel propaganda has joined hands with it and found a home in the embattled Muslim world. Something terrible has been born. What happened on September 11 is proof, as if we needed it, that people who threaten evil intend evil. This comes with the dawning awareness that weapons of mass destruction did not vanish with the Soviet Union; the knowledge that in fact they may pose a greater threat of actually being used in this century, if only in a limited fashion, is sinking in only now.

That a solution to one century's Jewish problem has become another century's Jewish problem is a cruel paradox. This tragedy has intensified to such a degree that friends, supporters of Israel, have wondered aloud to me if the time has come to acknowledge that the Israeli experiment has failed, that there is something in the enterprise itself that doomed it. This is the thinking of despair. I suppose one could wonder as much about America in the aftermath of the September 11 attacks, since many American values will now be challenged and since, in fighting a war, you always become a little like your enemy, if only in accepting the need to kill. I grew up at a time when sex education was considered essential but what might be called war education, what a country must do to survive, was looked upon with a kind of prudish horror. I suppose that will now change. In any event, Israel has been at war for fifty years. Without that context, clear judgment is impossible, especially by those accustomed to the Holocaust notion that Jews in war are nothing but helpless victims—a standard that can make images to the contrary seem aberrant.

I have a different way of looking at the Israeli experiment than my friends who wonder about its failure. It is connected to how I look at the fate of European Jewry. When the Jews of Europe were murdered in the Holocaust, one might have concluded that European Judaism failed—to defend itself, to anticipate evil, to make itself acceptable to the world around it, to pack up and leave. But one could also conclude in a deeper way that Christian Europe failed—to accept the existence of Jews in their midst, and it has been marked ever since, and will be for all time, with this blot on its culture. Israel is a test of its neighbors as much as its neighbors are a test for Israel. If the Israeli experiment fails, then Islam will have failed, and so will the Christian culture that plays a shaping role in that part of the region.

I am fearful of sounding as though I believe that the Holocaust is going to replay itself in some simplified fashion—that my childhood fantasy for my father is true for me, and it is I who am straining to hear Hitler's voice break over the radio. I do not. Israel has a potent, modern army. But so does the

United States, and it has proved vulnerable to attack, raising other fears. The United States spans a continent, and its survival is not in doubt. But experts who warn us about American vulnerability refer to areas the size of entire states that will become contaminated if a nuclear reactor is struck by a plane. Israel is smaller than New Jersey.

I am aware that an obsession with the Holocaust is seen as somehow unbecoming and, when speaking of modern politics, viewed almost as a matter of bad taste if not bad history. I do not wish to elide Israel's political flaws by invoking the Holocaust. But that very reluctance has been exploited and perverted in a way that makes me disregard it. "Six million Jews died?" the mufti of Jerusalem, a Palestinian Authority appointee, remarked last year. "Let us desist from this fairy tale exploited by Israel to buy international solidarity." (The utterance is particularly egregious because the mufti's predecessor paid an admiring visit to Hitler in 1941.) The demonizing language that is used about Israel in some of the European press, and about Jews in the Arab press, is reminiscent of Europe in the 1930s. I grew up thinking I was living in the post-Holocaust world and find it sounds more and more like a pre-Holocaust world as well.

Ten years ago, I interviewed Saul Bellow in Chicago and in the course of the interview asked him if there was anything he regretted. He told me that he now felt, looking back on his career, that he had not been sufficiently mindful of the Holocaust. This surprised me because one of his novels, *Mr. Sammler's Planet,* is actually about a Holocaust survivor. But Bellow recalled writing *The Adventures of Augie March*—the grand freewheeling novel that made his reputation—in Paris in the late 1940s. Holocaust survivors were everywhere, Bellow told me, and, as a Yiddish speaker, he had access to the terrible truths they harbored. But, as Bellow put it, he was not in the mood to listen. "I wanted my American seven-layer cake," he told me.

He did not wish to burden his writing at that early moment in his career with the encumbering weight of Jewish history. *Augie March* begins, exuberantly, "I am an American."

I, too, want my American seven-layer cake, even if the cake has collapsed a little in recent weeks. There is no pleasure in feeling reclaimed by the awfulness of history and in feeling myself at odds with the large universalist temper of our society. Thinking about it makes me feel old, exhausted, and angry.

In the Second World War, American Jews muted their separate Jewish concerns for the good of the larger struggle to liberate Europe. I understand the psychological urge to feel in sync with American aims. But Israel sticks out in this crisis as European Jewry stuck out in World War II, forcing a secondary level of Jewish consciousness, particularly because the anti-Zionism of the Arab world has adopted the generalized anti-Semitism of the European world.

The danger to America, which has already befallen us, and the danger to Israel, which so far remains primarily rhetorical, are, of course, connected. And though it is false to imagine that if Israel did not exist America would not have its enemies, people making the link are intuiting something beyond the simple fact that both are Western democracies.

In *Cultures in Conflict: Christians, Muslims, and Jews in the Age of Discovery,* Bernard Lewis points out that after Christians reconquered Spain from the Muslims in the fifteenth century, they decided to expel the Jews before the Muslims. The reason for this, Lewis explains, is that although the Jews had no army and posed far less of a political threat than the Muslims, they posed a far greater theological challenge. This is because Jews believed that adherents of other faiths could find their own path to God. Christianity and Islam, which cast unbelievers as infidels, did not share this essential religious relativism. The rabbinic interpretation of monotheism, which in seeing all human beings as created in God's image recognized their inherent equality, may well contain the seeds of the very democratic principles that the terrorists of September 11 found so intolerable.

Is it any wonder that in the minds of the terrorists and their fundamentalist defenders, Americans and Jews have an unholy alliance? Expressing my separate Jewish concerns does not put me at odds with our pluralistic society—it puts me in tune with it, since it is here of all places that I am free to express all my identities—American, Jewish, Zionist. And if Jews kicked out of Spain clung, at peril of death, to a religion with such an ultimately inclusive faith in the redeemable nature of humanity, who am I to reject that view? Perhaps the optimistic American half of my inheritance isn't at odds with the darker Jewish component after all. In this regard, the double consciousness that has burdened my response to our new war need not feel like a division. On the contrary, it redoubles my patriotism and steels me for the struggle ahead.

PAUL BERMAN

Something's Changed

Bigotry in Print. Crowds Chant Murder

I.

FEARS THAT ONLY YESTERDAY seemed absurd or silly begin to seem reasonable and more than reasonable. Thoughts that might have seemed inconceivable even two months ago become not just conceivable but spoken out loud. Crowds chant utter wildness on the street. In this way, the clouds grow blacker before our eyes. Very small clouds, you may say. Still, the transformation takes place at stupendous speed. Not everyone notices. The failure to notice constitutes a small black cloud in itself.

In Washington last month, a crowd of demonstrators gathered to celebrate the modern protest rituals of the anti-globalization movement. Only, this time, the radical opposition to globalization turned into radical opposition to Israel. A portion of the crowd chanted "Martyrs, not murderers." I suppose that many of the individuals in that part of the crowd would have explained that, in mouthing their *m*'s, they intended only to promote the cause of Palestinian rights, which is surely a worthy cause. But their chant was not about Palestinian rights. It was about mass murder.

I doubt that the streets of Washington have ever seen such

an obscene public spectacle, at least not since the days of public slave auctions, before the Civil War. Three months ago, I imagine, the demonstrators themselves would never have dreamed of shouting such a slogan. I don't want to suggest that everyone at the anti-globalization demonstration shared those sentiments. But everyone at the anti-globalization demonstration willy-nilly ended up shoulder to shoulder with people who did feel that way. Anti-globalization protests have never been like that before.

That same month, in New York, the annual Socialist Scholars Conference assembled at the East Village's venerable Cooper Union, where Abraham Lincoln gave one of his most famous speeches. The Socialist Scholars Conference is an annual meeting of a few thousand people, most of them intellectuals of some sort. The conference has always resembled an ideological bazaar, with every ridiculous left-wing sect selling its sacred texts, side by side with sober European social democrats and American liberals.

But this year a novelist from Egypt sat on one of the panels and stated her approval of the suicide bombers. To be sure, most people at the Socialist Scholars Conference would condemn random mass murders. But there is nothing new in condemning mass murder. This year, the new event was that someone supported it, and the rest of the participants, the rank and file Socialist Scholars, sat in comradely assemblage as the argument was advanced, and someone even spoke out in the panelist's defense. The newness in this event has to be remarked.

II.

I could cite a dozen other instances where, in the last few weeks, someone in a city like New York or Washington, London or Paris, has argued or chanted in favor of mass murder—someone who has never done such a thing in the past, in settings that have never heard such arguments before, or at least not in many years. What can explain the sudden development? It is a consequence, of course, of the Israeli incursion into the West Bank—or, rather, a consequence of how the Israeli incursion has been interpreted by an immense number of people all over the world.

One of the most prominent of those interpretations has looked on the incursion as Nazism in action, which is to say, as an event of extreme and absolute evil, requiring the most extreme and absolute counter-measures. In the last few months, Israel itself has been routinely compared to Nazi Germany, and Ariel Sharon to Adolf Hitler. Exactly why large numbers of people would arrive at such a comparison is not immediately obvious. In its half-century of existence, Israel has committed its share of serious crimes and even a few massacres (though not lately, as it turns out). But the instances of Israeli military frenzy or criminal indiscipline are not especially numerous, given how often Israel has had to fight.

There has never been a hint of an extermination camp, nor anything that could be compared in grisliness with any number of actions by the governments of Syria, Iraq, Serbia, and so forth around the world. Israel's wars have created refugees, to be sure; but Nazism's specialty was precisely *not* to create refugees. If Israel nonetheless resembles Nazi Germany, the resemblance must owe, instead, to some other factor, to some essence of the Israeli nation, regardless of the statistics of death and displacement.

The notorious old United Nations resolution (voted up in 1975 and repealed in 1991) about Zionism and racism hinted at such an essence by saying, in effect, that Israel's national doctrine, Zionism, was a doctrine of racial hatred. But why would anyone suppose that, like Nazi Germany, Israel has been built on a platform of hatred? The founding theorists of Zionism in the nineteenth and early twentieth centuries did not escape the prevailing doctrines of their own time, but their theories were chiefly theories of Jewish national revival and self-defense. They were not theories about the inferiority or hatefulness of anyone else, not even Judaism's worst enemies of the past, the Christian churches of Europe. Why, then, the accusation about hateful essences and Zionist doctrine? This is something that is very rarely explained.

In these last weeks, though, one of the world's most celebrated writers did stand up to discuss the hateful essence and its nature. The writer was José Saramago, the Portuguese novelist who won the Nobel Prize in literature in 1998. Saramago was part of an international group of writers who traveled to Ramallah to observe the Israeli siege of Yasser Arafat's compound. And, having observed the situation, Saramago came up with the same comparison as Breyten Breytenbach and any number of other people, lately. (It is fairly amazing how many otherwise serious writers have ended up choosing the same tiny set of images to apply to the Jewish state.) The situation at Ramallah, in Saramago's estimation, was "a crime comparable to Auschwitz." To the Israeli journalist who asked where the gas chambers were, Saramago gave his much-quoted reply, "Not yet here." But he also explained himself more seriously and at length in the April 21 issue of *El País,* a Madrid newspaper read and respected all over the Spanish-speaking world.

III.

Israel, in Saramago's view, has pursued immoral and hateful policies during its entire history. And why has Israel done so? Perhaps for the same reasons that other countries have pursued hateful, immoral, expansionist policies? Not at all. Saramago traced Israel's policies to biblical Judaism. He pointed to the story of David and Goliath, which, though commonly pictured as a tale of underdog triumph, is actually the story of a blond person (David's blond hair seemed to catch Saramago's attention) employing a superior technology to kill at a distance a helpless and presumably non-blond person, the unfortunate and oppressed Goliath. Today's events, in Saramago's fanciful interpretation, follow the biblical script precisely, as if in testimony to the Jews' fidelity to tradition. He writes:

> The blond David of yesteryear surveys from a helicopter the occupied Palestinian lands and fires missiles at unarmed innocents; the delicate David of yore mans the most powerful tanks in the world and flattens and blows up what he finds in his tread; the lyrical David who sang praise to Bathsheba, incarnated today in the gargantuan figure of a war criminal named Ariel Sharon, hurls the "poetic" message that first it is necessary to finish off the Palestinians in order later to negotiate with those who remain.

Saramago must have been ablaze, writing these lines.

Intoxicated mentally by the messianic dream of a Greater Israel which will finally achieve the expansionist dreams of the most radical Zionism; contaminated by the monstrous and rooted "certitude" that in this catastrophic and absurd world there exists a people chosen by God and that, consequently, all the actions of an obsessive, psychological and pathologically exclusivist racism are justified; educated and trained in the idea that any suffering that has been inflicted, or is being inflicted, or will be inflicted on everyone else, especially the Palestinians, will always be inferior to that which they themselves suffered in the Holocaust, the Jews endlessly scratch their own wound to keep it bleeding, to make it incurable, and they show it to the world as if it were a banner. Israel seizes hold of the terrible words of God in Deuteronomy: "Vengeance is mine, and I will be repaid." Israel wants all of us to feel guilty, directly or indirectly, for the horrors of the Holo-

caust; Israel wants us to renounce the most elemental critical judgment and for us to transform ourselves into a
docile echo of its will.

Israel, in short, is a racist state by virtue of Judaism's
monstrous doctrines—racist not just against the Palestinians, but against the entire world, which it seeks to manipulate and abuse. Israel's struggles with its neighbors, seen
in that light, do take on a unique and even metaphysical
quality of genuine evil—the quality that distinguishes Israel's struggles from those of all other nations with disputed borders, no matter what the statistics of death and
suffering might suggest.

Saramago, shrewder and more sophisticated than the crowds
in the Washington streets or the panelist at the Socialist Scholars Conference, did condemn the suicide bombers. He did so in
two throwaway sentences at the end of his essay, sneeringly,
with his own expressive ellipsis:

"Ah, yes, the horrendous massacres of civilians caused by
the so-called suicide terrorists. . . . Horrendous, yes, doubtless;
condemnable, yes, doubtless, but Israel still has a lot to learn if
it is not capable of understanding the reasons that can bring a
human being to turn himself into a bomb." And so, the deliberate act of murdering random crowds turns out to be the fault of
the murdered—or, rather, of the monstrous and racist doctrines of their religion, which is Judaism.

I don't want to leave the impression that *El País* is a newspaper full of editors and writers who share those views. The
newspaper right away published a commentary by a philosopher named Reyes Mate, who carefully explained that Nazi
analogies tend to downplay the true meaning of Nazism, and a
second commentary by the American writer Barbara Probst
Solomon, a regular correspondent for *El País,* who skillfully
pointed out that Saramago had written an essay not about the
actually existing Israel and its policies but about "the Jew that is

roiling around in his head." There was, then, a balance in *El País:* one essay that was anti-Semitic, and two that were not.

Still, something was remarkable in seeing, in this day and age, a fulmination against Judaism for its intrinsic hatefulness, written with the savage energy of a Nobel Prize winner, published in one of the world's major newspapers. Surely, this, too, like the crowd in Washington and the panel discussion in New York, marks something new in our present moment.

IV.

You may object that, in pointing to the anti-globalists in the Washington streets and the Socialist Scholars in New York, I have focused on a radical left whose spirit of irresponsibility isn't news. As for Saramago, isn't he renowned for his Stalinist politics, for being a dinosaur from the 1930s? But the new tone that I refer to, the new attitude, is anything but a monopoly of the radical left. In this age of Jean-Marie Le Pen there is no point even mentioning the extreme right. For the new spirit has begun to pop up even in the most respectable of writings, in the middle of the mainstream—not everywhere, to be sure, and not even in most places, but in some places, and not always obscure ones. The new spirit has begun to pop up in a fashion that seems almost unconscious, even among people who would never dream of expressing an extreme or bigoted view, but who end up doing so anyway.

A peculiar example appears in an essay called "Israel: The Road to Nowhere," by the New York University historian Tony Judt, which ran as the lead article in the May 9, 2002, issue of *The New York Review of Books*. Professor Judt is a scholar of French intellectual history, well-known and much-praised (by me, for instance, in a review in *The New Yorker*) for his willingness to examine, among other themes, the moral obtuseness of Jean-Paul Sartre and his followers a half-century ago. In his new essay Judt blames Prime Minister Ariel Sharon for failing to understand that, sooner or later, Israel will have to negotiate with the Palestinians, who cannot be expected to abandon their hope for national independence. Judt despairs of Sharon, but he calls on the United States to play a larger role, and he does hold aloft a hope. Everyone in the Arab-Israeli struggle has suffered over the years, but Judt points out that in recent years the world has seen many examples of enemy populations reconciling and living side by side—the French and the Germans, for instance, or, on a still grander scale, the Poles and the Ukrainians, whose mutual crimes in the 1940s surpassed anything that has taken place between Arabs and Israelis.

That is the gist of his essay, at least ostensibly, and it seems to me unexceptionable, if perhaps a little one-sided.

v.

But the remarkable aspect of Judt's essay is not the ostensible argument. It is the set of images and rhetorical devices and even the precise language that he has chosen to use. His single most emphatic trope is a comparison between Israel and French Algeria, and between the current fighting and the Algerian War. A discussion of French Algeria begins the piece, and French Algeria pops up repeatedly, and its prominence in his argument raises an interesting question, namely, Does Israel have a right to exist? The Algerian War was fought over the proposition that French Algeria, as a colonial outpost of the French imperialists, did not, in fact, have a right to exist. Most of the world eventually came to accept that proposition. But if Israel resembles French Algeria, why exactly should Israel and its national doctrine, Zionism, be regarded as any more legitimate than France's imperialism?

That particular question can be answered with a dozen arguments—the nativist argument (Zionism may have been founded to rescue the European Jews, but in the past fifty years it has mostly ended up rescuing the native Jews of the Middle

East instead), the social justice argument (the overwhelming majority of Israel's Jews arrived essentially as refugees), the social utility argument (if not for Israel, which country or international agency would have raised a finger on behalf of the supremely oppressed Jews of Ethiopia and many other places?), the democratic argument (democratic states are more legitimate than undemocratic ones), and so forth.

But it has to be recognized that, starting in the 1960s, ever larger portions of the world did begin to gaze at Israel through an Algerian lens. Arafat launched his war against Israel in 1964, in the aftermath of the Algerian War but well before the Israelis had taken over the West Bank and Gaza, and his logic was, so to speak, strictly Algerian—a logic that regarded Israel as illegitimate per se. The comparison between Israel and French Algeria has served as one more basis for regarding Zionism as a doctrine of racial hatred—a doctrine, from this point of view, not much different from the old French notion that France had every right to conquer any African country it chose. Judt cannot share that view of Zionism, given his expressed worry about Israel's survival. Someone who did share the view would regard Israel's demise as desirable.

Still, his essay emphasizes the Algerian analogy. And then, having underlined that comparison, Judt moves along to the argument that in recent times has tended to replace the one about French Algeria, now that the Algerian War has faded into the past. The newer argument compares Israel to the white apartheid Republic of South Africa, where a racist contempt for black Africans was the founding proposition of the state. Back in the days of apartheid, friends of social justice around the world had good reason to regard the white Republic of South Africa as illegitimate.

Judt, on this note, observes that, "following fifty years of vicious repression and exploitation, white South Africans handed over power to a black majority who replaced them without violence or revenge." And he asks, "Is the Middle East so different? From the Palestinian point of view, the colonial analogy fits and foreign precedents might apply. Israelis, however, insist otherwise." But are the Israelis right in their insistence? He says, "Most Israelis are still trapped in the story of their own uniqueness"—his point being, presumably, that the Israelis are wrong. But then, if Israel does in some profound way resemble apartheid South Africa, would it be right to boycott the Zionist state, just as South Africa was boycotted? One does not boycott a state merely because of some objectionable policy or other. Nobody boycotts Turkey because it mistreats the Kurds, nor Egypt because it drove out nearly its entire Jewish population.

But if a state is racist by nature, if racism is its founding principle, as was the case in apartheid South Africa, then a boycott might well be justified, with the hope of abolishing the state entirely. Now, Judt cannot possibly regard Israel as any more comparable to apartheid South Africa than he does to French Algeria, given his concern that Israel continues to exist. Still, he does note that a new movement is, in fact, afoot to boycott Israel. He writes, "The fear of seeming to show solidarity with Sharon that already inhibits many from visiting Israel, will rapidly extend to the international community at large, making of Israel a pariah state." Do the "many" who feel inhibited from visiting Israel merit applause for their moral consciences? Or should those people be seen as so many José Saramagos, smug in their retrograde bigotries? Judt refrains from comment, but his tone implies that he regards the "many" as more reasonable than not.

He does say about some future resolution of the conflict, "There will be no Arab right of return; and it is time to abandon the anachronistic Jewish one." That is a curious comment, in the context of these other remarks. The Arab "right of return" means the right of Palestinians to return to their original, pre-1948 homes in Israel, a right that, if widely exercised, would bring about the end of Israel as a Jewish state. That is why, if Israel is to survive, "there will be no Arab right of return." But what is the Jewish "right of return"? That phrase can only mean what is expressed and guaranteed by Israel's Law of Return, to wit, Israel's commitment to welcome any Jew from around the world who chooses to come.

What would it mean for Israel to abandon that commitment? It would mean abandoning the Zionist mission to build a shelter for oppressed Jews from around the world, which is to say, Zionism itself. It would mean abandoning Israel's autonomy as a state—its right to draw up its own laws on immigration. Judt cannot be in favor of Israel doing any such thing. But those throwaway remarks and his choice of comparisons and analogies make it hard to know for sure.

VI.

His essay, all in all, seems to have been written on two levels. There is an ostensible level that criticizes Israel, although in a friendly fashion, with the criticisms meant to rescue Israel from its own errors and thereby to help everyone else who has been trapped in the conflict; and a second level, consisting of images and random phrases (the level that might attract Freud's attention), which keep hinting that maybe Israel has no right to exist. It is worth looking at the religious images and references in Judt's essay. There are two of these, and they express the two contradictory levels with a painful clarity.

In his very last lines, Judt urges the Israelis to treat the Palestinian public with dignity and to turn quickly from war to peace negotiations. And, in order to give a pungency or fervor to his exhortation, he concludes by quoting a famous rabbinical remark, "And if not now, when?" He ends, that is, on a warm note of Judaism, which is plainly a sympathetic tone to adopt—a call for Israel to adhere to Judaism's highest traditions of morality and good sense. Yet, at another point he strikes a Christian note, and of the weirdest sort.

Judt wonders about Sharon, "Will he send the tanks into the Galilee? Put up electric fences around the Arab districts of

Haifa?" Judt complains that Israel's intellectuals are not mount-ing a suitable opposition to this kind of aggression. He de-scribes the intellectuals and their failure to oppose in these words: "The country's liberal intelligentsia who, Pilate-like, have washed their hands of responsibility." That is, Judt com-pares Israel's liberal intellectuals to Pontius Pilate, who took no responsibility for killing Jesus. That is a very strange phrase to stumble across in an essay on the Middle East. Freud's eye-brows rise in wonder. The phrase is worth parsing. If Israel's liberal intellectuals are Pontius Pilate, who is Sharon? He must be the Jewish high priest who orders the crucifixion. Who is Jesus? He can only be the people whom the high priest is set-ting out to kill—namely, the suicide bombers. Surely Judt can-not mean that the Palestinian terrorists are God.

But then, it does seem odd that, a couple of lines down, Judt turns to the word "terrorist" and doubts its usefulness. "'Terror-ist,'" he writes, "risks becoming the mantra of our time, like 'Communist,' 'capitalist,' 'bourgeois,' and others before it. Like them, it closes off all further discussion." Words do turn into meaningless slogans. Still, is it so unreasonable, at a moment when the astounding series of mass murders in Israel is still going on, to speak of "terrorists," that is, of people who delib-erately set out to kill randomly? The suicide bombers are, in fact, terrorists, by any conventional definition of the term. Judt cannot mean to let those people off the hook, and in one por-tion of his essay he sternly condemns them. Yet in the passage that follows the remark about Pontius Pilate he ends up com-menting, "terror against civilians is the weapon of choice of the weak." Presumably he means that the Palestinian bombers are weak and have had no alternative way to claim their national rights—though he doesn't explain why the "weak" would have turned to their "weapon of choice" precisely in the aftermath of former Prime Minister Ehud Barak's offer to create the Pales-tinian state in Gaza and on almost all of the West Bank.

About José Saramago, I do believe, on the basis of the essay in *El País,* that the winner of the 1998 Nobel Prize has gotten hung up on the Jew roiling in his head, in Barbara Solomon's phrase. Not for one moment do I believe anything of the sort about Tony Judt. I can imagine that Judt chose to write about Pontius Pilate for the simplest and most natural reasons. The notion that the suicide bombers are sacred figures fulfilling a divine function, combined with the notion that Israel's Jews are evil demons, has swept the world in the last few months. Even the notion that the Jews are guilty of deicide, which is Christian in origin, has in recent times spread to the Muslim world. The new young president of Syria expressed that very notion to the Pope, on the occasion of the Pope's visit.

But, once these ideas have been picked up by events and have been sent flying through the air like body parts in a terrorist attack, they can easily land anywhere, and a writer whose anger has gotten out of hand can end up making use of those notions, strictly by mistake. Doubtless a main lesson to be drawn from Judt's essay is that even the most brilliant of university professors, lacking training and experience in journalism, may fail to command the most workaday of journalistic skills—the skill that allows a cooler-headed newsroom pro to write to deadline in tense times without losing control of the nuances and hidden meanings of his own copy.

Losing control of his own rhetoric and nothing worse than that was, in Judt's case, surely the error. For just as most people in the anti-globalism movement would never chant in favor of suicide bombers (even if some people did chant in favor), and just as most of the Socialist Scholars would never support the terrorists (even if one of the honored panelists did), and just as a modern, high-minded newspaper like *El País* would not care to publish anti-Semitic demagoguery (even if it did publish such a work), Judt, I am confident, had no intention of indulging in anti-Zionism and certainly no intention of sacralizing the terrorists or demonizing the Jews (even if that is the inference of what he ended up writing).

Yet it is the unintended inferences that seem to me the most frightening of all. To go out and fight against bigots and racists of all sorts, the anti-Semites and the anti-Arab racists alike, seems to me relatively simple to do, even in these terrible times. It is not so easy to put up a fight against a wind, a tone, against an indefinable spirit of hatred that has begun to appear even in the statements of otherwise sensible people.

But that is what we are up against. The little accidents and odd behaviors do add up. The new wind is definitely blowing. A few months ago no one was chanting for murder. In those days it was pretty unusual to stumble across diatribes against Judaism or anti-Semitic phrases in the intellectual press. But look what has happened. Something has changed.

DAVID BROOKS

It's Back

AFTER JOE LIEBERMAN COMPLETED his unsuccessful campaign for the vice-presidency, I pretty much concluded that anti-Semitism was no longer a major feature of American life. I went around making the case that the Anti-Defamation League should close up shop, since the evil they were organized to combat had shrunk to insignificance.

Now I get a steady stream of anti-Semitic screeds in my e-mail, my voicemail, and my mailbox. It transpired that I couldn't have been more wrong. Anti-Semitism is alive and thriving. It's just that its epicenter is no longer on the Buchananite right, but on the peace-movement left.

"Hello. I'm a grandmother from Minnesota. I want to thank you for taking my call," a voicemail on my machine began recently. When you hear a message like that you sort of settle back and prepare for some civil sentiment. Then it continued. "I just wanted to know: Are you related to Paul Wolfowitz and Ari Fleischer? I can usually smell you people. . . ." At that point I deleted the thing.

But it's like that week in and week out. And I'm best known for appearances on PBS and NPR, which surely have the most civilized audiences in the land. Nor is this a fringe phenomenon. Lawrence Kaplan recently wrote an op-ed in *The Wash-*

ington Post, gathering some of the highly questionable state-ments politicians and columnists have made over the past few weeks, accusing Jews of dual loyalty and worse. I occasionally get reports about conversations at sophisticated Washington dinner parties that turn into gripe sessions about the Israeli agents who have grabbed control of President Bush's brain. Accusing Jews of twisting U.S. policy to suit Israel is the same as accusing Catholics of taking orders from the Pope. It's also logically absurd, since Israelis are far more concerned about Iran and Syria than Iraq. But it's become commonplace nonetheless.

Not long ago I was chatting with a prominent Washington figure in a greenroom. "You people have infested everywhere," he said in what I thought was a clumsy but good-hearted man-ner. He listed a few of "us": "Wolfowitz, Feith, Frum, Perle." I've never met Doug Feith in my life and Wolfowitz and Perle I've barely met. Yet he assumed we were tight as thieves. After a few minutes of jibing I finally pointed out that there were many non-Jews who support the president's policy against Iraq. I mentioned Bob Kerrey. "He's a shabbas goy. He's got a lot of Jewish money supporting that school," he shot back. Shabbas goys are Christians who perform tasks for observant Jews on Saturdays.

I am the last person who used to suspect people of anti-Semitism. I was never really conscious of it affecting my life until the last few weeks. But now I wonder. I watched a town meeting in northern Virginia a few weeks ago. A Vietnam vet got up to rail against U.S. policy on Iraq, which he said was engineered by "Paul Wolfowitz and Daniel Pearl." He got the wrong Pearl. He accidentally mentioned somebody who was beheaded for being American and Jewish. But the crowd didn't seem to notice. They roared with approval and slapped him on the back as he made his way from the microphone. Why didn't he say Cheney, Rumsfeld, Rice, and Powell were organizing the

Bush administration policy? They're higher ranking officials than Wolfowitz and actually members of the administration, unlike Perle. Would the crowd have roared as wildly if he'd mentioned Rice and Powell, I wondered, or did the words Wolfowitz and Perle somehow get their juices flowing?

It's not just the things people say. It's the things that are now socially acceptable. The leftist group ANSWER has a long and well-documented record of anti-Zionist statements so extreme and inflammatory that they are truly offensive. (Not to mention a record of supporting murderers and tyrants that is appalling and inhumane.) When the thousands gathered for the peace rally ANSWER co-organized on the Mall in Washington, I figured most of the marchers didn't really know the true nature of the group. But now principled liberals and many others have exposed its vicious and Stalinoid nature. And the peace marchers don't mind! They still flocked to the ANSWER-organized marches last weekend. The fact that the Jewish liberal Michael Lerner wasn't permitted to speak didn't bother them either! Would they march at peace rallies organized by the KKK or the American Nazi Party, groups that are about as despicable as ANSWER? Is all hatred now socially acceptable if it is organized in the cause of "peace"?

I mentioned that I barely know Paul Wolfowitz, which is true. But I do admire him enormously, not only because he is both a genuine scholar and an effective policy practitioner, not only because he has been right on most of the major issues during his career, but because he is now the focus of world anti-Semitism. He carries the burden of their hatred, which emanates not only from the Arab world and France, but from some people in our own country, which I had so long underestimated.

BARBARA AMIEL

Islamists Overplay Their Hand
But London Salons Don't See It

[This December 2001 column, which came to be known for a French diplomat's obscenity-studded description of Israel, was one of the first dramatic indications of how anti-Semitism had become, if not acceptable, common (in every sense of the word) in elite social circles in London.]

IN A COLUMN in last week's *Spectator,* Petronella Wyatt noted that "since September 11 anti-Semitism and its open expression has become respectable at London dinner tables."

This is an accurate observation and cannot be avoided by simply staying at home.

Recently, the ambassador of a major EU country politely told a gathering at my home that the current troubles in the world were all because of "that shitty little country Israel."

"Why," he asked, "should the world be in danger of World War Three because of those people?"

At a private lunch last month, the hostess—doyenne of London's political salon scene—made a remark to the effect that she couldn't stand Jews and everything happening to them was their own fault.

When this was greeted with a shocked silence, she chided her guests on what she assumed was their hypocrisy. "Oh come on," she said, "you all feel like that."

Once that remark would have cost her license as a serious

political hostess, but clearly she believes the zeitgeist is blowing her way.

The editor of a major British newspaper came to our home, and I can tell Petronella Wyatt that it can be just as awkward with good friends at lunch as it is with strangers at dinner.

The editor is a decent man but his paper habitually blames Israel's "opposition to peace" for the problems in the Middle East and lectures them to negotiate. "But, look," he was asked, "Arafat does not believe in the right of the Jewish people to a state. How can the Israelis negotiate in that situation?"

The editor replied with disarming honesty: "You have put your finger on the weak point in our argument."

All this is not as bad as it seems. True, these remarks are exceptionally painful for some British Jews who feel beleaguered aliens in their own land. For myself, it merits only a shrug.

One is irritated when, as last October, the community hall of a north London synagogue burned down in what police labeled a racist arson attack and the matter barely rated a mention except in the Jewish press.

The Monday after the triple suicide bombings in Israel that killed 26 and injured around 200, the *Evening Standard* turned to Charles Glass, an old anti-Israel hand. Glass wrote: "Palestinians kill Israelis. Israelis kill Palestinians. Who killed first? No one remembers and it does not matter."

For the past twenty-five years, I've watched sad-faced Israeli activists trudge around Western capitals with heavy hearts beating under ill-fitting suits. They carry folders of transcripts and videotapes to document the misrepresentations in the press and the moral hypocrisy of the world towards Israel.

They want to win the war of ideas on its merits. Their attention to detail in translating the hate literature of the Middle East and the hate-filled speeches of its leaders is commendable.

It's enlightening to read, for example, their studies of Syrian and Palestinian Authority school textbooks that explain to young schoolchildren that the Jews are a people made up of murderers and thieves.

It is sad to learn that such textbooks are used by the UN in its schools for Palestinian refugees. But something new is "blowin' in the wind."

Today, after years in the media desert, Israel's experts and front-line activists are slowly finding some media doors opening to them. They may think it is their own perseverance. But I think it is the daisy cutter effect.

For years, I said that Jews were out of fashion and I understood why. The world was sick of the Middle East problem: why should it be inconvenienced by the cost and the ripple effect of terrorism?

The West defeated the Third Reich and we Jews were no longer in need of a lifeboat: indeed, today we would probably be safer just about anywhere rather than the Middle East. But events in the past year or so changed the equation and our rehabilitation has begun. The Arab/Muslim world overplayed its hand.

Their first wrong move was the rejection of prime minister Ehud Barak's offer in 2000. Even if you looked at that proposal from an Arab point of view and believed that a Palestinian state comprising 95 percent of the West Bank and a shared Jerusalem was not sufficient, you couldn't possibly argue that such a deal should be rejected out of hand.

The second mistake was launching the Al-Aqsa intifada after rejecting that deal. Eventually, the world saw that it was not Ariel Sharon's walk on the Temple Mount that caused the new intifada (a walk pre-cleared with the Muslim authorities) but Arafat's decision to escalate violence for tactical reasons.

The greatest error of all was when bin Laden, acting in the name of the Arab/Muslim world, decided—with a total incomprehension of what this would entail—to blow up Lower Manhattan and blow it up at a time when the American administration was in the hands of Bush, Cheney, and Rumsfeld and not Clinton and Gore.

The Arab street remained silent at best or cheered the WTC bombing even as some of their leaders made ritual condemnations of it. Almost overnight, a blindfold fell off America's eyes. Appeasement didn't work.

The problem was not Israel's intransigence, nor even the conflict that comes from Israel's existence: the problem is Islamism.

Islam itself is split between Islam as a religion that can be essentially peaceful—endorsing the qualities of charity and mercy—and militant Islam (Islamism), which is intolerant and expansionist. Islam periodically goes into this expansionary phase and is now in one.

That is why in the past few years some mosques in the West have seen violent incidents, including murders, as radical mullahs fight moderates for supremacy. Militant Islam wants to be the dominant force in the world.

Its crusade has Muslims fighting Christians in Indonesia, Sudan, and Pakistan. Christians in Lebanon have largely fled. Muslim fights Muslim in Algeria. Islamism has been on the move all right, but it hasn't a chance now, because it finally woke up America.

It took the blowing up of three planes on an airstrip outside Jordan by Palestinian terrorists in 1970 to turn the world's attention to the Palestinian question. One regrets to say that it has taken a lot more violence to get the world to focus on the true nature of Islamism.

Powerful as the truth may be, it needs a nudge from 16,000-pound daisy cutter bombs once in a while. The Arab/Muslim world's intransigence comes into sharper focus when we see the Americans liberate Afghanistan from the Taliban in six weeks and a cornered Arafat unable to go to the bathroom without the risk of being blown into the next world.

Nothing succeeds like powerful bombs, as bin Laden explained in his latest video release. "When people see a strong horse and a weak horse, by nature they will like the strong horse," he said.

"Some of the media said that in Holland, in one of the centers, the number of people who accepted Islam during the days that followed the operations [attacks on the WTC and the Pentagon] were more than the people who accepted Islam in the past 11 years."

Bin Laden understands the power of a successful show of force all right, though he seems slow to grasp that America's horses are stronger than his.

Don't worry, Petronella. It is both sad and true that the consequences of super-liberalism led to suicide bombers and intifadas in Israel and to the attacks in America. But the U.S. has shown it is no paper tiger.

All those people bad-mouthing the Jews and Israel will quiet down. You are looking at the tail end of the train, but the engine has already turned a corner and is going in the opposite direction.

Nothing succeeds like success. America is driving this train and the world will get on board—though the last carriage may be those London dinner parties.

HAROLD EVANS

The View from Ground Zero
The Index Lecture

[*This was initially a talk, given at the Hay-on-Wye Literary Festival in September 2002, and represents one of the earliest comprehensive responses in the U.K. to worldwide post–9/11 anti-Semitism.*]

SEPTEMBER 11 HAS BEEN hard for us to explain to our children Isabel, ten, and George, fifteen, harder than anything in their lives, because we couldn't understand it ourselves.

Now we know. The Jews did it.

- The day the two airliners hit the twin towers, 4,000 Jews who worked there did not show up or called in sick because they had been secretly tipped off by Israel's Mossad to stay away that day.
- Israeli secret police advised Sharon not to travel to New York on September 11.
- Actually, no passengers were in the planes that hit the towers. They were aircraft operated by remote control from a secret downtown Mossad office.
- Five Israelis were caught filming the smoking rubble from their office building; but you never heard about this because it was hushed up by the FBI on orders from Washington. There were so many television and other pictures of the

planes hitting the towers and the towers falling only because cameras had been pre-positioned round the site.
• It was the same at the Pentagon. All Jews were absent that day when the plane struck.

The purpose of this vast and brilliant 9/11 Israeli conspiracy is clearer now than it was. It was a plot to vilify Muslims, to pave the way for a joint Israeli-U.S. military operation not just against Osama bin Laden and the Taliban but also Islamic militants in Palestine.

Could anybody believe this rubbish? Yes, millions and millions and millions did. And still do and we should hesitate to call them stupid. A Gallup Poll survey released in March this year questioned people in nine predominantly Islamic countries—Pakistan, Iran, Indonesia, Turkey, Lebanon, Morocco, Kuwait, Jordan, and Saudi Arabia representing about half the world's Muslim population. Some 67 percent found the attacks morally unjustified, which is something—why not 100 percent?—but they were also asked whether they believed reports that groups of Arabs carried out the attacks. Only in West-aligned Turkey was the answer yes, but it was a close 46 to 43 percent. In all the other eight Islamic countries, the populations rejected the idea that Arabs or Al Qaeda were responsible. The majorities are overwhelming in Pakistan, Kuwait, Iran, and Indonesia—in Pakistan only 4 percent believe the hijack killers were Arabs. Repeat, that is a poll just a couple of months ago, after millions of words from reporters, and exultant videos from the Osama bin Laden show. Of course, some of you know those videos were produced by Rent-a-Mullah, Inc., a CIA shadow company operating out of Maryland. But please keep it to yourself. . . .

Who could be crazy/malign/misguided enough to disseminate this odious invention as the truth? you may ask; there has been no consistent effort to find out. The short answer is the millenarians, imams, editors, columnists, government ministers, in every one of the non-democratic countries of the Arab and Islamic world, and on the West Bank.

But it is not confined to those closed societies where there is no freedom of the press. Sheikh Muhammad Gemeaha lived on New York's Upper West Side when he was in the United States for the Cairo Center of Islamic Learning at al-Azhar University and he explained to us dummies that "only the Jews" were capable of toppling the World Trade Center. If the conspiracy became known to the American people, said Sheikh Gemeaha, "they would have done to Jews what Hitler did." It is to be found too among Muslim groups in Paris and London, and among a tiny number of American youth. One of the most malevolent sources of activity is a body called the Associated Students of San Francisco State University allied with the General Union of Palestinian Students and the Muslim Student Association.

Pakistan's cooperation in the Afghanistan war was a little tricky for General Musharraf because the fact of the Israeli-American conspiracy to frame Arabs for 9/11 has been a running theme in most of the country's Urdu-language newspapers. *The Nation,* the leading daily published in Lahore, Islamabad, and Karachi, headlined a typically straight unqualified assertion:

MOSSAD BEHIND ATTACKS

The newspaper *Ad-Dustour* in moderate Jordan elaborated: The Twin Towers attack was "the act of the great Jewish Zionist mastermind that controls the world's economy, media and politics."

This Mossad conspiracy is being endlessly recycled. Thomas Friedman, the *New York Times* columnist, reported this month that it was an article of faith in Indonesia, the pivotal Southeast Asia state with the world's largest Muslim population. The week I was asked to give this talk, Dr. Y. Alaridi opined in the

English language *Syria Times:* "Has the CIA asked the Israeli Mossad if they had any idea about the September 11 tragedy before it happened? Sir, please forgive my rudeness, by the way, who does rule America?" There is no end to the paranoia. In an interview with Arab television only last week, a British spokesman was asked to prove that the 9/11 attacks were *not* carried out by the CIA.

How could people be so susceptible to misinformation? Well, conspiracy theories simplify a complex world. They have the advantage that the absence of evidence is itself proof of plot: missing records at Pearl Harbor, missing bullets in Dallas, missing bodies in Jenin. Preconceptions are outfitted in fantasy. Contradiction by authority is mere affirmation of the vastness of the plot: so he's in it, too. Conspiracy and rumor bloom especially where the flow of news and opinion is restricted and especially where illiteracy is high, as it is in Pakistan where the *madrassa*s (schools) devote all their attention to religious indoctrination—the only developing country, I think, where literacy rates are falling. Syed Talat Hussain, the prominent Pakistani journalist, was frank about it: "In a country where there is a void of information, newspapers resort to rumours. In addition, there is an abiding tradition in the Pakistani print media deliberately to prove that whatever goes wrong is the work of the Jews and the Hindus." But there is another explanation for the potency of the poison today. It is the aura of authenticity provided by technology, by the Internet. John Daniszewski of the *Los Angeles Times* asked an editor of *The Nation* in Islamabad, Ayesha Haroon, why they blamed Israel. "It is quite possible that there was deliberate malice in printing it," she admitted, but she went on: "I also think it has to do with the Internet. Somebody in Canada, the United States, or the UK is sitting there and makes up something and sends it to us. And when you see something on a computer, you tend to believe it is true." Here in the new magic is a source of much of our mis-

ery. An Indonesian just back from visiting the Islamic fundamentalist stronghold of Jogjakarta told Friedman how alarmed
he was by the tide running for Jihad against Christians and
Jews. What is frightening, he said, is an insidious digital divide.
"Internet users are only 5 per cent of the population—but these
5 per cent spread rumours to everyone else. They say, 'He got
it from the Internet.' They think it's the Bible."

But what about these 4,000 Jews? The figure of 4,000 got
into circulation because some years ago somebody guessed
that's how many Israelis there were in the city. The fact is Jews
and Israelis did what everybody did on September 11: they
showed up for work and died along with Muslims and Christians and Buddhists. The four children of Deborah Kaplan, en-
gineer, know too well that nobody tipped off their mother.
Allan Schwartzstein, equities trader, and father of two, died
wearing the watch he had received for his bar mitzvah fifteen
years before. He was named after an uncle killed in Israel in
1948. The uncle's body was never found and neither was
Allan's. His high-level connections in Israel did not help Hagay
Shefi, the technologist son of the Israeli brigadier general Dov
Shefi. He was speaking at the Risk Waters conference and
never had a chance on the 106th floor.

The smear that defiles the dead, that millions perceive as
reality, owes its original currency, astonishingly, to one website.
The story got legs because it fitted the story line of Jewish mas-
terminds and because very few people in media regarded it seriously enough to take note of, still less, eviscerate. One dotcom
reporter who did investigate, Bryan Curtis of Slate, first discovered the fiction surfacing on a site called Information Times on
September 12. It began tentatively saying the "terrorist government of Israel could not be ruled out as the suspect" and then
supposition congealed. At 6:26 A.M. on September 17 it sub-
stantiated the plot with the headline that 4,000 Jews were
spared execution by their compatriots. And the source for this

devastating charge seems to be Al-Manar Television in Lebanon, which exists "to stage an effective psychological warfare with the Zionist enemy" and gives frequent airtime to the terrorist group Hezbollah. So I thought I would call Information Times in Washington to ask whether they had the slightest qualms about making such a play of an unchecked story from such a source. They were hard to find. Directory assistance had no entry for Information Times, Info Times, or the editor listed on its website, a Wizard of Oz by the name of Syed Adeeb. Mr. Curtis also tried. The Press Club told him it had no such tenant; email messages were bounced back. When I spoke to Curtis this week, he told me he had been bombarded by anti-Semitic responses. He also got a threatening legal letter but when Slate's lawyers tried to reply, the evanescent litigants were on the lam again. But Information Times is still peddling its wares on the web and you will get the flavor if I read you a few of the thirty-one stories I found at the top of their list on May 16:

1306: Expose Lobbyists who Support Israeli Terrorism
1307: Powell cunningly encourages Genocide of Arabs
1309: Thomas Friedman is a violent extremist
1310: US REP Says Bush Junta behind 9/11 attacks
1313: Dumb Foxy Blonde Utters Israeli Propaganda
1316: Hindu Terrorists Raped and Burned Women
1322: Bush Imposes Criminal Dictator on Pakistan
1325: Bush Changes Our Name to US of Israel
1334: Israelis with bomb material arrested in Washington

Once upon a time Mr. Adeeb, and his shy sponsors, would be sending out smudged cyclostyled sheets that would never see the light of day. But now the mysterious Mr. Adeeb and others like him have a megaphone to the world, with this spurious authenticity of electronic delivery. Mr. Cordell Hull in the thirties of print and radio complained that a lie went halfway round the world before truth had time to put its trousers on; nowadays it has been to Mars and back before anyone is half awake. It is extraordinary how seductive it is. After 9/11, I heard that Palestinians had been filmed dancing joyously in the street, but that AP had for some reason not circulated the video.

Then I came across "the truth" on the Web. Here is what I read, capitalization as in the text:

> All around the world we are subjected to 3 or 4 huge news distributors and one of them is CNN. One set of images showed Palestinians celebrating the bombing out on the streets, eating some cake and making funny faces for the camera. Well THOSE IMAGES WERE SHOT BACK IN 1991. THOSE ARE IMAGES OF PALESTINIANS CEL-EBRATING THE INVASION OF KUWAIT! It is simply unacceptable that a super power of communications as CNN uses images which do not correspond to reality. This is a crime against public opinion. The truth is that the U.S. has shown no respect for other countries in the last decades.

Sounds right. One recalls Yasser Arafat led the Palestinians in support of Saddam in the Gulf War so perhaps the film in 2001 was indeed of 1990 celebrations of his invasion of Kuwait, or perhaps they erupted on the street when he launched Scud missiles against the hated Israelis.

What was CNN doing airing a decades-old film? Didn't it realize it would make Americans angry with the Palestinians?

Well, they weren't doing anything of the kind.

The web site exposé was itself a fraud. The film was not archive footage misapplied to a current event. It was shot on Black Tuesday, September 11, by a Reuters TV crew in East Jerusalem and supplied to CNN in the normal way—as testified both by Reuters and CNN. The internal evidence supports CNN's rebuttal: the video included comments from a Palestinian praising Osama Bin Laden, unknown on the Jerusalem street in 1990, and in the background were automobiles made after 1991.

So how did the lie get round the world? A student named Marcio A.V. Carvalho, at Universidad Estatal de Campinas-Brasil (Unicamp), was told by someone that a professor at another university had the CNN tape and could prove it false. Carvalho plugged the news into the email list of a discussion group he joined on the web. When members of the group got excited for more details, he went back to his contact and to the professor—who denied having the tape. Carvalho told his email list he had no more details. Later, following the CNN rebuttal, both the university announced regrets that one of its students had promulgated a falsehood, but by this time it had assumed an inflated life of its own. Carvalho disowned his Frankensteins; a hacker, he said, attacked his email domain and sent out distorted articles under his name.

I have reported this fragment in a little detail to show what we are up against today. We could be in this tent the rest of the week if we tried to find our way through the labyrinth of cognitive dissonance to assess the potential repercussions. On those who ingested the fraud alleging fraud, on those who caught up with it, on the different interpretations likely to be made by a viewer in America, in Europe, in the Middle East. But one thing is certain: whatever else they do, allegations of misreporting like this aggravate the dangers for journalists and TV crews—like Christiane Amanpour, who is with us tonight—bravely venturing into areas of tension, risking arrest by the authorities, a stray bullet, or violence from the street, the asylum of ignorance. I have lost three colleagues and friends this way. At the end of the line of incendiary lies, there is the life of a reporter, just trying to do his job, like Danny Pearl tortured and butchered because he was a Jew and a reporter, led into a trap by a graduate of a British university.

THE TIDAL WAVE OF ANTI-SEMITISM

We have to look very hard in the distorting mirrors of the Middle East for the absolute knowledge of Enlightenment presumptions. But the Internet, for all its elephant traps, does enable us at least to know to an unprecedented degree what is being retailed, what people are thinking and being told. Before I lift the lid an inch or two on this Pandora's box, you are entitled to know where I am coming from. I see Israel, for all its warts, and its origins in terrorist violence against the British, as the parliamentary democracy envisaged by the famous editor of *The Guardian*, C. P. Scott, when in 1917 he introduced Chaim Weizmann to Lloyd George and A. J. Balfour. That led to the Balfour declaration for a Jewish national home. At the same time, I have never hesitated whenever I thought Israel was failing to live up to its ideals or being intransigent in negotiation. At the *Sunday Times*, I was the subject of a great deal of criticism for documenting in detail cases of ill treatment of Arabs held prisoner on the West Bank by the Israeli military. I believe occupation is inevitably an ugly and humiliating thing. Israel would be well advised to stop building settlements; indeed as some peace groups in Israel suggest, it might be possible to break the cycle of violence by formally withdrawing from an abandoned settlement and letting it be known that more will follow if the gesture is reciprocated.

But none of the Palestinians' grievances can justify what they are doing today. Nothing, I believe, nothing, can justify that random murder of Israeli citizenry, wherever they are—in pre-'67 Israel, or the West Bank or Gaza. And nothing can justify the anti-Semitism that foments such terrorism. It is a big dark shadow on the world, and it is not simply a consequence of the Palestinian conflict, as conventional media portrays it— insofar as it portrays it at all, which is scandalously little. The leading authority on anti-Semitism, the author and scholar Professor Robert Wistrich, Neuberger Professor at the Hebrew University in Jerusalem, judges that today's level of anti-Semitism is unprecedented, and anyone who makes the most cursory examination cannot fail to be stunned. The effluent is from official sources and newspapers in Arab states, from schools and government-funded mosques, from Arab columnists and editorial writers, cartoonists, clerics, and intellectuals, from websites that trail into an infinity of iniquity. Hostility to Israel is pumped into millions of homes every day by the pan-Arab TV satellite channel, Al-Jazeera. It is said to be "objective." At the start of the Afghan campaign, it gave twice as much airtime to Bin Laden and his supporters as the coalition. Recently, it showed its priorities very clearly by giving an easy ride to the anti-Semitic Le Pen and a rough ride to Tony Blair. The appearance of modernity in the Arab media is illusory. More important than the presence of the hardware is the absence of the software, the notion of a ruggedly independent self-critical free press. CNN will film American bomb damage in Afghanistan. Al-Jazeera and the Middle East stations would never dream of talking to the orphans and widows whose loved ones were blown apart by a suicide bomber. An Arab critic of America and the coalition is always given the last word.

Wherever you apportion the balance of blame on the emotive issue of Palestine, vertigo is surely induced by seeing the ghost walk again: the specter of anti-Semitism that haunted Europe in the thirties to its ghastly fulfillment is now revived whole in the Arab media and in some of the European press, too. Certainly, in too much of European dialogue, Israel is supported, in Lenin's words, like a rope supports a hanging man. Outright anti-Semitism is not a common feature, and there may be a token gesture to the right of Israel to exist, but much Middle East reporting falls into the impartiality trap. It gives equal weight to information from corrupt police states and proven liars as to information from a self-critical democracy.

The pious but fatuous posture is that this is somehow fair, as if truth existed in a moral vacuum, something to be measured by the yard like calico. Five million Jews in Israel are a vulnerable minority surrounded by 300 million Muslims, who for the most part are governed by authoritarian regimes, quasi–police states, that in more than fifty years have never ceased trying to wipe it out by war and terrorism. They muzzle dissent and critical reporting, they run vengeful penal systems, they have failed in almost every measure of social and political justice from the rights of women to fair trials and freedom of the press, they deflect the frustrations of their streets to the scapegoat of Zionism, and they breed and finance international terrorism. Yet it is Israel that is regarded with skepticism and sometimes hostility. Take the battle of Jenin. *The Guardian* was moved to write the editorial opinion that Israel's attacks on Jenin were "every bit as repellent" as Osama bin Laden's attack on New York on September 11. Every bit? Every bit as repellent? Did we miss something? Was there some American provocation of Osama comparable to the murder of nineteen Israelis at Passover? Was something going on in the World Trade Center as menacing as the making of bombs in Jenin, known to Palestinians as Suicide Capital?

The presumption in the Jenin feeding frenzy in print and in hours and hours of television was that the Palestinian stories of 3,000 killed and buried in secret mass graves must be true, yet the main spokesman Saeb Erekat has been shown time and time again to be a liar. Human Rights Watch now puts the death toll at a total of 54, and on their count 22 civilians—the Israelis say 3. Some Palestinian militants in fact claim Jenin as a victory in the killing of 23 Israeli soldiers.

Of course, the press had a duty to report the Palestinians' allegations; it was entitled to raise questions and express alarm in the editorial columns. But truth did not lie in the balance between competing statements, and it was ill-served by hysteria. Big stories like this demand rigor in the reporting, restraint in the language, scrupulous care in the headlining, proper attribution of sources, and above all a sense of responsibility: "Genocide" is too agonizing when real for it to be devalued by its use as small change. Benjamin Pogrund is one of the bravest journalists I have ever met. He has practiced and defended the freedom of the press with his life all his life. He risked prison and beating bringing blacks and whites together during apartheid; he is doing something like that now in Israel promoting dialogue between Jews and Arabs in the West Bank, and he told me last week that the unskeptical reporting of Jenin made his hair stand on end.

LET ME REJECT the sophistry that to question such matters is to excuse everything done under the guise of protesting anti-Semitism. It is not anti-Semitic to raise questions about Jenin, no more than it is anti-press to raise questions about the reporting. It is not anti-Semitic to protest ill treatment of Palestinians. It is not anti-Semitic to consider whether Sharon's past belies his promises for the future. It is not anti-Semitic to deplore the long occupation, though originally brought by Arab leaders in instigating and losing three wars.

It *is* anti-Semitic to vilify the state of Israel as a diabolical abstraction, reserving tolerance for the individual Jew but not the collective Jew; it *is* anti-Semitic to invent malignant outrages; it *is* anti-Semitic to consistently condemn in Israel what you ignore or condone elsewhere; it *is*, above all, anti-Semitic to dehumanize Judaism and the Jewish people so as to incite and justify their extermination. That is what has been done thousands and thousands of times over on a preposterous scale.

Anti-Semitism on the scale it is today is something relatively new in the Islamic world. There was more tolerance for Jews in the Islamic empire than ever there was in Christian Europe. I was aware, as we all are, that Israelis are unpopular because of the prolonged occupation of the West Bank and Gaza.

What I did not realize until I began looking into it for this talk was how frenzied, vociferous, paranoid, vicious, and prolific— underscore prolific—the new anti-Semitism is, and how little this fact has been reported, analyzed, and commented on in the West by press, academia, church, and governments. Yes, every- one threw up their hands in horror about Le Pen—it is always satisfying to find fault with the French!—but Europe turns a blind eye to worse. A single skinhead assault on a synagogue in Europe is news, but not the unremitting daily assault on Jews waged from Morocco to Cairo to Damascus, from Baghdad to Teheran, the Gaza Strip to Karachi. The media in the Middle East is an open sewer. Let's not get trapped in a game of moral equivalency. In terms of abuse Muslims altogether suffer noth- ing comparable to the incessant warfare now. Twenty years ago Israeli school textbooks were disfigured by stereotypes of Arabs as treacherous, mendacious, stupid, and murderous. But not now. They have cleaned up. Israelis and Arabs have worked to good effect together here.

But the Palestinian Authority uses European money to run a stream of hate propaganda through the schools, the mosques, on television and radio, in political rallies and summer camps. They film little girls singing their dedication to martyrdom. The degree of infection was manifest at Al-Najah University in the city of Nablus where the students put on an exhibition en- titled "The Sbarro Café Exhibition."

The Sbarro café was the pizza parlor where on August 9 a Palestinian suicide bomber murdered fifteen people taking a meal. The exhibit, according to the Associated Press and Israeli media, included pizza slices and body parts strewn across the room. The walls were painted red to represent scattered blood.

It is hard looking for sanity to put in the picture. I found it in the Department of Psychiatry at Ein Shams University in Cairo. Here is Dr. Adel Sadeq, who is also chairman of the Arab Psychiatrists' Association, on suicide bombings:

As a professional psychiatrist, I say that the height of bliss comes with the end of the countdown: ten, nine, eight, seven, six, five, four, three, two, one. When the martyr reaches "one" and he explodes he has a sense of himself flying, because he knows for certain that he is not dead. It is a transition to another, more beautiful world. None in the Western world would sacrifice his life for his homeland. If his homeland is drowning, he is the first to jump ship. In our culture it is different. . . . This is the only Arab weapon there is and anyone who says otherwise is a conspirator.

Next patient, please!

The Muslim world's relentless caricatures of the Jew are boringly on the same one note; Jews are always dirty, hook-nosed, money-grubbing, vindictive, and scheming parasites. They are barbarians who deliberately spread vice, drugs, and prostitution and poison water. Among the fabrications:

• Israeli authorities infected by injection 300 Palestinian children with HIV virus during the years of the intifada (charge by Nabil Ramlawi, March 17, 1997, at the UN Commission on Human Rights, Geneva).
• Israel poisoned Palestinians with uranium and nerve gas. (Charge by Yasser Arafat at the 2001 World Economic Forum. Clips to show victims racked by convulsions and vomiting were fabricated by the Palestinian Authority, reports Fiamma Nirenstein.)
• Israel is giving out drug-laced chewing gum and candy intended to make women sexually corrupt and to kill children (Egyptian and Jordanian news stories).
• Jews use the blood of gentiles to make matzos for Passover (*Al-Ahram*, Cairo). In the Saudi government daily *Al-Riyadh* on March 12 this year, Dr. Umayma Ahmad Al-Jalahma of King Faisal University in Al-Dammam, de-

scribing the Jewish holiday of Purim, offered us this: "The blood of Christian and Muslim children under the age of 10 must be used. . . . Let us now examine how the victims' blood is spilled. For this, a needle-studded barrel is used . . . , with extremely sharp needles set in it on all sides. [These] pierce the victim's body from the moment he is placed in the barrel.

These needles do the job, and the victim's blood drips from him very slowly. Thus, the victim suffers dreadful torment—torment that affords the Jewish vampires great delight . . ."

• This April the state-funded San Francisco students I mentioned have put out a poster of a baby "slaughtered according to Jewish rites under American license."

Incredibly, the Arab and Muslim media, and behind them their states, have resurrected that notorious Bolshevik forgery, "The Protocols of the Elders of Zion." This supposedly occult document, which reads like something discarded as too ridiculous for the script for Mel Brooks' *The Producers,* is the secret Zionist plan by which satanic Jews will gain world domination. It has had more scholarly stakes through its heart than the umpteen re-enactments of *Dracula,* but this bizarre counterfeit is common currency in the Muslim world. A multi-million thirty-part series was produced in Egypt by Arab Radio and Television. With a cast of 400! And not as satire.

It is "The Protocols" that inspire Hamas, the Islamic Resistance Movement, to teach their children that the Jews control the world's wealth and mass media. According to Hamas—and who will be there in the classroom or on the street to raise a question?—Jews deliberately instigated the French and Russian revolutions, and World War I, so that they could wipe out the Islamic caliphate and establish the League of Nations "in order to rule the world by their intermediary." When I checked the website Palestine Watch, by the way, to check on what they were telling the world about Israeli propaganda, I drew a blank, but there it described Hamas as seeking nothing other than peace with dignity, forbearing to mention the small matter that Hamas is dedicated to the destruction of the state of Israel.

HOLOCAUST

Apart from the volume and intensity of the multi-media global campaign, there has been an ominous change in political direction. Arab frustration with the recognition of the state of Israel after World War II has for decades been expressed as "why should the Arabs have to compensate the Jews for the Holocaust perpetrated by Europeans?"

Today the theme is that the Holocaust is a Zionist invention. It is expressed with a vehemence as astounding as the contempt for scholarship.

A typical columnist in *Al-Akhbar,* the Egyptian government daily, on April 29: "The entire matter [the Holocaust], as many French and British scientists have proven, is nothing more than a huge Israeli plot aimed at extorting the German government in particular and the European countries. I personally and in the light of this imaginary tale complain to Hitler, even saying to him, 'If only you had done it, brother, if only it had really happened, so that the world could sigh in relief [without] their evil and sin.'"

Hiri Manzour in the official Palestinian newspaper: "the figure of six million Jews cremated in the Nazi Auschwitz camps is a lie," a hoax promoted by Jews as part of their international "marketing operation."

Seif al-Al Jarawn in the Palestinian newspaper *Al-Hayat Al-Jadeeda:* "They concocted horrible stories of gas chambers which Hitler, they claimed, used to burn them alive. The press overflowed with pictures of Jews being gunned down . . . or being pushed into gas chambers. The truth is that such malicious persecution was a malicious fabrication by the Jews."

Clearly here is a consistent attempt to undermine the moral

foundations of the state of Israel, and it is espoused by a number of supposedly moderate people. The former president of Iran, Ali Akbar Hashemi-Rafsanjani, had this to say on Tehran Radio: "One atomic bomb would wipe out Israel without trace while the Islamic world would only be damaged rather than destroyed by Israeli nuclear retaliation."

The brilliance of the whole campaign of anti-Semitism is its stupefying perversity: the Arab and Muslim media and mosque depict Israelis as Nazis—even the conciliatory Barak and the hawkish Sharon are alike dressed up in swastikas with fangs dripping with blood—but media and mosque peddle the same Judeophobia that paved the way to Auschwitz. How can you talk to someone who conducts all discourse standing on his head screaming? People in the West who adopt the same murderous metaphor for Israel, and I have heard it often on this visit, may be regarded as a joke in their own country, but that is not where the action is. They are moral idiots but they lend [credibility] to malevolent liars in the Middle East.

BY COMPARISON with the phantasmagoria I have described, it seems a small matter that without exception Palestinian school textbooks supplied by the Palestinian Authority, and funded by Europe, have no space in the maps for the sovereign state of Israel, no mention of its five million people, no recognition of the Jews' historic links to Jerusalem.

What many people in Europe do not realize is that while the Palestinian claim to a state might be reasonably supported, the cause is being exploited with "Jew" as a code word for extremist incitement of hatred of America and the West. Dr. Ahmad Abu Halabiya, former rector of the Islamic University in Gaza, speaks the message: "Wherever you are, kill the Jews, the Americans who are like them, and those who stand by them."

This is Jihad. It is aimed at us all, at Europeans who "look like" Americans because they believe in liberal democracy and are infected by American culture. But its first victims are the Palestinians and the frustrated masses of the Muslim world. Their leaders have led them into ignominy in three wars. They have failed to reform their corrupt and incompetent societies, failed in almost every measure of social and political justice, from the rights of women to fair trials and freedom of the press. It is no surprise that the Arab Street is angry. It is convenient to deflect the despair and anger of the Street to Israel and the Jews who supposedly control the West, but terror and hate have a way of poisoning the very society they are supposed to be helping. See Algeria, see Ireland. When Bernard Lewis observed sixteen years ago that anti-Semitism was becoming part of Arab intellectual life "almost as much as happened in Nazi Germany," he added the comforting thought that it lacked the visceral quality of Central and East European anti-Semitism, being "still largely political and ideological, intellectual and literary," lacking any deep personal animosity or popular resonance, something cynically exploited by Arab rulers and elites, a polemical weapon to be discarded when no longer required.

But that was before the Palestinians signed on for suicide bombings, before the full force of the tidal wave I have sketched, before 9/11. Habits of mind tending to sanction terror are becoming ingrained in the Muslim world, sanctioned by the lethargy and prejudice in Europe: those Palestinians who danced for joy on 9/11 and those students who staged the grisly exhibition of pizza parlor murders were not Al Qaeda, but their acceptance of terror as a substitute for politics does not augur well for the future of Palestine as a separate state or the possibilities of peaceful political dialogue in any of the Arab states.

WHAT CAN BE DONE?

The instant and prolific dissemination of incitement is not just an issue in the Middle East. Campaigns of mutual animosity between India and Pakistan underlie the menacing brinksmanship of the moment. I believe that leaders of the media in this age of the Immediate Big Lie/the Complex Half Truth have more than a responsibility neutrally to record countervailing statements; they have a responsibility to seek out falsehood, promote objective truth, and nurture political discourse. Mr. Jonathan Steele wrote in *The Guardian* that New York today is like Brezhnev's Moscow because nobody dares question the party line on the war on terrorism. Perhaps nobody *wants* much to question it. As an unknowing prisoner in the gulag, I have to say, however, that Mr. Steele dramatized a good point. Patriotism running high can run amok, its natural passions exploited in times of crisis to justify encroachments on freedom of speech and free inquiry. That is happening to some extent now in the United States with the Vice President suggesting that it is unpatriotic to investigate the intelligence blunders that preceded 9/11. He has it exactly upside down.

SOME THINGS communicators might do:

1. Locate the poison bottles I have described—and others —and take the initiative to label them for what they are. Not just for the sake of the West or Israel. Fundamentalist regimes will be more onerous for the ordinary people; see Iran, see Afghanistan.

2. Expose deceptive websites. Run "Lies Coming Your Way" features when inflammatory stories are running. Promote corrective websites: I would mention the Daily Howler, which nails with great comic gusto the sins of the wayward press in America. Barbara and David P. Mikkelson at snopes.com make lacerating fun of a multiplicity of rumors. I also commend the world of bloggers, or blogworld, as the *U.S. News & World Report* columnist John Leo calls it. Bloggers are opinionated folk concerned with public

affairs who log on the Web every day to correct falsehood. InstaPundit, run by Glenn Reynolds, a law professor, is a fine example.

3. Promote higher professional standards of journalism between adversaries. *The Guardian* has just staged a splendid initiative in bringing Palestinians and Israelis to hear counsel from old antagonists in Ireland on how to break out of a cycle of anarchy and nihilism. It must be warmly congratulated. I propose that *The Guardian* present Index with the birthday gift by helping it to sponsor meetings between editors and writers from the warring ideologies of the Middle East—all the Arab countries and Israel, and editors and television correspondents who report on them in the Western media. They would meet for mutual criticism, not so much to solve the political problems, as to agree on a civilized professional framework in which differences can be reported, devoid of hate and lies, and perhaps to achieve some greater understanding of their responsibilities to objective truth. Thirty years ago in the International Press Institute we found that adversaries' meetings such as that helped to defuse tensions then dangerously high between Greece and Turkey and India and Pakistan.

4. Fourth and finally, all of us should have as much care with the explosive power of words as Heathrow does with our luggage. Words like . . .

Martyrs/war crimes/massacres/
Nazis/atrocities/genocide

As Churchill said, words are the only things that last forever. We cannot think morally without a reverence for the meaning of words. Take just that one noun, "martyrs." There have been close on one hundred suicide bombings in

Israel. They are deluded youth and hired killers, paid by the Saudis and the Iraqis and organized under the Palestinian Authority—until Arafat's recent attempt to distance himself on the high moral ground that they are bad for Palestine's "image." Of course, Palestinians can call their bombers "martyrs" if they choose; but the rest of us should respect the classical integrity of the meaning of the word "martyr," someone who gives up his own life to save others—not randomly to kill babes in arms, old men in wheelchairs, mothers and fathers going their innocuous ways. To describe the assassins as "martyrs," which a headline I saw recently did, is to be emotionally complicit in what classical Islam itself regards as a double transgression, suicide and murder.

Thank you for your forbearance during a long and no doubt depressing catalogue of hatred and falsehood. To sum it all up, I would like to call in aid an objective truth noted by my most celebrated predecessor as the editor of *The Times*. Sir William Haley, addressing the staff on the day he retired, left them with this thought, as I do with you tonight:

> There are things which are bad, and false, and ugly, and no amount of specious casuistry will make them good, or true, or beautiful.

LAWRENCE SUMMERS

Address at Morning Prayers

Memorial Church, Harvard University,
September 17, 2002

I SPEAK WITH YOU TODAY not as president of the university but as a concerned member of our community about something that I never thought I would become seriously worried about—the issue of anti-Semitism.

I am Jewish, identified but hardly devout. In my lifetime, anti-Semitism has been remote from my experience. My family all left Europe at the beginning of the twentieth century. The Holocaust is for me a matter of history, not personal memory. To be sure, there were country clubs where I grew up that had few if any Jewish members, but not ones that included people I knew. My experience in college and graduate school, as a faculty member, as a government official—all involved little notice of my religion.

Indeed, I was struck during my years in the Clinton administration that the existence of an economic leadership team with people like Robert Rubin, Alan Greenspan, Charlene Barshefsky, and many others that was very heavily Jewish passed without comment or notice—it was something that would have been inconceivable a generation or two ago, as indeed it would have been inconceivable a generation or two ago that Harvard could have a Jewish president.

Without thinking about it much, I attributed all of this to progress—to an ascendancy of enlightenment and tolerance. A view that prejudice is increasingly put aside. A view that while the politics of the Middle East was enormously complex, and contentious, the question of the right of a Jewish state to exist had been settled in the affirmative by the world community.

But today, I am less complacent. Less complacent and comfortable because there is disturbing evidence of an upturn in anti-Semitism globally, and also because of some developments closer to home.

Consider some of the global events of the last year:

There have been synagogue burnings, physical assaults on Jews, or the painting of swastikas on Jewish memorials in every country in Europe. Observers in many countries have pointed to the worst outbreak of attacks against the Jews since the Second World War.

Candidates who denied the significance of the Holocaust reached the runoff stage of elections for the nation's highest office in France and Denmark. State-sponsored television stations in many nations of the world spew anti-Zionist propaganda.

The United Nations–sponsored World Conference on Racism—while failing to mention human rights abuses in China, Rwanda, or anyplace in the Arab world—spoke of Israel's policies prior to recent struggles under the Barak government as constituting ethnic cleansing and crimes against humanity. The NGO declaration at the same conference was even more virulent.

I could go on. But I want to bring this closer to home. Of course academic communities should be and always will be places that allow any viewpoint to be expressed. And certainly there is much to be debated about the Middle East and much in Israel's foreign and defense policy that can be and should be vigorously challenged.

But where anti-Semitism and views that are profoundly anti-Israel have traditionally been the primary preserve of poorly educated right-wing populists, profoundly anti-Israel views are increasingly finding support in progressive intellectual communities. Serious and thoughtful people are advocating and taking actions that are anti-Semitic in their effect if not their intent.

For example:

Hundreds of European academics have called for an end to support for Israeli researchers, though not for an end to support for researchers from any other nation.

Israeli scholars this past spring were forced off the board of an international literature journal.

At the same rallies where protesters, many of them university students, condemn the IMF and global capitalism and raise questions about globalization, it is becoming increasingly common to also lash out at Israel. Indeed, at the anti-IMF rallies last spring, chants were heard equating Hitler and Sharon.

Events to raise funds for organizations of questionable political provenance that in some cases were later found to support terrorism have been held by student organizations on this and other campuses with at least modest success and very little criticism.

And some here at Harvard and some at universities across the country have called for the university to single out Israel among all nations as the lone country where it is inappropriate for any part of the university's endowment to be invested. I hasten to say the university has categorically rejected this suggestion.

We should always respect the academic freedom of everyone to take any position. We should also recall that academic freedom does not include freedom from criticism. The only antidote to dangerous ideas is strong alternatives vigorously advocated.

I have always throughout my life been put off by those who heard the sound of breaking glass in every insult or slight, and conjured up images of Hitler's Kristallnacht at any disagreement with Israel. Such views have always seemed to me alarmist if not slightly hysterical. But I have to say that while they still seem to me unwarranted, they seem rather less alarmist in the world of today than they did a year ago.

I would like nothing more than to be wrong. It is my greatest hope and prayer that the idea of a rise of anti-Semitism proves to be a self-denying prophecy—a prediction that carries the seeds of its own falsification. But this depends on all of us.

PART TWO

SOMETHING OLD, SOMETHING NEW

BEREL LANG

On the "the" in "the Jews"
or, From Grammar to Anti-Semitism

THE SEVERAL TONGUE-TWISTING "the's" in my title are
less difficult to manage than the problem they conceal.
For there is a conceptual, cultural, and, finally, moral issue that
bears directly on anti-Semitism in the common linking of the
definite article "the" and Jews—that is, in "the Jews." I don't
mean to claim that anti-Semitism would not have occurred or
would now disappear if only its initiators and apologists paid
more attention to grammar. But when a common and super-
ficially innocent use of the definite article in statements about
Jews turns out to be not innocent at all but in effect anti-
Semitic, we need to consider more closely how and why that
happens. Whether the linguistic usage originated as a cause or
only a symptom of anti-Semitism hardly matters; it has in time
served both functions, and it has thus also, from both direc-
tions, extended the reach of ideology to grammar. Since ideology flourishes, furthermore, mainly by concealment, to bring
into the open this secret role of the "the," trivial as it seems,
may thus also contribute to undermining the many-layered
foundation of anti-Semitism.

The usage under suspicion here is the phrase "the Jews"—
and if the particular use of that phrase criticized is not its only

one, it is distinctive. As, for example—most famously—in: "The
Jews killed Jesus." Or, more currently, "The Jews control Hollywood"—or again, as in the aftermath of the recent controversy
about the "neighbors" in the Polish town of Jedwabne: "In
1939, after the Russians entered [Jedwabne], the Jews took
over all the offices, including the town hall."* The general
intent behind these statements might be inferred, but for the
moment—since we're talking first about grammar not psychology—I propose to put the questions of motive aside in order to
examine the difference between the statements themselves and
what they would mean if they appeared *without* the definite
article that each of the statements cited include; that is, the
common reference in each of them to "*the* Jews."

Consider, for contrast, the shortened versions of those same
statements with the definite article omitted: "Jews killed Jesus,"
"Jews control Hollywood," "In 1939, after the Russians entered
[Jedwabne], Jews took over all the offices, including the town
hall." The difference between the first and the second groups of
statements is clear. Both groups of statements assert that certain people "killed Jesus," "control Hollywood," and "took over
all the [Jedwabne] offices"—*and* that those people were or are
Jews. The first group of statements, however, goes one step further—implying that not only were or are the people responsible for the acts described Jews, but that they acted collectively
or in concert, among themselves and as part of a larger whole.
That is, as *the* Jews. Not just as some Jews, then, but as a corporate body, expressing a common purpose or will. To deny
this last implication would make the definite article in the sentence quite misleading—since there would then be nothing
definite for the "definite" article to refer to.

Admittedly, anyone making the statements in the first

---

* Senator Jadwiga Stolarska, in the Polish Senate, September 13, 2001. Cited in
Anna Bikont, "Seen from Jedwabne," *Yad Vashem Studies* XXX, 2002, p. 8.

group is unlikely to believe that every Jew alive at the time mentioned played a part in the act or disposition mentioned. But the main point of the statements is that "*the* Jews" (as a group) are responsible for that action even if it was more immediately the work of only a few of them. A collective will is thus presupposed, and so also, of course, a common responsibility, both of these now ascribed to "the" Jews. Not just "this one Jew" or "those several Jews," but the Jews as a group.

Each of the first set of statements, then, has two parts. The first part is a straightforward claim that those responsible for a certain act are or were Jewish; the second is the implied claim of a collective purpose motivating the act. Neither of these assertions is itself necessarily anti-Semitic; the test of truth is possible for both—measured by evidence to which the speaker already lays claim. To be sure, the second assertion in the second part echoes a well-worn anti-Semitic theme: the contention of a conspiracy of sorts among "the" Jews as a group. But this claim, too, is subject to proof or disproof, even if the purveyors of its best-known appearances have rarely troubled themselves with that issue. (The forged "Protocols of the Elders of Zion" remains a paradigmatic representation for this view of "the" Jewish conspiracy.)

It might be objected to my characterization so far that the phrase "the Jews" need not mean *all* Jews. On a variant reading, "The Jews killed Jesus" might refer only to a sub-group within the larger one—perhaps to the Jews then living in Palestine, at a time when many Jews lived elsewhere. But even in this more restrictive interpretation—which is not how the statement is typically understood—a common purpose would be posited among *those* Jews, with that claim then having to be demonstrated (as it rarely is). In this sense, Nazi anti-Semitism, for all its pseudo-science, had the systematic "advantage" of biologizing race. The conspiracies alleged by the Nazis (as, e.g., among Jewish Bolsheviks and/or Jewish capitalists) did not require any specific evidence of covert meetings or documents, since the genetic features, which in their view made Jewish character dangerous, would also account for the nefarious ways in which that group purpose would be realized. (That this "foundation" posed serious problems for a "scientific" genetic theory did not faze the Nazis who, from their earliest answer to the question of "Who is a Jew?" onward, relied on a social rather than a biological basis for their "racial" definition.) In social and historical terms, of course, anyone familiar with Jewish history and communal life would find implausible the claim of a single or even a common purpose or will among the diverse groups historically identified as Jewish. The conceptual and practical difficulties in proving all claims that assume the existence of corporate "persons" or intentions are greater still here; indeed, since there has been no central or coordinated authority in the two thousand years of post-exilic Judaism, it is difficult to understand what such a claim would even mean.

Perhaps this line of reasoning may encounter the objection that the term "the Jews" does not necessarily designate a collective or corporate Jewish will at all. What in some contexts serves as a collective or substantive noun may in others be shorthand for a group of individuals as individuals—who may, for instance, share certain beliefs but not because of any prior collective design. "The Jews are monotheists," for example, implies not that every Jew believes in one God, but that Biblical or traditional or "essential" Judaism claims that tenet. So also "The Jews in the U.S. have an average educational level of three years of college"—from which a certain characteristic can be inferred of a hypothetical individual, not a group plan or even a common feature of all individual Jews. Such references to "the Jews" are common enough—but they are also readily distinguished from the use challenged here. On the second, "individualist" use, there is no difference in meaning between statements in which "*the* Jews" appears and versions of the same statements in which the "the" is omitted. And this is clearly not true for the first group. There is, I hope to have shown, a difference—in ideological terms, a large one—between saying that "The Jews killed Jesus" and its shortened counterpart, that "Jews killed Jesus."

A QUESTION REMAINS, to be sure, of why *either* of the two pairs of statements should be asserted at all. And indeed, nothing said so far touches the question of the truth or falsity of any of the statement cited, whether in the first or the second versions. I have been trying to show only how ideology makes its way into such an apparently innocuous phrase as "the Jews." But if "the" is the primary culprit here, it is not the only one. For there is a substantive question which goes beyond grammar in asking what basis there could be in such statements for referring to the Jews at all. On the assumption that there is ordinarily an evident connection between the subject and the predicate of a sentence, it would be reasonable to ask why "Jews," let alone "*the* Jews," should appear in the statements noted. Is the statement that "Jews control Hollywood" meant to explain the types of film that Hollywood produces? Hollywood's financial success? The popular culture of which Hollywood films are part? Any of these, and many other, meanings are possible—but a question to which they are all subject is what relevance the role of Jews (or "the Jews") has to whatever they assert: why the reference at all?

A standard Jewish joke makes the point here (sometimes cited as a "Holocaust joke" but more broadly applicable and apparently much older in origin):

A: "The Jews are responsible for the economic crisis" (or the Crucifixion or the plague).
B: No, it is the Jews and the bicycle riders.
A: Why the bicycle riders?
B: Why the Jews?

The issue being made explicit here is that in the pairs of statements cited, not only is no evidence offered for the roles they ascribe to the Jews as Jews, but there is no acknowledgment of this even as an issue. Even if it could be proven that the people responsible for the crucifixion or who control Hollywood were (or are) Jews—and putting aside the complicating issue of exactly who is to count as a Jew or not—the substantive question remains of what importance this "proof" would have: what difference does it make? This is to ask why it would be *relevant* to know that the people who control Hollywood or who killed Jesus or who took control of the municipal offices of Jedwabne were Jews? The implication of identifying them as Jews is that it somehow adds to understanding the act (perhaps also of other general social or cultural issues). But does it? To allege that members of a certain group have power disproportionate to their numbers, or that members of the group were responsible for a particular historical act, would warrant the identification only if a connection could be shown between the group-identity and the event. But what, we ask, is the connection here?

It is probably true, for example—and let us for argument's sake assume—that the people who "killed Jesus" were less than six feet tall. Would the claim itself be worth making? It might, one supposes, have some interest as bearing on the average heights of people at the particular time and place—in contrast to the average heights of people at other places or times. But unless one also supposed a connection between those heights and the act of killing Jesus, the conjunction would seem random or arbitrary and, in any event, trivial even if true: what difference could it make? The fact itself seems to have little to do with explaining the circumstances of Jesus's execution— unless, of course, one built on it a verdict of continuing guilt through subsequent generations of everyone less than six feet tall.

Nor, in the same way, do we learn very much about Hollywood in finding that the studio heads who shaped or now "control" it were (or are) Jews—except, again, as a kind of anthropological stereotype, with all the excesses and dangers that stereotypes inevitably convey. Does it contribute to understanding film as a medium? The "entertainment" industry? Perhaps as much (but how much is that?) as the finding that the automobile industry, at approximately the same time, was developed by Midwestern Protestants—except who has ever commented on that? This does not mean that something substantial *might* not be illuminated by the reference—for example (in the case of the crucifixion), the evolving negative attitude towards capital punishment within Judaism as that would have figured in the trial and execution of Jesus as a co-religionist. Or, in the case of Jedwabne, as Polish Jews, because of their system of education, were either better or less qualified for certain types of work outside the community itself. Such connections might indeed turn out to be historically significant, and if so, they might also have occasioned the statements cited here as examples—but in fact no such connections have been demonstrated, and more important, the very issue of proof has typically been ignored.

In practice, of course, claims that "The Jews killed Jesus," even when reduced to only "Jews killed Jesus," have usually been cited not in historical studies of the relation between early Christianity and Rabbinic Judaism, but as the basis for a charge of deicide—and this, as a matter of corporate and thus continuing Jewish responsibility. That charge is intelligible, however, only if "the" Jews of Jesus's time, whether in Jerusalem or elsewhere, not only acted in concert with each other but also implicated future generations of Jews—a collective "the" on a large scale indeed. The claim that "the Jews" "took over" the municipal offices when the Russians arrived in Jedwabne may have fewer metaphysical implications than the charge of deicide, but neither is it meant to be part of an analysis of social class or municipal governance in Poland during World War II. The reference is clearly intended to explain, if not to justify, the massacre in Jedwabne of members of the Jewish populace by their non-Jewish Polish "neighbors" after the Nazis, in 1941, had driven out the occupying Russians. In this way, then, and perhaps predictably, ideology centered in the grammatical "the" links up with ideology in a much broader framework.

Again, no link to anti-Semitism is *entailed* in any of the statements cited. As truth is the measure of all supposedly descriptive statements, so here too; thus, the claims remain questions rather than assertions until tested by the evidence. Furthermore, applying the phrase "the Jews" presupposes acceptance of the notion of a collective will (and responsibility)—first, in general, and then, in particular reference to Jews as a group. In point of fact, to be sure, we know that the "the" in "the Jews" has often been summoned as a locution to the cause of anti-Semitism. And even if the locution has at times been used spontaneously or unconsciously, this would not make its connotation insignificant—or, for that matter, unintentional. In this way, a slight grammatical gesture turns out to be no less weighted ideologically than many of ideology's more blatant pronouncements. Expressions of language or reasoning are sometimes viewed as "beyond ideology": neutral with respect to social causes or even personal interests. Undoubtedly, certain uses of language warrant this exemption—but the specific connection between ideology and grammar in the "the" of "the Jews" is too clear to be denied.

ROBERT S. WISTRICH
The Old-New Anti-Semitism

T HE TWENTIETH CENTURY may well be seen by future historians as the age *par excellence* of ideological politics. Millions were slaughtered on the altar of false messianisms and their salvationist logic, and in some places the killing still continues unabated. In the totalitarian nightmare of the last century, the secular political religions of Nazism and Marxist-Leninism undoubtedly occupy a special place. So, too, does the oldest and darkest of ideological obsessions—that of anti-Semitism—for which over a decade ago I coined the term "the longest hatred."

For Adolf Hitler, in particular, anti-Semitism was the axis and *raison d'être* of the Nazi movement he created. His dream of global hegemony was overcome only through the combined military might of the United States, the British Empire, and the Soviet Union. Nazism as a vital force in world politics was indeed destroyed in the flames engulfing Berlin at the end of April 1945, but the anti-Jewish poison it spread to far-flung corners of the globe has yet to be eradicated. The legacy has proven to be especially potent in the former Soviet Union and the Arab-Islamic world, where anti-Semitism is once again acquiring a potentially lethal charge. There is currently a culture of hatred that permeates books, magazines, newspapers, sermons, video-cassettes, the Internet, television, and radio in the Arab Middle East which has not been seen since the heyday of Nazi Germany. Indeed, the dehumanizing images of Jews and Israel that are penetrating the body politic of Islam are sufficiently radical in tone and content to constitute a new "warrant for genocide." They combine the blood libel of medieval Christian Europe with Nazi conspiracy theories about the Jewish drive for "world domination" and slanderous Islamic quotations about Jews as the "sons of apes" and donkeys.

The Quranic motifs began to grow in importance after the Iranian Revolution of 1979, along with virulent anti-Americanism. In the Islamic demonology, both America and Israel are now bonded together as "Satanic forces" that threaten the core identity, values, and existence of Islam. This has been especially the case since the beginning of the Palestinian Al-Aqsa intifada in the autumn of 2000 and the massacres of September 11, 2001. Not only did an astonishing number of Muslims seek to place the responsibility for this mass murder onto the Jews, but Israel, more than ever, was execrated as a dagger of the West poised to strike at the heart of the Muslim Arab world. In the anti-Semitic script, America itself is depicted as being run by Jews malevolently determined to subvert and destroy Islam. This chorus of voices has grown even shriller with the American war on Iraq, a conflict that has led to an ever closer twinning of anti-American, anti-Israeli, and anti-Semitic sentiment in western Europe as well as the Islamic world. Driven by this ideology, Islamists see the fingerprints of the all-powerful Zionist lobby everywhere, spreading its tentacles and deadly lies, draining the life-blood of Arabs and Muslims, gratuitously inciting war against Iraq, and carrying out its sinister plans for global control. The current popularity of "The Protocols of the Elders of Zion"—a forged Russian document from the beginning of the twentieth century in which many Muslims appear to believe—is frightening testimony to the power of such myths. The recent television series in Egypt dramatizing the "Protocols" and their fantasy of "Jewish world domination" is a mark of how deeply this anti-Semitic virus has already penetrated the thinking of political Islam.

Fundamentalist and oil-rich Saudi Arabia, the same soil from which Osama bin Laden and his Al-Qaeda movement have sprung, is a major hotbed of the type of Muslim jihad that specifically calls for the terrorist murder of Jews and Christians. Government dailies even print gory nonsense about the "well-established fact" that "Jews spill human blood for their holiday pastries." But a no less anti-Semitic outlook holds sway in more secular Arab societies such as Egypt, Syria, Iraq, and Jordan. This hysteria cannot be adequately understood in terms of the Arab-Israeli conflict. Certainly, the cause of Palestine has periodically been hijacked by radical Islamists and pan-Arabists in order to broaden their political support in the Muslim world. But the "Jewish question" in radical Islam (as with its Western totalitarian predecessors) is not centered on Palestine, and certainly does not see Palestine as a purely territorial issue amenable to rational bargaining. The ideological anti-Semitism that characterizes Islamist thinking is driven by something else: an irrational belief that history itself is determined by the evil machinations of the Jewish people. In this respect the Islamists seem to be directly following the Nazi model, with its fixation on a mythical Jewish power that strives for global hegemony. Of course, the two models and the two situations are not identical, and the context has changed as well. The "Jewish question" radically changed its contours with the establishment of a Jewish state and Israeli military power in the Middle East. Nonetheless, the creation of Israel could not, on its own, blunt the potential of anti-Semitism as a global phenomenon. It seems rather to have attenuated its force for about two decades, even while a new version of the problem metastasized. Zionism in effect has shifted the focus of postwar anti-Jewishness to an assault on the dominant collective representation of contemporary Jewish existence—the State of Israel itself. Since 1948, the major ideological and political threat to the survival of the Jewish nation gradually switched from Europe to the Arab-Islamic world, fueled by a politicidal "anti-Zionist" ideology whose main thrust has always been the destruction of Israel as an independent state.

THE EUROPEAN LEGACY

To grasp the origins of the demonology behind contemporary Islamist versions of anti-Semitism, one needs to be aware of its characteristics as they first crystallized at the end of the nineteenth century. Fin-de-siècle European anti-Semitism was deeply pessimistic. It was obsessed with the "decadence" of Christian and "Aryan" civilization, supposedly in thrall to a newly emancipated and "victorious" Jewry. From the radical journalist Wilhelm Marr's prophecy of *Finis Germaniae* (1879) to Edouard Drumont's *La Dernière Bataille* (1889) and the Teutonomaniac Houston S. Chamberlain's *Foundations of the 19th Century* (1899), we find the same specter of Jewish power and gentile demise invoked by a new class of best-selling publicists and populist intellectuals. The anti-Semites inhabited a murky fantasy-world imbued with quasi-apocalyptic visions of European decline, colored by occult sectarianism and permeated with notions of retributive punishment on a cosmic scale. They elaborated negative millenarianism in secular garb—a "reactionary modernism" that reluctantly adapted to democratic mass politics and class conflict while preaching a backward-looking utopia based on pre-modern feudal or even tribal models. In this fin-de-siècle world of economic disorientation, rapid social change, and eroding traditional values, populist anti-Semitic movements arose that became the seedplot of Nazism. They were especially powerful in the decaying Austro-Hungarian Empire, where the young Hitler acquired the "granite-like foundations," as he called them in *Mein Kampf,* of his Welt-anschauung. The main elements of twentieth-century ideological anti-Semitism were already in place by 1914, when Hitler was twenty-five years old. These elements included: the beliefs that nationalism was an irresistible force and that race was a secular equivalent of Destiny or Providence; the fear of pollution by alien, inferior races; the angst provoked by Marxist class struggle and the leveling tendencies of mass society; and the hatred, nourished by movements of the radical Right and Left, of capitalism, modern urban civilization, and liberal democracy.

European anti-Semites usually shared a belief in occult, sinister forces working to undermine social hierarchy, order, authority, and tradition. They were alarmed by the spiritual vacuum induced by the declining hold of Christianity, and especially by the working classes' attraction to apocalyptic, revolutionary Marxism. Above all, they shared an obsession with the mythological figure of the satanic, ubiquitous, immoral, and all-powerful Jew. Here was, as Richard Wagner put it, the "plastic demon of modern civilization," whose unquenchable will to destroy gentile society lay behind all negative processes of change, providing a coherent explanation for the resulting anomie. "All comes from the Jew, all returns to the Jew." This classic formula of Edouard Drumont in 1886 exemplified the delirious causality embraced by modern anti-Semites. The principle of evil is not in ourselves; it comes from outside. It is the product of conspiracy and devilish forces whose incarnation is the mythical Jew. The mass slaughter of World War I, with its destruction of traditional elites, collapse of established monarchies, and sudden flurry of revolutionary coups in central Europe (above all the Bolshevik triumph in Russia, whose autocracy had been the fountainhead of the ancien régime in Europe), immeasurably envenomed and radicalized anti-Semitism. The massacres of Jews by the White Armies during the Russian Civil War (1918–20), the fierce anti-Semitic backlash against Jewish participation in the German and Hungarian revolutions, and the juxtaposition of the "Jewish" and "Red" perils in east-central Europe were all alarming signals of growing extremism.

These events greatly encouraged the mass dissemination of nineteenth-century anti-Semitic stereotypes and ideologies. The climate was ripe for a far more effective translation of conspiracy theories into political praxis than had been the case before World War I. German defeat in that war, crushing economic reparations imposed by the Allies, the resultant loathing for the democratic West, the devastating inflation of 1923, chronic political instability in the Weimar Republic, growing fear of communism, and the ravages of the Great Depression were so many milestones on the road to Nazism. From each one, the sense of helplessness grew, and the longing to blame someone or something for it grew with it. Nazi anti-Semitism thus sprang from popular fears, and at the same time stoked and organized them.

THE NAZI-ARAB NEXUS

Nazi doctrines exerted considerable fascination on the Arab world during these years. Both pan-Arabism and pan-Islamic ideologies in the Middle East looked to Hitler's Germany as a model for national unification, a counterweight to Western imperialism and a source of revolutionary dynamism. Anti-Semitic and anti-British feelings (which anticipated some of the anti-Americanism rampant today) created a powerful sense of affinity between German Nazis and Arab nationalists in Egypt, Syria, and Iraq. A former Syrian Ba'athi leader, recalling the atmosphere of the late 1930s, wrote:

> We were fascinated by Nazism, reading its books and the sources of its thinking, particularly Nietzsche, Fichte and Chamberlain. And we were the first who thought about

translating *Mein Kampf.* We, who lived in Damascus, could appreciate the tendency of the Arab people to Nazism which was the power which appealed to it. By nature, the vanquished admires the victorious.

Arab nationalists, radicals, and Islamic militants were clearly influenced by the anti-liberal and anti-Western spirit of fascism, its emphasis on youth, its pattern of organization, and, above all, its cult of power. In Iraq, the Director-General of Education, Dr. Sami Shawkat, told students in Baghdad in the autumn of 1933: "There is something more important than money and learning for preserving the honor of a nation and for keeping humiliation at bay. That is strength. . . . Strength, as I use the word here, means to excel in the Profession of Death."

Seventy years later, Saddam's Iraq provided a sinister confirmation of this outlook in its determination to develop weapons of mass destruction and its readiness to use them against internal as well as external enemies. The idolization of power, together with the totalitarian mystique of the nation, was already developed by many Arab radicals in the 1930s and 1940s. Their visions of grandeur were exacerbated by a feeling of deep malaise, and even trauma, which the encounter with Western civilization had inflicted upon Arab society. The Muslim Brotherhood, founded in 1928 by Hasan al-Banna in Egypt, represented the pristine anti-Western and fundamentalist version of this backlash. From the outset, the jihadists around al-Banna developed the cult of the leader and preached fascist doctrines of "unity and discipline" and "martial strength and military preparedness." Like Ahmad Hussein's Young Egypt movement of the late 1930s, they were militantly anti-Zionist and anti-Semitic, supporting the boycott and harassment of the Jewish community in Egypt.

The Muslim Brothers, with their vision of a *judenfrei* Palestine as a rallying-point for removing all Western influences from the Middle East, belonged to the first wave of Islamic fascism. The second wave, which swelled after the Six Day War, had as its leading ideologue one Sayyid Qutb, a revolutionary Egyptian intellectual executed by Nasser only a year before the Arab defeat. For Qutb and his followers, the invasion of Western culture had thrown Muslims back into a state of pre-Islamic barbarism (*jahīliyya*) dominated by social chaos, sexual permissiveness, polytheism, apostasy, and idolatry. His notorious text of the early 1950s, *Our Struggle with the Jews,* portrayed the Jews as the "eternal enemies" of Muhammad and the Islamic community who used Christianity, capitalism, and communism as weapons in their war to subvert the Muslim religion. The Islamists of today have faithfully followed Qutb in attributing Marxism, psychoanalysis, sociology, materialism, sexual depravity, and the destruction of morals and the family to "Jewish" influence. In this cultural war, they see Zionism and Americanism as kindred expressions of an existential threat to Muslim identity.

ANTI-SEMITISM TODAY

Today, the identity crisis affecting millions of Muslims is spawning its own brand of Islamic neo-fascism. That crisis is accentuated by accelerating urbanization, overpopulation, and endemic poverty, as well as the prevalence of suffocating dictatorships throughout the Arab world. Without the bogeymen of America and Israel, however, Arab despots would be hard put to explain to their own peoples why the modern world is passing them by. Why is Cairo infinitely poorer than Tel Aviv? Why is heart surgery so much better in London than in Damascus? Why do Arab immigrants prefer Los Angeles or Detroit to Baghdad or Beirut?

The crushing of dissent, the repression of women, the scale of mass illiteracy and underdevelopment, and the oil riches of corrupt ruling elites provide part of the answer. For decades, authoritarian Arab regimes turned the bitter feelings of humiliation and rage among the masses against the "colonialist" West. The Islamists have continued in this vein, adding their own paranoid suspicions of modern secular civilization. Fear of apostasy fuses with hatred of America, Jews, and non-Muslims in general. Rank homophobia and a fiercely puritanical, repressive vision of veiled and enslaved womanhood are added to the mix. Indeed, European fascism, for all its male-oriented warrior barbarism, was almost liberating in its attitudes toward women compared with the Taliban or Saudi Wahhabism. Militarism, the glorification of force, and a nihilistic cult of death are, however, traits that Nazis, fascists, and Islamists share completely in common. The morbid addiction to destruction and revenge drives them to paint the world red with blood in their mad rush to introduce utopia in the here-and-now. Added to this is the totalitarian belief, very much shared by Stalinists, in the all-encompassing power of propaganda, party organization, and terror—a mystique reinforced by the seemingly limitless manipulative possibilities of modern technology joined to ideological dogma. The individual is considered totally malleable and subordinate to the revolutionary cause, whether it be "living space," "racial purity," the "Arab Renaissance," the "classless society," or the jihad. Promethean doctrines, to which human life is so eagerly sacrificed, can only be vindicated by the success of a global revolution that grants political hegemony to true believers in the cause. Whether millions die in the attempt is irrelevant in the light of either the eternal laws of nature and history or the will of God.

Totalitarian anti-Semitism reached its genocidal extreme with Hitler's ideology and a political praxis that, though it grew up on Christian soil, was ultimately determined to replace and supplant Christianity. National Socialism was racial politics carried out under the sign of the Apocalypse, in which the global struggle between the "Aryan" world and Jewry stood at the center of a closed system of thought. Anti-Semitism was transformed into a crucial lever in the restructuring not only of Nazi Germany but of the entire international order—initially as a weapon for undermining Hitler's domestic adversaries and then for subverting or neutralizing opposition to his policies abroad. Hitler emphasized that the destruction of world Jewry was a precondition for restoring the natural hierarchy within the nation and between the races. The Darwinian racism that he espoused was not the root of his anti-Semitism; it was simply the "scientific" language he employed to give more credibility to his eschatological political agenda. Its deeper sources lay in a pseudo-religious, Manichean vision of a world in which "the Jew" was the negative wellspring and dark side of history driving mankind relentlessly toward the abyss.

Nazi ideology led to acts of murderous race-cleansing of varying kinds during World War II, but only the Jews were singled out for total extermination. The war against them was conceived as an apocalyptic *Vernichtungskrieg* for global hegemony. What Hitler did was to transform the demonological fantasies of both Christian and anti-Christian anti-Semitism into a practical political program on a universal scale. The choice of the target grew out of centuries of Christian teaching that had singled out the Jews as a deicidal people. But the Shoah was a modernized high-tech version of "Holy War" carried out by totalitarian atheists. These atheists consciously sought to eradicate both the Enlightenment legacy of reason and the entire Judeo-Christian tradition of ethics.

The topography and lexicography of post-Holocaust anti-Semitism changed dramatically after 1945, yet the essential elements of ideological continuity have been remarkably tenacious. Today, the geographical center of gravity is neither Germany nor the European continent (despite the alarming revival of old prejudices) but the Arab-Muslim world and its diasporic offshoots. Anti-Jewish rhetoric in the new millennium tends to be Islamic, anti-globalist, and neo-Marxist far more than it is Christian, conservative, or neo-fascist. Whether the assault comes from the far Left or Right, from liberals or fundamentalists, its focus now is above all the collective Jew embodied in the State of Israel. Despite the incessant hair-splitting over the need to separate anti-Zionism and anti-Semitism, this has in recent decades become a distinction without a meaningful difference. Whatever theoretical contortions one may indulge in, the State of Israel is a Jewish state. Whoever wants to defame or destroy it, openly or through policies that entail nothing else but such destruction, is in effect practicing the Jew-hatred of yesteryear, whatever their self-proclaimed intentions.

THE SOVIET LEGACY

The case of Soviet communism is particularly interesting in this regard. In 1931, Josef Stalin officially denounced anti-Semitism as "zoological," a form of cannibalism. This was formally consistent with the original internationalist policy of Marxist-Leninism and the older communist view of anti-Semitism as a reactionary tool of the ruling classes to divert attention away from the class struggle. By 1949, however, Stalin was beginning to sound like Adolf Hitler when it came to "the Jewish question." He adopted the classic Nazi mythology of "rootless cosmopolitanism" and applied it to Soviet Jews. Stalinist accusations which developed out of this slogan followed the pattern of the "Protocols of the Elders of Zion." This had an obvious propaganda value in Soviet Russia, as it did in all of the East European satellite countries that fell under communist control in the late 1940s, where anti-Semitism already enjoyed great popularity. The fictitious "world conspiracy" invented by the Stalinists offered a suitable backdrop for totalitarian claims to world rule alongside the crusade against Wall Street, capitalism, and imperialism.

Stalin's shift toward the Nazi paradigm became transparent

in the Slansky show trial in Czechoslovakia (1952–53), which proceeded as if all Jews were potentially Zionists and all Zionist groups were "agents" of American imperialism. This was followed by the extinction of Soviet Jewish culture and a planned "final solution" of the "Jewish question" by mass expulsion to Siberia. This disaster was averted only by Stalin's sudden death (on Purim, incidentally) fifty years ago.

Under Nikita Khrushchev's somewhat erratic but bold de-Stalinization policy, there was a temporary respite, though Soviet adventurism in the Third World and domestic campaigns against religion ensured that prejudices against Israel, the Jews, and Judaism continued to fester. After the Israeli victory in the Six Day War, a new Soviet-style version of the "Protocols" emerged behind a thin veneer of Marxist-Leninist verbiage. Relentless Communist Party propaganda unleashed a massive campaign portraying Zionism as "Fascist," "Nazi," "racist," driven by "hatred toward all peoples" and a "chosen people" superiority complex. It was no accident that Moscow played such a major role in masterminding the infamous UN resolution equating Zionism with racism.

These ideological fictions had little to do with the actual policies of the Jewish state. They assumed the existence of a dark Jewish conspiracy, linked to America and freemasonry, that sought planetary domination. The Zionist goals were allegedly to overthrow the communist systems in the USSR and Eastern Europe, to dominate the economy of the largest capitalist states, and to liquidate national-liberation movements throughout the Third World. The so-called Zionist "bourgeoisie" aimed to reduce the Arabs and the Third World to servitude. The "socialist" camp, led by the USSR, saw itself as the main obstacle to this perfidious design.

By the 1970s, Zionism was considered one of the darkest forces of world reaction, an ideology and an organization no less dangerous than Hitlerism and "Aryan" racism. History was rewritten by Soviet propagandists to make Zionism the source of inspiration for the Nazis! It was even branded as an active agent of "collaboration" in the German implementation of the Holocaust. In the Brezhnev era of Soviet expansion, "anti-Zionist" anti-Semitism became a cardinal feature of the official chauvinist ideology. This was the first major political campaign to totally defame Zionism as the incarnation of evil and to discredit the Torah as a book of hatred, preaching genocide. The Jewish religion was systematically slandered as a teaching of racial exclusion and its messianic ideals smeared as a justi-fication for *Lebensraum*. As in contemporary Islamic and Arab literature, the grand sweep of Jewish and Zionist history was twisted into a narrative of pure criminality, sadism, and im-morality.

The Soviet anti-Semitic demonology of Zionism did not immediately collapse with the fall of communism. In the early 1990s, the so-called "Red-Brown" alliance of neo-Stalinists and Russian ultra-nationalists, animated by their belief in the inter-national Zionist conspiracy, continued to preach anti-Jewish doctrines of hate. The alliance claimed that Jews controlled the channels of mass communication throughout the world, in-sisted that they had deliberately ruined Russia through the Communist Revolution, and proclaimed that Jewish oligarchs were now delivering the nation into the hands of a rapacious cosmopolitan clique working on behalf of American imperial-ist designs. This was the credo of Vladimir Zhirinovsky, who, ten years ago, won a quarter of all ballots cast in the Russian elections. Depicted in the media as the Russian Hitler, he spe-cialized in ethnic slurs against Balts, Armenians, Caucasians, and blacks as well as Jews; he established close ties with the German and Austrian radical Right (including neo-Nazis) and talked openly of restoring a Greater Russian dominion. Just as he execrated Jews and Zionists, so he identified strongly with Arab nationalist dictators like Saddam Hussein.

PAN-ARABIST AND ISLAMIST VERSIONS

The Russian communist model, like that of German Nazism, was an important formative influence in Saddam's version of Ba'athism. The Iraqi leader grew up in the framework of this dogmatic ideology, which not only glorified the Arabs as a "master race" but also emphasized the need for relentless struggle and perpetual revolution in the name of the pan-Arab cause. Saddam imbibed his radical nationalism from Michel Aflaq, a Greek Orthodox Christian born in Damascus who had turned his back on all Western ideas to create the Arab Renaissance in the 1940s. In the Aflaqian concept, the Arab nation was the culmination of spiritual perfection, far superior in its traditions and culture to the superficiality of Western civilization. But Arab unity would remain a dream without sacrifice, conflict, martyrdom, and bloodshed.

Saddam adopted Aflaq's highly charged ideological style while accentuating the Leninist party structures of Ba'athism in order to consolidate his grip on power. He embraced a quasi-mystical view of the Arabs which assumed that an exalted eschatological mission had been assigned to them by God himself. Saddam added to this belief a tremendous emphasis on the will to power, the need to crush a world of enemies, to prepare for endless war and perpetuate the revolution as a sacred task of the Ba'ath Party. For the Iraqi leader, there was never any question about his right to murder "inferior" groups such as the Kurds or anyone defined as an internal "enemy" of the regime. It was also an axiom that America and its civilization must be humiliated. It was no less self-evident to him that the "Zionist entity" must be eradicated.

For the Ba'athis, Israel was always an artificial "implant" in the Middle East, a multi-tentacled "octopus," a "deadly cancer" or an "AIDS virus" to be burned up, as Saddam Hussein publicly threatened to do shortly before the first Gulf War. Only two years ago he declared on Iraqi television: "Palestine is Arab and must be liberated from the river to the sea and all the Zionists who emigrated to the land of Palestine must leave." The fact that Saddam filled his speeches with references to Nebuchadnezzar (the Babylonian ruler who destroyed the first Jewish Temple) and Saladin demonstrated not only megalomania but also his determination to destroy the Jewish State and teach the Western "Christian" Crusaders a lesson they would never forget. In Saddam's totalitarian version of pan-Arabism, Jews were by definition "outsiders," "aliens," and enemies of the Arab nation. Hence it is no surprise to find that Israelis are completely dehumanized as murderers, criminals, and the scum of the earth in Iraqi (as well as in Syrian) Ba'athi literature. Wiping out Israel meant expelling or killing a collection of "rootless nomads" who stole a land that was not their own. For Islamic fundamentalists, the "liberation of Palestine" is no less of an ideological and political imperative than it is for the Ba'athis, but it is also a "war of civilizations" in a more far-reaching and even apocalyptic sense. In their confrontation with Israel and Zionism, the Islamists appeal to a 1,400-year-old history and repeatedly invoke Quranic precedents. Muhammad's war with the Jews in seventh-century Arabia is for them a vitally important guideline for the present. But this return to the distant past has not prevented Islamists from borrowing extensively from the much execrated Western culture's most extreme anti-Semitic motifs. Thus, fundamentalist Muslims have enthusiastically revived the blood libel of medieval Christianity and adopted the scenario of a "final struggle" with the Jews as part of their Islamic *Heilsgeschichte*.

The September 11, 2001, attack on America escalated such trends to new heights of defamation. The Al-Qaeda assault on the World Trade Center in New York was not only a declaration of war against the greatest metropolis of international capitalism. It was also seen by its perpetrators as a blow against the nerve-center of "world Jewry." There is a line of continuity running from Hitler to Ramzi Yousef, who planned the World Trade Center bombings of 1993, and Mohamed Atta, who masterminded the 9/11 atrocity. The Islamo-fascists, like the Nazis before them, are genuinely convinced that a corrupt America is in Jewish hands. Hence, the jihad to liberate Muslims across the world from oppression and injustice is simultaneously anti-American and anti-Jewish. It is also viscerally opposed to liberalism, individualism, and modernity as such. It goes without saying that the Islamists reject laissez-faire principles in economics, politics, and culture. It is axiomatic that they deeply despise the political liberties of the West, such as freedom of speech, freedom of thought, and freedom of association and assembly. In these respects they often find common ground with anti-globalist leftists and right-wing radicals in the West today, who concentrate all their spleen on the "sins" of America and Israel while dismissing the threat posed by international terrorism.

In its attitude toward the Jews, Islamic fundamentalism displays many parallels with Nazism and Stalinist communism as well. The identification of Judaism with threatening forces of modernity such as secularism, capitalism, liberalism, and moral lassitude is a pattern that applies to each of these ideologies. There is the same obsession with Jews as a revolutionary, subversive, and corrosive force; with their hidden, occult, manipulative activities; with their boundless "materialism" and abstract rationalism and its imagined undermining of "sacred values" like family, nation, and state. Global conspiracy theories reappear in fundamentalist Islam in apocalyptic colors reminiscent of those favored by its Christian and post-Christian totalitarian predecessors. In the Manichean struggle of the Forces of Light, Goodness, and Truth against those of darkness, evil, and falsehood, it is clear that the Jews are a spearhead of the Devil's legions. Sixty years ago, Haj Amin al-Husseini, the leader of the Palestinian Arab national movement (who spent much of World War II in Berlin), insisted that there were strong ideological parallels between Islam and National Socialism. By way of example, he pointed to a common authoritarianism, anti-communism, Anglophobia, and hatred of the Jews. His speeches would often begin with anti-Jewish quotations from the Quran. In March 1944, speaking on Radio Berlin, he called on the Arabs to rise up: "Kill the Jews, wherever you find them. This pleases God, history, and religion." A few months earlier, celebrating the friendship and ideological links between the German Nazis and Arabs, Haj Amin expressed his admiration for the way "they [the Germans] have definitively solved the Jewish problem." In the light of what has been happening in the past two years, one has to ask if anything fundamental has changed. Neither Yasir Arafat, the Fatah Al-Aqsa Brigades, Hamas, Islamic Jihad, nor Hizballah differ from Haj Amin in their desire to see the eradication of Israel and its replacement by a "liberated" Palestine. Like the global jihadists of Al-Qaeda, Palestinian Islamists are driven by a violently anti-Western and anti-Jewish religious fanaticism. Israel and the Jews are perceived as an existential threat to Muslim culture and collective identity. The Jewish state is theologically and ontologically intolerable because no "protected people" (*dhimmi*s) can exercise state sovereignty on what is defined as "sacred Muslim territory." This is understood as an affront to the "God-given right" of Muslims to enjoy exclusive political hegemony in *dar al-Islam* (the House of Islam). This outlook is shared by millions of Sunni and Shi'a Muslims, conservative Wahhabi Saudis, Iranian Ayatollahs, Al-Qaeda, Hizballah, Hamas, the Muslim Brotherhood, Islamic Jihad, and many secular Arab nationalists, despite the many differences among these groups. But the Islamist ideology remains the most intransigent of all the totalitarian options since it insists that permanent war—the jihad—must be waged against "infidels" until the Day of Judgment. No strategic compromise is possible with the American or Israeli "devils," let alone with Muslim "heretics" (i.e., normal, pious Muslims). There can certainly be no "normalization" with a Jewish state, since its very existence is the symptom of the malaise, decadence, and corruption in Islam as it is practiced today.

As was the case with Nazism, only the comprehensive and decisive defeat of these dark and irrational forces in the Islamic world can clear the road for peace in the Middle East and a genuine "dialogue of civilizations." Saddam's defeat will undoubtedly be a powerful blow in that cause, not only by eliminating the specter of deadly weapons in the hands of a ruthless dictator and stopping bonuses for the suicide-killers in the Palestinian territories and Israel, but by destroying one of the historic patrons of global terrorism. But this is also a war of ideas as much as it is a military and political confrontation. Its long-term success will depend on a dramatic awakening of the moderate and rational forces within the Arab-Muslim world, forces that have hitherto been strangled by the terrible legacies of totalitarianism, jihad, and anti-Semitism. Hopefully, that long-term reformation of Islam will begin in the aftermath of the Iraq War, even if its fruits may take time to mature.

We see that Nazism, communism, radical pan-Arab nationalism, and Islamism share a remarkably similar demonology of the Jew. Each of these modern ideologies declared war in different ways on Judeo-Christian and Enlightenment values and sought, or is seeking, the downfall of Western liberal democracy. They all share the same penchant for conspiracy theories of history, society, and civilization, as well as the same closed system of beliefs, addiction to mystical or salvationist politics, and will to power. In the case of the jihadist, the return of anti-Semitism also needs to be seen as a powerful backlash against Western and Israeli visions of a "new Middle East," as well as the rejection of a new world order, a global economy,

"normalization" with the Jewish state, and the idea of a negotiated peace. Indeed, "world Zionism" is today perceived as the
driving force behind globalization ("Americanization") much
as a century ago "international Jewry" was depicted by European anti-Semites as the satanic engine of finance capitalism
and supranational cosmopolitanism. The new anti-Semitism
eagerly scavenges this arsenal of older images which, since the
onset of modernity, have stereotyped the Jews as a dangerously
mobile, rootless, abstract, and transnational mafia uniquely
tuned to exploit capitalist economy and culture. The protean
caricature of the Jew has been given a new lease on life by the
contemporary Islamist apostles of jihad. Israel and Jewry have
become their great surrogate in the holy war against America
and the corrupt modern world of *jahiliyya*. Uncle Sam, so to
speak, has coalesced with Shylock into a terrifying specter of
globalization that threatens to swamp the world of Islam.

One can see this syndrome clearly at work in the ongoing
radicalization of Pakistan, where obscurantist, intolerant, and
misogynist Islamist parties were the biggest winners in the
October 2002 elections. This Sunni Muslim nuclear-armed
state has become increasingly Islamicized in the past two decades. Its Wahhabi influenced and funded private Islamic
educational system has been thoroughly penetrated by a fundamentalist creed in which hatred of Western civilization,
Jews, and Hindus is matched only by loathing for Shi'a Muslims. Such fanaticism produced the murder of *Wall Street Journal* reporter Daniel Pearl in January 2002 (both a Jew and an
American). It stokes the fantastic conspiracy theories, so widely
believed in Pakistan, that the Mossad engineered the 9/11 massacre, and it carries with it the danger of a nuclear confrontation with India. Pakistani "anti-Semitism" has no connection to
the empirical world or Israelis and Jews as real people. It is a
pure ideological product of totalitarian Islam—paid for and
nurtured by the House of Saud.

A century ago, partisans of the radical Right and Left first began to converge in a common hatred of "materialist" values represented by international capitalism. They discovered in political anti-Semitism a powerful new weapon against the liberal, democratic order. The German Social Democrat August Bebel once called this kind of bigotry the "socialism of fools." However, like so many others on the Left and in the liberal center, he hugely underestimated the genocidal potential of this ideology once it was harnessed by ruthless totalitarian parties or movements. The simplistic belief that, thanks to technological and scientific progress, the twenty-first century would usher in universal peace across the globe has proven to be no less naive. Today, in the context of a far more media-saturated and globalized village, anti-Semitism (often masquerading as anti-Americanism and anti-Zionism) has recharged its batteries with a vengeance.

In the Islamic world (and increasingly in western Europe), it has become a dangerous form of auto-intoxication and self-destruction—the intellectual equivalent of the suicide bomb. In the first half of the twentieth century, many good-hearted, rational people refused to accept that such highly irrational beliefs could be taken seriously by many people. They were wrong. This is an error well worth avoiding in the first half of the twenty-first century.

BEREL LANG

Self-Description and the Anti-Semite: Denying Privileged Access

I N A RECENT REVIEW of a comprehensive history of Europe, the reviewer pointed out certain blatant distortions in the book's account of European Jewish history—but concluded that since the book's author had denied being anti-Semitic, *this* explanation of the distortions could be ruled out: "On that matter," the reviewer wrote, "we have to take the author at his word."* In a letter to the editor (published, no doubt, because of its brevity), I asked a simple question about this conclusion: "Why?" The question seemed to me obvious, not only as it applied to that book's author, but to any writer or speaker who asserts that he or she is not anti-Semitic or an anti-Semite. It is not that self-descriptions of this sort should not count as evidence *at all*, but that they are at most only partial evidence (in both senses: fragmentary and self-interested) to be considered in judging the presence or absence of anti-Semitism.

On the surface, this thesis will seem no more than a commonplace. After all, a large number of public figures who by any reasonable measure were clearly anti-Semitic have, for a

---

* Norman Davies, *Europe: A History* (Oxford: Oxford University Press, 1996); reviewed by Tony Judt, *The New Republic*, October 27, 1997.

variety of reasons, explicitly rejected that description. (I think here, at an extreme, of Eichmann's memorable line, that he had "nothing personal" against the Jews.) Such denials, when confronted by independent and contradictory evidence, are no more persuasive or interesting than other mistaken or deceptive self-descriptions, which are, after all, a familiar part of our moral and psychological landscape. But a conceptual issue is at stake here that goes more deeply into the ascription of anti-Semitism than the fact that certain anti-Semites (like many other people) may lie or deceive themselves about their private feelings.

The issue I refer to here is part of a broader one in the theory of knowledge; it concerns assertions which claim "privileged access"—that is, the group of statements made by speakers who are supposedly in a position of special (in the event, final) authority so far as concerns their truth or falsity. In the statement, "I feel warm," for example, the speaker might of course be lying because of a wish to deceive the person(s) being addressed. But putting this possibility aside (it applies, after all, to *any* statement), we would not ordinarily consider responding to that statement by disagreeing: "No, you're mistaken; you *don't* feel that way." And we would not venture this response even if everyone else in the room had just been commenting on how cold the room was. (Someone might suggest that the person who "felt warm" was ill [or ironic], but these are different matters.)

The presumption at work here is that where feelings are concerned, it is the bearer of the feelings who knows best—not only best but definitively; they're his or her feelings, after all, nobody else's. Even if someone lies about those feelings to others, it is still the person who feels them who knows better than anyone else what those feelings truly are. But does this same authority of "privileged access" extend to a person's judgment of being anti-Semitic? It is just this claim that the book-reviewer referred to above implied, and it is also just this claim that analysis of the concept of privileged access in matters of self-description demonstrates to be unwarranted.

To be sure, the question cannot be avoided here of exactly what actions or words, and how many of them, are required to meet the "standard" of anti-Semitism; there is an evident problem as well in applying that single term to individuals as distant from each other in the expressions of their anti-Semitism as (for example) Hitler and T. S. Eliot. It is also clear that as for any theoretical criteria applied to practical circumstance, there will be boundary-line cases about which doubts remain; there is no simple litmus test to produce immediate and certain findings. One point that does emerge clearly, however, against the background of the concept of privileged access is that the "title" of anti-Semite cannot be ascribed either exclusively or decisively as a function of feelings, not even as the measure of a *disposition* to act or to speak in a certain way. The reasons for this view should now be apparent: For one thing, as already noted, if anti-Semitism were judged on that basis, then the "feeler" of anti-Semitic feelings would indeed have the last word on his own status. And more than this, not feelings alone, and not even words, are in fact decisive for such judgment; they can be assessed only in conjunction with the actions that accompany them, and these, too, can be judged only in a context of the whole.

The positive side of this argument adds still greater weight to the negative side, as pertinent not only to issues of anti-Semitism but to the status of self-descriptive statements in general. It is commonly recognized, for example, that other people are at times more accurate interpreters of our actions than we are ourselves: we often intend (or believe we intend) to say or to do one particular thing—and discover when someone else points it out to us that we have done or said something quite different. Even at the level of intention, the person whose intentions they are is not necessarily the only or the best judge. We are all familiar with apologies or excuses that end with the phrase "but my intentions were good." And here, too, the audience, especially if they have heard the same refrain from the same person many times before, might well be skeptical. It is not only that people sometimes deliberately misrepresent their intentions, but that at times they are not the best or even good judges of what those intentions are.

If anti-Semitism then is not simply a set of feelings or a state of mind (to which privileged access *would* hold the key); and if, furthermore, people can sometimes be mistaken about what exactly the intentions behind their actions are—then it should not be surprising to find that someone could deny being anti-Semitic, and yet be judged from the outside, by others, to be just that. Required for this reversal of judgment is no more than what is required for any judgment of someone's state or condition: the gathering of evidence. This would of course *include* self-descriptions by the person being judged, but also much more: accounts of conduct and actions (including other words) in which the person has engaged.

It is only by such broader criteria, for example, that the cliché that recurs in self-descriptive denials of anti-Semitism— "But some of my best friends are Jews"—can be understood as not at all inconsistent with being anti-Semitic. There is nothing in the concept of anti-Semitism to prevent the anti-Semite from making exceptions for *some* Jews; when that happens, it is just *because* they were exceptions—which invariably means that they are not like the "others," that is, like the much greater majority of Jews—that the anti-Semite accepts them. But for us to be able in this way to override the denial of being anti-Semitic requires the possibility of appealing to other external evidence, not to the person's words alone, and certainly not to the person's feelings about Jews. For this, again, is the point: anti-Semitism is not only or decisively a state of mind or a psychological disposition. For one thing, no one has clear access to these (not even the person whose they are); and for another thing, by themselves, so long as they do not manifest themselves in words or actions, they hardly count as anti-Semitic or anti-anything. Where anti-Semitism matters is in the acts or conduct for which the concept (and term) stand. And although the person responsible for those actions may well also provide an interpretation of them, that remains but one account among several possible ones.

This skeptical analysis of statements in the form, "I am not an anti-Semite," has the odd consequence that someone might say that he or she *was* an anti-Semite—but turn out to be mistaken about *that*. We might prove, in other words, that also this self-description was, on balance, without a basis in fact—for here, too, there is no privileged access: If we have rejected privileged access in this area as such, that rejection would apply no matter what a particular self-description asserted. Such instances as these are rare, of course; when they do occur, they appear more as a parody or ironic joke than anything else. But the possibility cannot be ruled out (I've known at least one person like this, a good friend, in fact), and it is in any event a small price to pay for understanding the basis on which we feel entitled to reject the much more common claim of privileged access as it is used to support denials of being anti-Semitic. If anti-Semites were as transparent in their denials as was the English author/diplomat Harold Nicolson when he wrote that "Although I loathe anti-Semitism, I do dislike Jews," we would have no need for this, or indeed for any, clarification. And certainly for many instances of anti-Semitism, self-descriptions and acts appear in close harmony; nobody is in doubt about the fact itself. But there are also instances of denial which base themselves on the claim of privileged access—and there is no need, I have argued, to accept those denials, certainly not at face value.

GABRIEL SCHOENFELD

Israel and the Anti-Semites

H AS A NEW and potent form of anti-Semitism come to life in the world? If so, what does it portend?

Let us for the moment bracket off the Muslim world. The evidence of anti-Jewish hatred in that immense pocket of humanity has been copiously documented and is simply too overwhelming to warrant extended discussion. The more interesting question concerns Europe—a continent, it was widely assumed, effectively inoculated against a toxin that a mere half-century ago had reduced it to ruin and that, in the decades since World War II, had been confined to obscure recesses of political life.

Events over the past months suggest otherwise. It was only this past February that Hillel Halkin, writing in *Commentary* about an "accumulating record of actual anti-Semitic incidents" around the world, cautioned that evidence of a substantial resurgence in Europe was so far only "circumstantial." Since then, the continental landscape has begun to shift with astonishing speed.

The immediate occasion for the shift was, of course, Israel's incursion into the West Bank in late March and April. That military operation was precipitated by the daily terror within Israel itself that had been going on for many months and that culminated in the bombing of a hotel ballroom in Netanya in which 29 Israelis perished and more than 140 were injured while sitting at their seder tables on the first night of Passover. To put an end to this relentless campaign of terror, Israel's national-unity government dispatched the army into Palestinian cities and camps to uncover and destroy bomb factories and to apprehend those responsible for the mass killings of Israeli civilians. "In the month of March, we lost the lives of more than 126 persons," explained Israel's dovish foreign minister, Shimon Peres; "we did not have any other alternative."

Though the incursion did not achieve all of its objectives, one visible result, at least as long as Israel's forces remained in place, was the near-total cessation of terrorist attacks inside the country. Another was the seizure of a trove of intelligence information, including documents confirming (to anyone who still doubted it) that Yasir Arafat, Israel's ostensible partner in the Oslo peace process and a man richly subsidized by the European Union, was in possession of arms forbidden to him by the Oslo accords and was personally funding and directing the civilian bombing missions of at least one armed unit, the Al Aqsa Martyrs Brigade.

That sectors of Europe would be critical of any Israeli military action against Arafat's Palestinian Authority, even one so self-evidently defensive in character, was hardly a surprise; the cause of Palestinian statehood is, after all, a cherished item on the European diplomatic and political agenda. But the scale and the venom of the reaction, on both the elite and the popular level, were something else again. At least we can now see things as they are.

Let us begin at the popular level, where there has been, first of all, a rash of physical attacks on Jewish symbols, Jewish institutions, and Jews themselves. The list of such violent incidents from the first two weeks of April alone is too long to summarize adequately.

In the Ukrainian capital of Kiev, for example, some fifty youths chanting "Kill the Jews" descended on a synagogue on a Saturday evening, broke twenty windows, and beat the rector of the religious school with stones. In Greece, Jewish cemeteries were vandalized in what the press termed "anti-Jewish acts of revenge," and the Holocaust memorial in Salonika, a city whose 50,000 Jews were rounded up and deported to Nazi death camps in 1943, was defaced with Palestinian slogans. In Slovakia, Jewish cemeteries were desecrated in what an official described as the "biggest attack on the Jewish community since the Holocaust."

In peaceful, democratic, law-abiding Western Europe—a part of the world that for the past half-century has prided itself on the degree of personal safety it affords its inhabitants—the story was similar. One scene of violent anti-Israel demonstrations was Holland, where protestors hurled rocks and bottles and small roving bands used stones and bicycles to shatter store windows in the heart of Amsterdam. In neighboring Belgium, five firebombs were tossed into a synagogue in a working-class district of Brussels, and a Jewish bookstore was severely damaged by arsonists; a synagogue in Antwerp was firebombed with Molotov cocktails, and in the same city a travel agency specializing in trips to Israel was also set alight.

In Germany, two Orthodox Jews were beaten while strolling on Berlin's chic Kurfuerstendamm, the heart of the city's shopping district. A woman wearing a star-of-David necklace was attacked in the subway. Jewish memorials in Berlin were defaced with swastikas; a synagogue was spray-painted with the words "Six Million Is Not Enough. PLO." Anti-Israel demonstrators hurled bricks through windows as they marched.

In England, reported the *London Express,* "race-hate attacks on the Jewish community have soared." In the first ten days of April there were fifteen anti-Semitic incidents, including eight physical assaults. Most of the attacks in England were on Jews walking alone, set upon and beaten by small roving bands. At least two of the victims required hospitalization.

France was the epicenter of aggression. Gangs of hooded men descended on Jewish victims and struck them with iron clubs. Buses carrying Jewish schoolchildren were stoned. Cemeteries were desecrated. Synagogues, Jewish schools, student facilities, and kosher stores were defaced, battered, and firebombed. On April 1, the Or Aviv synagogue in Marseille was burned to the ground, its prayerbooks and Torah scrolls consumed by flames; it was one of five synagogues in France attacked. The first half of the month saw "nearly 360 crimes against Jews and Jewish institutions," according to the French interior ministry—amounting, in the words of *The New York Times,* to "the worst spate of anti-Jewish violence" in France since World War II.

Some observers have drawn comparisons between this violent crime wave and Kristallnacht—the pogrom unleashed by the Nazis against German Jews on November 9 and 10, 1938. Unlike in the 1930s, however, there was no organized power behind the assaults, let alone a government, and in every European country the police, so far as one knows, did their duty (though the political authorities often stood aside until matters threatened to get out of control). Still, physical violence against Jews has undeniably become a pan-European phenomenon, visible in every country north and south, east and west. Everywhere one turns, moreover, this physical violence has been accompanied, and abetted, by an explosion of verbal violence.

The themes are also the same everywhere. Israel, a country victimized by terrorism, stands accused of perpetrating terrorism; the Jews, having suffered the most determined and thoroughgoing genocide in history, stand accused of perpetrating genocide. The language in which these accusations are leveled is extravagantly hateful, drawn from the vocabulary of World War II and the Holocaust but entirely and grotesquely inverted, with the Jews as Nazis and their Arab tormentors in the role of helpless Jews.

Still sticking to the popular level, events in early April were once again particularly instructive. In the course of two weeks, anti-Israel street demonstrations took place not only in every major European capital but in hundreds of minor cities and towns. In Tuzla, a town in Bosnia, some 1,500 demonstrators carried placards reading "Sharon and Hitler, Two Eyes in the Same Head" and "Israel—the Real Face of Terrorism." In Dublin, Ireland, the banners, several featuring Nazi swastikas superimposed over stars of David, read "Stop the Palestinian Holocaust" and "Jerusalem: Forever Beloved, Forever Palestinian." In Barcelona, Spain, demonstrators carried placards inscribed "Israel Murderer; USA Accomplice," and "No to Genocide." In Paris, the posters read "Hitler Has a Son: Sharon"; in Belgium, "Hitler Had Two Sons: Bush and Sharon." In Salonika, a solidarity concert was staged under the slogan "Stop the Genocide Now—We Are All Palestinians." In Bilbao, Spain, thousands marched through the streets chanting "No to Zionist terrorism." In Berlin, the placards read "Stop the Genocide in Palestine" and "Sharon is a Child Murderer." In cities and towns across France, "Death to Jews" and "Jews—murderers" were refrains heard at a multitude of rallies.

The catalog is infinitely expandable, for not only is it incomplete in itself but the passage of each day has brought new acts of violence, new demonstrations, and new and more vicious slogans. Who is behind all this street-level activity?

Actual physical violence against Jews has been, for the most part, the work of Muslims. According to the French ministry of the interior, the perpetrators have generally been "Arab youths from North African countries." Arriving from societies where hatred of Jews is fostered by government, government-controlled media, and radical clerics, these immigrants are fed a rich and stimulating diet from the Arab and European Arab-language press, whose brand of anti-Semitism is as hallucina-tory as anything ever peddled by Julius Streicher in the Nazi organ *Der Stürmer.*

Some of this fare stems ultimately from Saudi Arabia, a great and unceasing fount of wild anti-Jewish vitriol. *Al-Riyadh,* a government-controlled newspaper in that country, has, for example, parlayed a twist on an ancient libel to excite and ter-rify its readers—the Jewish use of the blood of Gentile adoles-cents not for Passover matzah but for Purim pastry:

> Let us now examine how the victims' blood is spilled. For this, a needle-studded barrel is used; this is a kind of bar-rel, about the size of the human body, with extremely sharp needles set in it on all sides. [These needles] pierce the victim's body, from the moment he is placed in the barrel.
>
> These needles do the job, and the victim's blood drips from him very slowly. Thus, the victim suffers dreadful torment—torment that affords the Jewish vampires great delight as they carefully monitor every detail of the blood-shedding with pleasure and love that are difficult to com-prehend.*

And so forth. The lesson that readers are supposed to draw from this ghastly fantasy is likewise inflammatory: a Saudi cleric enjoined his Muslim brothers in a recent government-sponsored sermon "not to have any mercy or compassion on the Jews, their blood, their money, their flesh. Their women are yours to take, legitimately. God made them yours. Why don't you enslave their women? Why don't you wage jihad? Why don't you pillage them?"

The fact that Islamic immigrants are behind most of the

*Translated by the Middle East Media Research Institute, available at www.memri.org.

physical attacks on European Jews hardly suggests that the problem is easily containable. Thanks to Europe's welcoming immigration policies, and to their own high fertility, Muslims are now a significant demographic factor on the continent. If in 1945 they numbered fewer than a million, today they are more than fifteen million, with some two million in England, more than four and a half million in France, three million in Germany, nearly a million apiece in Italy, Spain, and Holland, and the remainder scattered across more than a dozen other countries. They are, of course, a heterogeneous population, and most of them are no doubt neither in the grip of radical Islam nor susceptible to appeals to violence. But some significant number of them are, and the challenge they pose can only grow.

In any case, if Muslims have taken the lead in perpetrating physical violence, others have enthusiastically joined in or blazed the way when it comes to incitement and verbal abuse. The various demonstrations illustrate this well. Thus, at the event in Dublin, organized by a group known as the Ireland-Palestine Solidarity Campaign, half the demonstrators were reportedly Irishmen. Similarly, in Brussels, not only Arab students but representatives of Belgian social and political organizations took part, including the Catholic movement Pax Christi, the Belgian Socialist party, and the Belgian Green party. The solidarity concert in Salonika was organized by, among others, two Greek trade-union bodies; the dean of Athens University also lent his support, issuing a statement condemning Israel for its "continuing cruel violation in Palestine of human rights." In Barcelona, where some 10,000 people turned out, unions, political parties, and nongovernmental organizations campaigned against Israeli "genocide" and set fire to a star of David. In France, at the rallies where chants of "death to the Jews" were heard, one could find, according to Agence France-Presse, not only the Muslim Students of France and the Committee of Moroccan Workers but also officials of various trade unions and members of the Revolutionary Communist League, the Greens, and the French Communist party, along with officials of the Human Rights League. In the front ranks was José Bové, the French Luddite formerly known for vandalizing McDonald's hamburger outlets.

But these events at street level are only the beginning; it is in the world of politics and elite opinion that the nature of the burgeoning movement of European anti-Semitism becomes fully clear. And anti-Semitism is, incidentally, the right and the only word for an anti-Zionism so one-sided, so eager to indict Israel while exculpating Israel's adversaries, so shamefully adroit in the use of moral double standards, so quick to issue false and baseless accusations, and so disposed to invert the language of the Holocaust and to paint Israelis and Jews as evil incarnate.

A mild (in relative terms) expression of this current could be found in a petition being circulated among European academics. Passing over in silence the suicide bombings that were devastating Israeli civilian life, not to mention the eighteen months of unremitting violence that were Arafat's answer to Prime Minister Ehud Barak's offer of 97 percent of the territory of the West Bank and the division of Jerusalem, the statement denounced Israel's government as "impervious to moral appeals" and then called for a moratorium on grants by European educational institutions to Israeli scholars and researchers. (The reason, one assumes, was their tacit complicity in genocide.) Among the hundreds of signers of this meretricious document were scholars from institutions of higher learning in virtually every country of the continent, including the famed British Darwinist, Richard Dawkins.

Similarly in Norway, where in 1994 the Nobel committee had awarded its peace prize to Yitzhak Rabin, Shimon Peres, and Yasir Arafat. At that time, one honest member of the committee, Kaare Kristiansen, had resigned in protest, rightly calling Arafat a terrorist unworthy of this award. Now, however, other members, one of them a Lutheran bishop, said they wanted to strip not Arafat but Shimon Peres of the prize; his crime—participating in a government that was violating the "intention and spirit" of the award. Not to be outdone, the leader of the Socialist Left party demanded reparations from Israel for destroying Palestinian infrastructure paid for by Norwegian aid money—never mind that this sort of subsidized "infrastructure" regularly shelters armed Palestinian terrorists and their activities.

In Denmark, a Lutheran bishop delivered a sermon in Copenhagen Cathedral likening Ariel Sharon to the biblical King Herod, who ordered the death of all male children in Bethlehem under the age of two; Denmark's foreign minister, Per Stig Moller, branded Israel's anti-terror incursion a "war against a civilian population." The Portuguese writer José Saramago, a Nobel laureate in literature, delivered himself of this delicacy: "We can compare what is happening on the Palestinian territories with Auschwitz."

In Germany, Norbert Bluem, a minister under former chancellor Helmut Kohl, called Israel's offensive in the West Bank a "limitless war of annihilation," while Juergen Moellemann, an official of the Free Democrats, openly defended Palestinian violence against Jews: "I would resist too, and use force to do so . . . not just in my country but in the aggressor's country as well." Wrote one commentator in the *Suddeutsche Zeitung:* "It's been a long time since the hatred of Jews—once disguised as anti-Zionism—has been as socially acceptable in Germany as it is today."

In Italy, *La Stampa,* the liberal daily, resurrected the oldest Christian anti-Semitic canard of all: deicide. A cartoon depicted the infant Jesus looking up from his manger at an Israeli tank and pleading, "Don't tell me they want to kill me again."

From voices in the Vatican, utter indifference to the murder of Jews was coupled with the charge that the Jews themselves were committing genocide. "Indescribable barbarity" was the phrase of Franciscan officials in Rome describing Israel's attempt to arrest Palestinian terrorists who had taken shelter in the Church of the Nativity in Bethlehem. In the hallowed "land of Jesus," complained the Vatican daily *L'Osservatore Romano,* Israel was exhibiting an "irritating haughtiness" and engaging in "aggression that turns into extermination."

If France has led Europe in anti-Semitic violence, Great Britain may be where the elite expression of anti-Semitic ideas has been most uninhibited. (In his February *Commentary* article, Hillel Halkin memorably quoted the columnist Petronella Wyatt: "Since September 11, anti-Semitism and its open expression has become respectable at London dinner tables.") Thus, Claire Rayner, the president of the British Humanist Association, asserted in April that the notion of Israel as a homeland for the Jewish people was "a load of crap"; by contrast, the suicide bombings of Israeli restaurants and buses were both understandable and justifiable: "If you treat a group of people the way Palestinians have been treated they will use the only weapon they have, which is their individual lives."

More established figures voiced sentiments fully as bizarre as Claire Rayner's and, if anything, nastier. Last autumn, the highly regarded British novelist and biographer A. N. Wilson had "reluctantly" announced in the (London) *Evening Standard* that the state of Israel no longer had a right to exist. More recently, he used his talents to accuse the Israeli army of the "poisoning of water supplies" on the West Bank, thereby availing himself of another time-honored canard, traceable back to the fourteenth century and repeated on countless occasions since then to justify the mass murder of Jews.

Wilson is a self-described "unbelieving Anglican" who is certainly well aware of the shameful history of Christian reli-

gious anti-Semitism to which he was now making his own signal contribution. Tom Paulin is a professor at Oxford, an arts
commentator for the British Broadcasting Corporation, and a
poet whose recent verse includes a lament for a small Palestinian boy "gunned down by the Zionist SS." "I never believed that
Israel had the right to exist at all," Paulin told the Egyptian
Al-Ahram Weekly in April, and Jews from Brooklyn who have
settled in the West Bank "are Nazis, racists. . . . They should be
shot dead."

To *Al-Ahram*, Paulin is that "rare thing in contemporary
British culture, 'the writer as conscience.'" Some Europeans apparently agree with this judgment. *The Irish Times* found him
"a rigorous respecter of language" who "does not dilute his
words" while remaining free of any trace of personal prejudice.
Chiming in, A. N. Wilson called him a "brilliant scholar and literary critic" and noted that "many in this country and throughout the world would echo his views on the tragic events in the
Middle East."

On this last point, at least, Wilson may be right. One could
devote many more pages to, for example, the malevolent myth-
making of the British and European press in reporting on the
"massacre" of Palestinians in Jenin, where the Israelis aimed for
"the near-total destruction of the lives and livelihoods of the
camp's 15,000 inhabitants," according to the *Evening Standard*.
A "crime of especial notoriety," blared *The Guardian* about an
operation that cost the lives of over two dozen Israeli reservists
in an effort, successful but hideously costly, to eliminate terrorists while avoiding civilian Palestinian casualties. Or one could
dwell on the reflexive hatred of the Jewish state that now
appears to be rife within the Anglican Church: "Whenever I
print anything sympathetic to Israel," admits the editor of the
church's official newspaper, "I get deluged with complaints that
I am Zionist and racist." Or one could quote again from the
many examples adduced by Halkin and freely available in the
public prints and on the web. But we must once again move on.

The Palestinians who insisted that there was an Israeli massacre in Jenin surely had their reasons for fabricating such a claim. Those reasons are no doubt related to hatred of Jews per se—for such hatred exists, abundantly. But they are also closely related to the tactics of the Palestinian struggle, which has successfully relied on the readiness of many in Europe (and elsewhere) to accept such fabrications at face value, to spread and amplify them while ignoring all contrary evidence, and to pillory Israel on the basis of lies that they themselves have tended and fed.

Where this eager readiness comes from is another question. A considerable literature has been devoted to plumbing the nature of Europe's enduring "Jewish problem," and the current flare-up has already given rise to a fresh round of theorizing about its root causes, old and new. Among the factors regularly adduced, at least by those willing to acknowledge that it is a problem, are the seemingly indelible brand that has been left on European consciousness by centuries of ubiquitous anti-Semitic myths; hatreds rooted in Christian theological concepts; a deep-seated psychological need to lighten the burden of European guilt for the Holocaust by defaming its victims posthumously; a no less pressing need to atone for European colonialism and imperialism by casting Israel as the world's worst colonial power; and on and on. One can spin more theories with ease and find evidence to support each of them, for anti-Semitism is a disease with no single cause.

But one salient fact about the picture I have been painting is this: there is a clear fit between anti-Israel or anti-Jewish hatred and the general ideological predispositions of the contemporary European Left. As historical trends go, this is relatively new. For most of the last century, what predominated in Europe was the racialist and nationalist anti-Semitism of the Right, fused with and colored by Christian theological teachings. Today, though the neo-Nazis and the Holocaust deniers occupy their accustomed place, and though anti-Semites figure among the constituents of Jörg Haider in Austria and Jean-Marie Le Pen in France, the anti-Semitism in swiftest motion is the left-wing strain, the strain that loathes the Jews not on explicitly racialist or religious grounds but on "universalist" ones.

This tradition, too, has a long and ignoble history, from the Enlightenment's Voltaire (who regarded the Jews as "the most abominable people in the world") through socialism's Karl Marx (to whom Polish Jews were the "filthiest of all races"), through seven decades of Soviet Communism with its pro-Arab foreign policy and its harshly oppressive attitude toward Soviet Jewish citizens, through the New Left, through the German and Italian terrorism of recent decades and the post-60's alignment of the Left with the cause of Palestinian "liberation." Today, a new chapter is being written. There are, to be sure, neo-Nazis to be found among those burning the star of David and chanting obscene slogans against the Jewish state in the streets of Europe; but the ranks are more heavily composed of environmentalists, pacifists, anarchists, anti-globalists, and socialists. "I have difficulties with the swastika," said a member of Belgium's Flemish-Palestine Committee at an April demonstration, registering by his perturbance the anomaly of that Nazi symbol amid the placards of his ideological comrades.

The pattern continues in the upper reaches of European politics. True, anti-Semitic impulses cannot always be readily disentangled from the many other considerations that govern political behavior—like raw electoral calculations in a continent with many Muslims and (except for France) very few Jews. But surely it is significant that among Europe's governing bodies, it is the political Left that has been leading the charge against Israel. It was Germany's Social Democratic–Green coalition government that this past April, in the midst of Israel's battle for survival, and despite its much vaunted "special relationship" with the Jewish state, opted to halt further exports of spare parts for the Merkava tank. It was France's socialist

foreign minister, Hubert Vedrine, who in April publicly casti-
gated American Jews for being so "intransigent" as to fail to
make "the switch toward peace." When the European Parliament passed a resolution on April 10 calling for trade sanctions
against Israel, it was propelled forward by Europe's Liberal
Democrat and Green parties, with the Socialists denouncing
Israel in the most perfervid tones of all.

If one moves even higher up the rungs of political life, into
the multilateral institutions that shape the world polity and in
which the Europeans have invested so much of their diplomatic capital, the die is cast from the same mold. (The degree
to which the United Nations has turned itself into an anti-
Semitic mob warrants an extended essay of its own.) Thus,
when the UN Human Rights Commission passed a resolution
in April condemning Israel for "war crimes," "acts of mass killing," and an "offense against humanity," while simultaneously
backing without reservation the "right of the Palestinians to
resist," the European countries voting in favor included the socialist or Left-coalition governments of France, Belgium, Sweden, and Portugal, with centrist Spain and right-wing Austria
joining in. Outside of Europe, needless to say, every left-wing
dictatorship in the world voted in support of the resolution, including that shining protector of human rights, the People's
Republic of China.

It would be unfair to leave the subject of Europe without
noting the courageous efforts of those in England, France, Italy,
and Germany who have stood up to or spoken back to the
anti-Semites. Perhaps foremost among them lately has been
the Italian writer Oriana Fallaci, who in a lengthy and impassioned indictment published in the weekly *Panorama* declared,
in part:

> I find it shameful . . . that state-run television stations [in
> Italy] contribute to the resurgent anti-Semitism, crying

only over Palestinian deaths while playing down Israeli deaths, glossing over them in unwilling tones. I find it shameful that in their debates they host with much deference the scoundrels with turbans or kaffiyehs who yesterday sang hymns to the slaughter at New York and today sing hymns to the slaughters in Jerusalem, at Haifa, at Netanya, in Tel Aviv.

I find it shameful that the press does the same, that it is indignant because Israeli tanks surround the Church of the Nativity in Bethlehem, that it is not indignant because inside that same church two hundred Palestinian terrorists well armed with machine guns and munitions and explosives (among them are various leaders of Hamas and Al-Aqsa) are not unwelcome guests of the monks (who then accept bottles of mineral water and jars of honey from the soldiers of those tanks).

But these exceptions are notorious because they are exceptions. Elsewhere, and especially on the cultural and political Left, Europeans have tended to speak in a very different voice.

What about here, in the United States? Mercifully, anti-Semitism on these shores lacks Europe's rich traditionalism. Violent attacks on Jews have been exceedingly rare in our history, and although genuine social movements have at times been built—most famously by Father Charles E. Coughlin in the 1930s—on anti-Jewish hostility, the few attempts to harness this hostility to electoral purposes have all come to naught. The question is, under what circumstances might this change?

One relatively new factor in the American equation, as in the European, is a sizable Muslim influx. Reliable numbers remain hard to come by: a U.S. Department of State fact sheet offers a figure of six million, which is almost certainly much too high, while other estimates range from two to four million. But there is no disagreement that the Muslim population has grown dramatically in recent decades, or that this growth has already affected Jewish security. If physical attacks on Jews and Jewish institutions once came mostly from right-wing or nativist groups, now they come increasingly from Arab militants. One of the most well-known such attacks was the murder of Ari Halberstam, a Hasidic schoolboy, shot in 1994 by Arab gunmen while traversing the Brooklyn Bridge.

The years since 1995—years in which, according to the Anti-Defamation League's annual survey, anti-Semitism as a whole declined in America—also witnessed an upsurge of violent incidents connected to the Middle East and in most cases perpetrated by Arabs. This was especially pronounced after the beginning of the latest intifada in September 2000. Within months, at least 34 incidents—primarily vandalism and arson but including physical attacks on individuals—were reported in New York State alone.

Heightened security after September 11 seems to have brought about a decrease in violence of this kind, but lately the pace has picked up again. In Berkeley, California, for example, "Jewish residents have been attacked on the streets," *The Daily Californian* reported in late April. The university's Hillel society building was defaced with anti-Semitic graffiti, and the city's largest synagogue has received a stream of threats, including one in which a telephone caller said that all Jews should be "annihilated" and "holocausted." The mayor has proposed creating a special police unit to deal with the rash of death threats against Jews and bomb scares at synagogues.

But mention of Berkeley, one of the most advanced academic locales in the country, should remind us that no more than in Europe are anti-Semitic attitudes here limited to Arabs or Muslims, or to the uneducated. Rather, they have found a home in what are presumably the most enlightened precincts of society. "Die Jew. Die, die, die, die, die, die. Stop living, die, die, DIE! Do us all a favor and build yourself [an] . . . oven," were the words in a student newspaper at Rutgers. "How have

Judaism, the Jews, and the international forces all permitted Zionism to become a wild, destructive beast capable of perpetrating atrocities?" are the words of a tenured professor of sociology at Georgetown, a leading American university. In many elite universities, radical professors have joined with Arab students to compel their institutions to divest from the "apartheid" state of Israel. One need only scan the dozens of names of distinguished faculty sponsors of such initiatives to grasp that a significant movement is gathering force.*

The political address of this movement is once again on the Left. True, the nefarious reach of "world Zionism" has long been a favorite theme of American white supremacists like David Duke, just as it has been of the British Holocaust-denier David Irving. But even in its more genteel incarnations, as in the now-marginalized Patrick J. Buchanan, this brand of anti-Semitism is in relative eclipse, whereas on the Left it has become the glue of a new coalition. The environmentalists and anarchists who in past years satisfied themselves by hurling rocks through the windows of Starbucks coffee shops have now joined forces with Arab radicals to calumniate the Jewish state. "Hey, hey! Ho, ho! IMF has got to go!" was one slogan at an April rally in Washington, D.C. The other was "Sharon and Hitler are the same. Only difference is the name."

Among the most active elements of the Left-Arab alliance are, sad to say, a number of Jews. For years, figures like Noam Chomsky and his acolyte Norman Finkelstein have traded in extreme denunciations of Israel, to relatively little effect.† Of late, they are finding greater traction. The principal activity of a new organization called "Jews for Peace in Palestine and Israel" is organizing rallies in support of the PLO. "There are

---

*Typical is the initiative at Princeton; see www.princetondivest.org/faculty.htm.
†In a December 2001 lecture delivered in Beirut, Lebanon, Finkelstein likened Israeli actions to "Nazi practices" during World War II, albeit with some added "novelties to the Nazi experiments."

many American Jews who are flat-out embarrassed by the fact
the prime minister of Israel is guilty of war crimes," says its
executive director, Josh Ruebner. Rabbi Michael Lerner, editor
of *Tikkun* magazine, and dozens of his associates, including
Chomsky and such non-Jewish luminaries as the black activist
professor Cornel West, recently placed a full-page ad in *The
New York Times* in which, in classic anti-Semitic form, either
Ariel Sharon or one of his "supporters" was presented in a cartoon caricature as a hook-nosed, evil-looking Jew, the state of
Israel was characterized as a "Pharaoh," and Israeli soldiers
were likened to Nazis blindly "following orders" in "a brutal
occupation" that "violates international law, human rights, and
the basic ethical standards of humanity."

In the decades before World War II, a mass of anti-Semitic
rhetoric, from "The Protocols of the Elders of Zion" through
Mein Kampf and beyond, helped prepare the intellectual and
cultural groundwork for the catastrophe that followed. Today,
the ceaseless denunciations of Israel on the part of the international Left, including some of its most respected and respectable spokesmen, cannot help striking one as possessing
the seeds of a macabre replay. What George F. Will has called
the "centrality of anti-Semitism" to the current Middle East crisis may yet develop the potential of transforming that crisis
into (to quote Will again) "the second—and final?—phase of
the struggle for a 'final solution' to the Jewish question."

European leaders would heatedly abjure any such objective;
yet in their hands, the anti-Israel and anti-Jewish campaign has
generated real momentum. The European states are militarily
weak, but they have other levers of power to exercise. They
have already played a major role in Israel's political and diplomatic isolation, and they could conceivably attempt to strangle
it economically by means of the boycotts and sanctions they
have threatened to impose. By virtue of their influence in international organizations, and through the moral cachet they

continue, however unaccountably, to deploy in centers of elite opinion elsewhere around the world, they have been instrumental in chipping away at Israel's very legitimacy.

One does not wish to exaggerate. Today's virulent anti-Semitism is, in part, an epiphenomenon of the Israel-Arab conflict—or, more accurately, of Israel's effort to withstand the Arab determination to destroy it. To the degree that Israel succeeds in thwarting or turning aside that determination, the rhetoric may abate, and explicit anti-Semitism may diminish. (By contrast, the perception of Jewish weakness has historically always fed the appetite of anti-Jewish aggression.) But there is also no denying that the new anti-Semitism has taken on a life of its own, gathering strength from long-repressed theological hatreds suddenly given license to emerge, from all sorts of misplaced social resentments that have nothing to do with the Jews, and (to judge from the Left-Arab coalition) from broader ideological agendas in which Israel is a mere stand-in, a conveniently vulnerable target for those not yet willing or able to take on the mighty United States.

One small but very disturbing sign of the headway being made by the new anti-Semitism is the speculation that has suddenly sprung up in the most disparate places about the possibility of a world without Israel—as if it were a perfectly ordinary prospect for a thriving democracy of nearly five million Jews simply to disappear. That a leader of Hamas like Ismail Abu Shanab should contemplate the extinction of Israel is understandable; that he should feel comfortable in talking about it publicly—"There are," he has amiably explained, "a lot of open areas in the United States that could absorb the Jews"—tells us a good deal about what has come to be considered permissible discourse in the presence of reporters. But then, Tom Paulin and A. N. Wilson have followed close behind—and similar sorts of thoughts, suitably qualified, have even appeared under the bylines of avowed friends of the Jewish state here at home.

As one of them, Richard John Neuhaus, has lately written, while personally disclaiming any such sentiment, even to "wish that Israel 'would cease to exist' is . . . not necessarily a wish to destroy the Jews, since one might at the same time hope that the minority of the world's Jews living in Israel would find a secure home elsewhere, notably in the U.S." Such are the tortuous rationalizations to which the swell of worldwide anti-Semitism has led.

Great shocks, as we know from the last century, can produce political flux beyond all foresight. In the last years the world has been subjected to a series of such shocks, September 11 being the greatest, and more may well be on the way. Where their repercussions will end no one can yet say, but the concomitant and hardly accidental revival of the ancient fear and hatred known as anti-Semitism must make one tremble. The story of twentieth-century Europe, wrote the historian Norman Cohn in the concluding words of *Warrant for Genocide*, his 1966 study of European anti-Semitism in the years before World War II, is a story of how a "grossly delusional view of the world, based on infantile fears and hatreds, was able to find expression in murder and torture beyond all imagining. It is a case history in collective psychopathology, and its deepest implications reach far beyond anti-Semitism and the fate of the Jews."

Those words remain frighteningly relevant today.

PART THREE

ONE DEATH,
ONE LIE

One Death

JUDEA PEARL

This Tide of Madness

The World Must Stand Against the Evil That Took My Son's Life

TOMORROW WILL MARK the first anniversary of the day the world learned of the murder of my son Daniel Pearl, a reporter for this newspaper. It is time to step back and reflect on the significance of this tragedy.

Much has been written on the new challenges that Danny's murder represents to international journalism. But relatively little attention was given to one aspect of the motives of the perpetrators, specifically to the role of anti-American and anti-Semitic sentiments in the planning and execution of the murder. In fact, what shocked and united people from all over the world was the nature of those motives.

The murder weapon in Danny's case was aimed not at a faceless enemy or institution, but at a gentle human being—one whose face is now familiar to millions of people around the world. Danny's murderers spent a week with him; they must have seen his radiating humanity. Killing him so brutally, and in front of a video camera, marked a new low in man's inhumanity to man. People of all faiths were thus shocked to realize that mankind can still be dragged to such depths by certain myths and ideologies.

Danny was killed because he represented us, namely the ideals that every civilized person aspires to uphold—modernity, openness, pluralism, freedom of inquiry, truth, honesty, and respect for all people. Decent people of all backgrounds have consequently felt personally targeted in this crime, and have been motivated to carry on Danny's spirit.

Reactions to Danny's death varied from community to community. In Pakistan, many have condemned the murder as a barbaric act carried out by a minority of fanatics at the fringe of society, while some find absolution in assuming that Danny was a spy. Sadly, anti-Semitism and sympathies with the perpetrators, as revealed in the trial of Omar Sheikh, seem to be more widespread than openly admitted. The trial itself is at a puzzling standstill, with no date set for an appeal decision. In Saudi Arabia, the murder video has been used to arouse and recruit new members to terrorist organizations. In Europe, Danny's murder has been condemned as an attack against journalism, while the anti-American, anti-Jewish sentiments were played down considerably. This is understandable, considering the anti-American and anti-Western sentiment echoed in editorials in some respectable European newspapers.

In contrast, Danny's captors concentrated on his Jewish and Israeli heritage. Evidently the murderers were confident that Danny's Jewish connections were sufficient to license the gruesome murder they were about to commit. Such a brazen call to condone the killing of a human being by virtue of his religion or heritage is strongly reminiscent of the horrors perpetrated by Nazi Germany.

In a world governed by reason and leadership, one would expect world leaders to immediately denounce such racist calls before they become an epidemic. However, President Bush was the only world leader to acknowledge the connection between Danny's murder and the rise of anti-Semitism: "We reject the ancient evil of anti-Semitism whether it is practiced by the killers of Daniel Pearl or by those who burn synagogues in France." No European head of state rose to John F. Kennedy's "Ich bin ein Berliner" with the morally equivalent statement "Today, I am a Jew."

Not surprisingly, our unguided world has seen an alarming rise of anti-Semitic activity in the past year. Tens of millions of Muslims have become unshakably convinced that Jews were responsible for the September 11 attack. Egypt's state-controlled television aired a forty-one-part program based on the notorious anti-Semitic book "The Protocols of the Elders of Zion," and Egyptians were fed another fantasy, that Jews are plotting to take over the world. Syria's defense minister, Mustafa Tlas, released the eighth edition of his book, *The Matzah of Zion*, in which he accuses Jews of using the blood of Christians to bake matzah for Passover. And on the sideline, while these flames of hatred were consuming sizable chunks of the world's population, traditionally vocal champions of anti-racism remained silent.

Against this tide of madness the world is about to remember Daniel Pearl—a Jew, a citizen of the world, and a dialogue maker who formed genuine connections among people of different backgrounds. In Danny's spirit, we have asked every community that plans to commemorate the anniversary of his death to invite a neighboring synagogue, mosque, church, or temple of different faith to join in a prayer for a sane and humane world, a world free of the hatred that took Danny's life. Interfaith memorials will take place, starting tonight, in Los Angeles, New York, Toronto, London, and Jerusalem, with additional services planned world-wide.

We hope that the combination of multifaith attendance, joint statements against intolerance, and the unifying global spirit of the day will serve as catalysts for building alliances against the rising tide of fanaticism, dehumanization, and xenophobia.

THANE ROSENBAUM

Danny Pearl

IN THE MIDDLE EAST, where martyrdom is measured only in human sacrifice, where human bombs are indistinguishable from human remains, where the sound of an explosive is both an anthem and an alarm, where the future of the Palestinian people is mortgaged all too cheaply for the price of shrapnel, and where a slice of pizza can be a final meal or what's still grasped at the end of a severed arm—in short, in a region so grisly, why is the murder of Daniel Pearl a special reminder of what it means to be a Jew in an unspeakably horrible post–September 11 world?

"I'm a Jewish American. I come from a . . . on my father's side . . . a family of Zionists. My father's Jewish. My mother's Jewish. I'm Jewish. My family follows Judaism. We've made numerous family visits to Israel. In the town of B'nei Brak in Israel, there's a street called Haim Pearl Street, which was named after my great-grandfather, who was one of the founders."

Those are not my words. They were the final words of Daniel Pearl. But they weren't his words, either. He was forced to say them by his captors right before he was decapitated. And all of it was videotaped, not as a ransom note, because their hostage was dead, but as a scripted ritual murder, complete with a script for Pearl to recite, a passion play performed by those far too passionate about who this particular victim was.

Since these were the words of the murderers, it's fair to ask what was intended by this communication. Surely they could have killed Pearl without the cameras rolling, without his having to read these molesting lines of dialogue before his head was severed and held aloft like a trophy. Why did his murderers go through all this choreography when a simple bullet would have done nicely? In lieu of giving Pearl his last rites, they treated themselves to a party over his spilled blood.

There has been much written about the ethical and journalistic values that were either tarnished or elevated by making the entire video of the execution available over the Internet. I don't have a strong view of whether *The Boston Phoenix* performed a morally transgressive act, or whether they simply, in relying on the killers' own archival instincts, reported the news in the most graphically accurate way possible.

What I do know is that such matters of taste and judgment are ultimately a distraction from a more central point. The video offered a new development in the Daniel Pearl story. Its newsworthiness was not that a murder had taken place. That was old news. Daniel Pearl was dead. That we already knew. But what we didn't know, and perhaps this was something we needed to know, was that Pearl's murder wasn't designed as a simple death, not just another routine casualty in an exponentially escalating Middle East, Persian Gulf body count. These men were obviously hardened killers, desensitized to human loss. They are not natural tear-shedders. Had Pearl pleaded for mercy, it surely wasn't forthcoming. They were inured to death, and yet somehow this death among others was a special one, rousing them from the complacency of their usual endeavors, enough to make a show out of it.

Daniel Pearl's murder had to be recorded and preserved, if not for posterity, then as a kind of prurient, hard-porn reminder of the special hate for Jews that animates the consciousness and convictions of his murderers. The video, more than anything else, speaks not only to the execution, but goes beyond it, to an entirely different type of crime, one done to the spirit—the murder of the soul. It is this crime, as much as the decapitation, that depravedly speaks to what was inside the hearts of the men who killed him.

But first, a lesson from another era worth recalling at this time. The Nazis, in addition to everything else that might be said about them, were geniuses at genocide. They knew that the body was beside the point. In order for there to be a true final solution, it wasn't enough to merely exterminate Jews physically. It was equally necessary for them to be divested of dignity, to be reduced to hollow men and women, empty of spirit and life. All those forced separations, the branding of those yellow stars, the humiliation that came from shaved heads and numbered arms, the prolonging of imminent death. These acts of torture were yet another dimension in the Nazis' death strategy: the defilement, the extinguishing of hope, the erasure of identity, the starvation of the spirit. Soon the soul would die; the body would follow. Had the Nazis killed no one, but instead had endlessly dehumanized Six Million Jews, would they not have been guilty of mass murder and genocide?

The Daniel Pearl execution video, and the shamefully barbaric acts that it recorded, is damning evidence of a similar pathology: the impulse to kill his spirit before even bothering with his body, to force him to reveal the only name, rank, and serial number that these people cared about—his Jewish parentage. And while he was indeed an American, he was going to receive a Jewish death. Make no mistake about it: Before he was killed, Daniel Pearl was first branded. And even after his death, the humiliation continued in the showcasing of his severed head.

The knife may have slit Pearl's throat, but the words that were forced out of his mouth were equal in their violence, an act of spiritual murder that preceded his physical death. He did not speak these words of Jewish identity proudly, because they were not his words. He would have perhaps chosen to say something else altogether. Instead these words were given to him as an alibi for his murderers, justification for their cause and the manner in which they carried it out. There was no remorse, but rather giddy and purposeful satisfaction.

This is the way it always is with murderous anti-Semitism: The persecutors are obsessed with their ideology or religion, and it reaches a boiling point of fanaticism. But they're not all that particular about the passions of their victims, whether they too are obsessed, in this case, with being Jewish. To the Nazis it didn't matter whether the gas was going into the lungs of practicing Jews or Jews who had never stepped foot inside a synagogue. These were deaths without any reprieve or pardon. All that mattered was that the victim was Jewish, regardless of how tenuous their connection was to the tribe, or how adamantly they claimed to fit in elsewhere.

It is not surprising that the Pearl family wished to highlight Danny's humanistic, universal impulses as a way to convince his killers that they had the wrong man. But his killers didn't care. Actually, they had the right man. It must have been a tremendous coincidence for them to learn that the Pearls had a street named after them in Israel. Indeed, his murderers had hit the hostage jackpot: a Jewish-American journalist with Zionist roots. But they would have killed him anyway, even if he had never been to Israel, even if he didn't know what a Zionist was. Daniel Pearl transcended the ranks of a mere prisoner. His murderers marked him for death because of one central truth in his biographical data: Stripped down to his essence, Daniel Pearl was a Jew.

But imagine this, if Daniel Pearl had been an American journalist and a practicing Catholic, would they have required him to recite his relevant church affiliation? And would they have had him beheaded? Whether one chooses to see the tape or not, the gory message is clear: all Jews are now Daniel Pearl.

SAMUEL G. FREEDMAN
Don't Look Away

SHORTLY AFTER WATCHING the video of Daniel Pearl's execution, I pulled out an anthology titled *Capture the Moment: The Pulitzer Prize Photographs*. There, spread across pages 80 and 81, was the photograph I could still recall nearly thirty years later. It showed a Vietnamese girl running, naked and howling, away from an explosion, her clothes incinerated by napalm. Unsparingly, the photograph shows her bony ribs, her sticklike arms, her gaping mouth, her genitals.

For that picture, an Associated Press photographer named Nick Ut won the Pulitzer Prize for spot news in 1973. Far from being some disengaged voyeur, Ut had been wounded three times in the war and lost a brother to it. And in the United States, his photograph came to symbolize all that was ceaselessly tragic and senselessly destructive about the Vietnam War.

Throughout the pages of *Capture the Moment*, in fact, I found many such photographs, all of them deemed worthy of journalism's highest award. There is Edward Adams' photo of a South Vietnamese general executing a Viet Cong lieutenant during the Tet Offensive of 1968. There is Greg Marinovich's shot of African National Congress fighters setting afire a spy from the rival Zulu Inkatha Freedom Party.

The two prizewinning photographs from 1994 cumulatively explain why the United States got into and out of the hu-

manitarian intervention in Somalia. The first, taken by Kevin
Carter of *The New York Times,* captures a vulture hunching behind a supine, emaciated child. The second, shot six months
later by Paul Watson of the *Toronto Star,* depicts the body of
an American serviceman being dragged through the streets of
Mogadishu.

It would not surprise me if every one of these photogra-
phers were widely reviled for being not merely sensationalistic
but inhumane. As if to address that very question, *Capture the
Moment* explains that Ut took the Vietnamese girl to the hospital and remained in contact with her for many years, that
Carter shooed away the vulture and, a few months after winning the Pulitzer, committed suicide, leaving a reader to wonder if it wasn't out of desperation or guilt arising from his own
images.

What I kept thinking, all along, is that this is what we, as
journalists, do. We intrude. We afflict. We reawaken slumbering
anguish. We assault the senses with images worthy of night-
mares. And we tell ourselves, not falsely, that we do this out of
a belief in the transforming power of knowledge, of what the
intellectual historian Anne Douglas called in a different vein
"terrible honesty."

The propaganda tape of Daniel Pearl's final words and decapitation deserves to be available on the Internet precisely because it is so shocking, so ghastly, so brutal, so barbaric. Has
The Boston Phoenix acted entirely out of moral conscience and
journalistic integrity in linking to the video from its Web site,
and running still photographs in its print edition, as its publisher Stephen Mindich would have us believe? I doubt it.
Three months after Pearl's murder, Mindich's decision smacks
of promotional genius as much as First Amendment principle.
But what honest journalist, covering a war or catastrophe, can
honestly deny the way ambition and social conscience com-
mingle in our souls?

Certainly, Mindich is right in his central thesis. In a way

that no article about Pearl's execution or even CBS News' edited, bloodless excerpt of the tape possibly can, the unexpurgated video on the Internet attests to the nature of America's enemy in the war against terror. The most unnerving seconds in the video are not those when a knife is dragged across Pearl's neck or a hand holds aloft his severed head. No, they are those when Pearl, voice shaky, intones the script that reveals the motive.

"I'm a Jewish American," he tells the camera. "I come from a, on my father's side, a family of Zionists. My father's Jewish. My mother's Jewish. I'm Jewish. My family follows Judaism. We've made numerous family visits to Israel. In the town of B'nei Brak in Israel, there's a street called Haim Pearl Street, which is named after my great-grandfather, who was one of the founders." After a few cursory comments about the Guantánamo Bay prisoners, Pearl returns to his captors' dogma about America's "unconditional support of the government of the state of Israel" and its "twenty-four uses of the veto power to justify the massacres of children."

All the while, the screen displays scenes of supposed Palestinian victims of Israel—infants with head wounds, a sobbing mother, a young man on his funeral bier. There comes the famous footage of a Palestinian boy and his father huddling amid a shootout in Gaza during the early days of the al-Aksa intifada. President Bush is shown shaking hands with Israeli Prime Minister Ariel Sharon. Almost as an afterthought, bombs explode, presumably from the American campaign in Afghanistan.

To see this film is to have little doubt that Daniel Pearl, while he may have been kidnapped as an American and a journalist, was slain as a Jew. And that recognition, that awful truth, as Mindich argues, has not adequately sunk in. For understandable reasons, Pearl's family and his employers at *The Wall Street Journal* made little or no mention of Pearl's religion and Israeli heritage while there was still hope for his negotiated release. Before and after Pearl's death, his wife and now widow, Mariane, has repeatedly emphasized his openness, his universalism. The statement released by Pearl's family, after they learned of his death, memorialized him as "a musician, a writer, a storyteller, and a bridge-builder . . . a walking sunshine of truth, humor, friendship, and compassion."

Who could doubt all that? And who could doubt the distress of Mariane Pearl after CBS aired its video excerpt, when she said, "It is beyond our comprehension that any mother, wife, father, or sister should have to relive this horrific tragedy." Rarely have I heard a rationale as loathsome as Mindich's contention that "if Daniel had his choice, he'd want it seen."

I'm sure that when I showed up at the doorstep of a family in Piscataway, New Jersey, a few mornings before Christmas 1977, knocking on a front door that was decorated like a giant, beribboned gift box, their choice would surely have been not to talk to a reporter about how their teenaged son had been shot to death the night before on his job as a drive-in bank teller. I'm sure the parents of a college student murdered during spring break in Fort Lauderdale felt the same way when I had to call them up on deadline for a comment.

But this is what we do. And just because Daniel Pearl was one of us, and we grieve for him in the way we rarely grieve for all those strangers we write about, is no reason to obscure the hideous truth of his murder. Nobody is being forced to click on that link. Nor is anyone likely to again be passively faced with it the way viewers of CBS News were.

Human nature wants us to forget the horrors we have seen, which is why they revisit us in our sleep, when our defenses are down. Cerebrally, we understand that al-Qaida is a hateful and ruthless foe, and just as cerebrally we want to achieve distance from what that means. Let us not forget, either, that in large parts of the Muslim world it is still assumed that the tape is some American or Israeli forgery, just as it is widely believed that the Mossad attacked the World Trade Center.

But when I look on Nick Ut's photograph today, all the revisionism about the Vietnam War instantly falls away, and I understand anew why it sickened this country. And just as surely, when I hear the quavering in Daniel Pearl's final, forced words and see the residual anguish on his death's head, when I am thrust up against the joyful sadism of his executioners, I know exactly why this war must be fought.

One Lie

Jeningrad

What the British Media Said

ISRAEL'S ACTIONS in Jenin were "every bit as repellent" as Osama bin Laden's attack on New York on September 11, wrote Britain's *Guardian* in its lead editorial of April 17.

"We are talking here of massacre, and a cover-up, of genocide," said a leading columnist for the *Evening Standard*, London's main evening newspaper, on April 15.

"Rarely in more than a decade of war reporting from Bosnia, Chechnya, Sierra Leone, Kosovo, have I seen such deliberate destruction, such disrespect for human life," reported Janine di Giovanni, the London *Times* correspondent in Jenin, on April 16.

Now that even the Palestinian Authority has admitted that there was no massacre in Jenin last month—and some Palestinian accounts speak instead of a "great victory against the Jews" in door-to-door fighting that left 23 Israelis dead—it is worth taking another look at how the international media covered the fighting there. The death count is still not completely agreed. The Palestinian Authority now claims that 56 Palestinians died in Jenin, the majority of whom were combatants according to the head of Yasser Arafat's Fatah organization in the town. Palestinian hospital sources in Jenin put the total number of dead at 52. Last week's Human Rights Watch report also said

52 Palestinians died. Israel says 46 Palestinians died, all but three of whom were combatants. Palestinian medical sources have confirmed that at least one of these civilians died after Israel withdrew from Jenin on April 12, as a result of a booby-trapped bomb that Palestinian fighters had planted accidentally going off.

Yet one month ago, the media's favorite Palestinian spokespersons, such as Saeb Erekat—a practiced liar if ever there was one—spoke first of 3,000 Palestinian dead, then of 500. Without bothering to check, the international media just lapped his figures up.

The British media was particularly emotive in its reporting. They devoted page upon page, day after day, to tales of mass murders, common graves, summary executions, and war crimes. Israel was invariably compared to the Nazis, to al Qaeda, and to the Taliban. One report even compared the thousands of supposedly missing Palestinians to the "disappeared" of Argentina. The possibility that Yasser Arafat's claim that the Palestinians had suffered "Jeningrad" might be—to put it mildly—somewhat exaggerated seems not to have been considered. (Eight hundred thousand Russians died during the 900-day siege of Leningrad; 1.3 million died in Stalingrad.)

Collectively, this misreporting was an assault on the truth on a par with *The New York Times*'s Walter Duranty's infamous cover-up of the man-made famine inflicted by Stalin on millions of Ukrainians in the 1930s.

There were malicious and slanderous reports against Israel in the American media too—with Arafat's propagandists given hundreds of hours on television to air their incredible tales of Israeli atrocities—but at least some American journalists attempted to be fair. On April 16, *Newsday*'s reporter in Jenin, Edward Gargan, wrote: "There is little evidence to suggest that Israeli troops conducted a massacre of the dimensions alleged by Palestinian officials." Molly Moore of *The Washington Post* reported: "No evidence has yet surfaced to support allegations by Palestinian groups and aid organizations of large-scale massacres or executions."

Compare this with some of the things which appeared in the British media on the very same day, April 16: Under the headline "Amid the ruins, the grisly evidence of a war crime," the Jerusalem correspondent for the London *Independent,* Phil Reeves, began his dispatch from Jenin: "A monstrous war crime that Israel has tried to cover up for a fortnight has finally been exposed." He continued: "The sweet and ghastly reek of rotting human bodies is everywhere, evidence that it is a human tomb. The people say there are hundreds of corpses, entombed beneath the dust."

Reeves spoke of "killing fields," an image more usually associated with Pol Pot's Cambodia. Forgetting to tell his readers that Arafat's representatives, like those of the other totalitarian regimes that surround Israel, have a habit of lying a lot, he quoted Palestinians who spoke of "mass murder" and "executions." Reeves didn't bother to quote any Israeli source whatsoever in his story. In another report Reeves didn't even feel the need to quote Palestinian sources at all when he wrote about Israeli "atrocities committed in the Jenin refugee camp, where its army has killed and injured hundreds of Palestinians."

LEFT AND RIGHT UNITE AGAINST ISRAEL

But it wasn't only journalists of the left who indulged in Israel baiting. The right-wing *Daily Telegraph*—which some in the U.K. have dubbed the "Daily Tel-Aviv-ograph" because its editorials are frequently sympathetic to Israel—was hardly any less misleading in its news coverage, running headlines such as HUNDREDS OF VICTIMS "WERE BURIED BY BULLDOZER IN MASS GRAVE."

In a story on April 15 entitled HORROR STORIES FROM THE SIEGE OF JENIN, the paper's correspondent, David Blair, took at face value what he called "detailed accounts" by Palestinians that "Israeli troops had executed nine men." Blair quotes one woman telling him that Palestinians were "stripped to their underwear, they were searched, bound hand and foot, placed against a wall and killed with single shots to the head."

On the next day, April 16, Blair quoted a "family friend" of one supposedly executed man: "Israeli soldiers had stripped him to his underwear, pushed him against a wall and shot him." He also informed *Telegraph* readers that "two thirds of the camp had been destroyed." (In fact, as the satellite photos show, the destruction took place in one small area of the camp.)

The "quality" British press spoke with almost wall-to-wall unanimity. The *Evening Standard*'s Sam Kiley conjured up witnesses to speak of Israel's "staggering brutality and callous murder." The *Times*'s Janine di Giovanni suggested that Israel's mission to destroy suicide bomb–making factories in Jenin (a town from which at the Palestinians' own admission 28 suicide bombers had already set out) was an excuse by Ariel Sharon to attack children with chickenpox. The *Guardian*'s Suzanne Goldenberg wrote, "The scale [of destruction] is almost beyond imagination."

In case British readers didn't get the message from their "news reporters," the editorial writers spelled it out loud and clear. On April 17, the *Guardian*'s lead editorial compared the Israeli incursion in Jenin with the attack on the World Trade Center on September 11. "Jenin," wrote the *Guardian,* was "every bit as repellent in its particulars, no less distressing, and every bit as man-made."

"Jenin camp looks like the scene of a crime. . . . Jenin already has that aura of infamy that attaches to a crime of especial notoriety," continued this once liberal paper, which used to pride itself on its honesty—and one of whose former editors coined the phrase "comment is free, facts are sacred."

Whereas the *Guardian*'s editorial writers compared the Jewish state to al Qaeda, *Evening Standard* commentators merely compared the Israeli government to the Taliban. Writing on April 15, A. N. Wilson, one of the *Evening Standard*'s leading columnists, accused Israel of "the poisoning of water supplies" (a libel dangerously reminiscent of ancient anti-Semitic myths) and wrote "we are talking here of massacre, and a cover-up, of genocide."

He also attempted to pit Christians against Jews by accusing Israel of "the willful burning of several church buildings," and making the perhaps even more incredible assertion that "Many young Muslims in Palestine are the children of Anglican Christians, educated at St. George's Jerusalem, who felt that their parents' mild faith was not enough to fight the oppressor."

Then, before casually switching to write about how much money Catherine Zeta-Jones is paying her nanny, Wilson wrote: "Last week, we saw the Israeli troops destroy monuments in Nablus of ancient importance: the scene where Jesus spoke to a Samaritan woman at the well. It is the equivalent of the Taliban destroying Buddhist sculpture." (Perhaps Wilson had forgotten that the only monument destroyed in Nablus since Arafat launched his war against Israel in September 2000 was the ancient Jewish site of Joseph's tomb, torn down by a Palestinian mob while Arafat's security forces looked on.)

Other commentators threw in the Holocaust, turning it against Israel. Yasmin Alibhai-Brown, a leading columnist for *The Independent,* wrote (April 15): "I would suggest that Ariel Sharon should be tried for crimes against humanity . . . and be damned for so debasing the profoundly important legacy of the Holocaust, which was meant to stop forever nations turning themselves into ethnic killing machines."

Many of the hostile comments were leveled at the United States. "Why, for God's sake, can't Mr. Powell do the decent thing and demand an explanation for the extraordinary, sinister events that have taken place in Jenin? Does he really have to debase himself in this way? Does he think that meeting Arafat, or refusing to do so, takes precedence over the enormous slaughter that has overwhelmed the Palestinians?" wrote Robert Fisk in *The Independent.*

STAINING THE STAR OF DAVID WITH BLOOD

In the wake of the media attacks, came the politicians. Speaking in the House of Commons on April 16, Gerald Kaufman, a veteran Labour member of parliament and a former shadow foreign secretary, announced that Ariel Sharon was a "war criminal" who led a "repulsive government." To nods of approval from his fellow parliamentarians, Kaufman, who is Jewish, said the "methods of barbarism against the Palestinians" supposedly employed by the Israeli army were "staining the Star of David with blood."

Speaking on behalf of the opposition Conservative party, John Gummer, a former cabinet minister, also lashed out at Israel. He said he was basing his admonition on "the evidence before us." Was Gummer perhaps referring to the twisted news reports he may have watched from the BBC's correspondent Orla Guerin? Or maybe his evidence stemmed from the account given by Ann Clwyd, a Labour MP, who on return from a fleeting fact-finding mission to Jenin, told parliament she had a "croaky voice" and this was all the fault of dust caused by Israeli tanks.

Clwyd had joined a succession of VIP visitors parading through Jenin—members of the European parliament, U.S. church leaders, Amnesty International Secretary-General Irene Khan, Bianca Jagger, ex-wife of pop-music legend Mick Jagger. Clwyd's voice wasn't sufficiently croaky, though, to prevent her from calling on all European states to withdraw their ambassadors from Israel.

Not to be outdone by politicians, Britain's esteemed academics went further. Tom Paulin, who lectures in nineteenth- and twentieth-century literature at Oxford University, opined that the U.S.-born Jews who live on the west bank of the river Jordan should be "shot dead."

"They are Nazis, racists," he said, adding (though one might have thought this was unnecessary after his previous comment), "I feel nothing but hatred for them." (Paulin is also one of BBC television's regular commentators on the arts. The BBC says they will continue to invite him even after these remarks; Oxford University has taken no action against him.)

ONLY ONE WITNESS?

On closer examination, the "facts" on which many of the media reports were based—"facts" that no doubt played a role in inspiring such hateful remarks as Paulin's—reveal an even greater scandal. The British media appear to have based much of its evidence of "genocide" on a single individual: "Kamal Anis, a labourer" (*Times*), "Kamal Anis, 28" (*Daily Telegraph*), "A quiet, sad-looking young man called Kamal Anis" (*Independent*), and referred to the same supposed victim—"the burned remains of a man, Bashar" (*Evening Standard*), "Bashir died in agony" (*Times*), "A man named only as Bashar once lived there" (*Daily Telegraph*).

Independent: "Kamal Anis saw the Israeli soldiers pile 30 bodies beneath a half-wrecked house. When the pile was complete, they bulldozed the building, bringing its ruins down on the corpses. Then they flattened the area with a tank."

Times: "Kamal Anis says the Israelis levelled the place; he saw them pile bodies into a mass grave, dump earth on top, then ran over it to flatten it."

Evidently, as can be seen from the following reports, British journalists hadn't been speaking to the same Palestinian witnesses as American journalists.

Los Angeles Times: Palestinians in Jenin "painted a picture of a vicious house-to-house battle in which Israeli soldiers faced Palestinian gunmen intermixed with the camp's civilian population."

Boston Globe: Following extensive interviews with "civilians and fighters" in Jenin, "none reported seeing large numbers of civilians killed." On the other hand, referring to the deaths of Israeli soldiers in Jenin, Abdel Rahman Sa'adi, an "Islamic Jihad grenade-thrower," told the *Globe,* "This was a massacre of the Jews, not of us."

Some in the American press also mentioned the video filmed by the Israeli army (and shown on Israeli television) of Palestinians moving corpses of people who had previously died of natural causes, rather than in the course of the Jenin fighting, into graveyards around the camp to fabricate "evidence" in advance of the now-canceled U.N. fact-finding mission.

But if European readers don't trust American journalists, perhaps they are ready to believe the testimony given in the Arab press. Take, for example, the extensive interview with a Palestinian bomb-maker, Omar, in the leading Egyptian newspaper, *Al-Ahram.*

"We had more than 50 houses booby-trapped around the [Jenin] camp," Omar said. "We chose old and empty buildings and the houses of men who were wanted by Israel because we knew the soldiers would search for them. . . . We cut off lengths of main water pipes and packed them with explosives and nails. Then we placed them about four meters apart throughout the houses—in cupboards, under sinks, in sofas . . . the women went out to tell the soldiers that we had run out of bullets and were leaving. The women alerted the fighters as the soldiers reached the booby-trapped area."

Perhaps what is most shocking, though, is that the British press had closed their ears to the Israelis themselves—a society with one of the most vigorous and self-critical democracies in the world. In the words of Kenneth Preiss, a professor at Ben Gurion University: "Please inform the reporters trying to figure out if the Israeli army is trying to 'hide a massacre' of Palestinians, that Israel's citizen army includes journalists, members of parliament, professors, doctors, human rights activists, members of every political party, and every other kind of person, all within sight and cell phone distance of home and editorial offices. Were the slightest infringements to have taken place, there would be demonstrations outside the prime minister's office in no time."

ONLY AN INTELLECTUAL COULD BE SO STUPID

George Orwell once remarked to a Communist fellow-traveler with whom he was having a dispute: "You must be an intellectual. Only an intellectual could say something so stupid." This observation has relevance in regard to the Middle East, too.

So far only the nonintellectual tabloids have grasped the essential difference between right and wrong, the difference between a deliberate intent to kill civilians, such as that ordered by Chairman Arafat over the past four decades, and the unintentional deaths of civilians in the course of legitimate battle.

On both sides of the Atlantic, the mass-market papers have corrected the lies of their supposedly superior broadsheets. On April 17, the *New York Post* carried an editorial entitled "The massacre that wasn't." In London, the most popular British daily paper, *The Sun,* published a lengthy editorial (April 15) pointing out that "Israelis are scared to death. They have never truly trusted Britain—and with some of the people we employ in the Foreign Office why the hell should they?" Countries throughout Europe are still "in denial about murdering their entire Jewish population," *The Sun* added, and it was time to dispel the conspiracy theory that Jews "run the world."

The headline of *The Sun*'s editorial was THE JEWISH FAITH IS NOT AN EVIL RELIGION. One might think such a headline was unnecessary in twenty-first-century Britain, but apparently it is not.

One would hope that some honest reflection about their

reporting by those European and American journalists who are genuinely motivated by a desire to help Palestinians (as opposed to those whose primary motive is demonizing Jews) will enable them to realize that propagating the falsehoods of Arafat's propagandists does nothing to further the legitimate aspirations of ordinary Palestinians, any more than parroting the lies of Stalin helped ordinary Russians.

DR. DAVID ZANGEN

Seven Lies About Jenin

David Zangen views the film Jenin, Jenin

I WAS PRESENT at a private viewing of the film *Jenin, Jenin,* by Muhammad Bakri, at the Jerusalem Cinematheque. The limited audience included Lia van Leer, Director of the Cinematheque, and some journalists. At the end of the screening, I reacted by pointing out, one by one, the lies and lack of truth shown in the film. One of the participants responded furiously, "If you cannot accept the facts in the film, you apparently do not understand anything, and how can you be a doctor?" For a moment I forgot that I had been in Jenin last April, serving in the capacity of doctor for IDF forces in the area, while this esteemed viewer's information came, at best, from rumors. Bakri has woven together lies and half-truths so skillfully that it is difficult to withstand the temptation to be drawn into the distorted picture he has created.

I failed to convince the Cinematheque's management to cancel the screening. I was told that the images of destroyed houses are authentic and that, therefore, there is truth in the film, and that anyway, the film will be screened throughout the world. I was nevertheless invited to the film's Jerusalem premiere, and I went, so that I could use the opportunity to explain my position to the audience. Following are some of the points that I had hoped to raise.

1. The director of the hospital in Jenin, Dr. Abu-Rali, claims in the film that the western wing of the hospital was shelled and destroyed, and that the IDF purposely disrupted the supply of water and electricity to the hospital. The truth is that there never was such a wing and, in any case, no part of the hospital was shelled or bombed.

Indeed, IDF soldiers were careful not to enter the hospital grounds, even though we knew that they were being used to shelter wanted persons. We maintained the supply of water, electricity, and oxygen to the hospital throughout the course of the fighting, and helped set up an emergency generator after the electricity grid in the city was damaged.

Bakri himself is seen in the film wandering around the clean, preserved corridors of the hospital, but not in the "bombed" wing. I met him outside the auditorium and asked him if he had visited the western wing. At first he said no, and then immediately corrected himself. "Just a minute, you remember the glass that broke in the film—that was from there."

It is important to note that Abu-Rali is one of the "authorized sources" on which the claim of a "massacre" is based. At the beginning of the operation, he was interviewed on the TV station Al-Jazeera and spoke of "thousands of casualties."

2. Another impressive segment of the film is an interview with a seventy-five-year-old resident of Jenin who, crying bitterly, testified that he had been taken from his bed in the middle of the night and shot in the hand, and, when he failed to obey the soldiers' orders to get up, was shot again in the foot.

This same elderly man was brought to me for treatment after a clean-up operation in one of the houses used by a Hamas cell in the refuge camp. He had indeed sustained a slight injury to the hand and suffered from light abrasions on his leg (although certainly not a bullet wound). IDF soldiers brought him to the station for treating the wounded, and there he was treated, including by me.

One of the army doctors diagnosed heart failure, and we immediately offered to transfer him for treatment to the "Emek" Hospital in Afula. He requested to be treated at the hospital in Jenin since he was not fluent in Hebrew. After the Jenin hospital refused to admit him, we transferred him to Afula. He was in the internal medicine ward for three days and received treatment for heart problems and anemia, from which he suffered as a result of an existing chronic disease.

3. Another interviewee told the story of a baby hit by a bullet that penetrated the baby's chest, passed through its body, and created a large exit wound in its back. According to the information supplied in the film, the baby died after soldiers prevented his evacuation to hospital. However, the baby's body was never found. Furthermore, if such a wound had been in fact inflicted, it would have certainly been fatal, and evacuation to hospital would not have saved the baby's life. What was the baby's name? What happened to the body?

4. The same person also claimed that he used his finger to open an airway in a child's neck after he was wounded. Again, this is a total fabrication. It is impossible to perform such an operation with one's finger. This "witness" also told how tanks rolled over people, again and again, crushing them alive—this, too, never happened.

5. The film mentions mass graves in which the IDF put the Palestinians who were killed. All of the international or-

ganizations that investigated this matter are in agreement that a total of fifty-two Palestinians were killed in Jenin, and their bodies were turned over to the Palestinians for burial. Bakri did not even bother to show the location of these so-called mass graves.

6. The film claims that Israeli planes bombed the city. This is untrue. In order to avoid civilian casualties, only accurate gunfire from helicopters was used.

7. Another point worth noting is that Bakri was not in Jenin during the operation; he arrived two weeks after its conclusion. The destroyed area in the center of the city was filmed in such a way as to appear substantially bigger than it really was, and the posters of "martyrs" and Jihad slogans that covered the walls during the operation were all gone.

The film repeatedly manipulates visual images, showing tanks that had been photographed in other places juxtaposed artificially with pictures of Palestinian children. This is crude, albeit well-done, manipulation.

At the end of the screening, the hundreds of viewers awarded Bakri and the editor of the film with thunderous applause. Bakri turned to the audience and asked if there were any questions. I introduced myself, ascended the stage, and began to systematically list all the lies and inaccuracies in the film.

At first, there was a rustle in the crowd, and then boos and I was called a "murderer," "war criminal," and the like. Before I had even finished my second point, a man from the audience aggressively ascended the stage and tried to grab the microphone from my hand. I decided not to be dragged into violence. I let him take the microphone and walked off the stage. I was surprised that only a few spectators rose to the defense of freedom of speech and freedom of expression. I was amazed that the audience was not willing to hear the facts from someone who had physically been there.

It was painful for me as a man, a father, and a doctor to hear calls of "murderer" from my own people. I said that I hadn't murdered anyone, but the calls intensified. A powerful hatred was directed towards me. I had an unpleasant feeling that I haven't been able to shake.

I do not regret going to the Cinematheque that night, and I am certain that some people present did listen to me and that it changed their ideas a little about the "facts" they had just seen. I am also certain that there were other people who were chagrined at the intolerance demonstrated by the crowd. Still, the fact that they were a silent minority is hard for me to accept.

Permit me, therefore, to say what I did not succeed in saying to those hate-filled people that night. I am proud that I was part of the good and moral forces that operated in Jenin, regular and reserve soldiers with motivation and spirit who went out to destroy the infrastructure of terrorism at its capital. Many of the suicide bombers who murdered old people, women, and children in our city streets came from Jenin.

I am proud that we were there and fought, and proud also of our combat ethics. The camp was not bombed from the air, in order to prevent hurting innocent civilians; neither did we use artillery, although we knew of specific areas in the camp where terrorists were hiding out. The soldiers fought the terrorists, and only the terrorists. Before destroying a house from which heavy gunfire was being directed at our soldiers, several warnings were issued and every possibility was given for civilians to get out safely.

Our medical teams treated every wounded person, even if he had Hamas tattoos on his arms. At no stage was medical care withheld from anyone.

This heroic and at the same time moral fighting cost us dearly in the lives of the best of our fighters. We who were there, the soldiers who fell there, their families, and the IDF, don't deserve to be used by Muhammad Bakri to incite the world to murder and hatred.

TOM GROSS

The Massacre That Never Was

[Written after the "massacre" reports were discredited. Did the "massacre" reporters retract?]

THE STORY OF the British media and Jenin falls into three parts. First, there was the rush to judgment—judgment against Israel. Then there was the refusal to retract once the true facts became known. Finally, there is the continuing failure to publish adequate corrections of the original reports, even though the United Nations—which even Israel's fiercest critics don't accuse of being unduly sympathetic to the Jewish state—has officially confirmed that no massacre took place in Jenin in April, and that the majority of the fifty-two Palestinians killed there (along with twenty-three Israelis) were armed combatants.

Of course, journalists often get things wrong in the heat of the moment, and there isn't the space—or the need—to correct every mistake. But the extraordinary nature of the falsehoods disseminated during the battle of Jenin surely warrants a little introspection on the part of the journalists responsible. You would have thought they would have been moved to ask themselves how they came to harbor such unfair and unfounded views of Israel.

The language initially used by many reporters and commentators in the British media was sweeping and extreme.

Israel's actions in Jenin were "every bit as repellent" as Osama bin Laden's attack on New York on September 11, wrote *The Guardian* in its editorial of April 17. "We are talking here of massacre, and a cover-up, of genocide," wrote A. N. Wilson in the *Evening Standard,* on April 15. "Rarely in more than a decade of war reporting from Bosnia, Chechnya, Sierra Leone, Kosovo, have I seen such deliberate destruction, such disrespect for human life," reported Janine di Giovanni, in *The Times,* on April 16.

The "quality" press spoke with almost wall-to-wall unanimity, backing up their views with horror stories which have turned out to be complete fabrications. *The Daily Telegraph,* for example, ran headlines such as HUNDREDS OF VICTIMS "WERE BURIED BY BULLDOZER IN MASS GRAVE," and gave graphic and entirely false accounts of Palestinians being "stripped to their underwear, searched, bound hand and foot, placed against a wall and killed with single shots to the head."

Newspapers devoted page upon page, day after day, to tales of mass murders, common graves, summary executions, and war crimes. Israel was compared to the Nazis, to al Qaeda, and to the Taliban. One report even compared the thousands of supposedly missing Palestinians to the "disappeared" of Argentina.

The television coverage was, if anything, worse. The BBC's Orla Guerin cited Palestinians saying that Israelis troops "were scooping dead bodies with bulldozers" and that they had shot Palestinians dead "as they tended sheep."

But Guerin's language ("Israel is prepared to go all the way," Israel is committing "terror from above," "nothing is sacred" for Israel, and so on) reveals only one element of her misreporting. The choice of camera angles, her tone of voice, her facial expressions, the leading questions she asked of Palestinians ("Are you afraid he is going to die?" etc.)—all these gave viewers a very inaccurate picture of what was actually going on.

In comparison, little air time was given to the Israeli version of events, which was available, in meticulous detail, throughout the operation, and scant attention was paid to the twenty-three Israeli deaths in Jenin—still less to the fact that they were evidence of the dangers which the Israeli forces incurred in order to avoid collateral damage to Palestinian civilians. At the same time, Yasser Arafat's representatives were given ample opportunity to air their incredible tales of Israeli atrocities, while both TV and print journalists forgot to remind their viewers that Arafat's spokespeople, like those of the other totalitarian regimes that surround Israel, have a habit of lying a lot.

It is not as if the evidence wasn't there at the time. Some foreign journalists, especially Americans, presented an accurate picture. On April 16, for example, Phil Reeves in *The Independent* was reporting that "A monstrous war crime that Israel has tried to cover up for a fortnight has finally been exposed." On the same day, *Newsday*'s reporter in Jenin, Edward Gargan, wrote: "There is little evidence to suggest that Israeli troops conducted a massacre of the dimensions alleged by Palestinian officials." Molly Moore of *The Washington Post* reported: "No evidence has yet surfaced to support allegations by Palestinian groups and aid organizations of large-scale massacres or executions."

The *Los Angeles Times* reported that Palestinians in Jenin "painted a picture of a vicious house-to-house battle in which Israeli soldiers faced Palestinian gunmen intermixed with the camp's civilian population." Even Egyptian newspapers like *Al-Ahram* provided similar accounts. But not the British media— or, for that matter, the media elsewhere in Western Europe, who with very few exceptions were equally biased.

Few of us find it easy to admit that we have been wrong, so perhaps it is not surprising that apologies weren't forthcoming in April. But with the passage of time one might have hoped for some soul-searching, above all now that the UN report has officially concluded that no massacre took place and charged Palestinian militants with deliberately putting their fighters and equipment in civilian areas in violation of international law. Instead, the perpetrators have just dug themselves in deeper.

In an editorial last Friday (subtitled "Israel is still wanted for questioning"), *The Guardian* wrote: "Israel resorted to random, vengeful acts of terror involving civilians" and added "As we said last April, the destruction wrought in Jenin looked and smelled like a crime. On the basis of the UN's findings, it still does."

The editorial didn't make mention that the UN report—compiled with input from UN officials, the mayor of Jenin, five UN member states, private relief organizations, and international groups such as Amnesty International and Human Rights Watch—stated that the number of Palestinian civilians who died in Jenin was somewhere between 14 and 22, i.e., less than the 29 Israeli civilians killed in the Passover massacre, and the hundreds of others murdered by the 27 other suicide bombers dispatched from Jenin in the months that preceded Israel's incursion.

Likewise *The Independent*. On Saturday, the paper's chief Jerusalem correspondent, Phil Reeves, whose news reports from Jenin in April had extended to 3,000 words, wrote a comment piece on the subject. Reeves could have just said: "Sorry, *Independent* readers, for so badly misleading you."

But he didn't. Instead he offered up such excuses for his misreporting as: "My report that day—written by candle-light in the damaged refugee home in the camp, where we spent the night—was highly personalised."

In Israel, Reeves is known for the angry letters he dispatches to those publications which have charged him with bias—not just the rightist *Jerusalem Post,* but the leftist *Ha'aretz,* and the left-leaning *Jerusalem Report* magazine. Instead of being so dismissive of such a wide range of critics, perhaps Reeves should ask himself why his (unedited) news reports from *The Independent,* as well as those of Robert Fisk and some other British journalists, are regularly reproduced alongside articles by David Irving–style American Holocaust deniers in Arab newspapers such as *Asharq Al-Awsat.*

For those of us familiar with the working methods and attitudes of the international media in Israel (I reported there for British and American papers between 1995 and 2001), the rush to false judgment over Jenin came as no surprise. It fits into a deeper pattern of false reporting and systematic bias. But whatever the motives, the damage is likely to be long lasting. Myths have a way of living on, even when the true facts become known; and the myth of Jenin—the massacre that never was—may well continue to poison the atmosphere for years to come.

PART FOUR

THE
ULTIMATE STAKES:
THE SECOND-
HOLOCAUST DEBATE

PHILIP ROTH

Excerpt from *Operation Shylock*

[*In this excerpt from the novel, the "real" Philip Roth, in London, poses as a reporter who does a phone interview with the "imposter" Philip Roth in Jerusalem, where the imposter has been attempting to spread his doctrine of "Diasporism," using the real Roth's name and fame.*]

AFTER OUR DINNER that evening I told Claire that I was going off to my study at the top of the house to sit down again with Aharon's novels to continue making my notes for the Jerusalem conversation. But no more than five minutes had passed after I'd settled at the desk, when I heard the television set playing below and I picked up the phone and called the King David Hotel in Jerusalem and asked to be put through to 511. To disguise my voice I used a French accent, not the bedroom accent, not the farcical accent, not that French accent descended from Charles Boyer through Danny Kaye to the TV ads for table wines and traveler's checks, but the accent of highly articulate and cosmopolitan Frenchmen like my friend the writer Philippe Sollers, no "zis," no "zat," all initial *h*'s duly aspirated—fluent English simply tinged with the natural inflections and marked by the natural cadences of an intelligent foreigner. It's an imitation I don't do badly—once, on the phone, I fooled even mischievous Sollers—and the one I'd decided on even while Claire and I were arguing at the dinner table about the wisdom of my trip, even while, I must admit, the exalted voice of Reason had been counseling me, earlier that day, that doing nothing was the surest way to do him in. By nine o'clock that night, curiosity had all but consumed me, and curiosity is not a very rational whim.

"Hello, Mr. Roth? Mr. Philip Roth?" I asked.

"Yes."

"Is this really the author I'm speaking to?"

"It is."

"The author of *Portnoy et son complexe*?"

"Yes, yes. Who is this, please?"

My heart was pounding as though I were out on my first big robbery with an accomplice no less brilliant than Jean Genet— this was not merely treacherous, this was *interesting*. To think that he was pretending at his end of the line to be me while I was pretending at my end not to be me gave me a terrific, unforeseen, Mardi Gras kind of kick, and probably it was this that accounted for the stupid error I immediately made. "I am Pierre Roget," I said, and only in the instant after uttering a convenient nom de guerre that I'd plucked seemingly out of nowhere did I realize that its initial letters were the same as mine—and the same as his. Worse, it happened also to be the barely transmogrified name of the nineteenth-century word cataloger who is known to virtually everyone as the author of the famous thesaurus. I hadn't realized that either—the author of the definitive book of synonyms!

"I am a French journalist based in Paris," I said. "I have just read in the Israeli press about your meeting with Lech Walesa in Gdansk."

Slip number two: Unless I knew Hebrew, how could I have read his interview in the Israeli press? What if he now began speaking to me in a language that I had learned just badly enough to manage to be bar mitzvahed at the age of thirteen and that I no longer understood at all?

Reason: "You are playing right into his plan. This is the very situation his criminality craves. Hang up."

Claire: "Are you really all right? Are you really up to this? Don't go."

Pierre Roget: "If I read correctly, you are leading a movement to resettle Europe with Israeli Jews of European background. Beginning in Poland."

"Correct," he replied.

"And you continue at the same time to write your novels?"

"Writing novels while Jews are at a crossroads like this? My life now is focused entirely on the Jewish European resettlement movement. On Diasporism."

Did he sound *anything* like me? I would have thought that my voice could far more easily pass for someone like Sollers speaking English than his could pass for mine. For one thing, he had much more Jersey in his speech than I'd ever had, though whether because it came naturally to him or because he mistakenly thought it would make the impersonation more convincing, I couldn't figure out. But then this was a more resonant voice than mine as well, richer and more stentorian by far. Maybe that was how he thought somebody who had published sixteen books would talk on the phone to an interviewer, while the fact is that if I talked like that I might not have had to write sixteen books. But the impulse to tell him this, strong as it was, I restrained; I was having too good a time to think of stifling either one of us.

"You are a Jew," I said, "who in the past has been criticized by Jewish groups for your 'self-hatred' and your 'anti-Semitism.' Would it be correct to assume—"

"Look," he said, abruptly breaking in, "I am a Jew, period. I would not have gone to Poland to meet with Walesa if I were anything else. I would not be here visiting Israel and attending the Demjanjuk trial if I were anything else. Please, I will be glad to tell you all you wish to know about resettlement. Otherwise I haven't time to waste on what has been said about me by stupid people."

"But," I persisted, "won't stupid people say that because of this resettlement idea you are an enemy of Israel and its mission? Won't this confirm—"

"I am Israel's enemy," he interrupted again, "if you wish to put it that sensationally, only because I am for the Jews and Israel is no longer in the Jewish interest. Israel has become the gravest threat to Jewish survival since the end of World War Two."

"Was Israel ever in the Jewish interest, in your opinion?"

"Of course. In the aftermath of the Holocaust, Israel was the Jewish hospital in which Jews could begin to recover from the devastation of that horror, from a dehumanization so terrible that it would not have been at all surprising had the Jewish spirit, had the Jews themselves, succumbed entirely to that legacy of rage, humiliation and grief. But that is not what happened. Our recovery actually came to pass. In less than a century. Miraculous, more than miraculous—yet the recovery of the Jews is by now a fact, and the time has come to return to our real life and our real home, to our ancestral Jewish Europe."

"Real home?" I replied, unable now to image how I ever could have considered not placing this call. "Some real home."

"I am not making promiscuous conversation," he snapped back at me sharply. "The great mass of Jews have been in Europe since the Middle Ages. Virtually everything we identify culturally as Jewish has its origins in the life we led for centuries among European Christians. The Jews of Islam have their own, very different destiny. I am not proposing that Israeli Jews whose origins are in Islamic countries return to Europe, since for them this would constitute not a homecoming but a radical uprooting."

"What do you do then with them? Ship them back for the Arabs to treat as befits their status as Jews?"

"No. For those Jews, Israel must continue to be their country. Once the European Jews and their families have been resettled and the population has been halved, then the state can be reduced to its 1948 borders, the army can be demobilized, and those Jews who have lived in an Islamic cultural matrix for centuries can continue to do so, independently, autonomously, but in peace and harmony with their Arab neighbors. For these people to remain in this region is simply as it should be, their rightful habitat, while for the European Jews, Israel has been an exile and no more, a sojourn, a temporary interlude in the European saga that it is time to resume."

"Sir, what makes you think that the Jews would have any more success in Europe in the future than they had there in the past?"

"Do not confuse our long European history with the twelve years of Hitler's reign. If Hitler had not existed, if his twelve years of terror were erased from our past, then it would seem to you no more unthinkable that Jews should also be Europeans than that they should also be Americans. There might even seem to you a much more necessary and profound connection between the Jew and Budapest, the Jew and Prague, than the one between the Jew and Cincinnati and the Jew and Dallas."

Could it be, I asked myself while he pedantically continued on in this vein, that the history he's most intent on erasing happens to be his own? Is he mentally so damaged that he truly believes that my history is his; is he some psychotic, some amnesiac, who isn't pretending at all? If every word he speaks he means, if the only person pretending here is me. . . . But whether that made things better or worse I couldn't begin to know. Nor, when next I found myself *arguing*, could I determine whether an outburst of sincerity from me made this conversation any more or less absurd, either.

"But Hitler *did* exist," I heard Pierre Roget emotionally informing him. "Those twelve years *cannot* be expunged from history any more than they can be obliterated from memory, however mercifully forgetful one might prefer to be. The meaning of the destruction of European Jewry cannot be measured or interpreted by the brevity with which it was attained."

"The meanings of the Holocaust," he replied gravely, "are for us to determine, but one thing is sure—its meaning will be no less tragic than it is now if there is a second Holocaust and the offspring of the European Jews who evacuated Europe for a seemingly safer haven should meet collective annihilation in the Middle East. A second Holocaust is *not* going to occur on the continent of Europe, *because* it was the site of the first. But a second Holocaust could happen here all too easily, and, if the conflict between Arab and Jew escalates much longer, it will— *it must*. The destruction of Israel in a nuclear exchange is a possibility much less farfetched today than was the Holocaust itself fifty years ago."

"The resettlement in Europe of more than a million Jews. The demobilization of the Israeli army. A return to the borders of 1948. It sounds to me," I said, "that you are proposing the final solution of the Jewish problem for Yasir Arafat."

"No. Arafat's final solution is the same as Hitler's: extermination. I am proposing the alternative to extermination, a solution not to Arafat's Jewish problem but to ours, one comparable in scope and magnitude to the defunct solution called Zionism. But I do not wish to be misunderstood, in France or anywhere else in the world. I repeat: In the immediate postwar era, when for obvious reasons Europe was uninhabitable by Jews, Zionism was the single greatest force contributing to the recovery of Jewish hope and morale. But having succeeded in restoring the Jews to health, Zionism has tragically ruined its own health and must now accede to vigorous Diasporism."

"Will you define Diasporism for my readers, please?" I asked, meanwhile thinking, The starchy rhetoric, the professorial presentation, the historical perspective, the passionate commitment, the grave undertones . . . What sort of hoax *is* this hoax?

"Diasporism seeks to promote the dispersion of the Jews in the West, particularly the resettlement of Israeli Jews of European background in the European countries where there were sizable Jewish populations before World War II. Diasporism plans to rebuild *everything,* not in an alien and menacing Middle East but in those very lands where everything once flourished, while, at the same time, it seeks to avert the catastrophe of a second Holocaust brought about by the exhaustion of Zionism as a political and ideological force. Zionism undertook to restore Jewish life and the Hebrew language to a place where neither had existed with any real vitality for nearly two millennia. Diasporism's dream is more modest: a mere half-century is all that separates us from what Hitler destroyed. If Jewish resources could realize the seemingly fantastic goals of Zionism in even less than fifty years, now that Zionism is counterproductive and itself the foremost Jewish problem, I have no doubt that the resources of world Jewry can realize the goals of Diasporism in half, if not even one tenth, the time."

"You speak about resettling Jews in Poland, Romania, Germany? In Slovakia, the Ukraine, Yugoslavia, the Baltic states? And you realize, do you," I asked him, "how much hatred for Jews still exists in most of these countries?"

"Whatever hatred for Jews may be present in Europe—and I don't minimize its persistence—there are ranged against this residual anti-Semitism powerful currents of enlightenment and morality that are sustained by the memory of the Holocaust, a horror that operates now as a bulwark *against* European anti-Semitism, however virulent. No such bulwark exists in Islam. Exterminating a Jewish nation would cause Islam to lose not a single night's sleep, except for the great night of celebration. I think you would agree that a Jew is safer today walking aimlessly around Berlin than going unarmed into the streets of Ramallah."

"What about the Jew walking around Tel Aviv?"

"In Damascus missiles armed with chemical warheads are aimed not at downtown Warsaw but directly at Dizengoff Street."

"So what Diasporism comes down to is fearful Jews in flight, terrified Jews once again running away."

"To flee an imminent cataclysm is 'running away' only from extinction. It is running *toward* life. Had thousands more of Germany's fearful Jews fled in the 1930s—"

"Thousands more would have fled," I said, "if there had been somewhere for them to flee to. You may recall that they were no more welcome elsewhere than they would be now if they were to turn up en masse at the Warsaw train station in flight from an Arab attack."

"You know what will happen in Warsaw, at the railway station, when the first trainload of Jews returns? There will be crowds to welcome them. People will be jubilant. People will be in tears. They will be shouting, 'Our Jews are back! Our Jews are back!' The spectacle will be transmitted by television throughout the world. And what a historic day for Europe, for Jewry, for all mankind when the cattle cars that transported Jews to death camps are transformed by the Diasporist movement into decent, comfortable railway carriages carrying Jews by the tens of thousands back to their native cities and towns. A historic day for human memory, for human justice, and for atonement too. In those train stations where the crowds gather to weep and sing and celebrate, where people fall to their knees in Christian prayer at the feet of their Jewish brethren, only there and then will the conscience cleansing of Europe begin." He paused theatrically here before concluding this visionary outpouring with the quiet, firm pronouncement "And Lech Walesa happens to believe this just as strongly as Philip Roth does."

"Does he? With all due respect, Philip Roth, your prophecy strikes me as nonsense. It sounds to me like a farcical scenario out of one of your books—Poles weeping with joy at the feet of the Jews! And you tell me you are *not* writing fiction these days?"

"This will come to pass," he declared oracularly, "because it *must* come to pass—the reintegration of the Jew into Europe by the year 2000, not a reentry as refugees, you must understand, but an orderly population transfer *with an international legal basis, with restoration of property, of citizenship, and of all national rights.* And then, in the year 2000, the pan-European celebration of the reintegrated Jew to be held in the city of Berlin."

"Oh, that's the best idea yet," I said. "The Germans particularly will be delighted to usher in the third millennium of Christianity with a couple of million Jews holding a welcome-home party at the Brandenburg Gate."

"In his day Herzl too was accused of being a satirist and of making an elaborate joke when he proposed the establishment of a Jewish state. Many deprecated *his* plan as a hilarious fantasy, an outlandish fiction, and called him crazy as well. But my conversation with Lech Walesa was not outlandish fiction. The contact I have made with President Ceauşescu, through the chief rabbi of Romania, is no hilarious fantasy. These are the first steps toward bringing about *a new Jewish reality based on principles of historical justice.* For years now, President Ceauşescu has been selling Jews to Israel. Yes, you hear me correctly: Ceauşescu has *sold* to the Israelis several hundred thousand Romanian Jews for ten thousand dollars a head. This is a fact. Well, I propose to offer him ten thousand more dollars for each Jew he takes back. I'll go as high as fifteen if I have to. I have carefully studied Herzl's life and have learned from his experience how to deal with these people. Herzl's negotiations with the sultan in Constantinople, though they happened to fail, were no more of a hilarious fantasy than the negotiations I will soon be conducting with the dictator of Romania at his Bucharest palace."

"And the money to pay the dictator off? My guess is that to fund your effort you have only to turn to the PLO."

"I have every reason to believe that my funding will come from the American Jews who for decades now have been contributing enormous sums for the survival of a country with which they happen to have only the most abstractly sentimental connection. The roots of American Jewry are not in the Middle East but in Europe—their Jewish style, their Jewish words, their strong nostalgia, their actual, weighable history, all this issues from their European origins. Grandpa did not hail from Haifa—Grandpa came from Minsk. Grandpa wasn't a Jewish nationalist—he was a Jewish humanist, a spiritual, believing Jew, who complained not in an antique tongue called Hebrew but in colorful, rich, vernacular Yiddish."

Our conversation was interrupted here by the hotel operator, who broke in to tell him that Frankfurt was now on the line.

"Pierre, hold a second."

Pierre, hold a second, and I did it, *held,* and, of course, obediently waiting for him to come back on made me even more ludicrous to myself than remembering everything I'd said in our conversation. I should have taped this, I realized—as evidence, as proof. But of what? That he wasn't me? This needed to be *proved?*

"A German colleague of yours," he said when he returned to speak to me again, "a journalist with *Der Spiegel.* You must excuse me if I leave you to talk with him now. He's been trying to reach me for days. This has been a good, strong interview—your questions may be aggressive and nasty, but they are also intelligent, and I thank you for them."

"One more, however, one last nasty question. Tell me, please," I asked, "are they lining up, the Romanian Jews who are dying to go back to Ceauşescu's Romania? Are they lining up, the Polish Jews who are dying to return to Communist

Poland? Those Russians struggling to leave the Soviet Union, is your plan to turn them around at the Tel Aviv airport and force them onto the next flight back to Moscow? Anti-Semitism aside, you think people fresh from these terrible places will voluntarily choose to return just because Philip Roth tells them to?"

"I think I have made my position sufficiently clear to you for now," he replied most courteously. "In what journal will our interview be published?"

"I am free-lance, Mr. Philip Roth. Could be anywhere from *Le Monde* to *Paris-Match*."

"And you will be kind enough to send a copy to the hotel when it appears?"

"How long do you expect to remain there?"

"As long as the disassociation of Jewish identity threatens the welfare of my people. As long as it takes Diasporism to recompose, once and for all, the splintered Jewish existence. Your last name again, Pierre?"

"Roget," I said. "Like the thesaurus."

His laugh erupted much too forcefully for me to believe that it had been provoked by my little quip alone. He knows, I thought, hanging up. He knows perfectly well who I am.

RON ROSENBAUM

"Second Holocaust," Roth's Invention, Isn't Novelistic*

Blaming the Victims Back in Toxic Style in Civilized Europe

THE SECOND HOLOCAUST. It's a phrase we may have to begin thinking about. A possibility we may have to contemplate. A reality we may have to witness. Somebody has to think about the unthinkable, about the unbearable, and the way it looks now, it's at least as likely to happen as not. One can imagine several ways it will happen: the current, terrible situation devolves from slow-motion mutual slaughter into instantaneous conflagration, nuclear, chemical, or biological. Scenarios that remain regional. Scenarios that go global.

What is harder to imagine are ways in which it *won't* happen. A peace process? Goodwill among men? An end to suicidal fanaticism? In your dreams.

Instead we must begin to examine the variety of nightmare scenarios.

The Second Holocaust. It's a phrase first coined, as far as I

---

*Had the *Observer*'s narrow columns permitted, and had I had input into the original headline, it would have read: "Second Holocaust"? Roth's Phrase Isn't Necessarily Novelistic Fantasy Anymore."

know, by Philip Roth in his 1993 novel *Operation Shylock*. It's a novel which seemed incredibly bleak back then. And yet, re-examining Mr. Roth's use of the phrase "Second Holocaust" less than a decade later, even his darkest imaginings seem *optimistic* now. Especially when examined by the glare of burning synagogues in France.

I was reminded of Mr. Roth's Second Holocaust scenario when I came across an excerpt from *Operation Shylock* on the Web site of a Canadian blogger (www.davidartemiw.com) via the all-seeing InstaPundit.com.

Here's the crucial exchange between a character Roth calls the "Diasporist" and the novel's narrator:

"The meanings of the Holocaust," [says the Diasporist,] "are for us to determine, but one thing is sure—its meaning will be no less tragic than it is now if there is a second Holocaust and the offspring of the European Jews who evacuated Europe for a seemingly safer haven should meet collective annihilation in the Middle East.... A second Holocaust could happen here all too easily, and, if the conflict between Arab and Jew escalates much longer, it will—*it must*. The destruction of Israel in a nuclear exchange is a possibility much less farfetched today than was the Holocaust itself fifty years ago."

"The resettlement in Europe of more than a million Jews ... It sounds to me ... that you are proposing the final solution of the Jewish problem for Yasir Arafat."

"No. Arafat's final solution is the same as Hitler's: extermination. I am proposing the alternative to extermination [the return of the Jews from Israel to Europe]....

"You speak about resettling Jews in Poland, Romania, Germany? In Slovakia, the Ukraine, Yugoslavia, the Baltic states? And you realize, do you ... how much hatred for Jews still exists in most of these countries?"

"Whatever hatred for Jews may be present in Europe ... there are ranged against this residual anti-Semitism powerful currents of enlightenment and morality that are sustained by the memory of the Holocaust, a horror that operates now as a bulwark *against* European anti-Semitism. . . ."

Here, it is clear, is where Roth's darkest fantasy is too optimistic. Here is where we have to examine the dynamic going on in the mind of Europe at this moment: a dynamic that suggests that Europeans, on some deep if not entirely conscious level, are willing to be complicit in the murder of the Jews again.

The novel's narrator believes that there are in Europe "powerful currents of enlightenment and morality that are sustained by the memory of the Holocaust . . . a bulwark *against* European anti-Semitism, however virulent." It may be true in the case of *some* Europeans, although if so they have been very quiet about it. In fact, it seems that the memory of the Holocaust is precisely what *ignites* the darker currents in the European soul. The memory of the Holocaust is precisely what explains the one-sided anti-Israel stance of the European press, the European politicians, European culture. The complacency about synagogue burnings, the preference for focusing on the Israeli *response* to suicide bombers blowing up families at prayer, rather than on the mass murderers (as the suicide bombers should more properly be called) and those who subsidize them and throw parties for their families. . . .*

There is a horrid but obvious dynamic going on here: At some deep level, Europeans, European politicians, European culture is aware that almost without exception every European nation was deeply complicit in Hitler's genocide. Some manned the death camps, others stamped the orders for the transport of the Jews to the death camps, everyone knew what was going on—and yet the Nazis didn't have to use much if any force to make them accomplices. For the most part, Europeans *volunteered*. That is why "European civilization" will always be a kind of oxymoron for anyone who looks too closely

---

* [ellipsis in original]

at things, beginning with the foolish and unnecessary slaughters of World War I, Holocaust-scale slaughter that paved the way for Hitler's more focused effort.

And so, at some deep level, there is a need to blame someone *else* for the shame of "European civilization." To blame the victim. To blame the Jews. And the more European nations can focus one-sidedly on the Israeli response to terror and not to the terror itself, the more they can portray the Jews as the real villains, as Nazis, the more salve to their collective conscience for their complicity in collective mass murder in the past. Hitler may have gone too far, and perhaps we shouldn't have been so cowardly and slavish in assisting him, but look at what the Jews are doing.

Isn't it interesting that you didn't see any "European peace activists" volunteering to "put their bodies on the line" by announcing that they would place themselves in *real* danger—in the Tel Aviv cafés and pizza parlors, favorite targets of the suicide bombers. Why no "European peace activists" at the Seders of Netanya or the streets of Jerusalem? Instead, "European peace activists" do their best to protect the brave *sponsors* of the suicide bombers in Ramallah.

One has to put the European guilt complex not just in the context of complicity during World War II. One must also consider the malign neglect involved in the creation of the state of Israel. The begrudging grant of an indefensible sliver of desert in a sea of hostile peoples, to get the surviving Jews—reminders of European shame—off the continent, and leave the European peoples in possession of the property stolen from the Jews during the war. And that was when they didn't continue murdering Jews, the way some Poles did when some Jews were foolish enough to try to return to their stolen homes.

Someone remarked recently at the astonishing hypocrisy of European diplomats and politicians in supporting the Palestinian "right of return" when so many Europeans are still living in homes stolen from Jews they helped murder.

Make no mistake of it, the Palestinians are victims of history as well as the Jews. The last thing the nations of Europe wanted to do was the right thing, which would be to restore the Jews to their stolen homes, and so they acquiesced in the creation of a Jewish state and then did nothing to make it viable for either the Jews or the Palestinians, preferring to wash their hands of the destruction: let the Semites murder each other and blame the Jews, the Semites they were more familiar with hating.

And now it's so much easier for the Europeans to persecute the Jews, because they can just allow their own Arab populations to burn synagogues and beat Jews on the street *for* them. The way Hitler used the eager Croatians, for instance, as death-camp guards. Still, there's something particularly repulsive about the synagogue-burnings in France. I think in a way it goes a long way toward explaining why the Israeli government is acting the way it is now—with a little less restraint against those who murder their children. Yes, restraint: If Israel were to act with *true* ruthlessness to end the suicide bombings, they would tell the prospective bombers—who go to their deaths expecting that their families will celebrate their mass murders with a subsidized party and reap lucrative financial rewards courtesy of the Saudis and Saddam—that their families instead will share the exact same fate of the people the bombers blow up. That might put a crimp into the recruiting and the partying over dead Jewish children. But the Israelis won't do that, and that is why* there's likely to be a second Holocaust. Not because the Israelis are acting without restraint, but because they *are,* so far, still acting with restraint despite the massacres making their country uninhabitable.

Consider that remarkable Joel Brinkley story in the April 4

---

*In his "Hitler Is Dead" piece, Leon Wieseltier omits the words before the asterisk in this sentence. Just thought you'd like to know.

edition of *The [New York] Times,* in which the leaders of Hamas spoke joyfully and complacently of their great triumph in the Passover massacre and the subsequent slaughters in Jerusalem and Haifa. Two things made this interview remarkable. One was the unashamed assertion that they had no interest in any "peace process" that would produce a viable Palestinian state living side by side with a Jewish state. They only wanted the destruction of the Jewish state and its replacement with one in which "the Jews could remain living 'in an Islamic state with Islamic law.'"

That defines the reality that has been hidden by the illusion of hope placed in a "peace process." The Palestinians, along with their 300 million "Muslim brothers" surrounding the five million Jews, are not interested in a "negotiated settlement."

Israelis are forever being criticized for not negotiating, for not giving away enough of their security, but they have no one to negotiate with who doesn't, in their heart of hearts, want to exterminate their state and their people as well, if necessary.

The other thing that made the *Times* interview such a defining document was the description of its setting. The interview with one of the four directors of the Hamas mass murderers, a Dr. Zahar, was conducted in a comfortable home in which "Dr. Zahar, a surgeon, has a table tennis set in his vast living room for his seven children."

If the Israelis *were* as ruthless as the Europeans take great pleasure in calling them, there would be, let's say, no ping-pong playing for the murderer of their children.

Now let's talk further about the relationship between the first Holocaust and the next. The relationship between the European response to the first one and the likely Israeli response to the one in the making.

I think it might best be summed up by that old proverb: "Fool me once, shame on you. Fool me twice, shame on me."

The first time, when the Jewish people were threatened by

someone who called for their extinction, they trusted to the "enlightenment" values of the European people, as Philip Roth's character put it.

Civilized people wouldn't let something like that happen. Pogroms, well yes, but death camps, extermination? Never. They're transporting us to camps, yes, but what could it be, labor camps at worst? The world wouldn't let such a thing happen.

Well, the world did let it happen—with extraordinary complacency, a deaf ear, a blind eye, and not a little pleasure on the part of some. And it's clear from the reaction of Europe today that the world is prepared, is preparing itself, to let it happen again.

But I suspect that deep in the heart of most Israelis is the idea that this time we're not going to depend on others to prevent it from happening. We're not going to hope that the world will *care* that they're killing our children. This time, we won't go quietly; this time, if we go down, we'll go down fighting and take them with us and take more of them if we can, and the rest of the world be damned. Fool us twice, shame on us.

I feel bad for the plight of the Palestinians; I believe they deserve a state. But they had a state: They were part of a state, a state called Jordan, that declared war on the state of Israel, that invaded it in order to destroy it—and lost the war. There are consequences to losing a war, and the consequences should at least in part be laid at the feet of the three nations that sought and lost the war. One sympathizes with the plight of the Palestinians, but one wonders what the plight of the Israelis might have been had *they* lost that war. One doesn't envision spacious homes and ping-pong for their leaders.

But somehow the Israelis are told that they must trust the world—trust the European Union as guarantors of their safety, trust the Arab League's promises of "normal relations," trust the Saudis who subsidize suicide-bomber parties and ignore the exterminationist textbooks the Arab world tutors its children with. The Israelis must learn to make nice; the Jews must *behave* better with people who want to kill them. I don't think so.

As a secular Jew, I've always been more of a diasporist than a Zionist. I've supported the Jewish state, but thought that it was a necessary but not ideal solution with a pronounced dark side: The concentration of so many Jews in one place—and I use the word "concentration" advisedly—gives the world a chance to kill the Jews *en masse* again. And I also thought that Jews flourished best where they were no longer under the thumb of Orthodox rabbis and could bring to the whole world—indeed, the whole universe—the exegetical skills that are the glory of the people: reading the universe as the Torah, as Einstein and Spinoza did, rather than the Torah as the universe, as the Orthodox do.

But the implacable hatred of Arab fundamentalism makes no distinction between Jewish fundamentalists and Jewish secularists, just as Hitler didn't. It's not just the settlements they want to extirpate, it's the Jewish state, the Jewish people.

This is the way it is likely to happen: Sooner or later, a nuclear weapon is detonated in Tel Aviv, and sooner, not later, there is nuclear retaliation—Baghdad, Damascus, Tehran, perhaps all three. Someone once said that while Jesus called on Christians to "turn the other cheek," it's the Jews who have been the only ones who have actually practiced that. Not this time. The unspoken corollary of the slogan "Never again" is: "And *if* again, not us alone."

So the time has come to think about the Second Holocaust. It's coming sooner or later; it's not "whether," but *when*. I hope I don't live to see it. It will be unbearable for those who do. That is, for all but the Europeans—whose consciences, as always, will be clear and untroubled.

LEON WIESELTIER

Against Ethnic Panic

Hitler Is Dead

HAS HISTORY EVER TOYED so wantonly with a people as history toyed with the Jews in the 1940s? It was a decade of ashes and honey; a decade so battering and so emboldening that it tested the capacity of those who experienced it to hold a stable view of the world, to hold a belief in the world. When the light finally shone from Zion, it illuminated also a smoldering national ruin; and after such darkness, pessimism must have seemed like common sense, and a holy anger like the merest inference from life. But it was in the midst of that turbulence, in 1948, that the scholar and man of letters Simon Rawidowicz published a great retort to pessimism, a wise and learned essay called "*Am Ha-Holekh Va-Met*," "The Ever-Dying People." "The world has many images of Israel," Rawidowicz instructed, "but Israel has only one image of itself: that of an expiring people, forever on the verge of ceasing to be. . . . He who studies Jewish history will readily discover that there was hardly a generation in the Diaspora period which did not consider itself the final link in Israel's chain. Each always saw before it the abyss ready to swallow it up. . . . Often it seems as if the overwhelming majority of our people go about driven by the panic of being the last."

In its apocalyptic season, such an observation was out of season. In recent weeks I have thought often of Rawidowicz's mordant attempt to calm his brethren, to ease them, affectionately and by the improvement of their historical sense, out of their tradition of panic. For there is a Jewish panic now. The savagery of the Israeli-Palestinian conflict, the virulent anti-Zionism and anti-Semitism in the Arab world, the rise in anti-Jewish words and deeds in Europe: All this has left many Jews speculating morbidly about being the last Jews. And the Jews of the United States significantly exceed the Jews of Israel in this morbidity. The community is sunk in excitability, in the imagination of disaster. There is a loss of intellectual control. Death is at every Jewish door. Fear is wild. Reason is derailed. Anxiety is the supreme proof of authenticity. Imprecise and inflammatory analogies abound. Holocaust imagery is everywhere.

In the discussion of the atrocities that the Palestinians have committed against the Israelis, the subject is Hitler. "I am convinced that we are facing a threat as great, if not greater, to the safety and security of the Jewish people than we faced in the '30s," the head of a national Jewish organization announced in February. In *The New York Observer* in April, Ron Rosenbaum warned of "the Second Holocaust": "It's a phrase we may have to begin thinking about. A possibility we may have to contemplate." Indeed, "there's likely to be a second Holocaust. Not because the Israelis are acting without restraint, but because they are, so far, acting with restraint despite the massacres making their country uninhabitable." George F. Will admiringly cited Rosenbaum in a column that he called "'Final Solution,' Phase 2." "Here in Washington, D.C., a few blocks away, is the Holocaust Museum," William Bennett told the rally in support of Israel at the Capitol on April 15. "What we are seeing today, what Israel is feeling today, was not supposed to happen again." On the same occasion Benjamin Netanyahu compared Arafat to Hitler, and also to Stalin. ("We don't have to be afraid that the international community doesn't see eye to eye with us," he proclaimed at the Likud Party conference this week. "Did the international community see the danger of the Holocaust?") THE NEW KRISTALLNACHT, screamed the headline of a Jewish paper in New York about the Passover massacre in Netanya. "This is Kristallnacht transposed to Israel," wrote Charles Krauthammer in *The Washington Post.* And doves are as un- nerved as hawks. "As I've said before," Nat Hentoff told *New York* magazine, "if a loudspeaker goes off and a voice says, 'All Jews gather in Times Square,' it could never surprise me."

Call me a simple soul, but it could surprise me. The Jews that I see gathered in Times Square are howling at Nazis in Mel Brooks's kick lines. Hentoff's fantasy is grotesque: There is nothing, *nothing,* in the politics, the society, or the culture of the United States that can support such a ghastly premonition. His insecurity is purely recreational. But the conflation of the Palestinians with the Nazis is only slightly less grotesque. The murder of twenty-eight Jews in Netanya was a crime that fully warranted the Israeli destruction of the terrorist base in the refugee camp at Jenin, but it was not in any deep way like Kristallnacht. Solidarity must not come at the cost of clarity. Only a fool could believe that the Passover massacre was a prelude to the extermination of the Jews of Israel; a fool, or a person with a particular point of view about the Israeli- Palestinian conflict. If you think that the Passover massacre was like Kristallnacht, then you must also think that there cannot be a political solution to the conflict, and that the Palestinians have no legitimate rights or legitimate claims upon any part of the land, and that there must never be a Palestinian state, and that force is all that will ever avail Israel. You might also think that Jordan is the Palestinian state and that the Palestinians should find their wretched way there. After all, a "peace process" with the Third Reich was impossible. (Even if Chaim Weizmann once declared, about his willingness to enter into negotiations with Nazi officials, that he would negotiate with the devil if it would save Jews.) So the analogy between the Passover massacre and Kristallnacht is not really a historical argument. It is a political argument disguised as a historical argument. It is designed to paralyze thought and to paralyze diplomacy.

All violence is not like all other violence. Every Jewish death is not like every other Jewish death. To believe otherwise is to revive the old typological thinking about Jewish history, according to which every enemy of the Jews is the same enemy, and there is only one war, and it is a war against extinction, and it is a timeless war. This typological thinking defined the historical outlook of the Jews for many centuries. It begins, of course, with the Amalekites, the nomadic tribe in the Sinai desert that attacked the Israelites on their journey out of Egypt. "The Lord hath sworn that the Lord will have war with Amalek from generation to generation. . . . Thou shalt blot out the remembrance of Amalek from under heaven; thou shalt not forget it." From generation to generation: An adversarial role, a diabolical role, was created in perpetuity. And so Amalek became Haman (who actually was an Amalekite), who became the Romans, who became the Crusaders, who became Chmielnicki, who became Petlura, who became Hitler, who became Arafat. The mythifying habit is ubiquitous in the literature of the Jews. In some instances, it must not have seemed like mythifying at all. "A tale that began with Amalek," wrote the Yiddish poet Yitzhak Katznelson in the concluding lines of "The Song of the Murdered Jewish People" in 1944, not long before he died at Auschwitz, "and ended with the crueler Germans. . . ."

But it is mythifying, and the habit is back; and so a number of things need to be said about Amalek, and about the Amalekization of the present enemy. For a start, the prescription of an eternal war with Amalek was a prescription for the Jews to be cruel. Here is Rashi's brutal gloss, in the eleventh century in France, on the commandment to "blot out the remembrance": "Every man and every woman, every babe and every suckling, every ox and every sheep. The memory of Amalek cannot be said to survive even in an animal, such that someone could say, 'This animal once belonged to an Amalekite.'" This extreme of heartlessness was responsible for the most chilling sentence uttered by an Israelite in the Bible: "What meaneth then this bleating of the sheep in mine ears, and the lowing of the oxen which I hear?" That was what Samuel furiously demanded to know of the poignantly human Saul, the king who could not bring himself to slaughter his enemy completely. So if Amalek is waging a war of extermination against the Jews, the Jews are waging a war of extermination against Amalek. It was perhaps this pitilessness against which some (but certainly not all) medieval and early modern Jewish intellectuals revolted, when they wondered about the precise identity of Amalek in their own day, and proposed various kinds of symbolic action that would allow Jews to acquit themselves of the law about the erasure of the enemy, and deferred the application of the law to the messianic age. I wish also to record an extraordinary comment by Isaac Abarbanel, the thinker and statesman who failed to persuade the king and the queen of Spain to revoke the edict of expulsion in 1492 and promptly fled to Naples. The sin of the Amalekites, he explained, was that their aggression against the Israelites was groundless: "Amalek attacked them without reason. . . . For the Israelites possessed no land that the Amalekites coveted." It would appear that there is no place for Abarbanel in the Likud. For his implication is decidedly a moderate one. If the Israelites had possessed land that the Amalekites coveted, then this would not have been a war to the end of time. It would have been an ordinary war, a war that can be terminated in a peace.

But the real problem with typological thinking about history is that it is not historical thinking at all. It is ahistorical thinking. It obscures and obliterates all the differences between historical circumstances in favor of a gross, immutable, edifying similarity. It is an insufficiently worldly way to judge the world. For this reason, such thinking was overthrown in the modern period by Jews who decided that their myths would not ameliorate their misery; that there was not only one question and only one answer; that the entire universe was not their enemy and their enemy was not the entire universe; that the historical differences mattered as much as the historical similarities, because a change in history, progress, normality, tranquillity, was possible; that historical agency required historical thinking, that is, concrete thinking, empirical thinking, practical thinking, secular thinking. All these notions amounted to a revolution in the Jewish spirit, without which the Jewish national movement and the Jewish state could not have been brought into being. A historiosophy is not a strategy. The Jews taught themselves to attend not only to their fates, but also to their interests. That is to say, they taught themselves no longer to regard themselves as the last Jews. The lesson was called Zionism. The last Jews have nothing to do but fight or die; but Zionism has more to do. Israel was not created to destroy Amalek. Israel was created to deny Amalek.

Is Hamas Amalek? I have no idea. Also I do not care. It is bad enough that Hamas is Hamas. (Was Hitler Amalek? No, he was worse.) Anyway, Amalek is not all that justifies the use of force. But the important point is that Amalek justifies nothing but the use of force. There is no other solution to the Amalek problem. And that is why all this pessimism is not only intellectually sloppy, it is also operationally superfluous. It is a view of history that provides no foundation for Israeli restraint, and sometimes restraint is the intelligent policy. Consider this week's calamity. If Netanya was Kristallnacht, then Rishon Letzion was Kristallnacht. The villain in Netanya came from

Jenin, and Israel turned its might on Jenin. The villain in Rishon Letzion came from Gaza, but Israel is not turning its might on Gaza. Why not? The logic is the same. The answer, of course, is that this is not the logic of statecraft. If, as the Israeli press is reporting, there may be signs of flexibility on the Palestinian side, it is the duty of the Israeli government to stay its hand and have a look. These signs may be false; but too many people have perished not to take their measure. The exploration of opportunities for accommodation and understanding is a matter of both prudence and principle. It may be that Ariel Sharon, of all people, has comprehended this. As long as the prime minister of Israel continues to speak of the eventual establishment of a Palestinian state, Kristallnacht is over. (For Netanyahu, by contrast, every Nacht is Kristallnacht.)

The fright of American Jewry is owed also to a new recognition of the reality of anti-Semitism. Up to a point, this is as it should be: The happiness of the Jews in the United States certainly demands a regular refreshment of their awareness of evil. There is something a little odd, though, about the shock with which the news of European anti-Semitism has been met, since it is for the Jews the oldest news. There was one blessing, and one blessing only, that the Second World War conferred upon the Jewish people, and it is that the future of the Jewish people forever departed Europe. Anti-Semitism in Europe must be fought, but not with the confidence that this will be a European fight, too. European nationalism includes no conception of the multiethnic state. European culture is permeated with a contempt for otherness. Indeed, the moral incompetence of European culture with regard to otherness now falls more heavily upon Muslims than upon Jews.

The acknowledgment of contemporary anti-Semitism must be followed by an analysis of contemporary anti-Semitism, so that the magnitude of the danger may be soberly assessed. Is the peril "as great, if not greater" than the peril of the 1930s?

I do not see it. Jewish history now consists essentially in a competition for the Jewish future between Israel and the United States, between the blandishments of sovereignty and the blandishments of pluralism; it is a friendly competition, and by the standards of Jewish experience it is an embarrassment of riches. In many significant ways, the Jewish present is discontinuous with the Jewish past, and some of these discontinuities will stand among the finest accomplishments of Jewish history, though the ruptures were sometimes very bruising. The predicament of contemporary Jewry cannot be correctly understood except in terms of these saving discontinuities. Anti-Semitism has not disappeared, obviously; but Zionism was not premised on the expectation that anti-Semitism would disappear, it was premised on the expectation that anti-Semitism would *not* disappear, and in the United States the prejudice has never been granted political or philosophical legitimacy. (It was the legitimacy of Jew-hatred in European society that made it lethal.)

In Israel and in the United States, moreover, the Jews found not only safety, but also strength. The blandishments of pluralism in America have included the fierce and unembarrassed pursuit of Jewish interests, and so brilliantly that the American Jewish community has become the model for what an ethnic group can accomplish in such conditions of freedom. The blandishments of sovereignty in Israel have conspicuously included military power. Suicide bombs are sickening; but it is the Israelis who command an army and an air force, and also a nuclear arsenal. These instruments of warfare are themselves conclusions properly drawn from a severe history in which Jews lacked the means of self-reliance and self-defense. There is nothing vexing about the strength of the Jewish state, though there may be something vexing in the manner in which the Jewish state sometimes (but not often) exercises its strength. And military power has political purposes as well as military purposes. So Israel has adversaries, but Israel is stronger than its adversaries. That is why the real threat to Israel comes not from Jenin and Gaza, but from Baghdad and Tehran; not from booby-trapped casbahs, but from advanced missile technologies. But not even that threat, and it is grave, can be accurately compared to the plight of the Jews in Hitler's Europe. The comparison breaks down over more than the fact that this time the Jews have a spectacular deterrent. The Jews in the 1930s and 1940s were fighting, when they fought, for nothing more than a splendid death. They knew that the fight was futile, which makes their courage almost unbearable to contemplate. The Jews in Israel have no reason to believe that the fight is futile. And they are fighting for their home.

The fright of American Jewry is finally not very surprising, and not only because we are an "ever-dying people." To a degree that is unprecedented in the history of the Jewish people, our experience is unlike the experience of our ancestors: not only our ancient ancestors, but also our recent ones. It is also unlike the experience of our brethren in the Middle East. Their experience of adversity in particular is increasingly unrecognizable to us. We do not any longer possess a natural knowledge of such pains and such pressures. In order to acquire such a knowledge, we rely more and more upon commemorations— so much so that we are transforming the Jewish culture of the United States into a largely commemorative culture. But the identifications that seem to be required of us by our commemorations are harder and harder for us to make. In our hearts, the continuities feel somewhat spurious. For we are the luckiest Jews who ever lived. We are even the spoiled brats of Jewish history. And so the disparity between the picture of Jewish life that has been bequeathed to us and the picture of Jewish life that is before our eyes casts us into an uneasy sensation of dissonance. One method for relieving the dissonance is to imagine a loudspeaker summoning the Jews to Times Square. In the absence of apocalypse, we turn to hysteria.

In America, moreover, ethnic panic has a certain plausibility and a certain prestige. It denotes a return to "realism" and to roots. A minority that has agreed to believe that its life has been transformed for the better, that has accepted the truth of progress, that has revised its expectation of the world, that has taken yes for an answer, is always anxious that it may have been tricked. For progress is a repudiation of the past. Yes feels a little like corruption, a little like treason, when you have been taught no. For this reason, every disappointment is a temptation to eschatological disappointment, to a loss of faith in the promise of what has actually been achieved. That is why wounded African Americans sometimes cry racism and wounded Jewish Americans sometimes cry anti-Semitism. Who were we kidding? Racism is still with us. Anti-Semitism is still with us. The disillusionment comes almost as a comfort. It is easier to believe that the world does not change than to believe that the world changes slowly. But this is a false lucidity. Racism is real and anti-Semitism is real, but racism is not the only cause of what happens to blacks and anti-Semitism is not the only cause of what happens to Jews. A normal existence is an existence with many causes. The bad is not always the worst. To prepare oneself for the bad without preparing oneself for the worst: This is the spiritual challenge of a liberal order.

The Jewish genius for worry has served the Jews well, but Hitler is dead. The conflict between Israel and the Palestinians is harsh and long, but it is theology (or politics) to insist that it is a conflict like no other, or that it is the end. The first requirement of security is to see clearly. The facts, the facts, the facts; and then the feelings. Arafat is small and mendacious, the political culture of the Palestinians is fevered and uncompromising, the regimes in Riyadh and Cairo and Baghdad pander to their populations with anti-Semitic and anti-American poisons, the American government is leaderless and inconstant; but Israel remembers direr days. Pessimism is an injustice that we do to ourselves. Nobody ever rescued themselves with despair. "An ever-dying people is an ever-living people," Rawidowicz sagely remarked. "A nation always on the verge of ceasing to be is a nation that never ceases to be." It is one of the lessons that we can learn from the last Jews who came before us.

RUTH R. WISSE

On Ignoring Anti-Semitism

"HITLER IS DEAD." In April 1945, a headline containing those three words might have heralded the collapse of Nazi Germany and the beginning of the end of World War II. This past May, appearing on the cover of *The New Republic*, the same words ridiculed the "ethnic panic of the Jews." In the lead essay, Leon Wieseltier, the magazine's literary editor, charged that American Jews, spooked by the history of Jewish persecution, were stoking unwarranted and apocalyptic fears by comparing the Arab war against Israel with Hitler's earlier war against the Jews. The first requirement of security, he advised his readers, was not to imagine the worst on the basis of historical precedent but to "see clearly" the situation of the present.

The article provoked a number of rebuttals, and also a number of strong defenses. In the words of the historian Tony Judt, one of its defenders, Wieseltier had "elegantly dissected those *frissons* of existential angst in which some in the American Jewish community are wont to indulge themselves." Wieseltier's call for clarity is thus as good a starting point as any to ask whether we have made much progress since Hitler in understanding the political phenomenon that he represented.

Not that Hitler was by any means the first politician in Europe to fulminate against the Jews; but it is certainly true that no one before him had ever organized so radical a political platform. Still, during the years that he was consolidating his power, the majority of European Jews, unwilling or unable to fathom what his policy signified, or how it would be implemented, did not seem to fear him *sufficiently*. Rather than manifesting the kind of "ethnic panic" that Wieseltier ascribes to their American coreligionists today, they stand retrospectively accused by many historians of having minimized or ignored Hitler's menace until it was too late. Indeed, the same accusation has been extended to that generation's American Jews as well, who have been reproached for failing either to recognize the danger in time or to do what they could to help their beleaguered coreligionists.

We have, then, a variety of possibilities. It could be that the "panic" of today's Jews is an overcompensation for past negligence. It could be, contrarily, that the myopic Jews of the 1930s have finally been blessed with perfect vision, and that yesterday's Mister Magoo has become today's Ted Williams. Or it could simply be, as Wieseltier would have it, that Nazi anti-Semitism is so different in kind from the Arab variety that what would have been a proper response in the former case is improper in the latter. Since Wieseltier's article calls into question "the new recognition of the *reality* of anti-Semitism" (emphasis added), it would help to establish whether there is, today, a major threat to the Jewish people.

The Arab war against Israel has been going on since before the Jewish state was established in 1948, but lately there have been significant changes in its scope, its nature, and the degree of international support it enjoys. Until fairly recently, Arab rulers who exerted despotic or autocratic control over their populations kept the lid on armed aggression issuing from their territory. Now, however, radical ideologies and terrorist tactics against Israeli Jews seem to be dominating Arab politics as never before, while in liberal and academic circles everywhere in the West, as well as in the chancelleries of Europe, blame for this state of affairs has fallen largely on the state of Israel itself.

The avant-garde of anti-Israel radicalism has long been the Palestine Liberation Organization (PLO), the bastard offspring of the Arab world's insistence that the Palestinian people be kept demonstrably homeless as permanent evidence of Jewish culpability. The terrorist groups comprising the PLO, and their multiplying rivals, were given unique license by their fellow Arabs to intimidate, to extort, and to kill. Over time, they served their handlers superbly well, doing far greater harm to Israel than all the Arab military assaults combined.

Unlike the Germans who unleashed their war against the Jews under cover of a wider European conflict, the Arab nations, through the PLO, placed the destruction of Israel explicitly at the heart of their mission. The PLO's charter, a public document, defines the Jews as "not a people with an independent identity," branding them as colonial occupiers of land that belongs eternally to the Palestinian people, and their state as an illegitimate "entity" that needs to be eliminated. On these grounds, the PLO not only claimed the moral right to kill Jews but turned their murder into a sacred cause. And this, as the historian Michael Oren has pointed out, does mark one difference between German and Arab anti-Semitism, albeit a difference suggesting that the Arab variety is worse:

> For all the kudos discreetly given SS killers by the regime, Nazi Germany never publicly lionized them, never plastered their pictures on the streets, or openly encouraged children to emulate them. That kind of adoration for mass murderers can only be found, in abundance, among the Palestinians.

In the light of this adoration, indeed, it has become more and more difficult to maintain the distinction between anti-Semitism and anti-Zionism, with the latter defined as "merely" a political-territorial objection to the state of Israel as the home-land of the Jewish people. Rather, contemporary anti-Zionism has absorbed all the stereotypes and foundational texts of fascist and Soviet anti-Semitism and applied them to the Middle East. Every stratum of Arab society, from top to bottom, has been nourished on the myth of Israel's illegitimacy, and has been encouraged to express its loyalties through aggressive hostility to the Jewish people and its land.

The dissemination of anti-Jewish propaganda by and within Arab and Muslim societies has lately been swifter than the spread of the Internet. As anyone can discover by punching in the relevant keywords in any major library system, Arabic translations of all the major works of European anti-Semitism have been supplemented by an immense new body of original literature defaming Israel and the Jews. As long ago as 1986, Bernard Lewis could write in *Commentary* that certain Arab countries were the only places in the world "where hard-core, Nazi-style anti-Semitism is publicly and officially endorsed and propagated." Since then, Arab propagandists have been working hard to expand and revitalize the tradition. The sincerity and the steadfastness of this genocidal hostility, proliferating through the press, the visual media, literature, and the schools, are much greater in Arab lands than they ever were in pre-Hitler Europe—which had, after all, a contrary liberal tradition and at least the rudiments of a modern democratic culture. And now, thanks in part to Muslim immigrants, this same hostility has found its way back to the heartland of the very Europe where it originated.

Without citing all the other evidence that anti-Jewish politics is visibly on the rise in Europe, and even in scattered precincts in the United States,* I would therefore suggest that,

---

*The evidence has been abundantly documented. In *Commentary,* see, for example, Hillel Halkin, "The Return of Anti-Semitism" (February 2002); Gabriel Schoenfeld, "Israel and the Anti-Semites" (June 2002); and Michel Gurfinkiel, "France's Jewish Problem" (July–August 2002).

on the question of the threat itself, Wieseltier has things backward. So obvious is this threat that we should ask why the reality had to wait so *long* for its "new recognition." But there is an answer to that question as well, and it leads directly to the real gravamen of Wieseltier's article.

Palestinian bombings inside Israel and political/diplomatic assaults against the state's right to exist escalated dramatically after September 2000, when Yasir Arafat, unleashing the very kind of violence that under the Oslo accords he had solemnly undertaken to quell, launched the second Palestinian *intifada*. The first *intifada,* between 1987 and 1993, had claimed 160 Israeli lives. The second killed more than three times as many in twenty months, with thousands of wounded as a result of the explosives that had replaced the knives and stones that were the earlier weapons of choice.

But it was not until a year after the terrorist outbreaks in Israel that the American media and a significant proportion of American Jewry began to air anxieties about anti-Semitism. The reason clearly had to do with an intervening event: namely, September 11. President Bush set a new tone for the nation when he spoke before Congress of "a country awakened to danger and called to defend freedom." Although the President drew no analogy between the unprovoked assault on America and escalating Arab attacks against Israeli Jews, it was then that many observers began to think harder about the correspondence between the two types of terror.

At a Washington rally for Israel in April of this year, said to be the largest pro-Israel gathering ever held in the United States, most speakers, Jewish and non-Jewish alike, linked solidarity with Israel to America's war on terror. Representing the government of Israel, Deputy Prime Minister Natan Sharansky saluted the President's determination to wage a global battle against a common enemy. William J. Bennett, who in the wake of 9/11 had founded an organization called Americans for Victory Over Terrorism, pointed to the Holocaust Museum just a few blocks away and said: "What we are seeing today, what Israel is feeling today, was not supposed to happen again." Just as the attack on America had triggered memories of Pearl Harbor, the atrocities in Israel had begun to evoke the mass murders of European Jewry.

Drawing this analogy most insistently was the journalist and critic Ron Rosenbaum, who warned in *The New York Observer* of a possible "second Holocaust" at the hands of the Arabs should they ever get their hands on weapons of mass destruction. As for the origin of that ominous phrase, "second Holocaust," Rosenbaum traced it back to Philip Roth's 1993 novel *Operation Shylock*, where a character opines that "Arafat's final solution is the same as Hitler's: extermination," and then urges Israelis to seek safety in a Europe where (in the judgment of this same fictional character) memory of the Holocaust still acts as a bulwark against anti-Semitism.

Roth in 1993 was only toying with this incongruous idea. But Rosenbaum, ten years later, finds Roth's dark fantasy much too optimistic. Europe's own recent outbreaks of anti-Jewish violence persuade him that there is likely to be another attempt to destroy the Jewish people; the question for him is "not 'whether,' but *when.*"

This was the trigger that set off Wieseltier's tirade. He describes the emotional condition of American Jews in the following language:

> The community is sunk in excitability, in the imagination of disaster. There is a loss of intellectual control. Death is at every Jewish door. Fear is wild. Reason is derailed. Anxiety is the supreme proof of authenticity. Imprecise and inflammatory analogies abound. Holocaust imagery is everywhere.

As it happens, however, none of the evidence Wieseltier adduces in support of this claim can compete with the claim itself for sheer "excitability." Apart from the Washington rally, and a number of other initiatives to advocate Israel's cause and help the victims of terror there, American Jews have been going about their business as usual, manifesting no more visible panic than has been apparent among American citizens in general in the long months after 9/11. When Boston's Jewish Community Relations Council scheduled a rally last May to coincide with the day of Holocaust remembrance, it drew only about a thousand persons in a city of a quarter of a million Jews. The Jewish press has reported no protest suicides, no burning barricades, not even a canceled vacation.

What, then, explains Wieseltier's own overreaction? Primarily, his objection to any analogizing of European and Arab anti-Semitism would seem to rest less on issues of accuracy than on issues of political utility. In his analysis, invoking the Holocaust is a means of exaggerating the degree of hostility to Israel, and this in turn promotes and justifies a hard line against concessions to the Palestinians. The Nazi analogy, in short, denies the possibility of the "peace process." As Wieseltier writes:

> If you think that the Passover massacre [of twenty-eight Jews in Netanya] was like Kristallnacht [November 9, 1938, the night of multiple Nazi pogroms against the Jews of Germany], then you must also think that there cannot be a political solution to the conflict, and that the Palestinians have no legitimate rights or legitimate claims upon any part of the land, and that there must never be a Palestinian state, and that force is all that will ever avail Israel.

Is Wieseltier right about *this*? Have the Jews fallen victim to a self-fulfilling prophecy, missing the chance for reconciliation with today's Arabs by insisting on portraying them as yesterday's Nazis? After all, if it were possible to temper Arab hostility by, for example, withdrawing from the disputed territories and encouraging the creation of an Arab Palestinian state, might this not go a long way toward reaching the "peace" that Israel says it has been seeking for many long years? Would not a more forthcoming Jewish policy induce a more receptive Arab policy in turn?

The argument is, alas, all too familiar. It is exactly what produced the Oslo accords, which were designed to lead to the very settlement between Israelis and Palestinians that Wieseltier now envisions as if for the first time. In 1993, a mere nine years ago, the government of Israel invited Yasir Arafat back from exile and transferred administrative power over parts of the disputed territories to a newly appointed Palestinian Authority, expecting it to become the nucleus of an independent Arab state. At that time, the majority of American Jews, Wieseltier assertively among them, hailed the Oslo accords as the road to peace, and many actively lobbied Washington on behalf of the PLO.

The most revealing section of Wieseltier's narrative is thus the one that is missing. No one reading his words about ethnic panic would ever guess that American Jewish celebrants of the peace process had so recently danced the hora in honor of Yasir Arafat on the White House lawn. If there has indeed been a "loss of intellectual control," it is not the one that Wieseltier attributes to today's nervous Jews but that earlier orgy of hope, based as it was on political calculations that had no proven models, and on trust in those who had least earned it.

Wieseltier's failure even to mention a seminal course of events at such extreme odds with his own recitation of recent history suggests less an oversight than a cover-up, an attempt to dodge responsibility for a catastrophically misconceived policy. This is no doubt why some diehard champions of the Oslo "process" have so eagerly seized on his *New Republic* article. "A Bracing Response to Current Hysteria," exulted the columnist Leonard Fein, a founding member of Peace Now and, for over two decades, an enthusiastic promoter of concessions to

Arafat who has yet to account for the gap between his predictions and their results. Similar obeisance was paid by Tony Judt, who as an expert in modern European history has repeatedly likened Israel's occupation of the West Bank and Gaza to the French colonization of Algeria and attributed the lack of "credible Palestinian interlocutors" to Israel's own imperious behavior ever since its "hubris-inducing victory" of 1967.

To hold the Jews responsible for the aggression against them, as Judt does; to affirm the peaceful intentions of Arab terrorists, as Fein does; to transform American Jews who recently pimped for the PLO into paranoid hysterics of the Right, as Wieseltier does, is to disfigure political reality beyond recognition. Even if the Jews were the most rotten and misguided people on earth, they do not number 280 million in nationality (let alone one billion in religious affiliation); they have not organized *their* politics around the destruction of twenty-one Arab countries, or trained a generation of suicide bombers to achieve that goal; they have not used the United Nations as a medium for spreading a genocidal ideology around the globe, or their synagogues to preach "death to the Arabs!" Jews did not bomb America in the name of the Torah, or foment anti-Muslim sentiment throughout Europe.

It is certainly true that memories of the Holocaust and invocations of anti-Semitism can be used to justify militancy. They can also be used to justify pacifism, appeasement, and much else besides.

Which brings us to another point of similarity between "then" and "now"—namely, the agitation among intellectuals not only over the relative significance of political anti-Semitism but also over the uses to which it is allegedly put by Jews themselves. During the 1930s, in the pages of *The New Republic* and elsewhere, a few Jewish intellectuals did track the danger to Jews in Europe and in Palestine, warning, in Ludwig Lewisohn's words, of "the pathological bloodthirstiness of the Nazi anti-Semitic campaign." But Lewisohn's was a minority voice. Most intellectuals urbanely mocked such apocalyptic scenarios, and some of the Jews among them worried lest their co-religionists exploit the whole issue either to further Zionist ambitions in Palestine or to resuscitate an "archaic" Jewish religion.

Today, too, when deadlier forms of anti-Semitism are on the rise, there is massive intellectual resistance to acknowledging the threat, and most political analysts still treat anti-Semitism like a hiccup that will soon give way to regular breathing. Tony Judt writes that the solution to the Israel-Palestine conflict is in plain sight: "Israel exists. The Palestinians and other Arabs will eventually accept this; many already do." He states this conclusion as though it complied with some obvious and inexorable logic, though he might as well be saying that fish will fly because they have fins and will eventually use them.

As a European historian, Judt presumably knows that the Jews of Europe also "existed," and that by 1939 many, if not most, Germans and Austrians "already" accepted their existence. Nevertheless, a dedicated minority of motivated idealists was able to cleanse their countries of the blight within an astonishingly brief period of time. Today's situation is once again arguably worse: one no longer needs to hold mass rallies in Nuremberg to spread the sort of genocidal anti-Jewish propaganda that Egyptian television carries nightly to millions of homes, and preachers who call for holy struggle against Israel are no less committed than Judt is to *their* sense of the inevitable. This is not to say that the Arabs will succeed, any more than that the Germans and Austrians had to succeed; it means that one cannot dismiss anti-Semitism just because it offends one's sense of rational possibility.

Nor, on similar grounds, can one dismiss the possibility of Israel's physical defeat by its Arab and Muslim enemies just because its military power is for the moment unmistakably preponderant. Even greater powers—the United States, for one—

have been defeated in palpably unequal contests with lesser but more determined forces. The suicide bomber is a strategic weapon of immense effectiveness for those who feel they have expendable populations; more crucially still, the possession, imminent or actual, of weapons of mass destruction on the part of nations that have already declared their eagerness to use them against the Jewish state changes the regional balance of power definitively. And much as Israel may resemble the United States in other respects, it cannot lose a war to its enemies and necessarily expect to survive. Observers like Judt who point to Israel's defensive capabilities as evidence that it has little to fear from Arab aggression are playing a cruel game of loading up the donkey to see how much it can carry before it collapses.

Judt's views—I focus on them because they may be taken to represent the liberal academic consensus—are interesting in another respect as well: they illustrate how anti-Semitism makes inroads into the liberal mindset. In the years immediately following the creation of Israel, when Arab hostility was expected to give way "eventually" to recognition and acceptance, Israel was the beneficiary of widespread liberal sympathy. The question Western liberals posed to themselves was: how long would it take before the Arabs came to their senses, relinquished their intransigence, and accepted the reality of a Jewish state? But the paradoxical truth is that, the longer and more energetically the Arabs continued their aggression, the costlier it became for others—ideologically, as well as politically or militarily—to defend Israel. As the hostility escalated, it turned neutral onlookers not against the aggressors but against their intended victims.

Anti-Semitism offends Western sensibilities because it is not amenable to the kind of reasoning that we believe is innate in human beings. ("Israel exists. The Palestinians and other Arabs will eventually accept this; many already do.") In attacking

Jews, the anti-Semite also attacks, by proxy, the Western belief in tolerance, and the freedoms implicit in the Rights of Man. What is a good liberal to do? He knows hostility when he sees it, and he surely does not want it directed at himself. Since confronting Arab anti-Semitism would require confronting the entire Arab world, no less than confronting German anti-Semitism once meant confronting Germany itself, liberals and democrats find it much easier to blame the rising "anger" and "frustration" of the Arabs on *Israel's* intransigence, and to urge Israel to concede to them.

This helps explain why anti-Semitism began to be taken seriously only after the events of September 11. As long as Israel alone was being assaulted by terror and genocidal propaganda, there was little general credence in the idea that its destruction was the point at issue. But when nineteen homicidal Arabs coordinated a sophisticated attack on New York City and the Pentagon, it became harder to deny that something was afoot in the world that transcended "normal" international behavior. Once one is prepared to acknowledge that a given act of aggression is incommensurate with any offense that may have been given, terms like evil—and anti-Semitism—become permissible.

In the case of the so-called Arab-Israel conflict, to permit the concept of anti-Semitism into the discussion is to acknowledge that the origins of Arab opposition to the Jewish state are to be located in the political culture of the Arabs themselves, and that such opposition can end only if and when that political culture changes. For some supporters of the "peace process," this post–September 11 realization hit with the force of a revelation, and it has led to much salutary rethinking of former positions. For others, alas, it clearly remains a bridge too far.

"Is the peril 'as great, if not greater' than the peril of the 1930s? I do not see it," writes Leon Wieseltier. The determination not to see it is what has helped make the peril greater.

Consider the case of Michael Kamber, a correspondent of *The Village Voice* who had been reporting from Pakistan just before the disappearance of Daniel Pearl. When Kamber learned of Pearl's kidnapping, he knew for a certainty that Pearl would be murdered, and he was simultaneously shaken by the realization that he himself, being the son of a Jewish father, might just as easily have been the victim. After the murder was confirmed, Kamber filed a belated column, a kind of obituary-report about this land "where anti-Semitism flows as easily as water."

Kamber's column describes Pakistan as a country of 140 million inhabitants, 98 percent Muslim and 75 percent illiterate, all of whom seem to be obsessed with Jewish iniquity:

> In interviews conducted while I was there, government officials would occasionally veer off into long diatribes about the Jews; fundamentalist religious leaders, who educate hundreds of thousands of children in the country's *madrassa*s, spoke of little else. In Islamabad . . . an elderly mullah responsible for the education of hundreds of youngsters said, "To me [the bombing of the World Trade Center] seems the design of the Jewish lobby. The Jewish lobby wants to pit Islam against Christianity."

As Kamber tells the tale, Pakistan's uneducated populace, having no personal contact with Jews and no training in independent thought, takes its cues from religious and political authorities. Those authorities, unaccustomed to assuming any responsibility for the gross deficiencies of their society, blame the "Jews" for all that they need to explain away. No distinctions are made between Jews and Israel, or indeed between Israel and America—except when it is politically expedient to blame Jews for what is hateful about America, too. In such a climate, writes Kamber, now justifying his decision to hide his own half-Jewish identity, "to admit to being Jewish . . . would have been unthinkable."

This is a very significant admission. If the effect of anti-Semitism on Michael Kamber was to inhibit any mention of his Jewish identity to others while he was in Pakistan, its effect on his published journalism, up until this final act of intellectual penance, was to inhibit any mention of a huge and central fact of life in the society he was writing about. Western journalists are paid to report accurately on reality. But the very enormity of anti-Semitism—the fact that, in certain parts of the world, politicians and clerics turn abhorrence of Jews into an essential element of *their* reality—creates an inclination to turn away from it, if for no other reason than to retain the good will of the anti-Semites. Thus, in the name of maintaining "access," do American journalists affirm the power of dictators to control our putatively free and open press.

The problem transcends the case of Michael Kamber, and is again not a new one. When Arthur Hays Sulzberger took control of *The New York Times* in 1935, he seemed far more afraid of having it thought that he ran a "Jewish newspaper" than of the rise of Adolf Hitler. He believed that the threat of anti-Semitism was being used by some Jews as a political cover for a kind of nationalism he abhorred, and he instructed his city editor not to give "too much space" to the efforts of the American Jewish Committee to aid European Jews. When Zionist leaders charged him with failing to present the news impartially, he blamed *them* for turning him from a non-Zionist into an "anti-Zionist." In 1942 he wrote to Rabbi Abba Hillel Silver, chairman of the American Zionist Emergency Council, "I am opposed to Goebbels' tactics whether or not they are confined to Nazi Germany," equating Nazi pressure on the Jews of Germany with Rabbi Silver's pressure on him.

The effect of this was to upend the stated editorial principles of the *Times*. Ostensibly, the family wanted the paper to remain evenhanded and free of bias, by which it meant that it would not allow its own Jewish origins to dictate favorable coverage of the Jews. But in practice the paper carried this to the point of *creating* bias: lest it be accused of favoring the views of one side, it banned all letters to the editor concerning Hitler in the years that he was coming to power. The Ochs-Sulzbergers also believed that, since the Jews were not a people—the very claim that would one day be enshrined in the charter of the PLO—they were not in need of a Jewish homeland; and this, too, dictated a policy of minimizing anti-Semitism lest, by promoting sympathy for the Jewish plight, the *Times* play into the hands of Zionists.

Although the Ochs-Sulzberger families have since apologized for the "meager coverage" the *Times* gave to the Holocaust as it was unfolding, they have never made a connection between their prejudiced view of Jewish peoplehood and the paper's coverage of world news in general. They thus perpetuate the cycle of parochialization, as if the problem were one that affected only the Jews. But let us suppose for a moment that the publishers of *The New York Times* had acted truly without bias. They would then have responded to Hitler's virulent anti-Semitism as signaling a broader danger to everything precious to themselves and to America. They would have assiduously gathered information about Hitler's program of rearmament, as Winston Churchill tried to do once he became convinced that Hitler was planning to attack the West. They would have drawn daily attention to Germany's abuses of democratic freedoms, its perversion of the law, its abrogation of civil liberties. *And* they would have registered the way that Nazi anti-Semitism cloaked darker anti-democratic purposes behind an enmity directed against the Jews alone.

In brief, had the *Times* been truly neutral in reporting on Hitler's war against the Jews, it would have done a newspaper's proper job of ferreting out the painful but necessary truth about Hitler's war against the West. And the same holds true today, when embarrassment over Jewish causes still governs *Times* coverage of the Middle East and elsewhere, resulting in the same betrayal of professional standards. Had the *Times* been truly neutral, and doing its proper job, it would have long since reported in copious detail on the unmistakable signs of growing Arab extremism, an extremism that erupted with spectacular force in the attacks on America of September 11. The reluctance to expose dangers to the Jews suppressed recognition of much that threatened, and still threatens, the West.

Not that the *Times* is alone in this submission to anti-Semitic regimes. The same pattern prevails everywhere today in the academic community, which if anything is even more sensitive than the press to questions of "access." Scholars who work in politically controlled areas of research are rewarded for their sympathies and punished for their criticisms, sometimes in bizarre ways. A professor of ancient Middle East studies has told me that his German colleagues are embarrassed by Arabs in the places where they conduct research who congratulate them on what "they" did to the Jews; they dare not reveal their discomfort lest it prejudice their working relations with local personnel. More often, what begins as passive accommodation becomes active acquiescence. In American universities, the belief that Israel is to blame for the manifold failures of Arab society is by now such a corrupting feature of Middle East studies departments that it has assumed the status of a natural condition, like smog in Los Angeles.

Arab terrorism against Israel has exacerbated this situation without raising a peep from university administrations. Citing the difficulty of securing proper insurance coverage, Harvard recently followed the lead of other American universities in forbidding travel to Israel on Harvard funding. A longstanding archeological dig in Israel had to be abandoned this past summer, and students and faculty had to cancel programs of study and research—this, at the very moment when Harvard is promoting a new commitment to study abroad as a direct way of learning about the world.

Meanwhile, Jewish students attending American-sponsored Arabic programs in Arab countries have been instructed not to reveal their Jewishness and have been provided with false identities: a concession to Arab anti-Semitism that has neither been officially protested by any academic official nor brought to the attention of the American public. Thus do universities casually accede to policies of genocidal hatred, all the while proclaiming their dedication to multiculturalism, pluralism, and anti-discrimination.

What is it that, in the end, the record of anti-Semitism in Europe suggests? It suggests that the Jews are just the warm-up act to farther-reaching political ambitions. The ease with which Hitler was able to isolate the Jews, disenfranchise them, blackmail them, and begin persecuting them gave him the confidence to expand his conquests; he used the war against the Jews to encourage his followers to flex their muscles.

Anti-Semitism in this sense is not just a generic term for discrimination against Jews or even persecution of Jews. It is not just a means of scapegoating, though it is assuredly that. Nor is it merely a projection onto Jews of the desire to dominate, to "rule the world." More precisely than any of these, modern anti-Semitism achieved its power as a political instrument through its opposition to liberal democracy itself—as personified by the Jews.

Wilhelm Marr created the League of Anti-Semites in the 1870s to save Germany from what the Jews represented. "We have among us," he said, "a flexible, tenacious, intelligent, foreign tribe that knows how to bring abstract reality into play in many different ways." By "abstract reality," Marr meant everything the Jews could be made to stand for, summarized in the freedoms—religious, political, economic—that undergird modern democratic culture.

Marr's perception of the Jews as incarnations of modernity harnessed ancient prejudice to brand-new fears in societies that were in the process of losing their religious certainties and shedding many aspects of their traditional way of life, including the sense of security provided by autocratic rule. What some Europeans were certain was progress seemed to others a mortal danger, and politicians found that they scored well when they concretized those fears in the image of the ubiquitous Jews—a small, highly adaptive people with arguably the largest image on earth, a people desperately seeking acceptance and targetable at no political cost.

As the Jews were the practice range for anti-democratic and anti-liberal forces in pre-Hitler Europe, so in the second half of the twentieth century the state of Israel took the brunt of the Arab/Muslim war against Western democracy. But, unlike the Jews of Europe, the Jews of Israel toughened under the assault, at least initially. Having acquired the means of self-defense, the Jewish state seemed to grow stronger the more it was attacked. And for a long time, in a reverse dynamic to the process I have been describing, the democratic West as a whole reaped the benefit.

"We may never know how much time Israel bought for us in our decades of negligence," writes William Bennett, how many American lives it saved by its long-kept refusal to negotiate with or capitulate to terrorist murder and extortion, its resolve to use every means to track down, confront, and undo those who captured and killed its citizens, its crystalline message of defiance. What we do know is that all over the world, especially in the Soviet gulag and in the prisons of Eastern Europe, captive men gulped great draughts of hope whenever word filtered through of an act of Israeli rescue and punishment: palpable and too rare signals in those dark decades [of the cold war] that evil was not everywhere triumphant, everywhere accommodated, everywhere appeased.

Bennett is surely right that, apart from America itself, Israel still stands as the world's brightest model of national self-liberation based on ideals of individual responsibility and human freedom. Israel's ability to withstand Arab attempts to destroy it in one of the longest and most lopsided wars ever fought serves as an indelible testimony to the strength of democratic culture.

Israel *had* to be gritty; otherwise it would not exist. Nevertheless, in the 1990s it too began to tire under the perpetual assault. In systematic and sustained terrorism, the Arabs discovered the first weapon that really works against a democracy, destroying the trust, the openness, of an open society, and exploiting its precious freedoms to expose its acute vulnerability. Here once again Israel has served as a test case. How well *can* democracies withstand this new form of all-out foreign aggression? We know from the past that the West paid dearly for ignoring Hitler's war against the Jews. One can only hope it will not pay as dearly for having ignored or underestimated for so long the Arab war against Israel and the Jews.

PART FIVE

THE FACTS ON
THE GROUND
IN FRANCE

MARIE BRENNER

France's Scarlet Letter

> Street protests against American and British military action in Iraq have escalated into attacks by Muslim youths on Jewish demonstrators, sparking fears of a new wave of anti-Semitism across France.
>
> —London *Sunday Telegraph*, April 6, 2003

I T WOULD TAKE many months for David de Rothschild to realize that what was happening to Jews in France was a powerful predictor of a war that was coming down history's long stream. In May 2001, when he and a group of French business leaders arrived in Jerusalem for meetings with Prime Minister Ariel Sharon and members of his Cabinet, he reluctantly agreed to speak to a reporter from the *Jerusalem Post*. Then fifty-eight and the head of the French branch of his family's banking dynasty, he was just beginning to be aware of a wave of attacks on French Jews by French Muslims that would escalate into an unimaginable nightmare and affect France, the United States, and the Muslim and Jewish populations of both countries.

Rothschild was actively involved in Jewish organizations in France, but, as he told friends, he was not particularly *croyant,* or religious, by nature. In restaurants, however, if he overheard a conversation that struck him as anti-Semitic, he was known to walk over to the table and silently present his card. That day in Jerusalem, he did not yet comprehend how dangerous the situation in France had become. The facts were these: Between January and May 2001 there had been more than 300 attacks against Jews. From Marseille to Paris, synagogues had been destroyed, school buses stoned, children assaulted. Yet very few of the incidents had been reported in the French media, which have a distinctly pro-Palestinian tilt. So Rothschild was largely uninformed concerning the accurate numbers. He and his friends were still operating in a near vacuum, because of what is called in France *la barrière du silence,* which minimizes and mystifies reporting on French Jewish matters and the Middle East.

Rothschild would later be disturbed that he had not been made more aware faster of the degree of violence, which would be perceived outside France as the return of classic anti-Semitism and anti-Americanism and would infect France and much of Europe over the next two years. By the spring of this year, the number of hate crimes had risen above 1,000, and the relationship of the United States, poised to declare a war on Iraq, and France, implacably opposed to such a war, was glacial.

ABOUT SIX MILLION Muslims live in France, nearly 10 percent of the population, a potential voting bloc. In contrast, there are only about 650,000 Jews, but it is the third-largest Jewish population in the world, after Israel and the United States. The victims of the attacks appeared to live mostly in working-class areas in the *banlieues,* or suburbs, on the outskirts of Paris, a laboratory of assimilation where much of the unemployed Muslim population also lives. The situation, Rothschild later told me, was fraught with complexity. In addition to a large number of distinguished Arab intellectuals, France was also home to cells of terrorists, fundamentalist imams, and firms with strong business ties to Baghdad. When Rothschild arrived in Israel in May 2001, he had also left behind him another, subtler struggle, going on behind closed doors, between the establishment Ashkenazi Jews of central Paris and the *pieds-noirs,* French citizens formerly of North Africa, many of them lower-middle-class Sephardic Jews who live in the suburbs. The Sephardic communities in the Paris outskirts were the principal targets of anti-Western paranoia spewing up out of the Middle East. A widely shared position of the upper-class Jewish establishment in France was to let such things alone and not *jeter de l'huile sur le feu* (throw oil on the fire).

Rothschild and the Jewish intellectual establishment would be caught in the vise of a vicious debate at a time of intense political correctness in France. Their country was marginalized as a world power and owed billions of dollars by Iraq for the brisk trade between the two countries. In addition, before the 1991 Gulf War, France had been a major supplier of weapons to Iraq. Yet France trumpeted its moral superiority. By the time Rothschild saw the reporter from the *Jerusalem Post,* France was too busy "feeding the crocodile," as one historian remarked, to notice the danger that lurked within. In May 2001, Rothschild was worried principally about the growing popularity of Jean-Marie Le Pen, the far-right-wing candidate for president. Notoriously anti-Semitic—Hitler's gas chambers were a "minor detail" in World War II, he has said—Le Pen had won 15 percent of the vote in 1995 on an anti-foreigner hate platform, and was strong in the polls for the 2002 elections. Rothschild believed, he told the reporter in Jerusalem, that the wave of attacks was likely coming from "neo-Nazis, a hostile, aggressive, anti-Semitic, right-wing population, among which you may have some Moslems. But it's not being led by the Moslems."

Rothschild was careful with his language. "The Moslems who have chosen France live there normally, not with the aim of doing any terrorist activity," he said. "I promise you that in the last ten, fifteen years I haven't received any kind of anti-Semitic letter, any swastika, nothing like that. . . . Possibly because I am privileged, possibly because I live in a protected environment. . . . I personally do not feel anti-Semitism." Within hours of its publication, his comment would rocket through E-mails in the working-class areas of Paris and be talked about in catastrophic terms, inflaming an oddball activist cop who had taken the plight of France's Jews as his mission. It was but one small piece of a dilemma that would grow imperceptibly into a cataclysm as America and France came to a stunning break in their relationship on the eve of the U.S.-led war with Iraq. Rothschild was still trying to analyze the mystery that had led to an international crisis when he spoke on the phone with me this past March. His voice rose as he said, "Who was inhibited to talk? Why did it take so long? Whose fault was it? What was the reason?" He concluded sadly, "These are questions that are hard to answer."

I HAVE A STORY to tell. It begins on the northern outskirts of Paris in the town of Le Blanc–Mesnil in October 2000. Le Blanc–Mesnil is half a dozen stops on the Métro line from Charles de Gaulle Airport, a community of matchbox row houses with red tile roofs and cafés where the menu of falafel specialties is written in French and Arabic. It is inhabited by factory hands, accountants, teachers, and garment-industry workers. Along with Drancy, St.-Denis, and a cluster of other towns, Le Blanc–Mesnil is part of District 93, the "Red belt" historically governed by Communist mayors, where for years the underboil of ethnic hatred has been rumbling. Since the 1980s, thousands of Muslim immigrants have moved into the Red belt, a former outpost of French colonials and Sephardic Jews who had emigrated from Algeria, Tunisia, and Morocco decades earlier.

In October 2000, seven months before Rothschild visited Jerusalem, Sammy Ghozlan was home on Avenue Henri Barbusse in Le Blanc–Mesnil, planning the coming appearances of his dance bands. Ghozlan had just retired from the French police force after a long career as commissioner of the department of Seine–Saint-Denis. He was at the top of his game, known all over the Jewish community of Paris as *le poulet casher,* the kosher chicken, "poulet," like "flic," being slang for "cop." Ghozlan was a pied-noir reared in Algeria. His father had been a police officer in Constantine, a man of influence until suddenly one day he was not, and fled, like thousands of others, during the Algerian war. Sammy Ghozlan was obsessed with his Frenchness. He loved Voltaire and drank the best wines. Ghozlan's greatest passion was music; he had played piano and violin all his life, and had developed a Vegas-style Hasidic act into a thriving business, with two Sammy Ghozlan bands working the French Bar Mitzvah and wedding circuit. Ghozlan, as conductor, always wore a fresh tuxedo, a white satin scarf, and a perfectly pleated cummerbund. What little English he knew came from lip-synching to Wayne Newton and John Travolta. "I Will Survive" was his signature closer. He was deeply religious and would not pick up the telephone from sundown Friday until sundown Saturday.

EARLY IN HIS POLICE CAREER, Ghozlan had become a minor celebrity when he stopped the violence in the projects at Aulnay-sous-Bois, the next town over. He was like a detective in a film noir; his method was to negotiate, to suggest to his adversary that they were allies. He was convinced that success had come to him because he understood the nuances of the term *compte à régler* (a score to settle). For the exile, life in the banlieues was all about settling scores. Ghozlan had learned Arabic in Algeria and spoke it frequently in the streets so that he could put himself in the skin of the Arabs he had grown up with. "When the Arabs arrived in France, they were humiliated by the French," he said. "They were not appreciated. They suffered a lot because of that. This is the reason for their rage.

They want to take their revenge for the Algerian war." It was, he said, a way to show their identity.

On the night of October 3, 2000, Ghozlan was already missing police work, but his wife, Monique, had lectured him about not second-guessing or dropping in on the new commissioner of Seine–Saint-Denis. It was time to move on, she told him; he had no reason not to. He was making 5,000 euros per Bar Mitzvah and had months of bookings in France and Switzerland. Besides, mandatory retirement was not negotiable in France. At fifty-eight he was ready to hit the Sephardic European party circuit in his new life as not only *le poulet casher* but also the schmoozer and magnet for neighborhood crime gossip. He felt he had earned a festive third act, and he had all the celebrity he needed with a weekly show on 94.8 Judaiques FM radio. There, in his four-room office and studio up a narrow stairwell in the Fifth Arrondissement, close to the Panthéon and the Sorbonne, he could let fly, showcasing Jewish pop stars such as Enrico Macias, promoting the Ghozlan bands, and dispensing crime-protection advice to callers.

THAT SAME NIGHT at a two-room synagogue in Villepinte, a few towns away from Le Blanc–Mesnil, smoke billowed up from the kitchen and out the classroom windows of the religious school. Jacques Grosslerner, a leader of the Jewish community, immediately reached out to the most experienced person he could think of—Ghozlan. "There is a fire at Villepinte," Grosslerner told him. "Are you *au courant*?" It was ten o'clock. Ghozlan dialed the prefect of the district and repeated the question: "Are you *au courant*?" Then he got in his car and drove to Villepinte. The prefect reached Ghozlan on his cell phone. "It is nothing more than a trash fire," he told him. At the synagogue an hour later, however, Ghozlan ran into a detective he knew who told him, "It is no trash fire. We found six Molotov cocktails."

Ghozlan went right to work. He dug a plastic bag out of his

car and swept up bits of charred wood, blackened brick, and ash. Within months he would be on a collision course with the French police and several members of the establishment in Paris who ran major Jewish organizations. In Le Blanc–Mesnil, with no resources to draw on except his black plastic address book, Ghozlan was quickly enmeshed in the rising tide of what French Jewish intellectuals would tag "soft-wave anti-Semitism," a new form disguised as anti-Americanism and pro-Palestinianism. It would soon grow into a constant fear on the part of French Jews, a concern bordering on panic in synagogues across suburban America, and forums and articles in the American media. In Europe, however, terms recalling the Nazi era, such as Kristallnacht, were raised only occasionally, and then in a context that portrayed the Israelis as the new storm troopers. The title of an editorial in the New York *Daily News* was succinct: "The Poison's Back: Europeans Call It Anti-Zionism, but It's Really the Old Anti-Semitism."

Ghozlan could not foresee any of this as he quietly gathered soot and brick from Villepinte in the moonlight. But for the first time since he had escaped Algeria as a teenager— "You have three days to leave," an Algerian policeman had told his family—he was feeling an unease that bordered on dread. Over the next ten days, four more synagogues were burned in greater Paris, and nineteen arson attempts were reported against synagogues and Jewish homes and businesses. It occurred to Ghozlan that soon he might be back in police work. Within months he had set up a hot line and a one-man investigative unit called S.O.S. Truth and Security to monitor the trouble. He financed the operation with the money he made from the Ghozlan Hasidic bands.

ON THE AFTERNOON of October 7, 2000, Clément Weill-Raynal, a reporter and legal correspondent for the France 3 television network, was walking through the Place de la République when he saw hundreds of people massed for a demonstration. Paris is the city of demonstrations—there are so many that a caption in *The Economist* once satirized the French love of public display as "Another Day, Another Demo." At first Weill-Raynal tried to ignore the noise, the agitation, and the flags of Hezbollah, Hamas, and certain far-left organizations. "They were shouting, 'Death to the Jews! Kill the Jews! Sharon is a killer!' It was the moment when we had arrived at the point that I was afraid of for many years. The junction of leftists, pro-Palestinians, and Arabs had created a new form of anti-Semitism," Weill-Raynal said.

Anti-Semitism in France had been considered a right-wing phenomenon that historically had its roots in the Vatican and the libel of the greedy Jew as Christ-killer. It had fueled the crowds howling "Death to the Jews!" in the streets near L'École Militaire during the Dreyfus Affair in 1895, and seethed through Vichy with the deportation of 76,000 French Jews to the death camps. The new form of anti-Semitism, Weill-Raynal understood, was different: it was coming from the left, part of the movement known in France as *le néo-gauchisme,* and it was connected to the country's socialist politics and the difficulties of assimilating the large French Muslim population. It was camouflaged as anti-Israel politics, but the issue was immense and complex. Only in recent years has France recognized ethnic subcultures. It is illegal to count race or ethnicity in its census figures, and impossible to record accurate figures for its minorities. There is a spirit of universality in the school system, and a national curriculum. The Jewish issue was a dim, secondary preoccupation if it registered at all in French minds.

Although there were Jews on every level of political influence and intellectual stature in the country, the policy of modern France toward its Jews had been set during the time of Napoleon. "The Jews should be denied everything as a nation," remarked Count Stanislas de Clermont-Tonnerre in 1789, "but granted everything as individuals." Frenchness was what mattered. As one writer said to me, "I am French first, Jewish second." The most powerful Jews in France rarely identified themselves as Jews. To do so, one was being "Judeocentric," a term used with contempt. Additional complicating factors were a long-standing French-intellectual romantic attraction to Third World guerrillas, guilt over the slaughter in the Algerian war, and France's need for Iraq's oil and trading alliances from Saudi Arabia to Morocco. All of this was filtered through the thrum of dormant traditional anti-Semitism, which could be revived without much provocation. "Old wine in new bottles," one historian called it.

AFTER FIFTEEN YEARS at France 3, Weill-Raynal was well aware of the slanted coverage concerning the Palestinian-Israeli struggle. "We are not Israel," he told me. "The motto 'Jews is news' is a joke around here." Members of his family had been deported to the Nazi death camps from Drancy, but he was closer in spirit to the "assimilated" Jews of central Paris.

Weill-Raynal had been initiated early into an understanding of the barrier of silence in the media. The standard was set at *Le Monde,* which characterizes the Israeli settlers as "colons" (colonizers). In 1987, in the days after the first intifada—the fight waged in the West Bank and Gaza settlements—Weill-Raynal was told by his editors not to file reports on the Middle East.

"You are too biased," one told him.

"I asked them, 'How am I biased?' The answer was simple. I was Jewish."

The editor explained, "You cannot be fair."

"It is a story I know very well. I know the country. I know the people. I know the roots of the problem," Weill-Raynal said.

"No," the editor insisted. "You are too biased."

FRUSTRATED, WEILL-RAYNAL began to keep meticulous notes on Agence France-Presse, the wire service, a major source of information in the country. He immediately noticed an item the service used over and over to explain the violence in the Middle East, a controversial visit Ariel Sharon had made to the Temple Mount, the shrine known to Muslims as the Noble Sanctuary, in September 2000. "This ran again and again without any counterexplanation of the terrorist attacks or the provocation," Weill-Raynal said. "There was no subsequent reporting to place the visit in context. On the anniversary of the second intifada, they put out a revised report, and it was almost as biased. Now the news agency explained that, yes, in fact there were two versions of this incident—the Palestinian and the Israeli. It was as if it was inconceivable that the French might understand that there was a conflicting point of view."

Just days after the demonstration, Weill-Raynal received a barrage of phone calls from Sammy Ghozlan about the burning of a synagogue in Trappes. "This is very serious," Ghozlan said before he rang off to call *Le Parisien,* a tabloid that covers Paris and suburban news. Weill-Raynal knew Ghozlan as an activist and a minor local celebrity—the Sephardic Columbo with his Hasidic bands.

"What is this so-called synagogue burning at Trappes?" an editor had asked him.

"It is not 'so-called,'" Weill-Raynal had said. "It is an anti-Semitic attack."

"It was a true French moment," Weill-Raynal told me. "The editor immediately changed the subject and turned to the reporter next to me. He said, 'Georges, what are you working on?' The next day *Libération,* a left-wing paper, ran it on the front page. The editor came to me and said, 'You were right.'" But no assignment to report the attack was forthcoming.

As Weill-Raynal walked through the Place de la République that day, he was sickened by the screams of "Kill the Jews!" Hundreds of protesters crowded the streets in front of the Holiday Inn on the Right Bank. TV cameras focused on signs that read SHARON KILLER. For years, he says, he had accumulated reams of skewed reporting from Agence France-Presse. Returning to his apartment near the Place de la Bastille, he turned on the TV. "It was catastrophic," he said. "No one had reported what I saw, what I heard. No one had felt it was newsworthy to report 'Kill the Jews.'" Weill-Raynal realized that in all of Paris there was only one potential outlet for his dispatch, Judaiques FM. Jewish radio had arrived in Paris when the socialist government of the 1980s changed the licensing restrictions. The station, with a sizable audience in France, has become a powerful independent outlet of information for intellectuals and journalists. When I visited the studio, it seemed to be out of a different era. Just a few blocks from the Sorbonne, it could have been a radio station in wartime London or Nepal.

"How should we identify you?" the news announcer asked Weill-Raynal when he rushed in to make his report. "Suddenly I heard myself say, 'Clément Weill-Raynal, president of the Association of Jewish Journalists of the French Press.' It was the moment when I knew I had to declare myself as a Jew. I said, 'I want to get on and denounce a situation in Paris yesterday. The police were there. The Movement Against Racism and for Friendship Between People was there. They shouted "Kill the Jews!" in front of the statue of the République. This is a scandal. Nobody stopped it. No one has denounced it.' And you know, once in your life, you are the right man at the right time."

Just then Henri Hajdenberg, the president of Le Conseil Représentatif des Institutions Juives de France (CRIF), France's main Jewish organization, was in his car. His brother had been a backer of another Jewish station, and Hajdenberg often tuned in to Judaiques FM for the news. "He heard me on the radio," Weill-Raynal said. The next day, when Hajdenberg met with French president Jacques Chirac, he said, "Mr. President, I heard that demonstrators were shouting 'Kill the Jews!' at the Place de la République." As he left the Élysée Palace, Hajdenberg stopped to tell several reporters about the incident. "The president was shocked when I told him what had happened," Hajdenberg told them. Later a member of the French parliament asked Lionel Jospin, the prime minister, for an explanation, but Jospin refused to investigate the incident. Weill-Raynal said, "I asked the question 'Why has this taken days?' and the answer was 'It's not so simple.'"

I MET SAMMY GHOZLAN last September, a few days before the Jewish holidays. The Paris hotels were packed; the art dealers were in town for the antiques fair. As I left New York, Ed Koch, the former mayor of the city, had summoned his rhetoric against the French on his weekly radio show, angrily supporting boycotts. There were rumors of Jews wearing yarmulkes being beaten to death on the Champs-Élysées, and of killer apes unleashed to attack yeshiva boys. It was difficult to imagine that the Paris of *Amélie* had turned into *Badenheim, 1939*. Surely, I thought, this was shock-jock exaggeration.

Ghozlan was late for our meeting. I waited in a kosher pizzeria in the 19th Arrondissement, an area of shuls and Orthodox schools with a large Muslim population. Middle Eastern pastries glistened in the windows of the bakeries. The weather was warm, and the door of the pizzeria was open, so I could hear Ghozlan's voice before he actually walked in. *"Désolé, désolé,"* he mumbled like a chant as the door banged behind him. His white suit was rumpled; his gray Hush Puppies were scuffed. His reputation stuck out all over him. I knew he was thought to be—depending on who was offering an opinion—at the intersection of paranoia and truth, a one-man crime agency, and a folk hero of the banlieues. I scanned my American grid for a nuance to try to capture him, but the closest I could come was a tough, beat-up Yves Montand—hidden and canny, the receptacle of hundreds of lyrics memorized in the middle of the night, rehearsals, microphones, sound checks. Ghozlan had a clipped mustache, a low forehead, and thick dark hair; he was husky, but he moved with the agility of a dancer. He projected urgency, perpetual agitation. I imagined him leading his orchestra, a singing detective racing through lyrics at frenetic speed. The more time we spent together, the more I realized that what preoccupied him was his super-imposed scrim of the past, the fear that the Algerian war would be refought in Paris.

I followed him out of the restaurant to a pastry shop at the next corner. The owner of the pizzeria recognized him from TV and followed us out. *"Nous avons peur, Monsieur Ghozlan,"* he said. "We are being attacked every day." He stood very close to the retired policeman, as if proximity would provide safety. It was clear that he had no confidence in the local authorities. Ghozlan handed him the card for the hot line. "Call us," he said.

THE PASTRY SHOP was deserted. Ghozlan placed police dos-siers, files, and stacks of paper on a tray table of hammered Moroccan brass between us. He handed me a thick white plas-tic binder, the kind a high-school student might carry. In it were hundreds of reports, carefully written out by hand. At the top of each page were the words "S.O.S. Vérité-Sécurité" and, underneath, a box: "Formulaire de Déclaration." A 2002 report from the 10th Arrondissement read:

> I was in a taxi with my husband and I arrived in front of my building. I gave the money to the taxi driver and asked for a receipt and my husband went out of the car and I was waiting. She refused to give me the receipt and said, "You are a dirty Jew." And then she spit at me, *proférant des menaces en arabe* [threatening me in Arabic]. She took off in the car and beat me with clothes she had in the front seat. Then she told me that her sons would kill me. I tried to call for help, but the taxi was moving

too fast. At a red light, a young man saw me and came and helped me. He offered to be a witness. . . . The incident was shocking. Part of my family was deported to Auschwitz and did not come back. . . . And this is the first time something like this has happened to me. . . . Please do not mention my name. I am afraid that her sons will come to kill me.

A report from the town of Fontainebleau said, "Two 13-year-olds on their way to synagogue were hit with paddles. We will kill you." An insult hurled at a teacher: "When the Messiah comes, each Jew will have 10,000 goyim as slaves!" Another provocation at a different school: "Have you read The Protocols of the Elders of Zion? . . . Jews feast on the blood of non-Jewish children. They bake it in their matzohs. There is truth that they are all conspiring."

Ghozlan drew a diagram to explain an episode that had happened in Sarcelles, a fifteen-minute drive from Le Blanc–Mesnil. "There was a school bus . . . maybe you heard about it? They came, they attacked it. The schoolchildren were shocked and scared. I heard that the police said, 'It is expected because of what Israel does to the Palestinians. *C'est normal.*'"

His voice rose. "The president of France has said, 'There is no anti-Semitism in France.' What is the burning of the synagogue at Trappes? What are the Molotov cocktails thrown at the Jewish school in Créteil? And what are all of these?" He picked up the white plastic binder, flipped the pages, adjusted a pair of half-glasses on his nose, and began to read: "'Sale Juif' [dirty Jew] written on walls in Drancy. . . . Students wearing kippa attacked outside the schools. . . ."

OUT THERE. The phrase leapt at me from my first days in Paris. "We don't go out there," I was told at a dinner in a grand apartment in the 16th Arrondissement, and there was a whiff of contempt in the tone. "The attacks are all happening out there," said a doctor's wife, an active member of the Temple Beau Grenelle, which journalists and ministers attend.

I had come to investigate two questions: Had France become an anti-Semitic country? How would the policies of France affect the United States? I quickly sensed an odd, split-screen reality, a double narrative, two worlds of Paris, rarely colliding, trying to come to terms with a potential disaster. Anti-American best-sellers filled the windows of the bookshops on the Boulevard Saint-Michel. France was facing its fears of a République d'Islam on French soil. A work with a similar title was selling briskly in the stores, as was *Dreaming of Palestine*, a young-adult best-seller published by Flammarion glamorizing suicide bombers. Teachers in the suburbs have been shocked to discover girls in the bathroom praying to Mecca as if they were performing an illicit act rather than simply practicing their religion. Some of the classes were 70 percent Muslim. Seminars on how to teach history, particularly World War II, were held for teachers who had experienced violence in their classes when they brought up the subject of Hitler and the Jews. Gang rapes—another frequent problem in the working-class suburbs—occupied the school authorities. All over the banlieues, I heard the code of modern France— Judeophobia, Judeocentric, *anti-feuj,* a term from a pidgin French called Verlan, the protest language of the banlieues. "Feuj" is a backward spelling of "Juif."

Raising the subject of the hundreds of attacks on Jews was tricky business in central Paris. There was a moat around it, a moat full of alligators. It was impossible not to think I had somehow gone back in time to a world captured very well by Laura Hobson in her 1946 best-seller, *Gentleman's Agreement,* where the word "Jewish" was said in whispers. Every now and then some unpleasant remark would remind you that you were in the country that created the Dreyfus Affair, but mainstream

French Jews do not make waves. Occasionally I heard someone say, "This is not Vichy." It was a way to mute the drama of the alarming numbers, a method of self-reassurance that made the speaker seem above the fray of the statistics: Nothing to be alarmed about. The attacks were happening out there, as if that were Iceland, far away from the three-star restaurants and the Matisse-Picasso show at the Grand Palais.

"Out there" is, in fact, ten Métro stops from the Place de la Concorde. It is a territory of class identification, behind a Maginot Line of French snobbism and disconnection, a Gallic sense of the insider and the other. It contains towns that are full of memories of France's Vichy years—Drancy, where Simone de Beauvoir pushed food parcels through a barbed-wire fence to friends being deported to Auschwitz; Les Lilas, with its wedding-cake Hôtel de Ville, where Free French forces celebrated the Liberation.

NEWS TRAVELS FAST in the banlieues. All that autumn and into the winter of 2001 and the following year, the attacks intensified, linked in severity to the politics of the Middle East. In Le Blanc–Mesnil, Ghozlan was getting nowhere with the French police. He distributed his S.O.S. forms in schools, community centers, and synagogues, and installed another telephone line at home. On the weekends, volunteers from his synagogue and his daughters—one of them a lawyer who handles Arab divorce cases—helped him. He became increasingly harried. He had calls to make to the authorities, E-mails to send. The pages in his white notebook grew—stones thrown through windows, fires set in schools, boys wearing yarmulkes attacked at Métro stops. Several times a week he would leave his house in his gray Renault and drive the roads he had been traveling for years to the police headquarters of Seine–Saint-Denis. The small houses along the way were neatly appointed, with assists from the Republic, their decent façades disguising the lack of jobs within. He went to see the chief of police and began to hear such new euphemisms as *les desperados de cage d'escalier* (desperadoes of the stairwell) along with the traditional term *les voyous* (vandals). "Sauvageons," in Jean-Jacques Rousseau's sense of noble savages, had become a politically correct term for Arabs, along with "les jeunes" (the young).

"Look, Sammy," the chief told him, "they are doing the same things to the cops that they do to the Jews. They throw washing machines down from their apartments at police cars. They run into us." "I understood it," Ghozlan later told me. "They worried about appearing heavy-handed. There was a fear that they would be called thugs and Nazis. Several of my friends mentioned to me that they were afraid of creating a situation like in Los Angeles—another Watts."

That February, in Sarcelles, flaming objects were thrown into the Tiferet Israel School, destroying the building. In April, at Garges-les-Gonesse, firebombs were hurled at the synagogue. From Nice to Marseille, anti-Semitic mail was delivered. In the offices of CRIF, located in the Fifth Arrondissement several blocks from the popular food market on the Rue Mouffetard, an envelope arrived filled with white powder and a message: "The biological war against the Jewish lobby has begun."

IN LONDON in December 2001, in a now famous conversation at the publisher Conrad Black's, the French ambassador, Daniel Bernard, called Israel "that shitty little country" and refused later to apologize. Then, in Paris, a Hanukkah screening of a *Harry Potter* movie reserved by the Jewish National Fund was canceled by the theater because of fears of Muslim violence. Very few of these episodes were reported in the mainstream press, but E-mails bombarded the office of Abraham Foxman, the national director of the Anti-Defamation League, in New York. Foxman had long understood the delicacy of navigating within the French establishment. With a budget of $50 million, the ADL, headquartered in an eleven-story building across from the United Nations, has resources and a network of intelligence operatives that are inconceivable to most French Jewish officials. A little-known fact about French Jews is how underfunded their organizations are. Each year the Rothschild family contributes a significant amount of money to fund a myriad of budget requests—security guards, employees, operating expenses—to protect the Jews of France.

"What we are talking about here is the need to understand that Jewish France has been traditionally controlled by the Hofjuden, the Jews of the court," Shimon Samuels said to me the day we met. Samuels is an expert on the subject. He arrived in Paris from Jerusalem in 1980 and in 1988 set up an office of the Simon Wiesenthal Center, the organization responsible for tracking down many former Nazis. Trained in London and Jerusalem as a political scientist, Samuels was convinced that the new rise of Muslim fundamentalism had become a graver concern to the world than the capture and prosecution of octogenarians. He had the overview of a professor and used German words to describe the oddity of the French Jewish social structure. As the head of the Paris office of the Wiesenthal Center, he monitored potential terrorist and anti-Semitic activity throughout the world.

GETTING IN COMMUNICATION with Samuels is a daunting task. His E-mail cannot be accessed in many of the strange places he travels, and his cell-phone message system is often overloaded or impenetrable. E-mails I sent him bounced back to me, and I got used to phones that didn't ring and recordings that explained that Mr. Samuels was unable to receive messages. Much of his year is spent in zones of possible terrorist activity; he can "get by" in twelve languages. Rarely in Paris, he is a man in airplanes or at conferences in Third World countries. In Durban, where he participated in the U.N. World Conference

Against Racism in 2001, he was expelled from the room. Later he witnessed demonstrators marching to a synagogue screaming, "Hitler should have finished the job!" It is his occupation to monitor the hate surging up in Islamic-fundamentalist quarters. A tireless lobbyist, he has an ability to forge political compromises. With me, the phrase he used to describe French indifference concerning what was happening in their country was "the black box of denial," and he spoke of "the many-headed hydra" behind the attacks. He often sounded harried and snappish, the stern and rumpled professor who had no time for lengthy explanations. He understood that, for the establishment Jews of France, religion was secondary to their Frenchness. They maintained their status by being Hofjuden, skilled at *shah shtil,* the ability to whisper into the ear of the king.

Samuels is British and spent his early years in Warwickshire, in the English countryside, with a family that sent him to Sunday school. Coming home one afternoon, he and his cousin were attacked by local boys, who stoned them and tied them to a cross in a field. "Incredibly, I wiped the event from my mind, as if it didn't happen," he told me. Immediately after that, he rejoined his parents in London. Years later he visited his grandparents' grave, only to find that it had been desecrated. When he called the burial society to complain, he was told, "A storm destroyed it." "The storm stopped on the Jewish side of the cemetery?" he demanded. "Suddenly what happened to me as a child came back in excruciating detail," he said, "and I understood for the first time in my life why I do what I do."

SAMUELS DID NOT look forward to attending the CRIF annual dinner. CRIF always invited the prime minister and his Cabinet, and several hundred people attended the formal evening. For Samuels, the dinner was everything he disliked about working in France. A few months after his arrival in 1980, a bomb had been exploded outside the Rue Copernic synagogue in Paris. Four people walking in the neighborhood were killed. "Two innocent French persons were killed," the then prime minister, Raymond Barre, had remarked. He was widely criticized for the implication that Jewish victims were an altogether different species from the French. Before setting up the Wiesenthal office in Paris, Samuels had worked as the deputy director of a strategic political-science institute in Israel. By the end of the 1970s, he had begun to have a strong sense of the rise of terrorism in Islamic-fundamentalist sects.

In the winter of 2001, Samuels was having to navigate his own complex relationships within the French Jewish establishment, which was not ready to share fully his alarm at the attacks on Jews in the banlieues. Their focus was still on the traditional, Vichy model of historical right-wing anti-Semitism, and their concern centered on Jean-Marie Le Pen, who appeared to them to be a resurrection of the old hatreds. In 2002 he would pull roughly 20 percent of the national vote in the first round of the presidential election.

For Samuels, the differences between the old and new forms of anti-Semitism manifested themselves when he pressed the case for reparations for French victims of the Holocaust. "Jews should not be about money," a leader of a prominent Jewish organization told him. "It reinforces a negative stereotype." Samuels was told he was *un traître,* a traitor, and berated for his American pushiness in trying to collect restitution for victims. In the late nineties, Samuels assisted a team of New York lawyers pursuing a class-action lawsuit against French banks for hundreds of victims. The case had further established Samuels as a scrappy outsider, *trop américain,* in certain powerful circles. On the subject of the CRIF dinner, he was not hesitant about voicing his opinion. "The Jewish community should set itself as an objective that they do not need a dinner with the prime minister," he told me. "It sets in motion a set of political mortgages, where the prime minister has to give an accounting.

And the Jews, like in medieval times, come to the court with their pleas. It is humiliating . . . an event in which the community is put into the position of having to be a supplicant."

ALL THESE REASONS and more drew Shimon Samuels to Sammy Ghozlan. Samuels knew Ghozlan by reputation; he had been recruited during François Mitterrand's administration to help investigate the 1982 bombing at Jo Goldenberg's, a famous Jewish restaurant in the Marais district of Paris, and he had been the subject of a lengthy article in *Le Matin* magazine. The film director Alexandre Arcady had used the character of a Sephardic cop named Sammy in a Nazi-art-caper movie called *K,* based on a detective novel, but Samuels had never seen it or heard of the book. He knew of Ghozlan mainly through the flyers for his "grand orchestre de variétés" and the cards distributed at Bar Mitzvahs which showed Sammy posed behind drums in a tuxedo with his band, with "Groove, Funck, Hassidiques, Israélien . . . Oriental" written in bold yellow letters at the top. When the two men met at the CRIF dinner, Samuels mentioned his midlife attempt to learn to play the clarinet. "Ghozlan reminded me of a Pancho Villa type, very uncharacteristic of French Jews," Samuels later said. "He had no pretense of being an intellectual." Ghozlan told Samuels he had been incensed that the Jewish leadership had fought him when he took on the claimants' case against French banks. Samuels understood immediately that Ghozlan could be a useful ally. "He had come with the police background and was trying to do—with no real help!—exactly what we were doing, analyze documents, work his sources. . . . I thought the Jewish organizations had missed out on an effective intelligence operation in the banlieues." It would take months, however, for Samuels, forever circling the globe, to be able to forge an official relationship with the cop from the suburbs.

By the winter of 2001, the situation had become untenable.

The attack on the World Trade Center appeared to set off a fresh wave of violence. More and more, in the late afternoon, Monique Ghozlan would find her husband at the *consistoire,* which regulated synagogues and all aspects of Jewish life, giving interns and volunteers recommendations on how to take calls from attack victims.

Monique and Sammy live in a stone house behind a hedge, within walking distance of their small synagogue. The house is decorated with a collection of North African silver they brought from Algeria and family portraits, including one of Sammy's grandfather, who was once the chief rabbi of Algeria. At the turn of the twentieth century, the Ghozlans were orchardists who had large properties in the country. Monique, whom Sammy met when he was in the Boy Scouts, has pine-apple-blond hair and a perpetual tan. The daughter of a bar owner and the mother of three grown daughters and one son, she resembles the actress Dyan Cannon, with hair that cascades to her shoulders. As Sammy worked the phones in the late afternoon, Monique, home from her job teaching first grade, would cook couscous, fava beans, and fish—traditional Sephardic foods.

The Sephardim have a hermetic culture with entirely different rituals from those of Ashkenazi Jews. Considered by many to be more religious than their Eastern European counterparts, France's Sephardim never experienced massive pogroms or, for that matter, Europe's secular enlightenment; Spinoza was Sephardic, but there was no Sephardic Freud or Marx. Revered as "the muscle Jews" by the early Zionist leader Theodor Herzl, the Sephardim were thought to be free of the victim complexes of Eastern Europeans. "We are not always as educated, and we like to drink and have big parties, but we are not depressives," Sammy told me. In the small *shul*s on the outskirts, there is chaos during the service, with children running from family to family and men gossiping through the chanting of the Torah as if they were conducting business in a bazaar. Sephardic families are often large, and first cousins are permitted to marry. Since the Algerian war drove them to France in the 1960s, Sephardim can now be found at every level of education and accomplishment in French society—Nobel laureates, government ministers, distinguished intellectuals—and many of them have intermarried with Ashkenazi Jews. According to a recent survey, 70 percent of the Jews in France are Sephardic.

STILL, IT DID NOT take much to make Ghozlan see himself as an outsider, misunderstood by the French elite. He had a title, security adviser, which sounded impressive, but he had no office and no private phone. A special green telephone had been installed at the *consistoire,* and all calls received by volunteers were reported to Ghozlan. "I tried to bring the techniques of simple police interrogation," he said. "Ask the name, the address, the phone number, the place of the attack." He was often understandably frustrated. The idea that by the winter of 2001 this jerry-built detective agency was monitoring more than 200 incidents throughout France was shocking to Ghozlan. A rabbi had been beaten up, urine had been thrown at Jewish students on a playground, and fires had been set, yet few of the incidents were reported immediately to the police. It was detective work at its most primitive, on scraps of paper. Failure was unthinkable to Ghozlan, however, and he knew how to deal with the French bureaucracy. But lobbying through ethnic organizations was frowned upon in France and was considered an act with vulgar American overtones. The officials of many Jewish organizations were averse to such aggressive tactics.

At home Ghozlan had a large-screen television for his ninety-two-year-old mother, who lived with him. Ghozlan and his mother never missed an episode of *NYPD Blue,* dubbed into French, and it galled him that he was forced to operate without support or equipment of any kind. He looked for a storefront to use as a base for his operation, but he knew that that too would be primitive—two rooms tucked in the back of a Jewish center in an out-of-the-way arrondissement. On Fridays after his broadcast, he would drive to Rue Broca to check on his volunteers, only to find the interns had missed a call or were on an extended lunch break, indicating that they were oblivious to the seriousness of what seemed to them minor incidents. He began to seethe at the injustice and remembered every remark that seemed to diminish his work. One official told him, "There is no anti-Semitism unless someone dies."

Shortly after David de Rothschild made his remarks to the *Jerusalem Post,* Ghozlan's cell phone rang. When he learned that Rothschild had said there was no significant anti-Semitism in France and that neo-Nazis were most likely responsible for the attacks, Ghozlan erupted. "It was clear to me that Rothschild and the Ashkenazi Jews would never understand our situation. I wanted to start a Jewish security force," he told me.

As Jean-Marie Le Pen mounted his campaign in 2002, the tally of anti-Semitic attacks had risen to more than 350. The official line of the government continued to be "There is no anti-Semitism." "How can they say this with a straight face?" the reporter Christopher Caldwell would later demand in *The Weekly Standard.*

YOU GET TO THE HOUSE of Samuel Pisar, who is a survivor of Auschwitz, through an elaborate private entrance on the Square Foch. A grander address does not exist in Paris. Pisar made his fortune as an international lawyer; he was one of the last people to speak to the troubled media mogul Robert Maxwell before he went over the side of his yacht. He lives surrounded by Rothkos in a house of flawless modernity. Presidents Chirac and Mitterrand have often invited him to speak publicly on Jewish matters. As the attacks on Jews mounted, Pisar began to send frequent E-mails to Abraham Foxman in New York, reporting the endless debates raging privately in elite circles. Foxman had one word of advice: Mobilize. It was therefore up to Pisar to help galvanize a paralyzed French establishment that could equivocate with dexterity, extending arguments for months. In the period following the attack on the World Trade Center, Frenchmen began to speak of *"la benladenisation des banlieues."* They also noted that terrorist Zacarias Moussaoui, awaiting trial for his part in the 9/11 attacks, was a product of the banlieues, as were various terrorists arrested for attacks that had taken place from Strasbourg to Béziers, on the Belgian border.

Roger Cukierman often made his way to Square Foch to engage in lengthy discussions. Of all the Jewish officials in Paris, Cukierman, the head of CRIF, had the sharpest insights into the anti-Semitic problem, but he was cautious by nature. A former chairman of the Rothschild bank in Paris, he is often in Israel, where his son runs an investment house. Cukierman put the highest premium on respectability and did not want to be considered pro-Zionist. All that winter of 2002, behind closed doors within the elite Jewish community, a fierce struggle was going on.

"I urged Cukierman to go to the United States and see the great Jewish organizations," Pisar told me. "I wanted him to meet Abe Foxman, and the Bronfmans [founders of Seagram and patrons of many Jewish organizations], and I wanted him to learn how the American Jewish organizations handle these things." Pisar knew that Cukierman, despite his prestige in France, had never been totally free of worry as to how he was perceived. "After the Holocaust, European Jews carried with them the syndromes of the ghettos," Pisar said. "There were many Jews here who said, 'We have to do something,' but others said, 'Don't rock the boat.' In America they don't speak that way. No one says, 'Don't rock the boat.'" "I was very impressed by what I saw at the ADL," Cukierman told me. He had been in New York on many occasions, but the size and scope of the operation startled him. For starters, there was the outward symbol of the ADL's gray brick office building in the United Nations Plaza. Foxman's worldwide staff of intelligence agents shared information with the government, turned out press releases, put pressure on Congress, and had access to the leading editorial pages across the country. Cukierman and the group with him from Paris suddenly realized that Americans who happened to be Jewish felt wholly comfortable in their country and their communities. "When I got back," Cukierman said, "the first thing I did was to almost triple the budget of CRIF."

In February 2002, Cukierman submitted a searing and prophetic editorial to *Le Monde,* in the form of an open letter to President Jacques Chirac:

> The leaders of the country like to play down anti-Jewish acts. They prefer to see these as ordinary violence. We are deluged with statistics designed to show that an attack against a synagogue is an act of violence and not anti-Semitism. Some Jews who have lost touch with reality like to buttress their personal status by turning a deaf ear and a blind eye to danger, in order to curry favor with the public consensus. . . . Judicial authorities don't like to mete out strong punishment for acts of anti-Jewish violence, even when the perpetrators are caught red-handed: a three-month suspended sentence or nothing for an attack on a Jewish place of worship, compared to a year for burning a straw cottage in Corsica.
>
> Why this laxness? Because this violence, perpetrated by only one side, is linked to the conflict in the Middle East. Because too often Jew and Israeli mean the same thing. . . . Because the Muslim population is all-important. . . . Once again, we are the scapegoat. It's a part we no longer are prepared to play.

All over Paris, there was suddenly a flurry of activity—Shimon Samuels called it a derby race—as groups began to mobilize. As the election in which Le Pen was running neared its end, 200,000 protesters marched in the streets of Paris. The American Jewish Congress called for a boycott of the Cannes Film Festival. But the menace continued. Three men who burned a synagogue in Montpellier—identified as "Morad," "Jamel," and "Hakim"—were described by the prosecutor not as anti-Semites but as being "like a lot of petty delinquents, animated by a spirit of revenge, who try to ennoble their excesses by using a political discourse." Around the time Cukierman's editorial was published, individuals who broke into a synagogue in Créteil were given a three-month suspended sentence.

THERE ARE 130,000 police officers in France, according to Christopher Caldwell, but the police union is so strong that less than half of the force is assigned the beat, and only 10,000 are available for duty at any given time. Law-enforcement officials refer to the worst areas of the banlieues as *"zones de non-droit"* (lawless areas) and often refuse to go there. Even when police make arrests, according to Caldwell, liberal judges frequently let the criminals go, and 37 percent of the sentences are not carried out.

Victims are reluctant to be interviewed. You hear stories of people who named their attackers to the police and were later beaten up. It took me days to arrange to see a father whose two daughters were attacked in their school in central Paris. A well-known gerontologist, he insisted that I not use his name. I met him at his medical center, not far from the Marais. "My daughters were thirteen and fifteen and were surrounded by a group of students at school. A group of boys knocked them to the ground, covered them with food, and shouted, 'Dirty Jews.' What happened next was this: The attackers and other students threatened to kill the girls if they said anything, and for days my daughters received death threats." Two of the attackers were expelled, only to be reassigned to a school a short distance away, but the family kept receiving threats. At the end of the school year they moved to another arrondissement. "I could not put my daughters in any more danger," he said. "They completely changed. They had been close to so many diverse people in their school, and now they have pulled within themselves and just want to be with other Jewish students."

A history teacher named Barbara Lefebvre called Ghozlan's hot line when a student at her school insulted her. "I did not know where to turn," she told me. "I knew that no one in the school would address my concerns." One of the students had called her "a dirty Jew." "I went to one of the heads of the school and told her I was insulted as a teacher, a woman, a Jew, and a civil servant. I asked her to report it to the authorities, as I had done. She said, 'I do not have that power.'" Like the gerontologist, Lefebvre was concerned about reprisals and asked me not to identify her school. "Most of the school officials will say to the teachers, 'Don't talk about it.' It is to protect their reputation. Every pupil has a notebook with his picture in it. Many of the kids took their pictures off and put on the face of bin Laden. . . . And nobody said anything until a teacher saw it. They are afraid. But afraid of what? For those of us who have stepped forward, I say, we are not courageous. It is a duty."

Lefebvre told her story on the Jewish radio station and was contacted by another teacher, who used the pseudonym Emmanuel Brenner. A professor of history, Brenner developed a tutorial for teachers on how to teach World War II. "The problem of violence was so intense," he told me, "that I asked several of the teachers to compile their stories." He had collected them in a book called *Les Territoires Perdus de la République* (*The Lost Territories of the Republic*). *L'Express* had published an extract, but, Brenner told me, it was months before the book was mentioned by French television and *Le Monde*.

Only three of the seven teachers who contributed to the book used their own names. One, Iannis Roder, arrived at my hotel after school one day. "In my class, the students will not obey a woman," he said. "One child yelled at a woman whose name was Rabin, 'Jew! Jew!' I live with these children during the day, and when I tell my family about it, they are frightened. But when I talk to some journalists, they say, 'That can't be true.'" Roder said one reporter told him, "You are only seeing anti-Semitism because you are a Jew."

DRIVING TO TRAPPES, near Versailles, you pass housing projects where unemployed Muslims live. The small *shul* in town is down the block from one. Here, in October 2000, the synagogue was destroyed, and it is only slowly being rebuilt. There are black smoke marks all over the roof. "Arrests were made," the head of the Jewish community tells me. "Many people were questioned." But there was no prosecution. Later I visit the office of Ariel Goldmann, a criminal lawyer who has boxes of files concerning the incident. The authorities suggested that someone may have accidentally put a cigarette into a trash can, he says, shaking his head in disgust. Goldmann's father was the chief rabbi of Paris in the 1980s, and Goldmann often works on such cases pro bono. They are, he says, inevitably the same. Several blocks from Goldmann's office, I visit the lawyer William Goldnadel, whose clients include the Italian journalist Oriana Fallaci. "Who do you think was responsible for the pogroms in the Germany of the 1930s?" he asks. "Piano teachers? Professors? It is always the hooligans who are at the center of the violence."

Next I go to see Shmuel Trigano, the author of twelve books and part of a circle of influential thinkers that includes the philosopher Alain Finkielkraut, the writer Michel Gurfinkel, and the philosopher and activist Bernard-Henri Lévy. "I was outraged by what was going on here," he tells me, "and I began to keep a detailed list of all the attacks to publish in a new quarterly, which would document—in ways the French press was not doing—what was going on."

Trigano was not alone in his efforts to tabulate the attacks.

Dismayed by the pro-Palestinian bias in the French press, Elisabeth Schemla, a former managing editor of *L'Express,* hired a team of journalists and set up a Web site, Proche-Orient.info, to ensure objective reporting on the Middle East. The site, like the Jewish radio, has become mandatory for understanding the situation in France. The day I went to see Schemla, her deputy editor, Anne-Elisabeth Moutet, used the term *"tour de passe-passe"* (three-card monte) to explain the shuffles and contradictions involved in obtaining accurate information in France. CRIF and another group, S.O.S. Racisme, created by a moderate French Muslim group and a French Jewish student organization, were also investigating, and their efforts eventually galvanized the establishment. At the CRIF dinner in 2001, Roger Cukierman confronted the prime minister, telling him, he recalled, "'We are under attack as French citizens, and it is unacceptable.' That night I gave a list of more than 300 documented attacks to every one of the 700 guests." Cukierman was enraged by the French bureaucracy: according to police records, there were a mere 180 attacks.

"I WANT TO READ you something," Ghozlan said one night at his house. It was a letter from an uncle in Algeria, written in May 1962. He described being in the chic tourist area of Algiers in a crowd with many Spanish and Italian visitors:

> Massive gunfire erupted around us, the first victims fell, the ones on top of the others at our feet. Separated from my children, I was stuck between two lines of fire, one coming from the Rue d'Isly, and the other from the Rampe Bugeaud, just tens of meters apart, while the Muslim soldiers fired just meters away. . . . Then, with the bullets whistling by my ears, I called out for my children, who I couldn't find among the numbers of dead. . . . A miracle happened, [the children] had escaped and explained how a man jumped on top of them and took the bullets . . . try-

ing to protect his young son. . . . "You are too young to be assassinated by these bastards," he said.

Ghozlan's voice broke. "It was like this with all the families," Monique said. The uncle had later been killed in the Algerian war.

At the bottom of Ghozlan's character lurked a trip wire: he had his own score to settle. He felt condemned to repeat his history, and he recalled the phrase *"le cercueil ou la valise"* (the coffin or the suitcase), warning Jews in his homeland that they had only days to flee. The Cremieux decree had conferred French citizenship on Algeria's Jews in 1870, so at the height of the Algerian war, most Jews with government jobs left for France. The small-business owners fled to Israel.

Ghozlan's father's boss, the former Vichy official Maurice Papon, stationed in Algeria in the 1950s, would be tried in Bordeaux in 1997 and convicted of complicity in the arrests and internments of 1,690 Jews. At that time in Constantine, no one knew of Papon's past, but anyone working in the French police force operated in a shadowy zone of possible collaboration. As a child, Ghozlan knew Papon because his uncle was Papon's barber. Once, during a control operation, Ghozlan's father refused to kill a notorious leader of the Front de Libération Nationale (F.L.N.), a revolutionary group, because it was against his moral code. As a result of that, when the F.L.N. took over Algeria, it allowed Ghozlan and his mother and sister to leave. He took only a sweater, his high-school diploma, and a salami sandwich. "I watched the city as it became smaller. I couldn't imagine I would ever see it again."

GHOZLAN'S OPERATION, financed in part by the Wiesenthal Center, had a mandate to maintain a hot line for reports of attacks, but eventually Ghozlan himself began to act like a minister without portfolio and antagonize the authorities. Shortly after I arrived in Paris, Ghozlan organized a meeting in District 93 of all the Jewish leaders in that community and the chief of police. The tension in the little room was palpable. "You walk into the offices of the [assistant] mayor out here, and what is hanging there but the Palestinian flag," one Jewish leader said. The chief of police did not respond directly. "We believe we are all equal—churches, mosques, synagogues," he said. The Jewish leader countered by saying, "It is not the mosques that are being attacked." The meeting went on for hours as representatives from the Jewish community described the attacks to which they were routinely subjected. Such an event in an American city would likely have been covered in the press, but there was not a single French reporter in the room.

The day Papon, then ninety-two, was let out of prison, I spent the evening with Ghozlan at his house. He was extremely agitated, working two phones at once, dialing ministers and politicians, as he kept up a simultaneous conversation with me. "The mayor of Paris is coming to a demonstration I have organized at Drancy! And the chief of police. And the minister [of integration] Eric Raoult." He left long messages, giving the time of the demonstration and the names of the journalists he had invited. I had asked to hear him play at a Bar Mitzvah, and while he made and received calls, he projected a video of a party in a hotel ballroom. There he was in his tux, looking like Gilbert Bécaud at the Paramount, invoking old newsreels of cabaret performers during the Vichy era.

The next day I was at the CRIF office with Roger Cukierman when the telephone rang. Cukierman took the call and sounded annoyed. "I won't go myself, but I'll send a representative." When he hung up he said, "A man in the suburbs is organizing a demo."

"Do you mean Sammy Ghozlan?" I asked.

"Yes," he said. "He wants to get his picture in the newspaper all of the time."

"But isn't that good?" I asked. "Doesn't he serve a function by drawing attention to the situation in France?"

Cukierman snapped, "A totally negative function. . . . Whatever the subject, he jumps on it to get his own publicity."

BY LATE 2002, some American anti-war intellectuals were strongly criticizing the American Jewish organizations that were trying to call attention to the situation in France. As I left for France, in the fall, Susannah Heschel warned me, "If you write about any of these attacks, you will be used for fundraising purposes by the Jewish organizations." Heschel, the chairman of the Dartmouth Jewish Studies Program, is the daughter of the prominent Jewish scholar Rabbi Abraham Heschel. Along with Cornel West and Rabbi Michael Lerner, the editor of *Tikkun*, a liberal Jewish magazine, Heschel is a co-chair of Tikkun Campus Network, a college movement. By April of this year, however, Heschel, like Rothschild, felt that she had been misled by the lack of proper reporting. "The situation in France reminds me of the Dreyfus case. After he was found innocent, the Jews were blamed for getting him exonerated. . . . There was a clear failure of the French left to respond to Muslim anti-Semitism or to know how to criticize the victims of their own colonialism." Tony Judt, writing in a recent issue of *The New York Review of Books,* allowed that anti-Semitism is on the rise around the globe, but he cited the ADL's statistics on the number of reported American incidents, as if to imply an equivalency in the lifestyles of the middle-class American Jewish community and the Jews of the Parisian banlieues.

The new interior minister of France, a young man named Nicolas Sarkozy, had a clear sense of the terrorist activity in his country. On the Jewish high holy days, Sarkozy visited synagogues in the vicinity of the tony suburb of Neuilly, near the Bois de Boulogne. It is often said that Sarkozy's grandfather was Jewish—a figure of speech employed by Jews whose families, terrified for their lives, changed religions before or during World War II. "It is wrong that, fifty years after the Shoah, Jews have to be afraid how they think about Israel," he said. I followed him that day as he traveled with his wife, who wore a pink Chanel suit, and his deputy minister. Sarkozy was applauded in the tiny meetinghouses called *oratoires,* where, in the last century, assimilated Jews had gathered. Virtually no mention of his visits appeared in the press.

In February, Sarkozy announced that scores of potential terrorists had been arrested, and in April a Muslim *consistoire* was established. Many imams in France adhere to fundamentalism, which the demographer Michèle Tribalat and a coauthor have reported extensively on in *La République et l'Islam: Entre Crainte et Aveuglement (The Republic and Islam: Between Fear and Blindness).* The imams reported to Sarkozy's representatives that they would tell their followers the first law for Muslims is the religious law. Ghozlan had taken it on himself to try to negotiate with some of the more moderate imams, but certain Jewish organizations in France had put him on warning that he was overstepping his mandate. On the telephone, Shimon Samuels was philosophical when he told me, "Suddenly there are those who rejected Ghozlan in the beginning, but who are seeing that he is effective and what he's doing is important, and they want to take it over." If France accepted a role in the coming Middle East war, Samuels added, it would mean that the attacks that had been limited to the banlieues could escalate to bombs going off in supermarkets all over France.

I STAYED IN close communication with Ghozlan and Samuels through this past winter and into the spring. As the first bombs landed on Baghdad, Ghozlan was bracing himself for what might come next. He used the word *"ratonnade,"* and I asked him to define it. "It means that as an immigrant you are being attacked for being a separate identity." He feared, he said, a sinister new way of life, where people would abandon their common Frenchness and return to medieval tribalism, marooning themselves in their separate religions and ethnic inheritances.

In January, Samuels and the Wiesenthal Center announced a special UNESCO conference to address the issue of anti-Semitism—the first such conference in a decade. David de Rothschild offered his house for a reception for the world leaders who would attend. Trying to maintain a cosmopolitan overview, Rothschild told me, "If you fall into a depressed spiral and believe that there is no future and the French state is pro-Arabic, where does that lead but to wrong analysis and desperation?" In early April a new wave of anti-Semitism merged with France's anti-Israel politics and its outspoken disapproval of America's war. At demonstrations in Paris, not far from where Clément Weill-Raynal had heard the crowd cry "Death to the Jews" in October 2000, Stars of David were now intertwined with swastikas on banners. Nicolas Sarkozy's office dispatched marshals in white caps to keep the protests under control, but the new epidemic of violence grew—women clubbed in the street, rocks thrown through a synagogue window, another *shul* burned. One demonstrator told a reporter for *The New York Times,* "They are the targets. They are not welcome here because of what they did to our Palestinian brothers."

GHOZLAN'S CELL PHONE rang during a Bar Mitzvah he was attending. "It was a boy attacked during the demo. . . . He had approached a group carrying the Israeli and American flags intertwined with swastikas and told them they were not allowed to do that. . . . They beat him up." Ghozlan persuaded the young man to go to the police and took him to the Jewish radio station. It was clear that Ghozlan's dark prophecies had become reality. In the first week of April, *Le Monde* published a shocking poll, revealing that 30 percent of the French wanted Iraq to win the war. Mecca Cola was selling briskly all over the country, and Jacques Chirac suddenly had a new nickname on playgrounds in the banlieues: King of the Arabs. I had difficulty reaching Ghozlan and Samuels, and when I did, Samuels sounded as morose as Ghozlan had two years earlier. It had become impossible for the opinion-makers of France to distinguish between its NATO allies and Saddam's terrorists, he said. I mentioned the new poll to him. "You don't even know the full statistics they published," he said. "You really want to hear? Total of those disapproving of the American- and British-led intervention in Iraq: 78 percent. The city of Paris: 85 percent. The extreme left: 85 percent. The extreme right: 48 percent. Asked if they would be more supportive of the war if chemical weapons were used against American and British forces, 52 percent said no. Asked do you hope the U.S. wins, 33 percent said no."

I mentioned that I had been having trouble reaching Ghozlan. There was a reason, Samuels said; he and Ghozlan had that day decided to open an alternative headquarters in the Maison France-Israël headquarters on the Avenue Marceau, a few blocks from the Arc de Triomphe. Ghozlan's hot line was still going strong in the banlieues, but it was crucial that they also have a respected presence in central Paris. "The government has endorsed Saddam Hussein as a hero," Samuels said. "The genie has been let out of the bottle." The new police station would be one block from the main police headquarters. As American tanks rolled into Baghdad, there were signs that the French situation was not completely irrevocable. The cover story of the French newsmagazine *Le Point* was headlined: HAVE THEY GONE OVERBOARD?, a reference to the anti-American posturing of Jacques Chirac and his foreign minister, Dominique de Villepin. President Chirac, riding the popularity polls for his intractable opposition to the war, stayed mute even when the citizens of Baghdad openly embraced American forces, but his prime minister, Jean-Pierre Raffarin, attempted to redress the balance: "Being against the war does not mean that we want dictatorship to triumph over democracy."

The last time I spoke on the phone with Ghozlan, he sounded as frenzied as I had ever heard him. He had just learned of a new attack and was rushing to find out the details. In the first three months of this year, he told me, he had verified reports of 326 serious incidents in Paris alone.

PART SIX

THE SHIFT
FROM RIGHT
TO LEFT

MELANIE PHILLIPS
The New Anti-Semitism

WANT TO MAKE yourself really, really unpopular if you're a Jew? Try saying that the world is witnessing a terrifying firestorm of hatred directed at Israel and the Jewish people, in which the British and Europeans are deeply implicated.

Since it is now a given in many circles that Israel is a threat to the world equal to North Korea, and that Ariel Sharon is a cross between Martin Bormann and Hendrik Verwoerd, you will find yourself accused of using the Holocaust to avoid any criticism of Israel's behavior. Because, well, you know, you Jews always stick together and are mighty quick to deal that persecution card.

Anyone who holds that view may as well skip what follows. More objective and fair-minded souls, however, might be deeply alarmed to learn of the evidence provided at a recent conference on anti-Semitism and the media at the Vidal Sassoon International Centre for the Study of Antisemitism in Jerusalem.

This was scarcely a gathering of the Ariel Sharon fan club. Among academics and journalists from Israel, Europe, Britain, and America were several left-wingers and liberals who were deeply hostile to Israel's Likud government, believed that the settlements should be dismantled, and were troubled by the behavior of some of Israel's military. "There's no doubt that

Israel is committing human-rights violations on the West Bank," said Professor Yehuda Bauer, the distinguished Holocaust expert.

But there was equally no doubt, from what he and others said, that anti-Zionism is now being used to cloak a terrifying nexus between genocidal Arab and Islamist hatred of the Jews and deep-seated European prejudices.

Anti-Semitism is protean, mutating over the centuries into new forms. Now it has changed again, into a shape which requires a new way of thinking and a new vocabulary. The new anti-Semitism does not discriminate against Jews as individuals on account of their race. Instead, it is centred on Israel, and the denial to the Jewish people alone of the right of self-determination.

This is nothing to do with the settlements or the West Bank. Indeed, the language being used exposes as a cruel delusion the common belief that the Middle East crisis would be solved by the creation of a Palestinian state.

The key motif is a kind of Holocaust inversion, with the Israelis being demonized as Nazis and the Palestinians being regarded as the new Jews. Israel and the Jews are being systematically delegitimized and dehumanized—a necessary prelude to their destruction—with both Islamists and the Western media using anti-Zionism as a fig-leaf for prejudices rooted in both medieval Christian and Nazi demonology.

This has produced an Orwellian situation in which hatred of the Jews now marches behind the Left's banner of anti-racism and human rights, giving rise not merely to distortions, fabrications, and slander about Israel in the media but also to mainstream articles discussing the malign power of the Jews over American and world policy.

The Jerusalem conference heard chilling presentations about a phenomenon barely discussed in Britain: the virulent Arab and Muslim hatred of the Jews. This goes far beyond even the desire to finish off Israel as a Jewish state. Anti-Jewish hatred plays a crucial role in the fanatical jihadism that now threatens all of us in the West, pouring out in television programs, newspapers, and religious sermons throughout the Arab and Muslim world, and amounting to a new warrant for genocide.

The dominant message is that Jewish power amounts to a conspiracy to destroy Islam and take over the whole world. Truly mad theories circulate on Islamist Internet sites which have now convinced untold numbers of Arabs and Muslims that the Jews were behind both 9/11 and the *Columbia* space-shuttle disaster. Egyptian television transmitted a forty-one-part series which presented the notorious Tsarist forgery, the "Protocols of the Elders of Zion"—which purported to be a Jewish plot to control the world—as the truth. (This has prompted some Arab intellectuals to condemn such propaganda as both untrue and a tactical error, but these dissidents remain a small minority.) Meanwhile, Saudi media and religious sermons incite the murder of Jews.

According to the Arabic scholar Professor Menachem Milsom, this Arab and Islamist propaganda persistently dehumanized Jews by representing them as apes and pigs. A preacher at the totemic Haram mosque in Mecca said the Jews were "evil offspring," the "destroyers of God's word," "priest murderers," and the "scum of the human race." The medieval Christian blood libel—the claim that the Jews kill children and drink their blood—has surfaced time and again in prestigious Arab newspapers.

And Zionism was equated with Nazism; just as the Nazis believed in the superiority of the "Aryan" race, so Zionists [*sic*] believed they were the chosen people, which justified their own military expansion. This equation was not confined to a marginal few. Abu Mazen, said Milsom, the Palestinian Authority intellectual who is being talked about as Yasser Arafat's prime minister in a "reformed" administration, wrote as much in his doctoral thesis—in which he also said that the Zionists gave the Nazis permission to treat the Jews as they wished so long as this guaranteed their immigration to Palestine.

These sick outpourings are not so much religious or even fundamentalist doctrines as rooted in a fanatical totalitarian ideology. As Professor Bauer observed, the driving aim is the Islamic dictatorship of the world. Realization of this utopia necessitates the destruction of the foundation creeds of Western culture, Judaism and Christianity—and especially Israel, the supposed personification of Western global power-lust, which was planted as an incubus on Arab soil as a result of the Holocaust.

Holocaust denial is therefore central to Arab anti-Semitism, the prejudice which such historical falsehood has helped to forge a strategic alliance with Europe. For it absolves Europe of its guilt over the Jews, and replaces it with European guilt towards Arabs displaced as a result of the Holocaust.

Europe has waited for more than half a century for a way to blame the Jews for their own destruction. So instead of sounding the alarm over genocidal Islamist Jew-hatred, Europeans have eagerly embraced the Nazification of the Jews, a process which really got under way with Israel's disastrous invasion of Lebanon in 1982. This marked the beginning of the media's systematic inversion of Israeli self-defense as aggression, along with double-standards and malicious fabrications, which have nothing to do with legitimate (and necessary) criticism of Israel and everything to do with delegitimizing the Jewish state altogether in readiness for its dismantling.

So the conference heard about German accusations that Israel was using Nazi methods and (repeating a claim by Hamas) that the Monica Lewinsky scandal was a Jewish conspiracy against Bill Clinton. It heard of the Nazification of Israel in Sweden, where there were charges that the Israelis were exterminating the Palestinians, that the media were controlled by Jewish interests to suppress criticism of Israel, and that influential Jewish lobby groups were "spraying journalists with poison."

It heard that in France Jews were vilified and excluded from public debate if they challenged the lies being told about Israel. It was shown a devastating French film *Décryptage* (*Decoding*)—which has been playing to packed houses in Paris— about the obsessive malevolence toward Israel displayed by the French media. It was told about the way the British media described Israel's "death squads," "killing fields," and "executioners" while sanitizing Palestinian human bombs as "gentle," "religious," and "kind." It heard about the cartoon in the Italian newspaper *La Stampa* during the siege of the Church of the Nativity in Bethlehem, depicting an Israeli tank pointing a gun at the baby Jesus who is saying, "Surely they are not going to kill me again."

And of course there was Jenin, the so-called "massacre" or "genocide" reported as such by virtually the entire media, where in fact 52 Palestinians died, of whom more than half were terrorists, while Israel sustained (for it) the huge loss of 45 of its soldiers. This astonishing media distortion was conceded at the conference by the (extraordinarily brave) Palestinian politics professor Mohammad Dajani, who also observed that a distraught Palestinian public was—on this and other occasions—whipped up by biased and emotional Palestinian reporting which showed little concern for the truth. But the big lie of the Jenin massacre is now believed as fact, contributing to the belief that Israel is a criminal state.

Europeans have thus made themselves accomplices to an explicitly genocidal program. But an even more striking feature is that, while the old anti-Semitism still festers away among neo-Nazis, the new anti-Semitism is a phenomenon of their sworn enemies on the political Left. So, as the Canadian law professor

Irwin Cotler observed, we now have the mind-twisting situation where anti-Jewish hatred is harnessed to the cause of anti-racism and human rights, with Israel being compared to both Nazism and apartheid by those who define themselves against these ideologies. Such a travesty of the facts involves, of course, the implicit denial of the truth of those terrible regimes, quite apart from the prelude to annihilation created by such a lethal defamation of Israel. And even more counterintuitively, many Jews and Israelis on the Left also subscribe to this analysis— and even to the demonology of Israeli Nazism and apartheid— handing an effective weapon to those who dismiss the claim of a new anti-Semitism as Jewish paranoia or Islamophobia.

So what is the explanation for the Left's position? Partly, it's the old anti-imperialist and anti-West prejudice. Partly, it's the view that only the powerless can be victims; so Third World people can never be murderers, and any self-defense by Western societies such as Israel must instead be aggression. Partly, it's the postmodern destruction of objectivity and truth, which has ushered in the hegemony of lies. And partly, as the Left takes an axe to morality and self-restraint, it's a golden opportunity to pulverize the very people who invented the damn rules in the first place.

A left-wing Polish journalist at the conference, Konstanty Gebert, got the real point. The Left, he said, could not face the fact that they had totally misconstrued the Middle East because this would undermine their whole philosophy. This was founded on the premise that reason could reconcile all differences; all that was needed in Israel was an enlightened government for reason to prevail. The evidence that we are facing a phenomenon which is not susceptible to reason would destroy that world view. It would also give credibility to the hated Sharon, whose demonization is absolutely vital to the Left as a protection against the implosion of its whole ideological position.

So the evidence is being denied, and truth is being stood on its head. The result is the defamation of a people, the greater prospect of its destruction, and the disastrous failure of the populations of Britain and Europe to understand properly the threat that all free peoples now face.

DR. LAURIE ZOLOTH

Fear and Loathing at San Francisco State

[This was orginally sent out as an e-mail to friends of the author, but rapidly circulated and became an iconic eyewitness description of anti-Semitism on American campuses.]

TODAY, ALL DAY, I have been listening to the reactions of students, parents, and community members who were on campus yesterday. I have received e-mail from around the country, and phone calls, worried for both my personal safety on the campus, and for the entire intellectual project of having a Jewish Studies program, and recruiting students to a campus that in the last month has become a venue for hate speech and anti-Semitism.

After nearly seven years as director of Jewish Studies, and after nearly two decades of life here as a student, faculty member, and wife of the Hillel rabbi, after years of patient work and difficult civic discourse, I am saddened to see SFSU (San Francisco State University) return to its notoriety as a place that teaches anti-Semitism, hatred for America, and hatred, above all else, for the Jewish State of Israel, a state that I cherish.

I cannot fully express what it feels like to have to walk across campus daily, past maps of the Middle East that do not include Israel, past posters of cans of soup with labels on them of drops of blood and dead babies, labeled "canned Palestinian children meat, slaughtered according to Jewish rites under American license," past poster after poster calling out "Zionism = racism" and "Jews = Nazis."

This is not civic discourse, this is not free speech; this is the Weimar Republic with brown shirts it cannot control. This is the casual introduction of the medieval blood libel and virulent hatred smeared around our campus in a manner so ordinary that it hardly excites concern—except if you are a Jew, and you understand that hateful words have always led to hateful deeds.

SHOVED AGAINST THE WALL

Yesterday, the hatred coalesced in a hate mob. Yesterday's "Peace in the Middle East Rally" was completely organized by the Hillel students, mostly eighteen and nineteen years old. They spoke about their lives at SFSU and of their support for Israel, and they sang of peace. They wore new Hillel T-shirts that said "peace" in English, Hebrew, and Arabic.

A Russian immigrant, in his new English, spoke of loving his new country, a haven from anti-Semitism. A sophomore spoke about being here only one year, and about the support and community she found at the Hillel House. Both spoke of how hard it was to live as a Jew on this campus, how isolating, how terrifying. A surfer guy spoke of his love of Jesus, and his support for Israel, and a young freshman earnestly asked for a moment of silence.

And all the Jews stood still, listening as the shouted hate of the counter-demonstrators filled the air with abuse.

As soon as the community supporters left, the fifty students who remained—praying in a *minyan* for the traditional afternoon prayers, or chatting, or cleaning up after the rally, talking—were surrounded by a large, angry crowd of Palestinians and their supporters. But they were not calling for peace. They screamed at us to "go back to Russia" and they screamed that they would kill us all, and other terrible things. They surrounded the praying students, and the elderly women who are our elder college participants, who survived the Holocaust, who helped shape the Bay Area peace movement, only to watch as a threatening crowd shoved the Hillel students against the wall of the plaza.

I had invited members of my Orthodox community to join us, members of my Board of Visitors, and we stood there in despair. Let me remind you that in building the SFSU Jewish Studies program, we asked the same people for their support, and that our Jewish community, who pay for the program once as taxpayers and again as Jews, generously supports our program. Let me remind you that ours is arguably one of the Jewish Studies programs in the country most devoted to peace, justice, and diversity since our inception.

As the counter-demonstrators poured into the plaza, screaming at the Jews "Get out or we will kill you" and "Hitler did not finish the job," I turned to the police and to every administrator I could find and asked them to remove the counter-demonstrators from the Plaza, to maintain the separation of 100 feet that we had been promised.

The police told me that they had been told not to arrest anyone, and that if they did, "it would start a riot." I told them that it already was a riot.

Finally, Fred Astren, the Northern California Hillel director, and I went up directly to speak with Dean Saffold, who was watching from her post a flight above us. She told us she would call in the SF police. But the police could do nothing more than surround the Jewish students and community members who were now trapped in a corner of the plaza, grouped under the flags of Israel, while an angry, out of control mob, literally chanting for our deaths, surrounded us.

Dr. Astren and I went to stand with our students. This was neither free speech nor discourse, but raw, physical assault.

DOUBLE STANDARD

Was I afraid? No, really more sad that I could not protect my students. Not one administrator came to stand with us. I knew that if a crowd of Palestinian or Black students had been there, surrounded by a crowd of white racists screaming racist threats, shielded by police, the faculty and staff would have no trouble deciding which side to stand on.

In fact, the scene recalled for me many moments in the Civil Rights movement, or the United Farm Workers movement, when, as a student, I stood with Black and Latino colleagues, surrounded by hateful mobs. Then, as now, I sang peace songs, and then, as now, the hateful crowd screamed at me, "Go back to Russia, Jew." How ironic that it all took place under the picture of Cesar Chavez, who led the very demonstrations that I took part in as a student.

There was no safe way out of the Plaza. We had to be marched back to the Hillel House under armed SF police guard, and we had to have a police guard remain outside Hillel. I was very proud of the students, who did not flinch and who did not, even one time, resort to violence or anger in retaliation. Several community members who were swept up in the situation simply could not believe what they saw.

One young student told me, "I have read about anti-Semitism in books, but this is the first time I have seen real anti-Semites, people who just hate me without knowing me, just because I am a Jew." She lives in the dorms. Her mother calls and urges her to transfer to a safer campus.

Today is advising day. For me, the question is an open one: What do I advise the Jewish students to do?

POSTSCRIPT

The incident described here is, unfortunately, not in isolation. In the first few months of 2002, there have been over fifty documented cases of anti-

Semitic acts in and around the Bay Area. These include an attempted arson at a synagogue in Berkeley, and a synagogue in San Francisco that was fire-bombed.

The campus scene has been violent as well. In recent weeks at UC Berkeley, a brick was thrown through the Hillel windows, Hillel property was spray-painted with "Hate Jews," and a rabbi's son was beaten up, requiring stitches to his head.

TODD GITLIN

The Rough Beast Returns

T HE EMAIL SENT OUT last month by Laurie Zoloth, director of Jewish Studies at San Francisco State University,
was chilling on its face.

"I cannot fully express what it feels like to have to walk
across campus daily, past maps of the Middle East that do not
include Israel, past posters of cans of soup with labels on them
of drops of blood and dead babies, labeled 'canned Palestinian
children meat, slaughtered according to Jewish rites under
American license,' past poster after poster calling out 'Zionism
= racism' and 'Jews = Nazis,'" she wrote—and the details only
became more shattering from then on.

I read Zoloth's words with horror but not, alas, complete
amazement. Eleven years ago, during the Gulf War, across San
Francisco Bay, the head of a student splinter group at Berkeley
addressed a room full of faculty and students opposed to the
war, spitting out venomously, "You Jews, I know your names, I
know where you live."

The faculty and students in attendance sat stiffly and said
nothing. Embarrassed? Frightened? Or worse—thinking that it
wasn't time to tackle this issue, that it was off the agenda, an inconvenience.

Far more recently, two students of mine at NYU wondered

aloud whether it was actually true, as they had heard, that four thousand Jews didn't show up for work at the World Trade Center on September 11. They clearly thought this astoundingly crazy charge was plausible enough to warrant careful investigation, but it didn't occur to them to look at the names of the dead.

Wicked anti-Semitism is back. The worst crackpot notions that circulate through the violent Middle East are also roaming around America, and if that wasn't bad enough, students are spreading the gibberish. Students! As if the bloc to which we have long looked for intelligent dissent has decided to junk any pretense of standards.

A student movement is not just a student movement. It's a *student* movement. Students, whether they are progressive or not, have the responsibility of knowing things, of thinking and discerning, of studying. A student movement should maintain the highest of standards, not ape the formulas of its elders or outdo them in virulence.

It should therefore trouble progressives everywhere that the students at San Francisco State are neither curious nor revolted by the anti-Semitic drivel they are regurgitating. The simple fact that a student movement—even a small one—has been reduced to reflecting the hatred spewed by others should profoundly trouble anyone whose moral principles aim higher than simple nationalism—as should be the case for anyone on the left.

It isn't hard to discover the sources of the drivel being parroted by the students at San Francisco State. In the blood-soaked Middle East of Yasser Arafat and Ariel Sharon, in the increasingly polarized Europe of Jean-Marie Le Pen, raw anti-Semitism has increasingly taken the place of intelligent criticism of Israel and its policies.

Even as Laurie Zoloth's message flew around the world, even as several prominent European papers published scathing but warranted attacks on Israel's stonewalling of an inquiry into the Jenin fighting, the great Portuguese novelist José Saramago was describing Israel's invasion of Ramallah as "a crime comparable to Auschwitz."

In one of his long, lapping sentences, Saramago wrote in Madrid's *El País* (as translated by Paul Berman in *The Forward*, May 24):

> Intoxicated mentally by the messianic dream of a Greater Israel which will finally achieve the expansionist dreams of the most radical Zionism; contaminated by the monstrous and rooted "certitude" that in this catastrophic and absurd world there exists a people chosen by God and that, consequently, all the actions of an obsessive, psychological and pathologically exclusivist racism are justified; educated and trained in the idea that any suffering that has been inflicted, or is being inflicted, or will be inflicted on everyone else, especially the Palestinians, will always be inferior to that which they themselves suffered in the Holocaust, the Jews endlessly scratch their own wound to keep it bleeding, to make it incurable, and they show it to the world as if it were a banner. . . .

Note well: the deliciously deferred subject of this sentence is: "the Jews." Not the right-wing Jews, the militarist Israelis, but "the Jews." Suddenly the Jews are reduced to a single stick-figure (or shall we say hook-nosed?) caricature and we are plunged into the brainless, ruinous, abysmal iconography that should make every last reasonable person shudder.

The German socialist August Bebel once said that anti-Semitism was "the socialism of fools." What we witness now is the progressivism of fools. It is a recrudescence of everything that costs the left its moral edge. And, appallingly, it is this contemptible message the anti-Semitic students at San Francisco State chose to parrot.

We are not on the brink of "another Auschwitz," and to
think so, in fact, falsifies the danger. The danger is clear and
present, though not apocalyptic. It's no remote nightmare that
synagogues are bombed, including the one on the Tunisian
island of Djerba, famous for tolerance, an apparent al-Qaeda
truck bomb attack. This happened. It is no remote nightmare
that hundreds of Palestinian civilians died during Israeli incursions into the West Bank. This, too, happened. The nightmare
is that the second is being allowed to excuse and justify the first.

Laurie Zoloth wrote: "Let me remind you that ours is arguably one of the Jewish Studies programs in the country most
devoted to peace, justice, and diversity since our inception."

But anti-Semitism doesn't care. Like every other lunacy that
diminished human brains are capable of, anti-Semitism already
knows what it hates.

This is no incidental issue, no negligible distraction. A Left
that cares for the rights of humanity cannot cavalierly tolerate
the systematic abuse of any people—whatever you think of
Israel's or any other country's foreign policy. Any student
movement worthy of the name must face the ugly history that
long made anti-Semitism the acceptable racism, face it and
break from it.

If fighting it unremittingly is not a "progressive" cause, then
what kind of progress does progressivism have in mind? What
do you think?

ELI MULLER

Necessary Evils

(THURSDAY, FEBRUARY 20, 2003) It has been an unpleasant week to be Jewish at Yale. On Tuesday, Dean Pamela George published a column to the effect that it was no more inappropriate to invite rabid anti-Semite Amiri Baraka to speak than it was to invite former members of the Israeli military. That afternoon, Baraka spoke to a standing ovation. On Wednesday, Sahm Adrangi '03 informed readers of this page that condemnation of Baraka stemmed from the eagerness of Jews in the media to shield Israel from criticism ("Not Just Another Conspiracy Theory: Manipulating Anger"). For the next twenty-four hours, I watched more postings than I care to recall pile up on the *Yale Daily News* Web site, praising Sahm for his courage and denouncing Jews in the media for serving as Israeli shills. Hatred of Israel and its suspected apologists has never seemed more prevalent on this campus. In my years here I have heard unending discussion of whether anti-Zionism constitutes anti-Semitism. I have concluded that while the two are not identical, hatred of Israel constitutes a moral pathology in its own right, one that is still regarded as legitimate by many of my classmates. Some Jews will invariably denounce any criticism of Israel as anti-Semitic, using a powerful allegation as a barrier to dialogue. This pernicious tendency has contributed to the development of an equally false counter-proposition: that nothing you could say about Israel could possibly be anti-Semitic.

The truth is twofold: There are many things about the actions of the Israeli government that are deserving of criticism. On the other hand, some denunciations of the Israeli government are so hyperbolic, so wedded to a notion of Israel as an incarnation of the demonic, that they do constitute anti-Semitism. In other words, many negative things can and should be said about Israel's current policies without the speaker being subjected to charges of anti-Semitism. But when such remarks take on a reckless disregard for the factual, the proportional, or the right of individuals to be assessed on their own merits rather than on the basis of their ethnicity, such rhetoric begins to reek of bigotry.

For example, arguing that Israel should demolish all settlements in the West Bank and Gaza strip is far from anti-Semitic. Nor is it anti-Semitic to note the objective fact of the extent of Palestinian suffering. To suggest that Israel is an apartheid state, Nazi-like in its policies, intent on genocide or ethnic cleansing, however, is to bury the truth beneath the vilest of epithets. To demonize Israel in this way, to see it as a monster among the nations perpetrating "affronts to humanity," smacks of a level of hatred beyond the limits of criticism. Perhaps we ought not to call the condemnation of Israelis *qua* Israelis anti-Semitic, but it is nonetheless a form of fetishistic hatred, one which imputes the demonic to a state and its people such that the reality of the political entity disappears into a symbol of human evil.

The transformation of a real, complex nation into a scapegoat for the world's ills constitutes the essence of bigotry. This type of thinking transforms the social conscience into fuel for the smug hysteria of the ignorant and the dogmatic. What I sense in the ideology of Baraka's apologists is the notion that because Israel's defenders protest too much when confronted on the merits, any attack on Israel contributes to meaningful dialogue, no matter how scurrilous or devoid of merit. "The stanza on Israel by far doesn't constitute the main body of the poem. But that is where the attention was shifted, not by Baraka, but by certain members of the audience," wrote one student poster on the *Yale Daily News* Web site. "This debate is not about anti-Semitism, it's not about propaganda. It's about the Zionist supporters of Israeli occupation on campus refusing to accept any form of criticism of their cause."

How, I ask, does saying that the Israelis blew up the World Trade Center criticize the occupation? The underlying assumption seems to be that since American supporters of Israel are uncritical in their support for Israel, that any accusation against Israel is somehow an appropriate response to their intransigence. The hatred of Israel contained in such a sentiment is so virulent that I am at a loss to explain it. As a columnist, there is no empirical means of discovering how a significant number of my fellow students arrive at such extremes of prejudice. I suspect that antipathy to Israel stems from the automatic tendency to sympathize with the perceived underdog in any given conflict. A general aversion to the use of military force may also play a role in shaping campus attitudes toward Israel. Indeed, Adrangi and numerous posters cited Baraka's nod to the Rosenbergs, Rosa Luxembourg, and victims of the Holocaust in his poem as evidence to refute claims of anti-Semitism. It's worth noting that the philo-Semitic remarks only get applied to Jews as victims. For Jews who take up arms in their own defense, Baraka seems to have little room for sympathy.

Perhaps campus anti-Zionists are driven by an analogous impulse, by a distaste for power and the ethical complexities which come with it. If Jews were still powerless, stateless, and passive, perhaps people like Baraka would be as widely loathed at Yale as Ariel Sharon. But since Israel is not a mere collection of helpless victims but a real state with real flaws, capable of both great triumphs and profound injustice, it fails to merit collegiate sympathy. Sometimes I wonder, idly, what it would take to get these students to deal with the accomplishments and moral failings of the state of Israel in an even-handed, thoughtful way. But ultimately the genesis of anti-Zionist fanaticism at Yale is less important than the indisputable fact that such fanaticism exists. Its adherents are no anonymous horde but include friends, professors, and longtime colleagues. For better or for worse, they are my peers, and their bigotry an inextricable component of my Yale education.

MARK STRAUSS
Antiglobalism's Jewish Problem

THERE IS NO SHORTAGE of symbols representing peace, justice, and economic equality. The dove and the olive branch. The peace sign. The rainbow flag. Even the emblem of the United Nations. So why did some protesters at the 2003 World Social Forum (WSF) in Porto Alegre, Brazil, display the swastika?

Held two months prior to the U.S.-led attack on Iraq, this year's conference—an annual grassroots riposte to the well-heeled World Economic Forum in Davos—had the theme "Another World Is Possible." But the more appropriate theme might have been "Yesterday's World Is Back." Marchers among the 20,000 activists from 120 countries carried signs reading NAZIS, YANKEES, AND JEWS: NO MORE CHOSEN PEOPLES! Some wore T-shirts with the Star of David twisted into Nazi swastikas. Members of a Palestinian organization pilloried Jews as the "true fundamentalists who control United States capitalism." Jewish delegates carrying banners declaring TWO PEOPLES—TWO STATES: PEACE IN THE MIDDLE EAST were assaulted.

Porto Alegre provides just one snapshot of an unfolding phenomenon known as the "new anti-Semitism." Since the fall of the Berlin Wall, the oldest hatred has been making a global comeback, culminating in 2002 with the highest number of anti-Semitic attacks in twelve years. Not since Kristallnacht, the Nazi-led pogrom against German Jews in 1938, have so many European synagogues and Jewish schools been desecrated. This new anti-Semitism is a kaleidoscope of old hatreds shattered and rearranged into random patterns at once familiar and strange. It is the medieval image of the "Christ-killing" Jew resurrected on the editorial pages of cosmopolitan European newspapers. It is the International Red Cross and Red Crescent Movement refusing to put the Star of David on their ambulances. It is Zimbabwe and Malaysia—nations nearly bereft of Jews—warning of an international Jewish conspiracy to control the world's finances. It is neo-Nazis donning checkered Palestinian kaffiyehs and Palestinians lining up to buy copies of *Mein Kampf.*

The last decade had promised a different world. As statues of Lenin fell, synagogues reopened throughout Russia and Eastern Europe. In a decisive 111-to-25 vote, the U.N. General Assembly overturned the 1975 resolution equating Zionism with racism. The leader of the Palestine Liberation Organization shook hands with the prime minister of Israel. The European Union (EU), mindful of the legacy of the Holocaust and the genocidal Balkan wars, created an independent agency to combat xenophobia and anti-Semitism within its own borders. Confronted with a resurgence in hatred after what had seemed to be an era of extraordinary progress, the Jewish community now finds itself asking: Why now?

Historically, anti-Semitism has fluctuated with the boom and bust of business cycles. Jews have long been scapegoats during economic downturns, as a small minority with outsized political and financial influence. To some extent, that pattern still applies. Demagogues in countries engulfed by the financial crises of the late 1990s fell back on familiar stereotypes. "Who is to blame?" asked General Albert Makashov of the Communist Party of the Russian Federation following the collapse of the ruble in 1998. "Usury, deceit, corruption, and thievery are flourishing in the country. That is why I call the reformers Yids [Jews]." But other countries don't fit this profile. How, for instance, does one explain anti-Semitism's resurgence in Austria and Great Britain, which have enjoyed some of the lowest unemployment rates in Europe?

Rising hostility toward Israel is also a significant factor. The 2000 Al-Aqsa Intifada was more violent than its 1987 predecessor, as helicopter gunships and suicide bombers supplanted rubber bullets and stones. This second Intifada also marked the emergence of the Al-Jazeera effect, with satellite television beaming brutal images of the conflict, such as the death of twelve-year-old Palestinian Muhammed al-Dura, into millions of homes worldwide. In Europe, Muslim extremists took out their fury on Jews and Jewish institutions. Some in the European press, even as they dismissed anti-Jewish violence as random hooliganism or a political grudge match between rival ethnic groups, used incendiary imagery that routinely drew comparisons between Israel and the Nazi regime. This crude caricature of Israelis as slaughterers of the innocent soon morphed into the age-old "blood libel"—as when the Italian newspaper *La Stampa* published a cartoon depicting the infant Jesus threatened by Israeli tanks imploring, "Don't tell me they want to kill me again."

Then came the terrorist attacks of September 11, 2001. The U.S.–Israeli relationship—bound together by shared values, shared enemies such as Iran and Iraq, $2.7 billion a year in economic aid, and a powerful U.S. Jewish lobby—had allegedly brought down the wrath of the Islamic world and dragged the West into a clash of civilizations. This sentiment only deepened with U.S. military action against Iraq, when anti-Semitism bandwagoned on the anti-war movement and rising anti-Americanism. How else to explain a war against a country that had never attacked the United States, it was argued, if not for a cabal of Jewish neocon advisors who had hoodwinked the U.S. president into conquering Iraq to safeguard Israel?

But another element of the new anti-Semitism is often overlooked: The time frame for this resurgence of judeophobia corresponds with the intensification of international links that took place in the 1990s. "People are losing their compass," observes Dan Dinar, a historian at Hebrew University. "A worldwide stock market, a new form of money, no borders. Concepts like country, nationality, everything is in doubt. They are looking for the ones who are guilty for this new situation and they find the Jews." The backlash against globalization unites all elements of the political spectrum through a common cause, and in doing so it sometimes fosters a common enemy—what French Jewish leader Roger Cukierman calls an anti-Semitic "brown-green-red alliance" among ultra-nationalists, the populist green movement, and communism's fellow travelers. The new anti-Semitism is unique because it seamlessly stitches together the various forms of old anti-Semitism: the far right's conception of the Jew (a fifth column, loyal only to itself, undermining economic sovereignty and national culture), the far left's conception of the Jew (capitalists and usurers, controlling the international economic system), and the "blood libel" Jew (murderers and modern-day colonial oppressors).

FIRST THEY CAME FOR THE WTO

Jews have always aroused suspicion and contempt as a people apart, stubbornly resisting assimilation and clinging to their own religion, language, rituals, and dietary laws. But modern anti-Semitism made its debut with the emergence of global capitalism in the nineteenth century. When Jews left their urban ghettos and a small but visible number emerged as successful bankers, financiers, and entrepreneurs, they engendered resentment among those who envied their unfathomable success, especially given Jews' secondary status in society.

Some left-wing economists, such as French anarchist Pierre-Joseph Proudhon, depicted Jews as the driving force behind global capitalism. Other socialist thinkers saw their theories corrupted by the racism of the era. In 1887, German sociologist Ferdinand Tönnies published his classic work *Community and Society,* wherein he blamed capitalism for undermining society's communitarian impulses and creating a merchant class that was "unscrupulous, egoistic and self-willed, treating all human beings as his nearest friends as only means to his ends." A few years later, German social scientist Werner Sombart took Tönnies's theories to their next step and meticulously explained how Jews "influenced the outward form of modern capitalism" and "gave expression to its inward spirit." Sombart's book *The Jews and Economic Life* would influence an entire generation of German anti-Semitic authors, including Theodore Fritsch, who was honored by the Nazis as the *altmeister* ("old master") of their movement. Anti-Semitism would become the central defining ideology of the Third Reich, the "glue that held Nazism together," notes historian Robert Katz. "It delivered up the external enemy, 'international-finance Jewry,' by which Hitler succeeded in galvanizing and mesmerizing a Germany feeling itself victimized by otherwise less-definable outside forces."

Modern-day globalization—the opening of borders to the greater movement of ideas, people, and money—has stirred familiar anxieties about ill-defined "outside forces." Last June [2002], the Pew Research Center for the People and the Press published a survey conducted in forty-four countries revealing that, although people generally have a favorable view of globalization, sizable majorities of those polled said their "traditional ways of life" are being threatened and agreed with the statement that "our way of life needs to be protected against foreign influence." And many believe "success is determined by forces outside their personal control."

With familiar anxieties come familiar scapegoats. Today's financial crashes aren't on the same scale as the economic dislocations of the 1880s and 1930s. But, as the 1997 Asian crisis revealed, in an era of volatile capital flows, damaging financial contagion can sweep through nations in a matter of weeks. Countries in the developing world, who view themselves as victims of globalization, sometimes see conspiratorial undertones. Modern-day resentment against the perceived power of international financial institutions has merged with old mythologies. The nineteenth century had its Rothschilds; the current era has had Lawrence Summers and Robert Rubin at the U.S. Treasury Department, Alan Greenspan at the U.S. Federal Reserve, James Wolfensohn at the World Bank, and Stanley Fischer at the International Monetary Fund (IMF). Malaysian prime minister Mahathir Mohamad once lashed out against "Jews who determine our currency levels, and bring about the collapse of our economy." The spokesman for the Jamaat-i-Islami political party in Pakistan complained: "Most anything bad that happens, prices going up, whatever, this can usually be attributed to the IMF and the World Bank, which are synonymous with the United States. And who controls the United States? The Jews do." Economic chaos in Zimbabwe, where a once thriving Jewish community of 8,000 has dwindled to just 650, prompted President Robert Mugabe to deliver a speech declaring that the "Jews in South Africa, working in cahoots with their colleagues here, want our textile and clothing factories to close down."

Throughout the Middle East, where economic growth remains stagnant everywhere but Israel, Islamists and secular nationalists alike portray globalization as the latest in a series of U.S.–Zionist plots to subjugate the Arab world under Western economic control and erase its cultural borders. A former spokesman for the militant group Hamas warned in the early 1990s that if Arab governments accepted the Jewish state's existence, "Israel would rule in the region just as Japan dominates Southeast Asia, and all the Arabs will turn into the Jews' workers." Mainstream Arab media outlets, such as the Egyptian newspaper *Al-Ahram* and the Palestinian newspaper *Al-Ayyam,* publish columns that praise Osama bin Laden as the "man who says 'no' to the domination of globalization," and which cite "The Protocols of the Learned Elders of Zion"—the infamous nineteenth-century forgery of a purported blueprint for Jewish world domination—as hard evidence of globalization's true intent.

In the West, anxiety over globalization provides opportunities for far-right political parties, who exploit the fears of those who see their way of life threatened by migrants from the developing world and who believe their sovereignty is besieged by regional trade pacts and monetary union. Jörg Haider, the head of Austria's far-right Freedom Party, and Jean-Marie Le Pen, the leader of France's National Front Party—who both rode to electoral success on anti-immigrant, anti-Europe platforms—kept their anti-Semitic sentiments under wraps as they campaigned before the media. But other far-right organizations in Europe are not shy about pointing a finger at the "true culprits" behind their countries' woes. In Italy, the Movimento Fascismo e Libertà identifies globalization as an "instrument in the hands of international Zionism." In Russia and Eastern Europe, "brown" ultra-nationalists and "red" communist stalwarts have formed an ideological alliance against foreign investors and multinational corporations, identifying Jews as the capitalist carpetbaggers sacking their national heritage.

In their war against globalization, the browns on the far right have also found common cause with the greens of the new left. Matt Hale, the leader of the U.S. white supremacist World Church of the Creator, praised the 1999 antiglobalization protests in Seattle as "incredibly successful from the point of view of the rioters as well as our Church. They helped shut

278 THOSE WHO FORGET THE PAST

down talks of the Jew World Order WTO and helped make a mockery of the Jewish Occupational Government around the world. Bravo." To lure in activists planning to protest the 2002 G-8 summit in Calgary, the National Alliance—the largest neo-Nazi organization in the United States that maintains ties with white supremacist groups worldwide—set up a Web site called the Anti-Globalism Action Network, dedicated to "broadening the anti-globalism movement to include divergent and margin-alized voices."

Antiglobalization activists find themselves fighting a two-front battle, simultaneously protesting the World Trade Or-ganization (WTO), IMF, and World Bank, while organizing impromptu counter-protests against far-right extremists who gate-crash their rallies. A bizarre ideological turf war has bro-ken out. Nongovernmental organizations (NGOs) voice alarm about neo-Nazis "masquerading" as antiglobalization activists. On the Web site of the white supremacist Church of True Is-rael, an aggrieved Walter Nowotny retorts: "This accusation implies that we are late-comers to this movement and only associate with it to jump on a bandwagon that already has considerable momentum. But who are the real infiltrators and trespassers?"

History is repeating itself. As in the nineteenth century, the far right is plagiarizing left-wing dogma and imbuing it with racist overtones, transforming the campaign against the capitalist "New World Order" into a struggle against the "Jew World Order." The antiglobalization movement is, however, somewhat culpable. It isn't inherently anti-Semitic, yet it helps enable anti-Semitism by peddling conspiracy theories. In its eyes, globalization is less a process than a plot hatched behind closed doors by a handful of unaccountable bureaucrats and corporations. Underlying the movement's humanistic goals of universal social justice is a current of fear mongering—the IMF, the WTO, the North American Free Trade Agreement, and the

Multilateral Agreement on Investment (MAI) are portrayed not just as exploiters of the developing world but as supranational instruments to undermine our sovereignty. Pick up a copy of the 1998 book *MAI and the Threat to American Freedom* (wrapped in a patriotic red, white, and blue cover), written by antiglobalization activists Maude Barlow and Tony Clarke, and you'll read how "[o]ver the past twenty-five years, corporations and the state seem to have forged a new political alliance that allows corporations to gain more and more control over governance. This new 'corporate rule' poses a fundamental threat to the rights and democratic freedoms of all people." At an even more extreme end of the spectrum, the Web site of the Canadian-based Centre for Research on Globalization sells books and videos that "expose" how the September 11 terrorist attacks were "most likely a special covert action" to "further the goals of corporate globalization."

Unfortunately, conspiracy theories must always have a conspirator, and all too often, the conspirators are perceived to be Jews. It takes but a small step to cross the line dividing the two worldviews. "If I told you I thought the world was controlled by a handful of capitalists and corporate bosses, you would say I was a left-winger," an anarchist demonstrator told the online Russian publication *Pravda*. "But if I told you who I thought the capitalists and corporate bosses were, you'd say I was far right."

The browns and greens are not simply plagiarizing one another's ideas. They're frequently reading from the same page. In Canada, a lecture by anti-Semitic conspiracy theorist David Icke was advertised in lefty magazines such as *Shared Vision* and *Common Ground*. ("Canadians voted down free trade and we got it anyway," said one woman who saw the ads and attended the event. "So there has to be something to that.") Farright nationalists, such as former skinhead Jaroslaw Tomasiewicz, have infiltrated the Polish branch of the international antiglobalization organization ATTAC. The British Fascist Party includes among its list of recommended readings the works of left-wing anti-globalists George Monbiot and Noam Chomsky. A Web site warning of the dangers of "Jewish Plutocracy, Jewish Power" includes links to antiglobalization NGOs such as Corpwatch and Reclaim Democracy. The Dutch NGO De Fabel van de il-legaal withdrew in disgust from the anti-MAI movement when it learned that the campaign's activities were attracting the at-tention of far-right, anti-Semitic student groups. "By pointing to this so-called globalisation as our main problem, the anti-MAI activists prepare our thinking for the corresponding logi-cal consequence—the struggle for 'our own' local economy, and as a consequence also for 'our own' state and culture," the director of De Fabel warned. "Left-wing groups are spreading an ideology that offers the New Right, rather than the left, bright opportunities for future growth."

ANTI-GLOBALIZIONISM

The greens and the browns share another common cause: op-position to Israel. Given the antiglobalization movement's sym-pathy for Third World causes, it's not surprising that French activist José Bové took a break from trashing McDonald's res-taurants to show his solidarity with the Palestinian movement by visiting a besieged Yasir Arafat in Ramallah last year.

But, in the case of the new left, the salient question is not: What do antiglobalization activists have against Israel? Rather, it is important to ask: Why only Israel? Why didn't Bové travel to Russia to demonstrate his solidarity with Muslim Chechen separatists fighting their own war of liberation? Why are cam-pus petitions demanding that universities divest funds from companies with ties to Israel but not China? Why do the same antiglobalization rallies that denounce Israel's tactics against the Palestinians remain silent on the thousands of Muslims killed in pogroms in Gujarat, India?

Israel enjoys a unique pariah status among the anti-globalization movement because it is viewed as the world's sole remaining colonialist state—an exploitative, capitalist enclave created by Western powers in the heart of the developing world. "They're trying to impose an apartheid system on both the occupied territories and the Arab population in the rest of Israel," says Bové. "They are also putting in place—with the support of the World Bank—a series of neoliberal measures intended to integrate the Middle East into globalized production circuits, through the exploitation of cheap Palestinian labor."

Opposing the policies of the Israeli government does not make the new left anti-Semitic. But a movement campaigning for global social justice makes a mockery of itself by singling out just the Jewish state for condemnation. And when the conspiratorial mindset of the antiglobalization movement mingles with anti-Israeli rhetoric, the results can get ugly. Bové, for instance, told a reporter that the Mossad, the Israeli intelligence agency, was responsible for anti-Semitic attacks in France in order to distract attention from its government's actions in the occupied territories.

The consequences of embracing a double standard toward Israel are all too apparent at antiglobalization rallies. In Italy, a member of Milan's Jewish community carrying an Israeli flag at a protest march was beaten by a mob of antiglobalization activists. At Davos, a group of protesters wearing masks of Israeli prime minister Ariel Sharon and U.S. secretary of defense Donald Rumsfeld (wearing a yellow star) carried a golden calf laden with money. Worldwide, protesters carry signs that compare Sharon to Hitler, while waving Israeli flags where the Star of David has been replaced with the swastika. Such displays portray Israel as the sole perpetrator of violence, ignoring the hundreds of Israelis who have died in suicide bombings and the role of the Palestinian Authority in fomenting the conflict. And equating Israel with the Third Reich is the basest form of Holocaust revisionism, sending the message that the only "solu-tion" to the Israeli-Palestinian conflict is nothing less than the complete destruction of the Jewish state. Antiglobalization activist and author Naomi Klein has spoken out against such displays, but she is in the minority. The very same anti-globalization movement that prides itself on staging counter-protests against neo-Nazis who crash their rallies links arms with protesters who wave the swastika in the name of Palestin-ian rights.

Like the antiglobalist left, far-right activists have also em-braced their own form of anticolonialism. For them, global-ization is synonymous with "mongrelization," an attempt to mix races and cultures and destroy unique heritages. When the greens preach the virtues of "localization," a hearty "amen" echoes among the browns, who seek to insulate their countries against the twin evils of human migration and foreign capital. The far right sees nationalist movements and indigenous rights groups as allies in the assault against the multiculturalism of the new world order. And it sees the Palestinians, in particular, as a resistance movement against the modern-day Elders of Zion. American neo-Nazi David Duke summed up this worldview in an essay on his Web site: "These Jewish supremacists have a master plan that should be obvious for anyone to see. They consistently attempt to undermine the culture, racial iden-tity and solidarity, economy, political independence of every nation. . . . [They] really think they have some divine right to rule over not only Palestine but over the rest of the world as well."

IS ANOTHER WORLD POSSIBLE?

Commenting on the resurgence of anti-Semitic imagery in the Egyptian press, BBC correspondent Kate Clark noted that "if and when real peace comes, the Egyptian media are likely to forget their anti-Semitic line."

But, even if and when real peace comes, the conditions conducive to anti-Semitism aren't going away. The very existence of Israel offends those who view it as a colonialist aberration. Arab governments remain averse to serious economic and political reforms that would open their societies and lift their citizens out of poverty. War, terrorism, and recession may periodically slow the pace of globalization, but the movement of people and money around the world continues unabated. The anxieties that accompany global integration—the fear that nations are surrendering their cultural, political, and economic sovereignty to shadowy outside forces—will not simply disappear.

It is paradoxical that Jews should find themselves swept up in the backlash against globalization, since Jews were the first truly globalized people. The survival of Jewish civilization—despite two thousand years without a state and the scattering of its diaspora to nearly every nation on earth—undermines the claim that globalization creates a homogenized world that destroys local cultures. Jews accommodated, and at times embraced, the foreign cultures they lived in without sacrificing their identity. The golden age of Jewish learning was not in ancient Israel but in medieval Spain, where Jewish religious study, literature, and poetry flourished under the influence of Muslim scholars.

Given its long experience adapting to new contingencies, the Jewish community is confronting global anti-Semitism with global solutions. For the first time in its history, the state of Israel convened an international conference of Jewish leaders from around the world with the explicit objective of coordinating a strategy to confront the resurgence of anti-Semitism. Jewish NGOs, such as the Simon Wiesenthal Center (SWC) and the Anti-Defamation League, tirelessly publicize incidents of anti-Semitism and lobby governments worldwide. Responding to evidence that the problem had reached crisis proportions, the Organization for Security and Cooperation in Europe last June convened an unprecedented conference on anti-Semitism attended by representatives of fifty-five governments. Protests from the Israeli government and Jewish organizations compelled the United Arab Emirates to shut down a think tank, the Zayed International Centre for Coordination and Follow-Up, which had hosted a Saudi professor who alleged Jews used human blood to prepare "holiday pastries" and had issued a press release declaring "The Zionists are the ones who killed the Jews of Europe."

Jewish organizations are also becoming more of a presence in the antiglobalization movement. Last year, there were fears that the Johannesburg-hosted World Summit on Sustainable Development would turn into a replay of the ill-fated 2001 U.N. World Conference Against Racism in Durban, where anti-Semitic rhetoric culminated in a draft resolution adopted by the NGO forum singling out Israel as guilty of "genocide." The SWC urged 180 ecological organizations planning to attend Johannesburg to ensure the conference stayed on message. The responses were largely positive, reflecting the frustration of many Third World NGOs who felt that the controversy at Durban had overshadowed vital issues on their agendas.

And then there are the Jews within the antiglobalization movement itself. Many are drawn to the movement for the same reason that Jews have always been disproportionately represented in campaigns for social justice: the principle of *tikkun olam* (repairing the world). It imparts a commitment to care not only for the Jewish community but for all of society. The antiglobalization activists who are Jewish carry a unique burden in that they are made to feel like strangers even though they are passionately devoted to safeguarding the environment, advocating human rights, and promoting economic equality. But rather than abandoning the movement, they seek to wrest the agenda from the extremists who would exclude them. A measure of their success could be seen in the final day of the 2003 World Social Forum in Porto Alegre. While street protesters waved their swastikas, a small group of Jewish and Palestinian peace activists organized a series of workshops, funded by local Jewish and Palestinian communities in Brazil. The result was a joint statement, read to 20,000 cheering activists, calling for "peace, justice, and sovereignty for our peoples," and a Palestinian state existing side by side with Israel.

Some Jewish groups sympathetic to many of the antiglobalization movement's goals have mistakenly chosen to remain on the outside. Jewish voices need to be raised when the shouting of the militants threatens to drown out other issues. And *tikkun olam* imparts a mandate to counter demagogues in the developing world who scapegoat Jews and Israel as an excuse to perpetuate systems that keep their nations mired in poverty. In that spirit, Rabbi Joseph Klein told his congregation at a synagogue in Michigan last June, "We will have to develop a strategy that allows us to participate in the effort to bring social equity and economic justice to all people, while at the same time distancing ourselves from these newest purveyors of the 'Protocols.'" He concluded his sermon by quoting from *Pirkei Avot,* the Jewish book of ethics: "It is not for you to complete the work, but neither are you free to withdraw from it."

Terrorism Chic

A CURRENT LAMENT: You can't even blow up Jews these days without being labeled an anti-Semite.

That isn't funny, is it? But maybe a touch of the *noir* is in order, given the twisted state of discourse on the Arab-Israeli tragedy.

"Of course, the suicide bombings are terrible," one hears, "but the Palestinians are in despair over the occupation." Except . . . except so much. Except it is the peace camp in Israel, not the occupation, that has been destroyed by the insane Intifada. Except that the suicide bombings are not intended to end the occupation. They are intended to end Israel.

Some of my fellow liberals don't want to know that. In a state of denial that would alarm their therapists, they tune out the words of the terrorists themselves: no peace until the last Jew is driven out, not just from the West Bank, but from all of the land. Writing in *The Guardian,* Naomi Klein apparently hasn't processed this message. "The primary, and familiar, fear that [Israeli Prime Minister] Sharon draws on . . . is the fear that Israel's neighbors want to drive the Jews into the sea." As if that fear has no rational foundation.

For others on the left, in the romantic thrall of terrorist chic, the long and complex history of the Jews and the Arabs is displaced by theater—a fictionally constructed drama in which the Jews are the assigned villains, the Palestinians the assigned heroes. No need to learn history, ancient or recent, or to look closely at current events. Sufficient to cheer on the good guys, the Palestinians, whose every crime is explained and forgiven, and hiss at the bad ones, the Jews, whose every claim is negated and despised.

Amid all this, the anti-Semitic beast stirs, an unpleasant surprise to Klein. She is shocked—shocked!—to find Jew-haters among her colleagues of the left. The silence of her comrades in the face of synagogue and cemetery attacks, the revival of mad Jewish-conspiracy theories—aren't we all in the same struggle? Whence this unseemly visitation of the old hatred?

She thinks she knows: contemplating the burned façade of her own synagogue, she disapproves of the sign the Jews have erected there: "Support Israel: now more than ever." She thinks the sign should read, "Thanks for nothing, Sharon."

I think Klein's fellow congregants had it right.

Klein is concerned that Jews be approved of. Sharon is concerned that Jews live. The message of the Israeli counteroffensive: You won't terrorize us out of our state, you won't kill Jews without paying a price. I'm with Sharon on that one.

I was in Israel some decades ago, when all the Arab states were declaring the Three No's: No Peace, No Compromise, No Recognition of Israel. The first Jewish settlers, taking advantage of their enemies' rejectionism, established themselves— I believed unwisely—at Hebron. The Palestinians have suffered, partly because of their own awful leaders, partly because of my own people's failings. Yasser Arafat drove the Israeli peacemakers out of office, first Peres, then Barak. He wanted a violent uprising. He got it—and he got Sharon.

As to anti-Semitism, whether fueled by anti-Israel hatred, covered up by it, or standing on its own, here's my take: Anti-Semitism isn't the Jews' problem. Anti-Semitism is the anti-

Semite's problem. If you don't like Jews, fine with me. It's a free country—like and dislike whom you please. Stay away from me, though, because I'm a Jew. If you become a menace to me or my fellows, I'll defend myself against you, by whatever means necessary. Otherwise, feel free to enjoy your ignorance and your stupidity in peace.

The same goes for the trendy hate-Israel brigade. If you're one of these brain-dead lunkheads protesting fabricated stories of Israeli "massacres" while excusing the very real and deliberate massacres of Jews, then the distinction you imagine to exist between yourself and the anti-Semite is a false one. If you grant people license to murder my people, if you deny my people's right to defend itself against murder, your distinction has no sane meaning at all.

Innocent Palestinian civilians tragically died in the battle for the terror center of Jenin. So, equally tragically, did Israeli soldiers who gave their own lives in fighting the terror network that sends forth the murderers. But if you fit the above definition, in your repugnant moral calculus the Palestinians suffered "genocide," the Jews got what they deserved. Whatever your motive—if you even comprehend your motive—you are a purveyor of the blood libel, a carrier of hate and ignorance, a disgrace and a burden to the very people you claim to care about.

Let's pray for something better for all of us.

FIAMMA NIRENSTEIN

How I Became an "Unconscious Fascist"

IN 1967 I WAS a young communist, like most Italian young-sters. Bored by my rebellious behavior my family sent me to a kibbutz in the upper Galilee, Neot Mordechai. I was quite satisfied there, the kibbutz used to give some money every month to the Vietcong. When the Six Day War began, Moshe Dayan spoke on the radio to announce it. I asked: "What is he saying?" and the comrades of Neot answered: *"Shtuyot,"* silly things. During the war I took children to shelters; I dug trenches, and learned some simple shooting and acts of self-defense. We continued working in the orchards, but were quick to identify the incoming MiG-im and the outgoing Mirage-im, chasing one another in the sky of the Golan Heights.

When I went back to Italy, some of my fellow students stared at me as somebody new, an enemy, a wicked person who would soon become an imperialist. My life was about to change. I didn't yet know that, because I simply thought that Israel rightly won a war after having been assaulted with an incredible number of harassments. But I soon noticed that I had lost the innocence of the good Jew, of the very special Jew-ish friend, their Jew: I was now connected with the Jews of the State of Israel, and slowly I was put out of the dodecaphonic, psychoanalytic, Bob Dylan, Woody Allen, Isaac Bashevis Singer,

Philip Roth, Freud shtetl, the coterie that sanctified my Judaism in left-wing eyes.

I have tried for a long time to bring back that sanctification, and they tried to give it back to me, because we desperately needed each other, the Left and the Jews. But today's anti-Semitism has overwhelmed any good intention.

Throughout the years, even people that, like me, who had signed petitions asking the IDF to withdraw from Lebanon, became an "unconscious fascist" as a reader of mine wrote me in a letter filled with insults. In one book it was simply written that I was "a passionate woman that fell in love with Israel, confusing Jerusalem with Florence." One Palestinian told me that if I see things so differently from the majority, this plainly means that my brain doesn't work too well. Also, I've been called a cruel and insensitive human rights denier who doesn't care about Palestinian children's lives.

A very famous Israeli writer told me on the phone a couple of months ago: "You really have become a right-winger." What? Right-winger? Me? An old feminist human rights activist, even a communist when I was young? Only because I described the Arab-Israeli conflict as accurately as I could and because sometimes I identified with a country continuously attacked by terror, I became a right-winger? In the contemporary world, the world of human rights, when you call a person a right-winger, this is the first step toward his or her delegitimization.

The Left blessed the Jews as the victim "par excellence," always a great partner in the struggle for the rights of the weak against the wicked. In return for being coddled, published, filmed, considered artists, intellectuals, and moral judges, Jews, even during the Soviet anti-Semitic persecutions, gave the Left moral support and invited it to cry with them at Holocaust memorials. Today the game is clearly over. The Left has proved itself the real cradle of contemporary anti-Semitism.

When I speak about anti-Semitism, I'm not speaking of

legitimate criticism of the State of Israel. I am speaking of pure anti-Semitism: criminalization, stereotypes, specific and generic lies which have fluctuated between lies about the Jews (conspiring, bloodthirsty, dominating the world) to lies about Israel (conspiring, ruthlessly violent), starting most widely since the beginning of the second Intifada in September 2000, and becoming more and more ferocious since Operation Chomat Magen ("Defensive Shield"), when the IDF reentered Palestinian cities in response to terrorism.

The basic idea of anti-Semitism, today as always, is that Jews have a perverted soul that makes them unfit, as a morally inferior people, to be regular members of the human family. Today, this *Untermensch* ideology has shifted to the Jewish state: a separate, unequal, basically evil stranger whose national existence is slowly but surely emptied and deprived of justification. Israel, as the classic evil Jew, according to contemporary anti-Semitism, doesn't have a birthright, but exists with its "original sin" perpetrated against the Palestinians. Israel's heroic history has become a history of arrogance.

Nowadays, its narrative focuses much more on the Deir Yassin massacre than on the creation and defense of Kibbutz Degania; it focuses more and more on the suffering of the Palestinian refugees than on the surprise of seeing five armies in 1948 denying Israel's right to exist just after being established by the United Nations; much more on the Jewish underground resistance organizations, the Lechi and the Irgun, than on the heroic battle along the way to Jerusalem. The caricature of the evil Jew is transformed to the caricature of the evil state. And now the traditional hook-nosed Jew bears a gun and kills Arab children with pleasure.

On the front pages of European newspapers Sharon munches Palestinian children and little Jesuses in cradles are threatened by Israeli soldiers. This new anti-Semitism has materialized in unprecedented physical violence toward Jewish persons and symbols, coming from organizations officially devoted to human rights. Its peak occurred at the United Nations summit in Durban, when anti-Semitism officially became the banner of the new secular religion of human rights and Israel and Jews became its official enemy.

Jews, and the international community in general, have been caught unaware, and have failed to denounce the new trend of anti-Semitism. Nobody is scandalized when Israel is accused daily, without explanation, of excessive violence, of atrocities, of cruelty. Everybody is tormented about the necessity of painful attacks against terrorist nests, often located among families and children. Still, every country has the right to defend itself. Only the Jews in history have been denied the right of self-defense, and so it is today.

Why is the war on terrorism often looked upon as a strategic problem that the world still must solve (look at the U.S. war against Afghanistan and Iraq) and Israel is treated like a guilty defendant for fighting it? Is it not anti-Semitism when you act as if Jews must die quietly? Why is Israel officially accused by the human rights commission in Geneva of violating human rights, while China, Libya, Sudan, have never ever been accused? Why has Israel been denied a fixed place in regional groups in the UN while Syria sits in the Security Council? Why can everybody join a war against Iraq except Israel, despite the fact that Saddam has always threatened Israel with complete destruction? When sovereign states and organizations threaten death to Israel, why does nobody raise the question at the UN? Has Italy been threatened by France or Spain like those Iranian leaders who openly say that they will destroy Israel with an atomic bomb? And what is said when a large part of the world newspapers, TV, radio, and school textbooks recommend kicking the Jews out of Israel and killing them all over the world using terrorist bombers? The international community doesn't consider this a problem. Israel is an "Unterstate," denied the basic rights of every other state, to exist in honor and peace. The Jewish state is not equal.

Like the mythical Medusa, this new anti-Semitism has a face that petrifies anyone who looks at it. People don't want to admit it, don't even want to name it, because doing so reveals both the identity of its perpetrators and its object. Even Jews don't want to call an anti-Semite by his name, fearing disruption of old alliances. Because the Left has a precise idea of what a Jew must be, when Jews don't match its prescription, they ask: How do you dare being different from the Jew I ordered you to be? Fighting against terrorism? Electing Sharon? Are you crazy? And here the answer of Jews and Israelis is the same. We are still very shy, very concerned about your affection. So, instead of requesting that Israel become an equal nation and that Jews become equal citizens in the world, we prefer standing with you shoulder to shoulder, even when you have come out with hundreds, thousands, of anti-Semitic statements. We prefer to stand with you at Holocaust memorials cursing old anti-Semitism while you accuse Israel, and therefore the Jews, of being racist killers.

Let's take a well-known example: A famous Italian journalist, the former director of *Corriere della Sera,* was named president of RAI, which is a very important job. RAI is an empire that shapes Italian public opinion and manages billions of dollars. The nominee's last name, Mieli, is Jewish.

Mieli is a widely appreciated journalist and historian who enjoys enormous and well-deserved prestige. When he was appointed, the same night, the walls of RAI headquarters were filled with graffiti.

RAI means Radio Televisione Italiana—Italian Radio and Television. The graffiti authors wrote the word *raus* (get out!) over it. They drew a Star of David over the *A* of the word RAI, and transformed the acronym to "Radio Televisione Israeliana"—Israeli Radio and Television. The phrase is a perfect cross-section of what we are talking about: *Raus* and the use of the Star of David are the classic signs of traditional anti-Semitic contempt and hate, and the words "Radio Televisione Israeliana," putting Israel in the center of the picture, is a clear indication of how Israel is the focus of the left-wing anti-Semitic hate today.

Surprisingly, or perhaps predictably, such a blatant expression of anti-Semitism caused very little reaction from both the Italian authorities and the Italian Jewish community. The aggression and threat to such a famous intellectual gave rise to weak exclamations in a subdued tone and was treated like a minor issue in a debate centered on more relevant ones, such as the management of RAI and its political meaning.

Another meaningful episode: a group of professors at Ca Foscari University, the prestigious Venetian institution, signed a petition calling for a boycott of Israeli professors and researchers. The content of the document is totally irrelevant, but the reaction it provoked among the Jewish community is very interesting.

One prominent Venetian Jew, when asked for his opinion, said: "They're making a serious mistake. Those professors don't realize that they are reinforcing Sharon's policy with their boycott."

Such an absurd reaction is the clear proof of the failure, within the Jewish world, to understand this totally new type of anti-Semitism that focuses on the State of Israel. Another document, this time a letter by a group of professors at the University of Bologna "to their Jewish friends," was published with a very large number of signatures.

Here is an excerpt: "We have always considered the Jewish people an intelligent and sensitive one because they have been selected [that's right, selected!] by the suffering of persecution and humiliation. We have school friends and some Jewish students whom we have helped and educated, taking them to high academic levels, and today many of them teach in Israeli universities. We are writing because we feel that our love and appreciation for you is being transformed into a burning rage . . . we think that many people, also outside the university, feel the same. You have to realize that what was done to you in the past, you are now doing to the Palestinians . . . if you continue on this path, hatred for you will grow throughout the world."

The letter is an excellent summary of all the characteristics of the new anti-Semitism. There is the pre-Zionist definition of the Jewish people as one that suffers, has to suffer by nature, a people bound to bear the worst persecutions without even lifting a finger, and is, therefore, worthy of compassion and solidarity.

And there is the well-established, democratic, militarily powerful, and economically prospering State of Israel, which is the antithesis of this stereotype. The "new Jew" that tries not to suffer, and that, above all, can and wants to defend himself, immediately loses all his charm in the eyes of the Left.

But it was different before the map of the Middle East was painted in red by the Cold War and Israel was declared the long hand of American Imperialism. The rising newborn Israel, until the 1967 war, was built on an ideology that allowed and even obliged the Left to be proud of the Jews and the Jews to be proud of the Left, even when Israelis were fighting and winning hard wars.

The Jews that survived Nazi-Fascist persecution, the persecution of the Right, created a socialist state inspired by the values of the Left, work and collectivism, and by doing so, again sanctified the Left as the shelter of the victims.

In exchange for this, the Jews were granted legitimization. But in fact, the Jews were enormously important for the Left. The people of Israel were a living accusation of the anti-Semitism that marked the Holocaust, the Nazi-Fascist anti-Semitism; and now they were building collective farms and an omnipotent trade union! To some degree, this absolved Stalinist anti-Semitism, or gave it a much smaller importance than it really had. The Jews became indispensable for the Left: look at the passionate and paternalistic tone of the Bologna professors, as they seem to plead: "Come back, our dear Jews. Be ours again. Let us curse Israel together and then take a trip together to the Holocaust memorials."

But the contradiction has become even ontologically unbearable: How can you cry with the survivors for Jews killed by Nazis when the living Jews are accused to be Nazis themselves? Somebody on a European radio program said that after the diffusion of the images of Muhammed al Dura, Europe could finally forget the famous picture of the boy in the Warsaw ghetto with his hands raised. The meaning of this statement, often repeated in other forms, is obliteration of the Holocaust through the overlapping of Israel and Nazism, namely racism, genocide, ruthless elimination of civilians, women and children, an utterly unwarranted eruption of cruelty and the most brutal instincts. It means pretending to believe blindly, without investigation, the Palestinian version of a highly disputed episode and of many, many others; it means taking for granted the "atrocities" that the Palestinian spokespersons always talk about, and ignoring every proof or fact that doesn't serve this position.

Well, people can, and always did, take for granted the prejudices about Jews; everyone is free to think whatever he wants. But we, the Jews, must reserve our moral right to hold such people accountable: in our eyes, they will plainly be anti-Semites. We will have to say to them: when you lie or use prejudices and stereotypes about Israel and the Jews, you are an anti-Semite and I'll fight you.

We must not be intimidated by the professors who tell us in their letter: "We have helped you poor Jews lacking everything, a non-existent nation, in the Diaspora and in Israel, to keep you alive. Without us you are nothing. And therefore be careful: if you continue with your treachery we'll annihilate you. You don't exist if you don't know your place, and your place is nowhere." They'll say that it is a legitimate criticism about the State of Israel. The truth is that a big part of these criticisms are simply lies, just as when Suha Arafat claimed that Israel poisoned Palestinian waters, or when Arafat claimed that Israel uses depleted uranium against the Palestinian people, and that Israeli women soldiers show up naked in front of the Palestinian warriors to confuse them. It's just the same as when you say that the Israeli Army purposely shoots children or journalists.

As a journalist, I must mention the significant contribution of the mass media to this new anti-Semitism. Since the beginning of the Intifada, freedom-fighter journalists, grown in the Guevara and Fedayeen campus, have given the Israeli-Palestinian conflict some of the most biased coverage in the history of journalism. Here are the main problems that led to distorted reporting of the Intifada:

1. Lack of historic depth in attributing responsibility for its outbreak. In other words, failure to repeat the story of the Israeli offer of a Palestinian state and of Arafat's refusal, which, in essence, is a refusal to accept Israel as a Jewish state, and which continues the almost seventy-year-old Arab rejection of partition of the land of Israel between Arabs and Jews as recommended by the British in 1936, decided by the UN in 1947, and always accepted by the Jewish representatives.

2. Failure, right from the very first clashes at the checkpoints, to assign responsibility for the first deaths to the fact that, unlike in the first Intifada, in the second the IDF faced armed fighters hiding in the midst of the unarmed crowd.

3. Failure to recognize the enormous influence of the cultural pressure on the Palestinians from the systematic education in Palestinian schools and mass media, vilifying

Jews and Israelis and idealizing terrorist acts of murder and mayhem.

4. Describing the death of Palestinian children without identifying the circumstances in which they occurred. The equating of civilian losses of Israelis with those of the Palestinians, as if terrorism and war against it were the same thing, and as if intentional killing was the same as a deplored consequence of a difficult and new type of fight.

5. Using Palestinian sources to certify events, as if Palestinian sources were the most reliable. I am thinking of Jenin, of the unconfirmed reports that passed to printed pages or TV screens as absolute truth. In contrast, Israeli sources, which are very often reliable, are seen as subservient, prejudiced, and unworthy of attention, despite the country's aggressive free and open journalism, and the equally determined criticism of government policies by opposition parties, conscientious objectors, commentators, and journalists.

6. Manipulation of the order in which the news is given and of the news itself. The headlines give the number of Palestinians killed or wounded in most articles, at least in Europe, before describing the gunfights and their causes, and linger on the age and family stories of the terrorists. The purposes of the IDF actions, such as capturing terrorists, destroying arms factories or hiding places and bases for attacks against Israel, are rarely mentioned. On the contrary, Israel's operations are often described as completely uncalled for, bizarre, wicked, and useless.

7. Manipulation of language, taking advantage of the great confusion about the definition of "terrorism" and "terrorist." This too is an old issue, connected to the concept of freedom fighter, so dear to my generation.

A few days ago, at a checkpoint, I was doing some interviews. It soon became clear to me that the use of the word "terrorist" sounded to each one of my Palestinian interlocutors a capital political and semantic sin. The press has learned this very well: the occupation is the cause of everything, terrorism is called resistance and does not exist per se. Terrorists who kill women and children are called militants, or fighters. An act of terrorism is often "a fire clash," even when only babies and old men are shot inside their cars on a highway. It is also interesting to note that a young *shahid* is a cause of deep pride for the Palestinian struggle, but if you ask how a child of twelve can be sent to die and why young children are indoctrinated to do such acts, the answer is: "Come on, a child can't be a terrorist. How can you call a twelve-year-old boy a terrorist?"

This is perhaps the most crucial point: Given the fact that there is a ferocious debate on the definition of terrorism, it is widely accepted that terrorism is a way of fighting. This is a semantic and even substantial gift of the new anti-Semitism, where it is natural for a Jew to be dead. Namely, intentionally targeting civilians to cause fear and disrupt the morale of Israel is not a moral sin. It doesn't raise world indignation, and if it does, it hides in its folds some or much sympathy for the terrorist aggressor. What the European press fails to or doesn't want to understand is that Terror is a condemnable and forbidden way of fighting, regardless of the specific political goal it tries to achieve.

8.   The media have promoted the extravagant concept that the settlers, including women and children, are not real human beings. They present settlers as pawns in a dangerous game they choose to play. Their deaths are almost natural and logical events. In a way, they asked for it.

On the other hand, when a Hamas commander is killed, even though he obviously "asked for it," an ethical, philosophical debate arises, on the perfidy of extrajudicial death sentences.

This would certainly be a licit debate, were it not for the grotesque double standard on which the worldwide press bases it.

9.   Not to go overlooked is that censorship and corruption within the Palestinian Authority and the physical elimination of its political enemies are hardly ever covered.

The points listed above all point in one direction: Durban.

Here, the human rights movements that we will later find on the streets demonstrating against the war in Iraq chose Israel as their primary target and enemy. This choice constitutes a great success for Palestinian propaganda, but also a very serious signal of weakness from the movements themselves. The ideologically and politically cornered Left chose to adopt as universal a very controversial and sectarian struggle, marked heavily by terrorism. A Left incapable of confronting the capitalist globalization system decided to appoint the State of Israel as its main target. In a word, the Left decided to make Israel pay for what they think America should pay. Isn't this real cowardice?

In addition, there is the issue of how the UN and its outrageous policy have helped this process, and how Europe has coddled it because of its ancient sense of guilt toward Israel and its hate for the United States, Israel's friend and ally. This matter alone deserves an entire book.

Denouncing this new human rights anti-Semitism is psychologically a terribly arduous task for Israel and for Diaspora Jews.

It is even more difficult because between the Jews and the Left there is a divorce that the latter does not want. The Left wants to continue being considered the paladin of good Jews. It pretends to continue mourning the Jews killed in the Holocaust, crying together with the Jews shoulder to shoulder. And it does so because this gives it the moral authorization to go a second later and speak of the "atrocities" of Israel. After writing about the "atrocities" of Israel, the good European leftist will talk to you with vivacity about the fascinating shtetl culture and the sweetness of Moroccan Jewish dishes.

Until we break the silence, we, the Jews, give them the authorization to deny us the right to a nation of our own, and defend its people from unprecedented anti-Semitism.

Just as it curses Israel, the Left of human rights, of pacifism, of protest against the death penalty or war or racial and gender discrimination, also praises suicide terrorists and the caricatures of Sharon worthy of *Der Stürmer*. And none of its people will ever sit as a human shield in an Israeli coffee house or in a Jerusalem bus.

Still, this new anti-Semitism has a peculiar characteristic: It allows conversion. This kind of anti-Semitism, unlike Nazi anti-Semitism, is more like the older theological anti-Semitism, for it gives the Jews the option to renounce the devil (Israel, or sometimes Sharon). Whoever declares a sense of revulsion toward Israel's conduct is allowed to set foot again in the civil society, the one of common sense, civilized conversation, groups of good people full of goodwill that fight for human rights.

If we want to obtain something, if we decide that it is about time to fight, we must renounce "liberal" imposters. We have to know how to say that the free press is a failure when it lies, and that it does lie. We have to say that all human rights are violated when a people is denied the right of self-defense, and that right is denied to Israel. Human rights are also violated when a nation is subjected to systematic defamation and made a legitimate target for terrorists. We have to stop what we have accepted since the day the state was born, namely, that Israel be viewed as a different state in the international community.

Another very important point is that of all the parameters of anti-Semitism now used, one is the confusion between "Israeli" and "Jew." Supposedly, it is wrong to insinuate that the Jews act in the interests of the State of Israel and not their own state. The more a country confuses the two terms, the more anti-Semitic it is considered, and therefore one would imagine that the Jews combat this prejudice.

This is a serious conceptual error. Since the State of Israel, and along with it Jews, have been made the objects of the worst kind of prejudice, Jews everywhere should consider their being identified with Israel a virtue and honor.

They should assert that identification with pride.

If Israel is, and it is indeed, the focal point of anti-Semitic attacks, our attention must be concentrated there. We must measure the moral character of the person we are speaking to on that basis: if you lie about Israel, if you cover it with bias, you are an anti-Semite. If you're prejudiced against Israel, then, you're against the Jews.

This doesn't mean criticizing Israel and its policies is forbidden. However, very little of what we hear about Israel has to do with lucid criticism. Prejudice and bias, not Sharon's personality, is the major reason for criticism. The self-defined critics are not the pious interlocutors for the Jews that they pretend to be. So we must tell them: From now on you cannot use the human rights passport for free; you cannot use false stereotypes. You must demonstrate what you assert: that the army ruthlessly storms poor Arab villages that have nothing to do with terrorism; that it shoots children on purpose; that it kills journalists with pleasure. You cannot? You called Jenin a slaughter? Then you are an anti-Semite, just like the old anti-Semites you pretend to hate. You have to convince me that you are not an anti-Semite, now that we know that you do not condemn terrorism, that you have never said a word against the contemporary caricatures of hooked-nosed Jews with a bag of dollars in one hand and a machine gun in the other.

Israel is in shock over the new anti-Semitism. All the theories that claimed classic anti-Semitism would abate with the creation of the State of Israel and that, in the long run, it would be extinguished have been destroyed. Furthermore, Israel has actually become the sum of all the evil, the proof that the Protocols and the blood libels were right. The Palestinians are turned into Jesus, crucified; the war in Iraq or in Afghanistan waged by the United States is part of the Jewish plan of domination. Jews all over the world are threatened, beaten, even killed to pay the price of Israel's existence.

Israel and the Jews have today only one certainty: Now that Jews have their own means of defense, a new Holocaust is no longer possible. Still we have to pass from the idea of our possible physical elimination to that of possible moral elimination. The only way to face this threat is to fight fearlessly, on our own terrain, using all the historic and ethical weapons that Israel possesses. No shame, no fear, and no sense of guilt.

Israel has the chance to prove itself for what it really is: the outpost of the fight against terrorism and the defense of democracy. That is no small thing. But we the Jews pose as victims and hide from this chance because using it puts us in conflict with our ancient sponsors and their legitimization. We have to realize that legitimization is really in our own hands and we never used it.

The watchword of the Jews should be "Jewish pride," in the sense of pride in our history and national identity, wherever we are.

Jewish pride means that we have to claim the unique identity of the Jewish people and its right to exist. We must act as though it has never been acknowledged, because today, once again, it no longer is. In defending this identity we have to be, as Hillel Halkin says, as tough as can be and as liberal as no one else is.

No left and no right. We won't give the Left the power to decide where we stand. We will decide our alliances by ourselves, according to the actual position of our potential partners.

PART SEVEN

THE DEICIDE
ACCUSATION

NAT HENTOFF

Who Did Kill Christ?

L ENNY BRUCE USED TO TELL, in his act, about a Jew who
was weary not only of being called a Christ killer but of
occasionally being punched in the mouth by disciples of the
Prince of Peace. Finally, this beleaguered Jew put a note in his
cellar, where it could easily be found. He wanted to absolve all
other Jews. It said: "I did it. Morty."

This question of the Jews' responsibility for the crucifixion has considerable resonance for me because I grew up in
Boston, then the most anti-Semitic city in the country, and lost
some teeth after being punched in the mouth by young hooligans whose after-dark sport was invading our ghetto and bash-
ing Jews to avenge that deicide.

My mother told me that in the Old Country, when she
was a girl and word spread that the cossacks were coming,
her mother popped her into the oven, which fortunately was
not lit.

Therefore, I have become much interested in a story out of
Washington about a Jewish conservative journalist, Evan Gahr,
who has left three leading conservative institutions after charging Paul Weyrich with anti-Semitism. Weyrich, a founder of the
contemporary conservative movement, was at one point its
most successful fundraiser.

Thomas Edsall broke the story in the April 21 *Washington Post*. He cited an April 13 Paul Weyrich commentary, "Indeed He Is Risen!" on Weyrich's Free Congress Foundation's Web site.

The Weyrich statement, e-mailed to supporters, said, "Christ was crucified by the Jews who had wanted a temporal ruler to rescue them from the oppressive Roman authorities. Instead God sent them a spiritual leader to rescue them from their sins and despite the fact that Jesus Christ, the Son of God, performed incredible miracles, even raised people from the dead, He was not what the Jews had expected so they considered him a threat. Thus He was put to death."

In his article, Edsall quoted Evan Gahr, who had criticized Weyrich on the *American Spectator* Web site. Gahr called Weyrich "a demented anti-Semite" for that resurrection of Jews as Christ killers.

In Edsall's *Washington Post* article, there was further reaction from Marc Stern, a constitutional lawyer at the American Jewish Congress, whom I consult on establishment-clause cases, and Eugene Fisher, director of Catholic-Jewish relations for the National Conference of Catholic Bishops.

Stern noted that, through the centuries, the "blood libel" that we Jews were the ones who killed Christ had ignited pogroms.

And Fisher declared that Weyrich's accusation "is exactly the type of collective guilt on the Jewish people that the Second Vatican Council specifically condemned in the declaration *Nostra Aetate,* October 28, 1965." He added that last year, while in Israel, Pope John Paul II made clear that the Catholic Church is "deeply saddened by the hatred, acts of persecution, and displays of anti-Semitism directed against the Jews."

In the May 15 *Wall Street Journal,* David Novak, who teaches Jewish studies at the University of Toronto, noted that Weyrich is a deacon in the Catholic Church, which "has officially repudiated the old charge that the Jews, even the Jews of today, are responsible for Christ's death."

Novak added that "the greatest modern Christian theologian, Karl Barth," emphasized that "Jesus' death on the cross is atonement for the sins of all humans, even the sins of his followers. Thus, for Christians to deny their complicity in the death of Jesus, by shifting sole blame to the Jews, is to deny their own need for atonement."

And the head of the Anti-Defamation League, my friend Abe Foxman, with whom I often debate—but not this time—said of Paul Weyrich's assertion that "such destructive myths stated as fact may well reinforce the bigotry of the ignorant and uninformed, potentially leading to hateful anti-Semitic acts."

Like the removal of my teeth. But I do not call that a hate crime. Thirty days for assault would have been fine. No extra prison time.

On his Free Congress Web site, Paul Weyrich wrote on April 24 that Evan Gahr's charge "is absolutely amazing to me and shows how far down the road to political correctness we have come in our society." (And this response shows that one conservative can accuse another of political correctness.)

About his indictment of the Jews, Weyrich said, "This is historical fact. Are we now to be forbidden to mention historical fact? . . . I was merely quoting Scripture. Scripture is truth. And the truth shall set you free."

Evan Gahr's accurate description of what Weyrich wrote in "Indeed He Is Risen!" has set him free of all his writing and research assignments at three conservative organizations. Gahr has been removed from the list of contributing writers at the American Enterprise Institute's magazine and barred from using its office facilities. The Hudson Institute, where Gahr had been a senior fellow, fired him.

Gahr, who had been writing for David Horowitz's *Front-Page* [magazine] Web site, has also been fired by that very paladin of free speech, who so vigorously attacked those college newspaper editors who refused to run the Horowitz ad denouncing reparations for slavery.*

I have read the explanations these conservative warriors have given for letting Gahr go, and I have talked with the Hudson Institute. They all claim that Gahr was fired for other reasons. He does not believe this, nor do I. My congratulations to Linda Chavez, head of the Center for Equal Opportunity, who is not afraid of free speech and has brought in Gahr as an adjunct scholar.

If any of the conservative magazines or high-profile conservative intellectuals have spoken up for him, I haven't seen it. Stanley Crouch wrote about Gahr and Weyrich in the May 4 *Daily News*. But Stanley is not a conservative. He's part of the world of jazz, where free expression is the lodestar.

As Stanley writes: "Dissension in the ranks is a crime among hard-core ideologues, from far right to the far left."

---

*Gahr subsequently sent an e-mail to David Horowitz (who has denied the attack on Weyrich was the reason Gahr is gone from *FrontPage*), in which Gahr states: "I know full well that Weyrich has never advocated, suggested or implied that anybody should harm Jews."

PETER J. BOYER

The Jesus War: Mel Gibson's Obsession

O NE RAINY WEDNESDAY AFTERNOON this summer, I made
my way to the Sony Building, on Fifty-fifth Street and
Madison Avenue, where, through the accommodation of a
friend in the entertainment business, I attended a private
screening of *The Passion*, Mel Gibson's unfinished film about
the final hours and Crucifixion of Jesus of Nazareth. I didn't
know quite what to expect. I'd heard that some people had
been so moved by the film that they openly wept, and that
others were rendered speechless. I knew, too, that a group of
religion scholars and Jewish activists had condemned Gibson
and his film as dangerous and anti-Semitic, based upon their
reading of a *Passion* screenplay. That afternoon, Gibson, wearing jeans, a Hawaiian shirt, and a pair of leather clogs, perched
on a table at the front of the room and explained that he was
still editing the film, and that the version we were about to see
was quite rough. There were a couple of dozen people in the
small screening room, two or three of them in clerical attire.
Gibson joked a bit, then said, "Let's get started." He took a
place in the back row as the lights dimmed.

The dark screen filled with the printed words of prophecy
from the Old Testament Book of Isaiah, written four hundred
years before Christ: "He was wounded for our transgressions;

he was crushed for our iniquities. By his stripes we are healed."
There was, in the two hours that followed, much wounding
and crushing, and, when the lights came back up, there was
some wiping away of tears. I found the film riveting and quite
disturbing, and I was struck by an insistent memory from a
Jesus movie from my childhood, George Stevens's *The Greatest
Story Ever Told*. In the final scene, the risen Jesus, wispily played
by Max von Sydow in a pageboy haircut, levitates in the clouds
as a heavenly choir sings the "Hallelujah Chorus." Gibson had
undertaken *The Passion* with the avowed purpose of contra-
vening the overwrought piety of such conventions, and in that,
certainly, he had succeeded. Gibson's resurrected Christ rises
in the tomb with a steely glare, and then strides purposefully
into the light, to the insistent beat of martial drums. With that,
Gibson's Passion story, and perhaps even, the controversy that
has attended it, became clear. Gibson had once said that he
wasn't interested in making a religious movie, and in *The Passion* he hadn't. He was making a war movie.

Ten days later, I arrived at Gibson's Icon Productions,
which is housed in an unremarkable office building on Wilshire
Boulevard in Santa Monica, across from a fast-food Mexican
restaurant. Nothing about the place hints of show business
until the elevator opens onto an entry wall covered with large
movie posters from Icon's pictures (*What Women Want, Maver-
ick*). As I announced myself to a young woman at the reception
desk, the telephone rang. It was the producer Harvey Weinstein. "He'll get back to you," the receptionist said, and I was es-
corted down a winding corridor to the editing room, where
Gibson sat on the far end of a sofa, facing an Avid digital editing console. A white legal pad rested on his lap, containing
notes for possible editing changes he'd jotted down during his
last screening of the film. Gibson's editor, John Wright, was
manipulating the images of Pontius Pilate with a mouse and a
keyboard as Pilate pronounced judgment upon Jesus.

Gibson's story line reflects the basic Christian narrative of Christ's Passion, as it is laid out collectively in the Gospels of Matthew, Mark, Luke, and John. Jesus of Nazareth is a Jewish carpenter in Roman-controlled Palestine, who preaches a message of love and forgiveness, with an increasingly messianic subtext. During the Passover season, he enters the Holy City of Jerusalem, where he is welcomed by adoring crowds who hail him as the long-promised Messiah, bringing deliverance and a new kingdom. But Jesus is considered dangerous by the Jewish high priests, who conspire to arrest and try him, and then deliver him to the Roman prefect Pilate for execution, on the ground of treason against Rome. Jesus knows that his fate is the Cross, and briefly wishes to avoid it ("Oh, my Father, if it be possible, let this cup pass from me"); but he also knows that God, his father, sent him into the world for the very purpose of dying, as a sacrifice for the redemption of all mankind.

Gibson has said that his script for *The Passion* was the New Testament, and that the film was directed by the Holy Ghost. Movie audiences, though, will doubtless see in it the hand of the man who directed *Braveheart.* On one level, Gibson, who has been working on the film for more than a year, perceives the Passion as a heroic action story, and the principal quality he hoped to instill in it was the power of realism. "I wanted to bring you there," he says, "and I wanted to be true to the Gospels. That has never been done."

In that regard, Gibson made two key decisions. He cast the film without brand-name movie stars, in order to avoid the illusion-puncturing celebrity recognition that afflcted the old epics. Jesus is played by James Caviezel, whose biggest prior role was in *The Count of Monte Cristo,* and Monica Bellucci, of *The Matrix Reloaded* (and rapidly becoming better known), is Mary Magdalene. Gibson also had the actors' lines translated into Aramaic (the vernacular of ancient Palestine), Hebrew, and Latin. His purpose, he says, was not only to achieve authenticity but also to avoid the audience disconnect that might result from hearing two-thousand-year-old Biblical characters speaking perfect modern (or even King James') English. He initially didn't intend to have subtitles, either. "I've always wanted to make a Viking movie," Gibson, who is forty-seven, explains. "You've got Alfred the Great in Wessex, this English king, saying, 'All the Danes are coming up the river here, we've got to defend ourselves.' And these guys hop off the boats and they're all hairy and they're scary and they've got axes, and some of them are berserkers and they're doing flips and twirls and they just wanna rape and kill, you know? But if they start coming out with 'I want to die with a sword in my hand' and 'Oh, fair maiden,' that would be like—you know, you don't believe them. If they come out with low, guttural German, they are frightening. They are terrifying. They're like demons from the sea. So that's what the language thing did for me. It took something away from you—you had to depend upon the image."

It is not surprising, perhaps, that in the service of realism the signal trait of *The Passion* is its relentless violence. When Gibson directed the Oscar-winning 1995 film *Braveheart*, about the folkloric Scots hero William Wallace, he reshot only one scene—and that was in order to more graphically depict the image of enemy horses impaling themselves upon sharpened wooden stakes. Violence is Gibson's natural film language, and his Jesus is unsparingly pummeled, flayed, kicked, and otherwise smitten from first to last. After his arrest in the Garden of Gethsemane by Jewish temple guards, Jesus is dragged in shackles to the high priests. By the time he arrives, he has been beaten, knocked down, and thrown off a bridge. His right eye is swollen shut. ("I didn't want to see Jesus looking really pretty," Gibson said. "I wanted to mess up one of his eyes, destroy it.")

When the Romans take over, things get worse. Gibson studied the details of Roman crucifixion, reading, among other sources, a famous clinical investigation of the practice, "On the Physical Death of Jesus Christ," published in *The Journal of the American Medical Association* in 1986. That study explained why crucifixion inspired the word "excruciating": "Scourging produced deep stripe-like lacerations and appreciable blood loss, and it probably set the stage for hypovolemic shock. . . . The major pathophysiologic effect of crucifixion was an interference with normal respiration." Gibson seems to have relied heavily upon this study, which describes the Roman tools of punishment ("The usual instrument was a short whip . . . with several single or braided leather thongs of variable lengths, in which small iron balls or sharp pieces of sheep bones were tied at intervals"), the choreography of the infliction ("The man was stripped of his clothing, and his hands were tied to an upright post [and] the back, buttocks, and legs were flogged either by two soldiers . . . or by one who alternated positions"), and its severity (scourging "was intended to weaken the victim to a state just short of collapse or death"). All these elements are directly reflected in Gibson's film.

Gibson has been told by friendly audiences that *The Passion* is several measures too violent, that seeing Jesus subjected to such protracted scenes of brutality will have a numbing effect upon audiences, detaching them from Christ's pain. Gibson acknowledges that possibility, but then adds that the event in question "was pretty nasty." As I watched Gibson work on his film in the editing room, I noticed that the picture had changed since I'd seen it in New York. He said that it was shorter, partly because he had trimmed some of the violent scenes (but not by much). He called the editing process "the final rewrite" of the picture, but he seemed not altogether pleased by some of the cuts he had made, including one he made before the New York screening. The antagonist in Gibson's vision is plainly the Jewish high priest Caiaphas, played by an Italian actor who can seem a bit of a ham as he cajoles the ambivalent Pilate into executing Jesus. Finally, an exasperated Pilate relents and condemns the prisoner, but, according to the Gospel of Matthew, he first makes a show of his own guiltlessness by publicly washing his hands. In Matthew, that gesture is followed by a shout from the crowd: "His blood be on us, and on our children." This passage, which is depicted only in Matthew, is one of the sources of the notion of collective Jewish guilt for the death of Jesus. Gibson shot the scene, but with Caiaphas alone calling the curse down. Wright, Gibson's editor, strongly objected to including even that version. "I just think you're asking for trouble if you leave it in," he said. "For people who are undecided about the film, that would be the thing that turned them against it."

Gibson yielded, but he has had some regrets. "I wanted it in," he says. "My brother said I was wimping out if I didn't include it. It happened; it was said. But, man, if I included that in there, they'd be coming after me at my house, they'd come kill me."

He was referring to his critics, activists at such organizations as the Anti-Defamation League and the Simon Wiesenthal Center, as well as some academics, who worry that Gibson will draw too much upon a literal reading of the Gospels, and not enough upon contemporary scholarship that seeks to distance Jews from culpability in the Crucifixion. Gibson says that some of his friends asked him whether he's making an anti-Jewish movie; he's heard that someone from one of his hangouts, the Grand Havana Room, a Beverly Hills smoking club, said that he'd spit on him if he ever came in again. When he has shown the film to associates in the industry, he feels that they are looking for anti-Semitism. He says that is one of the reasons he finally decided to include subtitles in the picture, to make it clear that some of the Jews portrayed in the film are sympathetic figures. "You've just got to have them," he says. "I mean, I didn't think so, but so many people say things to me like 'Why aren't there more sympathetic Jews in the crowd?'

Well, they're there! But you've got to really point it out to them, and subtitles can do that." He goes on, "It's just amazing to me how one-eyed some people are about this thing. I mean, it's like a veil comes down and they just can't see it. For instance, did you know that one of the priests helps take his body down from the Cross? It's there! Nobody sees it. They can only view it from one eye."

It frustrates Gibson that others don't see *The Passion* as he does, but it does not surprise him. It is not an accident that Gibson set the terms of *The Passion* the way he did, from the first scene, where Jesus stomps a snake to death, to the last, where the risen warrior is called to battle. Gibson's fiercest detractors see in him a medieval sensibility, an accusation that he would not necessarily find objectionable. He has a Manichaean view of the world, in which all of human history is the product of great warring realms, the unseen powers of absolute good and total evil. He believes in the Devil as fully as he believes in God; that is why his career has evolved to *The Passion,* and it is how he accounts for the opposition that the film has aroused.

The editing session was interrupted late in the afternoon by an urgent summons from a colleague in an office down the hall, where a television monitor was tuned to CNN. The anchor Paula Zahn was interviewing two guests on the subject of Gibson's film and its alleged anti-Semitism. Both of the guests, the conservative film critic Michael Medved and William Donohue, the president of the Catholic League, had seen the movie, and vigorously defended it. Medved said that the press, in repeating the charges against Gibson and his film, was once again showing itself to be irresponsible; Donohue said that Gibson and his project had been unfairly associated with the eccentric views of Gibson's father, who in a *New York Times* column was accused of being a "Holocaust denier." In all, it was a victory for Gibson's side, but when the segment concluded Gibson was enraged. "That's bullshit," he said.

He went on, "I don't want to be dissing my father. He never

denied the Holocaust; he just said there were fewer than six million. I don't want them having me dissing my father. I mean, he's my father."

Gibson is clearly pained by the fact that Hutton Gibson, who is eighty-five, has been dragged into the *Passion* controversy, not least because it presents Gibson with the unwelcome choice of distancing himself from his father—which he adamantly will not do—or suffering by association the most toxic sort of social taint.

Hutton Gibson is a devout Catholic who, as a young seminarian, had aspirations to a missionary priesthood. When the Second World War began, he joined the service, abandoned plans for the clergy, and eventually married. The couple lived in a series of small towns in the lower Hudson Valley, where Hutton worked as a railroad brakeman until, after an injury, he went on disability. He and his wife, Ann, had eleven children, and the loss of his job posed a strain; but in 1968 Hutton, an autodidact with a ferocious literary appetite, appeared on the game show *Jeopardy!* and won what was then a huge pot of money—twenty-five thousand dollars. Mel, the middle child, was twelve. Hutton, flush with the prize money, moved the family to Australia.

At the time, Catholics like Hutton Gibson were reeling from the doctrinal convulsions created by the Second Vatican Council, the Church's sweeping effort, propagated over a three-year period, to modernize. Suddenly, many of the old verities, from the profound to the trivial, were gone—including fish on Friday and, most lamentably to many, the Latin Tridentine Mass. The most dramatic of Vatican II's reform impulses was its ecumenism, which declared that all Christians, not just Roman Catholics, were members of the Body of Christ. The council's final session, in 1965, included the declaration known as the Nostra Aetate, formally reconciling Christians and Jews and condemning the idea of Jews as "cursed by God."

"True, the Jewish authorities and those who followed their lead pressed for the death of Christ," the document declared. "Still, what happened in His passion cannot be charged against all the Jews, without distinction, then alive, nor against the Jews of today. Although the Church is the new People of God, the Jews should not be presented as rejected or accursed by God, as if this followed from the Holy Scriptures."

The first Christians were, of course, Jews, and considered themselves such; however, their insistence upon the godhead Jesus was, from the Judaic perspective, theologically irreconcilable. Historic anti-Semitism, premised partly on the idea of collective Jewish guilt in the death of Christ, came with the conversion of Rome. The Church fostered such anti-Semitism for centuries (doctrinally encouraging the "curse" interpretation of the blood passage from Matthew), leading to expulsions, ghettos, and forced conversions. When, after the Reformation, official anti-Semitism became a culturally (rather than a theologically) driven policy, the Church continued to countenance it. That was the history that the reconciliation decree of Vatican II meant to redress, and it was why the current Pope, John Paul II, prayed at Jerusalem's Western Wall for God's forgiveness for "the behavior of those who in the course of history have caused these children of Yours to suffer."

The council's reforms bitterly divided the Church, reflecting, to a large degree, the divisions caused by the social movements in the contemporary secular culture. Church progressives embraced the reforms, and, as reform hardened into new orthodoxy, bureaucracies sprang up in the Church which were devoted to interfaith relations. But other Catholics were dismayed by the sudden, drastic changes, arguing that the Church's immutability through the ages was one of its institutional strengths. Most of those Catholics, however discomfited, eventually accommodated themselves to Vatican II; still others left the Church. But some of those who were most appalled at what they saw as a cult of modernity corrupting the Church remained intensely faithful. These Traditionalists, as they called themselves, declared themselves the True Church, and defied the reforms of Vatican II, as well as the authority of the Pope who convened the council, John XXIII, and of all who have occupied St. Peter's chair since.

Traditionalists—the *Times* has put their number at a hundred thousand, but other estimates vary widely—observe the Latin Tridentine Mass (performed by a priest facing the altar, with his back to the congregants), require women to cover their heads in church, do not allow laypeople to serve the Eucharist, and do not eat meat on Fridays. Some Traditionalists, attempting to explain what they see as Vatican apostasy, have inclined toward conspiracy theories. Some blamed a Communist plot, others the old Catholic antagonist Freemasonry, and others, inevitably, saw the hand of the Jew (the Devil working in each). Hutton Gibson was one of those Catholics who felt alienated from their Church, and found their way to Traditionalism. As he grew old, he found his way to dark theories to explain the world. He told a *Times* reporter that the Second Vatican Council was "a Masonic plot backed by the Jews," and that the Holocaust was a tragedy that had been hyped out of proportion, which brought leverage against such institutions as the Catholic Church.

Mel Gibson briefly considered the priesthood himself, before he discovered acting, and, with *Mad Max*, *Gallipoli*, and *The Year of Living Dangerously*, quickly became a star. In 1980, he married Robyn Moore, an Australian dental nurse; they have seven children. Gibson says that he never doubted God, but, as his father was wrestling with the Church and his own career bloomed and took him to Hollywood, he grew distant from his faith. His acting success brought fame and more money than he had imagined possible; when he got a chance to direct, he won an Oscar.

But in his middle thirties Gibson slipped into a despair so

enveloping that he thought he would not emerge. "You can get pretty wounded along the way, and I was kind of out there," he says. "I got to a very desperate place. Very desperate. Kind of jump-out-of-a-window kind of desperate. And I didn't want to hang around here, but I didn't want to check out. The other side was kind of scary. And I don't like heights, anyway. But when you get to that point where you don't want to live, and you don't want to die—it's a desperate, horrible place to be. And I just hit my knees. And I had to use the Passion of Christ and wounds to heal my wounds. And I've just been meditating on it for twelve years."

Gibson returned to his faith with the zeal of a reformed backslider, and the faith he returned to was the faith he had known as a boy, the faith of his father. "Believe me," he says of the rigors of Traditionalist worship, "every other brand of everything is easier than what I do." When he was in Rome making *The Passion,* Gibson attended Mass every day—which was a challenge, because he had to find a priest (preferably one ordained before Vatican II) who would say the Tridentine Mass. He brought one priest from Canada, and when that one had to return home he found a French Traditionalist living in England who agreed to minister to him.

At home in California, Gibson worshipped until recently at a Traditionalist church some distance from their house in Malibu. Then he decided that he had the means, and the motivation, to make worship a bit easier. He determined to build his own chapel, a Traditionalist church called Holy Family, in the hills near his home.

When Gibson is trying to understand the antagonism that his project has excited, he characteristically conjures his scenario of the great spiritual realms, unseen but ever warring over humankind. "I didn't realize it would be so vicious," he says of the criticism. "The acts against this film started early. As soon as I announced I was doing it, it was 'This is a dangerous thing.'

There is vehement anti-Christian sentiment out there, and they don't want it. It's vicious. I mean, I think we're just a little part of it, we're just the meat in the sandwich here. There's huge things out there, and they're belting it out—we don't see this stuff. Imagine: There's a huge war raging, and it's over us! This is the weird thing. For some reason, we're important in this thing. I don't understand it. We're a bunch of dickheads and idiots and failures and creeps. But we're called to the divine, we're called to be better than our nature would have us be. And those big realms that are warring and battling are going to manifest themselves very clearly, seemingly without reason, here—a realm that we can see. And you stick your head up and you get knocked."

More temporal forces are also at work, those enduring enmities rooted in the great social and political divides of the 1960s. The culture wars that resulted are felt in American life still, in the media, in politics, and, as the anguished split over homosexuality in the Episcopal Church currently attests, in religion. In the dispute over Gibson's film, the familiar advocates have reflexively assumed their usual stations, even though the dramatic form at issue—the Christian Passion play—is so obscure in the secular age that many Americans, perhaps most, would not likely be able even to describe it. That *The Passion* became the subject of such contention a year before its planned release, however, was an accident—not of politics, or even of religion, but of real estate.

When Gibson decided to build a church, he bought sixteen acres of land in the community of Agoura Hills, through an entity he controls called the A. J. Reilly Foundation. Some local homeowners objected to the project as it made its way through the zoning process. One homeowner suggested that his son, a freelance journalist named Christopher Noxon, write about the church. The resulting article, published by *The New York Times* on March 9, 2003, created three salient impressions: that

Gibson's faith is a "strain of Catholicism rooted in the dictates of a 16th-century papal council and nurtured by a splinter group of conspiracy-minded Catholics, mystics, monarchists and disaffected conservatives"; that Gibson's father is representative of this paleo-Catholic strain; and that Mel Gibson's movie about the Crucifixion may serve as a propaganda vehicle for such views. Noxon attended Mass in the new church, and noted that the service rituals were "remarkably" like those he remembered from childhood.

The *Times* story caught the attention of a group of activists, scholars, and clerics who make up what is known as the interfaith community. Within the Church, these are the progressives and their spiritual heirs who advocated for Vatican II, and, in the years since, they have invested their careers in making ecumenism an important discipline unto itself. Doctrine is promulgated on how the Christians regard the Jews, and guidelines govern the presentation of Jews and Judaism in liturgical teaching, preaching, Biblical interpretation, and dramatic depictions of Christ's Passion. In this last regard, the interfaith committee of the national Bishops Conference issued, in 1988, a list of criteria to be followed when dramatizing the Passion, warning of the historical dangers in the form and urging that "anything less than [an] 'overriding preoccupation' to avoid caricaturing the Jewish people, which history has all too frequently shown us, will result almost inevitably in a violation" of Vatican II principle.

The interfaith community would not have been comforted by the news that Mel Gibson was basing his movie upon the Gospels, even if he weren't a Traditionalist Catholic. On the contrary, using the Gospels as the source would be cause for alarm; it is held that the Gospels, read alone, contain potentially dangerous teachings, particularly as they pertain to the role of Jews in the Crucifixion. "One cannot assume that by simply conforming to the New Testament, that anti-Semitism will not be promoted," a group of Catholic ecumenist scholars declared, regarding Gibson's film. "After all, for centuries sermons and passion plays based on the New Testament have incited Christian animosity and violence toward Jews."

After reading the *Times* story about Gibson's church and film, one leading Catholic ecumenist, Dr. Eugene Fisher, talked to an old friend from years of interfaith work, Abraham Foxman, the head of the Anti-Defamation League. Foxman was equally alarmed by the Gibson project, and had written to Gibson, seeking assurances that the movie "will not give rise to the old canard of charging Jews with deicide and to anti-Semitism." Fisher and Foxman agreed to convene a small ad-hoc group of likeminded colleagues, and to offer Gibson their help in making his film conform to contemporary doctrine.

The group comprised nine members, mostly Catholic scholars who are, like Fisher, specialists in Christian-Jewish relations. Fisher also invited into the group a respected Boston University professor, Paula Fredriksen, who would present Gibson with a different set of problems to consider. Fredriksen's specialty is the study of the historical Jesus. It is a relatively young field of inquiry, just two centuries old, and it is only in the past few decades that the discipline has assumed an authoritative voice.

Historical-Jesus scholars generally excuse themselves from the matter of Jesus' divinity, focusing instead upon Jesus the man—why he thought and behaved as he did—in the context of early-first-century Judaism. They concede that the four Gospels are probably the best (if not only) documents directly bearing upon the death of Jesus, but they depart from many Christians as to their origins and purpose. Ask Mel Gibson who wrote the Book of John, for example, and he would not hesitate to answer that it was St. John—that's why it's called "The Gospel According to John." Ditto Matthew, Mark, and Luke. "John was an eyewitness," Gibson says. "Matthew was there.

And these other guys? Mark was Peter's guy, Peter's scribe. And Luke was Paul's guy. I mean, these are reliable sources. These are guys who were around." The historical-Jesus scholars, however, are not so sure. "We do not know who wrote the Gospels," contends E. P. Sanders, of Duke University, who is the author of *The Historical Figure of Jesus,* and one of the pre-eminent scholars in the field. Sanders holds what is probably the consensus view, that the Gospels were written anonymously by early Church teachers, and were later assigned to the four evangelist saints, perhaps to bestow legitimacy.

The Gospel narratives generally concur on the essentials of Christ's Passion—the Last Supper, his betrayal by Judas Iscariot to Jewish leaders who were hostile to his messianic claims, his arrest in Jerusalem, an interrogation before the Jewish authorities, condemnation by Pilate, and crucifixion, followed by burial and resurrection. The accounts differ on particulars; Matthew and Mark, for instance, have Jesus interrogated before a full Sanhedrin trial, while John skips over the trial and has Jesus questioned at a high priest's residence before delivery to Pilate. In the view of historical-Jesus scholars, such differences invalidate the Gospels' strict historicity, and, therefore, any dramatization based literally upon them is deemed ahistorical. Many Christians, however, consider the Gospel narratives not contradictory but complementary. Regarding the interrogations to which Jesus was subjected, for example, they argue that the important fact is that there was some sort of Jewish legal proceeding, in which Jesus was effectively indicted. "The Gospels don't contradict one another," Gibson insists. "They mesh. There's a couple of places where, yeah, that's not quite the same scene. But they just complete parts of the story that the other guy didn't complete. That's all. They do not contradict one another. If you read all four of those, they mesh. Because if they didn't, you wouldn't have so many people hooked into this."

The study of the historical Jesus is a field inclined toward hermeneutical acrobatics, and its scholars routinely disagree not only with lay theologians but with each other. On the subject of Jewish involvement in the Crucifixion, for example, most historical-Jesus investigators believe that the Jewish high priests wanted Jesus dead, as the Gospels attest, and that the only question is why. Sanders believes it is because of Jesus' actions at the Temple during his Passover visit to Jerusalem, when he drove the money changers from the premises and overturned their tables. Fredriksen, though she is an admirer of Sanders, believes that the Temple scene probably didn't happen. She places the initiative of the Crucifixion entirely upon Pilate, almost to the point of absenting Jews from the scene altogether. Fredriksen's theory is that Jesus was so popular among the Jewish people (as evidenced by his triumphal entry into Jerusalem on the day Christians call Palm Sunday) that Pilate wanted him dead in order to teach Jews a lesson: Do not rebel.

In order to give informed advice to Gibson, Fisher and his group of scholars needed to see the film, or, at least, a script. When they approached Icon Productions in late March, however, they learned that Gibson was still in Italy, working on the film. Fisher then appealed to Father William Fulco, a Jesuit professor of classics and archeology at Loyola Marymount University, in Los Angeles, who had been hired by Gibson to translate the script into Latin, Aramaic, and Hebrew. Fisher sent along the Bishops Conference's guidelines for dramatizing the Passion, and Fulco assured him that Gibson's script committed no offenses. The scholars wanted to judge that for themselves, and asked for a copy of the script. Fulco said that the screenplay was not his to give. Icon did not respond to the request for a script. The scholars and Icon were at a standoff.

Then, in early April, Rabbi Yehiel Poupko, a Judaic scholar involved in interfaith work in Chicago, returned home to find a large, unmarked manila envelope at his front door. When

Rabbi Poupko opened it, he found a script that had no identi-fying title page. But Poupko realized that the script must be *The Passion,* and called up a friend in interfaith work, Father John Pawlikowski, who was one of Fisher's team of scholars. Paw-likowski asked to see the script, and Poupko sent it over.

Pawlikowski passed the script along to Fisher, who, plainly delighted by the development, made copies and sent them to each of the members of his panel on April 18—which hap-pened to be Good Friday. By e-mail, he informed Father Fulco that "the Easter Bunny came early to my office and delivered a copy of the script." Fisher attributed the mysterious appearance of the script to a "Biblical Deep Throat," and added that he had sent it along to the scholars "in time for their Good Friday meditations." Fisher's tone was solicitous; he told Fulco that "my own response is that with a couple of very minor adjust-ments, all is resolved."

But when the other scholars read the screenplay they were aghast. The script confirmed their worst fears about the Gibson project. Gibson seemed to be violating many, if not all, of the Bishops Conference's guidelines on dramatizing the Passion; the script included the scene from Matthew in which Pilate washes his hands of responsibility, and, worse, it had Caiaphas uttering the line "His blood be on us, and upon our children." The descriptive portions of the script, which do not necessar-ily reflect what gets filmed, were filled with inflammatory cues: Peter is "aware of the bloodthirsty nature of the rising chaos"; at the sight of the Cross, "the crowd's bloodthirst redoubles"; when Jesus is crushed by the weight of the Cross, the Roman guards holding the crowd back "have a difficult time restraining the impatient, predatory bloodthirst of the people"; and, most egregiously, as Jesus is reduced to a bloody mass, Caiaphas' eyes are "shiny with breathless excitement."

Now the tone of the scholars' dealings with Icon became openly adversarial. On Easter Monday, one member of the panel, Sister Mary Boys, a professor at the Union Theological Seminary, in New York, and an interfaith veteran, spoke to a *Los Angeles Times* reporter about the scholars' concerns that Gibson's film could incite anti-Semitism. Rabbi Eugene Korn, the head of the A.D.L.'s interfaith affairs, was quoted in the article as warning Gibson that he should not ignore the scholars' group. "If he doesn't respond, the controversy will certainly heat up," Korn said. "We are all very vigilant about things like this."

Gibson, who had returned to California, was furious. He began to hear negative comments from his friends in the industry, including the advice that he stay away from the Grand Havana Room. Three days after the article appeared, Gibson and his producer, Steve McEveety, had a telephone conversation with Eugene Fisher. According to notes taken by the Gibson team (Fisher won't comment), McEveety asked how the scholars could be trusted after they had gone public with negative comments based on a stolen script. He said that the whole thing felt a bit like extortion. Gibson said he found the article threatening, "a hatchet job." Fisher was again solicitous, saying that "this whole kind of thing I find very distasteful," and agreed that the implications of anti-Semitism were "absolutely untrue." He conceded that the fact that the script was stolen would "taint" any criticisms deriving from it, and said that Rabbi Korn "blew that one" by speaking to the press.

"You guys got ripped," Fisher said. But he defended the Anti-Defamation League as being a responsible group. He suggested that Gibson and his associates hear the scholars out.

"Whatever opinion you guys come up with are tainted notes," McEveety replied.

Meanwhile, the scholars worked on their suggestions, which they compiled into a report that they sent to Icon Productions in early May. The report, numbering eighteen pages, contained a long list of the film's transgressions, which "are embedded throughout the script." Contrary to the "very minor ad-justments" of which Fisher had spoken, the scholars' report said that Gibson's film would basically require a remake. "We believe that the steps needed to correct these difficulties will re-quire major revisions," the report stated.

For Fredriksen, one of the most dismaying elements of Gib-son's undertaking was his insistence that his film would be ac-curate. She notes that Gibson relied on an uninformed reading of the Gospels, as well as upon extra-scriptural Catholic litera-ture, such as the writings of two stigmatic nuns. "He doesn't even have a Ph.D. on his staff," she says.

Among the many errors that Gibson might have avoided had he followed the ecumenist guidelines is his portrayal of the two men who were crucified alongside Jesus as criminals. Al-though the men, described in Matthew and Mark, are identi-fied as "thieves" in the King James Version of the Bible, as "robbers" in the International and American Standard versions, and as "plunderers" in the original Greek, the Bishops Confer-ence prefers that they be identified as "insurgents."

Gibson is unconvinced by such scholarly interpretations. "They always dick around with it, you know?" he says. "Judas is always some kind of friend of some freedom fighter named Barabbas, you know what I mean? It's horseshit. It's revisionist bullshit. And that's what these academics are into. They gave me notes on a stolen script. I couldn't believe it. It was like they were more or less saying I have no right to interpret the Gospels myself, because I don't have a bunch of letters after my name. But they are for children, these Gospels. They're for chil-dren, they're for old people, they're for everybody in between. They're not necessarily for academics. Just get an academic on board if you want to pervert something!"

Gibson responded to the scholars through his attorney, who warned that they were in possession of a stolen script, and demanded its immediate return. What happened next placed

Eugene Fisher's panel of scholars in an awkward position. Fisher is the associate director of ecumenical and interreligious affairs for the United States Conference of Catholic Bishops, but he had acted on his own in forming the group. Fisher's standing (and the fact that he had used the Bishops Conference's letterhead in communicating with Icon) had lent the scholars' group an air of Church authority—an important element in that part of the public debate which emphasized Gibson's schismatic bent. Gibson and McEveety had been surprised to learn that Fisher's panel was an ad-hoc initiative, bearing no authority from the Church. After the Bishops Conference received the letter from Gibson's lawyer, it acted quickly to distance itself from the scholars and their report on Gibson's film. "Neither the Bishops' Committee for Ecumenical and Interreligious Affairs, nor any other committee of the United States Conference of Catholic Bishops, established this group, or authorized, reviewed or approved the report written by its members," the conference declared in June. Its counsel, Mark E. Chopko, advised the scholars to return the scripts to Icon, and issued an apology to Gibson. "We regret that 'this situation has occurred, and offer our apologies," Chopko wrote. "I have further advised the scholars group that this draft screenplay is not considered to be representative of the film and should not be the subject of further public comment. When the film is released, the USCCB will review it at that time."

The controversy, however, did not wane. The Anti-Defamation League issued no apology to Gibson, and the scholars stood by their report; some of them continued to criticize Gibson's film publicly. I arrived in California the day after *The New York Times* carried a front-page article on the dispute. The next morning, the paper published a column that criticized Gibson for refusing to show his film to Jewish leaders, such as Abraham Foxman, of the A.D.L. Gibson stewed all day, and by evening he had reached full pique. He was particularly aroused by the column, written by Frank Rich, which had argued that

Gibson's film could do real harm abroad, "where anti-Semitism has metastasized since 9/11," and which had accused Gibson's publicist, Alan Nierob, of using "p.r. spin to defend a Holocaust denier"—presumably, Gibson's father. Nierob, who is Jewish, and is the son of Holocaust survivors (and a founding member of the national Holocaust Museum), laughed it off. But Gibson called Nierob that evening, and apologized for "getting you into this."

Then Gibson expressed his feelings about Rich. "I want to kill him," he said. "I want his intestines on a stick. . . . I want to kill his dog." At this, Paul Lauer, Gibson's marketing man, who had been quietly engaged in deskwork, glanced at me, and calmly said, "The thing you have to understand is that the distance between Mel's heart and his mouth is greater than the distance between his imagination and his mouth. He is an artist, and he says these things, and his creative energy kicks in, and he comes out with these imaginative, wild things. But his heart . . ." He shrugged, and went back to work.

Gibson has half-jokingly remarked that *The Passion* may be a career-killer for him. If it is not, if it somehow manages to open, and even to succeed, it will be in no small measure owing to Lauer's efforts. Lauer, whose father is Jewish, is a practicing Roman Catholic who has often heard Gibson's Traditionalist views about the current Vatican (that the last "real" Pope predated Vatican II), and seems mostly unperturbed. More pressing, to him, is the difficult question of opening a movie that, even without the attacks against it, presents some formidable marketing problems: it is a religious film, whose actors speak their lines in two dead languages. Lauer has always known that the make-or-break audience for *The Passion* is the active Christian community, which could effectively kill the film if it discerned even a hint of blasphemy. As Paula Fredriksen has written in *The New Republic*, "evangelical Christians, in my experience, know their Scriptures very, very well."

For that reason, Lauer began to cultivate Christian groups

almost from the start. I first heard about *The Passion* from Billy Graham's public-relations man in Dallas, A. Larry Ross, who had seen the film in late May at the Icon offices. The evangelical reaction to the movie was almost uniformly enthusiastic. When the attacks on the film began, Icon was able to turn its marketing strategy into an effective counter-offensive. This summer, Lauer scheduled a series of screenings and appearances by Gibson before Christian groups and conservative columnists, who praised the film to their congregations and readers. "I can say *The Passion* is the most beautiful, profound, accurate, disturbing, realistic, and bloody depiction of this well-known story that has even been filmed," the nationally syndicated columnist Cal Thomas wrote in August. "Its message is not just for Christians, but for everyone. I doubt a better film about Jesus could be made." David Horowitz wrote in his Web log that "it is an awesome artifact, an overpowering work." Michael Medved said in a television appearance, "It is by a very large margin of advantage the most effective cinematic adaptation of a Biblical story I have ever seen."

I accompanied Gibson on several such appearances, and at each he was received with an enthusiasm that seemed to reach beyond the movie itself, to a deeply felt disaffection from the secular world; now an icon of that world was on their side. In Anaheim, Gibson showed a trailer of the film to a convention of the Full Gospel Business Men's Fellowship, and received a standing ovation. Afterward, the daughter of the organization's president laid hands on Gibson and asked Jesus to "bind Satan, bind the press, we ask you, Lord."

That same evening, Gibson made another appearance—the only one that seemed to make him nervous. It was a screening for three hundred and fifty Jesuits, who had gathered in an auditorium at Loyola Marymount University. After the film, Gibson took to the stage, and, shuffling his feet and staring at the ground, asked the priests if they had any questions. Gibson later explained the reason for his and Lauer's anxiety: "If anyone's gonna kill you, its' those guys, right? We're Catholics, right? We're scared of the Jesuits. Every good Catholic is." He needn't have been. Some of the Jesuits had eschatological concerns (Couldn't there be more of the risen Christ?), and one elderly priest wondered whether the subtitles might be made larger. The closest that anyone came to suggesting political correctness was when one priest toward the front urged that the language be more inclusive. "Rather than using 'Jesus, the son of man, maybe Jesus, the son of all'?" The other Jesuits booed him down, and the evening ended with another standing ovation.

The next morning, Robyn Gibson asked her husband not to read the newspaper until he had had his coffee. The *Los Angeles Times* had published a column, by Tim Rutten, that likened Gibson to "an unwholesomely willful child playing with matches. The immediate temptation may be to let the little brat learn the lesson that burnt fingers will teach." Gibson was still fuming when he reached his Icon office, where another special screening was scheduled, this one for the television evangelist Dr. Robert Schuller. The preacher's entourage arrived and took their places in the screening room, without Schuller, who had apparently got lost inside the building's corridors. While waiting for him, Gibson talked about the column, and observed, to general agreement, that "the *L.A. Times,* it's an anti-Christian publication, as is *The New York Times.*"

A moment later, Schuller walked in, with a book in his hand, which he presented to Gibson. It was a polemic called *Journalistic Fraud: How The New York Times Distorts the News and Why It Can No Longer Be Trusted,* by Bob Kohn.

"It hits the stores this week, and we expect it to be on the best-seller list," Schuller said. "And the author is very prominent, Bob Kohn, very wealthy . . . and Jewish."

"Hey! That's a great gift!" Gibson said, brightening. "Thank you."

After the film, Schuller said that he had watched carefully

for "who the Christ-killers were, and it was really the Romans." Mrs. Schuller wiped tears from her eyes, and said to Gibson, "You have a powerful masterpiece here."

Before leaving, Schuller faced Gibson and, his broadcaster's voice assuming the tone of prayer, pronounced his judgment on the film. "It's not your dream, this is God's dream," he said. "He gave it to you, because He knew you wouldn't throw it away. Trust Him."

The Christian groups, however, can't distribute the film, and Gibson has twenty-five million dollars of his own money at stake. Twentieth Century Fox has already said that it does not plan to take on *The Passion*. But word of mouth is everything in Hollywood, and Icon's strategy of selectively previewing the movie has played directly into the film community's native wish to be on the inside. Lauer has let it be known that he is planning several screenings over the coming months for selected people in the industry, a tactic that has only heightened interest in the film. Jeff Berg, the chairman and C.E.O. of International Creative Management, which represents Gibson and handles his distribution deals, is talking to several studios about a possible deal, among them Paramount, Warners, and Harvey Weinstein's Miramax. He has told them that he will show the film only to those studios which agree, in advance, to Icon's terms—an effort to weed out the merely curious.

"Inadvertently," Gibson says, "all the problems and the conflicts and stuff—this is some of the best marketing and publicity I have ever seen."

In his 1997 film *Conspiracy Theory*, Gibson played a paranoid New York taxi-driver who sees in everything around him the malign work of a dark, invisible hand. In the film's opening scene, Gibson's character is shown in a montage of taxi rides, in which he reveals his crazy notions to a series of bemused fares. "I mean, George Bush knew what he was saying when he said, 'New World Order,'" Gibson tells one rider. "Remember those three little words? 'New World Order'? Well, he was a thirty-third-degree Mason, you know." To a pair of nuns riding in the back seat, Gibson declares, "Hey, don't get me wrong, Sister, I'm sure your heart's in the right place, O.K.? But, you know, somebody's got to lift the scab, the festering scab, that is the Vatican." The scene is played as screwball comedy, and during the movie Gibson's character comes to believe something even loonier—that the government is trying to kill him, because he knows too much. The movie's twist, revealed at the end, is that Gibson's character is right—he's a former government assassin who had been part of a mind-control experiment. His conspiracy theories were true. In the movies, the technique is called "the slow reveal."

It has been an inside joke among some of Gibson's pals that the opening scene of *Conspiracy Theory* wasn't scripted, that Gibson just played it off the top of his head, employing dialogue reflecting his own views. By the end of my visit with Gibson, I realized that they weren't entirely kidding.

After the screening with Schuller, Gibson was scheduled to fly to Washington for an appearance at a gathering of the Knights of Columbus, the Catholic charity organization, and thence to more of Lauer's marketing stops. That evening, I joined Gibson for the trip East, along with Lauer and Danny Rafic, an Israeli film editor who is working on *The Passion*.

When Gibson was in Rome shooting the film, he told an Italian interviewer that he had felt moved by God's spirit to undertake the project. I asked him what he'd meant by that. How did he know that God wanted him to make *The Passion*?

"There are signals," he said. "You get signals. Signs. 'Signal graces,' they're called. It's like traffic lights. It's as clear as a traffic light. Bing! I mean, it just grabs you and you know you have to listen to that and you have to follow it. Like last night, you know?"

He reminded me of an incident that had occurred the night

before, as we were driving to Anaheim. Gibson was behind the wheel of his silver Lexus, negotiating the nightmarish traffic on the Santa Ana Freeway, when a car pulled in front of him and immediately hit the brakes. Gibson had seemed ready to unleash some invective, when he stopped and stared at the offending car's license plate. "Look! Look at what it says!" The car's license-plate holder bore the inscription "Psalm 91." Gibson said that on that very morning, after he'd been vexed by the *Los Angeles Times* column, one of his associates had urged him to read the ninety-first Psalm, and that he'd been moved to tears by it. ("A thousand shall fall at thy side, and ten thousand at thy right hand; but it shall not come nigh thee. . . . For he shall give his angels charge over thee, to keep thee in all thy ways.")

"It was weird," Gibson said. "Those are signals, all right?"

He then told me about something that had happened when he was building his church. He had wanted to fill the place with antique candlesticks and such, and he'd had a hard time finding them. He was in Philadelphia shooting a picture, and someone told him about a man who had a storehouse of old church items. Gibson called the man, and asked if he was willing to sell any of the stuff. The man, considering his celebrity customer, was reluctant. "Not if you're gonna put it in a disco, or fornicate on it," he said. Gibson talked to him for a while, and convinced him of the purity of his intent. They did business, and just before Gibson left the man pulled something out, and offered it to Gibson as a gift. It was a small, faded piece of cloth. "What is it?" he asked. The man told him that he had a special devotion to a nineteenth-century Augustinian nun, Anne Catherine Emmerich, and that the cloth was a piece of her habit.

As it happened, Emmerich had special meaning to Gibson as well. Emmerich was an impoverished Westphalian farm girl who had visions at an early age. She was so pious that when she joined a convent, at the age of twenty-eight, she was considered odd even there. Eventually, she began to experience ecstasies and develop stigmata. Her experiences attracted Church inquiries, state suspicions, and popular curiosity, and ultimately the attention of the poet Clemens Brentano, one of the founders of the German Romantic movement. Brentano made his way to Emmerich, who was ailing, and who told him that she had been awaiting his arrival. He wrote down her visions, including detailed narratives from Christ's Passion, and published them after her death, in 1824, in a book called *The Dolorous Passion of Our Lord and Saviour Jesus Christ.* Six weeks after she died, Emmerich's body was disinterred, and was said to show no decay. In Catholic theology, ecstasies are considered a rare gift from God, and Emmerich is proceeding toward beatification.

When Gibson returned to his faith, he acquired, from a nunnery that had closed down, a library of hundreds of books, many of them quite old. He says that when he was researching *The Passion* one evening he reached up for a book, and Brentano's volume tumbled out of the shelf into his hands. He sat down to read it, and was flabbergasted by the vivid imagery of Emmerich's visions. "Amazing images," he said. "She supplied me with stuff I never would have thought of." The one image that is most noticeable in *The Passion* is a scene after Jesus' scourging, when a grief-stricken Mary gets down on her knees to mop up his blood.

I reminded Gibson, who carries the Emmerich relic in his pocket, that some of his critics have pointed out that Emmerich's depiction of Jews is inflammatory, thereby imputing anti-Semitism to Gibson's film. "Why are they calling her a Nazi?" Gibson asked. "Because modern secular Judaism wants to blame the Holocaust on the Catholic Church. And it's a lie. And it's revisionism. And they've been working on that one for a while."

We talked of the nature of Gibson's faith, and I asked him about an aspect of Vatican II which has not been much discussed in the debate over his film. One of the council's most significant acts was its Decree on Ecumenism, which declared that all Christians, even those outside the Catholic Church, "have the right to be called Christian; the children of the Catholic Church accept them as brothers." This effectively overturned the Catholic notion that the only true course to salvation was through the Catholic Church.

I told Gibson that I am a Protestant, and asked whether his pre–Vatican II world view disqualified me from eternal salvation. He paused. "There is no salvation for those outside the Church," he said. "I believe it." He explained, "Put it this way. My wife is a saint. She's a much better person than I am. Honestly. She's, like, Episcopalian, Church of England. She prays, she believes in God, she knows Jesus, she believes in that stuff. And it's just not fair if she doesn't make it, she's better than I am. But that is a pronouncement from the chair. I go with it."

With that, Gibson excused himself, and headed toward the galley of the plane, where an attendant had laid out supper. I glanced up at the video monitor at the front of the cabin, showing our progress on the journey to Washington. We were forty-five thousand feet over the high plains of Colorado, heading toward Kansas, according to the monitor, which displayed the name of the town shimmering faintly below us. It was a place called Last Chance.

The next morning, Gibson was rousingly received at the Washington Hilton ballroom by the Knights of Columbus. One of the group's leaders, in introducing Gibson, reminded the big crowd that the Knights had been called to battle before on such issues as abortion and prayer in school. "If there's going to be a fight, maybe we should not duck it," he said. "Maybe we should make sure that Mel Gibson gets a fair hearing in this." After the event, I thanked Gibson, and bade him farewell. When I arrived home in New York, I called Abraham Foxman, of the A.D.L. By then, Foxman's associate Eugene Korn had managed to see a screening of *The Passion*, at the Museum of Fine Arts in Houston. Afterward, the A.D.L. had issued another statement warning of its grave concern that the film "could fuel hatred, bigotry, and anti-Semitism."

I asked Foxman if he believed that Gibson was an anti-Semite. "Per se, I don't think that Mel Gibson is anti-Semitic," Foxman said. "I think that he is insensitive."

But what of *The Passion* itself, I asked. Is the film anti-Semitic? "The film, per se, is not anti-Semitic," Foxman said. The problem, he added, was that, as with any literal reading of the New Testament, its message of love could be twisted into something hateful. "The film can fuel, trigger, stimulate, induce, rationalize, legitimize anti-Semitism," Foxman said.

"You know, the Gospels, if taken literally, can be very damaging, in the same way if you take the Old Testament literally," Foxman went on. "It says, 'An eye for an eye and a tooth for a tooth.' Now, has the Jewish state, or have Jews, practiced the Old Testament by taking an eye for an eye? No. So a literal reading of almost anything can lead to all kinds of things."

Speaking with Foxman made me realize just what it was that Gibson had done in making *The Passion*. Gibson had said from the start that he was going to make a movie taken straight from the Gospels. Foxman was saying that, for better or worse, Gibson had done just that. In focusing on Gibson's Traditionalist Catholicism, some of his critics have created the expectation that *The Passion* is a medieval Passion play depicting Jews in horns drinking Christian blood. It is not that. Nor is it the attenuated dramatization that the Catholic scholars might have wished for. Gibson's *Passion* is a literalist rendering of the Gospels' account of Jesus' Passion, which makes it the ultimate Traditionalist expression.

That fact will eventually become evident, no doubt. By

then, *The Passion* may well be out of the theaters and playing on cable. That is the art of the slow reveal.

POSTSCRIPT

Because of an editing error in the original piece, part of the passage describing Hutton Gibson's view of the Holocaust was wrongly attributed to *The New York Times*. The passage in my original manuscript, describing the elder Gibson's view that the tragedy had been "hyped out of proportion," was based on my own reporting. The use of the word "tragedy" in reference to the Holocaust was my own, and was not meant to suggest Hutton Gibson's attitude toward the event. Indeed, in a similar passage, the *Times* employed the term "catastrophe" in describing the elder Gibson's Holocaust theories. While neither the *Times*'s writer nor I can read Hutton Gibson's heart, his theories about the Holocaust would not obviously indicate that he views the Holocaust as either tragic or catastrophic.

FRANK RICH

The Greatest Story Ever Sold

Then Gibson expressed his feelings about Rich. "I want to kill him," he said. "I want his intestines on a stick. . . . I want to kill his dog."
—*The New Yorker*, September 15, 2003

PETA MEMBERS may be relieved to learn that I do not have a dog.

As for the rest of Mel Gibson's threats, context is all: the guy is a movie star. Movie stars expect to get their own way. They are surrounded by sycophants, many of them on the payroll. Should a discouraging word somehow prick the bubble of fabulousness in which they travel, even big-screen he-men can turn into crybabies. Mr. Gibson's tirade sounded less like a fatwa from the Ayatollah Khomeini than a tantrum from Sinatra in his cups.

My capital crime was to write a column on this page last month reporting that Mr. Gibson was promoting his coming film about the crucifixion, *The Passion*, by baiting Jews. As indeed he has. In January, the star had gone on *The O'Reilly Factor* to counter Jewish criticism of his cinematic account of Jesus's final hours—a provocative opening volley given that no critic of any faith had yet said anything about his movie (and wouldn't for another three months). Clearly he was looking for a brawl, and he hasn't let up since. In the *New Yorker* profile, Mr. Gibson says that "modern secular Judaism wants to blame the Holocaust on the Catholic Church," a charge that Abraham H. Foxman, of the Anti-Defamation League, labels "classic anti-Semitism." Mr. Gibson also says that he trimmed a scene from *The Passion* involving the Jewish high priest Caiaphas because if he didn't do so "they'd be coming after me at my house, they'd come to kill me."

Who is this bloodthirsty "they" threatening to martyr our fearless hero? Could it be the same mob that killed Jesus? Funny, but as far as I can determine, the only death threat that's been made in conjunction with *The Passion* is Mr. Gibson's against me. *The New Yorker* did, though, uncover one ominous threat against the star: "He's heard that someone from one of his hangouts, the Grand Havana Room, a Beverly Hills smoking club, said that he'd spit on him if he ever came in again." Heard from whom? What is the identity of that mysterious "someone"? What do they smoke at that "smoking club"? Has the Grand Havana Room been infiltrated by Madonna's Kabbalah study group? I join a worried nation in praying for Mr. Gibson's safety.

His over-the-top ramblings are, of course, conceived in part to sell his product. "Inadvertently, all the problems and the conflicts and stuff—this is some of the best marketing and publicity I have ever seen," Mr. Gibson told *The New Yorker*. That's true—with the possible exception of the word "inadvertently" —and I realize that I've been skillfully roped into his remarkably successful p.r. juggernaut. But I'm glad to play my cameo role—and unlike Bill O'Reilly, who sold the film rights to one of his books to Mr. Gibson's production company, I am not being paid by him to do so.

What makes the unfolding saga of *The Passion* hard to ignore is not so much Mr. Gibson's playacting fisticuffs but the extent to which his combative marketing taps into larger angers. The *Passion* fracas is happening not in a vacuum but in an increasingly divided America fighting a war that many on both sides see as a religious struggle. While Mr. Gibson may have thought he was making a biblical statement, his partisans are turning him into an ideological cause.

The lines are drawn on seethepassion.com, the most elaborate Web site devoted to championing Mr. Gibson. There we're told that the debate over *The Passion* has "become a focal point for the Culture War which will determine the future of our country and the world." When this site criticizes the *Times,* it changes the family name of the paper's publisher from Sulzberger to "Schultzberger." (It was no doubt inadvertent that Mr. O'Reilly, in a similar slip last week, referred to the author of a *New Republic* critique of Mr. Gibson, the Boston University historian Paula Fredriksen, as "Fredrickstein.") This animus is not lost on critics of *The Passion.* As the A.D.L.'s Rabbi Eugene Korn has said of Mr. Gibson to *The Jewish Week,* "He's playing off the conservative Christians against the liberal Christians, and the Jews against the Christian community in general."

To what end? For the film's supporters, the battle is of a piece with the same blue state–red state cultural chasm as the conflicts over the Ten Commandments in an Alabama courthouse, the growing legitimization of homosexuality (Mr. Gibson has had his innings with gays in the past), and the leadership of a president who wraps public policy in religiosity and called the war against terrorism a "crusade" until his handlers intervened. So what if "modern secular" Jews—whoever they are—are maligned by Mr. Gibson or his movie? It's in the service of a larger calling. After all, Tom DeLay and evangelical Christians can look after the Jews' interests in Israel, at least until Armageddon rolls around and, as millennialist theology would have it, the Jews on hand either convert or die.

Intentionally or not, the contentious rollout of *The Passion* has resembled a political, rather than a spiritual, campaign, from its start on *The O'Reilly Factor*. Since the star belongs to a fringe church that disowns Vatican II and is not recognized by the Los Angeles Roman Catholic archdiocese, his roads do not lead to Rome so much as Washington. It was there that he screened a rough cut of the movie to conservative columnists likely to give it raves—as they did.

The few Jews invited to *Passion* screenings by Mr. Gibson tend to be political conservatives. One is Michael Medved, who is fond of describing himself in his published *Passion* encomiums as a "former synagogue president"—betting that most of his readers will not know that this is a secular rank falling somewhere between co-op board president and aspiring Y.M.H.A. camp counselor. When non–right-wing Jews asked to see the film, we were turned away—thus allowing Mr. Gibson's defenders, in a perfect orchestration of Catch-22, to say we were attacking or trying to censor a film we "haven't seen." This has been a constant theme in the bouquet of anti-Semitic mail I've received since my previous column about *The Passion*.

I never called the movie anti-Semitic or called for its suppression. I did say that if early reports by Catholic and Jewish theologians alike were accurate in stating that *The Passion* revived the deicide charge against Jews, it could have a tinderbox effect abroad. The authorities I cited based their criticisms on a draft of the movie's screenplay. (The most forceful critic of the movie has been Sister Mary Boys, of the Union Theological Seminary in New York.) I have since sought out some of those who have seen the movie itself, in the same cut praised by Mr. Gibson's claque this summer. They are united in believing, as one of them puts it, that "it's not a close call—the film clearly presents the Jews as the primary instigators of the crucifixion."

Mr. Gibson would argue that he is only being true to tradition, opting for scriptural literalism over loosey-goosey modern revisionism. But by his own account, he has based his movie on at least one revisionist source, a nineteenth-century stigmatic nun, Anne Catherine Emmerich, notable for her grotesque caricatures of Jews. To the extent that there can be any agreement about the facts of a story on which even the four Gospels don't agree, his movie is destined to be inaccurate. *People* magazine reports he didn't even get the depiction of the crucifixion itself or the language right (*The Passion* is in Latin, Aramaic, and Hebrew, not the Greek believed to have been the *lingua franca* of its characters). Like any filmmaker, Mr. Gibson has selectively chosen his sources to convey his own point of view.

If the film does malign Jews, should it be suppressed? No. Mr. Gibson has the right to release whatever movie he wants, and he undoubtedly will, whether he finds a studio to back him or rents theaters himself. The ultimate irony may be that Jews will help him do so; so far the only studio to pass on the movie is Fox, owned by a conservative non-Jew, Rupert Murdoch. But Mr. Gibson, forever crying censorship when there hasn't been any, does not understand that the First Amendment is a two-way street. "He has his free speech," Mr. Foxman says. "I guess he can't tolerate yours and mine."

As for Mr. Gibson's own speech in this debate, it is often as dishonest as it is un-Christian. In the *New Yorker* article, he says that his father, Hutton Gibson, a prolific author on religious matters, "never denied the Holocaust"; the article's author, Peter J. Boyer, sanitizes the senior Gibson further by saying he called the Holocaust a "tragedy" in an interview he gave to the writer Christopher Noxon for a *New York Times Magazine* article published last March. Neither the word "tragedy" nor any synonym for it ever appeared in that *Times* article, and according to a full transcript of the interview that Mr. Noxon made available to me, Hutton Gibson said there was "no systematic extermination" of the Jews by Hitler, only "a deal where he was supposed to make it rough on them so they would all get out and migrate to Israel because they needed people there to fight the Arabs. . . ." (This is consistent with Hutton Gibson's public stands on the issue; he publishes a newsletter in which the word Holocaust appears in quotes.)

Then again, Mel Gibson's publicist, Alan Nierob, also plays bizarre games with the Holocaust. He has tried to deflect any criticism of the Gibsons by identifying himself in both the *New York Post* and *The New Yorker* as "a founding member of the national Holocaust Museum." That's not a trivial claim. The founders of the United States Holocaust Memorial Museum in Washington are an elite donors' group specifically designated as such; they gave a minimum of a million dollars each and are inscribed in granite on the museum's wall. Mr. Nierob is not among them. Presumably he was instead among the 300,000 who responded to the museum's first direct-mail campaign for charter members. That could set you back at least 25 bucks.

Mr. Gibson has told the press that he regards *The Passion* as having actually been directed by the Holy Ghost. If the movie is only half as fanciful as its promotional campaign, I'd say that He has a lock on the Oscar for best director. A Jean Hersholt Humanitarian Award for Mr. Gibson himself, though, may be something of a reach.

POSTSCRIPT

Peter Boyer's September 15, 2003, article in *The New Yorker* contained at least three factual errors: 1) the malignant and false insinuation that the freelance journalist Christopher Noxon, who was assigned by *The New York Times Magazine* to write an article about Mel Gibson's sponsorship of a new church in Malibu, California, had a personal agenda in undertaking the story. (Mr. Boyer wrote: "Some local homeowners objected to [the construction of the church] as it made its way through the zoning process. One homeowner suggested that his son, a freelance journalist named Christopher Noxon, write about the church."); 2) the statement that Mel Gibson's personal publicist was a "founding member of the National Holocaust Museum" in Washington, D.C., which he was not;

and 3) the statement that Hutton Gibson, Mel Gibson's father, had told Mr. Noxon "that the Holocaust was a tragedy that had been hyped out of proportion," when Mr. Gibson had said nothing of the kind to Mr. Noxon.

Though I pointed out errors 2) and 3) in my subsequent *New York Times* column of September 21, 2003 (collected within these pages), *The New Yorker* has yet to publish a correction of any of them (as of this writing, January 2004). Now, Mr. Boyer has used this anthology as an occasion to state that one of these errors—Hutton Gibson's characterization of the Holocaust as a tragedy—was based on his "own reporting," rather than Mr. Noxon's, attributing the mix-up in *The New Yorker* to an "editing error," whatever that means. (Presumably, this errant sentence not only went through *The New Yorker*'s fact checkers but was read in galleys by Mr. Boyer.)

What is Mr. Boyer's "own reporting" on this question? He doesn't explain where Hutton Gibson is on record anywhere referring to the Holocaust as a tragedy. Apparently, we are supposed to take this assertion on faith.

For those who want actual reporting, here is an excerpt from the transcript of Christopher Noxon's taped interview with Hutton Gibson and his wife, Joye, for Noxon's *New York Times Magazine* article. Far from being "dragged" into the story about Mel Gibson, as Mr. Boyer writes, Hutton Gibson invited Mr. Noxon to visit him and interview him at length at his home in Cypress, Texas. Hutton Gibson is a public figure in his own right, the author of three books on Traditionalism, the publisher of a quarterly newsletter on that subject, an activist, and a talk-radio guest. As I wrote in my column, Hutton Gibson refers to the Holocaust in quotes in his newsletter, "The War Is Now!" Here he elaborates on his views about what he calls the "Holocaust."

CN: What about the concentration camps?

HG: They had to rebuild the whole thing. Who knows if it was there in the first place? They say the Germans blew it up. They blew up the plumbing and left the building there. It's physically impossible. Go and ask an undertaker who operates a crematorium or something like that what's it take to get rid of a dead body. It takes one liter of petrol and twenty minutes. Now, six million?

Joye: There weren't even that many Jews in all of Europe.

HG: Anyway there were more after the war than there were be-
        fore. They based it on one figure in the almanac—the figure
        of 1939, I think, showed six million two hundred thousand
        Jews in Poland. And after the war it showed two hundred
        thousand of them—therefore there were six million gone they
        must be dead. But they were gone everywhere.

        There's a fellow named David [*inaudible*] who went around
        to the Auschwitz Museum and they told him that—they had to
        rebuild that stuff. The only place where there was any concen-
        tration was . . . [*inaudible*] Yeah there were prison camps, but
        half the people who died in prison camps died from bomb-
        ings from the Allies.

        There was no systematic extermination, no. The idea was—
        what Hitler considered his Final Solution—was. . . . He made a
        deal where he was supposed to make it rough on them so
        they would all get out and migrate to Israel, because they
        needed people there to fight the Arabs and take up space.

        And then the people who coined the word—Shoah—
        according to the various newspapers he was released from
        three different prison camps within several months. Figure if
        they were going to exterminate anyone, they would have ex-
        terminated him.

        No I don't believe that for a minute. Because even so,
        there were any number of Polish that were there after the war
        too.

        That's something that will never be forgotten. If the world
        lasts ten million years they . . .

CN: So, Hitler was secretly working with the Jews?

HG: He was cooperating with the bigwigs to get the small fry to
        get out of Germany and go to Israel.

CN: The bigwigs were?

HG: The financiers . . . I notice your machine is running. In Ger-
        many you can go to jail for saying it didn't happen.

CN: You can go to Jail?

HG: Yeah. Because they tell us that they have no connection to
        the crucifixion of Christ. Because they weren't there. It's their

ancestors if anybody, not the current people. But look at the whole race. We're all involved in original sin. In Germany, they weren't there. They're forced to pay reparations. They have two sets of rules—one for them and one for us. They're not responsible for what their ancestors did, but we are responsible for what ours did. It's not our fault, because we didn't do it. The rest of the world didn't know anything about it.

CN: Will the movie that Mel is making clearly make that connection to who is responsible?

HG: The facts are clear. Those facts are the most well established in our history.

Why Peter Boyer wishes to whitewash Hutton Gibson's views about the Holocaust remains a mystery, as does *The New Yorker*'s silence about the perpetration of that whitewash in its pages.

January 9, 2004

PART EIGHT

SOME NEW FORMS
OF ANTI-SEMITISM

SIMON SCHAMA

Virtual Annihilation

[*This is a transcript of Professor Schama's talk at the YIVO Institute conference "Old Demons, New Debates: Anti-Semitism in the West," May 11, 2003.*]

HOW WAS MOTHER'S DAY this year? Mine didn't go so well. I called my mother; I say, "What's up?" "Three hundred and eighty-six headstones is what's up," she says: "Plashett Cemetery in Eastham, your Uncle Victor"–it's actually her Uncle Victor–my Great-Aunt Prissy–"perpetrators apparently arrested."

"A shock," I say then. "No, I'm not shocked by anything anymore," she says. And she's right. We certainly shouldn't be surprised that ancient paranoia has, after all, survived both the reasonings of modernity and the testimony of history. We live, after all, in a country and at a time when—so the opinion polls tell us—more people than not reject the scientific validity of the theory of evolution. (In some quarters, Darwinism is regarded, along with secular humanism, as another conspiracy of the Elders of Zion.) But then America is not the only country in which children are made precociously knowing while adults are made credulous. It was a French book that became a bestseller by asserting that the al-Qaeda attack on the Pentagon never happened and that photographs which suggested it had, had been digitally doctored by the CIA. Where once it was naïvely supposed that images never lie, the sovereign assumption of the digital age is that they never tell the truth. Truth morphs: Elvis is alive, the Mogen David is really the Satanic pentangle, there were no gas chambers at Auschwitz. And digital-communications technology, once imagined as a universe of transparent and perpetual illumination in which cancerous falsehoods would perish beneath a saturation bombardment of irradiating data, has instead generated a much murkier, verification-free habitat, where a Google-generated search will deliver an electronic page in which links to lies and lunacy appear in identical format as those to truth and sanity. But why should we ever have assumed that technology and reason would be mutually self-reinforcing, since a quick visit to "Stormfront" will persuade you that the demonic is in fact the best customer of the electronic.

It's only in America that we imagine history as a series of cultural supercessions, each one comprehensively victorious in the totality of its effacements. Thus, in this processional view of the past, Native American society is supposed to have been obliterated by colonialism, which in turn yields to individualist, capitalist democracy. Except, of course, it doesn't, not entirely— and much time is spent, and blood oft times is spilled, tidying up the inconvenient anachronisms. In Europe, on the other hand, especially at the end of the last century, so rigidly serial in approach to cultural alteration, it has been suspected to be not much more than textbook convenience.

In Europe, ghosts have an impolite way of muscling their way into times and places where they are unexpected, which is why, for example, the cultural emblem of the first great industrial society in the world, Victorian Britain, imprinted on railway-station designs and museums of arts, crafts, and science, was the medieval pointed arch. It was, to be sure, an emblem of resistance as much as validation. So the pointiest of the champions of Christian perpendicular, England and Scotland, Thomas Carlyle, unsurprisingly turns out to be the fiercest in his hatred of—his words—"niggers and Jews." The great and the good of Victorian Britain could take both the friends and the enemies of the machine age in its stride, so the age which fetishized rootedness, Victorian Britain again, while at the same time making fortunes by displacing mass populations, made, as it thought, the willfully deracinated, *le juif errant*, the special target of its disingenuousness. Bonjour, Monsieur Melmotte; hello, Henry Ford.

To GROW UP British and Jewish is by definition not to be especially confounded at the obstinacy of atavisms refusing to lie down in the tomb of their redundancy. The protean persistence of anti-Semitism came home to me early. I think I was seven when I first saw the writing on the wall. The wall in question was one of those crumbling redbrick affairs, blocking off a view of the tracks on the Fenchurch Street line connecting London with the Essex villages which lie in the north banks of the Thames Estuary, where my family lived. They were not quite suburban, these places, though Jewish businessmen, like my father, had moved there out of the burnt-out wreckage of the city in the East End, where they still kept warehouses and offices. They were part fishing villages, part dormitory suburbs, part seaside towns: yellow broom in the spring, blowsy cabbage roses in the summer, the smell of the unloading shrimp boats, the laden winkle carts—dangerously, excitingly *treif*—drifting over the tide. But every morning those Jewish businessmen would take the Fenchurch Street train—and one morning my father took me as far as the station—and there on that wall, in white letters faint and fugitive, but since the day was cloudy and gray as they always are on the Estuary, it seems, livid in the light, were just two cryptic letters.

P.J. Nothing more, not P.J. LOVES S.T., just the letters alone. So of course I asked my father, and remember him reddening briefly and telling me it was just some *chazerei*, old *chazerei*, and to forget about it; it didn't matter. Which of course made me more determined to decode the crypt. And it was, I think, my cheder teacher, Mrs. Marks, the same teacher who got me to dress up in miniature tuxedo as Mr. Shabbes (the eight-year-old bride was, of course, Mrs. Balabooster), who looked me in the eye and told me, "P.J. was 'Perish Judah.'" And that was a relic of some bad old days in the thirties, when the union of fascists and Arnold Leese's Britain had marched—not just in Stepney and Whitechapel and Mile End but right down to the end of the line, to where the Jews had dared penetrate the sanctum sanctorum of Englishness: pebble-dashed, herbaceous-bordered, tea-pouring Westcliff and Leigh-on-Sea.

P.J. SCARED THE HELL out of me, and not because it smelled faintly of Zyklon B. I'm not sure I knew much about that in '52, despite the missing relatives on my mother's side. My generation, born in the last years of the war—I was born in '45—would only get their crash course in Holocaust a little later: in the London shul library, where Lord Russell of Liverpool—*Scourge of the Swastika,* with its obscenely unsparing photography of bulldozed, naked bodies—opened and shut our eyes. But I had read *Ivanhoe*—indeed, I'd seen Elizabeth Taylor's *Rebecca*—and so the archaic, declamatory quality of P.J. spoke to me of the massacres at York, the canonization of Little Saint Hugh of Lincoln, Richard I's coronation pogrom in London, 1199. The persistence of the ugliest strain of medieval paranoia in my island culture seemed, while not exactly fish and chips, not something wholly alien from British tradition, notwithstanding Disraeli, *Daniel Deronda,* and the Victorian high hats and morning coats, which for some reason marked the official Shabbes morning dress of the notables of our synagogue. Some of the same writers I most enthusiastically read as a child—Hilaire Belloc, G. K. Chesteron, John Buchan, all of them armored warriors for holy tradition and for the sceptered isle—of course turned out a bit later, on closer inspection, to be the most relentless perpetuators of anti-Semitic demonologies.

There was, however, a moment of innocence when the

cheerfully technocratic Festival of Britain in 1951 did seem to announce the exorcism of barbarian phantoms. Never mind it coincided with the first panicky revival of racist fascism in Britain, mobilized against Caribbean immigration. We were told that technology, and especially new kinds of communications technology, would diffuse knowledge and that knowledge would chase away superstition, destitution, and disease. It would fall to our generation, the most confidently booming of the baby boomers, to make good on the promises of the Enlightenment of Voltaire, Franklin, and, above all, the cheerfully ill-fated Marquis de Condorcet. Modernism, started in the first half of the twentieth century, had somehow fallen foul of red-fanged tribalism, but we were the children of techne, of the dream machines of the *philosophes*. Not that anything like this was as yet either on our lips or our minds. I remember one of our history teachers at school, secondary school, who in fact bore a rather startling resemblance to Voltaire, say to our class of thirteen-year-olds, "Well, lads, we don't know what the rest of the twentieth century has in store, but I guarantee that two of the old bugbears are finally done for—revealed religion and ethnic chauvinism." So much for history's predictive power.

Looking so much like Voltaire as he did, he should perhaps have known better, since Voltaire, as we know from Arthur Hertzberg, Peter Gay, and many other scholars, was a prime case of a *philosophe* who thought one way and felt another, who positively nursed the worm in the bud; who believed in the transformative power of reason up to a point, and that point was where it concerned Jews. It was not just that Voltaire believed the condition of being able to treat Jews humanely was the mass abandonment of Judaism and his understandable pessimism this would ever happen. It was that, *au fond,* he believed that even if the Jews could be persuaded to discard what made them culturally Jews, there would always still be some sort of insuperable racial or even biological obstacle to true assimilation.

The notion that the benevolent illuminations of the Enlightenment would in due course be bound to eradicate superstition and prejudice—both those said to be held by the Jews and those undoubtedly held against them—was compromised, not just by the disingenuousness of some of its apostles but by the slightly mechanical nature of their prescience. What failed them was their dependence on wordiness, their belief in the inevitable and permanent supremacy of textual logic, their faith in the unconditional surrender of fables to the irrefutably documented proof. He who could command critical reading, and critical writing, would in such a world of logically driven discourse command the future. And that future would be one in which rational demonstration would always prevail over emotive spectacle—just as, the same epistemologists thought, the Protestant *logos* had vanquished Catholic charisma. But of course it hadn't. Nor did the Enlightenment banish the fairy tale so much as become, in the hands of the Brothers Grimm, its most psychologically aggressive reinventor. What would unfold in the age of the industrial machine which ensued was precisely, as Walter Benjamin accurately diagnosed, the astonishing capacity of technology to promote and project fantastic mythologies rather than banish them.

From the outset, of course, the machinery of sensationalist stupefaction—the dioramas and panoramas and Eïdophusikons— were the natural handmaid of the sublime and terrible. As Victorian Britain became more colonized by industry, so its public became greedier by spectacles of disaster, brought to them as visceral entertainment: the simulacra of Vesuvian eruptions, the collapse of the Tay Bridge, an avalanche in the Simplon. More ominously, the paradox of a modernist technology, co-opted to attack modernism, came at the hands of its most adroit practitioners, no longer so paradoxical. The D. W. Griffith who specialized in the manipulation of immense crowds and the apocalyptic collapse of imperial hubris was all of a piece with the chivalric romancer of the Ku Klux Klan. Mussolini could simultaneously embrace the piston-pump ecstasies of Marinettian futurism and the most preposterous Cinecittà-fabricated colossalism of Roman nostalgia. Ultimately, of course, Albert Speer would deliver for Hitler a cathedral of light where annihilationist rant would be bathed in arch of refulgence and Leni Riefenstahl would begin her epiphany with a kind of aerial cinematic annunciation: the angel of the *Totenkopf* moving through the skies, casting an immaculately shadowed simulacrum down on the ancestral sod.

From which it is surely just a hop, skip, and a click to the consummation of cyber-hatred, to the welcoming page of the Czech-based "Jewrats," where its designers, appreciative of their predecessors' knack for cutting-edge media, proudly declare, rather as if they were offering a year's warranty, that "National Socialism was always known for its all-round quality propaganda." At "Jewrats," you can not only download the old favorites *Der Ewige Jude, Triumph of the Will,* and *The Turner Diaries* and elegiac interviews with George Lincoln Rockwell but also try your hand at games like "SA Mann," "Rattenjagd," and "Ghetto Blaster."

Or try the homepage of "Resistance Records," if you've got a strong stomach, featuring a video game called "Ethnic Cleansing," whose champions, Terminator-style, are garbed as gladiators, whose targets, helpfully visualized at the top of the page lest casual visitors confuse them with Bosnian Muslims, are Julius Streicher caricatures of Jews, complete with standard-issue *Der Stürmer* extruded lips and hooked proboscis.

Just as Romantic Gothic Sensationalism fed on the victories which the optical scored over the textual, so the creative forte of the digital media has been the projection of electronic violence and encrypted runes. The most archaic motives of human culture, manichean battle, objects of occult veneration, ecstatic occasionally hallucinatory vision, all delivered in liquid crystal readouts, one kind of elemental plasma translated into another. The online game "Nazi Doom" is in fact just an adapted and slightly pirated version of the emphatically non-scientific Gothic space-fantasy games "Doom," "Final Doom," and the deliciously oxymoronic "Final Doom 2." The optimistic dream of the Enlightenment that technology and addictive fantasy would be in some sort of zero-sum-game relationship turns out, as Benjamin predicted again, to be precisely the opposite case.

I don't mean of course to say that the digital world is typified by the engineered delivery of the irrational, only that it is not exactly inhospitable to its propagation. Cyberspace is, of course, itself the work of much cerebration, but its most elaborate fabulists are devoted to the primacy of the visceral over the logical. They know their market. Against instantly summoned electronically pulsing apparitions, the Celtic crosses of the white power organizations like Aryan Resistance or Stormfront—the mid-'90s creation of the ex-Klansman Don Black, who hooked it up in federal prison and who created a digital thirteen-year-old wide-eyed boy as his ideal teenage apologist and recruiter. Against that, the patiently discursive modes of recent argument are handicapped, especially in competition for the attention of alienated adolescents, for whom the appeal of barbarian symbolism and occasionally barbaric action is precisely the rejection of bookishness. The ultimate Gothic fantasists, the murderers at Columbine, are known to have been visitors to these websites.

It's a commonplace now to observe with Jay Bolter that the triumph of the Web represents the overthrow, for good or ill, not just of linear narrative but of the entire system of Baconian inductive reasoning, with its explicit commitment to hierarchies of knowledge, tests of proof, and so on. The universe of deep cyberspace is akin to whatever lies way beyond the reassuringly orderly alignment of the planets in our own relatively parochial solar system. Instead, it launches the traveler along a pathway of links to indeterminate destinations, the wormholes of epistemology; and along the routes, the digital argonaut is exposed to a furiously oncoming welter of incoherently arrayed bodies of information. The engineers of hate sites know this, and depend on capturing the aimless surfer who might, for example, stumble on an ostensibly Orientalist health site called "Bamboo Delights"—including "The Skinny Buddha Weight Loss Method" and—be directed through a single link to the neo-Nazi "Police Patriot" site, both designed by "Jew Watch" and "Stormfront."

The Web is by its nature uncritically omnivorous. All it asks for is to be fed with information. It has the capacity to monitor its input only through the clumsy and ethically controversial means of censorship, so that, I'm told, in Germany when asked for sites responding to the word "Mengele," the Web will refuse to deliver them to the user. But the notion that any sites can somehow be scrutinized—much less policed for misinformation, fraud, and lies—is already both electronically and institutionally impossible. If you search Google or www.alltheweb.com for *The Protocols of the Elders of Zion,* you'll be greeted on the first page with many hundreds of entries, many of which are now devoted to reporting or debating the Egyptian television series *Horse Without a Rider,* which notoriously treated the *Protocols* as an historical event; not by the Anti-Defamation League or by YIVO or any other critical historically informed repudiation of the forgery, but by Radio Islam's invitation to download the entire foul and forged text, along with *The Jewish Conspiracy Against the Muslim World* and Henry Ford's (there he is again) *The International Jew,* or the anti–new world order ravings of Henry Makow, Ph.D., inventor of the word game "Scruples," as he tells us—his website is www.savethemales.com—and who regards Judaism as a mask to disguise the international hegemony of the Khazars. All of these will line up for the unwary, long before any sort of critical or historically responsible commentary is reached.

Nor could anything possibly be further away from the epistemological conventions according to which arguments are tested against critical challenges than the Net's characteristic form of chat, which overwhelmingly takes the form of call and response, to which there is never any resolution nor conclusion, merely a string of unadjudicated utterances and ejaculations. Digital allegiances can be formed there not through any sort of sifting of truth and falsehood but in response to or in defense against a kind of cognitive battering. And the virtual reality of the Internet, as Sherry Turkle, Les Back, and others have pointed out, has been a gift to both the purveyors and the consumers of paranoia. It offers an electronic habitat which is simultaneously furtive and exhibitionist, structurally molecular but capable, as the user is emboldened, of forming itself into an electronic community of the like-minded. It is perfectly engineered, then, for leaderless resistance and the Lone Wolf—the recommended model for zealous racists, neo-Nazis, and white-power warriors, hunting, like Timothy McVeigh, in solitude or small or temporarily linked packs. Instead of slogging up to the camp in Idaho or Montana, digital stormtroopers can assemble in their very own virtual Idaho, download the "Horst Wessel Lied," and electronically bond.

The Web is also, of course, a mine of useful information for the aspiring neo-Nazi, not just in the selection of human and institutional targets but about the resources needed to strike them. Everything from artisanal ammonium nitrate to the much more wired offensives against the race enemy, involving intensive electronic jamming known as "digital bombing," to targeted systems of electronic virus contamination and sabotage. Taken together, the five hundred or so websites in the United States built to proselytize for anti-Semitic and racist causes constitute a virtual universe of hatred, protean enough to hunker down or reach out as the moment and the need require, encrypting, when necessary, their most bilious messages so that they become accessible only to those with decrypting keys, a tactic of course adored by secrecy fetishists, or aggressively and openly campaigning when that seems to be the priority.

Once inside this net, you can log on to "Resistance Records" and download white-power music like Nordic Thunder, order CDs from the online catalog; you can link to the ostensibly more mainstream racist organizations, like the British National Party, who have just trebled their representation in British local government elections. You can reassure yourself that the "Holo-cost," as it's called, or the "Holo-hoax," never happened, and it's just another disinformation conspiracy designed to channel reparations to the ever-open mouth of the international conspiracy of Jew bankers. You can browse the *Christian Guide to Small Arms,* order up Nazi memorabilia or your Aryan Nations warm-up jacket, with all the ease of someone going shopping for Yankees souvenirs. And most ominously of all, out there in cyberspace you can act out games of virtual annihilation with none of the risks or consequences you might incur in the actual world of body space.

In the circumstances, it is perhaps reassuring that according to the best and most recent estimates of regular visitors and inhabitants of these kinds of sites, these may amount to no more than maybe 50,000 or 100,000 at most. It's possible to argue it is better that the paranoids lock themselves away in the black holes of cyberspace than act out their delusions in the world of real humanity. But that is of course to assume that "Stormfront" troopers and Aryan crusaders will never make the leap from clicking to shooting. And if there's anything we've learned from this peculiarly delusional moment in our history, it is that today's media fantasy may indeed turn into tomorrow's cultural virus. And in the world of wired terror, head counts are no longer any guide to the possibility of trouble, which comes, as we've learned to our cost, very much in single spies rather than battalions.

However abhorrent, I suspect the real threat posed by electronic hatred may not be in the hard core of rabidly delusional anti-Semites, who may, alas, may always be with us. It is rather from the electronic extension of the paranoid's style out to much bigger constituencies of the aggrieved, who see in its basic worldview—a global conspiracy of money, secularism, and sexual corruption—a perennial explanation for their own misfortune, for their sense of beleaguered alienation. The transpositions then become easy. For the Rothschilds, read Goldman Sachs and the IMF; for the Illuminati, read the Council on Foreign Relations. Henry Ford said of the *Protocols of the Elders of Zion*: "All I know is that it fits events." Nor is this habitual imprinting of the old template onto contemporary events a monopoly of Left or Right. In fact, *les extrêmes se touchent:* anti-globalizers meet the anti-immigrants; anti-Americanism meets America First; America First meets America Only.

What they share is a freshening and quickening of the rhetoric of violence, the poisoning of the airwaves as well as cyberspace. Ultra-chauvinist blowhards habitually demonize on air those whom they take as insufficiently patriotic as "scum" or "vermin," and who need, in whatever manner, to be locked up, deported, or generally done away with.

Who are these contaminating aliens lodged in the bloodstream of the body politic? Lovers of multilateralism, or the United Nations, any sort of faggoty liberal intellectual who professes a self-evidently diseased skepticism and who exercises a disguised but clawlike grip over the media. Jews? Goodness, no. Just people who happen to talk too much, think too highly of reason, and organize conferences.

JOSHUA MURAVCHIK

The Neoconservative Cabal

OVER THE LAST MONTHS, the term "neoconservative" has been in the air as never before in its thirty-year career. Try entering it in Nexis, the electronic database of news stories. Even if you were to restrict the request to stories containing "Iraq" and "Bush," the search will abort; the number of entries exceeds the program's capacity. Seven years after Norman Podhoretz, the conductor of the neocon orchestra, pronounced the demise of the movement in these pages [*Commentary*], neoconservatives are seen to be wielding more influence than ever before. For it is they who, notoriously, are alleged to have transformed George W. Bush beyond all recognition. At their hands, the President who as a candidate had envisioned a "humble" America—one that would reduce foreign deployments and avoid nation building—became a warrior chieftain who has already toppled two foreign governments and has laid down an ultimatum to others warning of a similar fate.

"The neoconservatives . . . are largely responsible for getting us into the war against Iraq," observes Elizabeth Drew in *The New York Review of Books*. "The neocon vision has become the hard core of American foreign policy," declares *Newsweek*. "They have penetrated the culture at nearly every level from the halls of academia to the halls of the Pentagon," frets *The*

New York Times, adding that "they've accumulated the where-withal financially [and] professionally to broadcast what they think over the airwaves to the masses or over cocktails to those at the highest levels of government." "Long before George W. Bush reached the White House, many of these confrontations [with other nations] had been contemplated by the neoconservatives," reveals the *National Journal.*

Overseas, where the policies attributed to the neocons are far more controversial than here, the tone is commensurately hotter. A six-page spread in the French weekly *Le Nouvel Observateur* described "les intellectuals neoconservateurs" as the "ideologues of American empire." The article ran under a banner headline: AFTER IRAQ, THE WORLD. In England, the British Broadcasting Company (BBC) aired an hour-long television special that began: "This is a story about people who want the world run their way, the American way, [and] . . . scare the hell out of people." The *Times* of London anxiously urged close British cooperation with the U.S. if only to gain the leverage needed to "spike the ambitions of U.S. neoconservatives."

Who makes up this potent faction? Within the administration, Deputy Secretary of Defense Paul Wolfowitz is usually identified as the key actor, together with Richard Perle, a member and until recently the chairman of the Defense Advisory Board. A handful of other high-level Bush appointees are often named as adherents of the neocon faith, including Undersecretary of Defense Douglas Feith, Undersecretary of State John Bolton, National Security Council staff member Elliott Abrams, and Vice Presidential aide Lewis "Scooter" Libby. The American Enterprise Institute (AEI, where I work), *The Weekly Standard* magazine, and William Kristol's Project for the New American Century—all three rent offices in the same building— are often described as constituting the movement's Washington command center. And then, of course, there is this magazine [*Commentary*], crucible of so much neoconservative thought.

The history of neoconservatism is less sensational than its

current usage implies. The term came into currency in the mid-1970s as an anathema—pronounced, by upholders of leftist orthodoxy, against a group of intellectuals, centered mostly in *Commentary* and the quarterly *The Public Interest,* who then still thought of themselves as liberals but were at odds with the dominant thinking of the Left. One part of this group consisted of writers about domestic policy—Irving Kristol, Daniel Patrick Moynihan, James Q. Wilson, Nathan Glazer—who had developed misgivings about the programs of the New Deal or Lyndon Johnson's Great Society. The other main contingent focused on foreign policy, and especially on the decline of America's position vis-à-vis the Soviet Union in the wake of the Vietnam war. The names here included, among others, Podhoretz, Jeane Kirkpatrick, and Eugene V. Rostow. Although, at first, most of these people resisted the label "neoconservative," eventually almost all of them acquiesced in it.

Today, many who are called neoconservatives are too young to have taken part in these debates while others, although old enough, followed a different trajectory in arriving at their political ideas. This would hardly matter if neoconservatism were an actual political movement, or if there were general agreement about its tenets. But few of those writing critically about neoconservatism today have bothered to stipulate what they take those tenets to be. For most, the term seems to serve as a sophisticated-sounding synonym for "hawk" or "hardliner" or even "ultraconservative."

For others, however, it is used with a much more sinister connotation. In their telling, neoconservatives are a strange, veiled group, almost a cabal whose purpose is to manipulate U.S. policy for ulterior purposes.

Thus, several scribes have concentrated on laying bare the hidden wellsprings of neoconservative belief. These have been found to reside in the thinking of two improbable figures: the immigrant American political philosopher Leo Strauss (1899–1973) and the Bolshevik military commander Leon Trotsky

(1879–1940). "Who runs things?" *The New York Times* asked, concluding that "it wouldn't be too much of a stretch to answer: the intellectual heirs of Leo Strauss" with whom the Bush administration is "rife." *The Boston Globe* ran a 3,000-word article claiming that "we live in a world increasingly shaped by Leo Strauss," while in a sidebar to its own feature story on the neocons, *Le Nouvel Observateur* introduced French readers to "Leo Strauss, Their Mentor."

Michael Lind, an American who writes for the British leftist magazine *New Statesman,* has been the most insistent voice invoking the name of Trotsky, or rather "the largely Jewish-American Trotskyist movement" of which, Lind says, "most neoconservative defense intellectuals . . . are products." Jeet Heer, who expounded the Straussian roots of neoconservatism in *The Boston Globe,* went on to disclose the Trotsky connection in Canada's *National Post.* ("Bolshevik's Writings Supported the Idea of Pre-emptive War," ran the subhead.) Others agreed about this dual connection. William Pfaff, in the *International Herald Tribune,* contributed one column on the influence of Leo Strauss and another linking Bush's foreign policy to the "intellectual legacy of the Trotskyism of many of the neoconservative movement's founders." In particular, in Pfaff's judgment, administration policy "seems a rightist version of Trotsky's 'permanent revolution.'"

Actually, neither line of genealogical inquiry is new. Eight years ago, in *Foreign Affairs,* John Judis derided my advocacy of "exporting democracy" as a kind of "inverted Trotskyism." As for Strauss, it was noticed as far back as the Reagan administration that a small number of the philosopher's former students had taken policy positions in the State and Defense departments. But the prize for the recent resuscitation of Strauss's name would seem to belong to the crackpot political agitator Lyndon LaRouche, who began to harp on it in speeches and publications months before any of the references I have cited above. LaRouche, who ceased using the pseudonym Lyn Marcus (a conscious derivation of Lenin Marx) when he vaulted from the far Left to the far Right, and who has served time in a federal penitentiary on charges of gulling elderly people out of their savings in order to finance his political movement, has fingered Strauss "along with Bertrand Russell and H. G. Wells" as the parties responsible for "steering the United States into a disastrous replay of the Peloponnesian war."

This preoccupation with ancestor-hunting may seem of secondary interest, but since it is typical of the way most recent "analysis" of neoconservative ideas has been conducted, it is worth pausing over for another moment.

For one thing, the sheer sloppiness of the reporting on the alleged Strauss-Trotsky connection is itself remarkable. Thus, *The New York Times* claimed extravagantly that AEI consists in its entirety of Straussians, whereas a little checking yields, out of fifty-six scholars and fellows, exactly two who would count themselves as Straussians and a third who would acknowledge a significant intellectual debt to Strauss; none of the three is in the field of foreign policy. The *Times* also identified Perle as a Straussian—which is false—while erroneously stating that he was married to the daughter of the late military strategist Albert Wohlstetter, whom it likewise falsely labeled a Straussian. Even after an initial correction (explaining that Perle had merely studied under Wohlstetter at the University of Chicago and had not married his daughter) and a second correction (acknowledging that Perle had never studied under Wohlstetter *or* attended the University of Chicago), the paper still could not bring itself to retract its fanciful characterizations of either Perle's or Wohlstetter's ties to Strauss. The paper also mischaracterized Podhoretz as an "admirer" of Strauss, which is true only in a very loose sense. Similar errors have infected the stories in other publications.

And Trotsky? Lind in his disquisition on "the largely Jewish-American Trotskyist movement" instanced seven pivotal neocon figures as the Bolshevik revolutionary's acolytes: Wolfowitz,

Feith, Libby, Bolton, Abrams, James R. Woolsey, and Perle. This was too much for Alan Wald, a student of political ideas and himself a genuine Trotskyist who pointed out that none of these men "ever had an organizational or ideological association with Trotskyism." Even more ludicrously, Lind characterized a series of open letters to the President published by the Project for the New American Century as "a PR technique pioneered by their Trotskyist predecessors"; whatever Lind may have had in mind by this phrase, genuine Trotskyists would be less interested in sending petitions to the President than in hanging him from the nearest lamppost.

In truth, I can think of only one major neocon figure who did have a significant dalliance with Trotskyism, and that was Irving Kristol. The dalliance occurred during his student days some sixty-odd years ago, and whatever imprint it may have left on Kristol's thought certainly did not make him a neoconservative on foreign policy, for in that area his views have been much more akin to those of traditional conservatives. During the 1980s, for example, Kristol opposed the "Reagan Doctrine" of support for anti-Communist guerrillas and belittled the idea of promoting democracy abroad.

But that brings us to the actual ideas of these two presumed progenitors of neoconservatism. Strauss, according to Jeet Heer, emerges from a close reading as a

> disguised Machiavelli, a cynical teacher who encouraged his followers to believe that their intellectual superiority entitles them to rule over the bulk of humanity by means of duplicity.

Similarly, Pfaff:

> An elite recognizes the truth . . . and keeps it to itself. This gives it insight and implicitly power that others do not possess. This obviously is an important element in

Strauss's appeal to American conservatives. . . . His real appeal to the neoconservatives, in my view, is that his elitism presents a principled rationalization for policy expediency, and for "necessary lies" told to those whom the truth would demoralize.

Neither Heer nor Pfaff offers a clue as to where in Strauss's corpus one might find these ideas, giving one the impression that they learned what they know of him from a polemical book by one Shadia Drury, who holds a chair in "social justice" at a Canadian university and who finds Strauss to be a "profoundly tribal and fascistic thinker." In any event, although Strauss did write about restrictions on free inquiry, notably in *Persecution and the Art of Writing,* his point was not to advocate persecution but to suggest a way of reading philosophers who had composed their work in unfree societies. Far from the authoritarian described by Heer and Pfaff, Strauss, a refugee from Nazi Germany, was a committed democrat whose attachment and gratitude to America ran deep and who, in the words of Allan Bloom (perhaps his most famous student), "knew that liberal democracy is the only decent and just alternative available to modern man."

Both Heer and Pfaff make Strauss out to be a Machiavellian, but both have the story upside down. If there is a single core point in Strauss's teachings, including his book on Machiavelli, it concerns the distinction between ancients and moderns; his own affinity—perhaps eccentric, certainly "conservative"—lay with the thought of the former, who were devoted to knowing the good, in contradistinction to the latter, who were more exclusively concerned with practical things. In this understanding, it was Machiavelli who initiated the philosophical break with the Platonic/Aristotelian tradition, a development that Strauss regarded as baneful. But reading political counsel into Strauss is altogether a misplaced exercise. He was not a politico but a philosopher whose life's work was devoted to deepening our understanding of earlier thinkers and who rarely if ever engaged in contemporary politics.

If Strauss's writing is abstruse, Trotsky by contrast is easy to understand, at least if one knows the basic formulas of Marxism. Nonetheless, those who invoke him as another dark influence on neoconservatism are no better informed than those who invoke Strauss. Lind and Pfaff and Judis all refer portentously to Trotsky's theory of "permanent revolution," apparently under the impression that by it Trotsky must have intended a movement to spread socialism from one country to another in much the same violent and revolutionary manner that neocons supposedly aim to disseminate their own brand of democracy around the world.

But the theory of permanent revolution was about other matters entirely. According to the late-nineteenth- and early-twentieth-century Marxists, the socialist revolution could unfold only some years after capitalism and the bourgeoisie had triumphed over feudalism in undeveloped countries like Russia; this meant that socialists had no choice but to support capitalism until it ripened and set the stage for revolution. From this prospect of deadly boredom, Trotsky rescued the movement by arguing for an immediate seizure of power in hopes of somehow telescoping the bourgeois and socialist revolutions into one seamless sequence. That was "permanent revolution."

As is the case with the Strauss-hunters, it is far from evident what any of this has to do with Iraq, terrorism, or promoting democracy. The neocon journalist Arnold Beichman put it sardonically and well: "STOP THE PRESSES: Trotsky . . . wouldn't have supported the Iraq war." On second thought he probably would have—on Saddam's side.

Finally, if the attempts to link neoconservatives to Strauss and Trotsky are based on misidentification and misconstruction, the fact that both linkages have been made—in some cases by the same writer—is stranger still. For it would be hard to come up with a more disparate pair of thinkers. Strauss's mission was to take us back by means of contemplation to the nearly lost past of classical antiquity. Trotsky's was to lead mankind by means of violent action to an unprecedented new society. The one aimed to rescue philosophy from ideology; the other was the consummate ideologue. How, exactly, does neoconservatism bear the earmarks of both of these projects simultaneously? No one has attempted to explain.

There is, however, one thing that Strauss and Trotsky did have in common, and that one thing may get us closer to the real reason their names have been so readily invoked. Both were Jews. The neoconservatives, it turns out, are also in large proportion Jewish—and this, to their detractors, constitutes evidence of the ulterior motives that lurk behind the policies they espouse.

Lind, for example, writes that neocons "call their revolutionary ideology 'Wilsonianism' . . . , but it is really Trotsky's theory of the permanent revolution mingled with the far-right Likud strain of Zionism." Lind's view was cited at length and with evident approval by the *National Journal,* which noted that he "isn't alone":

> Commentators from surprisingly diverse spots on the political spectrum [agree] that neocons took advantage of the attacks on the World Trade Center and the Pentagon to advance a longstanding agenda that is only tangentially related to keeping the United States safe from terrorism. In this view, America's invasion of Iraq and threatening of Syria have little to do with fighting terrorism, eliminating weapons of mass destruction, or promoting democracy. Instead, those actions largely have to do with settling old grievances, putting oil-rich territory into friendly hands, and tilting the balance of power in the Middle East toward Israel.

Elizabeth Drew made a similar point, if more opaquely:

> Because some . . . of the neoconservatives are Jewish and
> virtually all are strong supporters of the Likud party's poli-
> cies, the accusation has been made that their aim to "de-
> mocratize" the region is driven by their desire to surround
> Israel with more sympathetic neighbors. Such a view
> would explain the otherwise puzzling statements by Wolf-
> owitz and others before the [Iraq] war that "the road to
> peace in the Middle East goes through Baghdad." But it is
> also the case that Bush and his chief political adviser Karl
> Rove are eager both to win more of the Jewish vote in
> 2004 than Bush did in 2000 and to maintain the support of
> the Christian Right, whose members are also strong sup-
> porters of Israel.

Drew's use of the word "but" at the head of the last sentence
was no doubt designed to distance her from the accusation that
the neocons' motive is to serve the interests of Israel, even as
the words that follow the "but" only seem to confirm the
charge.

More explicit, and more egregious, was the hard-Left historian Paul Buhle, who wrote in *Tikkun* that "It is almost as if
the anti-Semitic Protocols of Zion, successfully fought for a
century, have suddenly returned with an industrial-sized grain
of truth"—that "truth" being, of course, that the hawkish policies of the neoconservatives are indeed tailored for Israel's
benefit.

Perhaps the most dramatic effort to expose the hidden Jewish interest underlying neocon ideas was the BBC-TV special
on America's "war party." It was aired on the program *Panorama,* which touts itself as the British equivalent of CBS's
60 Minutes, and the lead-in announced: "Tonight: Will America's Superhawks Drag Us into More Wars Against Their Enemies?" It did not take long for the meaning of the phrase "their

enemies" to become apparent. First, however, viewers were introduced to a rogues' gallery of neoconservative interviewees, each of them filmed at an unusually close angle with the head filling the entire screen for an eerie, repulsive effect. Freeze-frame stills of the subjects were also shown, shifting suddenly from color into the look of white-on-black negatives, while in the background one heard sound effects appropriate to a lineup on a police drama. By contrast, the interviewer, Steve Bradshaw, and a number of guests hostile to the neocons were shown mostly in appealing poses.

On the show itself, Perle was introduced as "the neocons' political godfather," a suggestive term whose implication was reinforced by a question put separately to him and another guest: "Are you a mafia?" As the camera panned over the building that houses AEI and the other arms of this "mafia," we heard from the announcer that here was where the "future is being plotted."

And what exactly is being "plotted"? The answer was foreshadowed early on when an unidentified woman-in-the-street said of the war in Iraq: "It seems like there's . . . another agenda that we're not really privy to and that is what concerns me most." Several minutes later, Bradshaw returned to the same motif: "We picked up a recurrent theme of insider talk in Washington. Some leading neocons, people whisper, are strongly pro-Zionist and want to topple regimes in the Middle East to help Israel as well as the U.S." To shed light on this "highly sensitive issue," he then turned to Jim Lobe, identified as a "veteran neocon watcher and longstanding opponent of anti-Semitism."

Lobe was used repeatedly as the show's resident expert. A reporter with the "alternative" media who prides himself on being a nemesis of neoconservatives, he has no special credentials as an "opponent of anti-Semitism," but the gratuitous compliment was there for a purpose—namely, to inoculate him and his hosts against the obvious charge of Jew-baiting. For that is indeed what came next. Bradshaw posed the leading question: "You think it's legitimate to talk about the pro-Israeli politics of some of the neoconservatives?" And Lobe, looking as Jewish as his name sounds, replied: "I think it's very difficult to understand them if you don't begin at that point." A few moments later, in a simulacrum of journalistic balance, Bradshaw allowed the Middle East specialist Meyrav Wurmser to deny any special neoconservative fidelity to Israel. Wurmser is an immigrant to the United States from Israel, and looks and sounds the part; she could not have been chosen with more care to verify the charge she was brought on to deny—that the neoconservatives are indeed a Jewish mafia, dragging both America and Britain into war after war for the sake of Israel.

If there is an element of anti-Semitism at work in some of the attacks on the neoconservatives—and there manifestly is—to call it such is not, alas, enough. Even outright canards need to be rebutted, tedious and demeaning though the exercise may be. So let us ask the question: is it true that neoconservatives are mostly Jews, and are they indeed working to shape U.S. policy out of devotion to the interests of the "Likud party" or of Israel?

Many neoconservatives are in fact Jews. Why this should be so is not self-evident, although part of the answer is surely that Jews, whenever and wherever they have been free to indulge it, exhibit a powerful attraction to politics and particularly to the play of political ideas—an attraction that is evident all across the political spectrum but especially on the Left. Indeed, the disproportionate presence of Jews in early Communist movements in eastern and central Europe became grist for the Nazis and other far-Right movements that portrayed Bolshevism as a Jewish cause whose real purpose was (yes) to serve Jewish interests. In reality, Trotsky and Zinoviev and the other Jewish Communists were no more concerned about the interests of the Jewish people than were Lenin and Stalin which is to say, not at all.

As it happens, the Jewish affinity with the Left may be one reason why neoconservatism boasts so many Jewish adherents: it is a movement whose own roots lie in the Left. But the same affinity is to be seen at work in many of the insinuations against Jewish neocons by leftists who are themselves Jews or who profess some Jewish connection. Michael Lind, for one, has gone out of his way to assert his own Jewish "descent," and *Tikkun* is in some self-professed sense a Jewish magazine. Even the BBC's assault on the neocons featured a Jewish critic in the starring role. So passionate are these Jews in their opposition to neoconservative ideas that they have not hesitated to pander to anti-Semitism in the effort to discredit them. What about their ulterior motives, one wonders?

It may sound strange in light of the accusations against them, but in fact the careers of leading neoconservatives have rarely involved work on Middle East issues. The most distinctive of Richard Perle's many contributions to U.S. policy lie in the realm of nuclear-weapons strategy. Elliott Abrams made his mark as a point man for President Reagan's policies toward Central America. Paul Wolfowitz's long career in government includes not only high office in the State and Defense departments but also a stint as ambassador to Indonesia during which he pressed for democratization harder than any of his predecessors.

These three, as well as the rest of the neocon circle, are and were hard-liners toward the USSR, China, Nicaragua, and North Korea. Is it any wonder that they held a similar position toward Saddam Hussein's Iraq? If Israel did not exist, which of them would have favored giving Hans Blix's team still more time, or leaving the whole matter in the hands of the UN? Are we to believe that the decades-long neoconservative campaign against Communism and anti-Americanism was a fantastically farsighted Rube Goldberg machine programmed to produce some benefit for Israel somewhere down the line?

The BBC claimed to have found a smoking gun, one that

others have pounced on as well. Bradshaw "In 1996, a group of neocons wrote a report intended as advice for incoming Israeli Prime Minister Benny [*sic*] Netanyahu. It called for . . . removing Saddam Hussein from power, an important Israeli strategic objective in its own right." Perle and Douglas Feith, the latter now a high official in Bush's Defense Department, were among those who had "contributed" to this paper.

Yet even if the BBC had characterized the document accurately, it would not imply what the BBC (and not the BBC alone) suggested it did. The Americans whose names appeared on the paper had long sought Saddam's ouster, an objective that was already, in 1996, the implicit policy of the Clinton administration. It would thus make more sense to say that, in preparing a paper for Netanyahu, they were trying to influence Israeli policy on behalf of American interests than the other way around. Indeed, most Israeli officials at that time viewed Iran, the sponsor of Hizballah and Hamas, as a more pressing threat to their country than Iraq, and (then as later) would have preferred that it be given priority in any campaign against terrorism.

To make matters worse, the BBC fundamentally misrepresented the nature of the document. Contrary to Bradshaw's claim, no "group of neocons" had written it. Rather, it was the work of a rapporteur summarizing the deliberations of a conference, and was clearly identified as such. The names affixed to it were listed as attendees and not as endorsers, much less authors.

In any case, although it is true that many neocons are Jews, it is also true that many are not. Kirkpatrick, Woolsey, Michael Novak, Linda Chavez, William J. Bennett—all are of pure neocon pedigree, while other non-Jews figuring prominently in current foreign-policy debates and today called neocons include Bolton, AEI president Christopher DeMuth, and Gary Schmitt of the Project for the New American Century. These Gentile neocons are no less strong in their support of Israel than are Jewish neocons, which suggests a stance growing not out of ethnic loyalty but out of some shared analysis of the rights and wrongs of the Arab-Israel conflict.

Just as it is undeniable that many neoconservatives happen to be Jews, it is undeniable that America's war against terrorism will redound to Israel's benefit as the biggest victim of terrorism. But the attacks on the World Trade Center and the Pentagon, taking at a stroke three thousand lives, pushed America pretty high up on the list of terror's victims. That blow, and the certain knowledge that the terrorists would try for even greater carnage in the future, drove us to war in 2001 just as Pearl Harbor had done in 1941.

That earlier decision by the United States suffused Winston Churchill with joy, for England was then on the front lines with the Nazis just as Israel is today on the front lines with terrorists. At the time there were those who said we were going to war for the sake of England. For that matter, there were some who said we were going to war for the sake of the Jews: the subject is perennial. Then, as now, they were wrong.

If any single episode exposes the famousness of the charge that neoconservative policies amount to Jewish special pleading, it was the 1990s war in Bosnia—the same conflict that served to crystallize a post–cold-war approach to foreign policy that might fairly be described as neoconservative. It had been in large part as a response to the Soviet challenge that neoconservatism took shape in the first place, so it is only natural that the end of the cold war should have invited the question Norman Podhoretz raised in 1996: was there anything left of neoconservatism to distinguish it from plain, unprefixed conservatism?

One answer to this question may have come as early as 1992, when hostilities first broke out in Bosnia and then-President George H. W. Bush dismissed them as a "hiccup," while Secretary of State James Baker declared: "We have no dog in that fight." These two were not heartless men, but they were exemplars of a traditional conservative cast of mind. The essence of the matter, as they saw it, was that Bosnia engaged little in the way of American interests, which in the conventional view meant vital resources, or strategic geography, or the safety of allies.

Then a movement coalesced in opposition to American inaction. Its leaders, apart from a handful of young foreign-service officers who had resigned from the State Department in protest and who carried no ideological labels, were almost all from neoconservative ranks. Perle, Wolfowitz, Kirkpatrick, and Max Kampelman were among those in the forefront. So ardent was I myself on the issue that Bosnia was the chief of several points impelling me to support Bill Clinton against Bush in 1992, a choice over which I would sing my regrets in these pages when Clinton turned out to care not a whit more about Bosnia than had the elder Bush.

It bears recalling that the Bosnian cause was championed by international Islamists, and that the Bosnians themselves had been part of the Croatian fascist state during World War II, infamous for its brutality toward Jews. Logically, then, if there was any "Jewish interest" in the conflict, it should have led to support for the Bush-Clinton position. But as the bloodletting wore on, neoconservatives, Jewish and non-Jewish alike, were much more likely than traditional conservatives to support intervention. Despite the occasional, prominent exception—neoconservative columnist Charles Krauthammer was an opponent of intervention, conservative Senator Bob Dole a supporter—the prevailing division on Bosnia demonstrated that a distinctive neoconservative sensibility, if not ideology, endured, or perhaps had been reborn, after the end of the cold war. It centered on the question of the uses of American power, and it was held even by some who had not made the whole journey from liberalism with the original neocons.

What is that sensibility? In part it may consist in a greater readiness to engage American power and resources where nothing but humanitarian concerns are at issue. In larger part, however, it is concerned with national security, sharing with traditional conservatism the belief that military strength is irreplaceable and that pacifism is folly. Where it parts company with traditional conservatism is in the more contingent approach it takes to guarding that security.

Neoconservatives sought action in Bosnia above all out of the conviction that, however remote the Balkans may be geographically and strategically, allowing a dictator like Serbia's Slobodan Milosevic to get away with aggression, ethnic cleansing, and mass murder in Europe would tempt other malign men to do likewise elsewhere, and other avatars of virulent ultranationalism to ride this ticket to power. Neoconservatives believed that American inaction would make the world a more dangerous place, and that ultimately this danger would assume forms that would land on our own doorstep. Thus it had happened throughout the twentieth century; and thus, in the fullness of time, it would happen again on September 11 of the first year of the twenty-first.

In addition to their more contingent approach to security, neoconservatives have shown themselves more disposed to experiment with unconventional tactics—using air strikes against the Serbs, arming the Bosnians or, later, the Iraqi National Congress. By contrast, conservatives of traditional bent are more inclined to favor the use of overwhelming force or none at all, and to be more concerned with "exit strategies." Still another distinguishing characteristic is that neoconservatives put greater stock in the political and ideological aspects of conflict.

A final distinction may reflect neoconservativism's vestigial links with liberalism. This is the enthusiasm for democracy. Traditional conservatives are more likely to display an ambivalence toward this form of government, an ambivalence expressed centuries ago by the American founders. Neoconservatives tend to harbor no such doubts.

With this in mind, it also becomes easier to identify the true neoconservative models in the field of power politics: Henry "Scoop" Jackson, Ronald Reagan, and Winston Churchill. These were tough-minded men who were far from "conservative" either in spirit or in political pedigree. Jackson was a Democrat, while Reagan switched to the Republicans late in life, as Churchill did from the Liberals to the Tories. All three were staunch democrats and no less staunch believers in maintaining the might of the democracies. All three believed in confronting democracy's enemies early and far from home shores; and all three were paragons of ideological warfare.

Each, too, was a creative tactician. Jackson's eponymous "amendments" holding the Soviet Union's feet to the fire on the right of emigration and blocking a second unequal nuclear agreement put a stop to American appeasement. Reagan's provocative rhetoric, plus his arming of anti-Communist guerrillas, paved the way to American victory in the cold war. Churchill's innovative ideas, which rightly or wrongly had won him disrepute in the first world war, were essential to his nation's survival in the second. Could this element in neoconservatism help explain why the cause of Israel, an innovative, militarily strong democracy, is embraced by all neoconservatives, non-Jews as well as Jews?

But this brings us back at last to the question of the neocons' alleged current influence. How did their ideas gain such currency? Did they "hijack" Bush's foreign policy, right out from under his nose and the noses of Richard Cheney, Colin Powell, Donald Rumsfeld, and Condoleezza Rice—all members of the same team that, to hear the standard liberal version, was itself so diabolically clever that in the 2000 election it had stolen the presidency itself?

The answer is to be found not in conspiracy theories but in the terrorist outrage of September 11, 2001. Though it constituted a watershed in American history, this event was novel not in kind but only in scale. For roughly thirty years, Middle

Eastern terrorists had been murdering Americans in embassies, barracks, airplanes, and ships—even, once before, in the World Trade Center. Except for a few criminal prosecutions and the lobbing of a few mostly symbolic shells, the U.S. response had been inert. Even under President Reagan, Americans fled in the wake of the bombing of the Marine barracks in Beirut, then the largest single attack we had suffered.

Terrorism, we were told, was an accepted way of doing politics in the Middle East. More than a handful of the region's governments openly supported it, and the PLO, an outfit steeped in terror, was the poster child of the Arab cause. Any strong response to this scourge would serve only to make the people of the region angrier at us, and generate still more terrorists.

On September 11, we learned in the most dreadful way that terrorists would not be appeased by our diffidence; quite the contrary. We saw—they themselves told us—that they intended to go on murdering us in ever larger numbers as long as they could. A sharp change of course was required, and the neoconservatives, who had been warning for years that terror must not be appeased, stood vindicated—much as, more grandly, Churchill was vindicated by Hitler's depredations after Munich.

Not only did the neocons have an analysis of what had gone wrong in American policy, they also stood ready with proposals for what to do now: to wage war on the terror groups and to seek to end or transform governments that supported them, especially those possessing the means to furnish terrorists with the wherewithal to kill even more Americans than on September 11. Neocons also offered a long-term strategy for making the Middle East less of a hotbed of terrorism: implanting democracy in the region and thereby helping to foment a less violent approach to politics.

No neoconservative was elevated in office after September 11, as Churchill had been to prime minister after the collapse of the Munich agreement, but policies espoused by neoconservatives were embraced by the Bush administration. Was this because Bush learned them from the likes of Wolfowitz and Perle? Or did he and his top advisers—none of them known as a neocon—reach similar conclusions on their own? We may have to await the President's memoirs to learn the answer to that narrow question, but every American has reason to be grateful for the result.

If these policies should fail, for whatever reason—including a recurrence of national faint-heartedness—then neoconservative ideas will no doubt be discredited. But this matters hardly at all compared with what we will have lost. For, if they fail, either we will then be at the mercy of ever more murderous terrorism or we will have to seek alternative methods of coping with it—methods that are likely to involve a much more painful and frightening course of action than the admittedly daunting one that still lies before us.

If, however, the policies succeed, then the world will have been delivered from an awful scourge, and there will be credit enough to go around—some of it, one trusts, even for the lately much demonized neoconservatives.

ROBERT JAN VAN PELT

Excerpt from *The Case for Auschwitz*

*The Influence of Literary Theory on the Origins of Holocaust Denial**

[*Professor van Pelt was a key historical witness for Deborah Lipstadt in the lawsuit David Irving launched against her, accusing her of falsely describing Irving as a Holocaust denier. The defense made the truth of the Holocaust the center of its presentation. Van Pelt's testimony on "the case for Auschwitz"—the case that it was in fact a camp designed for systematic gas-chamber extermination—helped win Ms. Lipstadt a definitive victory. Here he makes a conjecture about the culture of literary and intellectual relativism which, he believes, allowed Holocaust denial to flourish.*]

[David] Irving did not explicitly embrace negationism at the 1983 conference, but the occasion was to have far-reaching consequences: it marked his first encounter with hard-core negationist Dr. Robert Faurisson. That meeting began a process that would lead to Irving's 1988 endorsement of the Leuchter Report and, twelve years later, culminate in the libel trial in the Royal Courts of Justice.

Faurisson was a one-time lecturer in French literature at the University of Lyons–2. He had emerged from a school of literary interpretation known as New Criticism. This school went

---

*This subtitle is my addition for this excerpt; it was not in van Pelt's original.

back to the early 1940s, when two prominent American critics, Monroe C. Beardsley and William Kurtz Wimsatt, proposed that the contemporary approach of interpreting poems in their autobiographical, historical, political, or cultural contexts was bankrupt. Instead, a critic should read a poem as a verbal icon—an autonomous verbal structure—and foreclose any appeal to history, biography, or cultural context. Even the poet's intention did not matter when judging a poem. French student of literature Robert Faurisson adopted Beardsley and Wimsatt's ontologically grounded aesthetic isolationism but abandoned its pragmatic aim to encase it in a particularly dogmatic set of rules. His "Ajax method" (because "it scours as it cleans as it shines") centered on the proposition that while words may have more than one meaning if taken in isolation, they acquire one specific meaning only within a text. And while texts may generate different responses, this does not mean that they have different meanings. In short: "Texts have only one meaning, or no meaning at all." Refusing to consider any external evidence, the only access to truth was now to be through Faurisson's own technique of textual exegesis.

Faurisson's work would have remained a footnote in the history of postmodern literary theory if not for his desire to apply the "Ajax method" to the study of history. It was, at first sight, a natural extension of his activities. "The historian works with documents," declared a nineteenth-century French handbook on historical methodology in its opening sentence. And it concluded its opening paragraph with the succinct formula: "No documents, no history"—an adage which, incidentally, would inspire Faurisson to coin his own maxim: "No holes, no Holocaust." Langlois and Seignobos's classic *Introduction to the Study of History* (1897) stressed the importance of a critical approach to documents because "criticism is antagonistic to the normal bent of the mind." Writing in a time which clearly remembered how historians cultivated an "empty and pompous species of literature which was then known as 'history,'"

Langlois and Seignobos pressed their case that historians should not make easy assumptions about documents written a long time ago by people who may have used language differently. But they also wrote that contemporary documents could be taken at face value. Ignoring Langlois and Seignobos's observation that it was not necessary to apply the most rigorous internal criticism to contemporary documents because the author and the historian shared language and outlook, Faurisson condemned historians who habitually failed to "attack" the documents they were using and instead tried to fit those texts into their various contexts. In other words, historians sinned against the ground rule of Faurisson's theory of criticism, seemingly justified by Langlois and Seignobos, that nothing should distract from the exegesis of the sacrosanct "word on the page."

Faurisson's attempt to apply his rule of textual exegesis to history was ill founded. First of all, it was a clear example of the kind of hypercriticism against which Langlois and Seignobos had warned. "There are persons who scent enigmas everywhere, even where there are none. They take perfectly clear texts and subtilise on them till they make them doubtful, under the pretext of freeing them from imaginary corruptions. They discover traces of forgery in authentic documents." Applied without restraint, hypercriticism destroyed the possibility of history.

Furthermore, Faurisson's approach very clearly departed from Beardsley and Wimsatt's own method of exegesis, which applied only to poetry because in poems "all or most of what is said or implied is relevant." For the interpretation of "practical messages," the critic had to "correctly infer the intention." However, Faurisson had no qualms about launching his theory of literary criticism into a colonizing drive beyond the boundary of the poetic to treat historical texts as merely rhetorical, purely discursive operations that have no link to external evidence.

Faurisson was not the only one to dissolve the boundary between literature and history. In fact, a whole school arose which, under the banner of New Historicism, began to apply the lessons of adherents of New Criticism to the discourse of history. The new historicism claimed that the materials of historical investigation—chronicles, correspondence, bills, minutes, memoirs, court proceedings, eyewitness testimonies, and so on—were at an ontological level not different from, for example, poetry. Fair enough. Yet they also charged that the accounts historians wrought from those elements—their "histories"—were no different from poems or novels or epics. In effect, they erased the fundamental distinction between fact and fiction—a distinction that had in a rough-and-ready fashion defined the boundary between history and literature since the ancient Greeks.

Faurisson could be seen as just another exponent of post-structuralist historiography if not for the fact that he attempted to apply this theory to a unique ideological agenda. To be sure, many in the New Historicist camp had a mission of their own: to challenge the dominant understanding of history as just another hegemonic discourse. The New Historicists aimed to create a place in history for the hitherto repressed—that is, everyone who was not white, straight, or male. In other words, by dissolving "History" into "histories," they tried to reveal new riches hitherto suppressed under the totalitarian discourse that centered on a Whig interpretation of history as progress. Faurisson, however, had a different axe to grind: he did not desire to make our reading of the past more inclusive. To the contrary: he aimed to narrow history by scouring the Holocaust from the record. If the champions of New Historicism intended to increase the truth content of history by allowing different and contradictory "truths" to float simultaneously, Faurisson desired to use the same technique to debunk a central truth of contemporary history as a lie.

In this mission, Faurisson was inspired by another French ideologue, Paul Rassinier. Born in 1906, Rassinier had been a communist in his youth, but he was expelled from the party in 1932. A pacifist in the 1930s, Rassinier applauded the Munich agreement. He served in the French army in 1940, joined the French Resistance in 1942, and edited the clandestine magazine *La Quatrième République.* Arrested on November 29, 1943, by the Gestapo, he was deported to the concentration camp of Buchenwald in January 1944. After a period of quarantine there, he was brought to the concentration camp at Dora-Mittelbau, where he was imprisoned for fourteen months.

When Rassinier entered the camps he saw no basic difference between the democratic West, National Socialist Germany, and communist Russia, between the First World War and the Second. He was simply not prepared to acknowledge that the National Socialist regime was different or that its concentration camps were unique. "The problem of the concentration camps was a universal one, not just one that could be disposed of by placing it on the doorstep of the National Socialists." Rassinier believed that the horror of camp life was the result not of German policies but of the common practice, found in every country, of letting trusted inmates, who were referred to in the French penitentiary system as *Chaouchs,* run the prison on behalf of the jailers. "From morning to night, our *Chaouchs,* throwing out their chests, plumed themselves on the power that they said that they had to send us to the *Kréma-torium* for the least indiscretion and with a single word." According to Rassinier, the SS kept a distance and were even ignorant of what happened inside the camp. If they had involved themselves with the day-to-day lives of the inmates, the situation would have been better. After having formulated the thesis that the SS was really not in control and that all the horror of inmate life was due to the petty cruelty of the Kapos, Rassinier came to a logical conclusion: the atrocity stories about the use of the camps as factories of death could not be true, because these stories implied an organized system of terror that transcended the cruelty of the Kapos. To account for the fact that such stories circulated nevertheless, Rassinier postulated "the complex of Ulysses' lie, which is everyone's, and so it is with all of the internees." Camp inmates had an inborn need to exaggerate their suffering "without realizing that the reality is quite enough in itself."

After he was liberated in April 1945, Rassinier returned to France. He had no patience for or empathy with his fellow deportees who "came back with hatred and resentment on their tongues and in their pens." They were caught in "a treadmill of lies. . . . So it was with Ulysses who, during the course of his voyage, each day added a new adventure to his Odyssey, as much to please the public taste of the times as to justify his long absence in the eyes of his family." To Rassinier, the proof of the fact that the ex-inmates were lying was their constant return to the (to him) obviously absurd proposition that camps had been equipped with homicidal gas chambers. As time progressed, he became more and more obsessed with the issue of the gas chambers, which had ceased to be the result of mere "lies of Ulysses" and had become a massive fabrication created with a political aim in mind.

This shift in explanation from psychology to conspiracy was due to the notorious Kravchenko trial, which dominated the French media in the first half of 1949. In 1944, Victor Kravchenko, a top official of the Soviet delegation in Washington, D.C., defected to the West. In his best-selling book *I Chose Freedom* (1946), Kravchenko described the Soviet Union as a totalitarian nightmare in which the successes that had been trumpeted all around the world, especially the ruthless collectivization of agriculture, had been achieved through the application of terror backed by an extensive system of concentration camps. The Soviets and their communist allies in the West answered through a campaign of defamation against Kravchenko, which resulted, among other things, in an article published in the French magazine *Les Lettres Francaises*. It claimed that Kravchenko was too stupid to have written the book, and that his so-called revelations had been manufactured by American intelligence. In response, Kravchenko filed a libel suit against the magazine, and in early 1949 the trial began in Paris. It lasted for two months. In the end Kravchenko won, but many never surrendered the idea that the whole gulag had been an invention of the American intelligence service, designed to discredit the Soviet Union. Rassinier drew the conclusion that if the Russian concentration camps had been concocted in Washington, D.C., the stories about German extermination camps with large crematoria equipped with homicidal gas chambers must also have been the product of some propaganda apparatus.

Rassinier spent the rest of his life trying to debunk the myth of the camps. As a known Nazi sympathizer and anti-Semite, Faurisson was attracted to Rassinier's thesis that the Holocaust was a hoax and the gas chambers the stuff of legend. Exposed to an alleged deception of such dimensions, Faurisson lost his interest in sonnets, odes, and novels and began to subject accounts about Auschwitz to his "Ajax method." [. . .]

INDEED, ON HIS return home to France Faurisson became, once again, the center of public debate. In April 1980 the so-called Faurisson Affair was given new life with the publication of Serge Thion's 350-page-long book *Vérité historique ou vérité politique? La dossier de l'affaire Faurisson. La question des chambres à gaz* (*Historical Truth or Political Truth? The File of the Faurisson Affair—The Question of the Gas Chambers*). With the strong declaration of the thirty-five French historians published in *Le Monde* on February 21, 1979, Faurisson had become the underdog opposed by the defenders of the status quo. For the champions of the radical left, Faurisson became a hero of the search for a new cause that would unmask the hypocrisy of the bourgeoisie, and they began to fashion, in imitation of the Dreyfus Affair, a so-called Faurisson Affair. Those who rallied to Faurisson's side were the same radicals who believed that the reporting on the Cambodian genocide had actually served the interests of the establishment. "The West's best propaganda resource is Pol Pot's regime," Régis Debray observed in discussion with Noam Chomsky. "We needed that scarecrow." And Chomsky provided, together with Edward Herman, a lengthy analysis of the way the liberal press averted its eyes from the "terrorizing elites" at home and used the news of atrocities abroad to help maintain the political, social, and economic status quo. Thus, the atrocities ascribed to Pol Pot (or Stalin) allowed the elites in the United States to discredit every form of socialism as a highway to the Gulag and to resist the creation of national health insurance, the improvement of welfare programs, and the growth of the labor movement.

Contemporary atrocities were not the only ones to be exploited by the reactionary establishment. Hitler also proved a convenient "scarecrow." For the French ultra-Left of the 1970s, National Socialism had been the ultimate political emanation of capitalist society, created to stop the historically necessary advance of the working classes. As such, it was a tool of the bourgeoisie, the same bourgeoisie that shaped and dominated postwar liberal-democractic society. Yet the bourgeoisie denied the fundamental identity between liberal democracy and Hitler's regime, and their main argument was, as some ultra-Left ideologists had discovered, the Holocaust. The strategists of the proletariat formulated the thesis that the fundamental identity between the two political systems would become clear only if the Holocaust, the principal foil of capitalism, were to be removed from the historical record.

Finally intellectual fashion played into Faurisson's hands. The generation that began to dominate the intellectual world in the late 1970s had been the same that, ten years earlier, had seen its hopes of progress through radical change defeated. As the promise of change had not materialized, the students of 1968 felt that "history" had betrayed them and became skeptical of any "grand narrative" of historical development that led to some social, political, and economic resolution at the end. This, in turn, led to the conception of a different kind of understanding of the past, or, for that matter, of the present. Instead of one privileged narrative that told of the progress of God's people from fall to redemption or of the progress of (Western) civilization from cave to lunar colony or of the progress from slavery to freedom, the generation of 1968 formulated the idea that one should allow, paraphrasing Chairman Mao, a thousand parallel "histories" to bloom. And they carried on their banners Nietzsche's observation that objective reality is not accessible, that what we call truth is a "mobile army of metaphors, metonyms, and anthropomorphisms" in the service of political, social, and economic power. Armed with Nietzsche's slogan that one's obligation to truth was just one's pledge to lie herd-like according to a fixed convention, these revolutionaries stormed the bastille of the "grand narrative" which, so they believed, disenfranchised all but the (generally) white male carriers of "the idea." These radicals preached that one should stop searching for "the truth" and become engaged in recovering many alternative "truths," such as the histories of the underprivileged class (the common folk, slaves), gender (women), race ("colonials"), and so on. In short, in an effort to defeat the cultural imperialism of the West and the cultural arrogance of its intellectual tradition, historians began to practice a principled relativism that demanded an absolute suspension of judgment when faced with "otherness" or concepts expressed in such neologisms as "alterity," "illeity," and "*différance*." In seeking the stranger and the foreigner, they hoped to find themselves. As a result, many of the generation of 1968, who reveled in the rhetoric of "difference," "textuality," "incommensurable phrase-regimes," and the like, were fascinated by Faurisson—the ultimate stranger, the champion of an alternative history that was incommensurable with the hegemonic narrative of the Holocaust.

For example, philosopher Jean-François Lyotard became interested in the Faurisson Affair because it illustrated a number of difficult issues that arise when one accepts, as Lyotard does, that questions of historical truth and falsehood are wholly defined within the context of language games and the incommensurability of discourses. Lyotard argued that any attempt to dismiss Faurisson by pointing to the massive amount of evidence concerning Auschwitz or to Faurisson's mistakes in logic would deny the narrative "differend" between his and our version of events. Therefore one ought to encounter Faurisson by suspending judgment and see in him a champion of the war on totality. In arguing his case, Lyotard provided what remains the classic summary of Faurisson's logic. "His argument is: in order for a place to be identified as a gas chamber, the only eye-witnesses I will accept would be a victim of this gas chamber; now, according to my opponent, there is no victim that is not dead; otherwise, this gas chamber would not be what he or she claims it to be. There is, therefore, no gas chamber."

To Lyotard, Faurisson's submission that we can have no knowledge, no *evidence* of what actually occurred in the gas chambers at Auschwitz since there exist no survivors who can vouch for the facts as a matter of firsthand empirical witness had a philosophical significance. He did not, however, become one of Faurisson's champions. Others found sufficient reason to take a more active role. The prominent left-wing radical Serge Thion rallied to Faurisson's case, presenting his support as the logical consequence of his commitment to the principles of freedom of thought and his political activism on behalf of the unassimilable "Other." Faurisson was "by all standards, a man alone." Remarkably enough, Thion moved beyond accepting Faurisson as the stranger that must be embraced and actually assimilated Faurisson's point of view, categorically dismissing the great abundance of evidence that attests to the historical reality of the Holocaust. The confessions of Höss* and other SS men were without value. "Once one is prepared to imagine the situation of those defeated men, gambling with their own lives between the hands of their jailers, a paltry game in which truths and lies are the basic tokens in a tactic of survival, one will not be prepared to accept all their declarations as valid currency." A true defender of the underdog, be it the Algerians in their battle with the French Republic, the Vietnamese in their battle with the United States, or Faurisson in his battle with the establishment, Thion had no difficulty feeling sympathy for even men such as Höss or Frank when they were in the dock. To Thion, the Nuremberg War Crimes Tribunals had been not much different from the Stalinist show trials, and therefore they had no evidentiary value.

Within months after bringing Thion's book on the market, Faurisson published his *Mémoire en Defense—contre ceux qui m'accusent de falsifier l'histoire. La question des chambres à gaz* (*Testimony in Defense—Against Those Who Accuse Me of Falsifying History: The Question of the Gas Chambers*). The true significance of the book was to be found in Noam Chomsky's ill-advised preface. As we have seen, in 1979 Chomsky had signed a petition in support of Faurisson's academic freedom to challenge the inherited account of the Holocaust, and one thing had led to another. Entitled "Some Elementary Commentaries on the Right to the Freedom of Speech," Chomsky reviewed the reasons why he had signed the 1979 petition and dismissed the outcry that had resulted from it. He stated that he had often signed petitions on behalf of people whose ideas he found detestable—Russian dissidents who supported American policies in Indochina, for example—and observed that in those cases no one had raised an objection. "If someone had, I

---

*[Auschwitz commandant Rudolf Höss—*ed.*]

396 THOSE WHO FORGET THE PAST

would have regarded him with the same contempt that those who denounce the petition in favor of Faurisson's right deserve, and for the same reasons." Then Chomsky went on to contrast the freedom-loving practice in the United States with the stifling intellectual climate in France. Back home, he proudly stated, Arthur Butz ("whom one may consider the American equivalent of Faurisson") was not subjected to harassment, negationists had not been hindered in running an international conference, and the American Civil Liberties Union had defended the right of neo-Nazis to march through the largely Jewish town of Skokie, Illinois. The French, in other words, had much to learn. In his final paragraph, he addressed the tricky question of Faurisson's anti-Semitism. This did not remove the obligation to defend Faurisson. On the contrary: Chomsky declared that it made the defense of Faurisson more necessary. "It is exactly the right to express the most dreadful ideas freely that must be defended most rigorously."

The Chomsky preface initiated a second wave of publicity for Faurisson, which led, among other things, to a radio interview on December 17, 1980. Faurisson said that the alleged Holocaust was a historical lie that served a huge political and financial swindle that benefited the State of Israel at the expense of the German and Palestinian peoples. This statement led to Faurisson's indictment under France's Race Relations Law. At the same time Faurisson was also indicted under Article 382 of the civil code for willfully distorting history. Finally, Faurisson faced a libel suit initiated by French historian Léon Poliakov, whom Faurisson had accused of fabricating his sources with reference to an important historical document on the Belzec extermination camp. The first two trials certainly put Faurisson in the position of the Dreyfusian underdog persecuted by the system and brought him much publicity, even sympathy, especially when he was convicted in each case.

JUDITH SHULEVITZ

Evolutionary Psychology's Anti-Semite

[*This important essay sparked a long-running discussion on* Slate'*s website, which can be accessed at http://www.slate.msn.com/id/74139/ entry/74452/*]

W HAT SCARES PEOPLE about the trial going on in London over whether Jewish historian Deborah Lipstadt libeled Holocaust denier David Irving by calling him a liar is that British law requires Lipstadt to show that her statement was true. If she can't prove beyond a doubt that the Holocaust took place, Irving might win. That would be a devastating blow to historical accuracy if it happens, but Culturebox [the persona for the *Slate* feature of that name] thinks it won't. There's a lot of truth on Lipstadt's side, and very little on Irving's. Plus Lipstadt has one of the best lawyers in London and is planning to call several heavyweight scholars to testify. Irving, on the other hand, is acting as his own lawyer and so far has named very few witnesses and experts, none of whom anyone has ever heard of.

If Irving doesn't appear to be taking the necessary steps to win, why else might he have brought the lawsuit? For publicity, is the obvious answer—to air his own views, as well as those of his witnesses. And that's what scares Culturebox. Irving's claim that there were no gas chambers at Auschwitz is bad enough, but since it bears directly on the question of his truthfulness, it will be refuted on the spot. Irving's experts, on the other hand, are being called to testify on issues tangential to the case, and their twisted theories could well go unanswered. One expert, John Fox, the former editor of a British Holocaust journal, will probably argue that Lipstadt and the Jews are trying to shut down free discussion of the Holocaust. Irving's other expert is an American professor named Kevin MacDonald, whose ideas about Jews have almost no relevance to the case but represent the broadest, ugliest, and most vicious anti-Semitism passing for scholarship in this country today.

We know more or less what MacDonald will say on the stand, because he recently put a copy of his written statement to the British court on the Internet. . . . The bulk of MacDonald's testimony will be a summary of his three books about Jews: *A People That Shall Dwell Alone: Judaism as a Group Evolutionary Strategy* (Praeger, 1994); *Separation and Discontents: Toward an Evolutionary Theory of Anti-Semitism* (Praeger, 1998); and *The Culture of Critique: An Evolutionary Analysis of Jewish Involvement in Twentieth-Century Intellectual and Political Movements* (Praeger, 1998). Here is what he says in them—in Culturebox's words, not his (if you want to read MacDonald's own summary, here is the link: http://www.csulb.edu/~kmacd).

MacDonald's central thesis is that Judaism is best understood not as a religion but as a blueprint for an experiment in eugenics—a "group evolutionary strategy," he calls it—designed to maximize a single trait: intelligence. For thousands of years, he says, Jews have separated themselves from their neighbors, choosing to confine themselves to a closed society with strict rules against marrying outside the group. They have lived by policies of extreme group loyalty and obedience to rabbinical authority, which served to maintain their racial purity; and they practiced low-birth-rate, high-investment parenting, which is the royal road to a high group I.Q. They conferred social status (which brings along with it the most desirable women) on men according to their brilliance—indeed, says MacDonald, study of the Talmud was nothing more than a casuistic exercise meant to weed out the dim. Eventually, their highly developed genes for mental and verbal acuity, as well as their social aggression (also carefully bred-in), gave the Jews powerful tools that enable them to dominate neighboring ethnic groups in the endless war of all against all for food and resources.

In his second book, MacDonald explains why Jews have encountered so much anti-Semitism for so many years: It was justified. Gentiles reacted to Jews the way any group of animals on the veldt would when confronted with a group of superior animals likely to challenge them successfully for control of the available resources—they tried to destroy the Jews before the Jews destroyed them. Even the most extreme forms of anti-Semitism, such as Nazism, can be seen not as aberrations but as "a mirror image" of Judaism, with its emphasis on creating a master race. (MacDonald does not deny that the Holocaust occurred, but he appears to think it was rooted in an immutable biological chain reaction that the Jews set off.) Faced with the hatred of gentiles, Jews have often resorted to a "strategy of crypsis"—that is, they have pretended not to be Jews. Do the Jews themselves realize what they're up to? MacDonald goes back and forth on this point; one moment he'll chastise Jews for believing their own religious rationalizations, the next he'll explain that they can't help it—they're genetically "prone to self-deception."

In his third book, MacDonald takes on what he calls the "Jewish" intellectual movements of the twentieth century, from psychoanalysis to Marxism to "Boasian anthropology" and "the Frankfurt School of social research." His argument is that the ideas of secular Jewish intellectuals are merely a device to promote tolerance of the Jewish presence by gentiles—so that the Jews can more efficiently pursue their nefarious agenda of systematic breeding and control of resources. A good example of this is cultural anthropology: Its Jewish founder, Franz Boas, shifted the focus of anthropology away from Darwinism and eugenicism and toward the study of culture in order to bring an end to the criticism of Jews as a race. Even if an intellectual movement (such as liberalism) was founded by non-Jews, the minute Jews join it, they'll take it over, because their ancestral history predisposes them to form "highly cohesive groups": "Intellectual activity is like any other human endeavor: Cohesive groups outcompete individualist strategies." Ideas that MacDonald identifies as Jewish, he invariably finds to be not only subtly self-interested but also repellent by any ordinary (which is to say gentile) moral or intellectual standard. Freud "conceptualized himself as a leader in a war on gentile culture." When Stephen Jay Gould and Richard Lewontin expressed doubts about sociobiology back in the 1970s, their approach exemplified the kind of "skeptical thrust of Jewish intellectual activity" that results in Jewish "nihilistic anti-science."

Toward the end of the third book, MacDonald lays out his solution for restoring what he calls "parity" between the Jews and other ethnic groups: systematic discrimination against Jews in college admission and employment and heavy taxation of Jews "to counter the Jewish advantage in the possession of wealth."

It is not a coincidence that MacDonald spends much of his time in his third book attacking the enemies of Darwinism and sociobiology—or evolutionary psychology, as it is usually called today. MacDonald identifies himself as an evolutionary psychologist, and indeed, most prominent figures in the field would at least know his name. But, remarkably, to Culturebox's knowledge, no American evolutionary psychologist has publicly objected to his work. This is not to say that it has been celebrated. A man in his fifties, MacDonald is still an associate professor of psychology at a third-rate school, California State

University in Long Beach. [Note from Culturebox two days later: *She was wrong about this. He is in fact a full professor. My apologies for the error.*] But much more important to an academic than his title is his standing among his peers, and there MacDonald is on firmer ground: He's the secretary, archivist, newsletter editor, and executive board member of the professional organization the Human Behavior and Evolution Society (HBES), to which the majority of America's leading evolutionary psychologists belong. He edits a small journal called *Population and Environment.* And the three books summarized above appeared in a series edited by Seymour Itzkoff, a well-known if extremely conservative scholar of the genetics of intelligence at Smith College.

Are MacDonald's peers aware of what he's writing in the name of a field long accused of fostering—unfairly, many of them would say; by Jews, MacDonald would say—sexist and racist stereotypes? Do other evolutionary psychologists have an opinion on MacDonald? Culturebox called several well-known members of HBES, specifying in her voice messages that she was writing an article about MacDonald. Few returned her phone calls, but those who did said they'd never read his Jewish trilogy. Two leading scholars said they had read papers of his on other subjects and found them "muddled"; one academic said she had been forced to reject a paper by MacDonald on child development for an anthology she was editing. When Culturebox described the contents of MacDonald's books to them, they expressed extreme shock and said he contradicted the basic principles of contemporary evolutionary psychology. "The notion that Jews are a genetically distinct group doesn't make it on the basis of modern population genetics," said John Tooby, the president of HBES and a professor of anthropology at the University of California at Santa Barbara. Also, he said, "group-selection theory"—the idea that natural selection can occur at the level of a group (such as a bunch of Jews) as opposed to individuals—was debunked in the 1960s, and though some scholars are working to bring group-selection theory back, it remains a minority view.

Not everyone in the field is as critical as Tooby, however. A review praising MacDonald's first book appeared in the journal *Ethnology and Sociobiology* four years ago (the publication was in the process of being taken over by HBES at the time); the author, John Hartung, a professor at the State University of New York and a former secretary of HBES, concluded that the Holocaust, "the most enormous act of reactive racism ever perpetrated," had been misrepresented as an unjustified evil so as to cow non-Jews into looking the other way while Jews "purloin" land in Israel. According to *Lingua Franca,* which covered the incident, the only public reaction to Hartung's review was a "tepid" letter by the journal's editor saying he didn't realize that it could be offensive, and an outright defense of Hartung by HBES's then-president, Dick Alexander. As for MacDonald, the author of the book that inspired these remarks, there was little visible effort at the time to refute him or to challenge the appropriateness of having him serve in so many key positions.

On the contrary. MacDonald thanks several prominent evolutionary psychologists in the acknowledgments to his trilogy. Among them is David Sloane Wilson, the leading advocate of group-selection theory. What exactly these scholars did for MacDonald is unclear. (Wilson did not return Culturebox's phone calls.) But MacDonald appears to have given them an opportunity to have their names suppressed, because there are other scholars he says he could have identified but didn't: "Regrettably," he writes, they "have asked that their names not appear here."

Can we blame the field of evolutionary psychology for Kevin MacDonald? Intellectually speaking, no. Evolutionary psychology is a fairly new endeavor trying to overcome an extremely disturbing past, and you can't make serious scholars accountable for all the discredited notions their peers cling to. But we can hold specific academics responsible—Itzkoff comes to mind—and we can ask what on earth the officers of HBES were thinking when they allowed MacDonald to become such an active member of their organization. If the response to Hartung's review is any indication, they would probably say that they don't believe in censoring their members. But it is the job of a scholarly association not just to foster discussion but also to police the boundaries of its discipline. When this evolutionary psychologist and HBES officer testifies in the Irving trial, he is bound to get his counterparts in a lot of trouble. In many ways, they deserve it.

PART NINE

ANTI-ZIONISM
AND
ANTI-SEMITISM

JEFFREY TOOBIN

Speechless: Free Expression and Civility Clash at Harvard

[*This excerpt represents about half of a longer piece, the second half of which is devoted chiefly to matters of race at Harvard Law School.*]

A T THE BEGINNING of November, Rita Goldberg was among the members of the Harvard academic community to receive a routine e-mail announcement of a poetry reading —not, at first glance, the sort of thing to reawaken the somewhat musty issue of free speech on campus. The e-mail said merely that Tom Paulin, an Irish poet, would give a poetry reading, known as the Morris Gray Lecture, on November 14.

Goldberg occupies a humble professional niche at the university. She is a non-tenured lecturer in the literature concentration, which itself is a poor cousin to the larger and more powerful Department of English and American Literature and Language, the sponsor of the Paulin lecture. "I had lived in England for many years," Goldberg told me, "and I knew Paulin's work. He's on television all the time there, and I knew the kind of things he had said about Israel. I put his name in Google, and it didn't take long to see just how bad it was." Goldberg herself had little clout, but she knew a good deal about how universities worked and possessed some proximity to real power at Harvard. Her husband is Oliver Hart, the chairman of the Economics Department, and, as it happened, he was the host of the department's annual dinner, at the Fogg Art Museum on Thursday, November 7. Among the guests was Lawrence H. Summers, the president of Harvard, who had been a member of the Economics Department in the years before he went to Washington, where he ultimately became Secretary of the Treasury under President Clinton. Goldberg sought out Summers at the dinner and informed him of the invitation to Paulin. "I told him about Paulin's views," Goldberg recalled, "and he said, 'That sounds pretty bad,' but then he also said, 'Be careful. This is a free-speech issue, too.'"

The following morning, six days before Paulin was to speak, Goldberg sent an e-mail to Lawrence Buell, the chairman of the English Department. "Dear Larry," she began, "I'm writing in response to your invitation to come hear Tom Paulin on November 14. I assume that the people who selected him for the Morris Gray Lecture know about the reputation he has recently made for himself in the U.K., not only because of his poem 'Killed in Crossfire,' but also because of statements he has made in the press and on television." Goldberg quoted an interview that Paulin had given to *Al-Ahram Weekly*, an English-language newspaper in Cairo, in April. "That interview is notorious for several remarks," Goldberg wrote, "especially the closing one, in which he refers to Jewish settlers on the West Bank: 'They should be shot dead. I think they are Nazis, racists. I feel nothing but hatred for them.'" She also included a copy of the poem:

> *We're fed this inert*
> *this lying phrase*
> *like comfort food*
> *as another little Palestinian boy*
> *in trainers jeans and a white teeshirt*
> *is gunned down by the Zionist SS*
> *whose initials we should*
> *—but we don't—dumb goys—*
> *clock in that weasel word* crossfire

She noted further, "I'm reluctant to intrude on anyone's right to free speech or free access. But in the minds of many thoughtful people both in England and here in the U.S., Paulin's vitriolic attacks have crossed a certain boundary between civilized discourse and something much more sinister. You ought at least to attach a warning label to your announcement of the reading."

Buell and Goldberg exchanged e-mails over the Veterans Day weekend, and the department chairman said he had known nothing about Paulin's political views. The invitation had been made nearly a year earlier, by a committee of three English professors—Helen Vendler, the chair, and two poetry professors, Jorie Graham and Peter Sacks. (Paulin was invited after the publication of the "Crossfire" poem but before his interview with *Al-Ahram*.) As Goldberg recalled, "I suggested two things to Larry—that they disinvite him or at least that they disclose what he'd said about Israel." Goldberg sent a version of her e-mail to a friend at Harvard's Hillel, the campus Jewish organization, urging the group to join her protest to the English Department. That e-mail, in turn, was forwarded to friends around and beyond the university.

The reaction to the news about Paulin illustrated, in a small way, a larger truth—that conservatives have become Israel's most passionate supporters in the United States. Denunciations of the invitation to the poet began surfacing among several conservative Internet bloggers—among them Andrew Sullivan and opinionjournal.com, the online counterpart to *The Wall Street Journal* editorial page. As a result, over the long weekend waves of e-mail protests about the poetry reading fell down on members of the English Department. "It spread like wildfire," Goldberg said.

Struggling in the unfamiliar realm of public controversy, several faculty members in the English Department had the same idea—to talk to their colleague Elisa New. Specifically, they wanted to ask her what Summers thought the department should do about the invitation to Paulin. As most people at Harvard know, New, a forty-four-year-old American-literature scholar, has been dating Summers, who is forty-eight, for more than a year. However, New had the same answer for everyone who asked about the president's views. "If you want to know what Larry Summers thinks, you should ask Larry Summers," she said. So, on Monday night, Lawrence Buell called Summers to ask him what to do.

The president of Harvard works in an elegant, if snug, suite of offices on the ground floor of Massachusetts Hall, a brick building nestled in the Yard. (The top floors of Mass Hall are a freshman dormitory.) In appearance, Summers has never betrayed his academic roots; his outfit on the morning I met with him included a tweed jacket, an open-necked shirt, and casual pants, all in clashing shades of blue. He propped his feet, which were shod in brown work shoes with thick rubber soles, on a glass coffee table, and talked about academic freedom. A big, shambling man, Summers has a provocative conversational style, which seems to involve disagreeing with every proposition that is put to him. For many at Harvard, that style, like Summers himself, has been unnerving.

Since Summers became Harvard's twenty-seventh president, in 2001, he has rejected the reticent, university-focused manner of his predecessor, Neil Rudenstine, in favor of a broader and more opinionated mode, one notably hostile to campus pieties. Many have welcomed the return of a Harvard president to national debates, but there is little question, too, that Summers has sometimes been ill-served by his own pugnacity. For instance, an early confrontation with the Afro-American Studies scholar Cornel West (the precise nature of which remains in dispute) led to West's decampment, last summer, for Princeton. On most issues, Summers, as an economist, is given to a straightforward weighing of pros and cons, and that includes free speech.

"There is enormously broad latitude for people to be able to invite people who they wish to the Harvard campus, for them to be able to be heard without disruption, and for there not to be censorship," Summers told me. "That is the premise on which successful research universities operate, and it's basically a policy that works because of the fallibility of human judgment." Summers went on to say that there are times when it probably would be sensible to censor speech "but no one is smart enough or wise enough to be the censor. Anytime one has an urge to censor something, one needs to think that there are plenty of people who thought advocacy of gay rights was a superb idea for censorship, that criticism of the Vietnam War, or advocacy of Marxist notions, was a superb notion for censorship. It is central to the kind of community we are that censorship not be a part of what the community is."

In light of these beliefs, one might assume that Summers would have a simple view of the invitation to Paulin: let him speak. But Summers himself has been especially outspoken on the subject of Israel and anti-Semitism, so it was not surprising that the chairman of the English Department wanted to take his pulse. In a widely noted speech on September 17, Summers took to the pulpit of Memorial Church, the symbolic center of the university, and said, "I speak with you today not as president of the university but as a concerned member of our community about something I never thought I would become seriously worried about—the issue of anti-Semitism." Harvard's first Jewish president—"identified but hardly devout," as he described himself—said that anti-Semitism had been remote from his own experience, but "there is disturbing evidence of an upturn in anti-Semitism globally." Moreover, he continued, "profoundly anti-Israel views are increasingly finding support in progressive intellectual communities. Serious and thoughtful people are advocating and taking actions that are anti-Semitic in their effect if not their intent." As examples, Summers cited European academics who shun contact with Israeli colleagues, the eviction of Israeli scholars from an international literary journal, and the demands for universities to remove from their investment portfolios companies that do business with Israel. Summers had never heard of Tom Paulin before November, but it appeared that the poet was just the kind of anti-Semite—in effect, if not in intent—that the university president had targeted in his speech.

Buell and Summers spoke on the night of Veterans Day, but there is some dispute about what the Harvard president said. Both Buell and a person familiar with Summers's recollection of the conversation agree that Summers had both an official answer and a personal response to the Paulin invitation. "As president of the university, my judgment is that the English Department should do what it sees fit to do and thinks is best in the situation," Summers said. But Buell and the Summers camp disagree about what else the president said. Summers, according to the person familiar with his version, thought the idea that no one knew about Paulin's views was preposterous, even if it happened to be true. Second, Summers thought it would look bad to withdraw the invitation. But, third, if the reading did go forward, the department should find a way to dissociate itself from Paulin's views about Israel. Buell took issue with this characterization of Summers's statement but declined to elaborate. Clearly, though, whatever Summers's intent, he succeeded in leaving a mixed message with Buell—one in keeping with the one that the Harvard president left around this time with William C. Kirby, the dean of the faculty of arts and sciences, that the Paulin matter had kicked up "kind of a shit storm."

Generations of Harvard freshmen once took their meals at the stolid brick pile known as the Union, but the old McKim, Mead & White structure has recently been renovated into the Barker Center for the Humanities, and on Tuesday morning, November 12, the offices of the English Department there were the center of the shit storm. As Robert Kiely, a longtime faculty member and former chairman of the department, recalled, "Over that long weekend, we got an avalanche of messages and e-mail raising the question as to how could the English Department invite such a person. The quote in the Cairo newspaper—'They should all be shot'—that was the key statement."

Before deciding what to do—Paulin was due to arrive in Cambridge the following day and to speak on Thursday—the committee on the Gray Lecture, Vendler, Graham, and Sacks, could at least share some rueful laughter. Faculty members who never came to poetry readings were vowing to shun this one, too. By the standards of Harvard's English Department, the Gray Lecture was a modest honor, which provided the speaker with only travel expenses and a small honorarium. At least, the committee members noted glumly, they were likely to improve on the average of seventy or so people who usually showed up for poetry readings. Mostly, though, the members started answering a question that had suddenly become ubiquitous in Cambridge: Who the hell was Tom Paulin?

Paulin is a fifty-three-year-old Irishman, a professor at Oxford University, who was spending the fall as a visiting professor at Columbia. He is a popular poet in England, where his work is widely praised and frequently anthologized. "Our committee deemed Paulin an important voice in contemporary Anglo-Irish poetry, and one that might be usefully added to the chorus of other voices reading at Harvard this year," Jorie Graham told me. Paulin has also sought to extend his franchise beyond poetry by becoming a familiar face of the political left outside the academic world, particularly on British television and radio. In his poetry, as well as in his literary criticism, Paulin often writes about politics, especially the Irish struggle against English occupation. Indeed, his views on Israel and Palestine form a kind of proxy for his views on England and

Ireland—oppressor and victim, occupier and dispossessed. Though Paulin has over the years spoken out against anti-Semitism, notably in an essay about T. S. Eliot, his virulent hostility to Israel, if not his precise language, reflects a common view among many European intellectuals.

But, without a Rita Goldberg stirring up trouble at Columbia, Paulin had enjoyed a quiet, almost protest-free fall teaching a course on Irish literature. "He was a terrific colleague—responsive, engaged, open-minded," James Shapiro, a professor of English at Columbia, said. "On the last day of class, after the Harvard story broke, a couple of students entered his class and started yelling about Israel. His students whipped out their cell phones and called security and then shoved the protesters out the door. You have to admire a teacher who commands that kind of loyalty."

Vendler, who had extended the invitation, had failed to reach Paulin over the weekend, so on Tuesday morning she tried him again. Vendler is one of Harvard's few University Professors, an elite within an elite, and an eminent literary critic of the old school, and she was plainly uncomfortable in the political maelstrom. (Declining to discuss the Paulin matter, she left me a message saying, with some disgust, "I write about poetry . . . , I don't write about chain letters.") As Graham recalled the events of that day, "We thought it would be a good idea to widen the scope of the event to include a question-and-answer session, or some kind of discussion, perhaps involving poetry and politics, or regarding the nature and effects of different kinds of 'speech.' We decided to ask Paulin—as he had only been invited to read from his work—whether he wished to include such an exchange after his reading." Vendler finally reached Paulin at Columbia, and after a short discussion they decided he would not speak at all at Harvard on November 14. Graham then called him and expressed her sorrow about the whole situation. "He"—Paulin—"said he was very sorry, but had 'no stomach for it.' He said he was tired of this whole thing, and that he just wanted some time while at Columbia—where he felt very comfortable—to get some work done," Graham said.

In his conversation with Vendler, Paulin agreed that the English Department would announce that the decision about the lecture had been made "by mutual consent." But consent to what? Paulin declined to discuss the matter, and he told friends that he had agreed only to a postponement of his appearance, not a cancellation. Vendler and the others on the committee have said that they, too, believed Paulin would ultimately give the reading. On that Tuesday, Buell posted an announcement on the English Department's Web site saying, "By mutual consent of the poet and the English Department, the Morris Gray poetry reading by Tom Paulin originally scheduled for Thursday November 14 will not take place. The English Department sincerely regret [*sic*] the widespread consternation that has arisen as a result of this invitation, which had been originally decided on last winter solely on the basis of Mr. Paulin's lifetime accomplishment as a poet." There was no suggestion that Paulin's lecture would ever take place.

That, at least initially, seemed fine with just about everyone at Harvard. Summers praised the English Department's decision. "My position was that it was for the department to decide," he said in a statement, "and I believe the department has come to the appropriate decision." Rita Goldberg, the unlikely initiator of the controversy, was astonished and delighted by the success of her electronic "chain letter." She said, "This was an honor for Paulin. Do you want to give this man this honor, when he has this history? This was an actual call to murder people. It's not a joke in wartime. Someone might take him up on it. It's incitement." As for Paulin himself, he had disavowed his call for the murder of the settlers months earlier, in a letter to the *Telegraph* of London. Since returning to Oxford in December, he has limited his public comments to a self-pitying poem, "On Being Dealt the Anti-Semitic Card," published in January in the *London Review of Books,* which referred to "the ones who play the a-s card -/of death threats hate mail talking tough/the usual cynical Goebbels stuff . . ."

Controversial speakers have been coming to Harvard for decades, and over the years there have been occasional unpleasant incidents, most memorably in 1966, when Robert McNamara, then Secretary of Defense, was noisily confronted during the Vietnam War. But Yasir Arafat, Malcolm X, the Shah of Iran, and scores of others have all spoken without incident. As Charles Fried, a professor at Harvard Law School, observed, "We've had Fidel Castro here, we've had Al Sharpton, we've had monsters, charlatans, and scoundrels." So why not Tom Paulin?

Fried had served as Solicitor General in the Reagan Administration and as a Republican appointee to the Massachusetts Supreme Judicial Court, and the Paulin matter roused his libertarian instincts. "I heard they were withdrawing the invitation because it caused 'consternation,'" Fried told me. "The reason that was given is they were disinviting him because people didn't like what he'd said. There's a difference between what you decide to listen to and what you silence. This is silencing."

Fried wrote a letter to the editor of the *Crimson,* the campus newspaper, and he recruited two law-school colleagues from a different end of the political spectrum, Alan M. Dershowitz and Laurence H. Tribe, to sign it with him. "By all accounts this Paulin fellow the English Department invited to lecture here is a despicable example of the anti-Semitic and/or anti-Israel posturing unfortunately quite widespread among European intellectuals," Fried wrote. "What is truly dangerous is the precedent of withdrawing an invitation because a speaker would cause, in the words of English department chair Lawrence Buell, 'consternation and divisiveness.' . . . If Paulin had spoken, we are sure we would have found ways to tell him and each other what we think of him. Now he will be able to lurk smugly in his Oxford lair and sneer at America's vaunted traditions of free speech. There are some mistakes which are only made worse by trying to undo them."

The law professors' letter—along with the controversy— prompted the English Department to call a meeting for the following Tuesday, to discuss the Paulin invitation. "The department, rightly, felt it has been misrepresented by the notion —untrue—that Paulin, because of statements and views attributed to him on the Internet, and then somehow distributed to selected media over the weekend, had been 'disinvited' by us," Jorie Graham said. At the meeting, on November 19, the thirty to forty senior and junior faculty members voted to reaffirm their own prerogatives. As Robert Kiely, the former department chair, recalled, "There was a unanimous reassertion that departments should be autonomous, free to invite whom they wish. And, after a long discussion, despite the unpleasantness of his views it was unanimous with two abstentions that the department should reinstate its invitation." So far, Paulin hasn't said whether he will come to Harvard after all.

MARTIN PERETZ

The Poet and the Murderer

"POETRY MAKES NOTHING HAPPEN," wrote W. H. Auden in a paradoxical homage to William Butler Yeats. But two poets—one an Oxford don, the other Saudi Arabia's ambassador to Britain—did make something happen last week. It was something ugly, but it was news.

Tom Paulin, a lousy but famous poet and a regular panelist on the BBC2 arts program *Late Review,* gave an interview to the Egyptian weekly *Al-Ahram* in which he said that "Brooklyn-born" settlers in Israel "should be shot dead. . . . [T]hey are Nazis. . . . [I] feel nothing but hatred for them." Paulin's venom toward Israel is nothing new. He once called its army the "Zionist SS" and charged that it systematically murders "little Palestinian boy[s]." In *Al-Ahram* he explained, "I can understand how suicide bombers feel. It is an expression of deep injustice and tragedy." He did, to be fair, express one scruple about the random butchery of innocent Israelis: He worried that the murders might not crush Israel's spirit. The attacks on Israeli "civilians, in fact, boost morale" among the Jews, admitted Paulin despairingly. If only the Jews would collapse in the face of terror and abandon their country to the people who want them dead.

But, as reported in the April 14 *Sunday Observer,* the other poet, Ghazi Algosaibi, Saudi Arabia's man in London for more than one decade, felt no need for such tactical caveats. Algosaibi, it is worth remembering, is one of Prince Abdullah's senior diplomats, the envoy of a monarch whose "peace plan" has elicited cheers throughout Europe. In the Arab world, Algosaibi is known as something of a poet himself. And he has at least once remarked that "[p]oetry is the soul of the Arabs." The ambassador's most recent verse was published in the London-based Arabic daily *Al-Hayat,* and it is called "The Martyrs." We know that it was not long in the writing, because "The Martyrs" is a paean to Ayat Akhras, the eighteen-year-old who detonated herself in a Jerusalem supermarket on March 29, taking two Israelis with her and maiming twenty-five others. Here's a snippet:

> *Tell Ayat, the bride of loftiness . . .*
> *She embraced death with a smile . . .*
> *While the leaders are running away from death,*
> *Doors of heavens are opened for her.*

And then, in case you missed the poet's meaning:

> *You died to honor God's word.*
> *(You) committed suicide?*
> *We committed suicide by living*
> *Like the dead.*

And finally, the United States as Satan:

> *We complained to the idols of the White House*
> *Whose heart is filled with darkness.*

The soul of the Arabs, indeed!

I am reminded by *The Daily Telegraph*'s Tom Payne of a line by Russian poet Osip Mandelstam about Stalin. "He rolls the executions on his tongue like berries." And, if they had their way with the Jews, so would Tom Paulin and Ambassador Algosaibi. But poets reflect politics; they do not make it. I do not know how many Arabs live in the United Kingdom. But some 15,000 of them marched from Hyde Park Corner to Trafalgar Square last Sunday in a protest that might have led you to believe it was Israelis who were dynamiting themselves to kill Palestinians—and not the reverse. The fatwa faithful from Bradford and Birmingham, Wolverhampton and London's Edgware Road, carried the flag that their cousins might have planted firmly in Palestine had Yasir Arafat not told Ehud Barak (and Bill Clinton) to fuck off.

The marchers brandished placards accusing Israel of genocide, specifically in Jenin. It will be a bitter pill for them, having conjured up gruesome holocaust images, to learn the truth: There were no more than 200 dead, and probably far less, in Jenin. Of course, any civilian death is a tragedy. But most of the Palestinian dead are not civilians; they are armed combatants. The civilian numbers are this low because of the scrupulousness of the Israel Defense Forces, whose troops risk their own lives so as not to kill innocents. You wouldn't know this from most of the British press. But, then, you wouldn't know it from much of the American press either.

The "Jenin massacre" is a case in point. The Palestinians claim the Israelis murdered hundreds of civilians in the city and buried them in "mass graves" to hide their heinous deeds. Their ideological partisans in the media parrot these assertions. Then your ordinary press stiff, having heard it from someone he had a drink with the night before—a nice-enough chap—reports it too. Suddenly, everybody is fuming about Israel's cover-up of a great atrocity. And, in Brussels and Paris, Oslo and Madrid, they are talking about trying Ariel Sharon for war crimes in front of the newly minted international criminal court. As Thomas Friedman admitted a bit shamefacedly in *From Beirut to Jerusalem,* one reason journalists repeat Palestinian lies, and fail to report Palestinian crimes, is fear—fear for their safety on the ground. But that doesn't quite explain those journalists who live in safe, far-off capitals and repeat the same hysterical, Israel-hating lies. To hear them tell it, Israel destroyed homes in Jenin just for the hell of it. But as even superdove Shimon Peres has noted, "There wasn't a house [in Jenin] that wasn't booby-trapped, and there was no way to neutralize the danger without demolishing the structure." And, of course, the Israelis, said Peres, "also encountered booby-trapped men, Palestinians who raised their hands to surrender while wearing explosive belts in an attempt to detonate themselves among our soldiers."

Well-intentioned European friends (and even some younger members of my own family) implore me to understand that it is the imagery of these tough Israelis with guns that is inciting anti-Semitism around the world. Yes, it is true; the killing of Jews can no longer occur with impunity and without consequence. But since the year 135 C.E., when Bar Kochba's second revolt against the Romans collapsed, Jews have almost always been without weapons. In the Middle Ages in Germany, they actually exchanged their right to bear arms for the promise of protection by the prince! (It was not long before they were slaughtered.) And so could we not say that this utter defenselessness was also a spur to anti-Semitism? Zionism strived for many ideals, some of which it has achieved. One of these is that Jews no longer go helplessly into the fire. So let us say that in this way we are like the gentiles: a normal community whose blood is not shed easily.

JONATHAN FREEDLAND

Is Anti-Zionism Anti-Semitism?

THERE ARE SOME QUESTIONS that need only be debated in the seminar room or lecture theater. There are others that battle it out on the wider university campus but also on the airwaves, in the newspapers, and, occasionally, even the streets. These questions have an importance that goes beyond mere intellectual or academic interest. They matter in the real world, with implications for individuals and even whole nations. This is one of those questions.

Does anti-Zionism equal anti-Semitism—sometimes, always, or never? That is the question. Occasionally it is argued head on. In 2002 the British Chief Rabbi, Jonathan Sacks, delivered a lecture on the resurgence of anti-Semitism, which sought, among other things, to delineate where one ended and the other began. In early 2003 the Oxford academic, Tom Paulin, answered those who had accused him of Jew-hatred with a poem, *On Being Dealt the Anti-Semitic Card*. In its own roundabout fashion, it too tried to argue that opposition to Zionism was distinct from loathing of Jews.

But most of the time the argument is not discussed so frontally. Instead it lies, implicit, beneath almost every row that pits Israel's friends against its critics. So when a university student union acts against a Jewish Society for its pro-Israel stance—a battle that seems to be played out on a British campus every year or so—the Jews complain of anti-Semitism, while their opponents claim mere anti-Zionism. Who is right and who is wrong hinges on our question: does anti-Zionism equal anti-Semitism?

In October 2002 this discussion spilled onto street level when the Stop the War coalition, together with the Muslim Association of Britain, marched in protest at a possible attack on Iraq. Jewish peace activists later complained that they had been "surrounded by hate-filled chanting and images in which anti-Israel and anti-Jewish imagery were blurred." They described posters with blood-curdling slogans; a handful of fellow marchers dressed in the garb of the suicide bomber—complete with Hamas-style "martyr's" headbands—even children, six or seven years old, brandishing toy Kalashnikovs, just like the shahids in those pre-bombing videos; and banners which linked, via an equals sign, the Star of David with the swastika. A fiery post-march exchange between these disappointed Jewish leftists and the demonstration organizers hinged on whether the Star of David was a Jewish symbol or an emblem of the Jewish state. Since it had been "co-opted" by Israel, and placed at the heart of the country's flag, said the Stop the War coalition, it was an Israeli totem. No, its history long predated the creation of the state in 1948, making it "an ancient symbol for all Jews everywhere," insisted the protesters. The dispute was not resolved but, once again, it turned on the same core question: is an attack on Israel an attack on all Jews?

But the arena where this argument has been slugged out most ferociously is not the campuses or the streets but the media. (Indeed, it often seems as if the principal form of identification with Israel currently practiced by Diaspora Jews is consumption of, and complaints about, the mainstream media's depiction of the Arab-Israeli conflict.) When Jewish viewers protest to the BBC or readers condemn, say, *The Guardian,* their objection is rarely confined to a quibble over accuracy. Whether stated explicitly or not, the complaint usually contains the accusation that the inaccuracy was committed *for a reason,* that the journalist or organization involved was biased against Israel and that that bias itself has a root cause—anti-Semitism. The media defense is consistent: "But we were only criticizing Israeli policy/the Israeli government/Ariel Sharon —we were not attacking Jews." Yet the viewers and readers experience it differently; they see or hear in the attack on Israel an attack on themselves. Once again, what's needed is a clear ruling on what counts as "mere" anti-Zionism and what crosses the line into anti-Semitism. Editors and broadcasters would certainly appreciate a universally-accepted, easy-to-use rule that would tell them which is which. They would like to know what counts as anti-Zionism (acceptable) and what is anti-Semitism (unacceptable), so that they could air a bit of the former while never being accused of the latter.

So pursuit of this debate will bring a double benefit. It should settle some currently vexing questions and, in the process, enable Jews to classify their adversaries with accuracy, separating mere critics from genuine enemies. But an inquiry into anti-Zionism and anti-Semitism promises a deeper reward, too. It cannot help but touch on much larger questions of Jewish identity. Are the Jews a nation or not? What is the nature of their connection to and claim on the land of Israel? To what extent has affinity with the Jewish state become fused with our very identity as Jews?

A useful starting point, as always, is with definitions. At one end of the dictionary lies *anti-Semite:* "*n.* a person who persecutes or discriminates against Jews." That seems clear enough. Now flip the book over and open the other end: Z for *Zionism.* "*n.* 1. a political movement for the establishment and support of a national homeland for Jews in Palestine, now concerned chiefly with the development of the modern state of Israel. 2.

a policy or movement for Jews to return to Palestine from the Diaspora."

That's a bit trickier, isn't it? You could stage a two-day seminar on either one of those definitions. (Anti-Zionists would certainly recoil from the second, with its acceptance that a Jewish move to Palestine constitutes a "return." Such is the sensitivity of this topic, it's all but impossible to craft even a sentence that will not be seen as biased by one side or other and, occasionally, both.) For our purposes, the Collins Dictionary was probably overzealous, saying more than it needed to. It's more helpful to stick with the initial definition it offered in its first clause: a movement for the establishment and support of a national homeland for Jews in Palestine. Loosely translated, Zionism represents nothing more than a belief in the right of a Jewish state in Palestine to exist. It says nothing about the borders of that state (that was, and remains to this day, an argument between different versions of Zionism). Nor does Zionism say anything about the nature, shape, or direction of that state (that, instead, is the realm of day-to-day Israeli politics). A belief in Zionism clearly does not relate to, let alone require support for, whichever government happens to rule Israel at any one time. It is a simple, ideological proposition: a Zionist believes in the Jewish state's right to exist, an anti-Zionist opposes it.

This should make life simpler. We can now happily remove from this discussion criticism of Ariel Sharon or of the post-1967 occupation of the West Bank and Gaza: such sentiments are more accurately described as anti-Likudism or anti-Sharonism. They are views that not only many Jews subscribe to, but also many Israelis and Zionists. Since such views do not, on their own, dispute Israel's right to exist, they cannot, in themselves, constitute anti-Zionism. If a hypothetical critic reviled everything Israel had done in practice since May 15, 1948, while upholding the right, in principle, of a Jewish state to exist in

Palestine, even he should not count as an anti-Zionist. He would be guilty of something we might want to call anti-Israelism, were it not such an ugly word.

A clear space should be opening up. While anti-Semitism is a blanket hatred of Jews, anti-Zionism is opposition to a specific idea—an opposition that began among, and which has always included, Jews. Judged like this, all those rows on campus and with the media should melt away: after all, on these definitions anti-Semitism and anti-Zionism stand miles apart, with barely any risk of confusion between the two. Fierce criticism of Israeli government policy, including opposition to the 35-year occupation, does not even meet the definition of anti-Zionism, let alone anti-Semitism. With these standards in mind, Jews should be able to see or read even the most withering assaults on current Israeli conduct on the BBC or in *The Guardian* without flinching: they are one thing, not the other.

Intellectually, that sounds right enough. But there are two threats to this neat separation of anti-Semitism from anti-Zionism and, indeed, criticism of Israel. The first is a matter of real-world practical expression; the second is located in the realm of ideas.

In the first category belong those critiques of Israel or Zionism which—judged strictly on their content—should not qualify as anti-Semitism at all, but which nevertheless have Jews reaching for their protective armor. Somehow Jews have sensed a foe, even when no outright hostility has been expressed. For example: I know of otherwise calm, reasonable people who insist that the reports a specific BBC Middle East correspondent files are unexceptionable in their content, but it doesn't matter: "You can tell from her voice that she's very 'anti.'" It's not what she says, *it's the way she says it.*

This should not count as a rational line of argument at all: people should surely be judged by what they say, not by their tone of voice. And yet Jews are not alone in applying such a de-

manding standard. I have heard black contemporaries denounce a white speaker whose crime had merely been to deliver a string of liberal platitudes. Yet something in his voice
had given him away: his black listeners had intuited that all the
nice talk concealed a set of outdated and condescending attitudes. They could not have offered proof to satisfy a court, but
somehow they just knew: in front of them was a mild, reform-
ing racist. In a neat reversal of the anti-Semite's old line about
being able to "sniff out a Jew from a hundred yards," so it seems
blacks can spot a racist, and Jews an anti-Semite, from an equal
distance.

In the latter case, the alarm goes off when criticism is
presented of Israel with an aggression, malice, or fervor the
speaker somehow lacks on all other topics. He is delivering the
very same list of anti-Sharon arguments you might serve up
yourself in a different context, but somehow it's not the same.
There is a zeal there, an almost gleeful pleasure in the flaws and
crimes of the Jewish state, that makes one suspect the worst:
maybe this person's passion is not really support for the Palestinians so much as hatred of Israel. You start wondering about
his motives. Of all the faraway conflicts in the world, why does
this one matter to him so much? It is nothing more than a
hunch. But just as gays enjoy a gay joke from Graham Norton,
but feel uncomfortable when the same gag is told by Bernard
Manning, so Jews can take even the bitterest criticism of Israel
from the pages of *Ha'aretz,* but feel twitchy when they read it
in, say, *The Independent.* Intentions are all.

For those seeking a clear way through this whole complex
business, don't worry: this is the grayest, most nebulous zone of
the debate. The rest does not rest on mere hunch and intuition,
but consists of more robust material. For, happily, there is more
to expression than inflection of voice and body language.
There are also the words, and tactics, people use.

The clearest collision comes when anti-Zionists, inadvertently or otherwise, deploy anti-Semitic language or imagery to press their case. In Britain the most straightforward example in recent memory occurred in 2002, when the *New Statesman* magazine ran a cover story on the perceived might of the "pro-Israel lobby." It showed a gleaming, brassy gold Star of David impaling a supine Union flag. The cover line read: *A Kosher Conspiracy?*

As the magazine later admitted in an apologetic editorial, they had "used images and words in such a way as to create unwittingly the impression that the *New Statesman* was following an anti-Semitic tradition that sees the Jews as a conspiracy piercing the heart of the nation." As it happens, the magazine had almost provided a service: their cover was a masterclass in how anti-Zionism becomes anti-Semitic when it expresses itself in the vernacular of the Jew-hater. Crammed onto a single sheet of paper was a virtual crash course in anti-Semitic iconography, including motifs that may well have been forgotten by much of the British liberal left which reads the *New Statesman*. The brassiness of the star conveyed ostentatious wealth; the defeat by the star of the British flag suggested an overmighty Jewry had won mastery over the humble, beleaguered UK; the use of kosher as a synonym for Jewish contained both street level crudity and a hint of cowardice, fighting shy of the J-word itself; and of course, the heart of the matter—conspiracy itself, with its ancient allegation that Jews are engaged in a secret plot to take over the world.

The *New Statesman* case was rare for being so egregious. Usually, this is a less open-and-shut business, one that not even all Jews agree on. The range of expressions which set Jewish antennae a-quiver can stretch from an unfortunate verb—a recent claim from leading anti-Zionist Paul Foot that pro-Israel forces were "bleating" had an unpleasant ring—to a problematic noun: why is it always the black "community" but the Jewish "lobby"?

Anti-Zionist tactics, as well as words, can have similarly highly-charged associations. The proposed academic boycott of Israel has aroused such a fierce Jewish response partly because it stirs a very specific memory for Jews: the boycott of Jewish shops and businesses under the Nazis in the 1930s. Supporters of the boycott loathe that link, and of course the two are not the same, but the emotional point still stands: like it or not, reasonable or not, that is the chord that a boycott strikes in Jewish hearts and minds.

Which makes it unsurprising that the most problematic of all anti-Zionist expressions is the equation of Israel, Zionism, and Jews with Hitler and Nazism. Nothing enrages Jews more, and no other move by an anti-Zionist is likelier to bring allegations of anti-Semitism. The critic Tom Paulin—whose poems have spoken of the "Zionist SS"—has learned this fact the hard way.

Does this style of anti-Zionist invective necessarily cross the line into anti-Semitism? Perhaps it is possible to imagine a very tight comparison of one specific aspect of Israeli conduct with an equally narrow item of Nazi policy that somehow did not feel like an assault on Jews—but it's hard to see what that might be. The more generalized comparisons, used rhetorically à la Paulin, strike most Jews as fundamentally anti-Jewish for these reasons. First, they are hyperbolic: no matter how bad Israel is, it is not the Third Reich. Second, they seem designed to cancel out the world's empathy for Jewish suffering in the 1930s and 1940s: under this logic, the Holocaust has now been "matched" by Israeli misbehavior, therefore the Jews have forfeited any claim they might once have had to special understanding. The world and the Jews are now "even." Third, and worse, the Nazi-Zionist equation does not merely neutralize memories of the Holocaust—it puts Jews on the wrong side of them. The logic of Paulin's position is that all the anger we feel toward Nazi brutality should not make us sympathetic to Jews but, on the contrary, compel us to redouble our efforts against the Zionists. After all, says Paulin, they are today's Nazis. Jews end up with the gravest hour in their history first taken from them—and then returned, with themselves recast as villains rather than victims. If anti-Zionists wonder why Jews find this anti-Semitic, perhaps they should imagine the black reaction if the civil rights movement—or any other vehicle of black liberation—was constantly equated with the white slave traders of old. It feels like a deliberate attempt to find a people's rawest spot—and tear away at it.

So much for the expressions of anti-Israel feeling which, as Jonathan Sacks has argued, can "shade into anti-Semitism." Let's assume that our hypothetical critic speaks with impeccable sensitivity to Jewish concerns. Let's assume, too, that his criticism is genuinely anti-Zionist, rather than a mere objection to the post-1967 occupation or to this or that Israeli administration. He rejects—to return to the Collins Dictionary—"the establishment and support of a national homeland for Jews in Palestine." Is he automatically an anti-Semite?

Some, including the lawyer and writer Anthony Julius, say yes. "Anti-Zionists deny Jews the right to exist collectively," they argue, which is a hair's breadth away from the anti-Semites' denial of the right of Jews to exist at all. This is a position with enormous implications. For if anti-Zionism can be identified with anti-Semitism, then that makes Jews and Zionism identical, too. To attack one is to attack the other; there is next to no space between them. This is not an absurd claim by any means. Jewish affinity with Israel is now so widespread and entrenched, across the political and religious spectrum, that it has indeed become a central part of Jewish identity. A 1995 survey by the JPR/Institute for Jewish Policy Research found just 3 percent of Anglo-Jewry had negative feelings toward Israel. For almost everyone else, the Jewish state has become inseparable from their Jewishness. As the novelist Howard Jacobson puts it, when Jews see an attack on Israel they see an attack on "a version of themselves." This should at least give the anti-Zionist pause: much as they may insist that they condemn only Zionists, not Jews, this is not how Jews themselves experience it. The Jewish people has made up its mind since 1945 and it has embraced Zionism. To stand against that idea now is to stand against a core Jewish belief.

Yet we should not use that fact to close down discussion. After all, it's still possible to disagree with someone, even on one of their most closely-held principles, without hating them. That should hold true for anti-Zionists, too: surely they should be allowed to disagree with Zionism without being branded a hater of Jews? Recall for a moment the Bundists, socialists, and communist Jews of the pre-Holocaust period who believed Jewish redemption would come through revolution rather than return: were they anti-Semites? Of course not. And what about the ultra-orthodox Jews who still hold that Jewish migration to Palestine represented a usurpation of God's role: it's up to the Messiah, not us, to create a Jewish state. Are these people anti-Semites? Again, no.

Yet these are not the grounds on which most non-Jews build their anti-Zionism. Rather they have different complaints —and it is here that Jews need to be subtle listeners. For some forms of anti-Zionism are different from others.

There is a variety of left anti-Zionism, for example, which sits alongside an avowed support for all other demands for self-determination. If there is a movement of national liberation, they'll back it—from Palestine to Scotland, northern Ireland to Catalonia. These people need to be asked a simple question: "if they support all these movements, why not the Jews?" Why are the Jews unique among the nations of the world in not deserving a state of their own? If no coherent answer comes back, it will be worth asking our anti-Zionist friend if his belief rests on no more sure foundation than simple discrimination against Jews—which is, of course, an element of anti-Semitism.

But he may have an answer. It may be that he says the Jews

are not a nation, and are therefore ineligible to claim national rights. Since Jews are defined by their religion, a Jewish state is no more defensible than a Protestant France or a Catholic Ireland. This belief is certainly wrong-headed. As we shall see, most Jews have made the shift toward a national, rather than purely religious, identity. Besides, as the Irish case illustrates, plenty of nationalisms are outgrowths of initially-religious groupings. But is it more than wrong-headed; is it anti-Semitic? It clearly denies the right of the Jews to define themselves: if Jews say they are a nation, what right does anybody else have to refuse them and insist they are this rather than that? If the right to self-definition is honored in every other case—Palestinians and Basques and Algerians are all allowed to describe themselves and chart their own destinies, but not Jews—then we are confronted, once more, with a straightforward case of discrimination. Unless the anti-Zionist has more to say, he is at least vulnerable to the charge of anti-Semitism.

What if he does have more to say? He might accept that Jews have a right to define themselves and that, as a nation, they have a right to self-determination—and then locate his objection elsewhere. He may say, first, that the unusual element in the Jewish case—the thing that separates it from the Catalan or Scottish or any other example—is that Jewish national liberation in Palestine could only ever be achieved at the expense of another people: the Palestinians.

For some anti-Zionists it is this simple fact which blocks the Zionist claim. If Palestine had indeed been the "land without a people for a people without a land," then there would be no reason to object. But Palestine was not empty. During the two millennia of Jewish exile a new community, even a new nation, arose there. For the Jews to have their national homeland another people would have to lose at least some of theirs. The simple, unavoidable fact of this dispossession is enough to make many write off Zionism as a moral enterprise.

Such a verdict is harsh, but is it anti-Semitic? Once again: not if applied evenly. If our anti-Zionist took the same hard line on all new societies founded by immigrants who displaced the earlier inhabitants, then he would be perfectly consistent. If he denied the right of, say, the United States, Australia, Canada, New Zealand, and whole swathes of Latin America to exist, then he would be immune to charges of anti-Semitism.

The reality, as we know, is that not many anti-Zionists take this option; not many show equal fervor in their denunciation of Washington, Sydney, or Wellington. Does this make them anti-Semites, for making such an exception of the Jewish state? That depends on whether you accept the anti-Zionist defense. It argues that there are some crucial differences in the Israeli case. First, this dispossession happened within living memory and that many of its direct victims are—unlike the native Americans, Aboriginals, and Maoris—still alive. Second, the current demand made by the dispossessed is not merely for equal treatment and rights—as it is in the United States, Australia, or New Zealand—but for national independence and statehood. It is this national character that gives the Zionist question its extra, more pressing dimension.

If this is persuasive, there is one more move our left anti-Zionist needs to make. He needs to show a consistent view that any landless people seeking a nation state would, like the Jews, be barred if their liberation entailed another's dispossession. If they are happy to agree to that, then one could hardly accuse them of anti-Jewish discrimination. Such a person is not making a special exception of the Jews, but rather of all peoples unlucky enough to seek a territory when they have none. The Roma people, should they desire a nation state, would be similarly blocked.

There is another line of anti-Zionist argument which should likewise not be instantly dismissed as anti-Semitism. There are some whose objection to the Jewish state is not so much to the displacement required to create it, as its inevitable nature once established. They say that a "Jewish state" is an ethnic construct, one which will always privilege one group of citizens over another. Its institutions, traditions, and national symbols will only ever include one section of the population—roughly 80 percent on current figures—and pointedly exclude the others. Just as if an Ireland formally designated a Catholic state would exclude and discriminate against Protestants and others, so a "Jewish state" necessarily makes second-class citizens of its non-Jews. To take one totemic example, a Jewish state must speak of the Jewish story—of exile and longing—in its national anthem. Yet how are Israel's one million Arab citizens to sing an anthem that is not about them at all?

The problem is intensified in the Zionist case because Jewishness represents what some scholars describe as a "closed" rather than "open" identity. Britishness or Americanness are open identities: merely living in the country long enough, or being born there, or acquiring citizenship, gives you membership. Jewishness is not like that. Israel's non-Jewish citizens cannot join the Jewish majority just by being there (the way, say, Britain's Jews have become British as a matter of course). Instead they would have to undergo a formal, religious conversion. This means that while Israeli status is open to all as a matter of citizenship, a fifth of the population can never feel fully Israeli as a matter of identity—for that would require identification with Israel as a Jewish state, a sentiment surely open only to Jews.

This brand of anti-Zionism, which questions Israel as a Jewishly-defined state, is probably best articulated by the Palestinian-Israeli member of Knesset, Azmi Bishara. Whether advocated by him or others, it would probably be a mistake instantly to label it anti-Semitic. So long as its exponents took a similarly harsh view of other ethnically defined states, there would be no discrimination claim to press.

Rather, Zionists may have to accept that, where proffered on principle rather than out of malice, these kinds of arguments deserve a serious answer. Both Bishara's critique of Israel as an ethnic state, and the more familiar denunciation of the upheavals of 1948, have to be confronted by those who believe in the idea, and morality, of a Jewish state.

So far that confrontation has tended to consist in questioning the premise, rather than engaging with the issue. Mainstream Zionists have rejected the allegations of dispossession in 1948—though that is becoming ever harder, thanks to Israel's own "new historians" who have done so much to uncover the "labor pains" that accompanied Israel's birth—and denied that there is anything remiss or discriminatory in Israeli democracy.

A tougher, but ultimately more rewarding response might be to admit these challenges to Zionism—and to work to craft a new Zionism that might be proofed against them. On the first matter, I have long believed that Israel should be strong enough to admit the reality of 1948—and to defend it all the same. Jews should turn to the anti-Zionists who claim that Zionism's moral claim was voided by the presence of another nation, and say: "In an ideal world, maybe. In an ideal world, perhaps national liberation would only be deemed possible when it does not entail another's dispossession. But this is not the ideal world. This is the real world, and in the middle of the twentieth century reality was all too clear to the Jewish people. We needed a home and we had every right to demand it—even if that meant forcing another people to share their land with us. Ours was the right of Amos Oz's drowning man reaching for a piece of driftwood: he is allowed to grab it, even to make another man budge up to share it. That was the nature of the Zionist crimes of 1948 (in 1967 we went further, not just asking our fellow drowner to share the driftwood—but forcing him off it and into the sea altogether). They were tough and people lost their homes, and for that Israel should make amends—through compensation, restitution, and commemoration. Let those four hundred villages that were emptied be named and marked, and let Palestinians remember what they see as the *naqba,* the catastrophe, their way. Israel and the Jews should have that reckoning with our recent past—but we don't have to renounce Zionism itself. We can still insist that the creation of a Jewish state was a moral necessity even if, like so many moral necessities, it was bought at a horribly high moral price."

The response to Bishara will require even more radical change. It necessitates what in Northern Ireland would be called an "equality agenda"—a raft of reforms in housing, employment, government spending, and the law to end discrimination against non-Jews. But it can't end there. Israel, and indeed the wider Jewish world, needs to work out a way that the country can still remain Jewish in character—a state for the Jews—without enshrining inequality forever. Bishara's slogan is "a state of all its citizens," which is indeed a description of most liberal democracies. Israel is currently a "Jewish state," with all the ramifications that entails. The challenge now is surely to find a place somewhere between those two, a position which would simultaneously allow Jews to feel their Zionist need has been met—that they have their own national home—and Arabs to feel like full members of the society in which they live. Could the winning formula be "a Jewish state of all its citizens," or is that too much of a fudge?

Either way, there is much to be done. Zionists need to stand firm against those critics who make an exception of Jews—who deny us the rights they would give everyone else—and whose language and methods, mistakenly or otherwise, play on the most gruesome memories of our past. Some anti-Zionists are anti-Semites and they should be fought like enemies.

But others are presenting us with a cogent challenge to our core values. They are asking the questions some of our long-lost fellow Jews—the Bundists, socialists, and anarchists—used to ask and would be asking now, had not so many of them been cut down a half-century ago. They are not unanswerable questions at all, but they need a response. We may not win over many of our enemies, but we shall make ourselves stronger. And there is no more Zionist project than that.

JUDITH BUTLER

The Charge of Anti-Semitism: Jews, Israel, and the Risks of Public Critique

---

> [P]rofoundly anti-Israel views are increasingly finding support in progressive intellectual communities. Serious and thoughtful people are advocating and taking actions that are anti-Semitic in their effect if not their intent.
>
> —address by Lawrence Summers, September 17, 2002

W HEN THE PRESIDENT of Harvard University declared that to criticize Israel at this time and to call on universities to divest from Israel are "actions that are anti-Semitic in their effect if not their intent," he introduced a distinction between effective and intentional anti-Semitism that is controversial at best. The counter-charge has been that in making his statement, Summers has struck a blow against academic freedom, in effect if not in intent. Although he insisted that he meant nothing censorious by his remarks, and that he is in favor of Israeli policy being "debated freely and civilly," his words have had a chilling effect on political discourse. Among those actions which he called "effectively anti-Semitic" were European boycotts of Israel, anti-globalization rallies at which criticisms of Israel were voiced, and fund-raising efforts for organizations of "questionable political provenance." Of local concern to him, however, was a divestment petition drafted by MIT and Harvard faculty members who oppose Israel's current occupation and its treatment of Palestinians. Summers asked why Israel was being "single[d] out . . . among all nations" for a divestment campaign, suggesting that the singling out was evidence of anti-Semitic intentions. And though he claimed that aspects of Israel's "foreign and defense" policy "can be and should be vigorously challenged," it was unclear how such challenges could or would take place without being construed as anti-Israel, and why these policy issues, which include occupation, ought not to be vigorously challenged through a divestment campaign. It would seem that calling for divestment is something other than a legitimately "vigorous challenge," but we are not given any criteria by which to adjudicate between vigorous challenges that should be articulated, and those which carry the "effective" force of anti-Semitism.

Summers is right to voice concern about rising anti-Semitism, and every progressive person ought to challenge anti-Semitism vigorously wherever it occurs. It seems, though, that historically we have now reached a position in which Jews cannot legitimately be understood always and only as presumptive victims. Sometimes we surely are, but sometimes we surely are not. No political ethics can start from the assumption that Jews monopolize the position of victim. "Victim" is a quickly transposable term: it can shift from minute to minute, from the Jew killed by suicide bombers on a bus to the Palestinian child killed by Israeli gunfire. The public sphere needs to be one in which both kinds of violence are challenged insistently and in the name of justice.

If we think that to criticize Israeli violence, or to call for economic pressure to be put on the Israeli state to change its policies, is to be "effectively anti-Semitic," we will fail to voice our opposition for fear of being named as part of an anti-Semitic enterprise. No label could be worse for a Jew, who knows that, ethically and politically, the position with which it would be unbearable to identify is that of the anti-Semite. The ethical framework within which most progressive Jews operate takes the form of the following question: will we be silent (and thereby collaborate with illegitimately violent power), or will we make our voices heard (and be counted among those who did what they could to stop that violence), even if speaking poses a risk? The current Jewish critique of Israel is often portrayed as insensitive to Jewish suffering, past as well as present, yet its ethic is based on the experience of suffering, in order that suffering might stop.

Summers uses the "anti-Semitic" charge to quell public criticism of Israel, even as he explicitly distances himself from the overt operations of censorship. He writes, for instance, that "the only antidote to dangerous ideas is strong alternatives vigorously advocated." But how does one vigorously advocate the idea that the Israeli occupation is brutal and wrong, and Palestinian self-determination a necessary good, if the voicing of those views calls down the charge of anti-Semitism?

To understand Summers's claim, we have to be able to conceive of an effective anti-Semitism, one that pertains to certain speech acts. Either it follows on certain utterances, or it structures them, even if that is not the conscious intention of those making them. His view assumes that such utterances will be taken by others as anti-Semitic, or received within a given context as anti-Semitic. So we have to ask what context Summers has in mind when he makes his claim; in what context is it the case that any criticism of Israel will be taken to be anti-Semitic?

It may be that what Summers was effectively saying is that the only way a criticism of Israel can be heard is through a certain acoustic frame, such that the criticism, whether it is of the West Bank settlements, the closing of Birzeit and Bethlehem

University, the demolition of homes in Ramallah or Jenin, or the killing of numerous children and civilians, can only be interpreted as showing hatred for Jews. We are asked to conjure a listener who attributes an intention to the speaker: so-and-so has made a public statement against the Israeli occupation, and this must mean that so-and-so hates Jews or is willing to fuel those who do. The criticism is thus given a hidden meaning, one that is at odds with its explicit claim. The criticism of Israel is nothing more than a cloak for that hatred, or a cover for a call for discriminatory action against Jews. In other words, the only way to understand *effective* anti-Semitism is to presuppose *intentional* anti-Semitism; the effective anti-Semitism of any criticism turns out to reside in the intention of the speaker as retrospectively attributed by the listener.

It may be that Summers has something else in mind; namely, that the criticism will be exploited by those who want to see not only the destruction of Israel but the degradation or devaluation of Jewish people in general. There is always that risk, but to claim that such criticism of Israel can be taken only as criticism of Jews is to attribute to that particular interpretation the power to monopolize the field of reception. The argument against letting criticism of Israel into the public sphere would be that it gives fodder to those with anti-Semitic intentions, who will successfully co-opt the criticism. Here again, a statement can become effectively anti-Semitic only if there is, somewhere, an intention to use it for anti-Semitic purposes. Indeed, even if one believed that criticisms of Israel are by and large heard as anti-Semitic (by Jews, anti-Semites, or people who could be described as neither), it would become the responsibility of all of us to change the conditions of reception so that the public might begin to distinguish between criticism of Israel and a hatred of Jews.

Summers made his statement as president of an institution which is a symbol of academic prestige in the United States, and although he claimed he was speaking not as president of the university but as a "member of our community," his speech carried weight in the press precisely because he was exercising the authority of his office. If the president of Harvard is letting the public know that he will take any criticism of Israel to be effectively anti-Semitic, then he is saying that public discourse itself ought to be so constrained that such statements are not uttered, and that those who utter them will be understood as engaging in anti-Semitic speech, even hate speech.

Here, it is important to distinguish between anti-Semitic speech which, say, produces a hostile and threatening environment for Jewish students—racist speech which any university administrator would be obliged to oppose and regulate—and speech which makes a student uncomfortable because it opposes a particular state or set of state policies that he or she may defend. The latter is a political debate, and if we say that the case of Israel is different, that any criticism of it is considered as an attack on Israelis, or Jews in general, then we have singled out this political allegiance from all other allegiances that are open to public debate. We have engaged in the most outrageous form of "effective" censorship.

The point is not only that Summers's distinction between effective and intentional anti-Semitism cannot hold, but that the way it collapses in his formulation is precisely what produces the conditions under which certain public views are taken to be hate speech, in effect if not in intent. Summers didn't say that anything that Israel does in the name of self-defense is legitimate and ought not to be questioned. I don't know whether he approves of all Israeli policies, but let's imagine, for the sake of argument, that he doesn't. And I don't know whether he has views about, for instance, the destruction of homes and the killings of children in Jenin which attracted the attention of the United Nations last year but was not investigated as a human rights violation because Israel refused to open its borders to an investigative team. If he objects to those actions, and they are among the "foreign policy" issues he believes ought to be "vigorously challenged," he would be compelled, under his formulation, not to voice his disapproval, believing, as he does, that that would be construed, effectively, as anti-Semitism. And if he thinks it possible to voice disapproval, he hasn't shown us how to do it in such a way as to avert the allegation of anti-Semitism.

Summers's logic suggests that certain actions of the Israeli state must be allowed to go on unimpeded by public protest, for fear that any protest would be tantamount to anti-Semitism, if not anti-Semitism itself. Now, all forms of anti-Semitism must be opposed, but we have here a set of serious confusions about the forms anti-Semitism takes. Indeed, if the charge of anti-Semitism is used to defend Israel at all costs, then its power when used against those who do discriminate against Jews—who do violence to synagogues in Europe, wave Nazi flags, or support anti-Semitic organizations—is radically diluted. Many critics of Israel now dismiss all claims of anti-Semitism as "trumped up," having been exposed to their use as a way of censoring political speech.

Summers doesn't tell us why divestment campaigns or other forms of public protest *are* anti-Semitic. According to him, some forms of anti-Semitism are characterized as such retroactively, which means that nothing should be said or done that will then be taken to be anti-Semitic by others. But what if those others are wrong? If we take one form of anti-Semitism to be defined retroactively, what is left of the possibility of legitimate protest against a state, either by its own population or anyone else? If we say that every time the word "Israel" is spoken, the speaker really means "Jews," then we have foreclosed in advance the possibility that the speaker really means "Israel." If, on the other hand, we distinguish between anti-Semitism and forms of protest against the Israeli state (or right-wing set-

tlers who sometimes act independently of the state), acknowledging that sometimes they do, disturbingly, work together,
then we stand a chance of understanding that world Jewry
does not see itself as one with Israel in its present form and
practice, and that Jews in Israel do not necessarily see themselves as one with the state. In other words, the possibility of a
substantive Jewish peace movement depends on our observing
a productive and critical distance from the state of Israel
(which can be coupled with a profound investment in its future
course).

Summers's view seems to imply that criticism of Israel is
"anti-Israel" in the sense that it is understood to challenge the
right of Israel to exist. A criticism of Israel is not the same,
however, as a challenge to Israel's existence, even if there are
conditions under which it would be possible to say that one
leads to the other. A challenge to the right of Israel to exist can
be construed as a challenge to the existence of the Jewish
people only if one believes that Israel alone keeps the Jewish
people alive or that all Jews invest their sense of perpetuity in
the state of Israel in its current or traditional forms. One could
argue, however, that those polities which safeguard the right to
criticize them stand a better chance of surviving than those
that don't. For a criticism of Israel to be taken as a challenge
to the survival of the Jews, we would have to assume not only
that "Israel" cannot change in response to legitimate criticism,
but that a more radically democratic Israel would be bad for
Jews. This would be to suppose that criticism is not a Jewish
value, which clearly flies in the face not only of long traditions
of Talmudic disputation, but of all the religious and cultural
sources that have been part of Jewish life for centuries.

What are we to make of Jews who *dis*identify with Israel or,
at least, with the Israeli state? Or Jews who identify with Israel,
but do not condone some of its practices? There is a wide range
here: those who are silently ambivalent about the way Israel

handles itself; those who only half articulate their doubts about the occupation; those who are strongly opposed to the occupation, but within a Zionist framework; those who would like to see Zionism rethought or, indeed, abandoned. Jews may hold any of these opinions, but voice them only to their family, or only to their friends; or voice them in public but then face an angry reception at home. Given this Jewish ambivalence, ought we not to be suspicious of any effort to equate Jews with Israel? The argument that all Jews have a heartfelt investment in the state of Israel is untrue. Some have a heartfelt investment in corned beef sandwiches or in certain Talmudic tales, religious rituals and liturgy, in memories of their grandmother, the taste of borscht, or the sounds of the old Yiddish theater. Others have an investment in historical and cultural archives from Eastern Europe or from the Holocaust, or in forms of labor activism, civil rights struggles, and social justice that are thoroughly secular, and exist in relative independence from the question of Israel.

What do we make of Jews such as myself, who are emotionally invested in the state of Israel, critical of its current form, and call for a radical restructuring of its economic and juridical basis precisely because we are invested in it? It is always possible to say that such Jews have turned against their own Jewishness. But what if one criticizes Israel in the name of one's Jewishness, in the name of justice, precisely because such criticisms seem "best for the Jews"? Why wouldn't it always be "best for the Jews" to embrace forms of democracy that extend what is "best" to everyone, Jewish or not? I signed a petition framed in these terms, an "Open Letter from American Jews," in which 3,700 American Jews opposed the Israeli occupation, though in my view it was not nearly strong enough: it did not call for the end of Zionism, or for the reallocation of arable land, for rethinking the Jewish right of return or for the fair distribution of water and medicine to Palestinians, and it did not

446 THOSE WHO FORGET THE PAST

call for the reorganization of the Israeli state on a more radically egalitarian basis. It was, nevertheless, an overt criticism of Israel.

Many of those who signed that petition will have felt what might reasonably be called heartache at taking a public stand against Israeli policy, at the thought that Israel, by subjecting 3.5 million Palestinians to military occupation, represents the Jews in a way that these petitioners find not only objectionable, but terrible to endure, as Jews; it is as Jews that they assert their disidentification with that policy, that they seek to widen the rift between the state of Israel and the Jewish people in order to produce an alternative vision of the future. The petitioners exercised a democratic right to voice criticism, and sought to get economic pressure put on Israel by the United States and other countries, to implement rights for Palestinians otherwise deprived of basic conditions of self-determination, to end the occupation, to secure an independent Palestinian state or to reestablish the basis of the Israeli state without regard to religion so that Jewishness would constitute only one cultural and religious reality, and be protected by the same laws that protect the rights of others.

Identifying Israel with Jewry obscures the existence of the small but important post-Zionist movement in Israel, including the philosophers Adi Ophir and Anat Biletzki, the sociologist Uri Ram, the professor of theater Avraham Oz, and the poet Yitzhak Laor. Are we to say that Israelis who are critical of Israeli policy are self-hating Jews, or insensitive to the ways in which criticism may fan the flames of anti-Semitism? What of the new Brit Tzedek organization in the United States, numbering close to 20,000 members at the last count, which seeks to offer a critical alternative to the American Israel Political Action Committee, opposing the current occupation and working for a two-state solution? What of Jewish Voices for Peace, Jews against the Occupation, Jews for Peace in the Middle East, the

Faculty for Israeli-Palestinian Peace, *Tikkun,* Jews for Racial and Economic Justice, Women in Black, or, indeed, Neve Shalom–Wahat al-Salam, the only village collectively governed by both Jews and Arabs in the state of Israel? What do we make of B'Tselem, the Israeli organization that monitors human rights abuses in the West Bank and Gaza, or Gush Shalom, an Israeli organization opposing the occupation, or Yesh Gvul, which represents the Israeli soldiers who refuse to serve in the Occupied Territories? And what of Ta'ayush, a Jewish-Arab coalition against policies that lead to isolation, poor medical care, house arrest, the destruction of educational institutions, and lack of water and food for Palestinians?

It will not do to equate Jews with Zionists or Jewishness with Zionism. There were debates among Jews throughout the nineteenth and early twentieth centuries as to whether Zionism ought to become the basis of a state, whether the Jews had any right to lay claim to land inhabited by Palestinians for centuries, and as to the future for a Jewish political project based on a violent expropriation of land. There were those who sought to make Zionism compatible with peaceful co-existence with Arabs, and those who used it as an excuse for military aggression, and continue to do so. There were those who thought, and still think, that Zionism is not a legitimate basis for a democratic state in a situation where a diverse population must be assumed to practice different religions, and that no group ought to be excluded from any right accorded to citizens in general on the basis of their ethnic or religious views. And there are those who maintain that the violent appropriation of Palestinian land, and the dislocation of 700,000 Palestinians, was an unsuitable foundation on which to build a state. Yet Israel is now repeating its founding gesture in the containment and dehumanization of Palestinians in the Occupied Territories. Indeed, the wall now being built threatens to leave 95,000 Palestinians homeless. These are questions about Zionism that should and must be asked in a public domain, and universities are surely one place where we might expect critical reflections on Zionism to take place. Instead, we are being asked, by Summers and others, to treat any critical approach to Zionism as effective anti-Semitism and, hence, to rule it out as a topic for legitimate disagreement.

Many important distinctions are elided by the mainstream press when it assumes that there are only two possible positions on the Middle East, the "pro-Israel" and the "pro-Palestinian." The assumption is that these are discrete views, internally homogeneous, non-overlapping, that if one is "pro-Israel" then anything Israel does is all right, or if "pro-Palestinian" then anything Palestinians do is all right. But few people's political views occupy such extremes. One can, for instance, be in favor of Palestinian self-determination, but condemn suicide bombings, and find others who share both those views but differ on the form self-determination ought to take. One can be in favor of Israel's right to exist, but still ask what is the most legitimate and democratic form that existence ought to take. If one questions the present form, is one anti-Israel? If one holds out for a truly democratic Israel-Palestine, is one anti-Israel? Or is one trying to find a better form for this polity, one that may well involve any number of possibilities: a revised version of Zionism, a post-Zionist Israel, a self-determining Palestine, or an amalgamation of Israel into a greater Israel-Palestine where all racially and religiously based qualifications on rights and entitlements would be eliminated?

What is ironic is that in equating Zionism with Jewishness, Summers is adopting the very tactic favored by anti-Semites. At the time of his speech, I found myself on a listserv on which a number of individuals opposed to the current policies of the state of Israel, and sometimes to Zionism, started to engage in this same slippage, sometimes opposing what they called "Zionism" and at other times what they called "Jewish" interests. Whenever this occurred, there were objections, and several people withdrew from the group. Mona Baker, the academic in Manchester who dismissed two Israeli colleagues from the board of her academic journal in an effort to boycott Israeli institutions, argued that there was no way to distinguish between individuals and institutions. In dismissing these individuals, she claimed, she was treating them as emblematic of the Israeli state, since they were citizens of that country. But citizens are not the same as states: the very possibility of significant dissent depends on recognizing the difference between them. Baker's response to subsequent criticism was to submit e-mails to the "academicsforjustice" listserv complaining about "Jewish" newspapers and labeling as "pressure" the opportunity that some of these newspapers offered to discuss the issue in print with the colleagues she had dismissed. She refused to do this and seemed now to be fighting against "Jews," identified as a lobby that pressures people, a lobby that had put pressure on her. The criticism that I made of Summers's view thus applies to Baker as well: it is one thing to oppose Israel in its current form and practices or, indeed, to have critical questions about Zionism itself, but it is quite another to oppose "Jews" or assume that all "Jews" have the same view, that they are all in favor of Israel, identified with Israel, or represented by Israel. Oddly, and painfully, it has to be said that on this point Mona Baker and Lawrence Summers agree: Jews are the same as Israel. In the one instance, the premise works in the service of an argument against anti-Semitism; in the second, it works as the effect of anti-Semitism itself. One aspect of anti-Semitism or, indeed, of any form of racism is that an entire people is falsely and summarily equated with a particular position, view, or disposition. To say that all Jews hold a given view on Israel or are adequately represented by Israel or, conversely, that the acts of Israel, the state, adequately stand for the acts of all Jews, is to conflate Jews with Israel and, thereby, to commit an anti-Semitic reduction of Jewishness.

In holding out for a distinction to be made between Israel

and Jews, I am calling for a space for dissent for Jews, and non-Jews, who have criticisms of Israel to articulate; but I am also opposing anti-Semitic reductions of Jewishness to Israeli interests. The "Jew" is no more defined by Israel than by anti-Semitism. The "Jew" exceeds both determinations, and is to be found, substantively, as a historically and culturally changing identity that takes no single form and has no single telos. Once the distinction is made, discussion of both Zionism and anti-Semitism can begin, since it will be as important to understand the legacy of Zionism and to debate its future as to oppose anti-Semitism wherever we find it.

What is needed is a public space in which such issues might be thoughtfully debated, and to prevent that space being defined by certain kinds of exclusion and censorship. If one can't voice an objection to violence done by Israel without attracting a charge of anti-Semitism, then that charge works to circumscribe the publicly acceptable domain of speech, and to immunize Israeli violence against criticism. One is threatened with the label "anti-Semitic" in the same way that one is threatened with being called a "traitor" if one opposes the most recent U.S. war. Such threats aim to define the limits of the public sphere by setting limits on the speakable. The world of public discourse would then be one from which critical perspectives would be excluded, and the public would come to understand itself as one that does not speak out in the face of obvious and illegitimate violence.

PART TEN

ISRAEL

DAVID MAMET

"If I Forget Thee, Jerusalem": The Power of Blunt Nostalgia

I AM READING IN JERUSALEM. I read, in *Azure*, a scholarly Israeli publication, an article by historian Michael Oren that Israeli opinion is split on Orde Wingate. Wingate was a Brit philosemite (the exception that, et cetera), creator of the doctrine of desert guerrilla warfare and godfather of the Israeli military. I read that the jury was still out on him, as he ate raw onions, strained his tea through his socks, and greeted guests in the nude. Now, as to particulars one and three, I have been guilty myself (though never in conjunction). As to particular two, I must ask, did he, in the absence of a strainer, improvise brilliantly with a pair of clean socks, or, did he (*disons le mot*) utilize the very socks in which he trod that desert land he was to aid in Making Free? But, perhaps, there are some doors History was never meant to open.

My accommodations in the Mount Zion Hotel are superb —two large picture windows overlook the Old City. To its left, modern Jerusalem, to the right, the Mount of Olives, East Jerusalem, and the descent to the Dead Sea. Looking east, before actual dawn, and just before sunset, the light is extraordinary. The Old City is the height of land—it rises from the sea to the Temple Mount and falls away to the Dead Sea and the desert.

A tour guide, a committed amateur archaeologist, gives me a tour of the south and east walls.

"Look up," he says, "what do you see?"

"The land rises and then falls away," I say.

He nods. "The clouds come in from the sea and deposit the rain at the highest point: the Old City. To its west, the land is tillable. To its east is desert. This is the division," he says. "This is the spot where . . ."

"Two cultures," I suggest.

"Not two cultures," he says, "but two *mentalities,* two *spiritualities* meet: the people in the land toward the sea, in biblical Canaan, were concerned with commerce, with trade, with agriculture. The people to the east, the people in the desert, were concerned with spirit, with visions. The two have always met in Jerusalem."

We walk toward the cemetery at the Mount of Olives. Below he shows me the City of David, that is, Jerusalem, as it existed at the turn of the common era. In those days, he says, it had more than 100,000 inhabitants. The July heat is killing me. It is not hard to imagine the relief of the desert traveler, coming to the high, watered ground. The cleansing, insistent influence of the desert to the Westerner does not need to be imagined; one feels it.

The Old City is fairly empty. It is usually, of course, steeved, if I may, with tourists and pilgrims. The current intifada has discouraged them. We stop for lunch in a Palestinian falafel place my friends recommend as the best around. We eat under a large poster showing the growth of Medina from the desert crossroads into the modern shrine. "Excuse me," I say, "but is it dangerous to be eating in a Palestinian restaurant?" I am assured that the proprietors, like most of their co-religionists in the Old City, are Israeli citizens and that they would not think of committing antisocial acts. I am puzzled to find this suggested suspension of human nature, and not gratified when, several weeks later, I find my friends' opinions proved too sanguine.

I am invited to Sabbath lunch in South Jerusalem, in a house one block from one of the latest bus bombings. My hosts are the Horensteins, close friends from Newton, Mass. I get out of the cab, and they greet me warmly. There is a group standing outside the front door, among them a nice-looking, obviously Christian gent, around my age. How like the Horensteins, I think, to extend their hospitality, to share their Jewish home with a non-Jewish friend.

The ringer is, of course, not him, but me. He is Michael Oren, the Horensteins' cousin, author of the piece on Wingate and, incidentally, of *Six Days of War: June 1967 and the Making of the Modern Middle East*. He is a scholar and saw the eponymous war (1967), and several others, as a paratrooper in the IDF. With him is his son, Yoram, an eighteen-year-old on half-day leave from his unit, an ultra-elite helicopter rescue squad in the IDF. The young man leaves, and Michael says, "When he came home last night, he was short one of his uniform shirts, so I lent him one of mine." This offhanded statement is the greatest expression of parental pride I have ever heard.

I am overcome by a sense of grief. We sit there, at the ritual meal, talking about Jerusalem, about the war—Michael's sister-in-law was killed in one of the recent bombings—about being Jewish.

To me, a Diaspora Jew, the question is constant, insistent, and poignant while in Israel. At this meal it is more than poignant, it is painful. How, I wonder, can I not be here; and how is it possible that I did not come here (as did Michael Oren) in my youth, and "grow up with the country," instead of wasting my time in show business? I am full of grief, as at a middle-aged meeting with the girl I did not marry.

Now, this blunt trauma of nostalgia is a dead giveaway, signaling not an inability to relive the past, but to face the present. The present, to me, consists in this: that I am an aging Diaspora Jew on a junket, and that my cheap feelings of personal loss could better be expressed as respect and homage.

Israel is at war and has been at war since its inception. Much contemporary opinion in the West is anti-Semitic. Before my trip, I was strolling through Newton. There, before me, was a broken-down Volvo of old, the vehicle of my brethren, the congenitally liberal. It was festooned, as are its kind, with every sort of correct exhortation: "Save James Bay," "Honor Diversity," and so on. A most interesting bumper sticker read: "Israel Out of the Settlements." Now this is a legitimate expression of free speech. Israel has been involved, as we know, in a rather protracted real estate dispute with several hundred million of its neighbors. This legitimate political expression, however, had all its S's transformed into dollar signs. Here we have, one would have supposed, a civilized person (one would assume that one could reason with the owner of a Volvo) sporting a slogan which could best be translated as "Hook-nosed Jews Die." My very airplane book, my refuge on the endless flight to Israel, is Tom Clancy's *The Sum of All Fears,* in which I find the major plot point, the misplacement, by Israel, of an atom bomb. As per Mr. Clancy, in this otherwise ripping yarn, the world is going to end because these lazy or distracted Mockies have committed a blunder no civilized folk would make.

It is—I cannot say "refreshing"—a relief to trade a low-level umbrage at anti-Israeli tripe for the reality of a country at war. Israel, at war, looks very much like Israel at peace. Life, as the phrase has it, goes on. Six thousand people have bought tickets to the opening night of the Jerusalem Film Festival. Nine thousand show up and are seated. We are in The Sultan's Pool, a natural open-air amphitheater, just under the walls of the Old City. Lia van Leer, the festival's founder and complete enchilada, asks me to accompany her to the podium to open the ball officially. I do so, in English, and add *"Shalom, chaverim"* ("Hello, companions"), thus exhausting my conversational Hebrew. And we watch Pedro Almodóvar's *Talk to Her,* with 9,000 mainly young Israelis. They laugh at the film, cordially boo the mayor, and, during the speeches afterward, smoke cigarettes, sitting under the open sky. Such beautiful young people. Even the old people here look young to me. But, then, I am in love.

I tour the sites of bombings on the Jaffa Road, accompanying Mayor Ehud Olmert. The tour ends at the house of Boris Schatz, the founder of the Bezalel School, the Jewish state's first school of art. Jimmy and Micah Lewensohn, his great-nephews, are my hosts. It is crammed with workbooks, plaques, sculptures, paintings, ceramics, weavings. Schatz, once court sculptor to the King of Bulgaria, had an unfortunate marital experience, around 1904, and it drove him back to his Judaism. Theodor Herzl enlisted him as the "First Artist of the Yishuv" (the pre-statehood settlement). Schatz came out to create a new Jewish art. Micah tells me that Schatz's wife, once a lover of Gorky, ended up screwing half the men in the Yishuv. It was, he said, like the Wild West. They went up to the Galilee on retreat, got whacked out on the native weeds, and it was one big orgy. These were disaffected youth, he said; they were, in effect, hippies, the early Zionists. Schatz dressed in a white djellaba, kept a pet peacock, and held court in the Galilee. Herzl comes up to see him, there he is: the peacock, half-naked girls, *Shabbos* dinner, and somebody's playing the flute. "And you *know*," Micah says, "the flute is prohibited on *Shabbos*."

So I am nostalgic for the days of '48, and Schatz's great-nephew is nostalgic for the 1910 Wild West, as he puts it, of the Galilee. "He was insane," Micah lovingly says of his great-uncle. "Here is the burial plaque he designed for Ben Yehuda. You will see he dated it 'In the Year Seven.'" He shrugs. Ben Yehuda died in '24, and Schatz reinvented the calendar to reflect "seven years since the Balfour Declaration."

In my study, in the United States, are two World War I posters. The images are identical, but the text of each is in a different language. They show a gallant squad of British soldiers in khaki, charging off. In the foreground, another soldier uses his bayonet to free a bound man. This man is a heavily bearded, tubercular, bowed endomorph in shirt sleeves. He has a hooked nose, essentially, a cartoon tailor of 1917. He gazes at the soldiers, whose ranks he will now join, and says, "You have cut my bonds and set me free. Now let me set others free." The superscription says, in the one poster in English, and in the other in Yiddish: "Jews the World Over Love Liberty, Have Fought, And Will Fight for It." And, below the pictured scene: "Britain Expects Every Son of Israel To Do His Duty—Enlist with the Infantry Reinforcements." Well, it is a various world.

Assimilated Western Jews say, "I don't like this Sharon," as if to refer to the prime minister simply as "Sharon" were to over-commit themselves. They are like the office assistant raised to executive status who immediately forgets how to use the fax machine. "This Sharon" indeed. Well, there are all sorts of Jews. One dichotomy is between the Real and the Imaginary. Imaginary Jews are the delight of the world. They include Anne Frank, Janusz Korczak, the Warsaw Ghetto fighters, and the movie stars in *Exodus*. These Jews delight the world in their willingness to die heroically as a form of entertainment. The plight of actual Jews, however, has traditionally been more problematic, and paradoxically, those same folk who weep at *Sophie's Choice* sniff at the State of Israel.

Here, in Israel, are *actual* Jews, fighting for their country, against both terror and misthought public opinion, as well as disgracefully biased and, indeed, fraudulent reporting. Here are people courageously going about their lives, in that which, sad to say, were it not a Jewish state, would, in its steadfastness, in its reserve, in its courage, rightly be the pride of the Western world. This Western world is, I think, deeply confused between the real and the imaginary. All of us moviegoers, who awarded ourselves the mantle of humanity for our tears at *The Diary of Anne Frank*—we owe a *debt* to the Jews. We do not owe this debt out of any "Unwritten Ordinance of Humanitarianism" but from a personal accountability. Having eaten the dessert, cheap sentiment, it is time to eat the broccoli. If you love the Jews as victims, but detest our right to statehood, might you not ask yourself "why?" That is your debt to the Jews. Here is your debt to the Jewish state. Had Israel not in 1981 bombed the Iraqi nuclear reactor, some scant weeks away from production of nuclear bomb material, all New York (God forbid) might have been Ground Zero.

I had two Tom Clancy books to while away the eons on the plane. One, as I say, was *The Sum of All Fears,* which I discarded on the trip out. Alone, in my Jerusalem hotel room, I turn to my second Clancy novel, *The Bear and the Dragon.* A subplot deals with the Chinese custom (reported by Clancy) of female infanticide. An American operative falls in love with a Chinese young woman and is informed of this crime and is, rightfully, horrified, as is Clancy. How can these little children be murdered? He writes, "If it were the Jews, the world would be Up in Arms." What can he mean? As the world was in 1941, when they rushed to the defense of six million innocents? Or as the world is today, in its staunch support of Israel's right to existence, and in opposition to the murder of its children? What *can* Clancy mean? *Is* there no beach novel to rest my overburdened sensibilities? Where do I belong? What will bring peace to the Middle East? Why has the Western press embraced anti-Semitism as the new black? Well, Jerusalem has been notorious, since antiquity, for inculcating in the visitor a sense not only of the immediacy but of the solubility of the large questions. I recommend it.

PHILIP GREENSPUN

Israel

THIS ARTICLE IS INTENDED for people who've grown weary and confused after exposure to the relentless media coverage of the conflict in and around Israel, often referred to as a "crisis." The questions to be answered include the following:

Why does the United States support the State of Israel?
Why do Arabs reject the State of Israel? (sub-question: "Are Arab Leaders Crazy?")
Why do Muslims hate Jews?
Why do Muslims hate the United States?
Why are the governments of the Middle East so unstable?
Why are the Palestinians so violent?
How have the Israelis survived for so long?
Is there really a crisis?
What can we, as average American citizens, do?

For answers we look back at history and at original sources where possible.

(I wrote this article because friends keep asking me for answers and opinions and it seemed better to lay it out in a coherent essay than provide piecemeal responses.)

WHY DOES THE UNITED STATES SUPPORT
THE STATE OF ISRAEL?

Israel and Egypt are America's largest recipients of foreign aid. Why should Americans want to spend their tax dollars supporting Israel and bribing the Egyptians into accepting peace on a continuous basis? Of what value is Israel to the United States? And if supporting Israel is such a great idea, how come the Europeans don't do it?

First let's look at what Israel is not. Israel is not a useful ally. We do not fight alongside the Israel Defense Forces in any battles. Nor does Israel fight any battles that we want fought on our behalf. The United States does not base troops or equipment in Israel. For its military adventures in the Middle East the United States has used aircraft carriers and bases in countries such as Egypt, Oman, Qatar, Saudi Arabia, Turkey, etc. The U.S. military is more powerful than the next fifteen countries' militaries combined. There is no conceivable conflict in which having Israeli assistance would mean the difference between victory and defeat.

Israel is not an important trading partner. In reports by country at the U.S. Census Bureau's Foreign Trade Statistics department (http://www.census.gov/foreign-trade/), Israeli trade is buried in "Other." The total volume of foreign trade with Israel was about $18 billion in 2002. This compares to $80 billion for Germany, $123 billion for China, $215 billion for Mexico, and $345 billion for Canada.

Supporting Israel in an effort to win over Jewish voters in the United States is not an obviously good strategy for a politician. The United States Department of State estimates that "by the year 2010, America's Muslim population is expected to surpass the Jewish population, making Islam the country's second-largest faith after Christianity" (http://usinfo.state.gov/usa/islam/fact2.htm). The Jews of America have declined in number to 5.2 million or less than 2 percent of the population. Politicians like rich people so you'd think that the fact that American Jewish households had a median income of $50,000 per year might give them more clout than the average American household with its $42,000 income (source: National Jewish Population Survey 2000–2001). However, the income differential fades into insignificance when you adjust for the fact that the median age among American Jews is 41 against 35 for the general population. Older people of any race or religion are more likely to have advanced degrees and career experience that lead to higher salaries. The bottom line is that an American political strategy of winning over Muslim voters by promising to liberate Palestine would seem to be roughly as effective as promising to support Israel.

Israel is not a sympathy case. Conventional wisdom in international politics is "Nations do not have friends. They have interests." Nonetheless the United States occasionally tries to help suffering people in foreign countries where it serves no apparent U.S. interest. Could Israel be one of these places? Compared to the average person on Planet Earth, Israeli citizens, including the 1.2 million Arabs (2000 census), live in a paradise of economic prosperity and equality with representative government with a functioning and powerful legal system. Looking just within the region we could find many folks more deserving of sympathy, starting with the slaves held in Sudan, Saudi Arabia, and the United Arab Emirates (www.iabolish. com). Or we could decide that charity begins at home; one can certainly find a lot more folks begging in the streets of Seattle and San Francisco than in Tel Aviv or Jerusalem.

What then has Israel done for the United States? The only concrete benefit that the State of Israel has provided to the United States is the absorption of millions of Jewish refugees from Europe, Arab countries, the former Soviet Union, and miscellaneous states such as Ethiopia. Most of these Jews would have preferred to live in the United States and in fact applied for admission to the United States. We were able to turn down their applications for immigration in good conscience. As long as the State of Israel exists, which grants automatic citizenship to any Jew who shows up, we can turn Jews away from our borders without risk of an embarrassing mass killing.

It was not always this way. During the 1930s the average European Christian had the following preferences:

1. [most preferred] Jews alive and well but living somewhere far away, e.g., North or South America
2. Jews dead
3. [least preferred] Jews living in Europe or somewhere else that would inconvenience Europeans

It is currently fashionable to demonize Adolf Hitler and the Germans who voted for him and his policies. However, it is worth pointing out that Hitler's original plan was not to kill Jews; he wanted to take their property and then kick them out of Europe. The United States and Britain, which together controlled the seas, were the largest obstacle to the German plan of expelling Jews. The United States would not accept Jewish immigrants. The British White Paper of May 1939, backed up by the British Navy, closed off Palestine. Under the White Paper no more than 75,000 Jews would be admitted to Palestine during the succeeding five years and after that all immigration would be at the discretion of Arabs. Nazi Germany's "Final Solution" was a solution to the problem of "there are no countries that are willing to accept Europe's Jews," not to the problem of "we really enjoy killing Jews and how can we kill as many as possible?"

Following the war, Americans changed their minds about Jews. Today the average American would probably express the following preference list:

1. Jews alive and well but living somewhere far away
2. Jews living in the United States
3. [least preferred] Jews dead

If the Arabs were to conquer Israel and fail to kill all of its citizens, there is a high probability that the Jewish survivors of that war would wash up on American shores. How happy would the average American gentile be to live alongside Russian and Middle Eastern Jews who don't share his culture, language, and values? A 2002 Anti-Defamation League study found that 17 percent of Americans agreed with a long list of classical anti-Jewish statements and an additional 35 percent agreed with "Jews have too much power in the business world" or "Jews have too much control and influence on Wall Street." Slightly more than 50 percent of Americans therefore are uncomfortable with the Jews that are already here. Rather than get into a national debate on whether more Jews can be tolerated on our shores, we send money and weapons to the Israelis. Imagine that you had a fat drunk cousin named Earl living in a trailer park in Louisiana. Would you rather send $250 every month to keep him in beer and pork rinds down there or let him come up and move into your guest room?

This preference shift occurring in America but not in Europe explains why the Europeans provide no financial support to the State of Israel. This is not because Europeans are stingy. European nations are the largest financial supporters of the Palestinian cause, providing more cash than the United States and far more than wealthy Arab countries such as Saudi Arabia (source: the "Building the State" section of www.pna.net). Europeans expect Jews fleeing Israel either to be killed or to settle in non-European countries.

Note that Europeans have demonstrated a willingness to pay money to keep immigrants out. Under German law ethnic Germans living in certain other countries (*volksdeutsche*) have the right to return to Germany and claim citizenship and various welfare benefits. There are approximately 300,000 *volksdeutsche* living in Kazakhstan. These are the remnants of a large ethnic German population that were once prosperous farmers in the Volga and who were exiled by Stalin to Kazakhstan in 1941. Their descendants do not speak German and don't have the skills or education to succeed in the German economy. So the German government tries to keep them happy right where they are through aid programs. Quoting from http://www.gtz.de/minderheiten/english/index.html: "The aim of the programme is to improve the living conditions of the German ethnic minority in Eastern Europe and Central Asia. It wants to provide an alternative to emigration and to encourage the German minorities to remain in their resident countries."

Israel's primary practical value to the United States is as a place that will accept immigrant Jews, of which the past decades have produced quite a few. In the 1940s and 1950s Arab governments and civilians emulated German policies from the 1930s. Rioting Muslims killed enough of their Jewish neighbors that the remainder fled. Arab governments required that the Jews leave any wealth or property behind. More than 600,000 Jews from Morocco, Iraq, Tunisia, Egypt, and other Arab countries sought asylum in the State of Israel. These folks spoke no English, had no money, lacked a modern education, and had no experience of participating in a democracy. Most Americans would not have wanted them as neighbors. You could say the same for the more than 1 million Russian Jews who emigrated to Israel between 1989 and 2002. Between the founding of Israel in 1948 and 2002, Israel absorbed a total of 2.93 million Jews from other countries (source: http://www.jafi.org.il/aliyah/aliyah/clock/table.html).

(Nor would the United States want to accept the forthcoming waves of Jewish emigrants. France is home to 5 million Muslims, a rapidly growing community whose native sons include

Zacarias Moussaoui, the "twentieth September 11 hijacker."
A rising tide of Muslim violence against Jews has sparked a
growing percentage of French Jews, Europe's largest community at 600,000, to think about emigration ["French Jews leave
home for Israel," BBC News, January 7, 2003]. Jewish population statistics show nearly one million Jews remaining in Russia
and Ukraine, countries with histories of anti-Jewish violence.
On balance it is probably reasonable to expect at least 1.5 million Jews to become refugees within the next fifty years.)

Israel has no practical value for the nations of Continental
Europe. The surviving descendants of Germany's 500,000 pre-
war Jews are not going to attempt to return to Berlin. Jews who
escaped from Morocco with the clothes on their back are not
going to want to try their luck in Poland (many of those Polish
Jews who tried to return to their homes following World War II
were murdered by mobs).

WHY DO ARABS REJECT THE STATE OF ISRAEL?

In the Web age it isn't necessary to speculate on why the Arabs
reject Israel. We can simply read what they've written on the
subject. Let's start with Article 22 of the Palestinian National
Charter [Covenant]:

> Zionism is a political movement organically associated
> with international imperialism and antagonistic to all ac-
> tion for liberation and to progressive movements in the
> world. It is racist and fanatic in its nature, aggressive, ex-
> pansionist, and colonial in its aims, and fascist in its meth-
> ods. Israel is the instrument of the Zionist movement, and
> geographical base for world imperialism placed strate-
> gically in the midst of the Arab homeland to combat the
> hopes of the Arab nation for liberation, unity, and prog-
> ress. Israel is a constant source of threat vis-a-vis peace in
> the Middle East and the whole world. Since the liberation
> of Palestine will destroy the Zionist and imperialist pres-

ence and will contribute to the establishment of peace in the Middle East, the Palestinian people look for the support of all the progressive and peaceful forces and urge them all, irrespective of their affiliations and beliefs, to offer the Palestinian people all aid and support in their just struggle for the liberation of their homeland.

Note that this is essentially the governing constitution for the Palestine National Authority, amendable only by a two-thirds vote of the Palestinian Congress. Not all Arab nations call for the destruction of Israel in their constitutions and yet most Arab countries have maintained a continuous declared state of war with Israel since 1948. To understand this fifty-five-year-long war it therefore becomes necessary to engage in a bit of analysis.

Israel occupies 20,330 square kilometers of land or roughly 0.23 percent of nearby Arab territory (see table at the end of this article). This percentage would be slightly larger if we excluded Iran, which is technically non-Arab but which has been at the forefront of the fight against Israel by training, financing, and arming Palestinians. This percentage would be much lower if we included the Arab states of North Africa such as Libya, Morocco, Algeria, Tunisia, etc. To put this into perspective, 0.23 percent of the Lower 48 United States is roughly equal to the southeastern corner of Florida (about one eighth of the state).

In some sense the State of Israel represents a tremendous achievement for the Arab countries. In exchange for a fraction of one percent of their territory they managed to expropriate the property of their Jewish citizens (estimated at between $13 and $30 billion in 1950 dollars) and expel approximately 870,000 Jews from their territories. Without incurring any of the bad publicity that afflicted Hitler, the Arabs managed to accomplish one of Nazi Germany's primary goals: creating a vast empire that was free of Jews. For the first time in 2,500 years an Arab could walk down the streets of Baghdad without encountering a Jew. Morocco and Algeria rid themselves of hundreds of thousands of Jews.

As impressive an achievement as concentrating the Jews from all the Arab countries into a tiny corner of the Arab world is, it would be yet more impressive to dump the Jews off somewhere in Christian territory, or perhaps to kill them all. This then becomes the challenge facing the modern Arab political leader.

Are Arab Leaders Crazy?

Let's step back for a moment and look at Arab political leadership. Americans tend to be smug about the superiority of our political system. We don't have politicians killing everyone in a town because they think the townsfolk won't vote for them (Syrian dictator Hafez Assad, Hama 1982; official government death toll 20,000 but human rights organizations estimate closer to 40,000), beheading citizens for expressing dissenting points of view (Saudi Arabia), declaring 40 percent of the government budget "missing" while building new villas and buying new Mercedes for their cronies (Yasser Arafat), etc. Does this make us morally superior to Arabs? Let's consider first that Arab leaders are not elected. People who live in an Arab country are *subjects* of the rulers. The job of an Arab leader is to figure out how the people can be made to serve him, not vice versa.

The closest analog in American society is the public corporation. The textbooks and some legal statutes say that the CEO and the Board are supposed to serve the interests of the shareholders. In practice the directors and top executives of American corporations siphoned off hundreds of billions of dollars of shareholder wealth into their personal bank accounts during the 1990s. Jack Welch in *Straight from the Gut* proudly states that during his twenty years as General Electric CEO the "em-

ployees," by which he means himself and some other top managers, went from 1 percent to 31 percent ownership of GE.
Rephrased, Jack and his golf partners stole 30 percent of GE
from the investors who owned the company in 1980. (The
most notorious Third World kleptocrat was Mobutu Sese
Seko, estimated to have diverted as much as $5 billion in funds
during thirty years of rule in Zaire [now the Congo]. Measured
against Congo's current annual GDP of $32 billion it would
seem that Mobutu's slice was much smaller than the GE executives'.)

There is no reason to expect an Arab dictator to behave
more altruistically than an American business executive. In fact,
the Arab leader who behaves out of self-interest violates no
trust or law, unlike his American CEO counterparts.

Suppose that you managed to seize power in an Arab country. What would your first order of business be? Dictatorship is
never a guaranteed long-term gig and therefore most people
have started by transferring all the money that they could find
into their personal Swiss bank accounts. Your second order of
business is ensuring the happiness of your subjects. You don't
actually care whether or not they're happy but you don't want
them rioting in the streets and interfering with the flow of cash
to Switzerland. Unless a subject is one of your cronies you can't
make him happy with money or improved material conditions
because you're moving all of the country's wealth into your
own pockets. What you *can* offer your subjects is pride. By continuing the fight against Israel your subjects can feel that they
are part of a noble effort that goes back to the seventh and
eighth centuries A.D. and that has been, on balance, a tremendous success.

Starting from their homeland in present-day Saudi Arabia
around the time of the death of Mohammed in A.D. 632, the
Arabs managed to conquer about half of the known world by
A.D. 750.

Islamic power and territory spread more gradually until the

fifteenth century when it began to decline relative to European Christendom. The Industrial Revolution in Europe reduced Arab power to a low point in the late nineteenth century when most Arab lands became colonial possessions of Britain and France. With the withdrawal of the Europeans and the rise in oil prices and production, Arabs have enjoyed a surge of increasing power throughout the second half of the twentieth century. Destroying the State of Israel would be a glorious milestone indeed in the Arab march of progress and your subjects will be happy to focus their attention on this goal rather than on the year-to-year economics of the nation.

Do you suppose that you would behave differently in this situation of absolute power? That you'd be unable to shake off your bourgeois roots and Western idea that government should serve the people? That unlike every Roman Emperor except Marcus Aurelius, you'd respond to absolute power by continuing to be a kind, generous, self-denying sort of human being?

Suppose that you made peace with Israel and withheld support from terrorists? In your country, as in every Muslim nation, there is a mosque funded by the Saudi Wahhabi sect where teenage boys are trained for the jihad. If they don't see you as part of the solution (war on the Great Satan [U.S.] and the Little Satan [Israel]) they will probably come to see you as part of the problem. Like Anwar Sadat, you may find yourself a target for assassination by an organized Islamic movement.

WHY DO MUSLIMS HATE JEWS?

Before we address the question of why Muslims hate Jews let us work on nomenclature and the broader question of why so many non-Muslims have also hated Jews through the centuries.

We will not use the term *anti-Semitism* in this article. The word was coined in 1879 by Wilhelm Marr to replace the then-current term *Judenhass,* which translates literally as "Jew-hatred." Marr hated Jews and conjectured that middle-class

Germans were turning away from the practice of Jew-hatred because the term for the activity sounded ugly. The neologism *anti-Semitism* was intended to sound more scientific and therefore make hatred of Jews more appealing to educated people in an industrial age.

Before considering why so many non-Muslims hate and have hated Jews, let's look at basic psychology research that has been done in this field. The classic experiment in this area is reported in *Intergroup Conflict and Cooperation: The Robbers Cave Experiment* (Muzafer Sherif et al., 1954; full text at http://psychclassics.yorku.ca/Sherif/). In 1949, Sherif divided 22 boys into two groups and took them to a 200-acre camp surrounded by Oklahoma's Robbers Cave State Park. The groups were set up in competition with one another and soon resorted to fighting and negatively stereotyping each other. Hating an out-group seems to make it easier for an in-group to function together. Moreover, inciting hatred can be beneficial to leaders.

For an example that is close to home, consider George W. Bush and his constant talk of a "war against Iraq." Militarily the term "war" does not make much sense. Using 5 percent of the American nuclear arsenal, Iraq could be wiped off the planet in five minutes. Limited to conventional bombs, the U.S. Air Force could reduce every Iraqi city to rubble within a few months, at little greater expense or risk to American lives than is currently entailed in the Air Force's training missions over Nevada. It doesn't make linguistic sense to talk about a "war" if there is no possibility of losing, but it does make political sense. If a president is in the middle of a war it is difficult to mount political opposition to that president without appearing disloyal and unpatriotic. Focusing media attention on a war prevents reporters from asking questions such as "How come William T. Esrey and Ronald LeMay, the two top executives at Sprint, deserved to get paid $311 million for their services to shareholders when the company's business and stock are in tatters? And then why is it fair that Joe Sixpack has to pay income tax but Esrey and LeMay didn't have to pay tax on their $311 million income? Would it have been fairer to divide the $311 million—equal to half of Sprint's 2002 profit—among the 13,000 workers that these guys laid off—$24,000 per worker— or possibly to the shareholders(!)?" (These gentlemen did pay a few million dollars to the accounting firm of Ernst and Young to participate in a tax shelter that the Internal Revenue Service is currently investigating and considering disallowing, in which case presumably Esrey and LeMay will join the folks in the February 7, 2003, *New York Times* story "Wealthy Suing Accountants Over Rejected Tax Shelters.") After the U.S. military crushes Iraq, a country that in 1990 had the same gross domestic product as West Virginia, George W. Bush will get a big boost in popularity for winning the war. Having Iraq as an enemy is apparently somewhat useful to the American people and very useful to America's leaders.

Why have the Jews through the centuries made such good all-purpose targets for hatred? It is difficult to understand how Jew-hatred started so let's focus on the factors that have made it endure: (1) concentration in residence, (2) concentration in occupation, (3) smallness in number, (4) military weakness.

Factor 1: concentration in residence. Until the early nineteenth century, when they were emancipated by Napoleon, the Jews of Europe were required to live in ghettos, separate from gentiles, by order of the Catholic Church. After emancipation, the Jews still tended to clump together if for no other reason than the requirement that at least ten men be assembled for morning prayers. In the United States, real estate covenants prohibiting the sale of property to Jews kept them to some extent separate from other Americans, at least from those in the ruling class (these covenants were gradually dismantled through legal action just before and after World War II). It is easier and more convenient to hate people if you don't have to live with them.

Considerably strengthening the effects of Factor 1 is the fact that people don't change their prejudices without direct personal contact with the object of those prejudices. For example, suppose that you've been taught negative stereotypes about black people. If you move into a middle-class neighborhood where half of your neighbors are black you'll probably begin to change your mind. But if you never meet a black person face-to-face, why would you ever change your mind? The phenomenon has also been demonstrated by those Europeans who express hatred of Jews in opinion polls despite the fact that they live in countries where all the Jews were killed in 1944. An Anti-Defamation League (ADL) study in 1998 concluded "The current survey shows that the most anti-Semitic Americans tend to have less contact with Jews in their day-to-day life than do other Americans."

Factor 2: concentration in occupation. Jews in Europe were prohibited from owning land or farming and encouraged to take up a variety of trades including money lending, an activity prohibited by scripture for Christians. This made it easy for Europeans to believe that Jewish bankers controlled the financial markets. Jews in the United States were excluded from universities by quotas. Jews weren't welcome in traditional industrial enterprises. For example, in the early 1920s Henry Ford was the most respected businessman on the planet, sort of like an über Bill Gates. He demonstrated his commitment to diversity in the workplace by publishing *The International Jew: The World's Foremost Problem,* a book that was a great inspiration to Adolf Hitler and early Nazi converts (if you Google the title you'll find the full text available on many Muslim sites worldwide). Jews looking for opportunity turned to new industries such as Hollywood and publishing. This made it plausible for Americans to believe that Jews controlled their media. Concentration in occupation among Jews reduces the likelihood that the average gentile will encounter a Jew at work and thereby have his or her prejudices contradicted.

Factor 3: smallness in number. Jews today number roughly 13 million worldwide. The peak of Jewish population was 1939 when the estimate was between 16 and 18 million. Close encounters, the only antidote to prejudice, are unlikely when the hated group is only 0.21 percent of the world population.

Factor 4: military weakness. Between the rise of the Roman Empire and 1948 the Jews were unable to achieve sovereign power in any region of the world and therefore were unable to build a military force. If you're going to hate a group and periodically inflict violence on them, it is best to pick a group that cannot retaliate.

The inherent virtues of hating an out-group plus these four factors were sufficient to fuel anti-Jewish violence throughout Christian Europe sponsored by the ruling class of the time. In medieval times this was primarily the Catholic Church and its local officials with secular authorities in the background. In modern times, up through the Holocaust, the primary sponsors of violence against Jews were secular officials with the Christian authorities in the background. The experience of Jews in the Islamic world was similar to the experience in Europe. State-sponsored murders of thousands of Jews were common in North Africa between the eighth and twelfth centuries; Arab mobs were responsible for most of the killings after 1800.

It is difficult to reach back through the mists of time to determine whether or not stirring up Jew-hatred was truly beneficial to the Catholic Church or various secular rulers. So let's start with Nazi Germany. Jew-hatred was one of the most successful programs of the Nazi party. Hating Jews galvanized the German people and helped in creating an economic boom through the 1930s. The Jews of Germany were pauperized, their wealth and property transferred to German gentiles, and profits spread among the government contractors who helped smooth the process along (see the book *IBM and the Holocaust* for just how willing American companies were to assist the German government, up to December 1941 and beyond). Foreign governments did not object to anti-Jewish measures such as the Nuremberg Laws of 1935. Germany's military and territorial ambitions ultimately resulted in negative consequences but her experience with Jew-hatred was almost entirely positive.

(Even those Germans directly involved in exterminating Jews were seldom punished. Participants in the Wannsee Conference, for example, where the Final Solution was planned, generally spent less than four years in prison—compare this to the minimum of five years in federal prison that you'll get today if you are caught with five grams of crack cocaine.)

Let us consider Jew-hatred in modern Europe. Opinion polls in countries such as Poland reveal that hatred of Jews has survived even where the Jews have not. British and French academics propose a cultural and scientific boycott against Israel, an echo of 1930s Germany in which university professors joined the Nazi party at a rate double that of the general population. What purpose does Jew-hatred serve in modern-day Europe? Nearly all European countries were home to enthusiastic participants in the murder of the Jews of Europe. This is a source of a certain amount of shame and bad publicity for Europeans. Suppose, however, that it were possible to demonstrate that Israel is the worst of the 300 nations on this earth? This justifies the killing of Europe's Jews to a large extent: "Just look at the rogue nation these Jews created when left to themselves." (The reasoning is a bit flawed because the vast majority of Israel's Jews come from Arab countries or Russia; the Europeans did such a thorough job of killing their Jews that we'll never know what kind of country they would have created.) A side effect of this desire to show how evil the state created by the co-religionists of the Jews whom they murdered is the European focus on Palestinians as a humanitarian cause. There may be billions of people in the world who are poorer and more oppressed than the Palestinians but they can't be held up as examples of how horrible Jews are and therefore get no mindshare and no assistance.

Jew-hatred in America is less prevalent and less violent than in Europe. As noted in the first section, a 2002 ADL study found that 17 percent of Americans were solid Jew-haters and 52 percent held some anti-Jewish beliefs. These numbers compare to 21 percent of Europeans holding the full range of stereotypes and a variable number by country proving mildly anti-Jewish, with the Spaniards topping the list at 71 percent. Americans generally are able to hold anti-Jewish stereotypes without feeling the need to take action. For example, the author has encountered quite a few Harvard Ph.D.s who express the belief that a conspiracy of Jewish financiers manipulates the U.S. economy (their doctorates are in humanities, not business). These university professors and non-profit organization administrators would not want to be seen at a Ku Klux Klan rally nor participate in a lynch mob but they'd be happy to join a boycott of the State of Israel. That only about half of Americans hold some of the same beliefs about Jews espoused by the Nazi party is comforting until one one reflects that Hitler was able to hold power in Germany with only 33 percent of the vote in 1932 and 44 percent in 1933.

We come finally to the original question of why Muslims hate Jews. These days it is mostly because they're taught to by their governments. The standard grade school curriculum in Muslim countries includes a healthy measure of Jew-hatred, much of it translated from materials first developed by Nazi Germany. State-run television in Muslim countries keeps the public fed with a constant stream of images of Israeli troops beating up Palestinians in the West Bank. Saudi-funded mosques complement the government-supplied material to the point that the average Malaysian Muslim, who has never been within five hundred miles of a Jew, might easily ascribe any of his problems to an international Jewish conspiracy and the rogue state of Israel.

A declining standard of living contributes to anger among the populace and the consequent search for scapegoats. The vast majority of Muslims live in Third World countries where any economic surplus is appropriated by the ruler's family and friends. Rather than investing the money in new machines for factories or productivity-enhancing technology, rich people in the Third World tend to sock money away in Swiss bank accounts or build themselves fabulous villas with fleets of imported cars and jets. The family that owns Saudi Arabia, for example, has reportedly transferred $1 trillion into foreign bank accounts, an amount nearly equal to the $1.1 trillion invested in capital goods during 2001 by all U.S. businesses; King Fahd spent $300 million on his August 2002 family vacation in Spain. Lack of re-investment of surplus results in slow or negative economic growth. Meanwhile the population in Muslim countries generally grows rapidly, e.g., 2 percent per year for Egypt, 2.5 percent for Jordan, and 2.9 percent for Saudi Arabia, compared to 0.1 percent per year for the average rich country (source: www.prb.org). If the Canadian economy grows 2 percent next year, for example, and the wealth is spread equally, the average person will have 1.7 percent more money to spend because the wealth need only be shared with 0.3 percent more people. If the Saudi economy were to do as well as it did in 2001 and grow 1.6 percent, the average Saudi would have a standard of living that was 1.3 percent lower, even if the new wealth were distributed equally.

(There is evidence that growth in the U.S. economy is governed by similar forces. In the late 1920s the share of wealth held by the top 1 percent of Americans rose to 45 percent. They built a lot of big fancy houses for themselves and the Great Depression followed. Between 1979 and 1997 the share of wealth for the top 1 percent of Americans rose from 20 percent to 40 percent. All of these rich people bidding against each other for waterfront property and Impressionist paintings has led to tremendous inflation in beach house prices and Sotheby's auctions while nobody can give away machine tools or improved information systems. In the 1950s a CEO made five to ten times the salary of the average worker and a company could pay out some of its profit in dividends, thereby encouraging further investment, and internally invest the rest in productivity improvements. In the 1990s a typical large company employed a long list of top executives earning one hundred to one thousand times the salary of their average worker. As in the case of the Sprint managers mentioned earlier, these amounts were often comparable to the company's total profits and therefore public corporations had a lot less to invest. The result was the recession that started in late 2000.)

Muslims have a Jew-hatred tradition that dates back at least a thousand years. Most Muslim countries expelled their Jews more than fifty years ago and consequently 99 percent of the world's Muslims will never meet a Jew face-to-face. Therefore it is reasonable to assume that Muslims will go on believing what they've been taught by their governments and mullahs. The worldwide Muslim population is estimated at between 1.2 and 1.4 billion. If we assume that the percentage of Muslims who really buy into what their leaders are telling them about Jews is equal to the percentage (33) of German voters who opted for Hitler in 1932, that works out to more than 400 million Jew-hating Muslims. This population constitutes an inexhaustible source of financial and physical support for anti-Jewish violence.

WHY DO MUSLIMS HATE THE UNITED STATES?

As with the preceding question we should step back and ask the more general question "Why does everyone hate the United States?" Everyone hates the United States because everything that goes wrong in the world today is the fault of the United States. Our military consists of 1.5 million highly trained people and tens of thousands of machines capable of getting them very quickly to where they are needed. Yet though we claim to be interested in justice and human welfare we generally don't bother to act to protect non-citizens. For example, impending genocide in Rwanda elicited the following quote from then-President Bill Clinton: ". . . I mention it only because there are a sizable number of Americans there and it is a very tense situation. And I just want to assure the families of those who are there that we are doing everything we possibly can to be on top of the situation to take all the appropriate steps to try to assure the safety of our citizens there." In other words, "We could use all of our airpower and troops to stop the Hutus from killing the Tutsis but instead we're going to airlift American citizens out and then move on to the next issue." An estimated one million people died.

Nobody is going to blame the Rwandan genocide on Ireland. They've only got 17,000 troops and a limited number of ships and cargo planes. Nobody is going to blame Denmark, with its 35,000 troops. But the U.S. military is strong enough to intervene anywhere in the world. People can blame, with some justification, anything that makes them unhappy on the United States.

Ask Joe Foreigner what upsets him most about the United States. Top on the list is the fact that the United States is too interventionist, swaggering cowboy-like with military power into complex international situations. Complaint #2, however, is that the United States failed to intervene in a particular situation that is near and dear to Joe's heart. They hate us because we are too interventionist . . . except when we're not interventionist enough. They also hate the United States because they're so weak and their government essentially serves at our government's pleasure. Consider how annoying it is to be an American voter, knowing that because you don't have $50 million you don't have any political power. Imagine how much more annoyed you'd be if you were a citizen of one of the European nations. Not only are your politicians corrupted by the local rich, but if your society wants to do something that is contrary to a sufficiently important U.S. desire, the U.S. military might invade and turn your country into a possession, ruled by a colonial viceroy.

Joe Third World Foreigner has even more reason to hate the United States than Joe European Foreigner. Most Third World governments have no plausible claim to legitimacy. They have power because they seized power and because the United States has chosen not to overthrow them. If Joe Third World Foreigner hates his rulers, who are presumably skimming whatever they can take out of his pocket, it is only natural for Joe to hate the United States for enabling his rulers to remain in power.

If Muslims hate the United States more than average it is probably simply because they have a longer than average list of things that are making them unhappy. Most Muslims are poor, getting poorer, and living under dictatorships in which they are essentially the personal property of the rulers. Most Muslims are exposed, at least via television, to a world in which women are permitted to show their heads in public, drive cars, and defy orders from their fathers and husbands. Most Muslims live in societies that lack the technological wherewithal to manufacture lightbulbs, much less the advanced weapons that will be necessary to overpower the infidels. And it can all be blamed on the United States.

WHY ARE THE GOVERNMENTS OF THE MIDDLE EAST SO UNSTABLE?

Today's most volatile Arab nations occupy land that was once part of the Ottoman Empire. The Sultan allied himself with Germany in World War I and as a consequence lost Syria, Palestine, Arabia, and Mesopotamia in the Treaty of Versailles (1919). France and Britain took possession of these territories and tried to make them into European-style nation-states. Note that the idea of a nation-state was relatively new at the time. Bismarck unified Germany in 1871 but most older Germans still identified more strongly with their principality, e.g., Bavaria, than with the German nation. The national anthem *Deutschland über Alles* ("Germany over all") was intended to encourage people to submerge their local affiliations. Italy was unified in 1870. Germany and Italy spent centuries on the path to unification, aided by literacy among their citizens, mass communications, railroads, and telegraphs.

The vast nation-states carved out in the Arab world by the British and French had very primitive communication infrastructures and a largely illiterate population. If you were friends with a European diplomat you might find that you and your family were given absolute power over an area one fifth the size of the United States (Saudi Arabia) or twice the size of Idaho (Iraq) and you could even ask that your new country be named after your family ("Hashemite Kingdom of Jordan" and "Saudi Arabia"). These regions might contain lots of mutually antagonistic tribes with linguistic, religious, and ethnic divisions. The first source of instability is that the nation-states of the Middle East in general did not encapsulate groups of people that had any real affinity for each other or common identity. Sudan, for example, contains a northern group of Muslim Arabs and a southern group of animist and Christian blacks. The primary interaction between these groups over the centuries has been the Arabs sweeping down to capture and enslave blacks. The British in 1956 decided that these two groups should be yoked together forever in one country and the result, according to BBC News, has been [that] "Unstable governments, civil war and widespread human rights abuses have afflicted the country ever since." The CIA Factbook notes that "Sudan has been embroiled in a civil war for all but 10 years of this period (1972–82). Since 1983, the war and war- and famine-related effects have led to more than 2 million deaths and over 4 million people displaced." The country is one quarter the size of the United States, the people lack a common language, religion, or race, the literacy rate is 46 percent, yet nobody is willing to say "Hey, maybe it was a mistake to carve this big a chunk out of the African continent as one country."

(Nigeria was a similar arbitrarily carved-out country with an Arab north and a Christian-indigenous south that has achieved a measure of stability. Muslim mobs killed thousands of Christians in the mid-1960s, leading the Christian Ibo [or "Igbo"] tribe to secede in the late 1960s, forming a new country called Biafra. The Muslim tribes controlled the Nigerian army and were therefore successful in overpowering the Ibo, which resulted in the deaths of an estimated one to three million Christians and the permanent exclusion of the Ibo from political power in the reunified nation. Muslim-Christian violence continues to claim hundreds of lives each year in Nigeria but the government and military have a firm grip on power and hence Nigeria is considered a successful example of decolonialization.)

A second factor contributing to instability is the fact that any tribal leader or military commander could claim just as much legitimacy to rule as the European-appointed dictator. No ruler sought or had the consent of his subjects. Iraq, originally granted by the British to the Hashemite family that also got Jordan, provides a typical example of coups and counter-coups.

A third factor contributing to instability is that agreements among peoples are impossible where there is no representative government. If the democratically elected government of the United States signs an agreement with the democratically elected government of Canada, one presumes that this agreement represents the will of both people. The agreement ought to survive even if the leaders who signed it have been replaced. This presumption does not make sense in the Arab world where every country is ruled by a dictator. The Ayatollah Khomeini did not feel bound to honor the deposed Shah's various treaties. If you seized power in Iraq tomorrow would you feel bound to honor Saddam Hussein's agreements with neighbors? An agreement in the Arab world is only good for as long as the two guys who signed it are still in power. (Note that this has painful implications for those Israelis who yearn for a negotiated peace; they could sign deals with every living Arab dictator but face a new war the instant that one of those signatories dies or is overthrown. For example, if they signed a peace treaty with Yasser Arafat today and Hamas took over the Palestinian leadership tomorrow, the war would be back on.)

WHY ARE THE PALESTINIANS SO VIOLENT?

If you want to know why Palestinians are violent, look in the mirror. Ask yourself if you'd be spending ten minutes thinking about the State of Israel or the disposition of Palestinians if not for their violence.

Most of the nations within the Middle East contain conquered people and conquerors. For an example right next door to the Palestinians, consider that the rulers and bulk of the population in Egypt are Arab conquerors who swept in from the southeast. The conquered indigenous people are the Copts, the descendants of the ancient Egyptians who built the pyramids and temples so familiar to tourists. The Copts converted to Christianity during the Roman Empire and have suffered from religious, political, and economic oppression for 1,300 years, ever since the Arab conquest. Copts are periodically murdered by Arab-Muslim mobs and generally the Arabs are not prosecuted for the killings. You could read about this in www.copts. net but you probably won't because the Copts are not violent.

At the Potsdam Conference the Allies granted Eastern European nations the right to expel their ethnic German citizens, i.e., people who had been living in these areas for generations but whose forebears were German and who spoke the German language. Roughly 12 million of these *volksdeutche* were in fact expelled, their property confiscated, and as many as two million may have been killed in the process. The surviving *volks-deutsche* settled in crummy houses in Germany and Austria and integrated themselves with those societies. If there were a Volksdeutsche Liberation Army murdering Czech, Polish, and Hungarian civilians the world might pay some attention to the injustices suffered by this group.

The 870,000 Jews expelled from Arab countries in the 1940s and 1950s similarly settled quietly in the United States, Europe, and Israel. They aren't out there blowing up Iraqi, Moroccan, and Algerian embassies or airplanes, which is why you probably never think about them.

The list of people who were displaced by the events of World War II and decolonization is endless. The only group that anyone pays attention to is the Palestinians. If the Palestinians were to stop blowing up airplanes and pizza shops people would stop paying attention.

Arab leaders don't care about non-violent Palestinians. As noted earlier, if you were an Arab leader there is no reason to care about your own subjects, much less members of very distant tribes. The only Arab nation that has ever offered Palestinians citizenship is Jordan; a Palestinian family that has lived in Egypt or Saudi Arabia for several generations will still be aliens with no right to permanent residence. Thus there are more than 4 million people officially classified as Palestinian refugees despite the fact that the final British census before the 1948 war found only about one million people of all religions living in Palestine. The primary agency for these stateless souls is the United Nations Relief and Works Agency for Palestine Refugees in the Near East (UNRWA). If you visit their Web site, http://www.un.org/unrwa/, you'll see that the United States and European nations provide almost all of the funding. Historically in fact the Western nations provided 100 percent of the funding for UNRWA, but in recent years Saudi Arabia has been shamed into chipping in. For 2002 the Saudis contributed $5.8 million, compared to a U.S. contribution of $120 million and Britain's $30 million. Most Arab countries contribute less than the cost of a new Mercedes automobile.

Violent Palestinians, by contrast, have no trouble getting support from fellow Arabs. In April 2002 the Saudi state television network ran a telethon that raised more than $100 million to aid the families of Palestinian suicide bombers (Associated Press, April 13, 2002). Iraq, which contributes nothing to UNRWA, has been donating roughly $10 million per year to the families of suicide bombers. Iran, another state that contributes nothing to UNRWA, sends weapons and money to anti-Israel groups such as Hezbollah and Yasser Arafat's army, most notably a 50-ton shipment of rockets and plastic explosives in January 2002 (notable because it was in violation of the agreements that Arafat had signed and because it was discovered and intercepted by the Israeli Navy).

The only way that a Palestinian can get his or her hands on a share of Arab oil wealth is by becoming a suicide bomber. "[Izzidene al Masri] lived with his 12 brothers and sisters and his parents in a neat, tile-floored house" (Knight-Ridder, April 1, 2002, on the Sbarro pizza shop bomber). If you lived in poverty it might make sense to trade your life for the knowledge that Saudi Arabians would support your parents, grandparents, and eleven siblings in comfort for the rest of their lives.

This kind of poverty is likely to endure because Palestinians combine a low level of education and a high level of illiteracy (30 percent) with perhaps the highest birthrate of any world population, estimated for 2001 at 5 percent per annum by passia.org. This means that Palestinians need to generate economic growth of 5 percent per year, and preserve that growth from kleptocratic politicians, merely to maintain their standard of living. For comparison, the most rapidly growing population with which most Americans are familiar is Mexico; its population is growing at an annual rate of 1.47 percent (CIA Factbook 2002). In the 1990s, according to the World Bank, the average country enjoyed a 2.5 percent annual growth rate. Even if they succeeded in liberating all of Palestine, the Palestinians would have a difficult time growing at any rate close to 5 percent per year. They'd have one of the most densely populated countries in the world, one of the poorest in natural resources, especially water, and a complete lack of industry.

It may be a mistake to look too deep into Palestinian poverty for the roots of Palestinian violence. For most violent Palestinians we need not conjecture as to the motivation for their violence because they've explained it in their own words. Here is an excerpt from the Palestinian National Charter, July 1–17, 1968:

> Palestine is the homeland of the Arab Palestinian people; it is an indivisible part of the Arab homeland, and the Palestinian people are an integral part of the Arab nation.
>
> Palestine, with the boundaries it had during the British Mandate, is an indivisible territorial unit. [Note that this would include the present-day country of Jordan, 70 percent of the land of the original British Palestine, split off and handed to Emir Abdullah in 1923.]
>
> Armed struggle is the only way to liberate Palestine.
>
> Commando action constitutes the nucleus of the Palestinian popular liberation war.
>
> The partition of Palestine in 1947 and the establishment of the state of Israel are entirely illegal, regardless of the passage of time, because they were contrary to the will of the Palestinian people and to their natural right in their homeland, and inconsistent with the principles embodied in the Charter of the United Nations; particularly the right to self-determination.

Source: http://www.yale.edu/lawweb/avalon/mideast/mideast.htm

Hamas has a Web site where they explain their goals:

> Hamas is a Jihadi (fighting for a holy purpose) movement in the broad sense of the word Jihad. It is part of the

Islamic awakening movement and upholds that this awakening is the road which will lead to the liberation of Palestine from the river to the sea.

[Settlement with the State of Israel] should not be allowed to happen because the land of Palestine is a blessed Islamic land that has been usurped by the Zionists; and Jihad has become a duty for Muslims to restore it and expel their occupiers out of their land.

Hezbollah also has a Web site (www.hizbollah.org) where they explain their objectives:

... Because Hezbollah's ideological ideals sees [*sic*] no legitimacy for the existence of "Israel" a matter that elevates the contradictions to the level of existence. And the conflict becomes one of legitimacy that is based on religious ideals. ... And that is why we also find the slogan of the liberation of Jerusalem rooted deeply in the ideals of Hezbollah. Another of its ideals is the establishment of the an [*sic*] Islamic Government. ...

Hezbollah also used one of its own special types of resistance against the Zionist enemy that is the suicide attacks. These attacks dealt great losses to the enemy on all thinkable levels such as militarily and mentally. The attacks also raised the moral [*sic*] across the whole Islamic nation. ...

Hezbollah also sees itself committed in introducing the true picture of Islam, the Islam that is logical. Committed to introduce the civilized Islam to humanity.

Note that if we take seriously the words of the Palestinian fighters we can ignore 99 percent of the journalism and punditry to which we are exposed. The guys with the guns have explained very clearly why they are fighting and under what conditions they will lay down their arms. Their reasons for fighting and their conditions for peace have nothing to do with day-to-day events.

HOW HAVE THE ISRAELIS SURVIVED FOR SO LONG?

The Arab war on Israel is now in its fifty-third year and the fact that the Israelis have hung on for so long is primarily a testament to spectacular Arab incompetence. Relying on an opponent's military incompetence is not a viable long-term strategy. The U.S. military exhibited spectacular incompetence at the beginning of World War II, losing battles where we outnumbered the Germans ten to one. Our enemies were not able to enter North America and prevent us from regrouping. Consequently we ultimately learned how to fight and prevailed. The Arabs are gradually moving into the modern age and learning how to use Western technology. Every year the Arabs sell a bit more oil and grow a bit wealthier. Additionally there are one billion non-Arab Muslims worldwide happy to devote a portion of their wealth and energy to the challenge of killing or otherwise removing the Jews in Israel. Every time an Arab army is defeated it can simply retreat back across the border and regroup to fight another year or another decade. At first glance, it is difficult to see how the Arabs have failed thus far and how they can continue to fail in the long run.

The last real fight between Arabs and Jews was the 1973 Ramadan War. In this war, called the "Yom Kippur War" by Westerners, Egypt and Syria attacked Israel, backed up with money, troops, tanks, and airplanes from Saudi Arabia, Kuwait, Iraq, Algeria, Tunisia, Sudan, Morocco, Lebanon, and Jordan, and came very close to winning. All of these countries have much larger economies and militaries than they did in 1973. All, except for Egypt and Jordan, remain in a state of declared war with Israel. In light of the example of the Ramadan War, the willingness of Anwar Sadat to sign a peace treaty with Israel back in 1978 seems either insane or an enormous triumph for the diplomacy of American President Jimmy Carter.

Perhaps there is a military and rational explanation for the 1978 peace treaty, however. The Israeli nuclear weapons program was in its infancy in 1973 when the Arabs launched their big war. The best estimates are that Israel had enough material to make three bombs. By 1978, however, Israel was estimated to have built between 100 and 200 atomic bombs, enough nuclear power to wipe out every town in Egypt, whose population is densely concentrated along the banks of the Nile River. Anwar Sadat, in command of a military without nuclear weapons, could no longer realistically hope to prevail in a conflict with Israel.

The nuclear balance of power has been shifting since 1978. Pakistan has the Bomb and long-range ballistic missiles. Wealthy Arab countries such as Saudi Arabia have been buying missiles from the Chinese and anyone else who will sell them. Ironically the Palestinians may save the physical lives of the Jews. If an Arab dictator were to succeed in acquiring nuclear weapons, dropping the Bomb on Israel would seem to be a quick and easy path to everlasting glory. The fact that the Palestinians are living in and among the Jews and would be killed alongside them might be the only thing that gives a nuclear-capable Arab pause. In 2002 there were 1.26 million Arabs who held Israeli citizenship and who lived within the 1948 boundaries of Israel, nearly 20 percent of the population. Most of the remainder of those officially classified as Palestinian refugees live in the West Bank, in Gaza, or in nearby Jordan.

Are the Palestinians adequate protection for the State of Israel? Islamic terrorists have demonstrated a willingness to kill co-religionists in the service of larger goals, e.g., when they brought down the World Trade Center and the Muslims working inside. Secular Arab leaders going as far back as Anwar Sadat have pronounced themselves willing to lose millions of their own soldiers in exchange for a victory over Israel. Given the lack of interest in Palestinian welfare by fellow Arabs over the decades it seems reasonable to conclude that the deaths of even several million Palestinians might come to be considered acceptable as the price of liberating the land.

Israel's nuclear arsenal is small and weak. The Israelis might be capable of wiping out neighboring capitals such as Cairo and Amman but not of surviving a first strike, deterring an Osama-bin-Laden–style foe, or of reaching a faraway enemy such as Saudi Arabia. On balance it would seem that the presence of the Palestinians amidst the Jews is currently the main deterrent against an Arab nuclear or biological attack.

Currently it seems as though Israel and its enemies have arrived at a standoff. However, taking the long view and keeping in mind that the Muslims can afford to lose a thousand battles while the Israelis cannot afford to lose even one, it seems worth considering what would transpire if the Muslims were to win. The published post-victory plans of the Arabs call for deporting all the Jews who weren't in Israel prior to 1947 back to where they came from. The most problematic subgroup therefore are the 600,000 Israeli Jews, and their descendants, who were expelled from Arab countries. Would the Arabs want them back in their homelands? Would a population that has grown up on a steady diet of Jew-hatred in their schools, mosques, and media accept Jews back in their midst?

CONCLUSION

Day-by-day newspaper accounts of violence in Israel are constructed to provide entertainment between advertising, not to illuminate. Fundamentally the facts are the following:

• Jews are not wanted in Europe or in Islamic countries.
• Although initially settled by some idealistic Zionists, Israel has become primarily a dumping ground for the world's unwanted Jews and this is its principal significance to non-Muslim countries.
• For dictators in Muslim nations, inculcating mass hatred of Jews has substantial political value; Israel's principal significance to Muslim countries is as a focus of popular hatred.

• For the dictators and subjects of Arab nations, the State of Israel takes on an additional significance as a place whose successful conquest would signify a resurgence of Arab power as exciting as the Arab conquests circa A.D. 700.

• Palestinian violence continues because it is yielding substantial material support from Arab and European nations, support that should lead to a gradual victory over the Jews and the liberation of all of Palestine.

Taking the long view, the State of Israel is most simply explained as a concentration camp for Jews. Starting in the 1930s the Europeans expropriated the property of their Jews and collected the physical bodies of those Jews in camps where they could be worked to death—the Nazis did not put healthy Jews into gas chambers but only those who had become exhausted by slave labor. In the 1940s and 1950s the remaining Jews of Central Europe were by and large sent to Israel while at the same time Arab nations expropriated the wealth of their 1,000- and 2,000-year-old Jewish communities and sent the physical bodies of the Jews to Israel (except for some thousands who were killed by mobs). In the last decades of the twentieth century the former Soviet Union began to export its Jewish population, though without the violence and confiscation that had accompanied Jewish migrations from Europe and Arab nations.

Historically most concentration camps for Jews have eventually turned into death camps and certainly there is no shortage of people worldwide trying to effect this transformation.

IS THERE REALLY A CRISIS?
(PRACTICAL IMPLICATIONS)

This article's primary practical value is intended to be in freeing you from the tyranny of the daily news. If there is a big news story from Israel, feel free to watch *The Simpsons*. Elected governments will come and go in Israel. Dictators will rise and fall among the Arab nations. Terrorists will kill civilians. The Israeli army will kill terrorists. American and European university professors will vent their Jew-hatred on Israelis and the Israeli government. Politicians and diplomats will negotiate. Peace agreements will be signed when a military stalemate is reached. War will resume when the Arabs believe that they have a new and useful military tactic. All of these events are insignificant against the larger background of history painted above and compared to the major events that will transpire when the Arabs score a major military breakthrough.

Referring to an Israeli-Palestinian "crisis" in a headline is a good way to sell newspapers but not an accurate description of a conflict that will enter its second century soon. The last significant event was the signing of the Israel-Egypt peace treaty on March 26, 1979. You could have missed every news report for more than two decades and yet be fully up to date on this crisis.

Events that would qualitatively change the situation in Israel include the following:

• Palestinian takeover of Jordan or establishment of a Palestinian state elsewhere.
• Islamic revolution in Egypt.
• Acquisition of nuclear weapons by a country ruled by Islamic fundamentalists (or a powerful independent group such as Al-Qaeda).

To build a strong military force for the ultimate liberation of all Palestine, the Palestinians must have their own sovereign state in which heavy weapons can be accumulated and large armies trained. This fact has not been lost on the neighboring governments. Between 1948 and 1967 the state of Jordan occupied the West Bank and prevented the Palestinians from forming their own state. Between 1967 and the present day the

State of Israel has occupied the West Bank and prevented the Palestinians from forming their own state. Lacking sovereignty the Palestinians have been unable to stop the Jordanian and Israeli armies from periodically rolling through their neighborhoods confiscating weapons and arresting terrorists, thus capping the number of effective fighters.

Start following the news if you hear that a sovereign Palestinian state has been established on the West Bank, because that is a required first step in any larger effort by Palestinians.

What would be the logical second step? Jew-haters worldwide like to cheerlead for a Palestinian takeover of the present State of Israel, but the reality is that a takeover of Jordan would be much easier and in fact this is where most Palestinian efforts to achieve sovereignty have been focused. Jordan offers five times the land area of Israel defended by a military that is considerably weaker. The majority of Jordan's citizens are Palestinian yet the country is ruled by foreigners, the Hashemite family of Mecca, who were defeated in their native land by the Bedouins under Ibn-Saud and were granted ownership of most of Palestine by Britain. Relations between Palestinians and the family have been strained ever since. A group of Palestinians organized King Abdullah's assassination in 1951 at the Al-Aqsa mosque on the Temple Mount. King Hussein, who was wounded in the attack that killed his father, fought a civil war with Yasser Arafat's PLO in 1970 resulting in the deaths of many thousands of Palestinians and the expulsion of all armed Palestinians to southern Lebanon (these fighters sparked off a fifteen-year civil war between Muslims and Christians in their new host country; more than 100,000 people were killed by their neighbors [plus a few thousand more when Israel invaded from 1982 to 1985]).

After Palestinian sovereignty the next important event to watch for is an Islamic revolution in Egypt, a country with a population of 70 million and an economy twice the size of

Israel's. Currently the population is kept under control by a 500,000-man military that has modernized its capabilities with $38 billion in U.S. military aid between 1978 and 2000. The army spends much of its time finding, torturing, and killing Islamic fundamentalists but still has plenty of energy left over to train for a big battle with Israel. If the Muslim Brotherhood manages to seize power in Egypt, the Israel Defense Forces could face their toughest challenges since the 1973 Ramadan War.

WHAT CAN WE, AS AVERAGE AMERICAN CITIZENS, DO?

Terrorism is funded by wealth. There are plenty of poor people in this world who hate the United States but we never hear from them because they can't afford airplane tickets, weapons, training, etc. When people get richer they buy more of all the things that they enjoy. If you give extra money to a group of French people you'll see that some is spent on fancy wine and cheese. Flip on the TV and watch Muslims worldwide celebrating the collapse of the World Trade Center or the destruction of the space shuttle *Columbia*. These are folks who will spend a portion of any new wealth on the killing of Americans. The principal source of Muslim wealth is oil. As a society the most effective way that we can protect ourselves from Muslim violence is by reducing our consumption of oil. They may still hate us but they will have less money to put their hatred into action.

Oil is an especially bad thing to buy and burn. Any country that earns most of its income from natural resource extraction is a place where it is easy for a ruling elite to transfer that income into its pockets. You don't need the consent or assistance of your subjects to strike a deal with a foreign oil company and watch them extract the product. Burning oil contributes to air pollution and atmospheric carbon dioxide, thus leading to global warming. "Roughly half the oil consumed in the U.S.

goes for cars and trucks," noted *The Wall Street Journal* on
March 18, 2003. The same article quotes Saudi Arabia's oil
minister, Sheik Ahmed Zaki Yamani, in 1981: "If we force
Western countries to invest heavily in finding alternative
sources of energy, they will. This will take them no more than
seven to ten years and will result in their reduced dependence
on oil as a source of energy to a point which will jeopardize
Saudi Arabia's interests."

If we were to tax oil to reflect its true military and environ-
mental cost, it would encourage investment in more fuel-
efficient technology. Half of our oil is burned up in cars and
trucks whose powerplants are scarcely different from the engine in a Model T Ford. One can build an engine with precise
computer-controlled solenoid-lifted valves rather than a sloppy
camshaft, but when gas is cheap it isn't worth the extra capital
cost (see "Why Not a 40-mpg SUV? Technology exists to double gas guzzlers' fuel efficiency. So what's the holdup?" in the
November 2002 *Technology Review*). Toyota and Honda show-
rooms offer hybrid cars that get fifty miles per gallon but at
current gas prices it takes years to recover the higher initial
investment. High-tech windmills are good enough that Denmark is able to generate 20 percent of its electricity from wind
power; in the United States it is slightly cheaper to take a fos-
silized dinosaur from Venezuela and light it on fire so that's
what we do. Would you invest in genetic engineering of bacte-
ria that could separate hydrogen fuel from water if you knew
that a Sheik in Riyadh could wipe out your company with the
stroke of a pen?

If you want to know who is funding terrorists, look in
the vanity mirror as you turn the key of your SUV. If you want
to stop funding terrorists, work for a $20-per-barrel tax on
imported oil and a $10-per-barrel tax on domestic oil, which
doesn't require an expensive military to defend but we still
want to discourage its use to curb pollution. The tax should be

phased in over five years, thus giving businesses and consumers time to replace inefficient older machines.

Terrorism is theater. Terrorism will taper off if people lose interest in news coverage of acts of terror. It is tough to ignore a spectacular event such as the destruction of the World Trade Center, but we can do our share by ignoring newspaper and television stories about run-of-the-mill terrorism. The Israeli-Palestinian conflict is like a traffic accident on Interstate 95: a tragedy for the handful of people involved that wouldn't have affected the rest of us if we hadn't slowed down to gawk. The last couple of years have been the most violent and even so the number of people killed on both sides has been about 1,000 per year. Shouldn't this many deaths provoke our sympathy and interest? If we're motivated by humanitarian concerns, there are richer opportunities for saving lives right here at home. For example, the National Academy of Sciences estimated that between 50,000 and 100,000 Americans are killed every year by medical malpractice (*To Err Is Human: Building a Safer Health System,* Kohn et al., 2000). The National Highway Transportation Safety Administration reports that 41,821 people died in motor vehicle crashes in the United States in 2000, at a cost to the economy of $230.6 billion, not including intangibles such as physical pain or reduced quality of life. Many of these deaths could be prevented with simple engineering, information system, and procedural improvements. If we want to be unselfish and help foreigners we might look at malaria, a preventable disease that kills between one and three million people each year.

Table of Middle Eastern Countries

	AREA (sq. km.)	POPULATION	DENSITY
Israel	20,330	6,029,529	297
Egypt	995,450	70,712,345	71
Lebanon	10,230	3,677,780	360
Jordan	91,971	5,307,470	58
Syria	184,050	17,155,814	93
Iraq	432,162	24,001,816	56
Iran	1,636,000	66,622,704	41
Saudi Arabia	1,960,582	23,513,330	12
Yemen	527,970	18,701,257	35
Oman	212,460	2,713,462	13
United Arab Emirates	82,880	2,445,989	30
Sudan	2,505,810	37,090,298	15
Total Middle East	8,659,895	277,971,794	32
Israel's percentage	0.23	2	
India	2,973,190	1,045,845,226	352
United States	8,000,000	280,562,489	35
0.23% of U.S.:	18,781		
Florida	151,670	16,396,515	108

Sources: Country areas and population from the CIA Factbook 2002; Florida data from US Census Bureau

SHALOM LAPPIN

Israel and the New Anti-Semitism

SINCE THE COLLAPSE of the Oslo peace process and the outbreak of the second intifada in September 2000, the Israeli-Palestinian conflict has generated an increasingly hostile view of Israel throughout Western Europe. Much of this reaction consists of sharp criticism of Israel's conduct in suppressing the Palestinian uprising in the Occupied Territories of the West Bank, Gaza, and East Jerusalem. To the extent that this response is directed at Israel's actions and policies, it is legitimate comment on the behavior of a state and its government. The severity of the criticism can, in part, be attributed to the fact that Israel is a relatively strong, developed country that is using its army to sustain the occupation of a large Palestinian population that is politically dispossessed and suffering economically. As the current violence has become increasingly brutal on both sides, the asymmetry of power between Israel and the Palestinians and Ariel Sharon's determination to entrench the occupation through settlement expansion while forcing the Palestinians into virtual capitulation have seriously undermined European support for Israel.

There are, however, good reasons for doubting whether all the hostility directed at Israel can be construed simply as opposition to its policies. The obsessive focus of European journalists and opinion makers on Israel's war with the Palestinians contrasts sharply with the relative indifference of (much) liberal opinion to other recent, as well as ongoing human rights violations on a significantly larger scale. Slobodan Milosevic's bloody campaigns in Bosnia and Kosovo attracted little if any organized protest in Europe until the United States initiated a NATO bombing campaign to force the Serbian army out of Kosovo in 1999. At that point, European peace groups launched a series of large protests against the intervention. The fact that many European Union countries actively collaborated with the Milosevic government during the Bosnian War and did virtually nothing to stop its onslaught produced no apparent outrage among most purveyors of progressive politics in these countries. While the mass murder of more than six thousand Bosnian Muslims in Srebrenica shocked some people, there was no demonization of Serbia, no calls for academic boycotts of Serbian universities. The International War Crimes Court in The Hague is prosecuting indicted Balkan war criminals, Milosevic foremost among them, while popular opinion in Europe, particularly on the left, has remained largely detached from the events that led to the court's creation.

Russia's unrestrained assault on Muslim separatists in Chechnya has been met with little more than occasional censure from human rights activists. It goes largely unreported and causes little if any concern in Europe. In both the Balkans and in Chechnya the level of violence and severe human rights abuses has been, to date, far higher than in the Israeli-Palestinian conflict. Although this doesn't justify Israel's actions in the territories, it does raise serious questions concerning the motivation behind some of the current hostility to Israel. Both the Balkans and Russia are natural areas of European interest. They are close to home and involve countries with which Western Europe is closely involved. Why, then, is there such a stark contrast between the relative calm with which the Balkan and Chechen wars have been received on one hand and the intense reaction to the Israeli-Palestinian conflict on the other?

One explanation for the current European view of Israel runs as follows: Israel was established as an act of compensation to the Jews on the part of Western countries burdened with the guilt of the Holocaust. This guilt allowed them to disregard the cost that Israel's creation inflicted on the Palestinians, who were innocent of the Holocaust. Now that several generations have passed and Israel has become a regional superpower, the Europeans no longer wish to relate to Israel as a nation of victims. They insist on redressing the dispossession of the Palestinians.

The historical claim on which this view is based is incorrect. The United Nations partition plan of 1947 that established Israel was adopted largely because of American and Soviet support. Neither the United States nor the Soviet Union suffered Holocaust guilt in 1947, nor should they have. They, together with Britain, were responsible for destroying Nazism and ending its genocide against the Jews. Stalin was staunchly anti-Zionist but supported the creation of Israel as a way of gaining political influence in a strategically important region still dominated by Britain. Truman remained undecided about partition until shortly before the vote, with both the State Department and the Pentagon split on whether or not to support the plan. Although historical and moral considerations seem to have played a role in Truman's decision, the desire to deepen American influence in the Middle East, displace Britain, and block Soviet penetration was probably the decisive factor in determining his position. Britain, the other major player in the partition debate, did its best to prevent the emergence of a Jewish state in Palestine. After the war it took the view that Jewish Holocaust survivors and refugees should be repatriated to the countries from which they had come. This included Polish Jews at a time when postwar pogroms were taking place in

Poland against returning survivors. Britain blocked the immigration of Jewish refugees to Palestine right up until the end of its mandate in 1948. It abstained from the UN partition vote, and it actively supported the Jordanian Legion in the 1948 war. It changed its policy and supported Israel only in the early 1950s. The idea that the creation of Israel was the product of Western guilt over the Holocaust is, then, largely unfounded.

Nonetheless, the idea that Israel was created through Holocaust guilt has gained widespread currency in Europe. This idea is used to impose moral conditions on Israel that are not generally applied to other countries. If Israel was created as an act of expiation for crimes against the Jews, so this reasoning goes, then its legitimacy depends upon its not oppressing other people. The idea of Israel as a conditional concession wrung from the West through Jewish suffering in Europe goes some way toward explaining the glee (relief?) with which Israel's more strident European critics insist on comparing its treatment of the Palestinians to the Nazi persecution of the Jews. The obvious perversity and inappropriateness of the comparison is the source of its attraction. Not only are the victims of the Nazis transformed into the oppressors, but the basis of their collective legitimacy is undermined. The power of the comparison has not been lost on Arab nationalists and Islamic fundamentalists, who invoke it regularly.

More significant than Holocaust fatigue in shaping European responses to the current Israeli-Palestinian conflict is, I suspect, the fear that militant anti-Western sentiment in the Islamic world will bring large-scale terrorist violence to Europe, as it did to the United States on September 11, 2001. With the end of the cold war and the creation of a more integrated European Union in the 1990s, West Europeans embraced a vision of prosperity and human rights promoted through an expanded framework of international institutions. The shock of September 11 and the Bush administration's aggressive, often unilateral "War on Terror" have replaced this optimism with a profound fear that Europe will once again be drawn into bloody ethnic conflicts that it thought belonged to its past. This danger is not only external. The existence of large communities of Muslim immigrants in Europe, where Islamic activism flourishes, turns this into a local issue. To the extent that Israel has become the focus of a massive wave of Islamic anger, many Europeans have come to see it as a major liability. They hold the country responsible for the terrorist threat that they wish to avoid. Intense European criticism of Israel is, in part, aimed at heading off this danger and purchasing security by deflecting Arab and Islamic hostility.

ISRAEL AS A JEWISH POLITY

But even granting the role of Holocaust fatigue and fear of Islamic terrorism as important factors in conditioning the current European reactions to the Middle East, there is another element that surfaces with increasing frequency in the discussion of Israel. That is a general discomfort with the notion of Israel as a Jewish polity. Even when Israel's right to exist is affirmed, a common complaint among both European and Arab critics is that Israel's characterization of itself as a Jewish country is exclusionary and racist. Although this criticism has always been raised by the anti-Zionist left, it is now often expressed as a mainstream view in the European media. We should consider it carefully.

Laws and institutions that reserve rights and privileges for one ethnic group while excluding others are indeed discriminatory and incompatible with liberal democratic values. Unfortunately, discriminatory legal structures do exist in certain parts of public life in Israel, specifically in the use and development of land owned by the Jewish National Fund (JNF), which accounts for most public land in the country. These restrictions date back to the pre-state era, when the JNF was the instrument through which the Jewish community in Palestine acquired land for settlement and development. Arabs are still excluded from leasing and building on this land.

The Law of Return is a more complex case. It grants the right of residence and citizenship to Jews (and immediate non-Jewish family members) from abroad. This law recognizes as extra-territorial nationals Jews living in the diaspora. It has approximate parallels in the nationality laws of other countries (China, Japan, the United Kingdom, Ireland, and Germany) that confer the right of citizenship or residence on people connected to the country by culture or descent. Unsurprisingly, the Palestinian Liberation Organization Charter proposes a similar law of return for Palestinians in the diaspora. For both Israeli Jews and Palestinians a law of return is regarded as a legal instrument for rehabilitating a nation of refugees in its national home. In general, laws that establish special rights for Jews derive from the formative period of the country when it was in the process of absorbing Jewish immigrants. Many Israelis of the liberal left who are committed to the existence of Israel as a Jewish country support the abolition of all these laws, with the possible exception of the Law of Return. Most Israelis regard the latter as still necessary for the protection of Jews living in unstable or repressive countries.

Critics of Israel who object to its identity as a Jewish state are, for the most part, not exercised by the fact that Iran and Saudia Arabia define themselves as Islamic states. They may reject their governments as theocratic and reactionary, but they do not regard these countries as illegitimate. They do not, in general, have problems with the religiously based partition of the Indian subcontinent between Pakistan and India, which took place at the same time as the creation of Israel. The implementation of this partition was accompanied by intense political violence that produced hundreds of thousands of refugees on both sides, most of whom have never returned to

their homes. Most significantly, they have no difficulty whatsoever with Arab states that purport to be both secular and Arab.
They see these states as natural political frameworks for the national groups that constitute their populations. The obvious
question, then, is why they have such difficulty with a country
that provides for the political independence of a Jewish population.

Assume the following utopian scenario. An enlightened liberal democratic government comes to power in Israel and
reaches a peace agreement with the Palestinians: a full withdrawal to (the equivalent of) the 1967 borders and the establishment of a Palestinian state. This government then proceeds
to eliminate all discriminatory legislation and institute a full
separation of religion and state. It implements reforms to integrate the Arab minority into the social and economic mainstream of the country. Israel would still be a Jewish country in
that it would have a decisive (80 percent) Jewish majority, its
culture and history would continue to reflect the experiences
and concerns of this majority, and its first language would remain Hebrew.

I suspect that many of its critics would continue to object to
Israel in this fully democratized format. These are the same
people who reject as racist the proposal advanced by some on
the Israeli left for a partition of Israel/Palestine along demographic lines; that is, that Israel should return as much territory
as possible to the Palestinians, including areas currently within
the green line that contain large numbers of Israeli Arabs.
Many reject a two-state solution and favor a single country,
"a secular democratic state of all its citizens." In fact, as they
must know, such a state would either dissolve into civil war or
become an Arab country with a subordinated Jewish minority.
What lies behind their critique is less a concern for secular
democracy than a deep hostility to the very idea of a Jewish
state, even when it is cast as political independence for a large

Jewish population under conditions of genuine democracy for all and equality for the non-Jewish minority. The objection to a Jewish polity of any sort in the territory of Israel/Palestine lies at the heart of Arab nationalist and Islamic hostility to Israel. It also informs much of the more extreme criticism of Israel that has recently entered the mainstream of political discourse in Europe.

The sense that much of the Arab and Islamic world simply cannot accept a Jewish political presence under any conditions has driven many Israelis to despair. After Oslo had raised hopes of a final peace agreement and reconciliation, the virulence of Palestinian and Arab hostility have persuaded a not insignificant part of the Israeli population that peace is impossible whatever concessions they make. This has produced a dangerous sense of helplessness and victimhood that effectively paralyzes the electorate into acquiescence in the brutal, expansionist policies of the right, even when most Israelis reject these policies. The specter of widespread European complicity in this challenge to Israel's basic legitimacy has further intensified its sense of isolation and reinforced de facto support for a disastrous right-wing adventure.

The rejection of a Jewish polity is closely related to a refusal to recognize the collective legitimacy of the Jews as a people who are entitled to a place among the nations of the world. This idea is deeply rooted in both European and Islamic sources. It has assumed a variety of religious and political forms in the past, and we may well be witnessing the emergence of a new version of this traditional theme.

MESSIANISM AND REPLACEMENT THEOLOGY

Late biblical and rabbinic Judaism introduced the idea of a messianic age in which peace and justice would be established for all humanity in real historical time. The concept of the messianic age is the result of a remarkable evolution from the demand for a national savior to deliver the people from external oppression (as in the period of the judges and the kings) to a universalist vision of a redeemer who ushers in a just social order. The messianic idea animated Jewish resistance to Roman occupation and sustained the Jews for centuries in the diaspora.

In appropriating the Jewish messianic vision, Christianity sought to replace the Jews as the heirs of the covenant with God within which this vision was defined. In order to achieve this expropriation it was necessary to portray the Jews as perverse nonbelievers who had forfeited their right to the covenant through their refusal to accept the Messiah. Jews were offered the choice of giving up their Jewish identity and joining the church in order to enter the New Covenant, or existing as a despised religious minority excluded from the social mainstream. It is important to recognize that orthodox Christian doctrine accorded the Jews a recognized role as an outcast community, in contrast to heretics, who were not tolerated at all. The marginality of Jews in the traditional Christian world was intended to emphasize the stigma that attached to their rejection of the new messianic order. The price for acceptance was, then, a total renunciation of Jewish life. The intensity of Christian anti-Semitism was due in part to the persistence of self-affirming Jewish communities in the midst of Christian societies, for these communities testified to the failure of the Christian messianic enterprise to displace its predecessor and so complete its universal project.

Islam also began its history with a failed overture to the Jews. Initially it received a positive response from Jewish tribesmen and rabbinic authorities in Arabia, who recognized the close affinity between the Prophet Muhammad's robustly monotheistic teachings and traditional Jewish belief. However, conflict soon developed when the Jews refused to give up their Judaism to embrace the new religion. The Jews, together with the Christians, were assigned the status of *el dhimmi*, a protected religious minority living on the fringes of Islamic society. Islam understands itself as incorporating the religious insights of both Judaism and Christianity while superseding them. Unlike Christian Europe, the Muslims did not regard the Jews as a threat to their hegemony, nor did they subject them to systematic, large-scale violence. However, the price that the Jews paid for refusing to accept Islam's messianic project was, again, existence in a marginalized community. Although their situation was far better than the one that they endured in the Christian world, there are obvious parallels between the positions that each society assigned them.

While traditional Islam does not recognize the legitimacy of any non-Islamic political power, the ongoing competition between Islamic and Christian empires that played out from the Middle Ages into the modern era forced pragmatic acceptance of non-Muslim rule in formerly Islamic territories such as Spain, Greece, and the Balkans. By contrast, the Jews never had collective political power at any point in this period, and so the question of accommodation with a Jewish political entity was not an issue. Similarly, Christian Europe had no need to deal with Jewish military or political power, and therefore the idea of a Jewish polity simply did not arise. In both Christian and Muslim domains the Jews were understood entirely as a dependent minority defined by its refusal to disband and join the new majority order.

SECULAR MESSIANISM AND THE EUROPEAN LEFT

With the emergence of secular civil societies in Western Europe following the French Revolution, Jews were offered the possibility of social and political emancipation without explicitly renouncing their Judaism. However, the conditions of this offer required that Jews enter the new social order on a strictly individual basis and abandon their view of themselves as constituting a people. The ideal recommended to them was full assimilation. Reconstitution as a religious denomination on the model of Christian churches would be tolerated. But to the extent that Jews insisted on retaining a connection to a collectivity, they would be stigmatized as an obstinately atavistic group clinging to an unwelcome foreign identity. Count Stanislas-Marie-Adélaide de Clermont-Tonnerre provided a particularly clear formulation of this view of the Jew in a civic society in his "Speech on Religious Minorities and Questionable Professions" delivered to the French National Assembly on December 23, 1789:

> We must refuse everything to the Jews as a nation and accord everything to Jews as individuals. We must withdraw recognition from their judges; they should only have our judges. We must refuse legal protection to the maintenance of the so-called laws of their Judaic organization; they should not be allowed to form in the state either a political body or an order. They must be citizens individually. But, some will say to me, they do not want to be citizens. Well then! If they do not want to be citizens, they should say so, and then, we should banish them. It is repugnant to have in the state an association of non-citizens, and a nation within the nation.

Where European liberalism insisted that Jews give up their involvement with a religiously defined collectivity as a condition for acceptance in the new civic democracy, the mainstream of the revolutionary European left refused to accept a culturally autonomous secular Jewish proletariat committed to class struggle alongside the working-class movements of other nations. The Jewish Labor Bund was persecuted by the Bolsheviks and then by Stalin. Trotsky and his followers also rejected it.

In contrast to the Zionists, the Bund did not seek the creation of a Jewish state, nor did it endorse a territorial solution to Jewish oppression in Eastern Europe. It envisioned the emergence of autonomous Jewish communal and cultural institutions within a socialist society. The Bund enjoyed widespread support in Poland and the Russian pale of settlement, where three to four million Jews constituted approximately 13 percent of the population. It argued that the Jewish population in Eastern Europe was an oppressed national minority that should be permitted to take its place among other peoples in the struggle for a just society. The left's problem with the Bund was not one of accepting a religious community in a secular society. The Bund's heresy was neither territorialism nor unacceptable ideas on the nature of socialism, but its demand that Jews be recognized as a people and permitted to sustain their language and their cultural institutions. The revolutionary left claimed to respect the rights of all peoples to self-determination and defended the rights of national minorities in other cases. Its refusal to apply these principles to Jews who sought to participate in the revolutionary movement as Jews exposes its thoroughgoing inability to cope with any form of Jewish collective life.

In effect both classical European liberalism and the revolutionary European left offered the Jews a secular version of the traditional Christian choice: either discard involvement with the Jewish people and achieve individual acceptance in a new liberated era or suffer stigmatization and marginalization as perverse holdouts against the mainstream. The choice expressly excluded the possibility of existing as a free nation among other nations.

Given that the view of the Jewish people as an illicit nation is so deeply ingrained in both religious and secular European culture, it is not surprising that assimilation failed to eliminate European anti-Semitism. Most Jews who adopted variants of this strategy soon found that their attempts to sever connections with collective Jewish life generated the suspicion that they had not fully renounced their forbidden loyalties. They were all the more threatening for having receded into the limbo of non-existence imposed upon them by classical liberals and revolutionary socialists. The issue was not simply Jewish collectivity but Jewish visibility. Leon Pinsker's critique of assimilation ("Auto-Emancipation," 1882) as a means of escaping oppression proved to be entirely correct.

A large part of the contemporary European left has inherited the liberal and revolutionary antipathy toward a Jewish collectivity, with Israel becoming the focus of this attitude. While acculturated Jewish intellectuals and progressive Jewish activists are held in high esteem, a Jewish country is treated as an illegitimate entity not worthy of a people whose history should have taught them the folly of nationalism. The current intifada is regarded as decisively exposing the bankruptcy not so much of a policy of occupation and settlement, but of the very idea of a Jewish polity, which could not but do otherwise than commit such misdeeds. These underlying attitudes are clearly expressed in Perry Anderson's extended editorial article "Scurrying Towards Bethlehem" (*New Left Review*, July–August, 2001). Anderson is at pains to show Zionism as a nationalist movement begotten in the sin of collaboration with European colonialism and sustained by continuing involvement with American imperialism. He envisages the de-Zionization of Israel as a necessary condition for a reasonable solution to the conflict. Interestingly, the fact that Arab nationalism and the various states that emerged from it were also deeply involved with European colonialist ventures plays no part in his story. Moreover, he does not regard Palestinian nationalism in particular and Arab nationalism in general as problematic phenomena. The former is understood solely as the engine of a progressive movement for national liberation. It seems, then, that the reasonable demands for graduation to a postnationalist politics and for a critique of historical myths apply exclusively to Israeli Jews. Palestinians and other Arab nationalists are exempt from these requirements as their national movements are inherently progressive, even if occasionally misguided in their formulations.

In the course of his article Anderson makes the important observation that Israel is unique as a settler state because its immigrants had no mother country in whose colonial interests they were dispatched. This insight should have alerted him to the important difference between the historical reasons that brought Israel into being and those that produced other immigrant-based settler countries, and hence to the inapplicability of a simple-minded analogy between Israel and these products of colonialism. Instead, he suggests that the power of Jewish economic and political influence in America has transformed the United States into an effective mother country for Israel. "Entrenched in business, government and media, American Zionism has since the sixties acquired a firm grip on the levers of public opinion and official policy toward Israel, that has weakened only on the rarest of occasions. Taxonomically, the colonists have in this sense at length acquired something like the metropolitan state—or state within a state—they initially lacked."

The specter of a Jewish-Zionist lobby/conspiracy that controls state power and the media, particularly in America, has become a significant theme in the writings of left-wing political journalists in Europe. So, for example, Robert Fisk ("I Am Being Vilified for Telling the Truth About Palestinians," *Independent*, December 13, 2000) and John Pilger ("Why My Film Is Under Fire," *Guardian*, September 23, 2002) insist that a powerful Zionist lobby operating in Britain but directed from America is working with considerable success to suppress all objective reporting and critical discussion of Israel. The January 14, 2002, issue of the *New Statesman* ran two articles on the Zionist lobby. The cover of the issue featured a large golden Star of David piercing the center of a British flag over the caption "A Kosher Conspiracy?" The first piece, by Dennis Sewell, concluded that the lobby, to the extent that it exists, is largely ineffective in stemming the tide of hostile reporting and comment on Israel. But the second article, by Pilger, repeated his claim of Zionist power in the British government and the press. It also included the comment that "Blair's meeting with Arafat served to disguise his support for Sharon and the Zionist project." For Pilger, then, Sharon's appalling policies are only derivative problems. The real target is the country as such, reduced to an ideological slogan as "the Zionist project." Peter Wilby, editor of the *New Statesman,* apologized for the offensive cover in an editorial that appeared in the February 11, 2002, issue. He explained that it had been innocently intended to attract attention on the newsstand. He did not address the obvious question of why a venerable publication of the Labor left should choose to use an image clearly reminiscent of Nazi iconography to promote its sales. It is too facile to dismiss this incident as a passing mistake of judgment. Sneering chatter of a powerful international Jewish lobby, once the stock in trade of fascist propaganda, has now become a staple of left-wing comment on Israel in the British and European press. By contrast, the activities of Arab, Muslim, and pro-Palestinian advocacy groups in the media and public discussion of the Middle East have gone largely unremarked. It is generally assumed, quite reasonably, that such groups have a natural role to play in debates on conflicts that concern them directly. Oddly, these assumptions do not extend to Jewish and Israeli advocacy groups.

The contrast between Europe and North America in this matter is clear. While by no means free of anti-Jewish prejudice, North America defines itself as an immigrant society in which ownership of the country is not the preserve of a single native group. Jews function like other immigrant communities, most of which have succeeded in developing hyphenated personae, easily combining their ethnic identities with their active presence in the mainstream of American life. It is not surprising, then, that public Jewish visibility and the notion of a Jewish polity seem to pose less difficulty in America than in Europe and the Middle East.

Although much of the criticism directed against Israel in the past two years of the intifada is legitimate if not always accurate, the growing hostility to the country stems, at least in part, from acute resistance to a Jewish polity and general difficulties with Jewish collective life. These attitudes are deeply rooted in the histories of both Europe and the Islamic world. The problem of distinguishing bigotry from reasonable opposition is difficult, given that in Israel the Jews are no longer dispossessed, but citizens of a powerful country with a large army that is now being used to sustain the occupation of another people. When considering the critical response to Israel it is reasonable to insist that it be accorded the same legitimacy and judged by the same principles as other countries. To require less of Israel is to allow it to claim rights that are denied to others. To demand more is to invoke a unique set of standards motivated by traditional prejudices. Both positions are unreasonable and must be resisted.

EDWARD SAID

A Desolation, and They Called It Peace

N OW THAT OSLO has clearly been proven the deeply flawed
and unworkable "peace" process that it really was from
the outset, Arabs, Israelis, and their various and sundry supporters need to think a great deal more, rather than less, clearly.
A number of preliminary points seem to suggest themselves at
the outset. "Peace" is now a discredited and fraudulent word,
and is no guarantee that further harm and devastation will not
ensue to the Palestinian people. How, after all the land confiscations, arrests, demolitions, prohibitions, killings that occurred unilaterally because of Israel's arrogance and power in
the very context of the "peace process," can one continue to
use the word "peace" without hesitation? It is impossible. The
Roman historian Tacitus says of the Roman conquest of Britain
that "they [the Roman army] created a desolation, and called it
peace." The very same thing happened to us as a people, with
the willing collaboration of the Palestinian Authority, the Arab
states (with a few significant exceptions), Israel, and the United
States.

Second, it is no use pretending that we can improve on the
current deadlock, which in the Oslo framework as it stands is
unbreakable, by returning to golden moments of the past. We
can neither return to the situation before the war of 1967, nor

can we accept slogans of rejectionism that in effect send us back to the golden age of Islam. You cannot turn the wheel back. The only way to undo injustice, as Israel Shahak and Azmi Bishara have both said, is to create more justice, not to create new forms of vindictive injustice, i.e., "They have a Jewish state, we want an Islamic state." On the other hand, it seems equally fatuous to impose total blockades against everything Israeli (now in fashion in various progressive Arab circles) and to pretend that that is the really virtuous nationalist path. There are, after all, one million Palestinians who are Israeli citizens: are they also to be boycotted, as they were during the 1950s? What about Israelis who support our struggle, but are neither members of the slippery Peace Now or Meretz or of the "great" Israeli Labor Party, led by Ehud Barak, widely presumed to be the murderer of Kamal Nasser and Abu Iyad? Should they—artists, free intellectuals, writers, students, academics, ordinary citizens—be boycotted because they are Israelis?

Obviously, to do so would be to pretend that the South African triumph over apartheid hadn't occurred, and to ignore all the many victories for justice that occurred because of non-violent political cooperation between like-minded people on both sides of a highly contested and moveable line. As I said in a recent article, we cannot win this struggle by wishing that all the Jews would simply go away, or that we could make everything become Islamic: we need the other *wilaya*s and the people within them who are partisan to our struggle. And we must cross the line of separation—which has been one of the main intentions of Oslo to erect—that maintains current apartheid between Arab and Jew in historic Palestine. Go across, but do not enforce the line.

Third and perhaps most important: there is a great difference between political and intellectual behavior. The intellectual's role is to speak the truth, as plainly, directly, and as honestly as possible. No intellectual is supposed to worry about whether what is said embarrasses, pleases, or displeases people in power. Speaking the truth to power means additionally that the intellectual's constituency is neither a government nor a corporate or a career interest: only the truth, unadorned. Political behavior principally relies upon considerations of interest —advancing a career, working with governments, maintaining one's position, etc. In the wake of Oslo it is therefore obvious that continuing the line propagated by the three parties to its provisions, Arab states, the Palestinian Authority, and the Israeli government, is political, not intellectual, behavior. Take for example the joint declaration made by Egyptians and Israelis (mostly men) on behalf of the Cairo Peace and Peace Now. Remove all the high-sounding phrases about "peace" and not only do you get a ringing endorsement of Oslo, but also of the Sadat–Begin agreements of the late '70s, which are described as courageous and momentous. Fine. But what does this have to do with Palestinians whose territory and self-determination were removed from those courageous and momentous Camp David documents? Besides, Egypt and Israel are still at peace. What would people think if a few Israelis and Palestinians got together and issued ringing proclamations about Israeli-Syrian peace that were meant to "appeal" to those two governments? Crazy, most people would say. What entitles two parties, one who oppresses Palestinians and the other who has arrogated the right to speak for them, to proclaim peaceful goals in a conflict that is not between them? Moreover, the idea of appealing to Israeli government, expecting solutions from it, is like asking Count Dracula to speak warmly about the virtues of vegetarianism.

In short, political behavior of this sort simply reinforces the hold of a dying succubus, Oslo, on the future of real, as opposed to fraudulent, American-Israeli peace. But neither, I must also say, is it intellectually responsible in effect to return to blanket boycotts of the sort now becoming the fashion in various Arab countries. As I said earlier, this sort of tactic (it is scarcely a strategy, any more than sticking one's head in the sand like an ostrich is a strategy) is regressive. Israel is neither South Africa, nor Algeria, nor Vietnam. Whether we like it or not, the Jews are not ordinary colonialists. Yes, they suffered the Holocaust, and yes, they are the victims of anti-Semitism. But no, they cannot use those facts to continue, or initiate, the dispossession of another people that bears no responsibility for either of those prior facts. I have been saying for twenty years that we have no military option, and are not likely to have one any time soon. Nor does Israel have a real military option. Despite their enormous power, Israelis have not succeeded in achieving either the acceptance or the security they crave. On the other hand, not all Israelis are the same, and, whatever happens, we must learn to live with them in some form, preferably justly rather than unjustly.

Therefore the third way avoids both the bankruptcy of Oslo and the retrograde policies of total boycotts. It must begin in terms of the idea of citizenship, not nationalism, since the notion of separation (Oslo) and of triumphalist unilateral theocratic nationalism, whether Jewish or Muslim, simply does not deal with the realities before us. Therefore, a concept of citizenship whereby every individual has the same citizen's rights, based not on race or religion, but on equal justice for each person guaranteed by a constitution, must replace all our outmoded notions of how Palestine will be cleansed of the others' enemies. Ethnic cleansing is ethnic cleansing, whether it is done by Serbians, Zionists, or Hamas. What Azmi Bishara and several Israeli Jews like Ilan Pape are now trying to strengthen is a position and a politics by which Jews and those Palestinians already inside the Jewish state have the same rights; there is no reason why the same principle should not apply in the Occupied Territories, where Palestinians and Israeli Jews live side by side, together, with only one people, Israeli Jews, now dominating the other. So the choice is either apartheid or it is justice and citizenship. We must recognize the realities of the Holocaust not as a blank check for Israelis to abuse us, but as a sign of our humanity, our ability to understand history, our requirement that our suffering be mutually acknowledged. And we must also recognize that Israel is a dynamic society with many currents—not all of them Likud, Labor, and religious—within it. We must deal with those who recognize our rights. We should be willing as Palestinians to go to speak to Palestinians first but to Israelis too, and we should tell our truths, not the stupid compromises of the sort that the PLO and PA have traded in, which in effect is the apartheid of Oslo.

The real issue is intellectual truth and the need to combat any sort of apartheid and racial discrimination, no matter who does it. There is now a creeping, nasty wave of anti-Semitism and hypocritical righteousness insinuating itself into our political thought and rhetoric. One thing must be clear, in my firm opinion: we are not fighting the injustices of Zionism in order to replace them with an invidious nationalism (religious or civil) that decrees that Arabs in Palestine are more equal than others. The history of the modern Arab world—with all its political failures, its human rights abuses, its stunning military incompetences, its decreasing production, the fact that, alone of all modern peoples, we have receded in democratic and technological and scientific development—is disfigured by a whole series of outmoded and discredited ideas, of which the notion that the Jews never suffered and that the Holocaust is an obfuscatory confection created by the elders of Zion is one that is acquiring too much, far too much, currency.

Why do we expect the world to believe our sufferings as Arabs if a) we cannot recognize the sufferings of others, even of our oppressors, and b) we cannot deal with facts that trouble simplistic ideas of the sort propagated by *bien-pensant* intellectuals, who refuse to see the relationship between the

Holocaust and Israel? Again, let me repeat that I cannot accept the idea that the Holocaust excuses Zionism for what it has done to Palestinians: far from it. I say exactly the opposite, that by recognizing the Holocaust for the genocidal madness that it was, we can then demand from Israelis and Jews the right to link the Holocaust to Zionist injustices toward the Palestinians, link and criticize the link for its hypocrisy and flawed moral logic.

But to support the efforts of Garaudy and his Holocaust-denying friends in the name of "freedom of opinion" is a silly ruse that discredits us more than we already are discredited in the world's eyes for our incompetence, our failure to fight a decent battle, our radical misunderstanding of history and the world we live in. Why don't we fight harder for freedom of opinion in our own societies, a freedom, no one needs to be told, that scarcely exists? When I mentioned the Holocaust in an article I wrote here last November I received more stupid vilification than I ever thought possible; one famous intellectual even accused me of trying to gain a certificate of good behavior from the Zionist lobby. Of course I support Garaudy's right to say what he pleases and I oppose the wretched Gayssot Law under which he was prosecuted and condemned. But I also think that what he says is trivial and irresponsible, and, when we endorse it, it allies us necessarily with Le Pen and all the retrograde right-wing fascist elements in French society.

No, our battle is for democracy and equal rights, for a secular commonwealth or state in which all the members are equal citizens, in which the concept underlying our goal is a secular notion of citizenship and belonging, not some mythological essence or an idea that derives its authority from the remote past, whether that past is Christian, Jewish, or Muslim. The genius of Arab civilization at its height in, say, Andalusia was its multicultural, multi-religious, and multi-ethnic diversity. That is the ideal that should be moving our efforts now, in the wake of an embalmed and dead Oslo, and an equally dead rejectionism. The letter killeth, but the spirit giveth life, as the Bible says.

In the meantime, we should concentrate our resistance on combating settlement (as described in an article I wrote [recently]) with non-violent mass demonstrations that impede land confiscation, on creating stable and democratic civil institutions (hospitals and clinics, schools and universities, now in a horrendous decline, and work projects that will improve our infrastructure), and on fully confronting the apartheid provisions inherent in Zionism. There are numerous prophecies of an impending explosion due to the stalemate. Even if they turn out to be true, we must plan constructively for our future, since neither improvisation nor violence is likely to guarantee the creation and consolidation of democratic institutions.

DANIEL GORDIS

Take Off That Mask

Jerusalem, Israel

Dear Jill,

When *The New York Times* carries a story about a student newspaper at the Jewish Theological Seminary refusing to print a D'var Torah,* something of interest is clearly happening. So, curious, I dug around the web a bit, found your submission, and read it with interest.

Given that JTS—hardly a bastion of rabid Zionism these days—had refused to publish it, I expected something really outrageous. But on the surface, it wasn't nearly as troubling as I'd expected. You're concerned about the fair treatment of Israeli Arabs. So am I. You're deeply troubled by the deaths of Palestinian civilians. So am I. You want Israel to be better. So do I.

So do many Israelis, Jill. Many of us are troubled by precisely the things that trouble you. That's why, for a while, I found myself feeling that the whole thing was a tempest in a teapot. OK, so it was a bit political for a D'var Torah, and a bit left. But still, why the outcry?

[* Torah-based commentary on current events criticizing Israel, by a rabbinical student, Jill]

But I read it again, and again. And over a couple of days, I found it making me more and more uncomfortable. So I asked myself, given that there is so much that I, like many Israelis, actually agree with in your piece, why does it leave me with such a feeling of discomfort? There are, I think, three dimensions of the epistle that strike me as troubling. I'd like to tell you why.

Before I do so, though, let me assure you that the critique that follows isn't about you. We've never met, though I look forward to doing so. My comments here aren't personal at all, but rather, are directed at a certain form of public discourse about Israel, which, I think, is reflected in your D'var Torah. What I'm addressing is a way of speaking about Israel that is found in the public utterances of groups like "Rabbinical Students for a Just Peace" (which you represent) and the American Jewish radical left, in general. Please read my letter in that spirit.

The first thing that troubles me about your piece is your certainty that Israel is simply wrong. Your tone implies that Israel has alternatives that are readily apparent to anyone with even a modicum of moral sophistication. Where I live, we muse on our predicament all the time; but unlike you, none of us can seem to think of any easy answers.

When the army accidentally killed two Jewish security personnel last week in a torrent of bullets, both the press and many of our friends began to wonder what that says about the behavior of the army in cases that we don't hear about, when the people being pursued are Palestinian, not Jews. The people we talked to over Shabbat (religious, and by no means anywhere near "left," if that will help dispel any stereotypes here) were deeply concerned. They were sad, perplexed.

But Jill, there's an enormous difference between our friends who live here and the American Jewish left you represent. Here in Jerusalem, we have those conversations in full knowledge that the alternative to this IDF "full court press" in the hills just outside our neighborhoods isn't obvious. For when the army lets up, our buses explode. When security measures are loosened just a bit, our children don't make it home from school. So we struggle, and we agonize.

But I don't feel any struggle in what you write. And your colleagues certainly don't agonize. You just assume that we're callous, that we're comfortable with all the results of our actions. You write as if Israel has made a choice to be evil. No, you don't say that, but that's what you imply. You imply that we're motivated by hate, by disregard for Arab life. Perhaps that's true of a small percentage of radical-fringe Israelis, but it's not the case for the overwhelming majority. Most of us are animated these days by something completely different.

This week is Purim. Today, the last school day before the Purim school vacation, thousands of kids went to school in costume. It's an amazing scene when you think about it—an entire city filled with dressed-up kids in the middle of one war, and on the eve of another [in Iraq]. But it's also a scene that infuriates me. Why? Because the police have told kids that they can't wear their Purim costume masks out on the streets—the possibility that a terrorist will use Purim as a chance to wear a disguise and blend into the city is too great. And because as I was driving across town today, there were hundreds of police guarding the kids on their parades, and closer to home, I saw my daughter's (high school) friends stationed with rifles along the street, also guarding their younger brothers' and sisters' class parades so that they're not blown up for the simple crime of trying to enjoy Purim.

Do you have any idea what the awareness, day after day, that someone is trying to gun down your kids does to you? No, you don't. Because if you did, you'd never have been able to write "I spent time sitting in cafés, having dinner with friends and former teachers, and wandering the streets of Jerusalem. Enjoying myself in West Jerusalem, I could easily forget about the difficult lives of Palestinians, Israeli Arabs, foreign workers and Jewish minorities." West Jerusalem is Disneyland, and East Jerusalem is hell, right?

No, Jill, wrong. True, there is much too much suffering in East Jerusalem and other Palestinian communities, but West Jerusalem is not the picnic your tourist visa led you to see. Raise children here. Send them off to school every day fully cognizant that someone out there is gunning for them, hoping against hope that the security forces get the "bad guys" (for that's exactly what they are, they're evil—or do you believe they're "freedom fighters"?) before they get our kids. Do that for a couple of years and then see if you can be in West Jerusalem and "easily forget about difficult lives." It's amazing what a few months of reality can do to Upper West Side idealism. Try to raise kids here for a few months, and then see how easy it is for you to write with such certainty that we're so obviously wrong, or that we have any real alternatives here.

If your certainty is my first concern, your naïveté is second. There's a small facet of this conflict that seems to have escaped your attention—this war isn't about territories, or settlements, or the Green Line. It's about Israel's existence. That's why the issue of refugees wasn't resolved at Camp David or in Taba. Israel couldn't compromise, because that would mean the end of a Jewish state. And the Palestinians wouldn't compromise, because the end of the Jewish state was exactly what they wanted.

And that's why I find myself bristling at your concern that your "visit [to Israel] would signal a tacit endorsement of the current Israeli government and of Israel's ongoing human rights violations." What's wrong with saying that? What's wrong is that it's dangerous and myopic.

Yes, it's dangerous. For the language of "ongoing human rights violations" is the language that the world used about South African apartheid, about Milosevic's Serbia and its ethnic cleansing, and now uses about Saddam's Iraq. And the world destroyed the first two, and is about to destroy the third. Is that what you want to happen to Israel? If it isn't, then it's time to recognize that the language you choose puts Israel into a category in which she doesn't belong, but to which the world is all too anxious to add her. In this world climate, responsible Jewish leadership requires watching the words you choose very carefully. Does your rabbinical school spend any time talking about responsible leadership?

Whatever you intend, you will be quoted and cited as evidence. Are you aware that you're featured and quoted on www.freepalestine.com? Do you really want to play into the hands of the French politically correct anti-Semites? Or the barbarian colonialist Belgians who have now decided to be the world's conscience? Do you really want to give tacit justification to the Norwegians who boycott Israeli goods, the British who refuse to invite Israeli academics to conferences, or the Italians who will not have Israeli artists (even politically left-wing performers) on their stages? Is that the tacit message you want to convey?

But lest you respond that I'm advocating that you hide the truth because the truth is dangerous in this case, rest assured that I mean nothing of the sort. Because what you and your colleagues write is not only dangerous; it is also myopic.

What strikes you as the moral high ground, as righteousness born of Jewish learning, strikes me as a wholly dysfunctional read of the situation on the ground. Has Israel done a variety of things in the past two and a half years that are not pleasant? Yes. Have grave mistakes been made? Absolutely. The army itself issued a report last week in which it stated that 18 percent of Palestinians killed in the conflict have been civilians. That's of deep concern to many people here.

But "Israel's ongoing human rights violations"? Do you really mean to compare Israel to South Africa and to Serbia? Did the apartheid regime publish statistics about the performance of its security forces? Did Milosevic? Where is your sense of balance, of proportion?

Yes, you and your "Rabbinical Students for a Just Peace" colleagues regularly and perfunctorily decry Palestinian terrorism. We've all read those pro forma utterances. But are you not aware that you've been sucked into a shocking sort of moral equivalency? Remember, if you can, whom we're fighting and what we haven't done. Have we blown up their restaurants in order to kill as many unarmed civilians as possible? Targeted their public transportation? Celebrated on our campuses after we blew their pizza parlors to high heaven? Rewarded the families of homicide bombers, and turned murderers into religious icons? Have we lynched, to the glee of hundreds standing outside, Palestinians who have made their way into Israel? Have we destroyed their religious sites as they did to Joseph's Tomb and Jericho's Shalom Al Yisrael Synagogue?

No matter how grievous some of the mistakes that the IDF may have made, and yes, there have been too many, do you really want to make this comparison? Do you really believe that it is a policy from the "top" that civilians are to be systematically killed? And be careful before you answer. Even if the policy is to play very serious hardball with the terror organizations in the knowledge that civilians will inevitably be killed, that's not the same thing as consciously and purposefully seeking to kill civilians. Don't we have the right to assume that future Jewish leaders will have the ethical and intellectual nuance needed to make this distinction?

No, I guess not. I suppose that it's of no interest to you that even the committed Israeli left has had to rethink its views in light of this war. Take Benny Morris, for example. Morris, one of the key figures among the Israeli New Historians, has done more than almost anyone to document the roles of the Hagganah and the early IDF in the expulsions of Arabs from their villages (among many other phenomena) during the War of

Independence. In doing so, he has aroused the ire of many centrist and right-wing Israelis. He, if anyone, would seem to be a committed leftist, devoted to settling this conflict and giving the Palestinians the home they deserve, right?

Right, except he looks around and realizes that there's no chance for that now. He reads the situation and realizes that this isn't about fairness, it's about our destruction. So, he's bagged that hope. Listen to him in his own words: "I have yet to see even a peace-minded Palestinian leader, as Sari Nusseibeh seems to be, stand up and say: 'Zionism is a legitimate national liberation movement, like our own. And the Jews have a just claim to Palestine, like we do.' . . . I don't believe that Arafat and his colleagues mean or want peace—only a staggered chipping away at the Jewish state." What would it take, Jill, to get the future leadership of the American Jewish community to understand what the Israeli left has had to learn?

The third quality of your D'var Torah that saddens me is the most subtle, but it may be the most important. I'll be personal here. When I read *Black Dog of Fate,* Peter Balakian's superb book about the Armenian genocide, I was sickened and appalled. There are scenes from that book that I still remember vividly, several years after having read it. The same with Philip Gourevitch's *We Wish to Inform You That Tomorrow We Will Be Killed with Our Families,* about the horrific genocides of Rwanda. I couldn't put either of those books down, and I think about them both, often.

But I'll be honest. They disgusted me and appalled me, but they didn't make me cry. Yet narratives from the Shoah do. Why? Was our suffering greater? I'm not a big believer in quantifying or comparing suffering. No, it's not that. I don't believe for a moment that our suffering matters more, or that our lives are more sacred. It's just that stories about my people, my family, my narrative, and yes—my country—move me more powerfully and intimately than stories about others.

Does that make me a lesser human being? I hope not. I think that it's simply a matter of—to use the phrase that Avishai Margalit uses so eloquently in his *The Ethics of Memory*—the difference between thick and thin relations. I have a much thicker set of relations with Jews—no matter where they are and who they are—than I do with Armenians or Rwandans. Most human beings are that way. It's part of the way we love, and it's part of the way we cope. We couldn't bear life if every human tragedy cut to the core of our being.

To my sadness, though, I don't feel that thickness of relationship when you write about your love for Israel. You say you love Israel, true, but in the very next sentence, you write that you could not "in good conscience, agree to preach unconditional support of a government that has long oppressed another people." Is that how you think of what's going on here? Of the myriad responsibilities the government has, and in the midst of everything the Jewish people is facing in this hour, that's your read of what Israel is? Your basic, instinctive reaction is that this country is now in the business of oppressing another people? You have every right to believe that, I suppose, but I see it in the business of trying to stay alive. If you see it as simply about oppression, then I see little difference between you and the rest of the world that would do us in, with no regard for the history that created us, or for the dream—however insufficiently fulfilled—that this homeland represents for us.

If you can write that it's time to "do teshuva [repentance] by reexamining the ways in which we speak and teach about Israel and by reconsidering our often unconditional support for the state," then we're not cut from the same national cloth. If that's how you feel, especially in these days, then it's a struggle for me to feel that we're part of the same people. "The state"? How neutral can someone get, Jill?

Be honest, Jill, you and your colleagues say it, but you don't mean that you love Israel. You might wish you loved Israel, or you might believe that you're supposed to love Israel, or you might love the myth of Israel on which so many of us were raised. But that's not what counts. You don't love the real Israel. That's where the American Jewish left has failed. It reminds me exactly of what Gershom Scholem wrote almost one-half century ago in response to Hannah Arendt on Eichmann. He accused her correctly, not of getting the facts wrong, but of lacking "ahavat Yisrael" ("the love of Israel"), that is, of the Jewish people as a whole and of its unique experience. Nothing's changed, has it?

As for me, I don't know how to think about the Jewish people today without Israel in some way at the core. That's not to say that every Jew ought to live here, or that Israel's perfect, or that criticism of Israel—by Jews or non-Jews—is always unacceptable. I don't believe any of those things.

But most of us know when someone loves us. We know it not just because of what they say, but because of what they choose not to say, and when they choose not to say it. We know they love us because of how they say what they say. We know they love us because they feel our pain, first and foremost, before they see our faults. That's what makes love real.

You're just not there. Take off your masks. You really don't love us. And because of that, you feel about us the way I feel about Rwandans. You're saddened and appalled when we're killed, but for too many of you, it's an intellectual thing, not a visceral, emotional, immediate one. We're other, removed, distant. So at a time when we need the partnership and support of all segments of American Jewish life more than ever, we have to admit that it's just not there to be had.

For the future of the Jewish people, Jill, that is about as sad as anything I could imagine.

I hope that your Purim in New York is a joyous one. Here in Jerusalem, we'll tell our kids that they can't wear their costume masks outside, even as we dust off their gas masks and get our sealed rooms ready. And if the siren goes off in the next few days or weeks and we have to go into those rooms while Scuds from Iraq or Katyushas from Hezbollah enclaves rain down, and we have to hold our kids on our laps and comfort them, I hope you'll forgive us if we don't have them read your D'var Torah.

You see, Jill, concern for the people trying to kill them is a luxury I suspect even our uncorrupted children won't have.

Purim Same'ach,

Daniel

PART ELEVEN

MUSLIMS

JEFFREY GOLDBERG
Behind Mubarak

THE MOHANDESSIN SECTION of Cairo is a fashionable district on the west bank of the Nile that contains a number
of embassies, boutiques, and American fast-food restaurants.
It also houses the Mustafa Mahmoud Mosque, which is named
after a physician and Islamic television personality who founded
it, twenty years ago. On Friday, September 21, I arrived at the
mosque just as the first worshippers were making their way
there, and the egalitarianism that is one of the great virtues of
the Muslim prayer service was evident: they were dark-skinned
and light, rich and poor; one man drove up in a blue Jaguar;
others, wearing grease-stained *galabiya*s and crude sandals, came
on foot, or by donkey cart. (Women, as is customary, prayed
apart, in another, smaller hall.) I had arranged to meet the
mosque's imam, Sheikh Nasser Abdelrazi. A slight, anxious
man, he preemptively offered up the observation that "Muslims
are gentle and Islam is peace."

Many in Cairo are on the defensive in the wake of the terror attacks on New York and the Pentagon. Greater Cairo, a
city of sixteen million people, is the intellectual capital of the
Arab world—home to its moviemakers, many of its great writers, and some of its most respected interpreters of Islam.
Muslim leaders here are sensitive to the image of their faith—

especially now, because Egyptians are among those allegedly involved in the attacks. Muhammad Atta, who is believed to have flown one of the hijacked planes into the World Trade Center, is the son of a middle-class Cairo lawyer. Ayman al-Zawahiri, a former leader of the Egyptian Islamic Jihad, a fundamentalist group that sought to turn Egypt into an Islamic state, is said to be second-in-command to Osama bin Laden, the Saudi exile who is suspected of directing the attacks.

I did not dispute the Imam's assertion, but the speaker at the service that Friday, Ahmed Youssef—an elderly, bespectacled professor at Cairo University, who joined us before the service got under way—did. "Look, what happened in New York is the work of a gangster mentality, but America must learn not to take the side of the aggressor," he said. "I hope America learns from this mistake before it makes another mistake."

In his view, the aggressor is Israel, which signed a peace agreement with Egypt almost twenty-three years ago. This historical fact is not immediately noticeable in Cairo, where the public obsession with Israel is overwhelming. Youssef said that the nineteen terrorists who on September 11 committed mass suicide in the course of committing mass murder engaged in an un-Islamic act. They killed civilians, which is *haram,* or forbidden, and they killed themselves, which is also *haram.* Only against Israel is it permissible to engage in a "martyrdom attack," he said, and this is because it is "only the Jews who kill innocent people." He added, "There are no Israeli civilians, only soldiers, so this is a legitimate tactic."

At this, Sheikh Abdelrazi blanched. "He is not speaking for the mosque," he whispered. The mosque, like all mosques in Egypt, ostensibly comes under the supervision of the government, whose position on suicide attacks against Israeli civilians is ambiguous. When I asked President Hosni Mubarak's chief spokesman, Nabil Osman, if his government condemns such attacks, he would say only, "One cannot condemn these acts without condemning the acts of the occupier."

I asked Sheikh Abdelrazi and Youssef if they believed that the Palestinian cause was the motivating factor in Muhammad Atta's alleged act.

"I don't know what happened in New York," Youssef said. "I don't have the answer."

The mosque's muezzin began calling the faithful to prayer. "God is Greater," he chanted, his voice carried by speakers across Arab League Street, beside the mosque. "I bear witness that there is no God but God. I bear witness that Muhammad is the messenger of God."

Some of the men who went to pray asked if I was a man of the Book; Christians and Jews, as monotheists, however flawed, still hold a certain status in Islam, and I was invited to perform the ablutions that would purify me for the prayer service. As we stepped outside to the fountain, where a great number of Muslims were already washing, an old man, sallow-skinned and stooped, moved our way, surrounded by courtiers.

"*He* has the answer," Sheikh Abdelrazi said, pointing to the mosque's founder, Mustafa Mahmoud himself. But Mahmoud hobbled into the mosque; the answer would wait until after prayers.

By now, two thousand or so worshippers had assembled. The Friday service was short, and the sermon lasted only a few minutes. In it, Youssef acknowledged that an injustice had been done in the United States but cautioned America to stay its hand. "Don't say that one should not kill civilians and then kill civilians yourself."

After prayer, Youssef found me and gave his interpretation of the differing outlooks of Christianity and Islam.

"In Islam, if I slap your cheek"—he slapped my cheek— "you should slap my other cheek. But in Christianity, Jesus says turn the other cheek. The U.S. is Christian, so why doesn't it turn the other cheek?"

The discussion was curtailed by the announcement that Mustafa Mahmoud was ready to meet with me. I made my way to an austere office where Mahmoud, who is eighty, was already sitting. "I understand you want the answer," Mahmoud said.

I said yes.

"Waco," he said. At my silent surprise, he went on, "The Branch Davidians attacked the World Trade Center, the McVeigh people. The Mossad gave them help. Did you know that the Israelis who work at the World Trade Center were told to stay home that day?"

He had learned this, he said, from research on the Internet.

"It is impossible for Osama bin Laden to do this," Mahmoud continued. "No Arab could have done this."

For moral reasons? I asked.

"No!" he said. "For technical reasons. Arabs are always late! They aren't coordinated enough to do this, all at once on four airplanes. What does Osama bin Laden know about American air travel, anyway? He lives in Afghanistan."

Mustafa Mahmoud is not a marginal figure in Egyptian society. He is an eminent surgeon and onetime Marxist who found religion; his popular television show, *Science and Faith*, explores the connections between religion and reason; a charitable organization that bears his name runs several clinics and hospitals in Cairo, including an eye institute that is reputed to be one of the most advanced in the Middle East.

Mahmoud told me that he is not sorry about the destruction of the World Trade Center. "Even Rome was a great empire once," he said. "This was an attack on American arrogance."

He said I could read more about his beliefs in a newspaper column that would appear the next day. In addition to his other achievements, Mahmoud regularly contributes articles to *Al-Ahram*, which is the largest and most respected daily newspaper in Egypt.

I later found, on the Internet, a translation of one of Mahmoud's columns, from late June. Its headline was ISRAEL—THE

PLAGUE OF OUR TIME AND A TERRORIST STATE. Much of the column is taken up with a recounting of the main points of the notorious turn-of-the-century tsarist forgery "Protocols of the Elders of Zion." "What exactly do the Jews want?" he wrote on June 23. "Read what the Ninth Protocol of 'The Protocols of the Elders of Zion' says: 'We have limitless ambitions, inexhaustible greed, merciless vengeance and hatred beyond imagination. We are a secret army whose plans are impossible to understand by using honest methods.'"

The image of Anwar Sadat and Menachem Begin joyously clasping hands with Jimmy Carter at the signing of the Egyptian-Israeli peace accord is indelible but misleading, because it did not herald a true peace between two peoples. It has been a cold peace, particularly on the Egyptian side. Israelis have visited Egypt by the thousands, but the Egyptian government has long discouraged its citizens from visiting Israel or doing business with Israelis. And since the latest outbreak of the Palestinian uprising, a year ago, and the attendant photographs of Israeli soldiers firing on Palestinian rock throwers, the relationship has turned frigid. Mubarak supports the peace treaty signed by his predecessor, Sadat—an American-aid package of two billion dollars a year fairly demands this of him—but he has discouraged the normalization of relations between the two states.

It is in the domain of the press that Mubarak's position is most evident. *Al-Ahram* is often described in the American press as a "semi-official" daily newspaper, but this may be an understatement. Its editor, two government officials told me, is chosen by President Mubarak, who also chooses the editors of other government newspapers and magazines. Even supposedly independent or opposition newspapers are said never to criticize the President. The one area in which they are given especially wide latitude is in criticizing Israel and, to a lesser extent, America.

One day last week, I visited the offices of the newspaper *Al-*

Usbu, an independent weekly that is distinctly anti-Israel and critical of ministers in the Mubarak government—though not, of course, of Mubarak himself. Its editor, Mustafa Bakri, who is in his forties, was in his office, watching Al-Jazeera, the Pan-Arabic cable channel. He was impeccably dressed, polite and deferential. I had wanted to meet him for some time, ever since I read a translation of a column in which he described a dream. The dream began with his appointment as one of Ariel Sharon's bodyguards, assigned to protect the Israeli Prime Minister at Cairo's airport, and in the column, which appeared in February, he wrote:

> The pig landed; his face was diabolical, a murderer; his hands soiled with the blood of women and children. A criminal who should be executed in the town square. Should I remain silent as many others did? Should I guard this butcher on my homeland's soil? All of a sudden, I forgot everything: the past and the future, my wife and my children and I decided to do it. I pulled my gun and aimed it at the cowardly pig's head. I emptied all the bullets and screamed. . . . The murderer collapsed under my feet. I breathed a sigh of relief. I realized the meaning of virility, and of self-sacrifice. The criminal died. I stepped on the pig's head with my shoes and screamed from the bottom of my heart: Long live Egypt, long live Palestine, Jerusalem will never die and never will the honor of the nation be lost.

Bakri offered me an orange soda, and talked of the attack on the World Trade Center. He spoke in terms that, in the current shorthand, are considered Nasserist, after Gamal Abdel Nasser, the revolutionary leader and Egypt's first President. Nasserism today combines populism, Pan-Arab socialism, and opposition to all relations with Israel. Nasserists also resent American economic influence.

"The new globalists want to impose American thinking on the Arabs," Bakri said. "This is a reaction to their thinking." Bakri blamed the September 11 attacks on the American right wing, with help from the Mossad. "Five Israelis were arrested the day before the attack outside the World Trade Center for taking pictures," he said, and added that he knew this from reading American newspapers. If America responds militarily to the attacks, he continued, "American targets will be legitimate targets of Arab anger."

I also went to the offices of *Al-Ahram* to talk about this phenomenon. I met with Abdel Monem Said Aly, the director of the Al-Ahram Center for Political and Strategic Studies, a respected moderate think tank attached to the newspaper. I asked him about the many anti-Israel and anti-American articles published in the official Egyptian press in the year leading up to the terror attacks. He himself has not disseminated anti-American ideas, and has fought the spread of conspiracy theories in Egyptian life.

"We have anti-Semitic papers and fanatics, yes, but these are garbage magazines," he said. "*Al-Ahram, Al-Akhbar,* these are very moderate newspapers. Sometimes they are highly critical of the U.S., but that does not mean that they're anti-American."

Nevertheless, *Al-Akhbar* this year has run opinion pieces defending Hitler. I found one of them translated on the Web site of the Middle East Media Research Institute, a watchdog organization based in Washington. "Thanks to Hitler, of blessed memory, who on behalf of the Palestinians took revenge in advance, against the most vile criminals on the face of the Earth," the *Al-Akhbar* columnist Ahmad Ragab wrote in April. "Although we do have a complaint against him, for his revenge was not enough."

Holocaust denial is a regular feature of *Al-Gomhuriya,* another government daily. Its deputy chief editor, Lotfi Nasif, sat with me in his windowless office in downtown Cairo last week and explained that the Holocaust is "an exaggeration" and that gas chambers are a product of the "Jewish imagination." He told me, "The crimes of the Zionists against the Palestinians far outweigh any of the crimes committed by the Nazis."

Colin Powell has frequently been denounced in the government press, sometimes in racial terms, and, shortly before the attacks in New York and in Washington, the *Al-Akhbar* columnist Mahmoud Abd Al-Munim Murad wrote, "The Statue of Liberty in New York Harbor must be destroyed because of . . . the idiotic American policy that goes from disgrace to disgrace in the swamp of bias and blind fanaticism." He also declared that "the age of the American collapse has begun." This is a not uncommon theme among members of the Egyptian intellectual class.

On one subject of international controversy—the use of suicide bombers against Israel—there is near unanimity: despite slight shades of difference, as seen at the Mustafa Mahmoud Mosque, most people agree that it is sometimes allowable. Some Islamic moderates believe that suicide attacks are doctrinally permissible only against Israeli soldiers; a more extremist position holds that all Israelis are legitimate targets.

Before September 11, American officials who worked closely with Egypt tried to downplay the role of anti-Israel and anti-American incitement in the local press. One of the few incidents that provoked a public American response came in 1998, when the newly appointed American Ambassador in Cairo, an Orthodox Jew named Daniel Kurtzer (who is now the Ambassador to Israel), was attacked in anti-Semitic terms in the Egyptian press.

Dennis Ross, who guided Middle East policy under the first Bush administration and was the chief Middle East negotiator for Bill Clinton, told me last week that he and others had underestimated the influence that the press and the imams had in creating a climate hostile to Israel and America.

"The media have been a kind of safety valve to release tensions, and you could even say that a safety valve is a legitimate way to approach such problems," Ross, who is now a distinguished fellow at the Washington Institute for Near East Policy, said. "But in doing so they appeased extremist sentiments rather than countering them. A climate has been created in which the practice of suicide attacks has come to be seen as legitimate. I'm concerned that there are those who say that if it's O.K. against Israelis, then it's O.K. against Americans."

When I summarized Ross's view to Muhammad El-Sayed Said, the deputy director of the Al-Ahram Center, he blamed Ross for the failure of the peace process. "Dennis Ross is behind it all," Said said. "The Americans should be blamed for the disaster we are in," he continued, referring to the collapsed peace process, and, indirectly, to the terror attacks on the United States. "There's an ambivalence about the World Trade Center. I saw so many people crying when they heard the news, but the other side of it is that many Egyptians saw this as a useful blow against American arrogance. The sense is that it will help the Americans learn that they, too, are vulnerable. That they are paying a price for their total support for Israel."

Egyptian political élites, unlike the makers of street opinion, do not suggest that Israel, either alone or in concert with American extremists, carried out the attacks, but they blame Israel for creating an atmosphere of despair which leads to terrorism.

Last Tuesday, I met with Amir Moussa, the secretary-general of the Arab League, which is housed in a palatial building on Tahrir Square, in the center of Cairo. Before being appointed secretary-general, Moussa served as President Mubarak's Foreign Minister. He is known as an outspoken critic of Israel. Moussa is a dapper man who, like many veteran diplomats, can speak at great length without giving much away. He said first that he hoped the World Trade Center would be rebuilt; then he outlined the current thinking of the Mubarak regime.

"There is a wide menu of cooperation," he said. "Countries will choose the areas where they can do best. All of us will fight terrorism, confront terrorism, but not necessarily by conducting a military campaign."

Moussa said that the World Trade Center attack should provide the impetus for America to "reassess" its Middle East alliances. "When it comes to the crunch, such as the Persian Gulf War, ten years ago, or the situation today, America has to sideline Israel," he said. "If Israel intervened on the side of America, it would be destructive to any coalition against terrorism." Many Arab governments have stated that they will not participate in a coalition in which Israel plays a part, and the Bush administration has agreed. Moussa said that Israeli behavior in the occupied territories is contributing to instability and unease throughout the Muslim world.

Last October, during a visit here to attend an Arab summit on the Palestinian uprising, I spent a morning with a Muslim cleric named Muhammad Sayed Tantawi. Tantawi is the highest-ranking cleric in Egypt, and an influential figure across the Sunni Islamic world. I met him in his office near Al-Azhar University, the venerable Muslim theological center, which he oversees. Tantawi is known as the Sheikh of Al-Azhar.

Tantawi was appointed by Mubarak, whose official photograph hangs in Tantawi's office. Sheikh Tantawi usually has taken the side of Islamic moderation and believes in interfaith dialogue, but he also supports the development of an Arab nuclear weapon. Last October, the Palestinian uprising was in its infancy; there had not been a wave of suicide bombings since 1997. But in the interview Tantawi forcefully addressed the issue of jihad. "If someone takes something from you by force, it is your right to take it back by force," he said. "This is a requirement of Islam. If the Israelis would stop transgressing

Muslim land, then there no longer would be a requirement to rise up and fight them."

I asked if Muslims were forbidden by Islamic law to engage in specific acts of retribution. "The killing of civilians is always wrong," he said. "Women, children. This is abhorrent to Islam."

Tantawi has since endorsed some suicide attacks against soldiers. In an interview earlier this year, he said, "The Palestinian youth who bomb themselves among people who fight against them are considered martyrs." Last week, though, he would not talk about suicide attacks. When I spoke to him briefly outside his office, he said only that he was sorry for the attacks on America, and he approved the notion of an international conference on terrorism. I noticed that he moved with a serious-looking security detail; men with submachine guns hanging under their jackets shadowed him through the building.

I asked one of Sheikh Tantawi's aides if there had been a specific threat against the Sheikh's life. No, he said, but added, "Egyptians are the victims of terrorism as well." He was referring to the anti-government campaigns of the 1990s, in which terrorists operated on behalf of two fundamentalist Muslim groups: the Egyptian Islamic Jihad and the Gama'a al-Islamiya. In this wave of terror, Egyptians and foreign tourists alike were murdered in a brutal campaign to convert Egypt into an Islamic state. Fundamentalists killed President Sadat in October of 1981, and they have tried to kill Mubarak as well. But the security around Tantawi suggests that they might want to kill him, too—and they could find, in a liberal interpretation of Tantawi's ruling favoring suicide attacks against "oppressors," a new and devastatating way to carry out their vision.

From an Islamic theological perspective, perhaps the most significant suicide attack to have taken place in the last two weeks occurred on September 9, in northern Afghanistan. Two men suspected to be operating under the command of Osama bin Laden blew themselves up along with the leader of the Afghan opposition, Ahmed Shah Massoud. It is one thing for Muslim extremists to martyr themselves while attacking infidels; it is quite another for them to begin defining religious Muslims such as Massoud as infidels. Even among the Islamic Jihad and Hamas clerics of the Gaza Strip, I never heard anyone justify the use of suicide bombers against Muslim targets.

For some fundamentalists, the Massoud murder seemed to have significantly shifted the boundaries of what is considered permissible. Some Islamic scholars, including those under Sheikh Tantawi's supervision at Al-Azhar, have argued that, if one could attack Israelis, one could also attack anyone who stands in the way of their vision of what the world should look like.

To better understand the thinking of Muslims who have killed fellow Muslims in holy war, I went to see Montasser al-Zayyat, the spokesman of the Gama'a al-Islamiya, which is the larger of Egypt's two fundamentalist terrorist groups. He is a lawyer and has represented, among others, his organization's spiritual leader, Sheikh Omar Abdel Rahman, who is in prison in America for plotting to blow up a number of New York landmarks, including the Holland and Lincoln Tunnels, the Empire State Building, and the United Nations.

When I arrived at a decrepit building in downtown Cairo, where al-Zayyat has his office, it was 9 P.M., and in his waiting room were several bearded men who were seeking an audience with him. They were noticeably hostile toward me, but I could not tell if they were upset by the presence of an American or by the fact that the American was jumping the line.

Al-Zayyat himself, a heavy featured, bearded man, was friendly, but, in the wake of the World Trade Center attacks, he was evasive. At a press conference in Cairo earlier this year, he had warned, "The U.S. will reap a bitter harvest if it continues humiliating Dr. Omar"—Sheikh Rahman. "The continuation of the Sheikh's abuse may result in an explosion of events targeted against U.S. interests. Sheikh Omar has many followers." That night, he said that his threats were not to be taken literally. "I'm very sorry for what happened in New York," he said.

Although Muslim fundamentalists in Egypt have been less visible since President Mubarak ordered a crackdown in the mid-nineties, they have been especially discreet over the last two weeks. The Gama'a al-Islamiya declared a ceasefire in 1999, but thousands of its members remain in jail. Like its rival, the ideologically similar Islamic Jihad, the Gama'a grew out of the Muslim Brotherhood movement, which for decades has been advocating the Islamization of Egyptian society. Unlike the Gama'a, which is illegal, the Muslim brothers exist in an ambiguous political state described to me by one government official as "illegal but tolerated."

The Egyptian Islamic Jihad is also illegal, and in any case seems to have transferred its operations to Afghanistan and merged with Osama bin Laden's Al Qaeda network, with the help of Jihad's Ayman al-Zawahiri. Though they represent rival organizations, al-Zayyat considers al-Zawahiri a friend.

"He's a very sensible man, a very quiet man," al-Zayyat said, when I asked him to describe al-Zawahiri. "When he speaks, you listen to him carefully."

I asked al-Zayyat what might have driven al-Zawahiri to help organize the American attacks. He replied that he had no knowledge of the attacks, and also said, "I'm not going to be a witness against my friend."

I had a final question: What is it about America that incites the fury of so many Islamists? I suggested that it is American values, especially as they relate to sex and the role of women in society, which Islamic conservatives abhor. "We have sex in Egypt," al-Zayyat said, laughing. Then he went on, "We don't have feelings of hatred toward the people of the U.S., but feelings of hatred toward the government of the U.S. have developed because you support Israel so blindly." At that moment, Montasser al-Zayyat's views seemed inseparable from those of Mubarak's spokesmen.

One evening, I met a friend, a member of the small Egyptian upper class, for drinks in a hotel by the Nile. Cairo isn't Islamabad: Muslims are free to drink alcohol, and there are movie theaters and belly dancing, although the percentage of women wearing traditional headscarves seems to have increased dramatically since I first visited, ten years ago. What people aren't encouraged to do is express interest in democratic reform. My friend asked that I not name him in anything I might write; he believes that the soft despotism of the Mubarak government is hardening, and he wants to stay out of jail. Earlier this year, a prominent sociologist and democracy advocate, Saad Eddin Ibrahim, was sentenced to seven years' hard labor on trumped-up charges, and, like the Egyptian peace camp, the number of those who support true democracy is purposefully shrinking from view.

We spoke about the Egyptian preoccupation with Israel. He is no friend of Israel—"I'm an Arab, how can I have warm feelings for such a place?" he said—but he believes that hatred of Israel, and, to a lesser extent, hatred of America, is fomented by the Mubarak regime as a diversion; as long as Egyptians think about Palestinians, they aren't thinking about themselves. "Egyptians live in just appalling conditions today," he said.

Per-capita income in Egypt is less than the per-capita income on the West Bank. Cairo is a tumultuous, decaying city with a wealthy élite and great masses of the destitute and the near-destitute. The universities are turning out thousands of graduates each year for whom there are no jobs. "The gap between rich and poor is widening, and what does the government give us? Hatred of the peace process." He ascribes to Mubarak's circle the ability to turn on and off anti-Western rhetoric.

All of this, he went on, is indirectly the fault of America, which gives Egypt two billion dollars a year in aid but demands little in return. "You allow them to manipulate you. Every time anti-American feelings appear here, Mubarak says, 'Support me or else you see what you'll get.' But the suppression and the corruption and the anti-democratic behavior will create much worse fundamentalism over time. Washington never stands up to them." He cited the imprisonment of the democracy advocate Saad Ibrahim, and said, "Look what they just did on the Queen Boat."

The boat in question, a well-known disco that allegedly attracted a gay clientele, was anchored a short distance from where we sat. ("Queen" is thought to refer to the wife of the deposed King Farouk.) Following a police raid of the vessel in May, fifty-three men were arrested for presumed homosexuality; these men are now on trial in Cairo. Two weeks ago, the first sentence was handed down: a seventeen-year-old received three years' hard labor.

"What does the U.S. do about this? Nothing," my friend said. The only prescription is the robust export of democratic values. "There's no Cold War anymore. You can't drive him into an alliance with the Soviets."

There are few Egyptian intellectuals who still argue publicly in favor of normalization with Jerusalem. They are despised, and for the most part quiet. One of them is Ali Salem, a playwright recently expelled from the Egyptian Writers' Union for making frequent visits to Israel and for assuming a pro-normalization stance.

I wanted to ask Salem, who is sixty-five years old and looks like the literary critic Harold Bloom, what had happened, but he said that he was interested in talking about "something deeper than that." We sat in a cafeteria not far from the Mahmoud mosque. Salem drank coffee and chain-smoked Marlboros. "History is cruel," he said. "It is trying to drag America backward. But I think in this case history is right."

He explained, "We here need to be more progressive, but

you need to take a step back. If the bureaucrats in your airports were just a little more paranoid, like us, it would be a different world. Really, America is a beautiful place: no one even asked why all these guys wanted flying lessons. You should learn to be suspicious. A little backwardness would be healthy."

I asked him to identify the cause of the attacks on America.

"People say that Americans are arrogant, but it's not true," he said. "Americans enjoy life and they are proud of their lives, and they are boastful of their wonderful inventions that have made life so much easier and more convenient. It's very difficult to understand the machinery of hatred, because you wind up resorting to logic, but trying to understand this with logic is like measuring distance in kilograms. These are people who are afraid of America, afraid of life itself. . . . These are people who are envious. To them, life is an unbearable burden. Modernism is the only way out. But modernism is frightening. It means we have to compete. It means we can't explain everything away with conspiracy theories."

Ali Salem paused to order another cup of coffee.

"Bernard Shaw said it best, you know. In the preface to *St. Joan,* he said Joan of Arc was burned not for any reason except that she was talented. Talent gives rise to jealousy in the hearts of the untalented."

Soon after seeing Ali Salem, I ran into Muhammad Atta's father, Muhammad al-Amir Atta, outside a downtown Cairo hotel. He was agitated, alternately aggressive and disconsolate. He had spent much of the week defending himself to reporters and defending his son. I asked him the same question: What, in his mind, lay behind the attack on the World Trade Center?

"The Mossad kidnapped my son and stole his papers," he told me. "Then they spread those papers out at the World Trade Center in order to make it seem like he did it."

BERNARD LEWIS

Muslim Anti-Semitism

[Published in June 1998]

WHAT HAS COME to be known as the peace process—the developing dialogue between the state of Israel on the one hand and the Palestinians and some Arab governments on the other—raised hopes that it would lead to a lessening of hostility and more specifically of anti-Semitism. In some quarters this did indeed occur. But in others the peace process itself has aroused a new Arab hostility to Jews, among both those frustrated by its slowness and those alarmed by its rapidity. As a result, anti-Semitism in recent years has conquered new territory and risen to a new intensity.

EUROPEAN INFLUENCE

European anti-Semitism, in both its theological and racist versions, was essentially alien to Islamic traditions, culture, and modes of thought. But to an astonishing degree, the ideas, the literature, even the crudest inventions of the Nazis and their predecessors have been internalized and Islamized. The major themes—poisoning the wells, the invented Talmud quotations, ritual murder, the hatred of mankind, the Masonic and other conspiracy theories, taking over the world—remain; but with an Islamic, even a Qur'anic twist.

The classical Islamic accusation, that the Old and New Testaments are superseded because Jews and Christians falsified the revelations vouchsafed to them, is given a new slant: the Bible in its present form is not authentic but a version distorted and corrupted by the Jews to show that they are God's chosen people and that Palestine belongs to them.[1] Various current news items—the scandal over Swiss banks accepting Nazi gold stolen from Jews, the appointment of Madeleine Albright as secretary of state, even the collapse of the Bank of Credit and Commerce International (BCCI)—are given an anti-Semitic slant. Jewish world plots—against mankind in general, against Islam, against the Arabs—have become commonplace.

One of the crimes of Israel and of the Zionists in these writings is that they are a bridgehead or instrument of American or, more generally, of Western penetration. For such, America is the Great Satan, Israel the Little Satan; Israel is dangerous as a spearhead of Western corruption. The more consistent European-type anti-Semites offer an alternative view: that America is the tool of Israel, rather than the reverse, an argument backed by a good deal of Nazi-style or original Nazi documentation. In much of the literature produced by the Islamic organizations, the enemy is no longer defined as the Israeli or the Zionist; he is simply the Jew, and his evil is innate and genetic, going back to remote antiquity. A preacher from Al-Azhar University explains in an Egyptian newspaper that he hates the Jews because they are the worst enemies of the Muslims and have no moral standards, but have chosen evil and villainy. He concludes: "I hate the Jews so as to earn a reward from God."[2]

The argument that "we cannot be anti-Semitic because we ourselves are Semites" may still occasionally be heard in Arab countries, though of course not in Turkey or Iran. But some of the more sophisticated spokesmen have become aware that to most outsiders this argument sounds silly or disingenuous. Some writers make a serious effort to maintain the distinction between hostility to Israel and Zionism and hostility to Jews as such. But not all. President Khatami of Iran, in his interview on CNN, pointed out—correctly—that "anti-Semitism is indeed a Western phenomenon. It has no precedents in Islam or in the East. Jews and Muslims have lived harmoniously together for centuries." A newspaper known to express the views of the "Supreme Guide" Khamenei rejected this statement as untrue: "The history of the beginnings of Islam is full of Jewish plots against the Prophet Muhammad and of murderous attacks by Jews . . . unequivocal verses in the Qur'an speak of the hatred and hostility of the Jewish people against Muslims. One must indeed distinguish between the Jews and the Zionist regime, but to speak in the manner we heard was exaggerated and there was no need for such a presentation."[3] The Egyptian director of a film about President Nasser reports a similar complaint by the late president's daughter. She objected to a passage in his film indicating that "Nasser was not against the Jews, but against Zionism, because she wanted to portray her father as a hero of the anti-Jewish struggle."[4]

Spokesmen of the government of Iran usually disclaim anti-Semitism; they refrain from overtly anti-Semitic phraseology and proclaim their readiness to tolerate Jews—of course within the limits prescribed by the Shari'a (Islamic law). This however does not prevent them from embracing the "Protocols of the Elders of Zion," the hundred-year-old Russian forgery alleging a Jewish plot to take over the world. These are frequently reprinted in Iran in book form and were even serialized in a daily newspaper "as a reminder to the reader."[5] Iranian networks also distribute copies of the "Protocols" internationally in various languages. In Egypt the "Protocols" formed the basis of an interview published in a popular Egyptian magazine with Patriarch Shenouda, head of the Coptic church.[6] The interviewer starts by introducing the Protocols as an authentic historical record and questions the patriarch, whose comments on Jews and Judaism seem to be based on the information supplied to him by the interviewer, and derived from the "Protocols" and another popular anti-Semitic forgery, the pseudo-Talmud.

ARAB OPPOSITION

Arab opposition to the peace process as such, or to the manner in which it is being conducted, is of three major types: political, economic, and Islamic.

I. Political

The first is basically a continuance of what went before— ideological polemic against Zionism and political warfare against the state of Israel. Ideological or political opposition as such is not based on prejudice, but it affects and is affected by prejudice.

This kind of opposition and the prejudice associated with it continue to flourish and even to spread in spite of, and in some quarters because of, the peace process. It has been aggravated by some of the actions of the new Israeli government and still more by the utterances of some of its followers. Israeli extremists cannot really be blamed for the anti-Semitic propaganda in the Egyptian and other Arab media, which had already reached high levels of scurrility before the change of government and policy in Israel in June 1996; they have, however, undermined the efforts of well-meaning Arabs to counter these campaigns.

An example of reporting and comments on the news may be seen in reports of the suicide bombing in Ramat Gan on July 24, 1995. This act was disclaimed, even denounced, by responsible Palestinian and other Arab leaders. It was acclaimed by many others, from the center and the left as well as in the fundamentalist Islamic press. A leading article in a Jordanian leftist weekly by its editor, Fahd ar-Rimawi, acclaims the heroism of the Hamas bomber who "sent seven Zionist settlers to hell and thirty others to the casualty wards" and goes on to denounce those who had condemned the attack as hypocrites or worse.[7] That Ramat Gan is near Tel Aviv, part of Israel since the foundation of the state, makes the description of its inhabitants as "Zionist settlers" the more noteworthy. The Jordanian fundamentalist Ziyad Abu Ghanima rails against those who "shed torrents of tears in mourning for filthy Jewish blood while sparing their tears when Palestinian or Lebanese blood is shed by the hands of the Jews, may God curse them."[8]

II. Economic

More dangerous than this old-guard resistance is a new active opposition to the peace process that arises from the process itself, from a fear that the prowess which the Israelis had demonstrated in the battlefield would be equaled or even exceeded in activities with which Jews are more traditionally associated—in the factory, the counting house, and the marketplace. A certain Israeli brashness and lack of understanding of the courtesies and sensitivities of Middle Eastern society have often exacerbated such fears.

According to this perception, Israel has changed its tactics. It has now switched from warlike to peaceful methods to pursue its nefarious design of penetrating and dominating the Arab world. Some see dark menace in every Israeli attempt at communication and cooperation. The expansion of trade links means economic exploitation and subjugation; the development of cultural links means the subversion and destruction of Arab-Islamic culture; the quest for political relations is a prelude to imperial domination. These fantasies, absurd as they may seem to the outsider or indeed to any rational observer, nevertheless command wide support in the Arab media and particularly in Egypt.

For exponents of this view, European anti-Semitism provides a rich reservoir of themes and motifs, of literature and iconography, on which to draw and elaborate. Shimon Peres's book, *The New Middle East*,[9] with its somewhat idyllic view of future peaceful cooperation between Israel and the Arab states for economic improvement and cultural advancement, has appeared in several Arabic translations. The purpose of these translations is indicated in the blurb of one of them, published in Egypt:

> When the Protocols of the Elders of Zion were discovered about two hundred years ago [*sic*] by a Frenchwoman [*sic*] and disseminated in many languages including Arabic, the international Zionist establishment tried its best to deny the plan. They even claimed that it was fabricated and sought to acquire all the copies in the market in order to prevent them from being read. And now, it is precisely Shimon Peres who brings the decisive proof of their authenticity. His book confirms in so clear a way that it cannot be denied that the Protocols were true indeed. Peres's book is the last but one step in the execution of these dangerous designs.[10]

The "Protocols" remain a staple, not just of propaganda, but even of academic scholarship. Thus, according to an article in an Egyptian weekly,[11] the University of Alexandria accorded the degree of master of arts to the writer of an important "scientific treatise" dealing with the economic role of the Jews in Egypt in the first half of the twentieth century. The description of this dissertation makes it clear that its author relied very heavily on the "Protocols" and on the methodology of research that they provided.

A campaign attacking Israeli agricultural techniques and products—the one area in which there has been real cooperation with Egypt—accuses the Israelis of selling hormonally altered fruit that kills men's sperm. (They also supposedly supply Egyptian women with hyper-aphrodisiac chewing gum that drives them into a frenzy of sexual desire.) Other stories accuse the Israelis (or simply "the Jews") of supplying Egyptian farmers with poisoned seeds and disease-bearing poultry "like time bombs";[12] of deliberately spreading cancer among the Egyptians and other Arabs by devising and distributing carcinogenic cucumbers and shampoos; of promoting drug consumption and devil worship; and of organizing a campaign to legalize homosexuality to undermine Egyptian society. A Syrian paper even claims that Arafat made peace because he himself is a Jew.[13]

III. Islamic

The strongest, most principled, and most sustained opposition to the peace process is offered in the name of Islam, especially by the government of Iran and its agencies, and by other Islamic parties and organizations. Islamic opposition has the considerable advantage of being ideologically formulated and logically consistent and of using familiar language to appeal to deep-rooted sentiments. This gives to arguments based on Islam far greater cogency and power than those based on nationality and race. Nevertheless, spokesmen for Islamic movements do not disdain to use racist arguments, and specifically, to draw on the rich resources of hatred provided by European anti-Semitism. Standard anti-Semitic themes have become commonplace in the propaganda of Arab Islamic movements like Hizbullah and Hamas, in the pronouncements of various agencies of the Islamic Republic of Iran, and even in the newspapers and other publications of Refah, the Turkish Islamic party whose head served as prime minister in 1996–97.

Most of these accusations are familiar and can be traced to their European sources. Others arise from local circumstances. Thus, for Turkish anti-Semites, the misdeeds of the Jews include the downfall of the Ottoman Empire and the recent troubles in Bosnia. In Iran, American sanctions and the resulting economic hardships are ascribed to sinister Jewish influences in Washington.

Other accusations are clearly transference or projection; for example, Israelis are allegedly told by rabbis that if they die while killing Palestinians they will go straight to paradise. Some are traditional Islamic accusations against the Jews, based on well-known passages in the Qur'an and *hadith* (sayings and actions attributed to the Prophet Muhammad). Some are borrowed or adapted from the standard armory of European anti-Semitism. Increasingly, the second and third motifs are combined.

REWRITING HISTORY

These different kinds of propaganda all share the technique of rewriting or obliterating the past, and in particular removing anything that might arouse compassion or evoke respect for the Jew. Standard themes include recasting ancient history, Holocaust denial, and equating Jews with Nazis.

Ancient history. The rewriting makes Jews disappear from the ancient Middle East. The historical museum in Amman tells through objects and inscriptions the history of all the ancient peoples of the region—with one exception. The kings and prophets of ancient Israel are entirely missing. I was able to find only three references to Jews. The first explains (in English) the inscription on the Mesha Stele as "thanking the Moabite god Chemosh for deliverance from the Israelites." (The Arabic explanation reads, "from the tyranny of the Israelites.") The second appears in an alcove containing the Dead Sea scrolls produced by a "Jewish sect." The third is a reference to "the militant Hasmonean Jews [who] established their own reign in Palestine and the northern part of Jordan. Most of the Greek cities welcomed the Roman army headed by General Pompey as a liberator from Jewish oppression."

Textbooks used in schools under the Palestinian Authority lack even these few allusions to ancient Jewish history. For them, the history of Palestine begins with the retroactively

Arabized Canaanites and jumps from them to the Arab conquest in the seventh century C.E., entirely omitting the Old Testament, its people, and their history.

Holocaust denial. Either the Holocaust never happened,
or if it did, it was on a small scale and—some add—the
Jews brought it on themselves. Another favorite line is that the
Zionists were the collaborators and successors of the Nazis.
This remarkable version of history commands increasing Arab
support, as is evidenced by the reception accorded to Roger
Garaudy, a French ex-Communist convert to Islam who has
published a book entitled *The Founding Myths of Israeli Politics.*[14] These myths are three: the religious myth of the Chosen
People and the Promised Land; the Holocaust myth of Jewish
extermination and Zionist anti-fascism; and the new myth of
the modern Israeli miracle, actually due to foreign money pro-
cured by Jewish lobbyists. Garaudy's sources include apologists
for Hitler, post-Zionist Israeli revisionists, and European anti-
Americanists.

Garaudy's Middle East tour in the summer of 1996 was a triumph. In Lebanon he was received by the prime minister and
the minister of education, in Syria by the vice president and several other ministers. He gave a number of highly publicized lectures and interviews in both countries and was welcomed by
major literary and other intellectual bodies. In Jordan and Egypt
he was not officially received but was welcomed with the same
or greater acclaim in literary circles. The government-sponsored
Arab Artists Union elected him an honorary member—the first
since the Federation was established more than twenty years
ago. The editor-in-chief of Egypt's semi-official *Al-Ahram* newspaper conferred a press prize on Garaudy in recognition of the
"fresh air" that he had contributed to the debate. He was even
invited to contribute a series of ten articles to an Arabic weekly
published in London by the BBC's Arabic service.[15]

Garaudy's welcome, however, was not unanimous. Some

fundamentalists, while approving his views on Israel, questioned his understanding of Islam. In Morocco he was acclaimed by some newspapers, but his public appearances were canceled. "The universities," said the minister of higher education, "will not open their gates to anti-Semites."

Jews as Nazis. Denying or minimizing the Holocaust facilitates another favorite theme—that Jews, far from being victims of the Nazis, were their collaborators who now carry on their tradition. Cartoons depicting Israelis and other Jews with Nazi-style uniforms and swastikas have now become standard. These complement the Nazi-era hooked noses and blood-dripping jagged teeth. The memory of both the Jewish victims and Arab admirers of the Third Reich is totally effaced. To maintain this interpretation of history, some measure of control is necessary, extending even to entertainment. *Schindler's List,* a film portraying the suffering of the Jews under Nazi rule, is banned in Arab countries. Even *Independence Day,* which has nothing to do with either the Nazis or the Middle East, was denounced in Arab circles because it has a Jewish hero, and that is unacceptable. The film won approval for release in Lebanon only after the censors had removed all indications of the Jewishness of the hero—the skullcap, the Hebrew prayer, the momentary appearance of Israelis and Arabs working side by side in a desert outpost. A Hizbullah press liaison officer explained his objection to the film. "This film polishes and presents the Jews as a very humane people. You are releasing false images about them."[16]

While visits to Arab bookshops or to religious bookshops in Turkey reveal a wide range of anti-Semitic literature, any kind of corrective is lacking. The Arab reader seeking guidance on such topics as Jewish history, religion, thought, and literature will find virtually nothing available. Some material on modern Israel (e.g., that produced by the former Palestine Research Center in Beirut) is reasonably factual. But most of what is available is either lurid propaganda or used as such. Translations from Hebrew are few and fall mainly into three categories: accounts of Israeli espionage, memoirs by Israeli leaders (Rabin, Peres, Netanyahu) with explanatory introductions and annotations, and writings by anti-Zionist and anti-Israel Jews.

SIGNS OF IMPROVEMENT

The peace treaties negotiated and signed between governments will remain cold and formal, amounting to little more than a cessation of hostilities, until peace is made between peoples. As long as a high-pitched scream of rage and hate remains the normal form of communication, such a peace is unlikely to make much progress.

But there are some signs of improvement, of the beginnings of a dialogue. Statesmen, soldiers, and businessmen have been in touch with their Israeli opposite numbers, and some of these contacts have so far survived the change of government in Israel. Intellectuals have proved more recalcitrant, but even among them, there have been signs of change. A few courageous souls have braved the denunciation of their more obdurate colleagues to meet publicly with Israelis and even on rare occasions to visit Israel.

A number of Arab intellectuals have expressed disquiet and distaste with the vicious anti-Semitism that colors so much of the debate on the Arab-Israel conflict. The trial of Roger Garaudy in Paris in February 1998 for a violation of the Loi Gayssot, making Holocaust denial a criminal offense in France, evoked strong reactions in the Arab world. In general, there was an outpouring of vehement moral and substantial material support. But there were some dissenting voices. In the first of a number of articles condemning the cult of Garaudy, Hazim Saghiya drew attention to the contrast between Western and Arab criticisms of the trial in Paris. Western critics took their stand on freedom of expression, even for odious ideas. Arab critics, he observed, have in general shown little concern for freedom of expression; it was Garaudy's ideas that they liked.[17] Several other writers in the Arabic press expressed disapproval of the cult of Garaudy, and more generally, of Holocaust denial.

There were other hopeful signs. In January 1997 a group of Egyptians, Jordanians, and Palestinians, including intellectuals, lawyers, and businessmen, met with a similar group of Israelis in Copenhagen and agreed "to establish an international alliance for Arab-Israeli peace." Their declaration is not confined to pious generalities but goes into detailed discussion of some of the specific issues at stake. Needless to say, the Arab participants in this enterprise were denounced and reviled by many of their colleagues as dupes, traitors, or worse.

A recent incident evoked disquieting memories of the rampage of the Egyptian gendarme Sulayman Khatir in 1985 when he shot at Israeli visitors, killing several and disabling nine of them. It also provided an encouraging contrast. On March 13, 1997, a Jordanian soldier, Ahmad Daqamsa, suddenly started firing at an Israeli girls' school outing, killing seven children and wounding several more before being overpowered by his comrades. In a gesture of contrition and compassion, King Husayn of Jordan a few days later crossed into Israel and called in person to offer his condolences to the bereaved families. Reactions in Jordan were mixed. Some of his people joined the Israelis in acclaiming this act of courage, human decency, and generosity of spirit. Others, while condemning the murders, thought the king's response excessive. Others again made the murderer's home a place of pilgrimage. But there was nothing comparable with the outpouring of support that, for a while, made Sulayman Khatir a popular national and even intellectual hero in Egypt.

Closer contact between the two societies may bring interesting, perhaps even valuable results. Israel with all its faults is an open, democratic society. A million Arabs are Israeli citizens; two million Palestinians have lived or are living under Israeli rule. Although this rule has often been harsh and arbitrary, by the standards of the region it has on the whole been benevolent. Two contrasting incidents illustrate a direction of possible change. During the intifada, a young Arab boy had his wrist broken by a baton-wielding Israeli soldier. He appeared next day, bandaged and in a hospital, denouncing Israeli oppression—on Israeli television. In 1997 a lawyer in Gaza submitted an article to a Palestinian journal describing the investigation by the Israeli police of the prime minister and other members of the Israeli government, and suggesting that similar procedures might be adopted by the Palestinian Authority. The editor of the journal did not publish the article but instead referred it to the attorney general who ordered the arrest and imprisonment of its author.

Growing numbers of Arabs see—and some even make—this point. It did not pass unnoticed that the only public investigation of the Sabra and Shatila massacre was a judicial inquiry held in Israel. No such inquiry was held in any Arab country. The principal perpetrator of the massacre, Elie Hubayqa, a Lebanese Christian militia leader at that time allied with Israel, subsequently went over to the Syrian side and has for some years past been a respected member of the Syrian-sponsored government in Beirut. The election for the Palestinian Authority held in January 1996, acclaimed as the freest and fairest held in the Arab world, contrasted the more sharply with the show election held a little earlier in Lebanon in the presence of a different neighbor.

The Royal Institute for Interfaith Studies in Amman, under the patronage of Crown Prince Hasan, is concerned with Judaism as well as with Islam and Christianity. It has invited Jewish scholars from Israel and elsewhere to contribute to its activities and to its English-language journal.[18] This attempt to present Jewish beliefs and culture in objective terms, even to allow Jews to speak for themselves, is rare, and perhaps unique, in the Muslim world.

The last word may be left to 'Ali Salim, one of the first Egyptian intellectuals who dared to visit Israel. He said: "I found that the agreement between the Palestinians and the Israelis was a rare moment in history. A moment of mutual recognition. I exist and you also exist. Life is my right; it is also your right. This is a hard and long road. Its final stage is freedom and human rights. It will not be strewn with roses but beset with struggle and endurance. One cannot make peace just by talking about it. There is no way to go but forward, to achieve peace with deeds and not just words."[19]

NOTES

[1] *Ash-Sha'b,* Jan. 3, 1997; *Al-Watan* (Muscat), Feb. 12, 1997.

[2] *Al-Ittihad,* Dec. 20, 1996.

[3] *Jumhuri-i Islami,* Jan. 8, 1998.

[4] *La Presse de Tunisie,* Jan. 26, 1998.

[5] Ettela'at published the "Protocols" in 1995 in more than 150 installments.

[6] *Al-Musawwar,* Dec. 27, 1996.

[7] *Al-Majd,* July 31, 1995.

[8] *Shihan,* July 29, 1995.

[9] Shimon Peres with Arye Naor, *The New Middle East* (New York: Henry Holt, 1993).

[10] Muhamad Hilmi 'Abd al-Hafiz, trans., *Ash-Sharq al-Awsat al-Jadid* (Alexandria: n.p., 1995).

[11] *Akhir Sa'a,* Dec. 25, 1996.

[12] *Ash-Sha'b* (Cairo), Mar. 14, 1997.

[13] *Ath-Thawra,* Oct. 4, 1995.

[14] *Les mythes fondateurs de la politique israelienne* (Paris: Samizdat, 1996).

[15] *Al-Mushahid as-Siyasi,* May 4, 11, 18, 25; June 1, 8, 15, 22, 29; July 6, 1997.

[16] *Al-'Ahd,* Nov. 15, 1996.

[17] *Al-Hayat,* Jan. 15, 1998.

[18] *Interfaith Newsletter,* Mar.–Sept. 1995; *Interfaith Monthly,* Sept. 1995.

[19] 'Ali Salim, *Rihla ila Isra'il* (Cairo: Akhbar al-Yawm, 1994), p. 8.

An Exchange Between
BERNARD LEWIS and
ABDELALEEM EL-ABYAD

September 1998

Dear Editor:

Writing about what he calls "Muslim Anti-Semitism" [*The Middle East Quarterly*, June 1998], Professor Bernard Lewis engages, as too often, in selective scholarship. He approaches his subject in a total vacuum. Sporadic phenomena of so-called Arab or Muslim anti-Semitism is not related to any wrong-doing by Israel or its supporters, or to the universally acknowledged fact of Palestinian victimization by an ethnic and a religious group that has suffered greatly at the hands of Hitler and other European anti-Semites.

Professor Lewis's sweep of accusations is really too wide, perhaps on purpose in order to obfuscate. No one could deny the existence, though very limited, of verbal manifestation of anti-Semitism in the Muslim world. Such manifestations, however, should be unequivocally condemned. But how much of this is really anti-Semitism in the well-established sense of the word, and how much of it is an expansion of indignation and frustrations against an Israeli policy of occupation, ethnic cleansing (1948 and 1967), settlers' behavior, etc.? The list is really very long.

Professor Lewis could have asked himself if Palestinian, Arab, and Muslim reaction would have been different if the occupier was Great Britain, Russia, or America. The professor of Islamic studies has never told us how Jewish extremists in Israel or in the United States perceive the Palestinians, the Arabs, and Muslims. The favorite slogans of these extremists, as is well known, are: "Death to the Arabs" and "The only good Arab is a dead Arab."

Allow me, Professor, to ask how you would describe the Jewish advocates of "transfer," which is a euphemism for ethnic cleansing. And Professor, which is really more nefarious: crude verbal expression of bias toward the enemy, or a consistent policy of annexations and total violation of human rights in the occupied territories?

I don't think there is enough space to respond to every piece of disinformation in Professor Lewis's piece. But I will refer to two examples he has given because they reflect on the cast of his scholarship. Professor Lewis is very proud of the fact that after the massacre of Shatilla and Sabra in Lebanon, there was an inquiry in Israel to determine Mr. Ariel Sharon's responsibility, something the professor is telling us could not happen in any Arab country.

As we recall, the massacre—it is true—was carried out with extreme brutality by Lebanese Phalangists who were trained and reviewed by then General Sharon's troops before they were set loose to do their mayhem. Incidentally, Professor, in this unprovoked invasion of Lebanon, 20,000 hapless Lebanese and Palestinians were murdered by Israel.

Another example touted by Professor Lewis is the banning of *Schindler's List* in many Arab countries. Personally, I'm against the banning. But the banning of this film could also be viewed against the very effective censorship exercised by Jewish activists of any film or television documentary sympathetic to the plight of Palestinians. In the 1960s and 1970s, when I used to live in New York City, all Soviet-bloc artistic shows, including classical operas, were banned from the city. The Soviets were perceived as pro-Arab. Cultural boycott remains a constant feature among Jewish activists to this day. We have a saying in Arabic which roughly translated means: "If you have no sense of shame, then every thing is possible."

The Egypt you have vilified in this article is the same Egypt that had provided a sanctuary to Sephardic Jews escaping the Inquisition and Jewish settlers in Palestine sharing German and Turkish persecution during 1914, World War I, etc. The Egyptian-Jewish community was part of the socio-economic elite, well-respected and highly trusted until Zionists started to foment disloyalty to Egypt among its members. The rest is well known.

Finally, Islam need not be apologetic about how it has treated its Jews. I thought you knew.

> Abdelaleem El-Abyad
> Press and Information Bureau
> Embassy of the Arab Republic
> of Egypt, Washington

Bernard Lewis replies:

Mr. El-Abyad's reply to my discussion of the new anti-Semitic campaign in some Muslim countries makes essentially three points: (1) it didn't happen; (2) it was justified; (3) the Jews themselves are as bad or worse.

Mr. El-Abyad concedes the existence of manifestations of anti-Semitism in the Muslim world, but dismisses them as "very limited" and "verbal." My article drew on an extensive range of newspapers and magazines in several countries, and relied exclusively, not on verbal, but on written and printed sources, none of which he has questioned.

Mr. El-Abyad complains that I did not discuss the various Israeli policies and actions which provoked Arab hostility. Indeed I did not discuss them, for precisely the same reason that

I did not discuss the innumerable Arabic books, articles, and other statements condemning these policies and actions. Israel is a state, Zionism an ideology, and it is perfectly legitimate to criticize the actions of the one and the doctrines of the other, without incurring any charge of prejudice or bigotry. My article is not concerned with such criticisms, but with something else—the appearance of racist anti-Semitism of the European type, attacking not just Israel and Zionism, but Jews in general, and using anti-Semitic themes such as Holocaust denial, the "Protocols of the Elders of Zion" and the plot to rule the world, and the innate, genetic, and eternal evil of the Jews. If Mr. El-Abyad really believes in the carcinogenic cucumbers, the fake Holocaust, the genuine "Protocols," and the rest, then his attempt to justify the anti-Semitic campaign that I described becomes, if not acceptable, then at least intelligible. If he does not, it is neither.

Mr. El-Abyad invites comparison with other occupations and conflicts. There have indeed been many, in Eastern Europe, in South Asia, in Africa, resulting in massacre and displacement on a vastly greater scale than in the Middle East. None of them, as far as I am aware, has produced this kind of vicious racist campaign.

Mr. El-Abyad's third argument, that the Jews are as bad or worse, relies on undocumented statements attributed to unnamed "extremists." There are certainly Jews in both Israel and the United States who harbor and give vent to such racist prejudices. But to compare the slogans of an extremist fringe with a campaign in which mainstream editors, authors, officials, and academic and religious dignitaries participate is, surely, somewhat misleading. The same may be said of Mr. El-Abyad's comparison of boycotts by one or another private group with the formal banning of a film by governments.

Mr. El-Abyad must surely be aware that there is now, in Israel, a school of writers, known as the "new historians," who have made a great effort to present, to Israelis, the Palestinian point of view of the events of 1948–49 and later. An episode in a nationally-produced television series, commemorating the 50th anniversary of the establishment of the State of Israel, did the same. These are criticized by many, in Israel and elsewhere, as excessively sympathetic to the Palestinian point of view— but they are published and broadcast. One of the sadder aspects of this whole problem is that so far one has looked in vain for any objective—let alone sympathetic—presentation in Arabic of a Jewish point of view on any of these matters. As the case of *Schindler's List* demonstrates, even compassion for Jews is banned.

In concluding my article I quoted some new voices from the Arab side, pleading for mutual tolerance and understanding. I can only regret that Mr. El-Abyad did not choose to add his voice to theirs.

It would be pointless to discuss a number of other basically irrelevant matters that Mr. El-Abyad raises, such as the movements of refugees into—and one might add out of—Egypt, the treatment of *dhimmi*s, etc. I would however like to correct two errors of fact. According to Mr. El-Abyad, I was "very proud" of the Israeli inquiry into Sabra and Shatilla, and I claimed that this "could not happen in any Arab country." I said nothing of the kind, merely that "no such inquiry was held in any Arab country"—by no means the same thing. I was of course referring specifically to the two Arab countries immediately affected, Syria and Lebanon. I found, and still find, it remarkable that neither of them held any public inquiry into a matter of such direct concern to them. And there is nothing in this wretched affair to cause pride to me or indeed to anyone else.

The other inaccuracy which I would like to correct is minor and personal. I am not and have never been a "Professor of Islamic Studies," nor would I regard the use of such a title by a non-Muslim as appropriate.

Mr. El-Abyad is, of course, entitled to his opinion of my scholarship, as I am entitled to my opinion of his diplomacy, but no useful purpose would be served by our exchanging views in this context. I should, however, like to thank him for the courtesy and moderation of his language, compared with most of the texts which I studied for my article.

December 1998

To the Editor:

In response to Bernard Lewis's fine article, "Muslim Anti-Semitism" [*MEQ*, June 1998], Abdelaleem El-Abyad's letter [*MEQ*, September 1998] contains three enduring misconceptions regarding Lebanon that require a response because it comes from seemingly so authoritative a source.

Mr. El-Abyad alludes first to what he calls Israel's "unprovoked invasion of Lebanon" in 1982. The head of his embassy's press and information bureau seems oblivious to the armed and belligerent Palestinian presence in Lebanon since 1968 that provoked the Israeli action. Successive Lebanese governments had urged Palestinian organizations in Lebanon to restrain and modify their reckless and irresponsible strategies in confronting Israel; their refusal to comply led to Lebanon's breakdown in 1975, two Israeli invasions in 1978 and 1982, the establishment of Israel's "security zone" in South Lebanon, hundreds of thousands of dead, wounded, and displaced Lebanese citizens, countless billions of dollars in destruction and losses to the Lebanese economy, and the eventual takeover of the country by Syria.

Second, Israel is hardly alone in having fomented violence in Lebanon; Egypt too was among the many neighboring countries that had a role in this. For example, the Egyptian-sponsored 'Ayn Jalut brigade of the Palestinian Liberation Army (PLA) participated in several sectarian massacres in Lebanon, including the destruction of the coastal city of Damur in 1976, resulting in the cold-blooded murder of hundreds of innocent civilians.

Third, on the question of the 1982 massacre in the Palestinian refugee camps of Sabra and Shatilla, Mr. Lewis accurately notes that the Israeli authorities had undertaken several investigations; neither the Syrians nor Palestinians did anything comparable, either on this occasion or in the scores of other massacres and atrocities in Lebanon in which they had roles. Worse, the two individuals—Elie Hobeika and Pierre Rizk—who shared command of the Lebanese Forces (Phalangists) at the time of the Sabra and Shatilla massacre have flourished in Syrian-controlled Lebanon. Hobeika has been one of the most trusted people in Lebanon by Damascus since at least 1985 and an influential minister in the Syrian-controlled Lebanese government since 1990. Rizk, who long collaborated with the PLO [Palestinian Liberation Organization] leadership, is currently reaping millions of dollars as a business front for Yasir Arafat and his wife Suha. Where are the Syrian or Palestinian inquiries into their leaderships' close connections to these two?

These errors are symptomatic of a larger problem. In an exchange of correspondence I had in late 1996 with Ahmed Maher El-Sayed, Egypt's ambassador to Washington, His Excellency would not acknowledge that Syria is an occupying force in Lebanon nor that there is a need for all foreign forces to withdraw from the country.

Time and again, in other words, the Egyptian Embassy in Washington engages in distortions when it deals with the Lebanese situation.

> Daniel Nassif
> Executive Director
> American Lebanese Institute

Abdelaleem El-Abyad replies:

Daniel Nassif's comments are extraneous to the determination of guilt in the Sabra and Shatilla massacre or to the central arguments in my letter to the *Middle East Quarterly*. The world's court of public opinion, including that in the United States, long ago had passed its verdict on this matter, as anyone can verify by revisiting coverage by leading American newspapers of this great tragedy.

Mr. Nassif is fully entitled to his views about Egypt, although they are shared neither by successive Lebanese governments nor [by] the overwhelming majority of Lebanese people who rightly believe Egypt to be their steadfast friend and ally. The many bonds that tie our peoples are too numerous to count. Nothing ever will sour this relationship.

Abdelaleem El-Abyad
Press and Information Bureau
Embassy of the Arab Republic of Egypt
Washington

TARIQ RAMADAN

Interreligious Dialogue

Excerpt from *Western Muslims and the Future of Islam*

[*This excerpt, a chapter called "Interreligious Dialogue," is distinctive for arguing, contrary to some interpretations of the Qur'an, that the Qur'an does not mandate conflict between Jews and Christians. Ramadan, a controversial and influential Muslim scholar, made careful footnoted references to the Qur'an.*]

THERE IS A very long tradition of interreligious dialogue. At various times in history, in very diverse contexts, people of various religions have engaged in interreligious exchanges to try to understand one another better; they have succeeded in gaining one another's respect and have managed not only to live but also to work together on shared endeavors. Today, we feel the need to engage even more in this process: Western societies' religious pluralism makes mutual knowledge essential. At the same time, technical developments have changed our view of the world, and daily images of societies and customs different from our own arouse our curiosity. More dramatically, acts of violence perpetrated in the name of religion challenge our awareness: how can such horror be justified in the name of religion? How can we understand it? How can we prevent it?

Many groups of specialists have been formed in recent years. At colloquia, conferences, and seminars, they meet to try to build bridges, discuss sensitive subjects, and prevent conflicts. With time, these specialists in dialogue have come to know one another and to enjoy excellent relationships founded on courtesy and respect. This is an important gain. Nevertheless, the problem remains that these are fairly closed circles whose members are not always in real contact with their own religious groups, and this makes it difficult to convey to the heart of each religious community the advances made in these numerous meetings. Moreover, whole sections of these communities are neither concerned with nor touched by the various dialogues that are taking place. Those who meet do not represent the various denominations, schools of thought, or tendencies of the adherents of their religion. Those who hold the most closed opinions, which in daily life are the cause of the real problem, never meet. Thus, we have, on both the national and international levels, a very uneven picture: dialogue is well under way between specialists from each religion who are more or less open-minded, while ordinary believers meet only rarely[1] and the most entrenched and radical views are never voiced. Common sense and logic would encourage us to hope for the opposite: the specialists do not, or no longer, really need dialogue, and it is within religious communities and between those with the most radical views that the debate should take place. It is a vicious circle: it is precisely because people do not know one another, or reject one another, that dialogue is impossible.

The responsibility of people involved in dialogue between religions is in fact doubly important: whether they have become specialists or are simply members of an interreligious group, it is vital that they play the role of mediators between their partners in dialogue and their coreligionists. It is a question of listening to the other side, challenging it and questioning it in order to increase understanding and then of getting involved in working within one's own community, informing, explaining, even teaching. At the same time, participants in dialogue should express their own convictions, clarify the place of their own sense of religion among other views held within their religious family, and respond as well as they can to the questions of their partners in dialogue. By acting in this way they create, between the various traditions, areas of trust, sustained by shared convictions and values that, even though they certainly do not bring the extremes together, do open real horizons for living together and at least allow ruptures to be avoided and conflicts better managed.

The need for interreligious dialogue is not in any doubt, but some people still do not understand its real usefulness and purpose. What exactly is it about? Does one want to convert the other? Can one get involved with a clear conscience? What is the real impact of these fine words about respect and living together when we look at how believers from each religion behave? Is there not a place for being doubtful or suspicious about the intentions of one or other side if we take the time to read the scriptural sources? These questions cannot simply be swept under the carpet. They are of primary importance, because, unless they are clearly and succinctly answered, we run the risk of having an outwardly agreeable dialogue that does not eliminate the mistrust and suspicion and that in the end leads nowhere. Let us try, from within the Muslim tradition, to suggest possible answers to these questions, beginning with the last.

THE ISLAMIC TRADITION AND
INTERRELIGIOUS DIALOGUE

We recall . . . that, according to Muslims, the last Revelation taught them to recognize all the books of the prophets who had gone before. They all had the same purpose: to remind human beings of the presence of the Creator and the finiteness of life on earth. The Islamic tradition's concept of humankind emerged through this teaching: after forgiving Adam his sin, God told men: "A guidance will certainly come to you from me. Those who follow my guidance will have nothing to fear and will not grieve."[2] This guidance is the series of Revelations that came throughout human history, each to confirm, complete, and correct the preceding.

NECESSARY DIVERSITY

So individuals, innocent and free, have to make their choices (either to accept or to reject the Revelation); there will necessarily be diversity among people, and so these three seemingly similar verses contain teachings that augment and complete each other: "Had God so willed, He would have united them [human beings] in guidance, so do not be among the ignorant"[3]; "If your Lord had so willed, everyone on earth would have believed. Is it for you to compel people to be believers?"[4]; "If God had willed, He would have made you one community but things are as they are to test you in what He has given you. So compete with each other in doing good."[5] The first verse instructs us that diversity is willed by the Transcendent, the second makes clear that, in the name of that will, compulsion in matters of religion is forbidden,[6] and the Revelation teaches that the purpose of these differences is to *test* us in order to discover what we are going to do with what has been revealed to us: the last commandment is to use these differences to "compete in doing good." Diversity of religions, nations, and peoples is a test because it requires that we learn to manage difference, which is in itself essential: "If God did not enable some men to keep back others, the world would be corrupt. But God is the One who gives grace to the worlds";[7] "If God did not enable some men to keep back others, hermitages, synagogues, chapels and mosques where the name of God is often called upon, would have been demolished."[8] These two verses give complementary information that is of prime importance: if there were no differences between people, if power were in the hands of one group alone (one nation, one race, or one religion), the earth would be corrupt because human beings need others to limit their impulsive desire for expansion and domination. The last verse is more precise with regard to our present discussion; it refers to places of worship to indicate that if there is to be a diversity of religions, the purpose is to safeguard them all: the fact that the list of places begins with hermitages, synagogues, and chapels before referring to mosques shows recognition of all these places of worship and their inviolability and, of course, respect for those who pray there. So, just as diversity is the source of our test, the balance of power is a requirement for our destiny.

Difference might naturally lead to conflict; therefore, the responsibility of humankind is to make use of difference by establishing a relationship based on excelling one another in doing good. It is vital that the balance of power be based not on a tension born of rejection or mutual ignorance but fundamentally on knowledge: "O people, we have created you from a male and a female, we have divided you into nations and tribes so that you might know one another."[9] Knowing the other is a process that is unavoidable if fear of difference is to be overcome and mutual respect is to be attained. So human beings live a test that is necessary for their nature but that they can—and must—master by making the effort to know and recognize those who are not of their tribe, their country, their race, or their religion.[10] Dialogue, particularly interreligious dialogue, is indispensable.

GENERAL PRINCIPLES OF DIALOGUE

All believers who participate in interreligious dialogue do so having been nourished by a faith or a conviction on the basis of which they understand themselves, perceive the world, and build relations with those around them. Their connection with Truth, with the beliefs of others, and with diversity in general is directly influenced by the content and nature of that faith or conviction. The centrality of *tawhid* in the message of Islam has been strongly emphasized. It is the principle on which the whole of Islamic teaching rests and is the axis and point of reference on which Muslims rely in dialogue. The intimate awareness of *tawhid* forms the perception of the believer, who understands that plurality has been chosen by the One, that He is the God of all beings and that He requires that each be respected: ". . . and say: 'We believe in what has been revealed to us and what has been revealed to you; our God and your God is the One.'"[11] It is out of this conviction that Muslims engage in dialogue, and this is assumed in forming relations with the other. What establishes difference from the other, and consequently the direction and terms of the dialogue that is to be built, is whether or not there is commitment to the expression of an absolute monotheism.[12] This is why the Qur'anic call to the Jews and Christians begins with: "O people of the book, come to agreed terms between us and you: that we worship none but God, that we do not attribute any associate to Him and that none of us takes other divinities apart from Him. If they turn away, say: 'Be witnesses that we are submitting ourselves [*muslimun*].'"[13] Firmly asserting this principle indicates that *tawhid* is the point of reference on the basis of which a Muslim engages in discussion: if there are differences on this central point, it is then necessary that dialogue be entered into and developed on the basis of shared values and teachings, since the last Revelation recognizes those that came before:[14] "God, there is no god but God. It is He who sent down the Book [the Qur'an] upon you [Muhammad] in all truth confirming what came before. And He sent down the Torah and the Gospel before as a guidance for people, and He sent down the Discernment [*al-furqan*] the Qur'an."[15] This recognition is fundamental and opens up the way for dialogue, which, although it forces us to see our differences, is bound to establish bridges between convictions and traditions.

The Qur'an not only issues a call to dialogue but is also insistent about the form it should take and the way in which it should be conducted. It should not simply be an exchange of information; it should also be a way of being and of speaking, an attitude: "And discuss with them in the best way,"[16] and again: "Do not discuss with the people of the Book except in the best of ways, apart from those who are unjust among themselves."[17] In this last verse, the restriction is not at all upon dialogue as such, but as it pertains to the repressive attitude some Jews and Christians adopted toward the Muslim community, which was at that time facing serious adversity. This contextualized approach is what gives meaning to the often quoted verse "You will certainly see that those most hardened in hostility toward the Muslims are the Jews and the polytheists and you will certainly see that those closest to you in affection are those who say: 'We are Christians,' because there are among them priests and monks who are not swollen with pride."[18] Here again, it is the attitude of people and potential partners in dialogue that is at issue, and not dialogue in itself. To those who choose to understand this contextualized teaching (warning us to be concerned about injustice, adversity, and the pride of human beings) as an absolute prohibition on dialogue, the Revelation replies clearly: "God does not forbid you from establishing relations of generosity and just behavior with those who have not fought against you over your religion and who have not evicted you from your dwellings. God loves those who act fairly."[19] This verse goes even further than all the others: if dialogue is necessary and if the way of speaking about oneself is important, we are here clearly called to establish relations of generosity and justice with all who respect our freedom of conscience and our human dignity. Dialogue is an act of conviction, of listening, of self-awareness, of self-knowledge, and of the heart: together, these qualities constitute wisdom.

VERSES INTERPRETED VARIOUSLY

When we speak of interreligious dialogue, it would not be honest to refer only to the verses we have quoted without mentioning a series of other passages in the Qur'an that can be equivocal and that are moreover variously interpreted by Muslim scholars. Some of the ulama of the literalist traditions read them restrictively, which basically does not leave any real room for discussion. A sincere involvement in dialogue must stop to consider these verses. Thus, one finds in the Qur'an verses that define Jews and Christians, even though they are among the "people of the Book," as *kuffar* (plural of *kafir*), most often translated as "infidels" or "miscreants": "They are certainly *in a state of denial*[20] [*kafara*], those who have said that God was the Messiah the son of Mary"[21] or again, "Those among the people of the Book and the polytheists who *have denied* [*kafaru*]."[22] According to the perspective of the majority of literalist scholars, this leaves no doubt as to their fate, especially since the Qur'an says explicitly: "Religion in the sight of God is Islam"[23] and again: "He who desires religion other than Islam will not find himself accepted and in the hereafter he will be among the losers."[24] Other verses seem to tell us that we should not trust Jews and Christians ("And the Jews and Christians will not be pleased with you unless you follow their religion")[25] or take them as allies except in extreme circumstances: "Let the believers [Muslims] not take as allies the deniers [*kafirin*] rather than believers; those who do so will receive no help from God, unless you feel yourselves to be in danger from them."[26] Such an avalanche of verses has the effect of causing perplexity and raises questions about whether any real place for dialogue remains, the more so since these same scholars clearly explain that they do not believe there is any virtue in discussion unless the intention is to convince the other party of the strength and truth of our arguments. Interreligious dialogue would then become a call to our truth, a *dawa* (call, invitation, preaching), with no meaning beyond that.

Here we are at the heart of the problem of the types of "reading" where the various schools of thought were described.

The advantage of the literalist reading over all the others is that it stops at the primary meaning of the text that, as soon as it is quoted, seems to make immediate sense and gives weight to the argument. No trouble is taken to work out a reading based on critical distance, contextualized interpretation, or determination of the meaning of a verse in light of the message as a whole. As a literalist, what I read is what was said, and God speaks through me as long as my quotations are from His word. It is nevertheless advisable to take each of the verses mentioned earlier and to try to discover whether the literalist reading is the only appropriate one.

It must be said, to begin with, that the Arabic notion of *kufr* or *kafir* has often been mistranslated, quite apart from the fact that many Muslims in the West use it as a definite insult. But the word has a neutral sense in the Islamic sciences, and it is clearly perceived at various levels. Without going into technical details here, we may say that, according to the root, the general meaning of *kafir* could be rendered as "a denier with a veiled heart": this refers to those whose original longing for the Transcendent[27] has been stifled, veiled, shut off in their hearts to the extent that they deny the presence of the Creator. But *kafir* may also indicate one who denies the evidence of the truth, like the satanic figure of Iblis in the Qur'an, who *knows* that God is, since he speaks to Him, but refuses to obey: "He [Iblis] refused, became proud and was among the deniers [*min al-kafirin*]."[28] To this must be added various kinds of negation, *kufr*, which are determined according to what is denied: God, the truth of the message, one of the pillars of faith, the nature of a particular commandment, and so on. So to apply the term *kafir* to Jews and Christians in a neutral sense is justified in that, in a quite natural way, they do not recognize the Qur'an as the last revealed book. They deny [*yakfuru*] the truth of the message and its Prophet, but this does not mean we may call them "miscreants" in the sense that their faith in God is not recognized, which would be an inaccurate assertion: this would be as senseless as to say that Iblis, who had a dialogue with the Most High, did not *believe* in Him and was a *miscreant*. This is neither logical understanding nor a consistent translation. We must add that it is never legitimate to use the word as an insult.

The verse indicating that the religion in the sight of God is Islam has caused a lot of ink to flow. Here again we are dealing with a question of interpretation. We know that in the Qur'an the word *islam* has two meanings. The first is universal and generic: all the elements are in "submission" to God because they respect the order of creation; in the same sense, all the revelations and prophets came with a message of the oneness of God and the need to "submit oneself" to Him. Thus, Abraham, well before the revelation of the Qur'an, is commanded by God: "And when his Lord said to him: 'Submit [*aslim*]!' he replied: 'I submit [*aslamtu*] to the Lord of the worlds.'"[29] The words *aslim* and *aslamtu* come from *islam* in the sense of recognition of the one God and acceptance of the obedience due to Him. The second meaning of the word *islam* is the religion whose text is the Qur'an and whose prophet is Muhammad. Literalist scholars have interpreted these verses giving the word the restricted meaning of the second definition, while the generic definition makes better sense of the Islamic message as a whole, which, apart from being the final revelation, identifies natural religion, one and unique throughout history, as the recognition of the existence of a Creator and conformance to His messages. This is also confirmed by the verse "Certainly those who have believed, the Jews, the Christians, and the Sabaeans, all those who have believed in God and in the last day of judgment and who have done good—they will have their reward from God. They will not be afraid and they will not grieve."[30] The generic meaning is clear here, and those scholars who have claimed that this verse has been abrogated [*mansukh*][31] pay no regard to the rule of abrogation, which specifies that only verses stipulating obligations or prohibitions (which may change in the course of revelation) can be abrogated but not information, which cannot be true one day and untrue the next. This verse is clearly giving information.[32]

The verse "The Jews and the Christians will not be pleased with you unless you follow their religion [*milla*]" is quoted at will in times of trouble or simply when people want to justify mistrusting some Jews or Christians. The verse is heard from mosque pulpits, in conferences, and at seminars, with the implication that it explains the attitude of Jews and Christians toward Muslims: their rejection of Islam, their double dealing, not to say deceitfulness, and colonization, proselytism, wars, Bosnia, Palestine, and so on. But that is not what the verse says: the phrase "will not be pleased with you" [*lan tarda anka*] translates here the idea of full and absolute satisfaction, expressed with the heart as well as the mind. For Jews and Christians convinced, like a Muslim, of the truth of their own message, complete satisfaction with the other is attained when the experience of faith and truth is shared. One has the feeling of living and sharing this essential element that gives meaning and light to one's life. This does not imply that in the absence of this full satisfaction one can live in and express only rejection, mistrust, and conflict. One can feel and manifest deep and sincere respect toward a human being with whom one does not share this full spiritual communion. It is a matter of being sincere and of recognizing the states of our souls and hearts. It is within our communities of faith that we live most deeply the fullness of the meaning of (*rida*) with the other who shares our truth, even if it is possible (though it is the exception rather than the rule) that we might experience a unique spiritual relationship with a woman or a man from another tradition. The Qur'an here is speaking only of the intimate and very natural inclination of people of faith toward one another.[33] At a deeper level, believers must be conscious that ultimately what they must seek before all else is to please God [*rida Allah*], not other people. It is good for believers to remember that the full satisfaction shared with their coreligionists is still only a stage along the way. Seeking the pleasure of God is a demanding path punctuated by testing stations, but this initiation is ultimately the only way that it is possible to become, in humility, fully content with oneself.

With regard to the verse referring to the seemingly impossible alliance with Jews and Christians, we have already referred to it. From the context of the verse, and others like it, we derive that Muslims are commanded in situations of potential conflict not to take deniers as allies against Muslims [*min dun al-muminin*],[34] that is to say, to make an alliance unjustly or treacherously in opposition to their spiritual community. It does not apply absolutely, and the following verse specifies clearly those with whom relations are banned: "God forbids you to turn in friendship toward [or take as allies] only such as fight against you because of your faith, and drive you forth from your homelands, or aid [others] in driving you forth: and as for those [from among you] who turn toward them in friendship [or alliance], it is they, they who are truly wrongdoers!"[35]

Here a word is needed on that concept of *dawa,* often translated as "preaching," "call," or "invitation to Islam" and which has thus come to express the missionary character of Islam. It cannot be denied that some Muslims, on the basis of a certain number of verses, are engaged in straightforward missionary activity, and in their minds dialogue is only a form of mission. To deny this would be dishonest. One must then look at how the Qur'an presents the act of "inviting" or "calling" to Islam. The verse that follows is well known: "Call [invite] to the path of your Lord using wisdom and good exhortation, and debate with them in the best of manner."[36] If we meditate on this verse, we understand that emphasis is put first on the

Muslim who "invites." He has to have acquired a certain wisdom, know to speak well, and have mastered the best way of expressing things: three injunctions bring together the requirements related to being a good speaker, the content of the message, and the way in which it must be delivered. In other words, to "invite" is first to "bear witness," as much by one's behavior as by the content and form of what one says, what the message of Islam is. It is not a matter of wanting to convert, because people's hearts are God's domain and secret. It is a matter of bearing witness, which is an invitation to remember and meditate. This meaning also is captured by another verse: "And thus have We willed you to be a community of the middle way, so that [with your lives] you might bear witness to the truth before mankind." [37] Interreligious dialogue should be a meeting of "witnesses" who are seeking to live their faiths, to share their convictions, and to engage with one another for a more humane, more just world, closer to what God expects of humanity.

At the end of this section, we note that the verses mentioned earlier are indeed variously interpreted. All religious traditions experience these differences, and, depending on the type of reading that is accepted, one may be open to dialogue or absolutely opposed to it. The nature of these difficulties has to be taken into account in order to avoid any illusions about the possible results of our meetings.

TOWARD EXACTING AND CONSTRUCTIVE DIALOGUE

The dialogue we engage in must be anything but complaisant. The lack of trust that permeates our Western societies and the situations of religious conflict throughout the world mean that our task must be far-reaching, exacting, and rigorous. First of all, dialogue must be based on mutual knowledge achieved by our seeking to make clear our shared convictions, values, and hopes, while clearly defining and circumscribing our specificities, our differences, and what may even be our disagreements.

This is what is done in most interreligious groups, and I believe it is necessary to move in this direction. But this will not be enough: we have already said that the majority of women and men engaged in this kind of meetings are rather open and ready for the encounter. It is crucial that they describe and explain what they really represent in their religious families—what trend, the extent of it, their relations with the community as a whole, and so forth. It is important to know to whom one is speaking; it is no less essential to know to whom one is not speaking, and why. Interreligious dialogue should make it possible for each partner better to understand the various theories, the points shared, the differences and conflicts that are present in other traditions. It is a matter first of not deluding oneself that the other "represents," for example, the *whole* of Hinduism, the *whole* of Buddhism, the *whole* of Judaism, the *whole* of Christianity, or the *whole* of Islam, and second of knowing what links and types of relations our partners have with their coreligionists.

To be involved in dialogue between religions while being completely cut off from the believers of one's own religion is problematic and can be illusory. Many "specialists" in interreligious dialogue, who go from conference to conference, are totally disconnected from their religious community, as well as from grass-roots realities. This might be conceivable if it were a matter of purely theological discussions, but in most cases, unfortunately, that is not the case.[38] How is it possible to have a real understanding of religious traditions and the dynamics that permeate them on the ground if those who dialogue are not actively involved in their communities? Again, how can one hope to influence believers more widely if the specialists' circle is isolated in an ivory tower and does not report back on the nature of its work to each of the respective religious communities?

So, two fundamental conditions for dialogue with the other

emerge: first, to commit oneself, as far as possible, to giving an account of the shared work to one's own faith community and second, in order to achieve that, to devote part of one's energy to opening up intracommunal dialogue, which will make possible the advancement of real pluralism. This dialogue is extremely difficult, sometimes much more difficult than interreligious dialogue itself, because discussion with one's nearest and dearest is so risky. This commitment is nevertheless essential if we want to break down internal ghettoes and sectarianism and try, within manageable limits, to respect one another more. It can never be said enough that intracommunal dialogue between Muslims is virtually nonexistent. Groups know one another, know how to identify one another and work out where they are in relation to one another, but then they immediately ignore one another, exclude one another, or insult one another, without any attempt at discussion. Within one religious understanding, one current of thought, divisions are maintained by intervening organizations. The culture of dialogue has practically abandoned Muslim communities and the respect for diversity, which always has been and should have continued to be their source of richness, has been replaced by dueling disagreements that contribute to maintaining the division, which causes their weakness. Some still tentative initiatives have taken off, but the movement must become more general and must naturally go alongside involvement in dialogue with other traditions.

Apart from getting to know one another, it is also necessary to establish relationships of trust and respect. Trust is lacking today: we meet often, listen sometimes, and distrust each other often. Trust needs time and support. The frequency and quality of meetings and the nature of the exchanges certainly help to create spaces for sincere encounter. However, it seems to me that four rules should be applied which may be quite demanding as preliminaries, but which are fundamentally constructive:

1. Recognition of the legitimacy of each other's convictions and respect for them;

2. Listening to what people say about their own scriptural sources and not what we understand (or want to understand) from them;

3. The right, in the name of trust and respect, to ask all possible questions, sometimes even the most embarrassing;

4. The practice of self-criticism, which consists in knowing how to discern the difference between what the texts say and what our coreligionists make of them, and deciding clearly what our personal position is.

These rules are essential. One cannot enter into dialogue if one does not recognize the legitimacy of other people's convictions. Not to share them is one thing, but not to recognize, deep in one's heart, their right to be is another. Nor is it fitting to try to become an exegete of one's partner's scriptures. This is not our role or our area of expertise. It is for our partners to tell us what they understand or what their coreligionists understand, from such and such a text. Reading the Torah or the Bible for a Muslim, the Qur'an for a Jew or a Christian, or the Bhagavad Gita for all three is certainly useful and necessary in order to try to understand others' convictions, but these readings should inspire meditation and questions, not a simplistic accusation. We must also give ourselves the right to dare to ask all the questions that occur to us. The answers may or may not be satisfying, they may or may not suit us, but they will have been clearly stated. Trust can be born only from this frankness and clarity: in the meantime, without the latter, courtesy is but artificial or even a masquerade. At a deeper level, these are all questions that help people to go further in understanding their own traditions. Looking for a way to give a deep explanation means making the effort to understand better. The relevance of the question to my partner in dialogue is a gift, an intellectual and spiritual tonic, because I learn to express better what I believe and so to understand more deeply the meaning of what I am. Finally, dialogue involves clarity and courage: our scriptural sources have sometimes been used, or have legitimized (and still legitimize) discourses, behavior, and actions toward others about which we need to make clear statements. This is not always easy, but it is nevertheless vital, and all the religious traditions should be involved in this self-criticism. Some see it as a kind of disloyalty toward their own community; it should instead be a matter of self-respect and dignity before God and each person's conscience.

SHARED INVOLVEMENT

Dialogue is not enough. Even if it is rigorous, even if it is necessary to give time to knowing, trusting, and respecting each other, even if we should take on ourselves the widest possible responsibility to report back, it is only one stage or one aspect of the encounter among the various religious traditions. In Western societies, it is urgent that we commit ourselves to joint action.

In dialogue, we soon realize that we hold a great number of convictions and values in common. We understand very quickly that we are facing the same difficulties and challenges. But we very rarely move outside these circles of reflection. Together we say "God," awareness, spirituality, responsibility, ethics, solidarity, but we live and experience, each one on one's own, the problems of education, transmission of spirituality, individualism, consumerism, and moral bankruptcy. In philosophical terms, we could say that we know one another in words but not *in action*. Our experience of fifteen years of joint action in South America, Africa, and Asia has convinced us not only that this path is necessary but that it is the only way to eventually change minds and build mutual respect and trust.

In the West, there are many shared challenges, first among them being education. How can we pass on to our children the sense of the divine, for the monotheistic faiths, or of spiritual practice for Buddhism, for example? In a society that pushes people to own, how are we to form individuals whose awareness of being illumines and guides their mastery of possession? Again, how are we to explain morality and boundaries, to pass on principles of life that do not confuse liberty with carelessness and that consider neither fashion nor quantity of possessions as the measure of goodness? All the religious and spiritual traditions are experiencing these difficulties, but we still see few examples of shared commitment to proposing alternatives. And there is so much to do—working together, as parents and as citizens, so that schools will provide more and more courses on the religions; suggesting ways of providing educational modules outside the school structures to teach the general population about the religions—their fundamental beliefs, particular topics, and social realities. Such modules need to be thought out together, not only by inviting a partner from the other religion to come to give a course as part of a program we have put together for and by ourselves. By way of example, the Inter-religious Platform in Geneva has launched an interesting "school of religions," and there is the Center for Muslim-Christian Studies, in Copenhagen, which, under the leadership of Lissi Rasmussen, is scored a first in Europe in establishing a real partnership within an institution promoting and practicing dialogue.

Acts of solidarity take place from within each religious family, but the examples of shared initiatives are rare. People sometimes invite others, but do not act in collaboration. One of the best testimonies that a religious or spiritual tradition can give of itself lies in acts of solidarity between its adherents and others. To defend the dignity of the latter, to fight so that our societies do not produce indignity, to work together to support marginalized and neglected people, will certainly help us know one another better but it will, above all, make known the essential message that shines at the heart of our traditions: never neglect your brother in humanity and learn to love him, or at least to serve him.

More broadly, we have to act together so that the body of values that forms the basis of our ethics is not relegated to such a private and secluded sphere that it becomes inoperative and socially dead. Our philosophies of life must continue to inspire our civil commitment, with all due respect to the supporters of a postmodernism whose aim seems to be to deny any legitimacy to all reference to a universal ethic. We need to find together a civil role, inspired by our convictions, in which we will work to demand that the rights of all be respected, that discriminations be outlawed, that dignity be protected, and that economic efficiency cease to be the measure of what is right. Differentiating between public and private space does not mean that women and men of faith, or women and men of conscience, have to shrink to the point of disappearance and fear to express themselves publicly in the name of what they believe. When a society has gone so far as to disqualify, in public debate, faith and what it inspires, the odds are that its system is founded only on materialism and ruled only by materialist logic—the self-centered accumulation of goods and profit.

We must dare to express our faith, its demands, and its ethics, to involve ourselves as citizens in order to make known our human concerns, our care for justice and dignity, our moral standards, our fears as consumers and televiewers, our hopes as mothers and fathers—to commit ourselves to do the best possible, together, to reform what might be. All our religious traditions have a social message that invites us to work together on a practical level. We are still far from this. In spite of thousands of dialogue circles and meetings, we still seem to know one another very little and to be very lacking in trust. Perhaps we must reconsider our methods and formulate a mutual demand: to behave in such a way that our actions, as much as possible, mirror our words, and then to act together.

NOTES

[1] Although it must be pointed out that more and more dialogue initiatives are aimed at the local level and in the United States and Europe unite believers from various religions.

[2] Qur'an 2:38.

[3] Qur'an 6:35.

[4] Qur'an 10:99.

[5] Qur'an 5:48.

[6] The Qur'an confirms this in a clear general rule: "No compulsion in religion" (2:256).

[7] Qur'an 2:251.

[8] Qur'an 22:40.

[9] Qur'an 49:13.

[10] Read and understood globally, these Qur'anic references bring together all the dimensions of "difference" among human beings: tribe, nation, race, religion.

[11] Qur'an 29:46.

[12] It does not mean that it would be impossible to dialog with pantheistic spirituality or Buddhism, but its ground and its focus would naturally be more essentially directed toward common moral values, ethical commitment.

[13] Qur'an 3:64.

[14] In the mind of Muslims, the Qur'an confirms, completes, and corrects the messages that came before it, and in this Muslims hold the same position that Christians hold toward the Jews. It is a position that is in itself perfectly coherent: to believe in a Book that comes later necessarily assumes that one considers that there is a deficiency or distortion in the former.

[15] Qur'an 3:2–3.

[16] Qur'an 16:125.

[17] Qur'an 29:46.

[18] Qur'an 5:82.

[19] Qur'an 60:8.

[20] Whether one translates this as "they are miscreants who . . ." or "they are infidels who . . ." depends on the sense one gives to *kafara*. We shall return to this.

[21] Qur'an 5:17.

[22] Qur'an 98:1. We find the same senses here: "who have done wickedly" or "who are infidels."

[23] Qur'an 3:19.

[24] Qur'an 3:85.

[25] Qur'an 2:120.

[26] Qur'an 3:28.

[27] See part I [of the whole book].

[28] Qur'an 2:34.

[29] Qur'an 2:131.

[30] Qur'an 2:62.

[31] On the strength of an opinion attributed to Ibn Abbas reported in al-Tabari's commentary (*tafsir*). It was said to be abrogated by 3:85, already referred to.

[32] After the revelation of the last message, those who had knowledge beforehand would be judged according to their sincerity in the search for truth. Only God is the judge of this, and no human being can declare another's destiny, or his own.

[33] The concept of "milla" used in this verse to express the idea of religion conveys the idea of "people's community of faith," a sense of belonging, much more than the word "din," which is "religion" or "concept and way of life" per se.

[34] In Qur'anic usage, the word *mumin* (bearer of faith) usually means *Muslim*.

[35] Qur'an 60:9.

[36] Qur'an 16:125.

[37] Qur'an 2:143.

[38] As I see it, interreligious debate cannot take place by way of a debate on theological questions. We often witness a choice between extremes; either the discussion is completely theological, or the theological aspect is totally ignored and people behave as if the cause of the problem were understood. Both approaches are, in my view, defective and illusory.

AMOS OZ
Two Middle East Wars

TWO PALESTINIAN-ISRAELI WARS have erupted in this region. One is the Palestinian nation's war for its freedom from occupation and for its right to independent statehood. Any decent person ought to support this cause. The second war is waged by fanatical Islam, from Iran to Gaza and from Lebanon to Ramallah, to destroy Israel and drive the Jews out of their land. Any decent person ought to abhor this cause.

Yasir Arafat and his men are running both wars simultaneously, pretending they are one. The suicide killers evidently make no distinction. Much of the worldwide bafflement about the Middle East, much of the confusion among the Israelis themselves, stems from the overlap between these two wars. Decent peace seekers, in Israel and elsewhere, are often drawn into simplistic positions. They either defend Israel's continued occupation of the West Bank and Gaza by claiming that Israel has been targeted by Muslim holy war ever since its foundation in 1948, or else they vilify Israel on the grounds that nothing but the occupation prevents a just and lasting peace. One simplistic argument allows Palestinians to kill all Israelis on the basis of their natural right to resist occupation. An equally simplistic counterargument allows Israelis to oppress all Palestinians because an all-out Islamic jihad has been launched against them.

Two wars are being fought in this region. One is a just war, and the other is both unjust and futile.

Israel must step down from the war on the Palestinian territories. It must begin to end occupation and evacuate the Jewish settlements that were deliberately thrust into the depths of Palestinian lands. Its borders must be drawn, unilaterally if need be, upon the logic of demography and the moral imperative to withdraw from governing a hostile population.

But would an end to occupation terminate the Muslim holy war against Israel? This is hard to predict. If jihad comes to an end, both sides would be able to sit down and negotiate peace. If it does not, we would have to seal and fortify Israel's logical border, the demographic border, and keep fighting for our lives against fanatical Islam.

If, despite simplistic visions, the end of occupation will not result in peace, at least we will have one war to fight rather than two. Not a war for our full occupancy of the holy land, but a war for our right to live in a free and sovereign Jewish state in part of that land. A just war, a no-alternative war. A war we will win. Like any people who were ever forced to fight for their very homes and freedom and lives.

AFTERWORD

CYNTHIA OZICK

The Modern *Hep! Hep! Hep!*

WE THOUGHT IT WAS finished. The ovens are long cooled, the anti-vermin gas dissipated into purifying clouds, cleansed air, nightmarish fable. The cries of the naked, decades gone, are mute; the bullets splitting throats and breasts and skulls, the human waterfall of bodies tipping over into the wooded ravine at Babi Yar, are no more than tedious footnotes on aging paper. The deportation ledgers, with their scrupulous lists of names of the doomed, what are they now? Museum artifacts. The heaps of eyeglasses and children's shoes, the hills of human hair, lie disintegrating in their display cases, while only a little distance away the visitors' cafeteria bustles and buzzes: sandwiches, Cokes, the waiting tour buses.

We thought it was finished. In the middle of the twentieth century, and surely by the end of it, we thought it was finished, genuinely finished, the bloodlust finally slaked. We thought it was finished, that heads were hanging—the heads of the leaders and schemers on gallows, the heads of the bystanders and onlookers in shame. The Topf company, manufacturer of the ovens, went belatedly out of business, belatedly disgraced and shamed. Out of shame German publishers of Nazi materials concealed and falsified the past. Out of shame Paul de Man, lauded and eminent Yale intellectual, concealed his early Nazi lucubrations. Out of shame Mircea Eliade, lauded and eminent

Chicago intellectual, concealed his membership in Romania's Nazi-linked Iron Guard. Out of shame memorials to the murdered rose up. Out of shame synagogues were rebuilt in the ruins of November 9, 1938, the night of fire and pogrom and the smashing of windows. Out of shame those who were hounded like prey and fled for their lives were invited back to their native villages and towns and cities, to be celebrated as successful escapees from the murderous houndings of their native villages and towns and cities. Shame is salubrious: it acknowledges inhumanity, it admits to complicity, it induces remorse. Naïvely, foolishly, stupidly, hopefully, a-historically, we thought that shame and remorse—world-wide shame, world-wide remorse—would endure. Naïvely, foolishly, stupidly, hopefully, a-historically, we thought that the cannibal hatred, once quenched, would not soon wake again.

It has awakened.

In "The Modern *Hep! Hep! Hep!*"—an 1878 essay reflecting on the condition of the Jews—George Eliot noted that it would be "difficult to find a form of bad reasoning about [Jews] which had not been heard in conversation or been admitted to the dignity of print." She was writing in a period politically not unlike our own, Disraeli ascendant in England, Jews prominent in liberal parties both in Germany and France. Yet her title points to something far deadlier than mere "bad reasoning." *Hep!* was the cry of the Crusaders as they swept through Europe, annihilating one Jewish community after another; it stood for *Hierosolyma est perdita* (Jerusalem is destroyed), and was taken up again by anti-Jewish rioters in Germany in 1819. In this single raging syllable, past and future met, and in her blunt bold enunciation of it, George Eliot was joining bad reasoning—i.e., canard and vilification—to its consequences: violence and murder. The Jews, she wrote, have been "regarded and treated very much as beasts hunted for their skins," and the curse on them, the charge of deicide,

was counted a justification for hindering them from pursuing agriculture and handicrafts; for marking them out as
execrable figures by a peculiar dress; for torturing them . . .
spitting at them and pelting them; for taking it certain that
they killed and ate babies, poisoned the wells, and took
pains to spread the plague; for putting it to them whether
they would be baptised or burned, and not failing to burn
and massacre them when they were obstinate; but also for
suspecting them of disliking their baptism when they had
got it, and then burning them in punishment of their in-
sincerity; finally, for hounding them by tens on tens of
thousands from their homes where they had found shelter
for centuries, and inflicting on them the horrors of a new
exile and a new dispersion. All this to avenge the Saviour
of mankind, or else to compel these stiff-necked people to
acknowledge a Master whose servants showed such be-
neficent effects of His teaching.

As an anti-Semitic yelp, *Hep!* is long out of fashion. In the
eleventh century it was already a substitution and a metaphor:
Jerusalem meant Jews, and "Jerusalem is destroyed" was, when
knighthood was in flower, an incitement to pogrom. Today, the
modern *Hep!* appears in the form of Zionism, Israel, Sharon.
And the connection between vilification and the will to undermine and endanger Jewish lives is as vigorous as when the howl
of *Hep!* was new. The French ambassador to Britain, his tongue
unbuttoned in a London salon, hardly thinks to cry *Hep!*; instead, he speaks of "that shitty little country." European and British scholars and academicians, their Latin gone dry, will never
cry *Hep!*; instead they call for the boycott of Israeli scholars
and academicians.

Even Martin Luther (though his Latin was good enough)
failed to cry *Hep!* Instead, he inquired:

What is to be done with this wicked, accursed race, which
can no longer be tolerated? The Talmud and the rabbis

teach that it is no sin to kill Christians, to break an oath to Christians, to rob and plunder them. The one and only aim of the Jews is to weaken Christianity. They have poisoned the springs, they have murdered Christian children for their blood for their rites. They are becoming too prosperous in Germany, and in consequence have become insolent. Then what is to be done? Their synagogues must be reduced to ashes, for the honor of God and of Christianity. Christians are to destroy the houses of Jews, and drive them all under one roof, or into a stable like gypsies. All prayer-books and copies of the Talmud are to be wrested from them by force, and their praying and even the use of God's name is to be forbidden to them under pain of death. Their rabbis are to be forbidden to teach. The authorities are to prohibit Jews from traveling, and to bar the roads against them. Their money must be taken from them. Able-bodied Jews and Jewesses are to be put to forced labor, and kept strictly employed with the flail, the axe, the spade. Christians are not to show any tender mercy to Jews. The emperor and the princes must be urged to expel them from the country without delay. If I had power over the Jews, I would assemble the best and most learned among them and, under penalty of having their tongues cut out, would force them to accept the Christian teaching that there is not *one* God, but *three* Gods. I say to you, the Jews do great evil in the land. If they could kill us all, they would gladly do so, aye, and often do it, especially those who profess to be physicians— they know all that is known about medicine in Germany; they can give poison to a man of which he will die in an hour, or in ten or twenty years; they thoroughly understand this art.

So much for sixteenth-century *Hep!*—a reprise, under the guise of Reformation, of three hundred years of abusive Christian power. But it foreshadows twentieth-century *Hep!* as well:

the flaming synagogues, the prohibitions, the expropriations, the looting, the forced labor, the phantasmagorical lies, the Stalinist doctors' plot, the bloodthirsty reversals of intent: "if they could kill us all, they would gladly do so."

Luther came late to these pious inspirations. Nearly all had their precedents in the Church he renounced; and even the medieval Church practiced mimicry. It was Pope Innocent III who implemented the yellow badge of ignominy (Hitler was no innovator, except as to gas chambers)—yet Innocent too was innocent of originality, since he took the idea from Prince Abu-Yusef Almansur, a Moroccan Muslim ruler of the thirteenth century. Post-Enlightenment France may be known for its merciless persecution of a guiltless Dreyfus, and for the anti-Jewish rioting it set off; and, more recently, for the gendarmes who arrested and deported the Jews of Paris with a zeal equal to that of the Germans. But Paris had seen anti-Jewish mobs before—for instance, in June of 1242, when twenty-four cartloads of Talmuds were set afire in a public square. And while elsewhere in France, and all through the Rhineland, the Crusaders were busy at their massacres, across the Channel the Archbishop of Canterbury was issuing a decree designed to prevent the Jews of England from having access to food.

All this, let it be noted, preceded the barbarities of the Inquisition: the scourgings, the burnings, the confiscations, the expulsions.

Any attempt to set down the record, early and late, of Christian violence against Jews can only be a kind of pointillism—an atrocity here, another there, and again another. The nineteenth-century historian Heinrich Graetz (as rationalist in temperament as Gibbon) summed up the predicament of Jews across the whole face of Europe:

If Jewish history were to follow chronicles, memorial books and martyrologies, its pages would be filled with bloodshed, it would consist of horrible exhibitions of corpses, and it would stand forth to make accusation against a doctrine which taught princes and nations to become common executioners and hangmen. For, from the thirteenth to the sixteenth century, the persecutions and massacres of the Jews increased with frightful rapidity and intensity, and only alternated with inhuman decrees issued by both Church and the state, the aim and purport of all of which were to humiliate the Jews, to brand them with calumny and to drive them to suicide. . . . The nations of Europe emulated one another in exercising their cruelty upon the Jews. . . . In Germany they were slain by thousands. . . . Every year martyrs fell, now in Weissenburg, Magdeburg, Arnstadt, now in Coblenz, Sinzig, Erfurt, and other places. In Sinzig all the members of the congregation were burnt alive on a Sabbath in their synagogue. There were German Christian families who boasted that they had burnt Jews, and in their pride assumed the name of *Judenbrater* (Jew-roaster).

And all this, let it again be noted, before the Shoah; before the Czarist pogroms and the Czarist fabrication of the "Protocols of the Elders of Zion"; before the exclusions, arrests, and gulag brutalities of the Soviet Union; before the shooting of the Soviet Yiddish writers in the basement of Moscow's Lubyanka prison; before the rise of contemporary Islamist demonization of Jews; before the eight-decades-long Arab assault on Jewish national aspiration and sovereignty; before the Palestinian cult of suicide bombing. Anti-Semitism feeds on itself from continent to continent, from Iceland to Japan: it scarcely requires living Jews. Its source is commonly taken to be the two supersessionist Scriptures that derive from Judaism—in Christianity, the Jews' cry (in the Gospel of Matthew) of "His blood be on us and on our children," the fount of the venomous deicide curse; in Islam, the unwillingness of Jews to follow Mohammed in the furtherance of a latter-day faith which accused the Hebrew Bible of distorting the biblical narratives that appear, Islam claims, more authoritatively and genuinely in the Koran.

But anti-Semitism originated in neither Christianity nor Islam. Its earliest appearance burst out in Egypt, in the fourth century B.C.E., during the reign of Ptolemy II, when Manetho, an Egyptian priest, in a polemic directed against the biblical account in Genesis and Exodus, described a people who "came from Jerusalem" as the descendants of a mob of lepers. Against the Hebrew text, which records Joseph as a wise and visionary governor, Manetho charged that Joseph defiled the shrines and statues of the gods and set fire to villages and towns. Nor did Moses liberate the Hebrews and bring them, under divine guidance, out of Egypt, from slavery to freedom. These offspring of lepers, Manetho declared, were ignominiously expelled, having savagely despoiled the country for thirteen years. Such calumnies soon infiltrated Hellenic literature. The Greeks, detecting no plastic representation of the divine order, were quick to name the Jews atheists—lazy atheists, since once in seven days they refrained from labor. The Greek scholar Mnaseas of Patara recycled an Egyptian myth (traces of it later turned up in Plutarch) which asserted that the Temple in Jerusalem harbored the golden head of an ass, the sole object of the Jews' worship. Another version had the Jews praying before an image of Moses seated on an ass while displaying a book containing laws of hatred for all humanity.

Greek enmity was most acutely encapsulated in the canard spread by Apion, whose contribution to the history of anti-Semitism is the infamously enduring blood libel. In its earliest form a Greek, captured by Jews, is taken to the Temple, fattened, and then killed; his entrails are ritually eaten in conjunction with an oath of hatred toward Greeks. Christian mythology altered Greek to Christian, usually a child, whose blood was said to be drained at Passover for the purpose of being baked into matzah. (A curious projection of the Eucharist's draught of blood.) From its Christian source, the blood libel leached into Muslim societies. It surfaced most recently in a Saudi newspaper, which fantasized Muslim blood in Purim cakes. Mustafa Tlal, the Syrian defense minister, is the author of *The Matzah of Zion,* which presents the 1841 Damascus blood libel as an established "Jewish ritual." And in a writing contest sponsored by the Palestinian Education Ministry, the winning entry, by a tenth-grader, described a Mother's Day gift an Israeli soldier brings to his mother: "a bottle of the blood of a Palestinian child he has murdered."

Current anti-Semitism, accelerating throughout advanced and sophisticated Europe—albeit under the rubric of anti-Zionism, and masked by the deceptive lingo of human rights—purports to eschew such primitivism. After all, Nazism and Stalinism are universally condemned; anti-Judaism is seen as obscurantist medievalism; the Vatican's theology of deicide was nullified four decades ago; Lutherans, at least in America, vigorously dissociate themselves from their founder's execrations; and whatever the vestiges of Europe's unregenerate (and often Holocaust-denying) Right may think, its vociferous Left would no more depart from deploring the Holocaust than it would be willing to be deprived of its zeal in calumniating the Jewish state. It is easy enough to shed a tear or two for the shed and slandered blood of the Jews of the past; no one will praise Torquemada, or honor Goebbels. But to stand up for truth-telling in the present, in a mythologizing atmosphere of pervasive defamation and fabrication, is not a job for cowards.

In the time of Goebbels, the Big Lie about the Jews was mainly confined to Germany alone; much of the rest of the world saw through it with honest clarity. In our time, the Big Lie (or Big Lies, there are so many) is disseminated everywhere, and not merely by the ignorant, but with malice aforethought by the intellectual classes, the governing elites, the most prestigious elements of the press in all the capitals of Europe, and by the university professors and the diplomats.

The contemporary Big Lie, of course, concerns the Jews of Israel: they are oppressors in the style of the Nazis; they ruthlessly pursue, and perpetuate, "occupation" solely for the sake of domination and humiliation; they purposefully kill Palestinian children; their military have committed massacres; their government "violates international law"; their nationhood and their sovereignty have no legitimacy; they are intruders and usurpers inhabiting an illicit "entity," and not a people entitled as other peoples are entitled; and so on and so on. Reviving both blood libel and deicide, respectable European journals publish political cartoons showing Prime Minister Sharon devouring Palestinian babies, and Israeli soldiers bayoneting the infant Jesus.

Yet the modern history of Jews in the Holy Land overwhelmingly refutes these scurrilities. It is the Arabs, not the Jews, who have been determined to dispose of a people's right to live in peace. Is there any point now—after so many politically willed erasures of fact by Palestinian Arabs, Muslim populations in general, and a mean-spirited European intelligentsia —to recapitulate the long record of Arab hostility that has prevailed since the demise of the Ottoman Empire? The Muslim Arab claim of hegemony (through divine fiat, possessive greed, contempt for pluralism, or all three) over an entire region of the globe accounts for the hundreds of Christian Arabs who have fled Bethlehem, Nablus, Ramallah, and all other places where Muslims dominate—a flight rarely reported. Unsurprisingly, the Christians who have not yet departed blame the Israelis for this displacement, not the Muslim extremists under whose threats of reprisal they live. As for the fate of Jews in the orbit of this self-declared Muslim imperium, the current roar of "resistance to occupation" is notoriously belied by the bloody Arab pogroms of 1920, 1921, 1929, 1936, and 1939, when there was no Jewish state at all, let alone any issue of "settlements." The 1929 attacks left Hebron, the site of an ancient and un-interrupted Jewish community, effectively *Judenrein*.

What use is there, in the face of brute political and cultural intransigence, to rehearse the events of 1948? In that year Arab rejection of an independent Palestinian state under the UN partition plan led to the invasion by five Arab armies intent on crushing nascent Jewish sovereignty; whole sections of Jerusalem were destroyed or overrun. Nineteen-forty-eight marked the second, though not the first or the last, Arab refusal of Palestinian statehood. The first came in 1937, when under the British Mandate the Peel Commission proposed partition and statehood for the Arabs of Palestine; the last, and most recent, occurred in 2000, when Arafat dismissed statehood in favor of a well-prepared and programmatic violence. (The flouting of the Road Map by Palestinian unwillingness to dismantle terror gangs will have counted as the Palestinians' fourth refusal of statehood; but the Road Map's callously criminalizing equation of civilian inhabitants of Jewish towns—settlements—with Palestinian murder of Jewish civilians is itself egregious.) After 1948, the Arab war against the Jews of Israel continued through the terror incursions of 1956, the Six-Day War of 1967, the Yom Kippur attacks of 1973, and the fomented violence of 1987, the so-called first intifada.

In short, for two-thirds of a century the Arabs have warred against a Jewish presence in "their" part of the world. The 1967 war in defense of Jewish lives (when affected Jews everywhere went into mourning, fearing catastrophe) culminated in Golda Meir's attempt to return, in exchange for peace, the territories which, in the spirit of partition, Israel had never sought to acquire, and had so unexpectedly conquered. The answer came at an Arab summit in Khartoum: no negotiations, no recognition, no peace. So much for the "crime" of occupation.

And though the Oslo accords of 1993 strove yet again for

negotiations, most energetically under Ehud Barak, both the Palestinian leadership and the Palestinian public chose killing over compromise—this time with newly conceived atrocities through suicide bombings, always directed against civilians, in buses, cafés, restaurants, supermarkets, or wherever Israelis peacefully congregate.

This is the history that is ignored or denigrated or distorted or spitefully misrepresented. And because it is a history that has been assaulted and undermined by world-wide falsehoods in the mouths of pundits and journalists, in Europe and all over the Muslim world, the distinction between anti-Semitism and anti-Zionism has finally and utterly collapsed. It is only sophistry, disingenuousness, and corrupted conscience that continue to insist on such a distinction. To fail to trace the pernicious consistencies of Arab political aims from 1920 until today, despite temporary pretensions otherwise, is to elevate intellectual negligence to a principle. To transmogrify self-defense into aggression is to invite an Orwellian horse-laugh. To identify occupation as Israel's primal sin—the most up-to-date *Hep!* of all—is to be blind to Arab actions and intentions before 1967, and to be equally blind to Israel's repeated commitments to negotiated compromise. On the Palestinian side, the desire to eradicate Jewish nationhood increases daily: it is as if 1948 has returned, replicated in the guise of fanatical young "martyrs" systematically indoctrinated in kindergartens and schools and camps—concerning whom it is cant to say, as many do, that they strap detonators to their loins because they are without hope. It is hope that inflames them.*

Perhaps the most bizarre display of international anti-Semitism was flaunted at Durban, during a UN conference osten-

---

*As I write, fresh news arrives—evidence of the fulfillment of one martyr's hope. An Israeli doctor and his twenty-year-old daughter have this day been blown up together in a café, where they had gone for a father-daughter talk on the eve of the young woman's marriage. She had been devoting her year of national service to the

sibly called to condemn "Racism, Discrimination, Xenophobia, and Related Intolerance." Plucked from the refuse heap, the old UN canard, "Zionism is racism," together with a determined Arab hijacking of the agenda, brought about the bitterest irony of all: a virulent hatred under the auspices of anti-hatred. At Durban the Jewish state was declared to have been conceived in infamy, Jewish representatives were threatened, and language was violated more savagely than at any time since the Nazi era. "Political language," said Orwell, "is designed to make lies sound truthful and murder respectable, and to give the appearance of solidity to pure wind." Yet the rant that emerged at Durban—those instantly recognizable snarls of anti-Semitism —hardly merited the term "political." It had the venerable sound of the mob: *Hep! Hep! Hep!*

Among the sophists and intellectuals, the tone is subtler. Here it is not Jewish lives that are put in jeopardy so much as it is Jewish sensibility and memory that are humbled and mocked. Pressing political analogies, however apt, are dismissed as "confused" or "odious." When history is invoked, it is said to be for purposes of coarse extortion: Israel is charged, for instance, with "using" the Holocaust as sympathetic coinage to be spent on victimizing others. In a *New York Times Magazine* piece called "How to Talk About Israel," Ian Buruma, alluding to Israel's 1981 demolishment of Iraq's nuclear installation, contends that "it might have been justified in many legitimate ways"—but he derides Menachem Begin's appeal to the memory of the one and a half million Jewish children who were annihilated by the applied technology of an earlier barbarous regime. Is the imagination's capacity to *connect* worthy of such

---

care of children with cancer; her ambition was to study medicine for the sake of such children. Her father was an eminent and remarkable physician, the tireless head of a hospital emergency room which tends the victims of terror attacks. He had just returned from the United States, where he was instructing American doctors in the life-saving emergency techniques he had pioneered. Father and daughter were buried on what was to have been the daughter's wedding day.

scorn, or is this how human beings ought to think and feel? Saddam Hussein's nuclear bomb was plainly a present danger to living Israeli children; and conscious of the loss of so many children within the lifetime of a generation, Jewish memory declines to be untender. Nor is the denigration of tenderness a pretty trait in itself, or a sign of rational objectivity. "The politics of the Middle East may be murderous," Buruma comments, "but it is not helpful to see them as an existential battle between good and evil." This suggests a popular contemporary form of liberal zealotry, very nearly the mirror-image of religious fanaticism—a great wash of devotedly obstinate indifference to the moral realities of human behavior and motivation, a willed inability to distinguish one thing from another thing. A switchblade is not a butter knife; the difference between them *is* "existential." And "not helpful" is one of those doggedly bland (yet contemptuous) jargonlike therapeutic phrases that reveals a mind in need of a dose of Dostoyevsky. Or of Mark Twain, who understood the real nature of what he dubbed "evil joy."

I would not wish to equate, in any manner or degree, the disparagement of Jewish memory and sensibility with anti-Semitism, a term that must be reserved for deadlier intentions. Disparagement is that much lighter species of dismissal that is sometimes designated as "social anti-Semitism," and is essentially a type of snobbery. Snobbery falls well short of lethal hatred—but it conveys more than a touch of insolence, and insolence in a political context can begin to be worrisome. It vibrates at the outer margins of "that shitty little country"; it is, one might say, not helpful.

Judith Butler, identifying herself as a Jew in the *London Review of Books,* makes the claim that linking "Zionism with Jewishness . . . is adopting the very tactic favored by anti-Semites." A skilled sophist (one might dare to say solipsist), she tosses those who meticulously chart and expose anti-Semitism's disguises into the same bin as the anti-Semites themselves. Having accused Israel of the "dehumanization of Palestinians"; having acknowledged that she was a signatory to a petition opposing "the Israeli occupation, though in my mind it is not nearly strong enough: it did not call for the end of Zionism"; and having acknowledged also that (explicitly) as a Jew she seeks "to widen the rift between the state of Israel and the Jewish people," she writes:

> It will not do to equate Jews with Zionists or Jewishness with Zionism. . . . It is one thing to oppose Israel in its current form and practices or, indeed, to have critical questions about Zionism itself, but it is quite another to oppose "Jews" or assume that all "Jews" have the same view; that they are all in favor of Israel, identified with Israel, or represented by Israel. . . . To say that all Jews hold a given view on Israel or are adequately represented by Israel, or, conversely, that the acts of Israel, the state, adequately stand for the acts of all Jews, is to conflate Jews with Israel and, thereby, to commit an anti-Semitic reduction of Jewishness.

One can surely agree with Butler that not all Jews are "in favor of Israel": she is a dazzling model of one who is not, and she cites, by name, a handful of "post-Zionists" in Israel proper, whom she praises. But her misunderstanding of anti-Semitism is profound; she theorizes rifts and demarcations, borders and dikes; she is sunk in self-deception. The "good" anti-Zionists, she believes, the ones who speak and write in splendidly cultivated English, will never do her or her fellow Jews any harm; they are not like the guttersnipe anti-Semites who behave so badly. It is true that she appears to have everything in common with those Western literary intellectuals (e.g., Tom Paulin and the late Edward Said) whose aspirations are indistinguishable from her own: that Israel "in its current form" ought to disappear. Or, as Paulin puts it, "I never believed that Israel had the right to exist at all." Tony Judt, a professor of European history, confirms this baleful view; writing in *The New York Review of Books*, he dismisses the Jewish state as—alone among the nations—"an anachronism."

Yet Butler's unspoken assumption is that consonance, or collusion, with those who would wish away the Jewish state will earn one a standing in the European, if not the global, anti-Zionist world club. To a degree she may be right: the congenial welcome she received in a prestigious British journal confirms it, and she is safe enough, for the nonce, in those rarefied places where, as George Eliot has it (with a word altered), it would be "difficult to find a form of bad reasoning about [Zionism] which had not been heard in conversation or been admitted to the dignity of print." In that company she is at home. There she is among friends.

But George Eliot's Zionist views are notorious; she is partial to Jewish national liberation. A moment, then, for the inventor of the pound of flesh. Here is Cinna, the poet, on his way to Caesar's funeral:

CITIZEN: As a friend or an enemy?
CINNA: As a friend.
CITIZEN: Your name, sir, truly.
CINNA: Truly, my name is Cinna.
CITIZEN: Tear him to pieces; he's a conspirator.
CINNA: I am Cinna the poet, I am Cinna the poet! . . . I am
    not Cinna the conspirator!
CITIZEN: It is no matter, his name's Cinna. . . . Tear him,
    tear him! Come, brands, ho! firebrands! Burn all!

And here is Butler, the theorist, on her way to widen the rift between the state of Israel and the Jewish people:

—As a friend, or as a Zionist?
BUTLER: As an anti-Zionist Jew.
—Tear her to pieces, she's a Jew.
BUTLER: I am Butler the anti-Zionist, I am Butler the anti-
    Zionist! I am not Butler the Zionist!

What's in a name? Ah, the curse of mistaken identity. How many politically conforming Jews will suffer from it, even as they toil to distance themselves from the others, those benighted Jews who admit to being "in favor of Israel"? As for that nobly desired rift, one can rely on *Hep!* to close it. To comprehend this is to comprehend anti-Semitism at its root. And to assert, as Butler does, that in the heart of this understanding lurks "the very tactic favored by anti-Semites" is not merely sophistry; not merely illusion; but simple stupidity, of a kind only the most subtle intellectuals are capable of.

The melancholy encounter with anti-Semitism is not, after all, coequal with Jewish history; the history of oppression belongs to the culture of the oppressors. The long, long Jewish narrative is in reality a procession of ideas and ideals, of ethical legislation and ethical striving, of the study of books and the making of books. It is not a chronicle of victimhood, despite the centuries of travail, and despite the corruptions of the hour, when the vocabulary of human rights is too often turned ubiquitously on its head. So contaminated have the most treasured humanist words become, that when one happens on a mass of placards emblazoned with "peace," "justice," and the like, one can see almost at once what is afoot—a collection of so-called anti-globalization rioters declaiming defamation of Israel, or an anti-Zionist campus demonstration (not always peaceful), or any anti-Zionist herd of lockstep radicals, such as ANSWER, or the self-proclaimed International Parliament of Writers, or the International Solidarity Movement, which (in the name of human rights) shields terrorists. Or even persons who are distinguished and upright. Rabbi Abraham Joshua Heschel, who marched at Selma, and who was impassioned in protesting the Vietnam war, appealed to his peace-and-justice colleagues to sign a declaration condemning the massacre of Israeli athletes by Palestinian terrorists at the 1972 Olympics. Too many refused.

It is long past time (pace Buruma, pace Butler) when the

duplicitous "rift" between anti-Zionism and anti-Semitism can be logically sustained. Whether in its secular or religious expression, Zionism is, in essence, the modern flowering of a vast series of diverse intellectual and pietistic movements, all of them steeped in the yearning for human dignity—symbolized by the Exodus from slavery—that has characterized Jewish civilization for millennia. Contempt and defamation from without have sometimes infiltrated the abject psyches of defeatist Jews, who then begin to judge themselves according to the prevailing canards. Such Jews certainly are *not* what is commonly called self-haters, since they are motivated by the preening self-love that congratulates itself on always "seeing the other side." Not self-haters, no; low moral cowards, rather, often trailing uplifting slogans.

Anti-Semitism is a foolish word; we appear to be stuck with it. "Semitism" has virtually no meaning. The Semites are a linguistic group encompassing Hebrew, Akkadian, Amharic, and Arabic. The argument one occasionally gets wind of—that Arabs, being Semites, cannot be charged with anti-Semitism, or that any objection to Arab political conduct is itself an instance of anti-Semitism—is nothing if not risible. Anti-Semitism (a term fabricated a century ago by a euphemistic German anti-Semite) signifies hatred of Jews, and hatred's easy corollary: a steady drive to weaken, to hurt, and to extirpate Jews.

Still, one must ask: why the Jews? A sad old joke pluckily confronts the enigma.

—The Jews and the bicyclists are at the bottom of all the world's ills.
—Why the bicyclists?
—Why the Jews?

—implying that blaming one set of irrelevancies is just as irrational as blaming the other. Ah, but it is never the bicyclists, and it is always the Jews. There are innumerable social, economic, and political speculations as to cause: scapegoatism; envy; exclusionary practices; the temptation of a demographic majority to subjugate a demographic minority; the attempt by corrupt rulers to deflect attention from the failings of their tyrannical regimes; and more. But any of these can burst out in any society against any people—so why *always* the Jews? A metaphysical explanation is proffered: the forceful popular resistance to what Jewish civilization represents—the standard of ethical monotheism and its demands on personal and social conscience. Or else it is proposed, in Freudian terms, that Christianity and Islam, each in its turn, sought to undo the parent religion, which was seen as an authoritative rival it was needful to surpass and displace.

This last notion, however, has no standing in contemporary Christianity. In nearly all Christian communities, there is remorse for the old theologically instigated crimes, and serious internal moral restitution, much of it of a very high order. But a salient fact remains, perhaps impolitic to note: relief has come through Christianity's having long been depleted of temporal power. Today's Islamists, by contrast, are supported and succored by states: Iran, Syria (and Lebanon, its vassal), Saudi Arabia, Sudan, Libya, Malaysia, Indonesia, Pakistan, Egypt (which suppresses its domestic extremists, while its official press, film industry, and other institutions encourage anti-Zionist incitements). Iranian weapons flood into Gaza, whether by sea or through tunnels from Egypt. Saudi Arabia not long ago unashamedly broadcast a telethon to collect millions to be sent to Palestinian terror gangs; it continues today as Hamas's chief funder. And though Saddam Hussein is finally gone, it will not be forgotten that he honored and enriched the families of suicide bombers. (I observe a telltale omission: those who deny any linkage between Iraq and terror universally discount Saddam's lavish payments to Hamas and Islamic Jihad.)

The riddle of anti-Semitism—why always the Jews?—

survives as an apparently eternal irritant. The German-Jewish philosopher Franz Rosenzweig, writing in 1916 (in italics) of *"hatred of the Jews,"* remarked to a friend, "You know as well as I do that all its realistic arguments are only fashionable cloaks." The state of Israel is our era's fashionable cloak—mainly on the Left in the West, and centrally and endemically among the populations of the Muslim despotisms. But if one cannot account for the tenacity of anti-Semitism, one can readily identify it. It wears its chic disguises. It breeds on the tongues of liars. The lies may be noisy and primitive and preposterous, like the widespread Islamist charge (doggerelized by New Jersey's poet laureate) that a Jewish conspiracy leveled the Twin Towers. Or the lies may take the form of skilled patter in a respectable timbre, while retailing sleight-of-hand trickeries—such as the hallucinatory notion that the defensive measures of a perennially beleaguered people constitute colonization and victimization; or that the Jewish state is to blame for the aggressions committed against it. Lies shoot up from the rioters in Gaza and Ramallah. Insinuations ripple out of the high tables of Oxbridge. And steadily, whether from the street or the salon, one hears the enduring old cry: *Hep! Hep! Hep!*

October 2003

ABOUT THE
CONTRIBUTORS

PART ONE: AWAKENINGS

JONATHAN ROSEN is the author of the novel *Eve's Apple* and of *The Talmud and the Internet: A Journey Between Worlds*. His essays and articles have appeared in *The New York Times, The New Yorker,* and *The American Scholar*. His new novel, *Joy Comes in the Morning,* will be published by Farrar, Straus & Giroux in the fall of 2004. He is editorial director of Nextbook, where he is creating a series of short books on Jewish subjects, in partnership with Schocken Books.

PAUL BERMAN writes on literature and politics for *The New Republic, The New York Times Book Review* and *Magazine, Dissent,* and other journals. He is the author of *Terror and Liberalism, The Passion of Joschka Fischer,* and *A Tale of Two Utopias: The Political Journey of the Generation of 1968*.

DAVID BROOKS was a senior editor at *The Weekly Standard* and a commentator on PBS's *News Hour,* and is now an op-ed columnist for *The New York Times*. He is the author of *Bobos in Paradise*.

BARBARA AMIEL is a columnist for the London *Telegraph*.

HAROLD EVANS is the former editor of the London *Sunday Times,* and the author of *The American Century*.

LAWRENCE SUMMERS was secretary of the Treasury in the Clinton administration and is currently president of Harvard University.

PART TWO: SOMETHING OLD, SOMETHING NEW

BEREL LANG, professor of humanities at Trinity College, is the author of *Act and Idea in the Nazi Genocide, Heidegger's Silence,* and *Holocaust Representation,* among other books.

ROBERT S. WISTRICH holds the Neuberger Chair for Modern European History at the Hebrew University of Jerusalem and is head of its International Center for the Study of Antisemitism. He is the author and editor of twenty-three books, several of which have won international awards. These include *Socialism and the Jews* (Oxford University Press, 1982); *The Jews of Vienna in the Age of Franz Joseph* (Oxford, 1989), which won the Austrian State Prize for Danubian History; and *Anti-Semitism, the Longest Hatred* (Pantheon, 1992), which received the H. H. Wingate Prize for nonfiction in the U.K. It was also the basis for the PBS film documentary, which Professor Wistrich scripted and co-edited. His most recent books are: *Hitler and the Holocaust* (Random House, 2001) and the edited volume *Nietzsche: Godfather of Fascism?* (Princeton, 2002).

GABRIEL SCHOENFELD is the senior editor of *Commentary* and the author of *The Return of Anti-Semitism*.

PART THREE: ONE DEATH, ONE LIE

JUDEA PEARL is the father of the late Daniel Pearl and president of the Daniel Pearl Foundation (www.danielpearl.org).

THANE ROSENBAUM, the former literary editor of *Tikkun*, is the author of *Second Hand Smoke, The Golems of Gotham,* and *The Myth of Moral Justice*. His articles appear in *The New York Times*, the *Los Angeles Times,* and *The Wall Street Journal*.

SAMUEL G. FREEDMAN, a professor of journalism at Columbia University, is the author most recently of *Jew vs. Jew: The Struggle for the Soul of American Jewry*.

TOM GROSS is former Middle East reporter for the London *Sunday Telegraph* and the New York *Daily News*. Gross maintains a weblist that reports on anti-Semitism in the media and politics.

DR. DAVID ZANGEN, head of the Pediatric Endocrine Service at Mt. Scopus Hadassah University Hospital in Jerusalem, was chief medical officer of a brigade in the Jenin area during Operation Defensive Shield.

PART FOUR: THE ULTIMATE STAKES: THE SECOND-HOLOCAUST DEBATE

PHILIP ROTH is one of America's most honored novelists. He is the recipient of the American Academy of Arts and Letters Gold Medal in fiction in addition to the Pulitzer Prize and National Book Award.

RON ROSENBAUM *see* "About the Editor."

LEON WIESELTIER is literary editor of *The New Republic*, author of *Kaddish*, and editor of *The Moral Obligation to Be Intelligent*, a selection of Lionel Trilling's essays.

RUTH R. WISSE, the Martin Peretz Professor of Yiddish Literature and professor of Comparative Literature at Harvard, is the author most recently of *The Modern Jewish Canon* (Free Press) and contributes to many journals.

PART FIVE: THE FACTS ON THE GROUND IN FRANCE

MARIE BRENNER is a special correspondent for *Vanity Fair* and the author of five books. Her piece on the Abner Louima incident won a Front Page Award and her report on tobacco whistleblower Jeffrey Wiegand was made into the film *The Insider*.

PART SIX: THE SHIFT FROM RIGHT TO LEFT

MELANIE PHILLIPS has been a columnist for the London *Times* and the London *Daily Mail*. She was awarded the Orwell Prize for journalism in 1996; her most recent book is *The Ascent of Women*.

DR. LAURIE ZOLOTH was director of the Jewish Studies Program at San Francisco State University when she wrote this e-mail. She now teaches at Northwestern University.

TODD GITLIN is a professor of journalism, culture, and sociology at New York University and the author of many books on media and society, including *Media Unlimited*.

ELI MULLER was a senior at Yale University when he wrote this column.

MARK STRAUSS is a senior editor at *Foreign Policy*.

BARRY ORINGER is a screen and television writer whose best-known works include *Ben Casey*, *I Spy*, and *The Fugitive*.

FIAMMA NIRENSTEIN is the Jerusalem correspondent for the leading Italian newspaper *La Stampa* as well as for the Italian magazine *Panorama*. Her work has appeared in many magazines and newspapers, including *Commentary* and *The New York Sun*. An author of several books about the Arab-Israeli conflict, she teaches history of the Middle East at the LUISS University in Rome, as a visiting professor. This article, which was posted on the Jewish World Review website, was first delivered as a speech at the YIVO

Institute conference "Old Demons, New Debates: Anti-Semitism in the West," May 11–14, 2003.

PART SEVEN: THE DEICIDE ACCUSATION

NAT HENTOFF is a columnist for *The Village Voice* and *The Progressive* and the author most recently of *The War Against the Bill of Rights,* among many other books. His work also appears in *Editor and Publisher* and the United Media Newspaper syndicate.

PETER J. BOYER has been a staff writer at *The New Yorker* since 1992. His stories have been included in the anthologies *Best American Crime Writing* and *Best American Science Writing.* As correspondent for the PBS documentary series *Frontline,* he has earned a Peabody Award and an Emmy. Boyer is currently at work on a nonfiction book for Random House.

FRANK RICH is a columnist at *The New York Times* and the author of the memoir *Ghost Light.*

PART EIGHT: SOME NEW FORMS OF ANTI-SEMITISM

SIMON SCHAMA, professor of art history at Columbia University, is the author of *Citizens, A History of Britain, Landscape and Memory, The Embarrassment of Riches: An Interpretation of Dutch Culture in the Golden Age,* and, most recently, *Rembrandt's Eyes.*

JOSHUA MURAVCHIK, a resident scholar at the American Enterprise Institute, is the author, most recently, of *Heaven on Earth: The Rise and Fall of Socialism.*

ROBERT JAN VAN PELT is a professor of architecture at the University of Waterloo, Canada. In addition to *The Case for Auschwitz: Evidence from the Irving Trial,* he is the co-author, with Debórah Dwork, of *Auschwitz: 1270 to the Present.*

JUDITH SHULEVITZ was editor of *Lingua Franca* and has been a columnist for *Slate* and *The New York Times Book Review.*

PART NINE: ANTI-ZIONISM AND ANTI-SEMITISM

JEFFREY TOOBIN is a staff writer at *The New Yorker* and the legal analyst for CNN. His books include *Too Close to Call: The 36-Day Battle to Decide the 2000 Election; A Vast Conspiracy: The Real Story of the Sex Scandal That Nearly Brought Down a President;* and *The Run of His Life: The People v. O. J. Simpson.*

MARTIN PERETZ is the editor-in-chief of *The New Republic*, and teaches at Harvard.

JONATHAN FREEDLAND has been a columnist at *The Guardian* (U.K.) since 1997, having served for four years as the paper's Washington correspondent. In 2002 he was named Columnist of the Year in the What the Papers Say Awards. Freedland is also the presenter of BBC Radio 4's history series *The Long View* and BBC 4's *The Talk Show*. He has written extensively on Israeli and Middle Eastern affairs. He also writes a monthly column for *The Jewish Chronicle* and is now at work on a book about identity, Jewishness, and the Middle East.

JUDITH BUTLER is Maxine Elliot Professor in Rhetoric and Comparative Literature at the University of California, Berkeley. Her book *Precarious Life* will be published by Verso in the spring of 2004.

PART TEN: ISRAEL

DAVID MAMET is one of America's leading playwrights and screenwriters and a recipient of the Pulitzer Prize and the Tony Award, among many others.

PHILIP GREENSPUN teaches at MIT, has authored textbooks on software and Web applications, and maintains a website on politics and economics at http://philip.greenspun.com/.

SHALOM LAPPIN is a professor in the Department of Computer Science at King's College London and a longtime supporter of the Israeli peace movement.

EDWARD SAID was a scholar and author who taught at Columbia University and wrote the influential study *Orientalism*. In addition, he was a leading advocate of the Palestinian cause. He died of leukemia in September 2003.

DANIEL GORDIS (www.danielgordis.org) is director of the Mandel Jerusalem Fellows and the author, most recently, of *If a Place Can Make You Cry: Dispatches from an Anxious State* (Crown).

PART ELEVEN: MUSLIMS

JEFFREY GOLDBERG is a staff writer and Middle East correspondent of *The New Yorker*. Before joining *The New Yorker*, he was a contributing writer to *The New York Times Magazine*, and also served as the New York bureau chief of *The Forward* and as a columnist for *The Jerusalem Post*. He began his career as a crime reporter for *The Washington Post*. Goldberg is the recipient of the International Consortium of Investigative Journalists' Award for Outstanding International Investigative Reporting and the National Magazine Award for Reporting, for his coverage of terrorism.

BERNARD LEWIS is the Cleveland E. Dodge Professor of Near Eastern Studies Emeritus at Princeton University and the author of *The Middle East: A Brief History of the Last 2,000 Years,* a National Book Critics Circle Award finalist; *The Emergence of Modern Turkey; The Arabs in History;* and *What Went Wrong?: Western Impact and Middle Eastern Response,* among other books. Lewis is internationally recognized as one of our era's greatest historians of the Middle East.

TARIQ RAMADAN is a Geneva-based scholar and lecturer and the author of *Western Muslims and the Future of Islam* (Oxford University Press).

AMOS OZ is the internationally acclaimed author of numerous novels and essays, which have been translated into over thirty languages. He is also one of the founders of Peace Now, and lives in Arad, Israel.

AFTERWORD

CYNTHIA OZICK is one of America's most admired novelists, essayists, and short story writers. Her most recent collection of essays, *Quarrel & Quandary,* won the National Book Critics Circle Award. Her new novel will appear in the fall of 2004.

SOURCE LIST

Jonathan Rosen, *The New York Times Magazine,* November 4, 2001

Paul Berman, *The Forward,* May 24, 2002

David Brooks, *The Weekly Standard,* February 2, 2003

Barbara Amiel, *The Telegraph,* December 17, 2002

Harold Evans, The Index Lecture (Hay-on-Wye Literary Festival), June 2, 2002

Lawrence Summers, Address at Memorial Church, Harvard University, September 17, 2002

Berel Lang (1), *Midstream,* May/June 2003

Robert S. Wistrich, *The National Interest,* Summer 2003

Berel Lang (2), Vidal Sassoon International Center for the Study of Antisemitism, Annual Report, 1999

Gabriel Schoenfeld, *Commentary,* June 2002

Judea Pearl, *The Wall Street Journal,* February 20, 2003

Thane Rosenbaum, *Tikkun,* November/December 2002

Samuel G. Freedman, Salon.com, June 12, 2002

Tom Gross (1), *National Review Online,* May 13, 2002

Dr. David Zangen, *Ma'ariv,* November 8, 2002

Tom Gross (2), Weblist, August 5, 2002

Philip Roth, from *Operation Shylock,* published by Simon & Schuster, 1993

Ron Rosenbaum, *The New York Observer,* April 15, 2002

Leon Wieseltier, *The New Republic,* May 27, 2002

Ruth R. Wisse, *Commentary,* October 2002

Marie Brenner, *Vanity Fair,* June 2003

Melanie Phillips, *The Spectator,* March 22, 2003

Dr. Laurie Zoloth, aish.com, May 9, 2002

Todd Gitlin, motherjones.com, June 27, 2002

Eli Muller, yaledailynews.com, March 1, 2003

Mark Strauss, *Foreign Policy,* November/December 2003

Barry Oringer, Pacific News Service, May 9, 2002

Fiamma Nirenstein, talk at YIVO Institute for Jewish Research, Conference on "Old Demons, New Debates: Anti-Semitism in the West," May 11–14, 2003

Nat Hentoff, *The Village Voice,* June 22, 2001

Peter J. Boyer, *The New Yorker,* September 15, 2003

Frank Rich, *The New York Times,* September 21, 2003

Simon Schama, talk at YIVO Institute for Jewish Research, Conference on "Old Demons, New Debates: Anti-Semitism in the West," May 11–14, 2003

Joshua Muravchik, *Commentary,* September 1, 2003

Robert Jan van Pelt, *The Case for Auschwitz: Evidence from the Irving Trial,* Indiana University Press, 2002

Judith Shulevitz, Slate.com, January 24, 2000

Jeffrey Toobin, *The New Yorker,* January 27, 2003

Martin Peretz, *The New Republic,* April 29, 2002

Jonathan Freedland, first published in *A New Anti-Semitism?: Debating Judeophobia in 21st-Century Britain,* Profile Books, October 2003

Judith Butler, *London Review of Books,* August 21, 2003

David Mamet, *The Forward,* December 27, 2002

Philip Greenspun, http://www.philip.greenspun.com

Shalom Lappin, *Dissent,* Spring 2003

Edward Said, *Al-Ahram Weekly* (online), June 25–July 1, 1998

Daniel Gordis, *Midstream,* May/June 2003

Jeffrey Goldberg, *The New Yorker,* October 8, 2001

Bernard Lewis (1), *The Middle East Quarterly,* June 1998

Bernard Lewis (2), *The Middle East Quarterly,* September 1998 and December 1998

Tariq Ramadan, from *Western Muslims and the Future of Islam,* Oxford University Press, October 2003

Amos Oz, *The Nation,* April 22, 2002

Cynthia Ozick, written for this volume, Sept.–Oct. 2003

PERMISSION CREDITS

Grateful acknowledgment is made to the following for permission to reprint previously published material:

Al-ahram: "A Desolation, and They Called It Peace" by Edward Said (June 25–July, 1998, issue #383). Reprinted by permission of *Al-ahram.*

Barbara Amiel: "Islamists Overplay Their Hand" by Barbara Amiel (*The Telegraph,* December 17, 2001). Copyright © 2001 by Barbara Amiel. Reprinted by permission of the author.

Paul Berman: "Something's Changed" by Paul Berman. This article was originally published in the *The Forward.* Reprinted by permission of the author.

Peter J. Boyer: "The Jesus War" by Peter J. Boyer (*The New Yorker,* September 15, 2003), copyright © 2003 by Peter J. Boyer. Reprinted by permission of the author.

Judith Butler: "The Charge of Anti-Semitism: Jews, Israel, and the Risks of Public Critique" by Judith Butler (*London Review of Books,* August 21, 2003). Reprinted by permission of the author.

Commentary: "Israel and the Anti-Semites" by Gabriel Schoenfeld (*Commentary,* June 2002). Reprinted by permission of *Commentary.*

Harry Evans & Associates: Speech entitled "Hay-on-Wye Speech" by Harry Evans. Reprinted by permission of Harry Evans.

Foreign Policy: "Antiglobalism's Jewish Problem" by Mark Strauss. Reprinted by permission of *Foreign Policy* (www.foreignpolicy.com).

Samuel G. Freedman: "Don't Look Away" by Samuel G. Freedman (Salon.com, June 12, 2002). Copyright © 2002 by Samuel G. Freedman. Reprinted by permission of the author.

Philip Greenspun: "Israel," by Philip Greenspun, which appeared in February 2003 on http://philip.greenspun.com. Reprinted by permission of the author.

ACKNOWLEDGMENTS

The idea for this book emerged from my conversations with my exceedingly wise friend Jonathan Rosen; the reality of it from the encouragement and insights of my singularly brainy and empathetic editor, David Ebershoff. I'm grateful as well for the strong support of Dan Menaker and Gina Centrello at Random House.

Valuable ideas for thinking about the subject and structure of the book were contributed by my thoughtful comrade David Samuels. And by my literary agent, Kathy Robbins, who offered her usual superb advice and moral support throughout the process—I am constantly amazed by her wisdom and clarity.

I was especially fortunate in having the counsel of Veronica Windholz, the gifted and dedicated senior copy editor at Random House. Also at Random House, I'm grateful for the advice and counsel of Laura Goldin and Amelia Zaleman, and for the enthusiasm of Lynne Martin. Thanks also to Kapo Ng for his elegant jacket design and to Dominique Troiano, David Ebershoff's assistant, for all the work she put in on the project.

A special word of undying gratitude to Cynthia Ozick, a writer I've always looked up to, for agreeing to write her remarkably eloquent and impassioned Afterword for this book.

And to all the contributors herein, my thanks for allowing me to include your thought-provoking work in this book.

My conversations with Craig S. Karpel, Tom Gross, Jeffrey Goldberg, Errol Morris, Berel Lang, Neal Kozodoy, Stanley Mieses, Paul Berman, Gabriel Schoenfeld, Nat Hentoff, Daniel Kunitz, Thane Rosenbaum, Rabbi Adam Mintz of Lincoln Square Synagogue, to name a few, were important in helping to clarify some of my ideas, and alerting me to essays I wanted to include.

I also owe a lot to the vigilance of webloggers such as Glenn Reynolds, Meryl Yourish, David Artemiw, Jeff Jarvis, Roger Simon, and, of course, Zachary and Mo of "Exposing the Exposer" (to name a few) in helping me keep in constant touch with the situation and the issues.

There are so many others who deserve credit for many forms of support that made it possible for me to put together a seven-hundred-page book:

Peter Kaplan and Arthur Carter at *The New York Observer* gave me the space and freedom to explore my ideas on this subject. Petra Bartosiewiecz, who was my editor there through much of this period, also came up with important suggestions for additions to this book. My current editor, Mario Russo, and all my other colleagues at the paper have my thanks as well.

All the smart people at Kathy Robbins's office—Kate Rizzo, Sandy Bontemps Hodgman, Teri Tobias, Diane Bijou, Sophie Landres, Sarah D'Imperio, and David Halpern—have played important roles in various capacities in helping put this book together.

Liz Groden of City-Secretarial.com has been indispensable, not just in assembling the manuscript but in Web-based research as well. Additional important research help came from Lisa Singh.

Among the many friends and colleagues who have been supportive in various ways while I was putting this together, I'd like to thank Betsy Carter, Gary Hoenig, Virginia Heffernan, Dr. Joseph Fetto, Faye Beckerman, Holly Staver, Noah Kimerling, Richard Horowitz, Sheldon Piekny, Deb Friedman, Fred Kaplan, Eve Babitz, Dora Steinberg, Mark Steinberg, Lauren Thierry, Jim Watkins, Helen Whitney, Jonathan Karp, Jonathan Schwartz, Drs. Paul and Marvin Belsky, Marie Brenner, Naomi Wax, Laura Frost, Daniel Ahn, Susan Kamil, Dan Kornstein, and David Livingstone.

And, as always, my wisest and most knowing counselor has been my sister, Ruth Rosenbaum.

My deepest apologies to those deserving people I've inadvertently left out: it's the nightmare of doing Acknowledgments; I'm sure a dozen more names will occur to me after this goes to press, but please accept my thanks and my chagrin.

INDEX

About the Editor

RON ROSENBAUM grew up on Long Island and graduated from Bay Shore High School and Yale. He left a graduate fellowship in the Yale English Department to write full-time. His essays and journalism have appeared in *The New York Times Magazine* and *Book Review, The New Yorker, Harper's, The Atlantic Monthly, Slate, Salon,* and other journals, and have been collected most recently in *The Secret Parts of Fortune* (Random House 2000/Harper Perennial 2001).

He spent more than ten years working on *Explaining Hitler,* an exploration and critique of postwar attempts to account for Hitler's crimes. Translated into ten languages, *Explaining Hitler* (Random House 1998/Harper Perennial 1999) was a *New York Times* Notable Book of the Year and was described by David Remnick as "a remarkable journey by one of the most original journalists and writers of our time."

He has taught nonfiction writing at Columbia's Graduate School of Journalism; he co-wrote the documentary *Faith and Doubt at Ground Zero* for PBS/*Frontline,* which won a Du Pont-Columbia University Award; and he writes a bi-weekly column for *The New York Observer.* He is currently working on a book about Shakespeare scholars and directors for Random House.